PLAYFAIR FOOTBALL ANNUAL 2010-2011

EDITED BY
GLENDA ROLLIN AND **JACK ROLLIN**

<u>headline</u>

First published in 2010
by HEADLINE PUBLISHING GROUP

1

Cataloguing in Publication Data is available from the British Library

ISBN 978 0 7553 6108 3

Typeset by Wearset Ltd, Boldon, Tyne and Wear

Printed and bound in Great Britain by Clays Ltd, St Ives plc

Headline's policy is to use papers that are natural, renewable and recyclable products and made from wood grown in sustainable forests. The logging and manufacturing processes are expected to conform to the environmental regulations of the country of origin.

HEADLINE PUBLISHING GROUP
An Hachette UK Company
338 Euston Road
London NW1 3BH

www.headline.co.uk
www.hachette.co.uk

CONTENTS

EDITORIAL

Once the dust of South Africa settled, the metaphorical tent pegs tapped, canvas folded and the fans dispersed to the four corners of the earth to await another four years for the trip to Brazil, the fact remained that England did not even reach the last eight. Ranked thereabouts by FIFA's quaint method of determining where every country stands once a month, it was a blow to discover where we were labelled with a one-over-the-eight hangover.

Ironically when the so called golden generation of players had once again failed to deliver in a major tournament, the youth of the country had enjoyed a welcome win in the UEFA Under-17 championships, beating Spain no less in the final. The Under-19 team were finalists in their similar competition and also qualified for the next tournament. While many of our youngsters often find opportunities of senior football quicker than their overseas counterparts, it was nonetheless an outstanding achievement.

Naturally in the wake of the defeat in South Africa, the suggestions to improve matters have been readily forthcoming from all quarters, few of which were even mentioned before the World Cup finals took place. Reducing the number of foreign players in the Premier League is once again the popular knee-jerk reaction to continued disappointment at the highest level.

At the start of 2009–10 one survey revealed that less than forty-two percent of 595 Premier League players were English. Of the foreign contingent no fewer than 68 different countries were represented. More than a hundred players from the Premier League and some from the Football League were sprinkled among the teams in South Africa. Six appeared in the final itself.

But one thought on this tack is what use is it to have young home grown players sitting on the bench – almost as many of them as are on the field of play in one team – when they could be playing themselves? Reserve team football has been confined to midweek almost universally and the big clubs have one squad for the first team, another for the reserves and a third for the Academy. However, the structure of the reserve format may soon change.

In this editorial last year it was pointed out that Germany's successes at various levels needed to be investigated to discover the pattern which has led to this being eliminated by our old foe. And of course Germany did not go on to win the 2010 trophy!

There is also far too much football outside of the normal league and cup fixtures. The growth of both the Champions League and now Europa League has meant that scant consideration is given to domestic cup tournaments. Even the FA Cup has lost much of its romance and indeed is being considered for midweek only, which would surely end its magic.

Football continues twelve months of the year. Before the end of the World Cup in South Africa the Champions League had started again. One of the England youth teams was involved in a tournament towards the end of July, too. Talk of a winter break to give players a rest is nonsensical because there is no guarantee when bad weather will strike, If the wrong weeks were chosen the matches would have to be squeezed in somewhere in an already crowded calendar.

At the grass roots level some progress has been made despite the background of a former Government which did nothing to encourage competitive sport and even eroded the actual playing areas where the youth of the country could actually participate in the game.

Immediately ahead is the start of Euro 2012 and a group which should be within our capabilities to qualify. The man in charge Fabio Capello has been given the green light to carry on regardless despite heavy criticism in the aftermath of the dismissal by Germany. In December we will also know whether football is really coming home for 2018.

Long before the World Cup kicked off in the southern hemisphere there had been calls for the introduction of technology to solve controversial goal line incidents. The finals in South Africa did little to dispel the feeling that one day some kind of electronic system must be installed either inside the goal posts or within the actual ball.

Apart from the most obvious blunder which sadly affected England's hope of equalising against Germany with the ball a foot at least over the line and clearly visible to cameras, there were enough goals either ruled out or allowed to stand where the scorer was clearly on or offside.

The ball used in the final tournament was not to everyone's liking – especially goalkeepers who discovered the flight of it in the air varied alarmingly. Many German clubs had used this Jabulana in the Bundesliga. The modern method whereby goalkeepers do not get their whole body behind the ball whenever possible did little to help their cause.

In the wake of the criticism which was launched over the England goal in particular, FIFA who had consistently refused to discuss the introduction of technology suddenly announced there would be changes to the system. We await the outcome with baited breath.

CLUB AND OTHER RECORDS 2009–2010

Blackpool
Becomes the 44th team to play in the Premier League.

Burton Albion
Jacques Maghoma becomes the most capped player for the club, appearing for DR Congo. Record League victory 6-1 v Aldershot T, 12 December 2009.

Chelsea
Frank Lampard increases his club record appearances to 80 of his 82 caps for England.
Ashley Cole wins his sixth FA Cup Winners medal (three with Arsenal) and also scores the 18,000th Premier League goal.
The club's championship-winning goals margin of 71 between those scored and conceded is another record.

Dagenham & Redbridge
Record Football League play-off score (6-0), semi-final first leg v Morecambe 16 May 2010. Josh Scott four goals in the same match; the best individual score in the competition.

Liverpool
Steven Gerrard becomes the club's most capped player with his 84th cap for England.
Jack Robinson at 16 years 250 days against Hull City on 9 May 2010 becomes the club's youngest League player.

Manchester United
Ryan Giggs continued his record as the only Premier League player to have scored at least one goal in each of the competition's seasons.

Millwall
Neil Harris adds to his club record by taking his total of goals to 114.

Morecambe
Record League victory 5-0 v Bournemouth, 12 December 2009.

Newcastle United
The club establishes a record for the Football League Championship since 1992–93 with an attendance of 52,181 v Ipswich Town on 24 April 2010.

Peterborough United
Craig Morgan becomes the club's most capped player with his 19th cap of 20 for Wales.

Reading
Kevin Doyle becomes the club's most capped player with his 26th cap of 35 for the Republic of Ireland before his transfer to Wolverhampton Wanderers.

Rochdale
Gary Jones adds to his club record number of League appearances, taking his total to 379.

Scunthorpe United
Grant McCann becomes the club's most capped player with 10 appearances for Northern Ireland out of a total of 28.

Wigan Athletic
Most capped players with Wigan Athletic: Kevin Kilbane, 22 appearances for Republic of Ireland and Henri Camara with 22 for Senegal, from their respective totals.

Wycombe Wanderers
Kadeem Harris becomes the youngest Football League player at 16 years 201 days v Yeovil Town on 26 December 2009.

Premier League
The first all-foreign starting line-up for both teams in the Premier League came in the match between Arsenal and Portsmouth on 30 March 2010.

England
Record score at under 19 level 7-1 v Slovenia, 27 July 2009.

Republic of Ireland
Shay Given and Kevin Kilbane equal the record number of international appearances, taking their totals to 103 each.

LEAGUE REVIEW AND CLUB SECTION

For Carlo Ancelotti in his first season in charge of Chelsea it must have been a dream come true. Moreover he had the traditional double of Premier League and FA Cup, the twin pots of gold of English football.

Chelsea saw off the other three in the so-called "Big Four" – namely Arsenal, Liverpool and Manchester United, scoring twelve goals and winning the six matches involved. Yet this was no comfortable campaign. Just one point separated Chelsea and United on the last day of the season. They both won United scoring four against Stoke City, Chelsea getting eight against Wigan Athletic.

Yet on 21 March the top of the table had United four points ahead with Chelsea, lying third with a game in hand. The crucial match was on 3 April at Old Trafford and with Wayne Rooney out injured, Chelsea won 2-1 to snatch a two point lead. Didier Drogba was top scorer in the Premier League with 29 goals.

Even second place can be a tremendous disappointment and Manchester United had just the Carling Cup success over Aston Villa for which to be thankful. Rooney missed half a dozen games with injury and it certainly cost him the leading scorer slot, though he finished with 26. Moreover there was no Champions League joy.

Ten points behind even United, inconsistent Arsenal, finished in third place. Briefly on Saturday night 20 March the Gunners were top. However, fourth place was something of a triumph for Tottenham Hotspur and earned them a place in the Champions League. Manchester City were edged out after a bright start which included a run of ten undefeated games with eight draws!

Aston Villa had thoughts of fourth place but the goals dried up at the turn of the year. Yet for Liverpool there was arguably the most disappointment of any team. Fernando Torres suffered from injuries and missed sixteen games. Even a second chance in the Europa League ended unsuccessfully after faltering in the Champions League. At season's end, Rafa Benitez departed Anfield, to be replaced in the summer with Roy Hodgson from Fulham who had taken the Craven Cottage club to the Europa League final, to lose just in added time to Atletico Madrid – a magnificent performance – rightly awarded as Manager of the Year.

Only two points behind their Mersey rivals, Everton had a better second half to the season and performed well enough in the Europa League. They finished the term with an unbeaten run of eleven games.

Birmingham City's meagre thirty-eight goals produced 50 points and ninth place. Twelve unbeaten matches into January was the highlight. Blackburn Rovers never managed a run of three consecutive wins and were involved in seven goalless draws.

Stoke City also found goal scoring a problem area, failing to average one per game, yet achieving 47 points and eleventh place.

For a team which suffered in mid-season, Sunderland was a surprise thirteenth, due mostly to others struggling. Darren Bent scored half of their goals.

Bolton Wanderers having captured Owen Coyle, Burnley's manager, had scratched around for goals on their own behalf. Sixteen times they were non-scorers, chiefly in the second half of the season again surviving through the adversity of more lowly life.

Newly promoted Wolverhampton Wanderers scraped together just thirty-two goals but again it guaranteed safety. Seventeen times they failed to score, yet beating Burnley on 20 December they were twelfth.

Wigan Athletic made to suffer by Chelsea as previously mentioned, found itself punished severely in another game when crashing 9-1 at Tottenham Hotspur on 22 November. Thirty-seven goals of their own succeeded in keeping just out of the relegation zone throughout.

But it was a close run outcome for West Ham United second from bottom at the half-way stage and hovering in peril, too, thereafter until two wins in the last five outings pulled them out of danger.

Not as fortunate was the fate of Burnley, Hull City and Portsmouth. Wins for all three were rarities. Newcomers Burnley began early beating Manchester United but won only three games in the second half of the season. Hull contrived just two more wins after the end of November and hit only thirty-four goals. Portsmouth in financial meltdown and with points deducted, remained rooted to the cellar, yet courageously reached the FA Cup final.

Newcastle United finished as Football League Championship winners, West Bromwich Albion as runners-up and Blackpool via the play-offs becoming the 44th team to play in the Premier League.

Down into League One went Sheffield Wednesday, Plymouth Argyle and Peterborough United. Up from League One came Norwich City and Leeds United plus Millwall from the play-offs. Into League Two fell Gillingham, Wycombe Wanderers, Southend United and Stockport County.

Their replacements were Notts County, Bournemouth, Rochdale and Dagenham & Redbridge who had been placed seventh but who came through the play-offs in some style. Trying life in the Blue Square Premier is Grimsby Town, but for Darlington it was a second experience. Returning to the Football League came Oxford United accompanied by Stevenage who had been denied access on a previous occasion.

BARCLAYS PREMIER LEAGUE 2009–2010

(P) *Promoted into division at end of 2008–09 season.*
(R) *Relegated into division at end of 2008–09 season.*

			Home				Away					Total					
	P	W	D	L	F	A	W	D	L	F	A	W	D	L	F	A	GD	Pts
1 Chelsea	38	17	1	1	68	14	10	4	5	35	18	27	5	6	103	32	71	86
2 Manchester U	38	16	1	2	52	12	11	3	5	34	16	27	4	7	86	28	58	85
3 Arsenal	38	15	2	2	48	15	8	4	7	35	26	23	6	9	83	41	42	75
4 Tottenham H	38	14	2	3	40	12	7	5	7	27	29	21	7	10	67	41	26	70
5 Manchester C	38	12	4	3	41	20	6	9	4	32	25	18	13	7	73	45	28	67
6 Aston Villa	38	8	8	3	29	16	9	5	5	23	23	17	13	8	52	39	13	64
7 Liverpool	38	13	3	3	43	15	5	6	8	18	20	18	9	11	61	35	26	63
8 Everton	38	11	6	2	35	21	5	7	7	25	28	16	13	9	60	49	11	61
9 Birmingham C (P)	38	8	9	2	19	13	5	2	12	19	34	13	11	14	38	47	–9	50
10 Blackburn R	38	10	6	3	28	18	3	5	11	13	37	13	11	14	41	55	–14	50
11 Stoke C	38	7	6	6	24	21	4	8	7	10	27	11	14	13	34	48	–14	47
12 Fulham	38	11	3	5	27	15	1	7	11	12	31	12	10	16	39	46	–7	46
13 Sunderland	38	9	7	3	32	19	2	4	13	16	37	11	11	16	48	56	–8	44
14 Bolton W	38	6	7	6	26	31	4	3	12	16	36	10	9	19	42	67	–25	39
15 Wolverhampton W (P)	38	5	6	8	13	22	4	5	10	19	34	9	11	18	32	56	–24	38
16 Wigan Ath	38	6	7	6	19	24	3	2	14	18	55	9	9	20	37	79	–42	36
17 West Ham U	38	7	5	7	30	29	1	6	12	17	37	8	11	19	47	66	–19	35
18 Burnley (P)	38	7	5	7	25	30	1	1	17	17	52	8	6	24	42	82	–40	30
19 Hull C	38	6	6	7	22	29	0	6	13	12	46	6	12	20	34	75	–41	30
20 Portsmouth*	38	5	3	11	24	32	2	4	13	10	34	7	7	24	34	66	–32	19

Portsmouth deducted 9 points.

LEADING GOALSCORERS 2009–2010

BARCLAYS PREMIER LEAGUE

	League	Carling Cup	FA Cup	Other	Total
Only goals scored in the same division are included.					
Didier Drogba *(Chelsea)*	29	2	3	3	37
Wayne Rooney *(Manchester U)*	26	2	0	6	34
Darren Bent *(Sunderland)*	24	0	1	0	25
Carlos Tevez *(Manchester C)*	23	6	0	0	29
Frank Lampard *(Chelsea)*	22	0	3	2	27
Jermain Defoe *(Tottenham H)*	18	1	5	0	24
Fernando Torres *(Liverpool)*	18	0	0	4	22
Cesc Fabregas *(Arsenal)*	15	0	0	4	19
Emmanuel Adebayor *(Manchester C)*	14	0	0	0	14
Gabriel Agbonlahor *(Aston Villa)*	13	2	1	0	16
Louis Saha *(Everton)*	13	0	0	2	15
Florent Malouda *(Chelsea)*	12	1	2	0	15
Dimitar Berbatov *(Manchester U)*	12	0	0	0	12
In order of total goals:					
Bobby Zamora *(Fulham)*	8	0	3	9	20

Other matches consist of European games, J Paint Trophy, Community Shield and Football League play-offs. Players listed in order of League goals total.

COCA-COLA CHAMPIONSHIP 2009–2010

		Home						Away						Total					
		P	W	D	L	F	A	W	D	L	F	A	W	D	L	F	A	GD	Pts
1	Newcastle U (R)	46	18	5	0	56	13	12	7	4	34	22	30	12	4	90	35	55	102
2	WBA (R)	46	16	3	4	48	21	10	10	3	41	27	26	13	7	89	48	41	91
3	Nottingham F	46	18	2	3	45	13	4	11	8	20	27	22	13	11	65	40	25	79
4	Cardiff C	46	12	6	5	37	20	10	4	9	36	34	22	10	14	73	54	19	76
5	Leicester C (P)	46	13	6	4	40	18	8	7	8	21	27	21	13	12	61	45	16	76
6	Blackpool¶	46	13	6	4	46	22	6	7	10	28	36	19	13	14	74	58	16	70
7	Swansea C	46	10	10	3	21	12	7	8	8	19	25	17	18	11	40	37	3	69
8	Sheffield U	46	12	8	3	37	20	5	6	12	25	35	17	14	15	62	55	7	65
9	Reading	46	10	7	6	39	22	7	5	11	29	41	17	12	17	68	63	5	63
10	Bristol C	46	10	10	3	38	34	5	8	10	18	31	15	18	13	56	65	−9	63
11	Middlesbrough (R)	46	9	8	6	25	21	7	6	10	33	29	16	14	16	58	50	8	62
12	Doncaster R	46	9	7	7	32	29	6	8	9	27	29	15	15	16	59	58	1	60
13	QPR	46	8	9	6	36	28	6	6	11	22	37	14	15	17	58	65	−7	57
14	Derby Co	46	12	3	8	37	32	3	8	12	16	31	15	11	20	53	63	−10	56
15	Ipswich T	46	8	11	4	24	23	4	9	10	26	38	12	20	14	50	61	−11	56
16	Watford	46	10	6	7	36	26	4	6	13	25	42	14	12	20	61	68	−7	54
17	Preston NE	46	9	10	4	35	26	4	5	14	23	47	13	15	18	58	73	−15	54
18	Barnsley	46	8	7	8	25	29	6	5	12	28	40	14	12	20	53	69	−16	54
19	Coventry C	46	8	9	6	27	29	5	6	12	20	35	13	15	18	47	64	−17	54
20	Scunthorpe U (P)	46	10	7	6	40	32	4	3	16	22	52	14	10	22	62	84	−22	52
21	Crystal Palace*	46	8	5	10	24	27	6	12	5	26	26	14	17	15	50	53	−3	49
22	Sheffield W	46	8	6	9	30	31	3	8	12	19	38	11	14	21	49	69	−20	47
23	Plymouth Arg	46	5	6	12	20	30	6	2	15	23	38	11	8	27	43	68	−25	41
24	Peterborough U (P)	46	6	5	12	32	37	2	5	16	14	43	8	10	28	46	80	−34	34

*Crystal Palace deducted 10 points. ¶ Blackpool promoted via play-offs.

COCA-COLA CHAMPIONSHIP

	League	Carling Cup	FA Cup	Other	Total
Peter Whittingham (Cardiff C)	20	2	1	2	25
Nicky Maynard (Bristol C)	20	1	0	0	21
Gary Hooper (Scunthorpe U)	19	1	0	0	20
Andy Carroll (Newcastle U)	17	0	2	0	19
Kevin Nolan (Newcastle U)	17	1	0	0	18
Michael Chopra (Cardiff C)	16	1	2	2	21
Gylfi Sigurdsson (Reading)	16	1	3	0	20
Charlie Adam (Blackpool)	16	1	0	2	19
Darren Ambrose (Crystal Palace)	15	2	3	0	20
Robert Earnshaw (Nottingham F)	15	0	0	2	17
Billy Sharp (Sheffield U on loan to Doncaster R) (Carling Cup goal for Sheffield U)	15	1	0	0	16
Danny Graham (Watford)	14	0	0	0	14

COCA-COLA LEAGUE 1 2009–2010

		Home					Away					Total						
	P	W	D	L	F	A	W	D	L	F	A	W	D	L	F	A	GD	Pts
1 Norwich C (R)	46	17	3	3	48	22	12	5	6	41	25	29	8	9	89	47	42	95
2 Leeds U	46	14	6	3	41	19	11	5	7	36	25	25	11	10	77	44	33	86
3 Millwall¶	46	17	5	1	48	15	7	8	8	28	29	24	13	9	76	44	32	85
4 Charlton Ath (R)	46	14	6	3	41	22	9	9	5	30	26	23	15	8	71	48	23	84
5 Swindon T	46	13	8	2	42	25	9	8	6	31	32	22	16	8	73	57	16	82
6 Huddersfield T	46	14	8	1	52	22	9	3	11	30	34	23	11	12	82	56	26	80
7 Southampton* (R)	46	15	5	3	48	21	8	9	6	37	26	23	14	9	85	47	38	73
8 Colchester U	46	15	5	3	37	21	5	7	11	27	31	20	12	14	64	52	12	72
9 Brentford (P)	46	9	12	2	34	21	5	8	10	21	31	14	20	12	55	52	3	62
10 Walsall	46	10	8	5	36	26	6	6	11	24	37	16	14	16	60	63	–3	62
11 Bristol R	46	13	3	7	32	30	6	2	15	27	40	19	5	22	59	70	–11	62
12 Milton Keynes D	46	10	5	8	31	28	7	4	12	29	40	17	9	20	60	68	–8	60
13 Brighton & HA	46	7	4	12	26	30	8	10	5	30	30	15	14	17	56	60	–4	59
14 Carlisle U	46	10	4	9	34	28	5	9	9	29	38	15	13	18	63	66	–3	58
15 Yeovil T	46	9	7	7	36	26	4	7	12	19	33	13	14	19	55	59	–4	53
16 Oldham Ath	46	7	7	9	23	28	6	6	11	16	29	13	13	20	39	57	–18	52
17 Leyton Orient	46	10	6	7	35	25	3	6	14	18	38	13	12	21	53	63	–10	51
18 Exeter C (P)	46	9	10	4	30	20	2	8	13	18	40	11	18	17	48	60	–12	51
19 Tranmere R	46	11	3	9	30	32	3	6	14	15	40	14	9	23	45	72	–27	51
20 Hartlepool U*	46	10	6	7	33	26	4	5	14	26	41	14	11	21	59	67	–8	50
21 Gillingham (P)	46	12	8	3	35	15	0	6	17	13	49	12	14	20	48	64	–16	50
22 Wycombe W (P)	46	6	7	10	26	31	4	8	11	30	45	10	15	21	56	76	–20	45
23 Southend U	46	7	10	6	29	27	3	3	17	22	45	10	13	23	51	72	–21	43
24 Stockport Co	46	2	6	15	21	51	3	4	16	14	44	5	10	31	35	95	–60	25

Southampton deducted 10 points, Hartlepool United deducted 3 points.

¶ *Millwall promoted via play-offs.*

LEADING GOALSCORERS 2009–2010

COCA-COLA LEAGUE 1

	League	Carling Cup	FA Cup	Other	Total
Rickie Lambert (Southampton)	30	1	2	3	36
(including one League goal for Bristol R)					
Billy Paynter (Swindon T)	26	2	1	0	29
Jermaine Beckford (Leeds U)	25	0	5	1	31
Grant Holt (Norwich C)	24	3	3	0	30
Lee Barnard (Southampton)	24	2	0	0	26
(Includes 15 League and 2 Carling Cup goals for Southend U)					
Steve Morison (Millwall)	20	0	2	1	23
Jordan Rhodes (Huddersfield T)	19	3	1	0	23
Charlie Austin (Swindon T)	19	0	0	1	20
Chris Martin (Norwich C)	17	0	4	2	23
Ian Harte (Carlisle U)	16	1	1	0	18
Luciano Becchio (Leeds U)	15	0	2	0	17
Charlie MacDonald (Brentford)	15	0	2	0	17
Adam Lallana (Southampton)	15	2	1	2	20

COCA-COLA LEAGUE 2 2009–2010

		Home					Away					Total						
		P	W	D	L	F	A	W	D	L	F	A	W	D	L	F	A	GD	Pts
1	Notts Co	46	16	6	1	58	14	11	6	6	38	17	27	12	7	96	31	65	93
2	Bournemouth	46	16	3	4	33	16	9	5	9	28	28	25	8	13	61	44	17	83
3	Rochdale	46	14	3	6	45	20	11	4	8	37	28	25	7	14	82	48	34	82
4	Morecambe	46	14	6	3	44	24	6	7	10	29	40	20	13	13	73	64	9	73
5	Rotherham U	46	10	9	4	29	18	11	1	11	26	34	21	10	15	55	52	3	73
6	Aldershot T	46	12	7	4	43	24	8	5	10	26	32	20	12	14	69	56	13	72
7	Dagenham & R¶	46	15	2	6	46	27	5	10	8	23	31	20	12	14	69	58	11	72
8	Chesterfield	46	14	3	6	38	27	7	4	12	23	35	21	7	18	61	62	–1	70
9	Bury	46	11	6	6	29	23	8	6	9	25	36	19	12	15	54	59	–5	69
10	Port Vale	46	8	8	7	32	25	9	9	5	29	25	17	17	12	61	50	11	68
11	Northampton T (R)	46	9	9	5	29	21	9	4	10	33	32	18	13	15	62	53	9	67
12	Shrewsbury T	46	10	6	7	30	20	7	6	10	25	34	17	12	17	55	54	1	63
13	Burton Alb (P)	46	9	5	9	38	34	8	6	9	33	37	17	11	18	71	71	0	62
14	Bradford C	46	8	8	7	28	27	8	6	9	31	35	16	14	16	59	62	–3	62
15	Accrington S	46	11	1	11	38	39	7	6	10	24	35	18	7	21	62	74	–12	61
16	Hereford U (R)	46	12	4	7	32	25	5	4	14	22	40	17	8	21	54	65	–11	59
17	Torquay U (P)	46	9	6	8	34	24	5	9	9	30	31	14	15	17	64	55	9	57
18	Crewe Alex (R)	46	7	4	12	35	36	8	6	9	33	37	15	10	21	68	73	–5	55
19	Macclesfield T	46	7	8	8	27	28	5	10	8	22	30	12	18	16	49	58	–9	54
20	Lincoln C	46	9	7	7	25	26	4	4	15	17	39	13	11	22	42	65	–23	50
21	Barnet	46	8	10	5	30	18	4	2	17	17	45	12	12	22	47	63	–16	48
22	Cheltenham T (R)	46	5	8	10	34	38	5	10	8	20	33	10	18	18	54	71	–17	48
23	Grimsby T	46	4	9	10	25	36	5	8	10	20	35	9	17	20	45	71	–26	44
24	Darlington	46	3	3	17	14	40	5	3	15	19	47	8	6	32	33	87	–54	30

¶ *Dagenham & R promoted via play-offs.*

COCA-COLA LEAGUE 2

	League	Carling Cup	FA Cup	Other	Total
Lee Hughes *(Notts Co)*	30	0	3	0	33
Brett Pitman *(Bournemouth)*	26	0	1	1	28
Adam Le Fondre *(Rotherham U)*	25	0	2	3	30
Chris O'Grady *(Rochdale)*	22	0	0	0	22
Shaun Harrad *(Burton Alb)*	21	0	1	0	22
Chris Dagnall *(Rochdale)*	20	0	0	0	20
Mark Richards *(Port Vale)*	19	2	0	1	22
Phil Jevons *(Morecambe on loan from Huddersfield T)*	18	0	1	0	19
Ryan Lowe *(Bury)*	18	0	0	0	18
Paul Benson *(Dagenham & R)*	17	0	1	4	22
Adebayo Akinfenwa *(Northampton T)*	17	0	0	0	17

BARCLAYS PREMIER LEAGUE

HOME TEAM	Arsenal	Aston Villa	Birmingham C	Blackburn R	Bolton W	Burnley	Chelsea	Everton	Fulham	Hull C
Arsenal	—	3-0	3-1	6-2	4-2	3-1	0-3	2-2	4-0	3-0
Aston Villa	0-0	—	1-0	0-1	5-1	5-2	2-1	2-2	2-0	3-0
Birmingham C	1-1	0-1	—	2-1	1-2	2-1	0-0	2-2	1-0	0-0
Blackburn R	2-1	2-1	2-1	—	3-0	3-2	1-1	2-3	2-0	1-0
Bolton W	0-2	0-1	2-1	0-2	—	1-0	0-4	3-2	0-0	2-2
Burnley	1-1	1-1	2-1	0-1	1-1	—	1-2	1-0	1-1	2-0
Chelsea	2-0	7-1	3-0	5-0	1-0	3-0	—	3-3	2-1	2-1
Everton	1-6	1-1	1-1	3-0	2-0	2-0	2-1	—	2-1	5-1
Fulham	0-1	0-2	2-1	3-0	1-1	3-0	0-2	2-1	—	2-0
Hull C	1-2	0-2	0-1	0-0	1-0	1-4	1-1	3-2	2-0	—
Liverpool	1-2	1-3	2-2	2-1	2-0	4-0	0-2	1-0	0-0	6-1
Manchester C	4-2	3-1	5-1	4-1	2-0	3-3	2-1	0-2	2-2	1-1
Manchester U	2-1	0-1	1-0	2-0	2-1	3-0	1-2	3-0	3-0	4-0
Portsmouth	1-4	1-2	1-2	0-0	2-3	2-0	0-5	0-1	0-1	3-2
Stoke C	1-3	0-0	0-1	3-0	1-2	2-0	1-2	0-0	3-2	2-0
Sunderland	1-0	0-2	3-1	2-1	4-0	2-1	1-3	1-1	0-0	4-1
Tottenham H	2-1	0-0	2-1	3-1	1-0	5-0	2-1	2-1	2-0	0-0
West Ham U	2-2	2-1	2-0	0-0	1-2	5-3	1-1	1-2	2-2	3-0
Wigan Ath	3-2	1-2	2-3	1-1	0-0	1-0	3-1	0-1	1-1	2-2
Wolverhampton W	1-4	1-1	0-1	1-1	2-1	2-0	0-2	0-0	2-1	1-1

2009–2010 RESULTS

	Liverpool	Manchester C	Manchester U	Portsmouth	Stoke C	Sunderland	Tottenham H	West Ham U	Wigan Ath	Wolverhampton W
	1-0	0-0	1-3	4-1	2-0	2-0	3-0	2-0	4-0	1-0
	0-1	1-1	1-1	2-0	1-0	1-1	1-1	0-0	0-2	2-2
	1-1	0-0	1-1	1-0	0-0	2-1	1-1	1-0	1-0	2-1
	0-0	0-2	0-0	3-1	0-0	2-2	0-2	0-0	2-1	3-1
	2-3	3-3	0-4	2-2	1-1	0-1	2-2	3-1	4-0	1-0
	0-4	1-6	1-0	1-2	1-1	3-1	4-2	2-1	1-3	1-2
	2-0	2-4	1-0	2-1	7-0	7-2	3-0	4-1	8-0	4-0
	0-2	2-0	3-1	1-0	1-1	2-0	2-2	2-2	2-1	1-1
	3-1	1-2	3-0	1-0	0-1	1-0	0-0	3-2	2-1	0-0
	0-0	2-1	1-3	0-0	2-1	0-1	1-5	3-3	2-1	2-2
	—	2-2	2-0	4-1	4-0	3-0	2-0	3-0	2-1	2-0
	0-0	—	0-1	2-0	2-0	4-3	0-1	3-1	3-0	1-0
	2-1	4-3	—	5-0	4-0	2-2	3-1	3-0	5-0	3-0
	2-0	0-1	1-4	—	1-2	1-1	1-2	1-1	4-0	3-1
	1-1	1-1	0-2	1-0	—	1-0	1-2	2-1	2-2	2-2
	1-0	1-1	0-1	1-1	0-0	—	3-1	2-2	1-1	5-2
	2-1	3-0	1-3	2-0	0-1	2-0	—	2-0	9-1	0-1
	2-3	1-1	0-4	2-0	0-1	1-0	1-2	—	3-2	1-3
	1-0	1-1	0-5	0-0	1-1	1-0	0-3	1-0	—	0-1
	0-0	0-3	0-1	0-1	0-0	2-1	1-0	0-2	0-2	—

COCA-COLA CHAMPIONSHIP

HOME TEAM	Barnsley	Blackpool	Bristol C	Cardiff C	Coventry C	Crystal Palace	Derby Co	Doncaster R	Ipswich T	Leicester C
Barnsley	—	1-0	2-3	1-0	0-2	0-0	0-0	0-1	2-1	1-0
Blackpool	1-2	—	1-1	1-1	3-0	2-2	0-0	2-0	1-0	1-2
Bristol C	5-3	2-0	—	0-6	1-1	1-0	2-1	2-5	0-0	1-1
Cardiff C	0-2	1-1	3-0	—	2-0	1-1	6-1	2-1	1-2	2-1
Coventry C	3-1	1-1	1-1	1-2	—	1-1	0-1	1-0	2-1	1-1
Crystal Palace	1-1	4-1	0-1	1-2	0-1	—	1-0	0-3	3-1	0-1
Derby Co	2-3	0-2	1-0	2-0	2-1	1-1	—	0-2	1-3	1-0
Doncaster R	0-1	3-3	1-0	2-0	0-0	1-1	2-1	—	3-3	0-1
Ipswich T	1-0	3-1	0-0	2-0	3-2	1-3	1-0	1-1	—	0-0
Leicester C	1-0	2-1	1-3	1-0	2-2	2-0	0-0	0-0	1-1	—
Middlesbrough	2-1	0-3	0-0	0-1	1-1	1-1	2-0	2-0	3-1	0-1
Newcastle U	6-1	4-1	0-0	5-1	4-1	2-0	0-0	2-1	2-2	1-0
Nottingham F	1-0	0-1	1-1	0-0	2-0	2-0	3-2	4-1	3-0	5-1
Peterborough U	1-2	0-1	0-1	4-4	0-1	1-1	0-3	1-2	3-1	1-2
Plymouth Arg	0-0	0-2	3-2	1-3	0-1	0-1	1-0	2-1	1-1	1-1
Preston NE	1-4	0-0	2-2	3-0	3-2	1-1	0-0	1-1	2-0	0-1
QPR	5-2	1-1	2-1	0-1	2-2	1-1	1-1	2-1	1-2	1-2
Reading	1-0	2-1	2-0	0-1	3-0	2-4	4-1	0-0	1-1	0-1
Scunthorpe U	2-1	2-4	3-0	1-1	1-0	1-2	3-2	2-2	1-1	1-1
Sheffield U	0-0	3-0	2-0	3-4	1-0	2-0	1-1	1-1	3-3	1-1
Sheffield W	2-2	2-0	0-1	3-1	2-0	2-2	0-0	0-2	0-1	2-0
Swansea C	3-1	0-0	0-0	3-2	0-0	0-0	1-0	0-0	0-0	1-0
Watford	1-0	2-2	2-0	0-4	2-3	1-3	0-1	1-1	2-1	3-3
WBA	1-1	3-2	4-1	0-2	1-0	0-1	3-1	3-1	2-0	3-0

2009–2010 RESULTS

Middlesbrough	Newcastle U	Nottingham F	Peterborough U	Plymouth Arg	Preston NE	QPR	Reading	Scunthorpe U	Sheffield U	Sheffield W	Swansea C	Watford	WBA
2-1	2-2	2-1	2-2	1-3	0-3	0-1	1-3	1-1	2-2	1-2	0-0	1-0	3-1
2-0	2-1	3-1	2-0	2-0	1-1	2-2	2-0	4-1	3-0	1-2	5-1	3-2	2-3
2-1	2-2	1-1	1-1	3-1	4-2	1-0	1-1	1-1	2-3	1-1	1-0	2-2	2-1
1-0	0-1	1-1	2-0	0-1	1-0	0-2	0-0	4-0	1-1	3-2	2-1	3-1	1-1
2-2	0-2	1-0	3-2	1-1	1-1	1-0	1-3	2-1	3-2	1-1	0-1	0-4	0-0
1-0	0-2	1-1	2-0	1-1	3-1	0-2	1-3	0-4	1-0	0-0	0-1	3-0	1-1
2-2	3-0	1-0	2-1	2-1	5-3	2-4	2-1	1-4	0-1	3-0	0-1	2-0	2-2
1-4	0-1	1-0	3-1	1-2	1-1	2-0	1-2	4-3	1-1	1-0	0-0	2-1	2-3
1-1	0-4	1-1	0-0	0-2	1-1	3-0	2-1	1-0	0-3	0-0	1-1	1-1	1-1
2-0	0-0	3-0	1-1	1-0	1-2	4-0	1-2	5-1	2-1	3-0	2-1	4-1	1-2
—	2-2	1-1	1-0	0-1	2-0	2-0	1-1	3-0	0-0	1-0	1-1	0-1	0-5
2-0	—	2-0	3-1	3-1	3-0	1-1	3-0	3-0	2-1	1-0	3-0	2-0	2-2
1-0	1-0	—	1-0	3-0	3-0	5-0	2-1	2-0	1-0	2-1	1-0	2-4	0-1
2-2	2-3	1-2	—	1-2	0-1	1-0	3-2	3-0	1-0	1-1	2-2	2-1	2-3
0-2	0-2	0-1	1-2	—	1-1	1-1	4-1	2-1	0-1	1-3	1-1	0-1	0-1
2-2	0-1	3-2	2-0	2-0	—	2-2	1-2	3-2	2-1	2-2	2-0	1-1	0-0
1-5	0-1	1-1	1-1	2-0	4-0	—	4-1	0-1	1-1	1-1	1-1	1-0	3-1
0-2	1-2	0-0	6-0	2-1	4-1	1-0	—	1-1	1-3	5-0	1-1	1-1	1-1
0-2	2-1	2-2	4-0	2-1	3-1	0-1	2-2	—	3-1	2-0	0-2	2-2	1-3
1-0	0-1	0-0	1-0	4-3	1-0	1-1	3-0	0-1	—	3-2	2-0	2-0	2-2
1-3	2-2	1-1	2-1	2-1	1-2	1-2	0-2	4-0	1-1	—	0-2	2-1	0-4
0-3	1-1	0-1	1-0	1-0	2-0	2-0	0-0	3-0	2-1	0-0	—	1-1	0-2
1-1	1-2	0-0	0-1	1-0	2-0	3-1	3-0	3-0	3-0	4-1	0-1	—	1-1
2-0	1-1	1-3	2-0	3-1	3-2	2-2	3-1	2-0	3-1	1-0	0-1	5-0	—

COCA-COLA LEAGUE 1

HOME TEAM	Brentford	Brighton & HA	Bristol R	Carlisle U	Charlton Ath	Colchester U	Exeter C	Gillingham	Hartlepool U	Huddersfield T
Brentford	—	0-0	1-3	3-1	1-1	1-0	0-0	4-0	0-0	3-0
Brighton & HA	3-0	—	2-1	1-2	0-2	1-2	2-0	2-0	3-3	0-0
Bristol R	0-0	1-1	—	3-2	2-1	3-2	1-0	2-1	2-0	1-0
Carlisle U	1-3	0-2	3-1	—	3-1	2-1	0-1	2-0	3-2	1-2
Charlton Ath	2-0	1-2	4-2	1-0	—	1-0	2-1	2-2	2-1	2-1
Colchester U	3-3	0-0	1-0	2-1	3-0	—	2-2	2-1	2-0	1-0
Exeter C	3-0	0-1	1-0	2-3	1-1	2-0	—	1-1	3-1	2-1
Gillingham	0-1	1-1	1-0	0-0	1-1	0-0	3-0	—	0-1	2-0
Hartlepool U	0-0	2-0	1-2	4-1	0-2	3-1	1-1	1-1	—	0-2
Huddersfield T	0-0	7-1	0-0	1-1	1-1	2-1	4-0	2-1	2-1	—
Leeds U	1-1	1-1	2-1	1-1	0-0	2-0	2-1	4-1	3-1	2-2
Leyton O	2-1	1-1	5-0	2-2	1-2	0-1	1-1	3-1	1-3	0-2
Millwall	1-1	1-1	2-0	0-0	4-0	2-1	1-0	4-0	1-0	3-1
Milton Keynes D	0-1	0-0	2-1	3-4	0-1	2-1	1-1	2-0	0-0	2-3
Norwich C	1-0	4-1	5-1	0-2	2-2	1-7	3-1	2-0	2-1	3-0
Oldham Ath	2-3	0-2	2-1	2-0	0-2	2-2	2-0	1-0	0-3	0-1
Southampton	1-1	1-3	2-3	3-2	1-0	0-0	3-1	4-1	3-2	5-0
Southend U	2-2	0-1	2-1	2-2	1-2	1-2	0-0	1-0	3-2	2-2
Stockport Co	0-1	1-1	0-2	1-2	1-2	2-2	1-3	0-0	2-2	0-6
Swindon T	3-2	2-1	0-4	2-0	1-1	1-1	1-1	3-1	0-2	2-1
Tranmere R	1-0	2-1	2-0	0-0	0-4	1-1	3-1	4-2	0-0	0-2
Walsall	2-1	1-2	0-0	2-2	1-1	1-0	3-0	0-0	3-1	2-1
Wycombe W	1-0	2-5	2-1	0-0	1-2	1-1	2-2	3-0	2-0	1-2
Yeovil T	2-0	2-2	0-3	3-1	1-1	0-1	2-1	0-0	4-0	0-1

2009–2010 RESULTS

Leeds U	Leyton O	Millwall	Milton Keynes D	Norwich C	Oldham Ath	Southampton	Southend U	Stockport Co	Swindon T	Tranmere R	Walsall	Wycombe W	Yeovil T
0-0	1-0	2-2	3-3	2-1	1-1	1-1	2-1	2-0	2-3	2-1	1-1	1-1	1-1
0-3	0-0	0-1	0-1	1-2	0-2	2-2	2-3	2-4	0-1	3-0	0-1	1-0	1-0
0-4	1-2	2-0	1-0	0-3	1-0	1-5	4-3	1-0	3-0	0-0	0-1	2-3	1-2
1-3	2-2	1-3	5-0	0-1	1-2	1-1	2-1	0-0	0-1	3-0	1-1	1-0	1-0
1-0	0-1	4-4	5-1	0-1	0-0	1-1	1-0	2-0	2-2	1-1	2-0	3-2	2-0
1-2	1-0	1-2	2-0	0-5	1-0	2-1	2-0	2-0	3-0	1-1	2-1	1-1	2-1
2-0	0-0	1-1	1-2	1-1	1-1	1-1	1-0	0-1	1-1	2-1	2-1	1-1	1-1
3-2	1-1	2-0	2-2	1-1	1-0	2-1	3-0	3-1	5-0	0-1	0-0	3-2	1-0
2-2	1-0	3-0	0-5	0-2	2-1	1-3	3-0	3-0	0-1	1-0	3-0	1-1	1-1
2-2	4-0	1-0	1-0	1-3	2-0	3-1	2-1	0-0	2-2	3-3	4-3	6-0	2-1
—	1-0	0-2	4-1	2-1	2-0	1-0	2-0	2-0	0-3	3-0	1-2	1-1	4-0
1-1	—	1-0	1-2	2-1	1-2	2-2	1-2	2-0	0-0	2-1	2-0	2-0	2-0
2-1	2-1	—	3-2	2-1	2-0	1-1	2-0	5-0	3-2	5-0	2-1	0-2	0-0
0-1	1-0	1-3	—	2-1	0-0	0-3	3-1	4-1	2-1	1-0	1-0	2-3	2-2
1-0	4-0	2-0	1-1	—	2-0	0-2	2-1	2-1	1-0	2-0	0-0	5-2	3-0
0-2	2-0	0-1	2-1	0-1	—	1-3	2-2	0-0	2-2	0-0	1-0	2-2	0-0
1-0	2-1	1-1	3-1	2-2	0-0	—	3-1	2-0	0-1	3-0	5-1	1-0	2-0
0-0	3-0	0-0	2-1	0-3	0-1	1-3	—	2-1	2-2	1-1	3-0	1-1	0-0
2-4	2-1	0-4	1-3	1-3	0-1	1-1	0-2	—	0-1	0-3	1-1	4-3	1-3
3-0	3-2	1-1	0-0	1-1	4-2	1-0	2-1	4-1	—	3-0	1-1	1-1	3-1
1-4	2-1	2-0	0-1	3-1	0-1	2-1	2-0	0-1	1-4	—	2-3	0-3	2-1
1-2	2-2	2-2	2-1	1-2	3-0	1-3	2-2	2-0	1-1	2-1	—	2-1	0-1
0-1	0-1	1-0	0-1	0-1	2-2	0-0	1-1	2-1	2-2	0-1	2-3	—	1-4
1-2	3-3	1-1	1-0	3-3	3-0	0-1	1-0	2-2	0-1	2-0	1-3	4-0	—

COCA-COLA LEAGUE 2

HOME TEAM	Accrington S	Aldershot T	Barnet	Bournemouth	Bradford C	Burton Alb	Bury	Cheltenham T	Chesterfield	Crewe Alex
Accrington S	—	2-1	1-0	0-1	2-0	0-2	2-4	4-0	2-0	5-3
Aldershot T	3-1	—	4-0	2-1	1-0	0-2	2-3	4-1	1-0	1-1
Barnet	1-2	3-0	—	1-1	2-2	1-1	0-0	1-1	3-1	1-2
Bournemouth	2-0	1-0	3-0	—	1-0	1-0	1-2	0-0	1-2	1-0
Bradford C	1-1	2-1	2-1	1-1	—	1-1	0-1	1-1	3-0	2-3
Burton Alb	0-2	6-1	2-0	0-2	1-1	—	0-0	5-6	2-2	1-2
Bury	0-2	1-2	2-0	0-3	2-1	3-0	—	0-1	2-1	3-0
Cheltenham T	1-1	1-2	5-1	0-1	4-5	0-1	5-2	—	0-1	0-4
Chesterfield	1-0	0-1	1-0	2-1	1-1	5-2	1-0	1-0	—	2-3
Crewe Alex	5-1	1-2	2-2	1-2	0-1	2-1	2-3	1-2	0-1	—
Dagenham & R	3-1	2-5	4-1	1-0	2-1	2-1	3-1	0-2	2-1	2-0
Darlington	0-0	1-2	1-2	0-2	0-1	1-0	0-1	1-1	2-3	0-1
Grimsby T	2-2	1-2	2-0	3-2	0-3	1-2	1-1	0-0	2-2	0-4
Hereford U	2-0	2-0	2-1	2-1	2-0	3-4	1-3	1-1	1-0	1-1
Lincoln C	2-1	1-0	1-0	2-1	2-1	0-2	1-0	1-1	2-1	1-1
Macclesfield T	0-0	1-1	1-1	1-2	2-2	1-1	2-0	1-0	2-0	4-1
Morecambe	1-2	1-0	2-1	5-0	0-0	3-2	3-0	1-0	0-1	4-3
Northampton T	4-0	0-3	1-3	2-0	2-2	1-1	1-1	2-1	0-0	2-2
Notts Co	1-2	0-0	2-0	2-2	5-0	1-1	5-0	5-0	1-0	2-0
Port Vale	2-2	1-1	0-2	0-0	2-1	3-1	0-1	1-1	1-2	0-1
Rochdale	1-2	1-0	2-1	0-0	1-3	1-2	3-0	0-1	2-3	2-0
Rotherham U	1-0	0-0	3-0	1-3	1-2	2-2	1-0	0-0	3-1	0-0
Shrewsbury T	0-1	3-1	2-0	1-0	1-2	3-1	1-1	0-0	1-1	2-0
Torquay U	2-1	1-1	0-1	1-2	1-2	2-3	1-1	3-0	2-0	1-1

2009–2010 RESULTS

Dagenham & R	Darlington	Grimsby T	Hereford U	Lincoln C	Macclesfield T	Morecambe	Northampton T	Notts Co	Port Vale	Rochdale	Rotherham U	Shrewsbury T	Torquay U
0-1	2-1	2-3	1-2	1-0	1-1	3-2	0-3	0-3	1-2	2-4	2-1	1-3	4-2
2-3	3-1	1-1	2-2	3-1	0-0	4-1	2-1	1-1	1-1	1-1	3-0	2-0	0-2
2-0	3-0	3-0	0-0	1-2	1-2	2-0	0-0	1-0	0-0	1-0	0-1	2-2	1-1
0-0	2-0	3-1	2-1	3-1	1-1	1-0	0-2	2-1	4-0	0-4	1-0	1-0	2-1
3-3	1-0	0-0	1-0	0-2	1-2	2-0	2-0	0-0	0-0	0-3	2-4	1-3	2-0
0-1	1-2	3-0	3-2	1-0	1-1	5-2	3-2	1-4	1-0	1-0	0-1	1-1	0-2
0-0	1-1	0-1	1-0	2-0	2-1	0-0	2-2	3-3	1-1	1-0	2-1	1-0	0-3
1-1	3-3	2-1	0-1	1-0	1-2	2-0	2-2	1-1	1-1	1-4	1-1	1-2	1-1
2-2	5-2	3-2	1-2	2-1	4-1	1-1	1-0	2-1	0-5	2-0	0-1	0-1	1-0
1-2	3-0	4-2	1-0	0-0	2-1	1-2	3-2	0-1	1-2	2-2	2-3	0-3	1-1
—	2-0	2-0	2-1	3-0	3-1	1-1	0-1	0-3	1-1	1-2	0-1	5-0	5-3
0-2	—	0-2	0-1	1-1	0-1	0-4	1-2	0-5	1-3	0-2	2-0	2-1	1-3
1-1	1-1	—	1-0	2-2	1-1	1-1	1-2	0-1	1-2	0-2	1-2	3-0	0-3
1-1	2-1	0-1	—	2-0	0-2	0-1	0-2	0-2	2-2	2-1	3-0	2-1	1-0
1-1	3-0	0-0	3-1	—	0-0	1-3	1-1	0-3	1-2	1-3	1-2	0-2	0-0
2-2	0-2	0-0	3-1	0-1	—	2-2	0-2	0-4	2-0	0-1	1-3	0-1	2-1
1-0	2-0	1-1	2-2	3-1	2-2	—	2-4	2-1	1-0	3-3	2-0	1-1	2-0
1-0	2-0	0-0	1-3	1-0	0-0	2-0	—	0-1	1-1	1-2	3-1	2-0	0-0
3-0	4-0	1-1	5-0	3-1	1-0	4-1	5-2	—	3-1	1-0	1-0	1-1	2-2
3-1	1-0	4-0	2-0	4-0	0-0	0-2	1-3	2-1	—	1-1	1-2	1-1	2-2
3-1	0-1	4-1	4-1	1-1	3-0	4-1	1-0	2-1	0-0	—	4-0	4-0	2-1
2-0	1-2	2-1	1-1	2-0	3-1	0-0	1-0	0-0	1-2	2-1	—	1-1	1-1
2-1	0-2	0-0	3-1	1-0	2-2	2-3	3-0	0-1	0-1	0-1	2-0	—	1-1
0-0	5-0	0-2	1-0	2-3	1-0	2-2	1-0	0-0	1-2	5-0	0-2	2-1	—

ACCRINGTON STANLEY   FL CHAMPIONSHIP 2

Player	Ht	Wt	Birthplace	D.O.B.	Source
Burton Alan (M)	6 0	11 00	Blackpool	22 2 91	Scholar
Dunbavin Ian (G)	6 2	10 10	Knowsley	27 5 80	Scarborough
Edwards Phil (D)	5 8	11 03	Kirkby	8 11 85	Wigan Ath
Grant Robert (M)	5 11	12 00	Blackpool	27 3 87	Scholar
Joyce Luke (M)	5 11	12 03	Bolton	9 7 87	Carlisle U
Kempson Darran (D)	6 2	13 00	Blackpool	6 12 84	Shrewsbury T
McConville Sean (F)	5 11	11 09	Burscough	6 3 89	Skelmersdale U
Miles John (F)	5 10	10 08	Fazackerley	28 9 81	Macclesfield T
Proctor Andy (M)	6 0	12 04	Lancashire	13 3 83	Gt Harwood T
Richardson Leam (D)	5 8	11 04	Blackpool	19 11 79	Leeds
Ryan James (M)	5 8	11 08	Maghull	6 9 88	Liverpool
Symes Michael (F)	6 3	12 04	Gt Yarmouth	31 10 83	Shrewsbury T
Turner Chris (F)	5 10	11 10	Manchester	12 8 87	Scholar
Winnard Dean (D)	5 9	10 04	Wigan	20 8 89	Blackburn R

League Appearances: Black, A. (1); Bouzanis, D. 12(2); Dunbavin, I. 27; Edwards, P. 46; Flynn, J. 6(2); Grant, R. 41(1); Joyce, L. 36(5); Kee, B. 15(22); Kempson, D. 40; King, C. 1; King, G. 3(5); Lees, T. 39; Martin, A. 7; McCarten, J. 1; McConville, S. 14(14); Miles, J. 32(4); Mullin, J. 1(2); Mullin, P. 4; Murphy, P. 5(5); Procter, A. 44; Richardson, L. 2; Ryan, J. 36(3); Symes, M. 39(2); Turner, C. 11(13); Winnard, D. 44.

Goals – League (62): Grant 14, Symes 13 (1 pen), Kee 9, Edwards 8 (5 pens), Procter 5, Miles 3, Ryan 3, Turner 2, Joyce 1, Kempson 1, King G 1, McConville 1, own goal 1.

Carling Cup (3): Grant 1, Mullin 1, Symes 1.

FA Cup (7): Symes 3, Grant 2, Miles 1, Ryan 1.

J Paint Trophy (7): Symes 2, Edwards 1, Grant 1, King G 1, Winnard 1, own goal 1.

Ground: The Fraser Eagle Stadium, Livingstone Road, Accrington, Lancashire BB5 5BX. Telephone: (0871) 434 1968.

Record Attendance: 4368 v Colchester U, FA Cup 1st rd, 3 January 2004.

Capacity: 5,057.

Manager: John Coleman.

Secretary: Hannah Bailey.

Most League Goals: 96, Division 3 (N) 1954–55.

Highest League Scorer in Season: George Stewart, 35, 1955–56 Division 3(N); George Hudson, 35, 1960–61, Division 4.

Most League Goals in Total Aggregate: George Stewart 136, 1954–58.

Most Capped Player: Romuald Boco, 19 (39), Benin.

Most League Appearances: Jim Armstrong, 260, 1927–34.

Colours: All red.

ALDERSHOT TOWN   FL CHAMPIONSHIP 2

Brown Aaron (D)	6 4	14 07	Birmingham	23 6 83	Truro C
Charles Anthony (D)	6 0	12 00	Isleworth	11 3 81	Barnet
Donnelly Scott (M)	5 8	11 10	Hammersmith	25 12 87	QPR
Halls John (M)	6 0	11 11	Islington	14 2 82	Brentford
Harding Ben (M)	5 10	11 02	Carshalton	6 9 84	Milton Keynes D
Herd Ben (D)	5 9	10 12	Welwyn	21 6 85	Shrewsbury T
Hudson Kirk (F)	6 0	10 10	Rochford	12 12 86	Bournemouth
Hylton Danny (F)	6 0	11 03	London	25 2 89	Youth
Morgan Marvin (F)	6 4	12 08	Manchester	18 4 83	Woking
Sandell Andy (M)	5 11	11 09	Calne	8 9 83	Salisbury C
Soares Louis (M)	5 11	11 05	Reading	8 1 85	Barnet
Straker Anthony (D)	5 9	11 11	Ealing	23 9 88	Crystal Palace

| Winfield Dave (D) | 6 3 | 13 08 | Aldershot | 24 | 3 88 | Youth |
| Young Jamie (G) | 5 11 | 13 00 | Brisbane | 25 | 8 85 | Wycombe W |

League Appearances: Blackburn, C. 36(6); Bozanic, O. 19(6); Brown, A. 12; Chalmers, L. 19(4); Charles, A. 32(1); Connolly, R. (3); Donnelly, S. 42(1); German, A. 2(1); Grant, J. 5(12); Halls, J. 10(6); Harding, B. 28(5); Henderson, S. 8; Herd, B. 33(1); Hinshelwood, A. 13(2); Hopkinson, B. (1); Howell, D. (3); Hudson, K. 24(10); Hylton, D. 5(16); Jackson, M. 18(4); Jaimez-Ruiz, M. 30; Masters, C. (1); Morgan, M. 36(4); Morgan, D. 8(1); Parrett, D. 4; Riza, O. (1); Sandell, A. 29; Soares, L. 28(8); Spencer, D. 3(9); Straker, A. 35(2); Winfield, D. 19(6); Young, J. 8(1).
Goals – League (69): Morgan M 15 (1 pen), Donnelly 13 (5 pens), Soares 7, Sandell 5 (1 pen), Charles 4, Hudson 4, Morgan D 4, Grant 3, Hylton 3, Bozanic 2, Straker 2, Winfield 2, Brown 1, Harding 1, Howell 1, Jackson 1, own goal 1.
Carling Cup (1): Morgan M 1 (pen).
FA Cup (3): Bozanic 1, Donnelly 1, Soares 1.
J Paint Trophy (2): Hudson 1, Soares 1.
Play-Offs (0).
Ground: The EBB Stadium at the Recreation Ground, High Street, Aldershot GU11 1TW. Telephone: 01252 320211.
Record Attendance: 19,138 v Carlisle U, FA Cup 4th rd (replay) 28 January 1970.
Capacity: 7,100.
Manager: Kevin Dillon.
Secretary: Bob Green.
Most League Goals: 83, Division 4, 1963–64.
Highest League Scorer in Season: John Dungworth, 26, Division 4, 1978–79.
Most League Goals in Total Aggregate: Jack Howarth, 171, 1965–71 and 1972–77.
Most Capped Player: Louie Soares, 3, Barbados.
Most League Appearances: Murray Brodie, 461, 1970–83.
Honours – Blue Square Premier League: Champions 2007–08. **Setanta Shield:** Winners 2008.
Colours: All red shirts with blue sleeves, red shorts with blue and white trim, red stockings with blue and red trim.

ARSENAL   FA PREMIERSHIP

Afobe Benik (F)			Leyton	12	2 93	Scholar
Almunia Manuel (G)	6 3	13 00	Pamplona	19	5 77	Celta Vigo
Arshavin Andrei (F)	5 8	9 11	St Petersburg	29	5 81	Zenit
Barazite Nacer (M)	6 2	13 01	Arnhem	27	5 90	Scholar
Bartley Kyle (D)	5 11	11 00	Manchester	22	5 91	Scholar
Bendtner Nicklas (F)	6 2	13 00	Copenhagen	16	1 88	Scholar
Bothelo Pedro (D)	6 2	12 00	Salvador	14	12 89	Salamanca
Clichy Gael (D)	5 9	10 04	Toulouse	26	7 85	Cannes
Coquelin Francis (M)	5 10	11 08	Laval	13	5 91	Laval
Cruise Thomas (D)	6 1	12 08	London	9	3 91	Scholar
Denilson (M)	5 10	11 00	Sao Paulo	16	2 88	Sao Paulo
Diaby Vassirki (M)	6 2	12 04	Paris	11	5 86	Auxerre
Djourou Johan (D)	6 3	13 01	Ivory Coast	18	1 87	Scholar
Eastmond Craig (D)	5 8	11 11	Wandsworth	9	12 90	Scholar
Eboue Emmanuel (D)	5 10	10 03	Abidjan	4	6 83	Beveren
Eduardo (F)	5 10	10 03	Rio de Janeiro	25	2 83	Dinamo Zagreb
Emmanuel-Thomas Jay (M)	5 9	11 05	Forest Gate	27	12 90	Scholar
Evina Cedric (D)			Cameroon	16	11 91	Scholar
Fabianski Lukasz (G)	6 3	13 01	Costrzyn nad Odra	18	4 85	Legia
Fabregas Francesc (M)	5 11	11 01	Vilessoc de Mar	4	5 87	Barcelona
Freeman Luke (F)	6 1	10 00	London	22	3 92	Gillingham

Name	Ht	Wt	Birthplace	Birthdate	Source club
Frimpong Emanuel (M)	5 11	10 07	Ghana	10 1 92	Scholar
Gibbs Kieran (M)	5 10	10 02	Lambeth	26 9 89	Scholar
Henderson Conor (M)	6 1	11 13	Sidcup	8 9 91	Scholar
Hoyte Gavin (D)			Waltham Forest	6 6 90	Scholar
Lansbury Henri (M)	6 0	13 04	Enfield	12 10 90	Scholar
Mannone Vito (G)	6 0	11 08	Desio	2 3 88	Atalanta
McDermott Sean (G)			Kristiansand	30 5 93	Scholar
Miquel Ignasi (D)			Barcelona	28 9 92	Scholar
Murphy Rhys (F)	6 1	11 13	Shoreham	6 11 90	Scholar
Nasri Samir (M)	5 9	11 11	Marseille	26 6 87	Marseille
Nordtveit Havard (D)			Vats	21 6 90	Vats 94
Ozyakup Oguzhan (M)			Zaandam	23 9 92	AZ
Perez Fran Merida (M)	5 11	13 00	Barcelona	4 3 90	Scholar
Ramsey Aaron (M)	5 9	10 07	Caerphilly	26 12 90	Cardiff C
Randall Mark (M)	6 0	12 12	Milton Keynes	28 9 89	Scholar
Rosicky Tomas (M)	5 11	11 06	Prague	4 10 80	Borussia Dortmund
Sagna Bakari (D)	5 10	11 05	Sens	14 2 83	Auxerre
Simpson Jay (M)	5 11	13 04	London	1 12 88	Scholar
Song Bilong Alexandre (M)	6 4	12 07	Douala	9 9 87	Bastia
Sunu Gilles (F)	5 11	11 00	Chateauroux	30 3 91	Scholar
Szczesny Wojciech (F)	5 10	11 11	Warsaw	18 4 90	Scholar
Traore Armand (D)	6 1	12 12	Paris	8 10 89	Monaco
Van Persie Robin (F)	6 0	11 00	Rotterdam	6 8 83	Feyenoord
Vela Carlos (F)	5 9	10 05	Mexico	1 3 89	Celta Vigo
Vermaelen Thomas (D)	6 0	11 11	Kapellen	14 11 85	Ajax
Walcott Theo (F)	5 9	11 01	Compton	16 3 89	Southampton
Watt Sanchez (M)	5 11	12 00	London	14 2 91	Scholar
Wilshere Jack (M)	5 7	11 03	Stevenage	1 1 92	Scholar

League Appearances: Almunia, M. 29; Arshavin, A. 25(5); Bendtner, N. 13(10); Campbell, S. 10(1); Clichy, G. 23(1); Denilson, 19(1); Diaby, V. 26(3); Djourou, J. (1); Eastmond, C. 2(2); Eboue, E. 17(8); Eduardo, 13(11); Fabianski, L. 4; Fabregas, F. 26(1); Gallas, W. 26; Gibbs, K. 3; Lansbury, H. (1); Mannone, V. 5; Merida Perez, F. (4); Nasri, S. 22(4); Ramsey, A. 7(11); Rosicky, T. 14(11); Sagna, B. 31(4); Silvestre, M. 9(3); Song Billong, A. 25(1); Traore, A. 9; Van Persie, R. 14(2); Vela, C. 1(10); Vermaelen, T. 33; Walcott, T. 12(11); Wilshere, J. (1).

Goals – League (83): Fabregas 15 (3 pens), Arshavin 10, Van Persie 9, Vermaelen 7, Bendtner 6, Diaby 6, Denilson 3, Gallas 3, Ramsey 3, Rosicky 3, Walcott 3, Eduardo 2, Nasri 2, Eboue 2, Merida Perez 1, Silvestre 1, Song Billong 1, Vela 1, own goals 6.

Carling Cup (4): Bendtner 1, Merida 1, Vela 1, Watt 1.

FA Cup (3): Denilson 1, Eduardo 1, Ramsey 1.

Champions League (26): Bendtner 5 (1 pen), Fabregas 4 (1 pen), Nasri 3, Arshavin 2, Eboue 2, Eduardo 2 (1 pen), Campbell 1, Denilson 1, Diaby 1, Gallas 1, Van Persie 1, Vermaelen 1, Walcott 1, own goal 1.

Ground: Emirates Stadium, Highbury House, 75 Drayton Park, Islington, London N5 1BU. Telephone (0207) 619 5003.

Record Attendance: 73,295 v Sunderland, Div 1, 9 March 1935 (at Highbury); 60,161 v Manchester U, FA Premier League, 3 November 2007. **Capacity:** 60,361.

Manager: Arsène Wenger.

Secretary: David Miles.

Most League Goals: 127, Division 1, 1930–31.

Highest League Scorer in Season: Ted Drake, 42, 1934–35.

Most League Goals in Total Aggregate: Thierry Henry, 174, 1999–2007.

Most Capped Player: Thierry Henry, 81 (123), France.

Most League Appearances: David O'Leary, 558, 1975–93.

Honours – FA Premier League: Champions – 1997–98, 2001–02, 2003–04. **Football League:** Division 1 Champions – 1930–31, 1932–33, 1933–34, 1934–35, 1937–38, 1947–

48, 1952–53, 1970–71, 1988–89, 1990–91. **FA Cup:** Winners – 1929–30, 1935–36, 1949–50, 1970–71, 1978–79, 1992–93, 1997–98, 2001–02, 2002–03, 2004–05. **Football League Cup:** Winners – 1986–87, 1992–93. **European Competitions: European Cup-Winners' Cup:** Winners – 1993–94. **Fairs Cup:** Winners – 1969–70.
Colours: Red shirts with white trim, white shorts, white stockings with red tops.

ASTON VILLA   FA PREMIERSHIP

Name			Birthplace			Club
Agbonlahor Gabriel (F)	5 11	12 05	Birmingham	13 10 86		Scholar
Albrighton Marc (M)	6 2	12 06	Sutton Coldfield	18 11 89		Scholar
Baker Nathan (D)	6 2	11 11	Worcester	23 4 91		Scholar
Beye Habib (D)	6 0	12 06	Paris	19 10 77		Newcastle U
Carew John (F)	6 5	15 00	Lorenskog	5 9 79		Lyon
Clark Ciaran (D)	6 2	12 00	Harrow	26 9 89		Scholar
Collins James M (D)	6 2	14 05	Newport	23 8 83		West Ham U
Collins James S (F)			Coventry	1 12 90		Scholar
Cuellar Carlos (D)	6 3	13 03	Madrid	23 8 81		Rangers
Davies Curtis (D)	6 2	11 13	Waltham Forest	15 3 85		WBA
Delfouneso Nathan (F)	6 1	12 04	Birmingham	2 2 91		Scholar
Delph Fabian (D)	5 8	11 00	Bradford	5 5 91		Leeds U
Devine Daniel (M)			Dublin	8 5 93		Scholar
Downing Stewart (M)	5 11	10 04	Middlesbrough	22 7 84		Middlesbrough
Dunne Richard (D)	6 2	15 10	Dublin	21 9 79		Manchester C
Forrester Harry (M)				2 1 91		Scholar
Friedel Brad (G)	6 3	14 00	Lakewood	18 5 71		Blackburn R
Gardner Gary (M)			Solihull	29 6 92		Scholar
Guzan Brad (G)	6 4	14 11	Home Glen	9 9 84		Chivas USA
Halfhuid Arsenio			Voorburg	9 11 91		Excelsior
Herd Chris (M)	5 9	11 04	Melbourne	4 4 89		Scholar
Heskey Emile (F)	6 2	13 12	Leicester	11 1 78		Wigan Ath
Hogg Jonathan (M)	5 7	10 05	Middlesbrough	6 12 88		Scholar
Lichaj Eric (M)	5 11	12 07	Denwers Grove	17 11 88		Chicago Magic
Lowry Shane (D)	6 1	13 01	Perth	12 6 89		Scholar
Milner James (M)	5 9	11 00	Leeds	4 1 86		Newcastle U
O'Halloran Stephen (D)	6 0	11 07	Cork	29 11 87		Scholar
Osbourne Isaiah (M)	6 2	12 07	Birmingham	5 11 87		Scholar
Parish Elliot (G)			Northampton	20 5 90		Scholar
Petrov Stilian (M)	5 11	13 05	Montana	5 7 79		Celtic
Reo-Coker Nigel (M)	5 8	12 03	Southwark	14 5 84		West Ham U
Salifou Moustapha (M)	5 11	10 12	Lome	1 6 83		FC Wil
Shorey Nicky (D)	5 9	10 08	Romford	19 2 81		Reading
Sidwell Steve (M)	5 10	11 00	Wandsworth	14 12 82		Chelsea
Siegrist Benjamin (G)			Basle	31 1 92		Scholar
Warnock Stephen (D)	5 7	11 09	Ormskirk	12 12 81		Blackburn R
Weimann Andreas (F)	6 2	11 13	Vienna	5 8 91		Scholar
Williams Derrick (D)			Germany	17 1 93		Scholar
Young Ashley (F)	5 6	9 06	Stevenage	9 7 85		Watford
Young Luke (D)	6 0	12 04	Harlow	19 7 79		Middlesbrough

League Appearances: Agbonlahor, G. 35(1); Albrighton, M. (3); Beye, H. 5(1); Carew, J. 22(11); Clark, C. 1; Collins, James M 26(1); Cuellar, C. 36; Davies, C. 2; Delfouneso, N. (9); Delph, F. 4(4); Downing, S. 23(2); Dunne, R. 35; Friedel, B. 38; Gardner, C. (1); Heskey, E. 16(15); Milner, J. 36; Petrov, S. 37; Reo-Coker, N. 6(4); Shorey, N. 3; Sidwell, S. 12(13); Warnock, S. 30; Young, A. 37; Young, L. 14(2).
Goals – League (52): Agbonlahor 13, Carew 10 (1 pen), Milner 7 (3 pens), Young A 5 (1 pen), Dunne 3, Heskey 3, Cuellar 2, Downing 2, Collins, James M 1, Davies 1, Delfouneso 1, own goals 4.

Carling Cup (13): Milner 4 (2 pens), Agbonlahor 2, Heskey 2, Young A 2, Downing 1, Warnock 1, own goal 1.
FA Cup (15): Carew 6 (4 pens), Delfouneso 2, Young A 2, Agbonlahor 1, Collins, James M 1, Cuellar 1, Delph 1, Petrov 1.
Europa League (2): Carew 1, Milner 1 (pen).
Ground: Villa Park, Trinity Road, Birmingham B6 6HE. Telephone (0121) 327 2299.
Record Attendance: 76,588 v Derby Co, FA Cup 6th rd, 2 March 1946.
Capacity: 42,582.
Manager: Martin O'Neill.
Secretary: Sharon Barnhurst.
Most League Goals: 128, Division 1, 1930–31.
Highest League Scorer in Season: 'Pongo' Waring, 49, Division 1, 1930–31.
Most League Goals in Total Aggregate: Harry Hampton, 215, 1904–15.
Most Capped Player: Steve Staunton 64 (102), Republic of Ireland.
Most League Appearances: Charlie Aitken, 561, 1961–76.
Honours – Football League: Division 1 Champions – 1893–94, 1895–96, 1896–97, 1898–99, 1899–1900, 1909–10, 1980–81. Division 2 Champions – 1937–38, 1959–60. Division 3 Champions – 1971–72. **FA Cup:** Winners – 1887, 1895, 1897, 1905, 1913, 1920, 1957. **Football League Cup:** Winners – 1961, 1975, 1977, 1994, 1996. **European Competitions: European Cup:** Winners – 1981–82. **European Super Cup:** Winners – 1982–83. **Intertoto Cup:** Winners – 2001, 2008.
Colours: Claret body, blue sleeve shirts, white shorts, sky blue stockings.

BARNET   FL CHAMPIONSHIP 2

Adomah Albert (F)	6 1	11 08	Harrow	13 12 87	Harrow Borough
Cole Jake (G)	6 2	13 00	Hammersmith	11 9 85	QPR
Devera Joe (D)	6 2	12 00	Southgate	6 2 87	Scholar
Hart Danny (M)	5 10	11 09	London	26 4 89	Boreham Wood
Hughes Mark (M)	5 10	12 05	Dungannon	16 9 83	Chester C
Kamdjo Clovis (D)	5 11	12 02	Cameroon	15 12 90	Reading
Lockhart-Adams Kofi (F)	6 1	12 13	London	9 10 92	Scholar
Vilhete Mauro (M)	5 8	11 09	Rio de Mauro	10 5 93	Scholar

League Appearances: Adomah, A. 37(8); Bolasie, Y. 14(8); Breen, G. 25; Butcher, C. 3; Charles, E. (3); Cole, J. 46; Deen, A. 12(4); Devera, J. 31(2); Deverdics, N. 4(12); Furlong, P. 31(7); Gillet, K. 31(6); Hart, D. (1); Hughes, M. 40(1); Hyde, J. 17(17); Hyde, M. 41; James, C. (2); Jarrett, A. 33(12); Kamdjo, C. 14(1); Leach, D. 12(1); Livermore, D. 11(3); Lockhart-Adams, K. (1); Lockwood, M. 19; McAllister, C. 4(1); Medley, L. (1); O'Flynn, J. 31(5); O'Neill, R. 11(4); Sawyer, L. 4(3); Sinclair, D. 2(1); Tabiri, J. 2(3); Upson, E. 5(4); Vilhete, N. 1(1); Wright, B. (3); Yakubu, I. 25.
Goals – League (47): O'Flynn 12 (3 pens), Hyde J 6 (1 pen), Adomah 5, Furlong 5, Bolasie 2, Hughes 2, Jarrett 2 (1 pen), Lockwood 2 (1 pen), Yakubu 2, Deen 1, Deverdics 1, Hyde M 1, Livermore 1, Sawyer 1, Sinclair 1, Upson 1, own goals 2.
Carling Cup (0).
FA Cup (5): O'Flynn 3 (1 pen), Hyde M 1, Yakubu 1.
J Paint Trophy (3): Hyde J 1, O'Flynn 1, Yakubu 1.
Ground: Underhill Stadium, Barnet Lane, Barnet, Herts EN5 2DN. Telephone 0208 441 6932.
Record Attendance: 11,026 v Wycombe Wanderers, FA Amateur Cup 4th Round 1951–52. **Capacity:** 5,345.
Manager: Mark Stimson.
Secretary: Andrew Adie.
Most League Goals: 81, Division 4, 1991–92
Highest League Scorer in Season: Dougie Freedman, 24, Division 3, 1994–95.
Most League Goals in Total Aggregate: Sean Devine, 47, 1995–99.
Most Capped Player: Ken Charlery, 4, St. Lucia.

Most League Appearances: Paul Wilson, 263, 1991–2000.
Honours – Football League: GMVC: Winners – 1990–91. **Football Conference:** Winners – 2004–05. **FA Amateur Cup:** Winners 1945–46.
Colours: All black with amber trim.

BARNSLEY   FL CHAMPIONSHIP

Adam Jamil (M)	5 10	10 00	Bolton	5	6 91	Scholar
Butterfield Jacob (D)	5 10	11 00	Manchester	10	6 90	Scholar
Colace Roberto (M)	5 10	11 07	Buenos Aires	6	1 84	Newells Old Boys
Devaney Martin (M)	5 11	12 00	Cheltenham	1	6 80	Watford
Doyle Nathan (M)	5 11	11 13	Derby	12	1 87	Hull C
Foster Stephen (D)	6 0	11 05	Warrington	10	9 80	Burnley
Gray Andy (F)	6 1	13 00	Harrogate	15 11	77	Charlton Ath
Hammill Adam (M)	5 11	11 07	Liverpool	25	1 88	Liverpool
Hassell Bobby (D)	5 10	12 00	Derby	4	6 80	Mansfield T
Hume Iain (F)	5 7	11 02	Brampton	31 10	83	Leicester C
Potter Luke (D)	6 2	12 07	Barnsley	13	7 89	Scholar
Preece David (G)	6 2	11 11	Sunderland	28	8 76	Odense
Steele Luke (G)	6 2	12 00	Peterborough	24	9 84	WBA
Thompson O'Neil (D)	6 4	13 00	Kingston	11	8 80	Notodden

League Appearances: Adam, J. (2); Anderson, 25(6); Bialkowski, B. 2; Bogdanovic, D. 20(9); Butterfield, J. 10(10); Campbell-Ryce, J. 8(5); Colace, R. 41; Devaney, M. 6(5); Dickinson, C. 27(1); Doyle, N. 32(2); El Haimour, M. 2; Foster, S. 42; Gray, A. 19(11); Gray, J. 1(4); Hallfredsson, E. 22(5); Hammill, A. 31(8); Hassell, B. 22(2); Hume, I. 17(18); Kozluk, R. 12(2); Macken, J. 27(4); Moore, D. 33(2); Noble-Lazarus, R. (2); Odejayi, K. 2(3); Potter, L. 12(2); Preece, D. 5(1); Rodriguez, J. 1(5); Shotton, R. 30; Sodje, O. (1); Steele, L. 39; Taylor, A. (1); Teixeira, F. 14; Thompson, O. 1; Trippier, K. 3.
Goals – League (53): Bogdanovic 11 (1 pen), Colace 7, Gray A 6 (1 pen), Hume 5 (1 pen), Hammill 4, Macken 4, Anderson 3, Hallfredsson 3, Foster 2, Butterfield 1, Dickinson 1, Hassell 1, Moore 1, Rodriguez 1, own goals 3.
Carling Cup (6): Bogdanovic 3 (1 pen), Anderson 1, Colace 1, Macken 1.
FA Cup (0).
Ground: Oakwell Stadium, Grove St, Barnsley, South Yorkshire S71 1ET. Telephone (01226) 211 211.
Record Attendance: 40,255 v Stoke C, FA Cup 5th rd, 15 February 1936. **Capacity:** 23,186.
Manager: Mark Robins.
Secretary: Albert Donald Rowing.
Most League Goals: 118, Division 3 (N), 1933–34.
Highest League Scorer in Season: Cecil McCormack, 33, Division 2, 1950–51.
Most League Goals in Total Aggregate: Ernest Hine, 123, 1921–26 and 1934–38.
Most Capped Player: Gerry Taggart, 35 (50), Northern Ireland.
Most League Appearances: Barry Murphy, 514, 1962–78.
Honours – Football League: Division 3 (N) Champions – 1933–34, 1938–39, 1954–55.
FA Cup: Winners – 1912.
Colours: Red shirts with white trim, white shorts, red stockings.

BIRMINGHAM CITY   FA PREMIERSHIP

Bent Marcus (F)	6 2	13 03	Hammersmith	19	5 78	Charlton Ath
Bowyer Lee (M)	5 9	10 12	Canning Town	3	1 77	West Ham U
Butland Jack (G)	6 4	12 00	Clevedon	10	3 93	Scholar
Carr Stephen (D)	5 9	11 13	Dublin	29	8 76	Newcastle U
Dann Scott (D)	6 2	12 00	Liverpool	14	2 87	Coventry C

Doyle Colin (G)	6 5	14 05	Cork	12 8 85	Scholar
Fahey Keith (M)	5 10	12 07	Dublin	15 1 83	Aston Villa
Ferguson Barry (M)	5 7	9 10	Glasgow	2 2 78	Rangers
Foster Ben (G)	6 2	12 08	Leamington Spa	3 4 83	Manchester U
Gardner Craig (M)	5 10	11 13	Solihull	25 11 86	Aston Villa
Jerome Cameron (F)	6 1	13 06	Huddersfield	14 8 86	Cardiff C
Jervis Jake (F)	6 3	12 13	Birmingham	17 9 91	Scholar
Johnson Roger (D)	6 3	11 00	Ashford	28 4 83	Cardiff C
Larsson Sebastian (M)	5 10	11 00	Eskilstuna	6 6 85	Arsenal
McFadden James (M)	6 0	12 11	Glasgow	14 4 83	Everton
McPike James (F)	5 10	11 02	Birmingham	4 10 88	Scholar
Michel (M)	6 0	11 05	Pola de Lena	9 11 85	Gijon
Murphy David (D)	6 1	12 03	Hartlepool	1 3 84	Hibernian
Mutch Jordon (M)	5 9	10 03	Birmingham	2 12 91	Derby Co
O'Connor Garry (F)	6 1	12 02	Edinburgh	7 5 83	
O'Shea Jay (M)	5 9	12 00	Dunlaoghdrie	10 8 88	Galway U
Parnaby Stuart (M)	5 11	11 00	Durham	19 7 82	Middlesbrough
Phillips Kevin (F)	5 7	11 00	Hitchin	25 7 73	WBA
Ridgewell Liam (D)	5 10	10 03	Bexley	21 7 84	Aston Villa
Sammons Ashley (M)	5 8	11 02	Solihull	10 11 91	Scholar
Shroot Robin (M)	5 9	11 05	London	26 3 88	Harrow Borough

League Appearances: Benitez, C. 21(9); Bowyer, L. 34(1); Carr, S. 35; Carsley, L. 3(4); Dann, S. 30; Fahey, K. 18(16); Ferguson, B. 37; Gardner, C. 10(3); Hart, J. 36; Jerome, C. 32; Johnson, D. (1); Johnson, R. 38; Larsson, S. 26(7); McFadden, J. 32(4); McSheffrey, G. 1(4); Michel, 3(6); O'Connor, G. 5(5); O'Shea, J. (1); Parnaby, S. 6(2); Phillips, K. 2(17); Queudrue, F. 6; Ridgewell, L. 30(1); Tainio, T. 5(1); Taylor, Maik 2; Vignal, G. 6(2).
Goals – League (38): Jerome 11, Bowyer 5, McFadden 5 (2 pens), Larsson 4, Phillips 4, Benitez 3, Ridgewell 3, Gardner 1, O'Connor 1, own goal 1.
Carling Cup (2): Bowyer 1, Carsley 1.
FA Cup (5): Ferguson 2, Benitez 1, Dann 1, Ridgewell 1.
Ground: St Andrews Stadium, Birmingham B9 4RL. Telephone (0844) 557 1875.
Record Attendance: 66,844 v Everton, FA Cup 5th rd, 11 February 1939.
Capacity: 30,079.
Manager: Alex McLeish.
Secretary: Julia Shelton.
Most League Goals: 103, Division 2, 1893–94 (only 28 games).
Highest League Scorer in Season: Joe Bradford, 29, Division 1, 1927–28.
Most League Goals in Total Aggregate: Joe Bradford, 249, 1920–35.
Most Capped Player: Maik Taylor, 50 (83), Northern Ireland.
Most League Appearances: Frank Womack, 491, 1908–28.
Honours – Football League: Division 2 Champions – 1892–93, 1920–21, 1947–48, 1954–55, 1994–95. **Football League Cup:** Winners – 1963. **Leyland Daf Cup:** Winners – 1991.
Auto Windscreens Shield: Winners – 1995.
Colours: Blue shirts with white trim, white shorts, blue stockings.

BLACKBURN ROVERS   FA PREMIERSHIP

Aley Zach (M)				17 8 91	Scholar
Andrews Keith (M)	6 0	12 04	Dublin	13 9 80	Milton Keynes D
Banton Jason (F)					Scholar
Bowen Jordan (M)					Scholar
Brown Jason (G)	5 11	13 03	Southwark	18 5 82	Gillingham
Chimbonda Pascal (D)	5 10	11 05	Les Abymes	21 2 79	Tottenham H
Diouf El Hadji (F)	5 11	11 11	Dakar	15 1 81	Sunderland
Doran Aaron (M)	5 7	12 00	Ireland	13 5 91	Scholar
Dunn David (M)	5 9	12 03	Gt Harwood	27 12 79	Birmingham C

Emerton Brett (M)	6 1	13 05	Bankstown	22 2 79	Feyenoord
Fielding Frank (G)	5 11	12 00	Blackburn	4 4 88	Scholar
Flynn Jonathan (D)	5 8	11 00	Belfast	18 11 89	Ballymena U
Givet Gael (D)	5 11	11 11	Arles	9 10 81	Marseille
Grella Vince (M)	6 0	12 06	Melbourne	5 10 79	Torino
Gunning Gavin (D)	6 0	12 06	Dublin	26 1 91	Scholar
Hanley Grant (D)	6 2	12 00	Dumfries	20 11 91	Scholar
Haworth Andrew (M)	5 11	11 10	Lancaster	28 11 88	Scholar
Hitchcock Tom (F)					Scholar
Hoilett David (M)	5 8	11 00	Ottowa	5 6 90	Scholar
Jacobsen Lars (D)	5 11	12 02	Odense	29 9 79	Everton
Jones Phil (D)	5 11	11 02	Preston	21 2 92	Scholar
Kalinic Nikola (F)	6 2	12 11	Olin	5 1 88	Hajduk Split
Khizanishvili Zurab (D)	6 1	12 08	Tbilisi	6 10 81	Rangers
Linganzi Amine (M)	6 1	10 00	Alger	16 11 89	Saint Etienne
N'Zonzi Steven (M)	6 3	11 11	Paris	15 12 88	Amiens
Nelsen Ryan (D)	5 11	14 02	New Zealand	18 10 77	DC United
Olsson Martin (D)	5 7	11 00	Sweden	17 5 88	Hogaborg
Pedersen Morten (F)	5 11	11 00	Vadso	8 9 81	Tromso
Rigters Maceo (F)	5 10	14 07	Amsterdam	22 1 84	NAC Breda
Roberts Jason (F)	6 1	13 06	Park Royal	25 1 78	Wigan Ath
Robinson Paul (G)	6 1	14 07	Beverley	15 10 79	Tottenham H
Salgado Michel (D)	5 9	11 11	Galicia	22 10 75	Real Madrid
Samba Christopher (D)	6 5	13 03	Creteil	28 3 84	Hertha Berlin
Santa Cruz Julio (F)	6 0	12 04	Asuncion	12 5 90	Cerro Porteno

League Appearances: Andrews, K. 22(10); Basturk, Y. 1; Brown, J. 3(1); Chimbonda, P. 22(2); Di Santo, F. 15(7); Diouf, E. 24(2); Dunn, D. 20(3); Emerton, B. 17(7); Gallagher, P. (1); Givet, G. 33(1); Grella, V. 10(5); Hanley, G. 1; Hoilett, D. 8(15); Jacobsen, L. 11(2); Jones, P. 7(2); Kalinic, N. 14(12); Linganzi, A. 1; McCarthy, B. 7(7); N'Zonzi, S. 33; Nelsen, R. 25(3); Olsson, M. 19(2); Pedersen, M. 27(6); Reid, S. 1(3); Roberts, Jason 15(14); Robinson, P. 35; Salgado, M. 16(5); Samba, C. 30; Warnock, S. 1.
Goals – League (41): Dunn 9 (2 pens), Roberts, Jason 5, Nelsen 4, Samba 4, Diouf 3, Pedersen 3, Givet 2, Kalinic 2, N'Zonzi 2, Andrews 1 (1 pen), Chimbonda 1, Di Santo 1, McCarthy 1, Olsson 1, own goals 2.
Carling Cup (16): Kalinic 4 (1 pen), McCarthy 3 (1 pen), Emerton 2, Pedersen 2, Dunn 1, Hoilett 1, Olsen 1, Reid 1 (pen), Salgado 1.
FA Cup (1): Kalinic 1.
Ground: Ewood Park, Blackburn, Lancashire BB2 4JF. Telephone (0871) 702 1875.
Record Attendance: 62,522 v Bolton W, FA Cup 6th rd, 2 March 1929. **Capacity:** 31,367.
Manager: Sam Allardyce.
Secretary: Andrew Pincher.
Most League Goals: 114, Division 2, 1954–55.
Highest League Scorer in Season: Ted Harper, 43, Division 1, 1925–26.
Most League Goals in Total Aggregate: Simon Garner, 168, 1978–92.
Most Capped Player: Henning Berg, 58 (100), Norway.
Most League Appearances: Derek Fazackerley, 596, 1970–86.
Honours – FA Premier League: Champions – 1994–95. **Football League:** Division 1 Champions – 1911–12, 1913–14. Division 2 Champions – 1938–39. Division 3 Champions – 1974–75. **FA Cup:** Winners – 1884, 1885, 1886, 1890, 1891, 1928. **Football League Cup:** Winners – 2002. **Full Members' Cup:** Winners – 1986–87.
Colours: Blue and white halved shirts, white shorts, blue stockings.

BLACKPOOL   FA PREMIERSHIP

Adam Charlie (M)	6 1	12 00	Dundee	10 12 85	Rangers
Almond Louis (F)			Blackburn	15 8 90	Scholar

Clarke Billy (F)	5 7 10 01	Cork	13 12 87	Ipswich T
Coid Danny (D)	5 11 11 07	Liverpool	3 10 81	Trainee
Crainey Stephen (D)	5 9 10 06	Glasgow	22 6 81	Leeds U
Demontagnac Ishmel (F)	5 10 11 05	London	15 6 88	Walsall
Eardley Neal (M)	5 11 11 10	Llandudno	6 11 88	Oldham Ath
Eastham Ashley (D)	6 3 12 06	Preston	22 3 91	Scholar
Euell Jason (F)	5 11 11 13	Lambeth	6 2 77	Southampton
Evatt Ian (D)	6 3 13 12	Coventry	19 11 81	QPR
Gilks Matthew (G)	6 3 13 12	Rochdale	4 6 82	Norwich C
Halstead Mark (G)	6 3 14 00	Blackpool	1 1 90	Scholar
Husband Stephen (M)	6 0 12 13	Dunfermline	29 10 90	Hearts
John-Baptiste Alex (D)	6 0 11 11	Sutton-in-Ashfield	31 1 86	Mansfield T
Ormerod Brett (F)	5 11 11 12	Blackburn	18 10 76	Preston NE
Rachubka Paul (G)	6 2 13 04	California	21 5 81	Huddersfield T
Southern Keith (M)	5 10 12 06	Gateshead	24 4 81	Everton
Taylor-Fletcher Gary (F)	5 11 12 06	Liverpool	4 6 81	Huddersfield T
Vaughan David (M)	5 7 11 00	Rhuddlan	18 2 83	Real Sociedad

League Appearances: Adam, C. 41(2); Bangura, A. 2(7); Bannan, B. 8(12); Bouazza, H. 11(8); Burgess, B. 20(15); Butler, A. 4(3); Campbell, D. 14(1); Clarke, B. 9(9); Coleman, S. 9; Crainey, S. 41; Demontagnac, I. 1(7); Dobbie, S. 6(10); Eardley, N. 22(2); Eastham, A. (1); Edwards, R. 19(2); Emmanuel-Thomas, J. 6(5); Euell, J. 23(10); Evatt, I. 35(1); Gilks, M. 26; Husband, S. 1(2); John-Baptiste, A. 42; Martin, J. 4(2); Nardiello, D. 1(4); Ormerod, B. 27(9); Rachubka, P. 20; Seip, M. 7; Southern, K. 43(2); Taylor-Fletcher, G. 26(6); Vaughan, D. 37(4).

Goals – League (74): Adam 16 (3 pens), Ormerod 11, Campbell 8, Burgess 6, Taylor-Fletcher 6, Dobbie 4, Euell 4, Evatt 4, John-Baptiste 3, Seip 2, Southern 2, Bannan 1, Bouazza 1, Clarke 1, Coleman 1, Emmanuel-Thomas 1, Vaughan 1, own goals 2.

Carling Cup (9): Burgess 2, Adam 1, Clarke 1, Demontagnac 1, Nardiello 1, Nowland 1, Taylor-Fletcher 1, Vaughan 1.

FA Cup (1): Ormerod 1.

Play-Offs (9): Campbell 3, Adam 2 (1 pen), Dobbie 1, Ormerod 1, Southern 1, Taylor-Fletcher 1.

Ground: Bloomfield Road, Seasiders Way, Blackpool FY1 6JJ. Telephone (0871) 221 953.

Record Attendance: 38,098 v Wolverhampton W, Division 1, 17 September 1955.

Capacity: 9,491.

Manager: Ian Holloway.

Secretary: Matt Williams.

Most League Goals: 98, Division 2, 1929–30.

Highest League Scorer in Season: Jimmy Hampson, 45, Division 2, 1929–30.

Most League Goals in Total Aggregate: Jimmy Hampson, 248, 1927–38.

Most Capped Player: Jimmy Armfield, 43, England.

Most League Appearances: Jimmy Armfield, 568, 1952–71.

Honours – Football League: Division 2 Champions – 1929–30. **FA Cup:** Winners – 1953.

Anglo-Italian Cup: Winners – 1971. **LDV Vans Trophy:** Winners – 2002, 2004.

Colours: Tangerine shirts with white trim, white shorts, tangerine stockings with white tops.

BOLTON WANDERERS   FA PREMIERSHIP

Al-Habsi Ali (G)	6 4 12 06	Oman	30 12 81	Lyn
Basham Chris (M)	5 11 12 08	Stafford	20 7 88	Scholar
Bogdan Adam (G)	6 4 14 02	Budapest	27 9 87	
Cahill Gary (D)	6 2 12 06	Dronfield	19 12 85	Aston Villa
Cohen Tamir (M)	5 11 11 09	Israel	4 3 84	Maccabi Netanya
Connolly Mark (D)	6 1 12 01	Monaghan	16 12 91	Wolverhampton W

Davies Kevin (F)	6 0 12 10	Sheffield	26 3 77	Southampton
Davies Mark (M)	5 11 11 08	Wolverhampton	18 2 88	Wolverhampton W
Davis Sean (M)	5 10 12 00	Clapham	20 9 79	Portsmouth
Elmander Johan (F)	6 1 11 13	Alingsas	27 5 81	Toulouse
Gardner Ricardo (D)	5 9 11 00	St Andrews	25 9 78	Harbour View
Harsanyi Zoltan (D)	6 1 12 00	Bratislava	1 6 87	Senec
Holden Stuart (M)	5 10 11 07	Aberdeen	1 8 85	Houston Dynamo
Hunt Nicky (D)	6 1 13 08	Westhoughton	3 9 83	Scholar
Jaaskelainen Jussi (G)	6 3 12 10	Mikkeli	19 4 75	VPS
Knight Zat (D)	6 6 15 02	Solihull	2 5 80	Aston Villa
Lainton Robert (G)	6 2 12 06	Ashton-under-Lyne	12 10 89	Scholar
Lee Chung Yong (M)	5 11 10 09	Seoul	2 7 88	FC Seoul
McCann Gavin (M)	5 11 11 00	Blackpool	10 1 78	Aston Villa
Muamba Fabrice (M)	6 1 11 10	Kinshasa	6 4 88	Birmingham C
Mustapha Riga (F)	5 10 11 00	Accra	10 10 81	Levante
O'Brien Andy (D)	6 2 11 13	Harrogate	29 6 79	Portsmouth
O'Brien Joey (M)	6 0 10 13	Dublin	17 2 86	Scholar
Obadeyi Temitope (F)	5 10 11 09	Coventry	29 10 89	Scholar
Ricketts Sam (D)	6 1 12 01	Aylesbury	11 10 81	Hull C
Samuel JLloyd (D)	5 11 11 04	Trinidad	29 3 81	Aston Villa
Sheidan Sam (M)	5 11 11 10	Manchester	30 11 89	Scholar
Shittu Dan (D)	6 2 16 03	Lagos	2 9 80	Watford
Steinsson Gretar (D)	6 2 12 04	Siglufjordur	9 1 82	AZ
Taylor Matthew (D)	5 11 12 03	Oxford	27 11 81	Portsmouth
Vaz Te Ricardo (F)	6 2 12 07	Lisbon	1 10 86	Scholar
Ward Daniel (F)	5 11 12 05	Bradford	11 12 91	Scholar

League Appearances: Basham, C. 2(6); Cahill, G. 29; Cohen, T. 26(1); Davies, K. 37; Davies, M. 5(12); Davis, S. 3; Elmander, J. 15(10); Gardner, R. 11(10); Holden, S. 1(1); Jaaskelainen, J. 38; Klasnic, I. 12(15); Knight, Z. 35; Lee, C. 27(7); McCann, G. 5(6); Muamba, F. 35(1); Mustapha, R. (1); O'Brien, A. 6; Ricketts, S. 25(2); Robinson, P. 24(1); Samuel, J. 12(1); Steinsson, G. 25(2); Taylor, M. 29(8); Ward, D. (2); Weiss, V. 3(10); Wilshere, J. 13(1).

Goals – League (42): Klasnic 8, Taylor 8 (3 pens), Davies K 7 (1 pen), Cahill 5, Lee 4, Cohen 3, Elmander 3, Gardner 1, Knight 1, Muamba 1, Wilshere 1.

Carling Cup (4): Cahill 1, Davies K 1, Davies M 1, Elmander 1.

FA Cup (7): Cahill 1, Davies K 1, Davies M 1, Elmander 1, Lee 1, Steinsson 1, own goal 1.

Ground: The Reebok Stadium, Burnden Way, Lostock, Bolton, Lancashire BL6 6JW. Telephone Bolton (0844) 871 2932.

Record Attendance: 69,912 v Manchester C, FA Cup 5th rd, 18 February 1933.

Capacity: 28,101.

Manager: Owen Coyle.

Secretary: Simon Marland.

Most League Goals: 100, Division 1, 1996–97.

Highest League Scorer in Season: Joe Smith, 38, Division 1, 1920–21.

Most League Goals in Total Aggregate: Nat Lofthouse, 255, 1946–61.

Most Capped Player: Mark Fish, 34 (62), South Africa.

Most League Appearances: Eddie Hopkinson, 519, 1956–70.

Honours – Football League: Division 1 Champions – 1996–97. Division 2 Champions – 1908–09, 1977–78. Division 3 Champions – 1972–73. **FA Cup:** Winners – 1923, 1926, 1929, 1958. **Sherpa Van Trophy:** Winners – 1989.

Colours: White shirts with blue body trim, blue shorts, white stockings.

AFC BOURNEMOUTH   FL CHAMPIONSHIP 1

Bartley Marvyn (M)	6 1	12 04	Reading	4 7 86	Hampton & Richmond B
Bradbury Lee (F)	6 0	12 07	Isle of Wight	3 7 75	Southend U
Cooper Shaun (D)	5 10	10 05	Newport (IW)	5 10 83	Portsmouth
Cummings Warren (D)	5 9	11 08	Aberdeen	15 10 80	Chelsea
Feeney Liam (M)	5 10	12 02	Hammersmith	24 1 87	Salisbury C
Fletcher Steve (F)	6 2	14 09	Hartlepool	26 7 72	Crawley T
Garry Ryan (D)	6 0	11 05	Hornchurch	29 9 83	Arsenal
Hollands Danny (M)	6 0	12 00	Ashford	6 11 85	Chelsea
Igoe Sammy (M)	5 6	10 00	Staines	30 9 75	Bristol R
Jalal Shwan (G)	6 2	14 02	Baghdad	14 8 83	Peterborough U
McQuoid Josh (M)	5 9	10 10	Southampton	15 12 89	Scholar
Molesley Mark (M)	6 1	12 07	Hillingdon	11 3 81	Grays Ath
Partington Joe (M)	5 11	11 13	Portsmouth	1 4 90	Scholar
Pearce Jason (D)	5 11	12 00	Hampshire	6 12 87	Portsmouth
Pitman Brett (M)	6 0	11 00	Jersey	31 1 88	St Paul's, Jersey
Robinson Anton (M)	5 9	10 03	Harrow	17 2 86	Weymouth

League Appearances: Bartley, M. 24(10); Bradbury, L. 43(1); Connell, A. 19(19); Cooper, S. 6; Cummings, W. 27(7); Edgar, A. 2(1); Feeney, L. 44; Fletcher, S. 31(14); Garry, R. 33(1); Goulding, J. 3(14); Guyett, S. 6(3); Hollands, D. 37(2); Igoe, S. 15(6); Jalal, S. 44; McQuoid, J. 9(20); Molesley, M. 10; Partington, J. 4(7); Pearce, J. 39; Pitman, B. 46; Robinson, A. 43(1); Stech, M. 1; Stockley, J. (2); Thomas, D. 1(1); Webb, G. (1); Wiggins, R. 19.
Goals – League (61): Pitman 26 (5 pens), Hollands 6, Connell 5, Feeney 5, Fletcher 4, Robinson 4, Igoe 2, Bradbury 1, Garry 1, Goulding 1, McQuoid 1, Molesley 1, Pearce 1, own goals 3.
Carling Cup (0).
FA Cup (4): Connell 2, Igoe 1, Pitman 1.
J Paint Trophy (3): Connell 1, Hollands 1, Pitman 1.
Ground: Dean Court, Kings Park, Bournemouth BH7 7AF. Telephone (01202) 726 300.
Record Attendance: 28,799 v Manchester U, FA Cup 6th rd, 2 March 1957.
Capacity: 10,375 (with temporary stand) 9,776 (without).
Manager: Eddie Howe.
Secretary: Neil Vacher (Football Administrator).
Most League Goals: 88, Division 3 (S), 1956–57.
Highest League Scorer in Season: Ted MacDougall, 42, 1970–71.
Most League Goals in Total Aggregate: Ron Eyre, 202, 1924–33.
Most Capped Player: Gerry Peyton, 7 (33), Republic of Ireland.
Most League Appearances: Steve Fletcher, 514, 1992–2007; 2008–09.
Honours – Football League: Division 3 Champions – 1986–87. **Associate Members' Cup:** Winners – 1984.
Colours: Red shirts with thin black vertical stripes, black shorts, black stockings.

BRADFORD CITY   FL CHAMPIONSHIP 2

Convey Matthew (G)	6 1	11 12	Oman	5 11 89	Scholar
Daley Omar (M)	5 7	10 03	Jamaica	25 4 81	Charleston Battery
Dean Luke (F)	5 9	11 00	Bradford	1 8 89	Scholar
Evans Gary (F)	6 0	12 08	Macclesfield	26 4 88	Macclesfield T
Hanson James (F)	6 4	12 04	Bradford	9 11 87	Guiseley
Horne Louis (M)	6 2	12 05	Bradford	28 5 91	Scholar
McLaughlin Jon (G)	6 2	13 00	Edinburgh	9 9 87	Harrogate Railway
Neilson Scott (M)	6 2	12 00	Enfield	15 5 87	

O'Brien James (M)	6 0	11 06	Dublin	28	9 87	
O'Brien Luke (D)	5 9	12 01	Halifax	11	9 88	Scholar
Osborne Leon (F)	5 10	10 10	Doncaster	28	10 89	Scholar
Ramsden Simon (D)	6 0	12 06	Bishop Auckland	17	12 81	Rochdale
Rehman Zesh (D)	6 2	12 08	Birmingham	14	10 83	QPR
Wetherall David (D)	6 3	13 12	Sheffield	14	3 71	Leeds U
Williams Steve (D)	6 4	13 04	Preston	24	4 87	Bamber Bridge

League Appearances: Bateson, J. 14(7); Bolder, A. 14; Boulding, M. 9(12); Boulding, R. (2); Brandon, C. 14(6); Bullock, L. 41; Clarke, M. 20(1); Colbeck, J. 3(2); Daley, O. 6(8); Dean, L. (1); Eastwood, S. 22; Evans, G. 38(5); Flynn, M. 41(1); Glennon, M. 17; Grant, G. 7(4); Hanson, J. 33(1); Harrison, R. (1); Horne, L. (1); Kendall, R. 2(4); McCammon, M. 2(2); McLaughlin, J. 7; Neilson, S. 18(5); O'Brien, L. 39(4); O'Brien, J. 15(8); O'Leary, S. 4(3); Oliver, L. 7; Osborne, L. 5(7); Ramsden, S. 30(1); Rehman, Z. 36(2); Sharry, L. (1); Thorne, P. 4(3); Threlfall, R. 17; Whaley, S. 5(1); Williams, S. 36(3).
Goals – League (59): Hanson 12, Evans G 11, Flynn 6, Williams 4, Boulding M 3, Brandon 2, Kendall 2, O'Brien J 2, Oliver 2, Rehman 2, Threlfall 2, Bolder 1, Bullock 1, Clarke 1, Daley 1, Neilson 1, O'Brien L 1, Ramsden 1, Whaley 1, own goals 3.
Carling Cup (0).
FA Cup (1): Boulding M 1.
J Paint Trophy (6): Flynn 2, Boulding M 1, Brandon 1, Hanson 1, Neilson 1.
Ground: Cral Window Stadium, Valley Parade, Bradford BD8 7DY. Telephone 01274 773 335.
Record Attendance: 39,146 v Burnley, FA Cup 4th rd, 11 March 1911. **Capacity:** 25,136.
Manager: Peter Taylor.
Football Club Secretary: Kath Brown.
Most League Goals: 128, Division 3 (N), 1928–29.
Highest League Scorer in Season: David Layne, 34, Division 4, 1961–62.
Most League Goals in Total Aggregate: Bobby Campbell, 121, 1981–84, 1984–86.
Most Capped Player: Jamie Lawrence, (24), Jamaica.
Most League Appearances: Cec Podd, 502, 1970–84.
Honours – Football League: Division 2 Champions – 1907–08. Division 3 Champions – 1984–85. Division 3 (N) Champions – 1928–29. **FA Cup:** Winners – 1911.
Colours: Claret and amber striped shirts with claret sleeves, black shorts, black stockings.

BRENTFORD   FL CHAMPIONSHIP 1

Bean Marcus (M)	5 11	11 06	Hammersmith	2	11 84	Blackpool
Bennett Alan (D)	6 2	12 08	Kilkenny	4	10 81	Reading
Blake Ryan (D)	5 10	10 10		8	12 91	Scholar
Cort Carl (D)	6 4	12 04	Southwark	1	11 77	Norwich C
Dickson Ryan (M)	5 10	11 05	Saltash	14	12 86	Plymouth Arg
Foster Danny (D)	5 10	12 10	Enfield	23	9 84	Dagenham & R
Hunt David (M)	5 11	11 09	Dulwich	10	9 82	Shrewsbury T
Legge Leon (D)	6 1	11 02	London	28	4 85	Tonbridge Angels
MacDonald Charlie (F)	5 8	12 10	Southwark	13	2 81	Southend U
Moore Simon (G)	6 3	12 02		19	5 90	Farnborough T
O'Connor Kevin (F)	5 11	12 00	Blackburn	24	2 82	Trainee
Osborne Karleigh (M)	6 2	12 08	Southall	19	3 88	Scholar
Saunders Sam (M)	5 6	11 04	London	29	10 82	Dagenham & R
Strevens Ben (M)	6 1	12 00	Edgware	24	5 80	Dagenham & R
Taylor Cleveland (M)	5 8	10 07	Leicester	9	9 83	Carlisle U
Weston Myles (F)	5 11	12 05	Lewisham	12	3 88	Notts Co
Wood Sam (M)	6 0	11 05	London	6	2 88	Bromley

League Appearances: Ainsworth, L. 1(8); Akinde, J. 2; Balkestein, P. 8; Balkestein, P. 6; Bean, M. 25(6); Bennett, A. 11(2); Blake, R. (1); Bostock, J. 9; Bull, N. 5(1); Cort, C. 16(12); Diagouraga, T. 20; Dickson, R. 26(1); Foster, D. 32(4); Grabban, L. 7; Hunt, D. 18(6); Kabba, S. 3(7); Legge, L. 28(1); MacDonald, C. 39(1); Moore, S. (1); Murphy, R. 1(4); O'Connor, K. 43; Osborne, K. 13(6); Phillips, M. 19(3); Price, L. 13; Saunders, S. 15(11); Smith, T. 8; Strevens, B. 20(5); Szczesny, W. 28; Taylor, C. 8(4); Weston, M. 32(8); Wilson, J. 13; Wood, S. 37(6).

Goals – League (55): MacDonald 15 (3 pens), Weston 8, Cort 6, Strevens 6, O'Connor 4 (3 pens), Hunt 3, Bostock 2, Dickson 2, Grabban 2, Legge 2, Wood 2, Balkestein 1, Saunders 1, Taylor 1.

Carling Cup (0).

FA Cup (8): MacDonald 2, Weston 2, Cort 1, Legge 1, O'Connor 1, Strevens 1.

J Paint Trophy (0).

Ground: Griffin Park, Braemar Road, Brentford, Middlesex TW8 0NT. Telephone (0845) 3456 442.

Record Attendance: 38,678 v Leicester C, FA Cup 6th rd, 26 February 1949. **Capacity:** 12,400.

Manager: Andy Scott.

Secretary: Lisa Hall.

Most League Goals: 98, Division 4, 1962–63.

Highest League Scorer in Season: Jack Holliday, 38, Division 3 (S), 1932–33.

Most League Goals in Total Aggregate: Jim Towers, 153, 1954–61.

Most Capped Player: John Buttigieg, 22 (98), Malta.

Most League Appearances: Ken Coote, 514, 1949–64.

Honours – Football League: Championship 2 Winners – 2008–09. Division 2 Champions – 1934–35. Division 3 Champions – 1991–92, 1998–99. Division 3 (S) Champions – 1932–33. Division 4 Champions – 1962–63.

Colours: White shirts with red sleeves and black trim underneath, four separated red vertical stripes on body, black shorts and stockings.

BRIGHTON & HOVE ALBION   FL CHAMPIONSHIP 1

Brezovan Peter (G)	6 6	14 13	Bratislava	9 12 79	Swindon T
Calderon Inigo (D)	5 10	12 02	Vitoria	4 1 82	Alaves
Cook Steve (D)	6 1	12 13	Hastings	19 4 91	Scholar
Crofts Andrew (D)	5 10	12 09	Chatham	29 5 84	Gillingham
Davies Craig (F)	6 2	13 05	Burton-on-Trent	9 1 86	Oldham Ath
Dicker Gary (M)	6 0	12 00	Dublin	31 7 86	Stockport Co
Dickinson Liam (F)	6 4	11 07	Salford	4 10 85	Derby Co
Dunk Lewis (D)			Brighton	21 11 91	Scholar
El-Abd Adam (D)	5 10	13 05	Brighton	11 9 84	Scholar
Elphick Tommy (M)	5 11	11 07	Brighton	7 9 87	Scholar
Holroyd Chris (F)	5 11	12 03	Macclesfield	24 10 86	Cambridge U
McNulty Jim (D)	6 1	12 00	Liverpool	13 2 85	Stockport co
Murray Glenn (F)	6 1	12 12	Maryport	25 9 83	Rochdale
Navarro Alan (M)	5 10	11 07	Liverpool	31 5 81	Milton Keynes D
Smith Jamie (M)	5 6	10 07	Leytonstone	16 9 89	Scholar
Tunnicliffe James (D)	6 4	12 03	Denton	17 1 89	Stockport Co
Walker Mitch (G)			St Albans	24 9 91	Scholar
Whing Andrew (D)	6 0	12 00	Birmingham	20 9 84	Coventry C
Wright Jake (D)	5 10	11 07	Keighley	11 3 86	Bradford C

League Appearances: Arismendi, D. 3(3); Barnes, A. 4(4); Bennett, E. 43; Brezovan, P. 20; Calderon, I. 19; Carole, S. 7(2); Caskey, J. (1); Cox, D. 9(12); Crofts, A. 44; Davies, C. (5); Davies, A. 7; Dicker, G. 33(9); Dickinson, L. 17(10); Dunk, L. 1; El-Abd, A. 33(2); Elphick, T. 43(1); Forster, N. 23(4); Hart, G. 1(16); Hawkins, C. (1); Hendrie, L. 6(2); Holroyd, C. 5(8); Hoyte, G. 16(2); Kuipers, M. 20; LuaLua, K. 9(2); McLeod, K. 2(3);

32

McNulty, J. 5(3); Murray, G. 25(7); Navarro, A. 31(5); Painter, M. 18(1); Smith, G. 5(1); Smith, J. 1(1); Thornhill, M. 3(4); Tunnicliffe, J. 17; Virgo, A. 20(5); Walker, M. 1; Whing, A. 9; Wright, M. 2(2); Wright, J. 4(2).

Goals – League (56): Forster 13 (1 pen), Murray 12 (2 pens), Bennett 7 (1 pen), Crofts 5, Barnes 4, Dickinson 4, Elphick 3, Dicker 2, Tunnicliffe 2, Calderon 1, El-Abd 1, Virgo 1, own goal 1.

Carling Cup (0).

FA Cup (12): Forster 3 (2 pens), Bennett 2, Crofts 2, Dickinson 2, Murray 2 (1 pen), Elphick 1.

J Paint Trophy (0).

Ground: Withdean Stadium, Tongdean Lane, Brighton, East Sussex BN1 5JD. Telephone (01273) 695 400 (admin offices 44 North Road, Brighton).

Record Attendance: 36,747 v Fulham, Division 2, 27 December 1958 (at Goldstone Ground).

Capacity: 8,850.

Manager: Gus Poyet.

Secretary: Derek J. Allan.

Most League Goals: 112, Division 3 (S), 1955–56.

Highest League Scorer in Season: Peter Ward, 32, Division 3, 1976–77.

Most League Goals in Total Aggregate: Tommy Cook, 114, 1922–29.

Most Capped Player: Steve Penney, 17, Northern Ireland.

Most League Appearances: 'Tug' Wilson, 509, 1922–36.

Honours – Football League: Division 2 Champions – 2001–02. Division 3 Champions – 2000–01. Division 3 (S) Champions – 1957–58. Division 4 Champions – 1964–65.

Colours: Blue and white striped shirts, white sleeves with blue trim, white shorts, white stockings.

BRISTOL CITY   FL CHAMPIONSHIP

Akinde John (F)	6 2	12 00	London	9	7 89	Ebbsfleet U
Campbell-Ryce Jamal (M)	5 7	12 03	Lambeth	6	4 83	Barnsley
Carey Louis (D)	5 10	12 09	Bristol	20	1 77	Trainee
Clarkson David (F)	5 10	10 03	Belshill	10	9 85	Motherwell
Collis Steve (G)	6 1	13 00	Barnet	18	3 81	Crewe Alex
Edwards Joe (D)	5 8	11 07	Gloucester	31	10 90	Scholar
Elliott Marvin (M)	6 0	12 02	Wandsworth	15	9 84	Millwall
Fontaine Liam (D)	5 11	11 09	Beckenham	7	1 86	Fulham
Gerken Dean (G)	6 3	12 08	Rochford	22	5 85	Colchester U
Hartley Paul (M)	5 8	10 05	Glasgow	19	10 76	Celtic
Haynes Danny (F)	5 11	12 04	London	19	1 88	Ipswich T
Henderson Stephen (G)	6 3	11 00	Dublin	2	5 88	Aston Villa
Jackson Marlon (F)	5 11	11 12	Bristol	6	12 90	Scholar
Johnson Lee (M)	5 6	10 07	Newmarket	7	6 81	Hearts
Maynard Nicky (F)	5 11	11 00	Winsford	11	12 86	Crewe Alex
McAllister Jamie (D)	5 10	11 00	Glasgow	26	4 78	Hearts
McCombe Jamie (D)	6 5	12 05	Scunthorpe	1	1 83	Lincoln C
Nyatanga Lewin (D)	6 2	12 08	Burton	18	8 88	Derby Co
Orr Bradley (M)	6 0	11 11	Liverpool	1	11 82	Newcastle U
Ribeiro Christian (D)	5 11	12 02	Neath	14	12 89	Scholar
Skuse Cole (M)	6 1	11 05	Bristol	29	3 86	Scholar
Sproule Ivan (M)	5 8	11 09	Castlederg	18	2 81	Hibernian
Williams Gavin (M)	5 10	11 05	Pontypridd	20	6 80	Ipswich T
Wilson Brian (D)	5 10	11 00	Manchester	9	5 83	Cheltenham T
Wilson James (D)	6 2	11 05	Newport	26	2 89	Scholar

League Appearances: Agyemang, P. 5(2); Akinde, J. (7); Basso, A. 4; Campbell-Ryce, J. 13(1); Carey, L. 36(1); Clarkson, D. 10(16); Elliott, M. 33(6); Fontaine, L. 31(5); Gerken,

33

D. 39; Hartley, P. 36(4); Haynes, D. 29(9); Henderson, S. 3; Iwelumo, C. 7; Johnson, L. 18(10); Maierhofer, S. 1(2); Maynard, N. 40(2); McAllister, J. 31(2); McCombe, J. 13(3); Nyatanga, L. 33(4); Orr, B. 38(1); Ribeiro, C. 5; Saborio, A. 11(8); Sawyer, G. 2; Skuse, C. 39(4); Sno, E. 16(8); Sproule, I. 8(22); Velicka, A. (1); Williams, G. 2(12); Wilson, B. 3.

Goals – League (56): Maynard 20 (1 pen), Haynes 7, Hartley 5 (3 pens), Clarkson 4, Sno 3, Carey 2, Fontaine 2, Iwelumo 2, Orr 2, Saborio 2, Skuse 2, Elliott 1, Johnson 1, McCombe 1, Nyatanga 1, Sproule 1.

Carling Cup (1): Maynard 1.

FA Cup (1): Williams 1.

Ground: Ashton Gate Stadium, Bristol BS3 2EJ. Telephone (0871) 222 6666.

Record Attendance: 43,335 v Preston NE, FA Cup 5th rd, 16 February 1935. **Capacity:** 21,804.

Manager: Steve Coppell.

Secretary: Michelle McDonald.

Most League Goals: 104, Division 3 (S), 1926–27.

Highest League Scorer in Season: Don Clark, 36, Division 3 (S), 1946–47.

Most League Goals in Total Aggregate: John Atyeo, 314, 1951–66.

Most Capped Player: Billy Wedlock, 26, England.

Most League Appearances: John Atyeo, 597, 1951–66.

Honours – Football League: Division 2 Champions – 1905–06. Division 3 (S) Champions – 1922–23, 1926–27, 1954–55. **Welsh Cup:** Winners – 1934. **Anglo-Scottish Cup:** Winners – 1977–78. **Freight Rover Trophy:** Winners – 1985–86. **LDV Vans Trophy:** Winners – 2002–03.

Colours: Red shirts with white trim, white shorts, red stockings.

BRISTOL ROVERS   FL CHAMPIONSHIP 1

Anthony Byron (D)	6 1	11 02	Newport	20 9 84	Cardiff C
Blizzard Dominic (M)	6 2	12 04	High Wycombe	2 9 83	Stockport Co
Clough Charlie (M)	6 0	12 04	Somerset	3 9 90	Scholar
Coles Danny (D)	6 1	11 05	Bristol	31 10 81	Hull C
Duffy Darryl (F)	5 11	12 01	Glasgow	16 4 84	Swansea C
Green Mike (G)	6 1	13 01	Bristol	23 07 89	Scholar
Hughes Jeff (D)	6 1	11 00	Larne	29 5 85	Crystal Palace
Lines Chris (M)	6 2	12 00	Bristol	30 11 85	Filton College
Osei-Kuffour Jo (F)	5 8	11 11	Edmonton	17 11 81	Bournemouth
Reece Charlie (M)	5 11	11 03	Birmingham	8 9 88	Scholar
Regan Carl (D)	5 11	11 12	Liverpool	14 1 80	Milton Keynes D
Richards Elliot (M)			New Tredegar	10 9 91	
Swallow Ben (M)			Cardiff	20 10 89	
Tyrrell James (D)	6 2	13 04	Oxford	26 4 89	Scholar
Williams Andy (F)	5 11	11 09	Hereford	14 8 86	Hereford U
Wright Mark (M)	5 11	11 00	Wolverhampton	24 2 82	Brighton & HA

League Appearances: Andersen, M. 39; Anthony, B. 37; Baldwin, P. 6; Blizzard, D. 22(12); Brown, W. 3(1); Campbell, S. 46; Coles, D. 36; Dickson, C. 10(4); Duffy, D. 15(15); Elliott, S. 21; Evans, R. 3; Forster, F. 4; Heffernan, P. 11; Hughes, J. 44; Hunt, B. (2); Jones, D. 17; Lambert, R. 1; Lescott, A. 23(1); Lines, C. 41(1); Osei-Kuffour, J. 42; Pipe, D. 5(2); Reece, C. 5(9); Regan, C. 32(3); Richards, Elliot (5); Swallow, B. 6(17); Williams, A. 18(25); Wright, M. 19(5).

Goals – League (59): Osei-Kuffour 14, Hughes 12 (7 pens), Lines 10, Dickson 4, Duffy 4, Heffernan 4, Williams 3, Lescott 2, Blizzard 1, Coles 1, Elliott 1, Lambert 1, own goals 2.

Carling Cup (3): Duffy 2 (1 pen), Elliott 1.

FA Cup (2): Duffy 1, Hughes 1 (pen).

J Paint Trophy (0).

Ground: The Memorial Stadium, Filton Avenue, Horfield, Bristol BS7 0BF. Telephone (0117) 909 6648.
Record Attendance: 9,464 v Liverpool, FA Cup 4th rd, 8 February 1992 (Twerton Park). 38,472 v Preston NE, FA Cup 4th rd, 30 January 1960 (Eastville). 12,011 v WBA, FA Cup 6th rd, 9 March 2008 (Memorial Stadium). **Capacity:** 11,626.
Manager: Paul Trollope.
Secretary: Rod Wesson.
Most League Goals: 92, Division 3 (S), 1952–53.
Highest League Scorer in Season: Geoff Bradford, 33, Division 3 (S), 1952–53.
Most League Goals in Total Aggregate: Geoff Bradford, 242, 1949–64.
Most Capped Player: Vitalijs Astafjevs, 31 (159), Latvia.
Most League Appearances: Stuart Taylor, 546, 1966–80.
Honours – Football League: Division 3 (S) Champions – 1952–53. Division 3 Champions – 1989–90.
Colours: Blue and white quartered shirts, white shorts, white stockings.

BURNLEY   FL CHAMPIONSHIP

Alexander Graham (D)	5 10	12 07	Coventry	10 10 71	Preston NE
Anderson Chris (M)	5 11	10 02	Burnley	2 10 90	Scholar
Bikey Andre (D)	6 0	12 08	Douala	8 1 85	Reading
Carlisle Clarke (D)	6 2	14 11	Preston	14 10 79	Watford
Cort Leon (D)	6 3	13 01	Bermondsey	11 9 79	Stoke C
Eagles Chris (M)	5 10	11 07	Hemel Hempstead	19 11 85	Manchester U
Easton Brian (D)	6 0	12 00	Glasgow	5 3 88	Hamilton A
Eckersley Richard (D)	5 9	11 09	Worsley	12 3 89	Manchester U
Edgar David (D)	6 2	12 13	Ontario	19 5 87	Newcastle U
Elliott Wade (M)	5 10	10 03	Southampton	14 12 78	Bournemouth
Fletcher Steven (F)	6 1	12 00	Shrewsbury	26 3 87	Hibernian
Fletcher Wes (F)	5 11	12 06	Ormskirk	28 2 90	Scholar
Fox Danny (D)	5 11	12 06	Crewe	29 5 86	Celtic
Harvey Alex-Ray (M)	5 7	10 09	Burnley	4 4 90	Scholar
Hoskin Benjamin (D)	5 11	11 02	Blackburn	8 10 90	Scholar
Jensen Brian (G)	6 4	16 09	Copenhagen	8 6 75	WBA
Kudiersky Nikolaus (D)	6 1	13 04	Tameside	15 2 91	Scholar
Long Kevin (D)	6 3	13 01	Cork	18 8 90	Cork C
Lynch Chris (D)	6 3	15 06	Blackburn	31 1 91	Chester C
MacDonald Alex (F)	5 7	11 04	Warrington	14 4 90	Scholar
Marney Dean (M)	5 10	11 09	Barking	31 1 84	Hull C
McCann Chris (M)	6 1	11 11	Dublin	21 7 87	Scholar
McDonald Kevin (M)	6 2	13 03	Carnoustie	4 11 88	Dundee
Mears Tyrone (D)	5 11	11 10	Stockport	18 2 83	Derby Co
Paterson Martin (F)	5 9	10 11	Tunstall	13 5 87	Scunthorpe U
Penny Diego (G)	6 6	12 00	Lima	22 4 84	Coromel Bolognesi
Rodriguez Jay (F)	6 0	12 00	Burnley	27 7 89	Scholar
Van der Schaaf Remco (D)	6 1	12 02	Ten Boer	28 2 78	Vitesse

League Appearances: Alexander, G. 33; Bikey, A. 26(2); Blake, R. 20(11); Caldwell, S. 12(1); Carlisle, C. 27; Cork, J. 8(3); Cort, L. 15; Duff, M. 10(1); Eagles, C. 20(14); Edgar, D. 2(2); Elliott, W. 34(4); Fletcher, S. 35; Fox, Danny 13(1); Gudjonsson, J. 1(9); Guerrero, F. (7); Jensen, B. 38; Jordan, S. 23(2); Kalvenes, C. 3(3); McCann, C. 7; McDonald, K. 15(11); Mears, T. 38; Nimani, F. (2); Nugent, D. 20(10); Paterson, M. 17(6); Penny, D. (1); Thompson, S. 1(19).
Goals – League (42): Fletcher 8, Alexander 7 (6 pens), Nugent 6, Elliott 4, Paterson 4, Thompson 4, Blake 2, Eagles 2, Bikey 1, Caldwell 1, Cork 1, Fox, Danny 1, McDonald 1.
Carling Cup (4): Fletcher S 3, Eagles 1.

FA Cup (2): Alexander 1 (pen), Fletcher S 1.
Ground: Turf Moor, Harry Potts Way, Burnley, Lancashire BB10 4BX. Telephone (0871) 221 1882.
Record Attendance: 54,775 v Huddersfield T, FA Cup 3rd rd, 23 February 1924.
Capacity: 22,610.
Manager: Brian Laws.
Football Secretary: Pauline Scott
Most League Goals: 102, Division 1, 1960–61.
Highest League Scorer in Season: George Beel, 35, Division 1, 1927–28.
Most League Goals in Total Aggregate: George Beel, 179, 1923–32.
Most Capped Player: Jimmy McIlroy, 51 (55), Northern Ireland.
Most League Appearances: Jerry Dawson, 522, 1907–28.
Honours – Football League: Division 1 Champions – 1920–21, 1959–60. Division 2 Champions – 1897–98, 1972–73. Division 3 Champions – 1981–82. Division 4 Champions – 1991–92. **FA Cup:** Winners – 1913–14. **Anglo-Scottish Cup:** Winners – 1978–79.
Colours: Claret shirts with blue sleeves, white shorts, claret stockings.

BURTON ALBION   FL CHAMPIONSHIP 2

Austin Ryan (D)	6 3	13 07	Stoke	15 11 84 Crewe Alex
Boertien Paul (D)	5 10	11 02	Haltwhistle	21 1 79 Walsall
Branston Guy (D)	6 1	15 01	Leicester	9 1 79 Kettering T
Corbett Andrew (M)	6 0	11 05	Worcester	20 2 82 Nuneaton B
Gilroy Keith (M)	5 10	10 12	Sligo	8 7 83 Darlington
Harrad Shaun (F)	5 10	12 04	Nottingham	11 12 84 Notts Co
Jackson Richard (D)	5 8	12 10	Whitby	18 4 80 Hereford U
James Tony (D)	6 3	14 02	Cardiff	9 10 78 Weymouth
Knowles James (F)	5 9	11 04	Sheffield	7 6 90 Scholar
Maghoma Jacques (M)	5 9	11 06	Lubumbashi	23 10 87 Tottenham H
McGrath John (M)	5 10	10 03	Limerick	27 3 80 Tamworth
Pearson Greg (F)	6 0	11 00	Birmingham	3 4 85 Bishop's Stortford
Penn Russell (M)	5 11	12 13	Dudley	8 11 85 Kidderminster H
Phillips Jimmy (M)	5 7	10 00	Stoke	20 9 89 Stoke C
Poole Kevin (G)	5 10	11 11	Bromsgrove	21 7 63 Derby Co
Walker Richard (F)	6 0	12 04	Sutton Coldfield	8 11 77 Bristol R
Webster Aaron (D)	6 2	12 02	Burton-on-Trent	19 12 80 Youth

League Appearances: Austin, R. 18; Boco, R. 3(5); Boertien, P. 33(1); Branston, G. 18(1); Brown, A. 1; Cadogan, K. 2; Corbett, A. 32(2); Edworthy, M. 1; Gilroy, K. 4(4); Goodfellow, M. (3); Harrad, S. 35(7); Jackson, R. 4(1); James, T. 42; Kabba, S. 18(5); Kelly, S. 2(2); Krysiak, A. 38; Maghoma, J. 24(11); Makofo, S. (2); McGrath, J. 44(1); Parkes, T. 21(1); Pearson, G. 24(18); Penn, R. 34(6); Phillips, J. 19(5); Poole, K. 5(1); Redmond, S. 3; Shroot, R. 4(3); Simpson, M. 20(4); Stride, D. 5(4); Taylor, C. 23(1); Thompson, O. 1(1); Walker, R. 10(7); Webster, A. 18(6).
Goals – League (71): Harrad 21 (4 pens), Pearson 14 (3 pens), Kabba 6, Penn 4, Taylor 4, Webster 4, Maghoma 3, Walker 3, Austin 2, Simpson 2, Boertien 1, Corbett 1, James 1, McGrath 1, Parkes 1, Phillips 1, own goals 2.
Carling Cup (1): Phillips 1.
FA Cup (3): Austin 1, Harrad 1 (pen), Maghoma 1.
J Paint Trophy (1): McGrath 1.
Ground: Pirelli Stadium, Princess Way, Burton-on-Trent, Staffordshire DE13 0AR. Telephone: (01283) 565 938.
Record attendance: 6,192 v Oxford U, Blue Square Premier, 17 April 2009.
Capacity: 6,350 (2,034 seated).
Manager: Paul Peschisolido.

Football Secretary: Fleur Robinson.
Most League Goals: 71, FL 2, 2009–10.
Highest League Scorer in Season: Shaun Harrad, 21, 2009–10.
Most Capped Player: Jacques Maghoma, 1, DR Congo.
Most League Appearances: John McGrath, 45, 2009–10.
Honours: Conference: Champions – 2008–09. **Southern League Cup:** Winners – 1964, 1997, 2000. **Northern Premier League:** Champions – 2001–02. **Northern Premier League Shield:** 1983. **Challenge Cup:** Winners – 1983. **Birmingham Senior Cup:** Winners – 1954, 1997. **Staffordshire Senior Cup:** Winners – 1956. **Midland Floodlit Cup:** Winners – 1976.
Colours: Yellow shirts with black insert, black shorts, black stockings.

BURY   FL CHAMPIONSHIP 2

Belford Cameron (G)	6 1 11 10	Nuneaton	16 10 88	Coventry C
Bishop Andy (F)	6 0 11 00	Stone	19 10 82	York C
Carlton Danny (F)	5 11 12 04	Leeds	22 12 83	Carlisle U
Cresswell Ryan (D)	5 9 10 05	Rotherham	22 12 87	Sheffield U
Futcher Ben (D)	6 7 12 05	Manchester	20 2 81	Peterborough U
Jones Mike (M)	5 11 12 04	Birkenhead	15 8 87	Tranmere R
Lowe Ryan (F)	5 10 12 08	Liverpool	18 9 78	Chester C

League Appearances: Baker, R. 7(7); Barry-Murphy, B. 46; Belford, C. 5(2); Bishop, A. 12(13); Brown, W. 41; Buchanan, D. 37(1); Carlton, D. 1(6); Cresswell, R. 24(4); Dawson, S. 45; Elliott, T. 7(9); Futcher, B. 29(3); Hewson, S. 1(6); Johnson, S. 1(3); Jones, M. 36(5); Lowe, R. 34(5); Morrell, A. 25(7); Nardiello, D. 6; Newey, T. 29(3); Parker, K. 2; Poole, J. 4(5); Racchi, D. 10(12); Robertson, J. 4; Rouse, D. 1(3); Scott, P. 26(4); Sodje, E. 39; Worrall, D. 34(6).
Goals – League (54): Lowe 18 (6 pens), Morrell 9, Jones 5, Dawson 4 (1 pen), Nardiello 4 (1 pen), Worrall 4, Bishop 3 (1 pen), Sodje 2, Baker 1, Barry-Murphy 1, Elliott 1, Robertson 1, own goal 1.
Carling Cup (0).
FA Cup (0).
J Paint Trophy (4): Jones 2, Racchi 1, Worrall 1.
Ground: Gigg Lane, Bury, Lancs BL9 9HR. Telephone (08445) 790009.
Record Attendance: 35,000 v Bolton W, FA Cup 3rd rd, 9 January 1960. **Capacity:** 11,669.
Manager: Alan Knill.
Secretary: Mrs Jill Neville.
Most League Goals: 108, Division 3, 1960–61.
Highest League Scorer in Season: Craig Madden, 35, Division 4, 1981–82.
Most League Goals in Total Aggregate: Craig Madden, 129, 1978–86.
Most Capped Player: Bill Gorman, 11 (13), Republic of Ireland and (4), Northern Ireland.
Most League Appearances: Norman Bullock, 506, 1920–35.
Honours – Football League: Division 2 Champions – 1894–95, 1996–97. Division 3 Champions – 1960–61. **FA Cup:** Winners – 1900, 1903.
Colours: Black and blue halved shirts, white shorts, black stockings.

CARDIFF CITY   FL CHAMPIONSHIP

Blake Darcy (M)	5 10 12 05	New Tredegar	13 12 88	Scholar
Bothroyd Jay (F)	6 3 14 11	Islington	7 5 82	Wolverhampton W
Burke Chris (M)	5 9 10 10	Glasgow	2 12 83	Rangers
Chopra Michael (F)	5 9 10 10	Newcastle	23 12 83	Sunderland
Dennehy Darren (D)	6 4 12 08	Republic of Ireland	21 9 88	Everton

Name			Birthplace			Previous Club
Feeney Warren (F)	5 8	12 04	Belfast	17	1 81	Luton T
Gerrard Anthony (D)	6 2	13 07	Liverpool	6	2 86	Walsall
Gyepes Gabor (D)	6 3	13 01	Hungary	26	6 81	Northampton T
Hudson Mark (D)	6 1	12 01	Guildford	30	3 82	Charlton Ath
Ledley Joe (M)	6 0	11 07	Cardiff	23	1 87	Scholar
Marshall David (G)	6 3	13 04	Glasgow	5	3 85	Norwich C
Matthews Adam (M)	5 10	11 02	Swansea	13	1 92	Scholar
McCormack Ross (F)	5 9	11 00	Glasgow	18	8 86	Motherwell
McNaughton Kevin (D)	5 10	10 06	Dundee	28	8 82	Aberdeen
McPhail Steve (M)	5 10	13 03	Westminster	9	12 79	Barnsley
Quinn Paul (D)	6 0	11 04	Wishaw	21	7 85	Motherwell
Rae Gavin (D)	5 11	10 04	Aberdeen	28	11 77	Rangers
Taiwo Soloman (M)	6 1	13 02	Lagos	29	4 85	Dagenham & R
Whittingham Peter (M)	5 10	11 06	Nuneaton	8	9 84	Aston Villa
Wildig Aaron (M)	5 9	11 02	Hereford	26	1 90	Scholar

League Appearances: Blake, D. 15(3); Bothroyd, J. 40; Burke, C. 38(6); Capaldi, T. 10(5); Chopra, M. 36(5); Comminges, M. (1); Enckelman, P. 3(1); Etuhu, K. 7(9); Feeney, W. 1(8); Gerrard, A. 39; Gyepes, G. 16; Hudson, M. 26(1); Kennedy, M. 25(5); Ledley, J. 27(2); Magennis, J. 1(8); Marshall, D. 43; Matthews, A. 24(8); McCormack, R. 21(13); McNaughton, K. 20(1); McPhail, S. 21; Morris, A. (1); Quinn, P. 16(6); Rae, G. 28(9); Scimeca, R. 2(2); Taiwo, S. 2(6); Whittingham, P. 41; Wildig, A. 4(7).

Goals – League (73): Whittingham 20 (7 pens), Chopra 16 (1 pen), Bothroyd 11, Burke 9, McCormack 4, Ledley 3, Gerrard 2, Hudson 2, Gyepes 1, Matthews 1, Rae 1, Wildig 1, own goals 2.

Carling Cup (6): Whittingham 2, Bothroyd 1 (pen), Chopra 1, Magennis 1, Rae 1.

FA Cup (7): Chopra 2, Bothroyd 1, Burke 1, McCormack 1, Whittingham 1, own goal 1.

Play-Offs (5): Chopra 2, Whittingham 2 (1 pen), Ledley 1.

Ground: Cardiff City Stadium, Leckwith Road, Cardiff CF11 8AZ. Telephone (0845) 365 1115.

Record Attendance: 62,634, Wales v England, 17 October 1959 (at Ninian Park); 26,055 ,v Leicester C, FL C Play-Off semi-final 2nd leg, 12 May 2010 (at Cardiff City Stadium). **Capacity:** 26,828.

Manager: Dave Jones.

Secretary: Jason Turner.

Most League Goals: 95, Division 3, 2000–01.

Highest League Scorer in Season: Robert Earnshaw, 31, Division 2, 2002–03.

Most League Goals in Total Aggregate: Len Davies, 128, 1920–31.

Most Capped Player: Alf Sherwood, 39 (41), Wales.

Most League Appearances: Phil Dwyer, 471, 1972–85.

Honours – Football League: Division 3 (S) Champions – 1946–47; Division 3 Champions – 1992–93. **FA Cup:** Winners – 1926–27 (only occasion the Cup has been won by a club outside England). **Welsh Cup:** Winners – 22 times. **Charity Shield:** Winners 1927.

Colours: Blue shirts with yellow trim, white shorts, white stockings.

CARLISLE UNITED   FL CHAMPIONSHIP 1

Name			Birthplace			Previous Club
Aldred Tom (D)	6 2	13 02	Bolton	11	9 90	Scholar
Bowman Ryan (F)	6 2	12 02	Carlisle	30	11 91	Scholar
Bridge-Wilkinson Marc (M)	5 6	11 00	Coventry	16	3 79	Bradford C
Collin Adam (G)	6 2	12 00	Carlisle	9	12 84	Doncaster R
Cook Andy (F)	6 1	11 04	Bishop Auckland	18	10 90	Scholar
Gillespie Mark (G)			Newcastle	27	3 92	Scholar
Harte Ian (D)	5 11	12 06	Drogheda	31	8 77	Blackpool
Hurst Kevan (M)	5 10	11 07	Chesterfield	27	8 85	Scunthorpe U

Kane Tony (D)	5 11 11 00	Belfast	29 8 87	Blackburn R
Keogh Richard (D)	6 0 11 02	Harlow	11 8 86	Bristol C
Madine Gary (F)	6 1 12 00	Gateshead	24 8 90	Scholar
Murphy Peter (M)	5 10 12 10	Dublin	27 10 80	Blackburn R
Offiong Richard (F)	5 11 12 02	South Shields	17 12 83	Hamilton A
Robson Matty (D)	5 10 11 02	Durham	23 1 85	Hartlepool U
Thirlwell Paul (M)	5 11 11 04	Springwell Village	13 2 79	Derby Co

League Appearances: Aldred, T. 4(1); Anyinsah, J. 20(8); Bowman, R. (6); Bridge-Wilkinson, M. 6(13); Clayton, A. 28; Collin, A. 29; Dobie, S. 24(15); Duffy, D. 7(1); Gillespie, M. (1); Harte, I. 45; Horwood, E. 31(1); Hurst, K. 30(3); Kane, T. 1(3); Kavanagh, G. 28(1); Keogh, R. 41; Livesey, D. 38; Madine, G. 6(14); Marshall, B. 11(9); Murphy, P. 12(4); Offiong, R. 2(13); Pericard, V. 10; Pidgeley, L. 17; Price, J. 8(1); Raven, D. 14(2); Robson, M. 39; Rothery, G. (1); Taiwo, T. 30(5); Taylor, C. 1; Thirlwell, P. 24(4).
Goals – League (63): Harte 16 (6 pens), Anyinsah 9, Dobie 5, Madine 4, Pericard 4, Price 4, Robson 4, Keogh 3, Marshall 3, Hurst 2, Kavanagh 2, Livesey 2, Clayton 1, Duffy 1, Offiong 1, Taiwo 1, Thirlwell 1.
Carling Cup (4): Dobie 2, Harte 1 (pen), Madine 1.
FA Cup (7): Hurst 2, Pericard 2, Anyinsah 1, Harte 1, Keogh 1.
J Paint Trophy (17): Dobie 3, Kavanagh 3, Robson 3, Clayton 2, Anyinsah 1, Bridge-Wilkinson 1, Hurst 1, Keogh 1, Madine 1, Murphy 1.
Ground: Brunton Park, Warwick Road, Carlisle CA1 1LL. Telephone (01228) 526 237.
Record Attendance: 27,500 v Birmingham C, FA Cup 3rd rd, 5 January 1957 and v Middlesbrough, FA Cup 5th rd, 7 February 1970. **Capacity:** 16,981.
Manager: Greg Abbott.
Secretary: Sarah McKnight.
Most League Goals: 113, Division 4, 1963–64.
Highest League Scorer in Season: Jimmy McConnell, 42, Division 3 (N), 1928–29.
Most League Goals in Total Aggregate: Jimmy McConnell, 126, 1928–32.
Most Capped Player: Eric Welsh, 4, Northern Ireland.
Most League Appearances: Allan Ross, 466, 1963–79.
Honours – Football League: Division 3 Champions – 1964–65, 1994–95; Championship 2 Champions – 2005–06. **Auto Windscreen Shield:** Winners 1997.
Colours: Blue shirts with white and red trim, white shorts, white stockings.

CHARLTON ATHLETIC   FL CHAMPIONSHIP 1

Bailey Nicky (M)	5 10 12 06	Hammersmith	10 6 84	Southend U
Elliot Rob (G)	6 3 14 10	Chatham	30 4 86	Scholar
Fleetwood Stuart (F)	5 10 12 07	Gloucester	23 4 86	Hereford U
Fofana Beko (F)		Ivory Coast	8 9 88	ASEC Mimosas
Llera Miguel (D)	6 3 13 12	Seville	7 8 79	Milton Keynes D
McLeod Izale (F)	6 1 11 02	Birmingham	15 10 84	Milton Keynes D
Moutaouakil Yassin (D)	5 10 11 05	Nice	18 7 86	Chateauroux
Racon Therry (M)	5 10 10 02	Villen've-St-Georges	1 5 84	Guingamp
Randolph Darren (G)	6 2 14 00	Dublin	12 5 87	Scholar
Richardson Frazer (D)	5 11 11 12	Rotherham	29 10 82	Leeds U
Semedo Jose (D)	6 0 12 08	Setubal	11 1 85	Sporting Lisbon
Sodje Akpo (F)	6 2 12 08	Greenwich	31 1 81	Sheffield W
Solly Chris (D)	5 8 10 07	Chatham	20 1 91	Scholar
Stavrinou Alex (M)	5 9 11 12	Harlow	13 9 90	Scholar
Wagstaff Scott (F)	5 10 10 03	Maidstone	31 3 90	Scholar
Youga Kelly (D)	5 11 12 06	Bangui	22 9 85	Lyon

League Appearances: Bailey, N. 43(1); Basey, G. 14(5); Borrowdale, G. 10; Burton, D. 35(4); Dailly, C. 44; Dickson, C. 1(4); Elliot, R. 33; Forster, N. 8; Gray, A. (2); Ikeme, C. 4; Jackson, J. 4; Llera, M. 23(2); McKenzie, L. (12); McLeod, I. 3(8); Mooney, D. 20(8);

Omozusi, E. 7(2); Racon, T. 36; Randolph, D. 9(2); Reid, K. 11(6); Richardson, F. 37(1); Sam, L. 40(3); Semedo, J. 35(3); Shelvey, J. 19(5); Sodje, S. 24(3); Sodje, A. 2(7); Sodje, A. 8(8); Solly, C. 2(7); Spring, M. 7(5); Tuna, T. (1); Wagstaff, S. 9(21); Youga, K. 18.

Goals – League (71): Burton 13 (5 pens), Bailey 12 (1 pen), Mooney 5, Llera 4, Reid 4, Sam 4, Shelvey 4, Sodje S 4, Wagstaff 4, Sodje A 3, Forster 2 (1 pen), McLeod 2, Sodje A 2, Dailly 1, Racon 1, Richardson 1, Semedo 1, own goals 4.

Carling Cup (0).

FA Cup (0).

J Paint Trophy (5): Bailey 1, McKenzie 1, McLeod 1, Tuna 1, Wagstaff 1.

Play-Offs (3): Burton 1, Mooney 1, own goal 1.

Ground: The Valley, Floyd Road, Charlton, London SE7 8BL. Telephone (020) 8333 4000.

Record Attendance: 75,031 v Aston Villa, FA Cup 5th rd, 12 February 1938 (at The Valley). **Capacity:** 27,111.

Manager: Phil Parkinson.

Football Secretary: Chris Parkes.

Most League Goals: 107, Division 2, 1957–58.

Highest League Scorer in Season: Ralph Allen, 32, Division 3 (S), 1934–35.

Most League Goals in Total Aggregate: Stuart Leary, 153, 1953–62.

Most Capped Player: Jonatan Johansson, 41 (103), Finland.

Most League Appearances: Sam Bartram, 583, 1934–56.

Honours – Football League: Division 1 Champions – 1999–2000. Division 3 (S) Champions – 1928–29, 1934–35. **FA Cup:** Winners – 1947.

Colours: Red shirts with white trim, white shorts, white stockings with red tops.

CHELSEA   FA PREMIERSHIP

Alex (D)	6 2	14 00	Niteroi	17 6 82	PSV Eindhoven
Anelka Nicolas (F)	6 1	13 03	Versailles	14 3 79	Bolton W
Bertrand Ryan (D)	5 10	11 00	Southwark	5 8 89	Scholar
Borini Fabio (F)	5 10	11 02	Bentivoglio	23 3 91	Bologna
Bosingwa Jose (D)	6 0	12 08	Kinshasa	24 8 82	Porto
Cech Petr (G)	6 5	14 03	Plzen	20 5 82	Rennes
Clifford Conor (M)	5 8	10 08	Dublin	1 10 91	Scholar
Cole Ashley (D)	5 8	10 08	Stepney	20 12 80	Arsenal
Cork Jack (D)	6 0	10 12	Carshalton	25 6 89	Scholar
Deco (M)	5 9	11 07	Sao Bernardo do Campo	27 8 77	Barcelona
Di Santo Franko (F)	6 4	13 01	Mendoza	7 4 89	Audax Italiano
Djalo Aliu (M)			Bissau	5 2 92	Scholar
Drogba Didier (F)	6 2	13 08	Abidjan	11 3 78	Marseille
Essien Michael (M)	5 10	13 06	Accra	3 12 82	Lyon
Gordon Ben (D)	5 11	12 06	Bradford	2 3 91	Scholar
Hilario (G)	6 2	13 05	San Pedro da Cova	21 10 75	Nacional
Hutchinson Sam (D)	6 0	11 07	Slough	3 8 89	Scholar
Ivanovic Branislav (M)	6 0	12 04	Sremska Mitreovica	22 2 84	Lokomotiv Moscow
Kakuta Gael (F)	5 8	10 03	Lille	21 6 91	Lens
Kalou Salomon (F)	6 0	12 02	Oume	5 8 85	Feyenoord
Lampard Frank (M)	6 0	14 01	Romford	20 6 78	West Ham U
Magnay Carl (D)	6 0	11 13	Durham	27 1 89	
Malouda Florent (M)	6 0	11 06	Cayenne	13 6 80	Lyon
Mancienne Michael (D)	6 0	11 09	Isleworth	8 1 88	Scholar
Matic Nemanja (M)	6 4	12 13	Sabac	1 8 88	Kosice
Mellis Jacob (M)	6 0	11 08	Nottingham	8 1 91	Scholar
Mikel John Obi (M)	6 0	13 05	Jos	22 4 87	Lyn
Mitrovic Marko (F)			Malmo	27 6 92	Malmo

Paulo Ferreira (D)	6 0	11 13	Cascais	18 1 79	Porto
Phillip Adam (F)			Carshalton	19 6 91	Scholar
Philliskirk Daniel (M)	5 10	11 05	Oldham	10 4 91	Scholar
Rajkovic Slobodan (D)	6 5	14 00	Belgrade	3 3 89	OFK Belgrade
Ricardo Carvalho (D)	6 0	12 04	Amarante	18 5 78	Porto
Sala Jacopo (M)			Bergamo	5 12 91	Scholar
Sebak Jan (G)	6 4	12 13	Plana	31 1 91	Scholar
Sinclair Scott (F)	5 10	10 00	Bath	26 3 89	Bristol R
Stoch Miroslav (F)	5 6	10 01	Nitra	19 10 89	Scholar
Sturridge Daniel (F)	6 2	12 00	Manchester	1 9 89	Manchester C
Taylor Rhys (G)	6 2	12 08	Neath	7 4 90	Scholar
Terry John (D)	6 1	13 08	Barking	7 12 80	Trainee
Tore Gokhan (M)	5 9	11 09	Cologne	20 1 92	Leverkusen
Turnbull Ross (G)	6 4	15 00	Bishop Auckland	4 1 85	Middlesbrough
Van Aanholt Patrick (D)	5 9	10 08	S'Hertogenbosch	3 7 88	Ajax
Van Homoet Jeffrey (D)			Rotterdam	13 11 91	Scholar
Walker Sam (G)	6 5	14 00	Gravesend	2 10 91	Scholar
Woods Michael (M)	6 0	12 07	York	6 4 90	Scholar
Zhirkov Yuri (M)	6 1	11 11	Tambov	20 8 83	CSKA Moscow

League Appearances: Alex, 13(3); Anelka, N. 31(2); Ballack, M. 26(6); Belletti, J. 4(7); Borini, F. (4); Bosingwa, J. 8; Bruma, J. (2); Cech, P. 34; Cole, A. 25(2); Cole, J. 14(12); Deco, 14(5); Drogba, D. 31(1); Essien, M. 13(1); Hilario, 2(1); Hutchinson, S. (2); Ivanovic, B. 25(3); Kakuta, G. (1); Kalou, S. 11(12); Lampard, F. 36; Malouda, F. 26(7); Matic, N. (2); Mikel, J. 21(4); Paulo Ferreira, 11(2); Ricardo Carvalho, 22; Sturridge, D. 2(11); Terry, J. 37; Turnbull, R. 2; Van Aanholt, P. (2); Zhirkov, Y. 10(7).

Goals – League (103): Drogba 29 (1 pen), Lampard 22 (10 pens), Malouda 12, Anelka 11, Kalou 5, Ballack 4, Cole A 4, Essien 3, Cole J 2, Deco 2, Terry 2, Alex 1, Ivanovic 1, Sturridge 1, own goals 4.

Carling Cup (8): Kalou 3, Drogba 2, Deco 1, Malouda 1, Paulo Ferreira 1.

FA Cup (17): Sturridge 4, Drogba 3, Lampard 3, Malouda 2, Anelka 1, Ballack 1, Kalou 1, Terry 1, own goal 1.

Champions League (12): Anelka 3, Drogba 3, Kalou 3, Essien 1, Lampard 1, own goal 1.

Community Shield (2): Lampard 1, Ricardo Carvalho 1.

Ground: Stamford Bridge, Fulham Rd, London SW6 1HS. Telephone (0871) 984 1955.

Record Attendance: 82,905 v Arsenal, Division 1, 12 October 1935.

Capacity: 41,841.

Manager: Carlo Ancelotti.

Secretary: David Barnard.

Most League Goals: 103, FA Premier League, 2009–10

Highest League Scorer in Season: Jimmy Greaves, 41, 1960–61.

Most League Goals in Total Aggregate: Bobby Tambling, 164, 1958–70.

Most Capped Player: Frank Lampard, 80 (82), England.

Most League Appearances: Ron Harris, 655, 1962–80.

Honours – FA Premier League: Champions – 2004–05, 2005–06, 2009–10. **Football League:** Division 1 Champions – 1954–55. Division 2 Champions – 1983–84, 1988–89. **FA Cup:** Winners – 1970, 1997, 2000, 2007, 2009, 2010. **Football League Cup:** Winners – 1964–65, 1997–98, 2004–05, 2006–07. **Full Members' Cup:** Winners – 1985–86. **Zenith Data Systems Cup:** Winners – 1989–90. **European Cup-Winners' Cup:** Winners – 1970–71, 1997–98. **Super Cup:** Winners – 1999.

Colours: Reflex blue shirts, reflex blue shorts, white stockings with blue trim.

CHELTENHAM TOWN   FL CHAMPIONSHIP 2

Bird David (M)	5 9	12 00	Gloucester	26 12 84	Cinderford T
Brown Scott P (G)	6 2	13 01	Wolverhampton	26 4 85	Bristol C

Duff Shane (D)	6 1 12 10	Wroughton	2 4 82	Juniors
Emery Josh (M)	5 6 10 10	Ledbury	30 9 90	Scholar
Gallinagh Andy (D)	5 8 11 08	Sutton Coldfield	16 3 85	Stratford T
Hayles Barry (F)	5 10 12 11	Lambeth	17 5 72	Leicester C
Haynes Kyle (D)	5 11 11 02	Wolverhampton	29 12 91	Scholar
Lee Jake (F)	6 0 12 07	Cirencester	18 9 91	Scholar
Lewis Theo (F)	5 10 10 12	Oxford	10 8 91	Scholar
Low Josh (M)	6 2 14 03	Bristol	15 2 79	Peterborough U
Pook Michael (M)	5 11 11 10	Swindon	22 10 85	Swindon T
Richards Justin (F)	5 11 11 00	Sandwell	16 10 80	Peterborough U
Watkins Marley (M)	5 10 10 04	London	17 10 90	Scholar

League Appearances: Almond, L. 2(2); Alsop, J. 21(20); Andrew, D. 9(1); Artus, F. 7; Bird, D. 35(2); Bozanic, O. 4; Brown, Scott P 46; Brown, Scott (1); Cox, S. 1; Denton, T. 1(1); Diallo, D. 17(1); Duff, S. 11; Eastham, A. 18(2); Elito, M. 12; Eyjolfsson, H. 4; Gallinagh, A. 35(4); Hammond, E. 14(10); Hayles, B. 23(16); Haynes, K. 6(7); Hutton, D. 14(11); Labadie, J. 11; Lee, J. (1); Lescott, A. 7(1); Lewis, T. 9(6); Low, J. 35(4); Marshall, B. 6; Pipe, D. 7(1); Pook, M. 31(4); Richards, J. 39(5); Ridley, L. 26(1); Rose, R. 1; Thornhill, M. 16(1); Townsend, M. 34; Watkins, M. 4(9).

Goals – League (54): Richards 15 (5 pens), Hayles 7, Pook 5, Alsop 4, Hammond 4, Low 4, Elito 3, Thornhill 3, Townsend 3, Marshall 2, Gallinagh 1, Ridley 1, Watkins 1, own goal 1.

Carling Cup (1): Hammond 1.

FA Cup (1): Lewis 1.

J Paint Trophy (1): Low 1.

Ground: The Abbey Business Stadium, Whaddon Road, Cheltenham, Gloucestershire GL52 5NA. Telephone (01242) 573 558.

Record Attendance: at Whaddon Road: 8,326 v Reading, FA Cup 1st rd, 17 November 1956; at Cheltenham Athletic Ground: 10,389 v Blackpool, FA Cup 3rd rd, 13 January 1934.

Capacity: 7,136.

Manager: Mark Yates.

Secretary: Paul Godfrey.

Most League Goals: 66, Division 3, 2001–02.

Highest League Scorer in Season: Julian Alsop, 20, Division 3, 2001–02.

Most League Goals in Total Aggregate: Martin Devaney, 38, 1999–2005.

Most Capped Player: Grant McCann, 7 (28), Northern Ireland.

Most League Appearances: Jamie Victory, 258, 1999–.

Honours – Football Conference: Champions – 1998–99. **FA Trophy:** Winners – 1997–98.

Colours: All red with white trim.

CHESTERFIELD   FL CHAMPIONSHIP 2

Allott Mark (M)	5 11 11 07	Middleton	3 10 77	Oldham Ath
Boden Scott (F)	5 11 11 00	Sheffield	19 12 89	IFK Marlehamn
Bowery Jordan (F)	6 1 12 00	Nottingham	2 7 91	Scholar
Breckin Ian (D)	6 2 13 05	Rotherham	24 2 75	Nottingham F
Downes Aaron (D)	6 3 13 00	Mudgee	15 5 85	Frickley C
Gray Dan (M)	6 0 11 00	Mansfield	23 11 89	Scholar
Gritton Martin (F)	6 1 12 02	Glasgow	1 6 78	Macclesfield T
Lee Tommy (G)	6 2 12 00	Keighley	3 1 86	Macclesfield T
Lester Jack (F)	5 9 12 08	Sheffield	8 10 75	Nottingham F
Lowry Jamie (D)	6 0 12 04	Newquay	18 3 87	Scholar
Malak Matt (G)	6 3 12 00	Doncaster	23 9 90	Scholar
Niven Derek (M)	6 0 12 02	Falkirk	12 12 83	Bolton W

| Page Robert (D) | 6 0 | 12 05 | Llwynpia | 3 | 9 74 | Huddersfield T |
| Talbot Drew (F) | 5 10 | 11 00 | Barnsley | 19 | 7 86 | Luton T |

League Appearances: Allott, M. 45; Artus, F. 2(1); Austin, K. 14(5); Boden, S. 5(30); Boshell, D. 3(6); Bowery, J. 2(8); Breckin, I. 41(1); Conlon, B. 15(4); Crossley, M. 4; Currie, D. 2(2); Demontagnac, I. 10; Djilali, K. 8; Downes, A. 7; Goodall, A. 17; Gray, D. 16(3); Green, D. 10; Gritton, M. 2(7); Hall, D. 5(2); Harsley, P. (3); Lee, T. 42; Lester, J. 27(2); Lewis, T. (1); Little, M. 12; Lowry, J. 13; Madine, G. 2(2); McDermott, D. 13(2); Morris, I. 7; Niven, D. 28(11); Page, R. 38(1); Perkins, D. 11(2); Picken, P. 20(1); Robertson, G. 8(2); Rundle, A. 12(4); Small, W. 24(3); Somma, D. 1(2); Talbot, D. 26(4); Whaley, S. 5(1); Whing, A. 9(2).
Goals – League (61): Lester 11, Conlon 7 (5 pens), Boden 6, Talbot 6, Lowry 5 (3 pens), McDermott 5, Small 4, Demontagnac 3, Allott 2, Green 2, Niven 2, Djilali 1, Downes 1, Gritton 1, Hall 1, Page 1, Perkins 1, Whaley 1, own goal 1.
Carling Cup (1): Currie 1 (pen).
FA Cup (1): Lester 1.
J Paint Trophy (9): Talbot 4, Small 2, Bowery 1, Currie 1 (pen), Lowry 1.
Ground: The Recreation Ground, Chesterfield, Derbyshire S40 4SX. Telephone (01246) 209 765.
Record Attendance: 30,968 v Newcastle U, Division 2, 7 April 1939. **Capacity:** 8,502.
Manager: John Sheridan.
Finance Director: Alan Walters.
Most League Goals: 102, Division 3 (N), 1930–31.
Highest League Scorer in Season: Jimmy Cookson, 44, Division 3 (N), 1925–26.
Most League Goals in Total Aggregate: Ernie Moss, 161, 1969–76, 1979–81 and 1984–86.
Most Capped Player: Walter McMillen, 4 (7), Northern Ireland; Mark Williams, 4 (30), Northern Ireland.
Most League Appearances: Dave Blakey, 613, 1948–67.
Honours – Football League: Division 3 (N) Champions – 1930–31, 1935–36. Division 4 Champions – 1969–70, 1984–85. **Anglo-Scottish Cup:** Winners – 1980–81.
Colours: Blue shirts with white trim, white shorts, white stockings.

COLCHESTER UNITED   FL CHAMPIONSHIP 1

Baldwin Pat (D)	6 3	12 07	City of London	12 11 82	Chelsea
Beevers Lee (D)	6 2	11 07	Doncaster	4 12 83	Lincoln C
Bender Thomas (M)	6 3	12 00	Harlow	19 1 93	Scholar
Cousins Mark (G)	6 1	11 03	Chelmsford	9 1 87	Scholar
Elito Medy (M)	6 2	13 00	Kinshasa	20 3 90	Scholar
Fox David (M)	5 9	11 08	Leek	13 12 83	Blackpool
Gillespie Steven (F)	5 9	11 02	Liverpool	4 6 84	Cheltenham T
Hackney Simon (M)	5 8	9 13	Manchester	5 2 84	Carlisle U
Heath Matt (D)	6 4	13 13	Leicester	1 11 81	Leeds U
Henderson Ian (F)	5 10	11 06	Thetford	25 1 85	Luton T
Ifil Phil (D)	5 10	12 02	Willesden	18 11 86	Tottenham H
Izzet Kem (M)	5 7	10 05	Mile End	29 9 80	Charlton Ath
Maybury Alan (D)	5 8	11 08	Dublin	8 8 78	Leicester C
O'Toole John (M)	6 2	13 07	Harrow	30 9 88	Watford
Odejayi Kayode (F)	6 2	12 02	Ibadon	21 2 82	Barnsley
Okuonghae Magnus (D)	6 3	13 04	Nigeria	16 2 86	Dagenham & R
Perkins David (D)	5 6	11 06	St Asaph	21 6 82	Rochdale
Platt Clive (F)	6 4	12 07	Wolverhampton	27 10 77	Milton Keynes D
Prutton David (M)	5 10	13 00	Hull	12 9 81	Leeds U
Reid Paul (D)	6 2	11 08	Carlisle	18 2 82	Barnsley
Thomas Joel (F)	6 1	12 04	Caen	30 6 87	Hamilton A
Tierney Marc (D)	5 11	11 04	Manchester	7 9 86	Shrewsbury T

Vincent Ashley (F)	5 10	11 08	Oldbury	26	5 85	Cheltenham T
White John (M)	5 10	12 01	Maldon	26	7 86	Scholar
Williams Ben (G)	6 0	13 01	Manchester	27	8 82	Carlisle U
Wordsworth Anthony (M)	6 1	12 00	London	3	1 89	Scholar

League Appearances: Baldwin, P. 6(1); Batth, D. 16(1); Beevers, L. 4; Bender, Thomas (1); Elito, M. (3); Fox, D. 15(3); Gillespie, S. 8(22); Guy, J. (1); Hackney, S. 9(8); Hammond, D. 2; Heath, M. 13(5); Henderson, I. 6(7); Ifil, P. 15(12); Izzet, K. 31(6); Lisbie, K. 35(6); Lockwood, M. 1; Maybury, A. 1(1); O'Toole, J. 30(1); Odejayi, K. 19(9); Okuonghae, M. 44; Payne, J. 2(1); Perkins, D. (5); Platt, C. 36(5); Prutton, D. 18(1); Queudrue, F. 3; Reid, P. 10(2); Ribeiro, C. 2; Thomas, J. (4); Tierney, M. 41; Vernon, S. 4(3); Vincent, A. 15(4); White, J. 38(1); Williams, B. 46; Wordsworth, A. 36(5).

Goals – League (64): Lisbie 13 (5 pens), Wordsworth 11, Odejayi 9, Platt 7, Fox 3, Prutton 3, Vernon 3, Vincent 3, Henderson 2, Ifil 2, O'Toole 2, Batth 1, Gillespie 1, Hackney 1, Perkins 1, own goals 2.

Carling Cup (1): Hackney 1.

FA Cup (5): Hackney 1, Gillespie 1, Odejayi 1, O'Toole 1, Platt 1.

J Paint Trophy (1): Platt 1.

Ground: Weston Homes Community Stadium, United Way, Colchester, Essex CO4 5UP. Telephone (01206) 755 100.

Record Attendance: 19,072 v Reading, FA Cup 1st rd, 27 November, 1948. **Capacity:** 10,000

Manager: John Ward.

Football Secretary: Caroline Pugh.

Most League Goals: 104, Division 4, 1961–62.

Highest League Scorer in Season: Bobby Hunt, 38, Division 4, 1961–62.

Most League Goals in Total Aggregate: Martyn King, 130, 1956–64.

Most Capped Player: Bela Balogh, 2 (9), Hungary.

Most League Appearances: Micky Cook, 613, 1969–84.

Honours – GM Vauxhall Conference: Winners – 1991–92. **FA Trophy:** Winners: 1991–92.

Colours: Royal blue and white striped shirts with white sleeves, royal blue shorts, white stockings.

COVENTRY CITY   FL CHAMPIONSHIP

Baker Carl (M)	6 2	12 06	Prescot	26 12 82	Stockport Co
Bell David (M)	5 10	11 05	Kettering	21 1 84	Norwich C
Clarke Jordan (D)	6 0	11 02	Coventry	19 11 91	Scholar
Clingan Sammy (M)	5 11	11 06	Belfast	13 1 84	Norwich C
Cranie Martin (D)	6 1	12 09	Yeovil	23 9 86	Portsmouth
Deegan Gary (M)	5 9	11 11	Dublin	28 9 87	Bohemians
Doyle Micky (M)	5 8	11 00	Dublin	8 7 81	Celtic
Eastwood Freddy (F)	5 11	12 04	Epsom	29 10 83	Wolverhampton W
Grandison Jermaine (D)	6 4	13 03	Birmingham	15 12 90	Scholar
Gunnarsson Aron (M)	5 9	11 00	Akureyri	22 9 89	AZ
Hussey Chris (D)	5 10	10 03	Hammersmith	2 1 89	AFC Wimbledon
Ireland Daniel (G)			Sydney	20 1 89	
Jeffers Shaun (F)	6 1	11 03	Bedford	14 4 92	Scholar
McIndoe Michael (M)	5 8	11 00	Edinburgh	2 12 79	Bristol C
McPake James (D)	6 2	12 08	Bellshill	2 6 84	Livingston
Osbourne Isaac (M)	5 9	11 11	Birmingham	22 6 86	Scholar
Turner Ben (D)	6 4	14 04	Birmingham	21 1 88	Scholar
Westwood Keiren (G)	6 1	13 10	Manchester	23 10 84	Carlisle U
Wood Richard (D)	6 3	12 13	Wakefield	5 7 85	Sheffield W

44

League Appearances: Baker, C. 14(8); Barnett, L. 19(1); Bell, D. 20(8); Best, L. 25(2); Cain, A. (2); Clarke, J. 6(6); Clingan, S. 32(2); Cork, J. 20(1); Cranie, M. 38(2); Deegan, G. 9(8); Eastwood, F. 21(15); Grandison, J. 1(2); Gunnarsson, A. 34(6); Hall, M. 7(1); Hussey, C. 1(7); Jeffers, S. (4); Konstantopoulos, D. 2(1); Madine, G. (9); McIndoe, M. 38(2); McKenzie, L. (1); McPake, J. 17; Morrison, C. 38(8); Osbourne, I. 12(3); Sears, F. 3(7); Stead, J. 9(1); Turner, B. 13; Van Aanholt, P. 19(1); Ward, E. 4(4); Westwood, K. 44; Wood, R. 22(2); Wright, S. 38.
Goals – League (47): Morrison 11 (1 pen), Best 9, Eastwood 8, Clingan 5, Wood 3, Bell 2, Deegan 2, Stead 2, Cranie 1, Gunnarsson 1, McIndoe 1, McPake 1, own goal 1.
Carling Cup (0).
FA Cup (2): Bell 1, Best 1.
Ground: The Ricoh Arena, Phoenix Way, Foleshill, Coventry CV6 6GE. Telephone (0844) 873 1883.
Record Attendance: 31,407 v Chelsea, FA Cup 6th rd, 7 March 2009 (at The Ricoh Arena); 51,455 v Wolverhampton W, Division 2, 29 April 1967 (at Highfield Road).
Capacity: 32,609.
Manager: Aidy Boothroyd.
Secretary: Pam Hindson.
Most League Goals: 108, Division 3 (S), 1931–32.
Highest League Scorer in Season: Clarrie Bourton, 49, Division 3 (S), 1931–32.
Most League Goals in Total Aggregate: Clarrie Bourton, 171, 1931–37.
Most Capped Player: Magnus Hedman, 44 (58), Sweden.
Most League Appearances: Steve Ogrizovic, 507, 1984–2000.
Honours – Football League: Division 2 Champions – 1966–67. Division 3 Champions – 1963–64. Division 3 (S) Champions 1935–36. **FA Cup:** Winners – 1986–1987.
Colours: Sky blue shirts with grey horizontal stripes, white shorts, sky blue stockings.

CREWE ALEXANDRA   FL CHAMPIONSHIP 2

Antoni Sarcevic (M)	5 10	11 00		13	3 92	Woodley Sports
Bailey James (M)	6 0	12 05	Bollington	18	9 88	Scholar
Brayford John (D)	5 8	11 02	Stoke	29	12 87	Burton Alb
Donaldson Clayton (F)	6 1	11 07	Bradford	7	2 84	Hibernian
Gardner Danny (F)	6 1	12 08	Manchester	30	11 89	Scholar
Grant Joel (F)	6 0	12 01	Hammersmith	26	8 87	Aldershot T
Jordan Connerton (M)			Lancaster	2	10 89	Lancaster C
Legzdins Adam (G)	6 1	14 02	Stafford	28	11 86	Birmingham C
Leitch-Smith AJ (F)	5 11	12 04	Crewe	6	3 90	Scholar
Martin Carl (D)	5 8	10 07	London	24	10 86	Wealdstone
Mellor Kelvin (D)	5 10	11 09	Copenhagen	5	4 90	Nantwich T
Miller Shaun (F)	5 10	11 08	Alsager	25	9 87	Scholar
Mitchel-King Mat (D)	6 4	13 02	Cambridge	12	9 83	Histon
Moore Byron (M)	6 0	10 06	Stoke	24	8 88	Scholar
Murphy Luke (M)	6 1	11 05	Macclesfield	21	10 89	Scholar
Patrick Ada (D)	6 0	13 05	Yaounde	14	1 85	Histon
Shelley Danny (D)	5 9	10 08	Stoke	29	12 90	Scholar
Tootle Matt (D)	5 9	11 00	Crewe	11	10 90	Scholar
Westwood Ashley (D)	5 10	11 00	Crewe	1	4 90	Scholar
Zola Calvin (F)	6 3	14 06	Kinshasa	31	12 84	Tranmere R

League Appearances: Ada, P. 16(2); Bailey, J. 20(1); Bogdan, A. 1; Brayford, J. 45; Button, D. 10; Collis, S. 1; Davis, H. (1); Donaldson, C. 28(9); Elding, A. 4(6); Gardner, D. (2); Grant, J. 41(2); Jones, B. 10(1); Legzdins, A. 6; Leitch-Smith, A. (1); Martin, C. 1(5); Miller, S. 22(11); Mitchel-King, M. 11(1); Moore, B. 13(19); Murphy, L. 24(8); O'Donnell, D. 27; Phillips, S. 28; Schumacher, S. 27(5); Shelley, D. 7(12); Stokes, C. 2; Tootle, M. 26(2); Verma, A. 5(2); Walton, S. 26(5); Westwood, A. 34(2); Worley, H. 21(2); Zola, C. 30(4).

Goals – League (68): Zola 15, Donaldson 13, Grant 9, Miller 7 (1 pen), Westwood 6, Schumacher 4, Moore 3, Murphy 3, Jones 2 (1 pen), Martin 1, Shelley 1, Tootle 1, Walton 1, Worley 1, own goal 1.
Carling Cup (1): Zola 1.
FA Cup (2): Grant 1, Zola 1.
J Paint Trophy (1): Zola 1.
Ground: The Alexandra Stadium, Gresty Road, Crewe, Cheshire CW2 6EB. Telephone (01270) 213 014.
Record Attendance: 20,000 v Tottenham H, FA Cup 4th rd, 30 January 1960. **Capacity:** 10,107.
Manager: Dario Gradi MBE.
Financial Operations Manager: Andrew Blakemore.
Most League Goals: 95, Division 3 (N), 1931–32.
Highest League Scorer in Season: Terry Harkin, 35, Division 4, 1964–65.
Most League Goals in Total Aggregate: Bert Swindells, 126, 1928–37.
Most Capped Player: Clayton Ince, 38 (79), Trinidad & Tobago.
Most League Appearances: Tommy Lowry, 436, 1966–78.
Honours – Welsh Cup: Winners – 1936, 1937.
Colours: Red shirts with white trim, white shorts, red stockings.

CRYSTAL PALACE   FL CHAMPIONSHIP

Ambrose Darren (M)	6 0	11 00	Harlow	29	2 84	Charlton Ath
Andrew Calvin (F)	6 0	12 11	Luton	19 12 86		Luton T
Cadogan Kieron (M)	6 4	12 07	Wandsworth	16	8 90	Scholar
Carle Nick (F)	5 9	12 04	Sydney	23 11 81		Bristol C
Clyne Nathaniel (D)	5 9	10 07	London	5	4 91	Scholar
Danns Neil (M)	5 10	10 12	Liverpool	23 11 82		Birmingham C
Davis Claude (D)	6 3	14 04	Kingston	6	3 79	Derby Co
Djilali Kieran (M)	6 3	13 02	London	1	1 91	Scholar
Hills Lee (D)	5 10 11 11		Croydon	3	4 90	Scholar
Lee Alan (F)	6 2	13 09	Galway	21	8 78	Ipswich T
McCarthy Patrick (D)	6 2	13 07	Dublin	31	5 83	Charlton Ath
N'Diaye Alassane (M)	6 4	14 02	Audincourt	25	2 90	Scholar
Pinney Nathaniel (F)	6 0	12 05	South Norwood	16 11 90		Scholar
Scannell Sean (F)	5 9	11 07	Cork	21	3 89	Scholar
Speroni Julian (G)	6 0	11 00	Buenos Aires	18	5 79	Dundee

League Appearances: Ambrose, D. 44(2); Andrew, C. 13(14); Butterfield, D. 36(1); Carle, N. 14(8); Clyne, N. 19(3); Danns, N. 41(1); Davis, C. 19(2); Derry, S. 46; Djilali, K. 2(6); Ertl, J. 29(4); Flahavan, D. 1; Fonte, J. 22; Hill, C. 43; Hills, L. 10(9); John, S. 7(9); Lawrence, M. 14(4); Lee, A. 33(9); McCarthy, P. 20; Moses, V. 14(4); N'Diaye, A. 12(14); Scannell, S. 11(15); Sears, F. 11(7); Smith, R. (5); Speroni, J. 45; Zaha, W. (1).
Goals – League (50): Ambrose 15 (1 pen), Danns 8, Lee 6, Moses 6, N'Diaye 3, John 2, Scannell 2, Andrew 1, Carle 1, Clyne 1, Djilali 1, Fonte 1, Hill 1, own goals 2.
Carling Cup (2): Ambrose 2 (1 pen).
FA Cup (10): Butterfield 3, Ambrose 3 (1 pen), Andrew 1, Danns 1, Ertl 1, Lee 1.
Ground: Selhurst Park, Whitehorse Lane, London SE25 6PU. Telephone (020) 8768 6000.
Record Attendance: 51,482 v Burnley, Division 2, 11 May 1979. **Capacity:** 26,225.
Manager: George Burley.
Assistant Secretary: Christine Dowdeswell.
Most League Goals: 110, Division 4, 1960–61.
Highest League Scorer in Season: Peter Simpson, 46, Division 3 (S), 1930–31.
Most League Goals in Total Aggregate: Peter Simpson, 153, 1930–36.
Most Capped Player: Aleksandrs Kolinko, 23 (83), Latvia.
Most League Appearances: Jim Cannon, 571, 1973–88.

Honours – Football League: Division 1 – Champions 1993–94. Division 2 Champions – 1978–79. Division 3 (S) 1920–21. **Zenith Data Systems Cup:** Winners – 1991.
Colours: Red and blue striped shirts, blue shorts, blue stockings.

DAGENHAM & REDBRIDGE   FL CHAMPIONSHIP 1

Antwi Will (D)	6 2	12 08	Epsom	19 10 82	Wycombe W
Arber Mark (D)	6 1	11 09	Johannesburg	9 10 77	Peterborough U
Benson Paul (F)	6 1	11 01	Rochford	12 10 79	White Notley
Bingham Billy (D)	5 11	11 02	London	15 7 90	Crystal Palace
Dean Harlee (M)	6 0	11 10	Basingstoke	26 7 91	Scholar
Doe Scott (D)	6 0	11 06	Reading	6 11 88	Weymouth
Gain Peter (M)	5 9	11 07	Hammersmith	11 11 76	Peterborough U
Green Danny (M)	5 11	12 00	Harlow	9 7 88	Northampton T
McCrory Damien (D)	6 2	12 10	Limerick	22 2 90	Plymouth Arg
Montgomery Graeme (M)	6 1	12 00	Dagenham	3 3 88	Wealdstone
Nurse Jon (F)	5 9	12 04	Barbados	28 3 81	Stevenage B
Ogogo Abu (D)	5 8	10 02	Epsom	3 11 89	Arsenal
Roberts Tony (G)	6 0	14 11	Bangor	4 8 69	QPR
Scott Josh (F)	6 1	12 00	London	10 5 85	Hayes & Yeading
Tejan-Sie Thomas (F)	5 6	11 08	London	23 11 88	Wingate & Finchley
Thomas Wesley (F)	5 10	11 00	Essex	23 1 87	Fisher Ath
Thurgood Stuart (M)	5 8	12 03	Enfield	4 11 81	Gillingham
Uddin Anwar (D)	6 1	13 07	London	1 11 81	Bristol R
Vincelot Romain (M)	5 9	11 02	Poitiers	29 10 85	Gueugnon
Walsh Phil (F)	6 3	13 04	Hartlepool	4 2 84	Dorchester T

League Appearances: Antwi, W. 19; Arber, M. 41; Benson, P. 45; Bingham, B. (2); Carlos, J. (1); Currie, D. 5(11); Day, J. 8; Dean, H. (1); Doe, S. 40(2); Folly, Y. 5(2); Gain, P. 43; Green, D. 45(1); Griffiths, S. 13; Lockwood, M. 4; McCrory, D. 20; Miller, A. 8; Montgomery, G. 4(13); Nurse, J. 30(8); Ofori-Twumasi, N. 8; Ogogo, A. 27(3); Pack, M. 17; Roberts, T. 46; Scott, J. 36(4); Spiller, D. 7(3); Taiwo, S. 4; Tejan-Sie, T. 1(2); Thomas, W. 3(20); Thurgood, S. 17; Uddin, A. 3(3); Vincelot, Romain 7(2); Walsh, P. (9).
Goals – League (69): Benson 17, Green 13 (3 pens), Scott 10, Nurse 7, Arber 4 (3 pens), Gain 3, Thomas 3, Montgomery 2, Ofori-Twumasi 2, Ogogo 2, Antwi 1, Griffiths 1, Pack 1, Vincelot, Romain 1, own goals 2.
Carling Cup (1): Scott 1.
FA Cup (1): Benson 1.
J Paint Trophy (1): Scott 1.
Play-Offs (10): Benson 4, Scott 4, Green 1, Nurse 1.
Ground: The London Borough of Barking and Dagenham Stadium, Victoria Road, Dagenham, Essex, RM10 7XR. Telephone (0208) 592 1549.
Record Attendance: 4,791 v Shrewsbury T, FL2, 2 May 2009. **Capacity:** 6,007.
Manager: John L. Still.
Secretary: Terry Grover.
Most League Goals: 77, FL 2, 2008–09.
Highest League Scorer in Season: Paul Benson, 28, Conference, 2006–07.
Most League Goals in Total Aggregate: 40, Paul Benson, 2007–.
Most Capped Player: Jon Nurse, 4, Barbados
Most League Appearances: Tony Roberts, 132, 2007–.
Honours – Conference: Champions – 2006–07. **Isthmian League (Premier):** Champions 1999–2000.
Colours: Red shirts with blue sleeves and red trim, blue shorts, blue stockings.

Arnison Paul (D)	5 10 10 12	Hartlepool	18 9 77	Bradford C
Barnes Corey (F)	5 8 10 08	Sunderland	1 1 92	Scholar
Burn Dan (D)		Blyth	9 5 92	
Byrne Richie (D)	6 1 12 04	Shamrock	24 9 81	
Gray Josh (F)	6 1 11 12	South Shields	22 7 91	Scholar
Lumsdon Chris (M)	5 11 10 06	Newcastle	15 12 79	Carlisle U
Main Curtis (F)	5 9 12 02	South Shields	20 6 92	Scholar
Miller Ian (M)	6 2 12 02	Colchester	23 11 83	Ipswich T
Moore Chris (M)	5 10 10 09	Newcastle	1 12 85	Whitley Bay
Purcell Tadgh (F)	5 11 12 02	Dundrum	9 2 85	Shamrock R
Smith Gary (M)	5 8 10 09	Middlesbrough	30 1 84	Brentford
Smith Michael (M)	5 11 11 03	Wallsend	17 10 91	Scholar
Waite Gareth (M)		Stockton	16 2 86	Spennymoor T

League Appearances: Arnison, P. 17(1); Bains, R. 3(1); Barnes, C. 4(2); Barnett, M. 4; Bennett, J. 3(1); Bower, M. 12(1); Burn, D. 2(2); Byrne, R. 2(2); Chandler, J. 12(2); Chisholm, R. 2(1); Collins, J. 5(2); Convery, M. 9(12); Cook, J. 4(1); Davis, D. 5; Deane, P. (10); Dempsey, G. 24; Devitt, J. 5(1); Diop, M. 18(5); Dowson, D. 6(4); Foster, S. 15(1); Gall, K. 9(1); Giddings, S. 22; Gray, J. 10(17); Groves, D. 8(8); Hall, D. 3; Harsley, P. 3; Hogg, J. 5; Hoult, R. 6; Jones, A. 1; Kane, T. 4; Knight, D. 7; Liversedge, N. 13; Lumsdon, C. 2; Madden, S. 13(2); Main, C. 12(14); Marshall, J. (3); McReady, J. 3(1); Miller, I. 40; Milne, A. 12(1); Moore, C. 8(3); Mulligan, N. 10(6); Plummer, M. 5(3); Porritt, N. 4(1); Purcell, T. 22; Redmond, S. 19; Smith, G. 32(2); Smith, J. 22(2); Smith, M. 3(4); Thomas, S. 7; Thorpe, L. 7(1); Waite, G. 14; Whelan, N. 2(1); White, A. 23(1); Windass, D. 3(3).
Goals – League (33): Purcell 9 (1 pen), Main 3, Collins 2, Diop 2, Gall 2, Arnison 1, Dempsey 1, Devitt 1, Dowson 1, Gray 1, Hogg 1, Miller 1, Mulligan 1, Smith G 1, Smith M 1, Thomas 1, Waite 1, White 1, own goals 2.
Carling Cup (0).
FA Cup (1): Diop 1.
J Paint Trophy (2): Convery 1, Thorpe 1.
Ground: Northern Echo Darlington Arena, Neasham Road, Hurworth Moor, Darlington DL2 1DL. Telephone (01325) 387 000.
Record Attendance: 21,023 v Bolton W, League Cup 3rd rd, 14 November 1960.
Capacity: 25,000.
Manager: Mark Cooper.
Secretary: Lisa Charlton.
Most League Goals: 108, Division 3 (N), 1929–30.
Highest League Scorer in Season: David Brown, 39, Division 3 (N), 1924–25.
Most League Goals in Total Aggregate: Alan Walsh, 90, 1978–84.
Most Capped Player: Franz Burgmeier, 7 (58), Liechtenstein.
Most League Appearances: Ron Greener, 442, 1955–68.
Honours – Football League: Division 3 (N) Champions – 1924–25. Division 4 Champions – 1990–91. **GM Vauxhall Conference:** Champions – 1989–90.
Colours: White shirts, black sleeves with white trim, black shorts with white trim, black and white hooped stockings.

DERBY COUNTY   **FL CHAMPIONSHIP**

Abalimba Medi (M)		Congo	30 9 91	Southend U
Addison Miles (D)	6 2 13 03	Newham	7 1 89	Scholar
Anderson Russell (D)	5 11 10 09	Aberdeen	25 10 78	Sunderland
Atkins Ross (G)	6 0 13 00	Derby	3 11 89	Scholar
Barker Shaun (D)	6 2 12 08	Nottingham	19 9 82	Blackpool
Buxton Jake (D)	6 1 13 05	Sutton-in-Ashfield	4 3 85	Burton Alb

Bywater Stephen (G)	6 2	12 08	Manchester	7	6 81	West Ham U
Commons Kris (M)	5 6	9 08	Mansfield	30	8 83	Nottingham F
Connolly Paul (D)	6 0	11 09	Liverpool	29	9 83	Plymouth Arg
Connolly Ryan (M)	5 10	10 06	Castlebar	13	1 92	Scholar
Croft Lee (M)	5 11	13 00	Wigan	21	6 85	Norwich C
Davies Steve (F)	6 0	12 00	Liverpool	29	12 87	Tranmere R
Deeney Saul (G)	6 1	11 07	Derry	23	3 83	Burton Alb
Green Paul (M)	5 9	10 02	Pontefract	10	4 83	Doncaster R
Hanson Mitchell (D)	6 1	13 07	Derby	2	9 88	Scholar
Hulse Rob (F)	6 1	12 04	Crewe	25	10 79	Sheffield U
Leacock Dean (D)	6 2	12 04	Croydon	10	6 84	Fulham
Mendy Arnaud (F)	6 3	13 10	Evreux	10	2 90	Rouen
Mills Greg (F)	6 2	13 00	Derby	18	9 90	Scholar
Moxey Dean (D)	6 2	11 00	Exeter	14	1 86	Exeter C
O'Brien Mark (D)	5 11	12 02	Dublin	20	11 92	Cherry Orchard
Pearson Stephen (M)	6 1	11 11	Lanark	2	10 82	Celtic
Porter Chris (F)	6 1	12 09	Wigan	12	12 83	Motherwell
Pringle Ben (M)	5 8	11 09	Newcastle	27	5 89	Ilkeston T
Savage Robbie (M)	5 11	11 00	Wrexham	18	10 74	Blackburn R
Varney Luke (F)	5 11	11 00	Leicester	28	9 82	Charlton Ath

League Appearances: Addison, M. 10(3); Anderson, R. 9(6); Ball, C. (1); Barker, S. 33(2); Buxton, J. 19; Bywater, S. 42; Campbell, D. 6(2); Commons, K. 11(9); Connolly, R. (1); Connolly, P. 17(4); Croft, L. 14(5); Cywka, T. 4(1); Davies, S. 7(11); Dickov, P. 10(6); Green, P. 30(3); Hendrie, L. 4(5); Hughes, B. 3; Hulse, R. 30(7); Hunt, N. 20(1); Johnson, L. 4; Leacock, D. 13(4); Livermore, J. 11(5); Martin, David J 2(9); Martin, David E 2; McEveley, J. 28(5); Mendy, A. (1); Mills, G. (2); Moxey, D. 27(3); Pearson, S. 34(3); Porter, C. 11(10); Pringle, B. 1(4); Savage, R. 45(1); Stoor, F. 10(1); Sunu, G. 6(3); Teale, G. 21(7); Tonge, M. 18; Varney, L. (1); Vaughan, J. 2; Vidal, J. (1).

Goals – League (53): Hulse 12 (1 pen), Barker 5, Porter 4, Campbell 3, Commons 3 (2 pens), Addison 2, Dickov 2, Green 2, McEveley 2, Savage 2, Teale 2, Tonge 2, Anderson 1, Buxton 1, Croft 1, Davies 1 (1 pen), Livermore 1, Martin, David J 1, Pearson 1, Sunu 1, own goals 4.

Carling Cup (1): Teale 1.

FA Cup (4): McEveley 2, Commons 1, Davies 1.

Ground: Pride Park Stadium, Derby DE24 8XL. Telephone (0871) 472 1884.

Record Attendance: Pride Park: 33,475 Derby Co Legends v Rangers 9 in a Row Legends, 1 May 2006 (Ted McMinn Benefit). Baseball Ground: 41,826 v Tottenham H, Division 1, 20 September 1969. **Capacity:** 33,597.

Manager: Nigel Clough.

Secretary: Clare Morris.

Most League Goals: 111, Division 3 (N), 1956–57.

Highest League Scorer in Season: Jack Bowers, 37, Division 1, 1930–31; Ray Straw, 37 Division 3 (N), 1956–57.

Most League Goals in Total Aggregate: Steve Bloomer, 292, 1892–1906 and 1910–14.

Most Capped Players: Deon Burton, 42 (59).

Most League Appearances: Kevin Hector, 486, 1966–78 and 1980–82.

Honours – Football League: Division 1 Champions – 1971–72, 1974–75. Division 2 Champions – 1911–12, 1914–15, 1968–69, 1986–87. Division 3 (N) Champions – 1956–57. **FA Cup:** Winners – 1945–46. **Texaco Cup:** Winners 1972.

Colours: White shirts with black trim, black shorts with white trim, white stockings with black trim.

DONCASTER ROVERS   FL CHAMPIONSHIP

| Brooker Stephen (F) | 6 0 | 14 00 | Newport Pagnell | 21 | 5 81 | Bristol C |
| Chambers James (D) | 5 10 | 11 11 | West Bromwich | 20 | 11 80 | Leicester C |

Clarke Robert (M)	5 5	10 10	Hull	30 4 91	Scholar
Coppinger James (F)	5 7	10 03	Middlesbrough	10 1 81	Exeter C
Dumbuya Mustapha (D)	5 7	11 00	Sierra Leone	7 8 87	Grays Ath
Fairhust Waide (F)	5 10	10 07	Sheffield	7 5 89	Scholar
Hayter James (F)	5 9	10 13	Newport (IW)	9 4 79	Bournemouth
Hird Samuel (D)	5 7	10 12	Askern	7 9 87	Leeds U
Lockwood Adam (D)	6 0	12 07	Wakefield	26 10 81	Yeovil T
Martis Shelton (D)	6 0	11 11	Willemstad	29 11 82	WBA
O'Connor James (D)	5 10	12 05	Birmingham	20 11 84	Bournemouth
Oster John (M)	5 9	10 08	Boston	8 12 78	Crystal Palace
Roberts Gareth (D)	5 8	12 00	Wrexham	6 2 78	Tranmere R
Shiels Dean (F)	5 11	9 10	Magherfelt	1 2 85	Hibernian
Stock Brian (M)	5 11	11 02	Winchester	24 12 81	Preston NE
Sullivan Neil (G)	6 2	12 00	Sutton	24 2 70	Leeds U
Webster Byron (D)	6 5	12 07	Leeds	13 3 87	SIAD Most
Wilson Mark (M)	5 11	12 00	Scunthorpe	9 2 79	Dallas
Woods Gary (G)	6 1	11 00	Kettering	1 10 90	Manchester U
Woods Martin (M)	5 11	11 13	Airdrie	1 1 86	Rotherham U

League Appearances: Chambers, J. 43; Coppinger, J. 38(1); Dumbuya, M. (3); Emmanuel-Thomas, J. 12(2); Fairhurst, W. 2(4); Fortune, Q. 3(3); Gillett, S. 10(1); Guy, L. 1(12); Hayter, J. 29(9); Heffernan, P. 6(11); Hird, S. 21(15); Lockwood, A. 10(6); Martis, S. 13(1); McDaid, S. (1); Mutch, J. 5(12); O'Connor, J. 33(5); Oster, J. 36(4); Roberts, G. 40(2); Shackell, J. 20(1); Sharp, B. 32(1); Shiels, D. 25(13); Smith, B. 1(1); Spicer, J. 9(11); Stock, B. 15; Sullivan, N. 45; Ward, E. 6; Webster, B. 1(4); Wilson, M. 29(6); Woods, M. 21(3).

Goals – League (59): Sharp 15 (2 pens), Hayter 9, Shiels 6 (1 pen), Emmanuel-Thomas 5, Coppinger 4, Woods M 4 (1 pen), Roberts 3, Fairhurst 2, Lockwood 2, Mutch 2, Fortune 1, Martis 1, Oster 1, Shackell 1, Ward 1, own goals 2.

Carling Cup (2): Coppinger 1, Woods M 1 (pen).

FA Cup (1): O'Connor 1.

Ground: Keepmoat Stadium, Stadium Way, Lakeside, Doncaster, South Yorkshire DN4 5JW. Telephone (01302) 764 664.

Record Attendance: 37,149 v Hull C, Division 3 (N), 2 October 1948. **Capacity:** 15,231.

Manager: Sean O'Driscoll.

Secretary: David Morris.

Most League Goals: 123, Division 3 (N), 1946–47.

Highest League Scorer in Season: Clarrie Jordan, 42, Division 3 (N) 1946–47.

Most League Goals in Total Aggregate: Tom Keetley, 180, 1923–29.

Most Capped Player: Len Graham, 14, Northern Ireland.

Most League Appearances: Fred Emery, 417, 1925–36.

Honours – Football League: Division 3 Champions – 2003–04. Division 3 (N) Champions – 1934–35, 1946–47, 1949–50. Division 4 Champions – 1965–66, 1968–69.

J Paint Trophy: Winners – 2006–07. **Football Conference:** Champions – 2002–03.

Colours: Red and white hooped shirts, red sleeves with black trim, black shorts with red trim, black stockings with red tops.

EVERTON   FA PREMIERSHIP

Agard Kieran (F)	6 2	14 00	Newham	10 10 89	Scholar
Akpan Hope (M)	6 0	10 06	Liverpool	14 8 91	Scholar
Anichebe Victor (F)	6 1	13 00	Nigeria	23 4 88	Scholar
Arteta Mikel (M)	5 9	10 08	San Sebastian	26 3 82	Real Sociedad
Baines Leighton (D)	5 8	11 00	Liverpool	11 12 84	Wigan Ath
Baxter Jose (F)	5 10	11 07	Bootle	7 2 92	Academy
Bidwell Jake (D)	6 0	11 00	Southport	21 3 93	Scholar

Name	Ht	Wt	Birthplace	Birthdate	Previous Club
Bilyaletdinov Diniyar (F)	6 1	11 11	Moscow	27 2 85	Lokomotiv Moscow
Cahill Tim (M)	5 10	10 12	Sydney	6 12 79	Millwall
Coleman Seamus (D)	6 4	12 00	Donegal	11 10 88	
Craig Nathan (M)			Bangor	25 10 91	Scholar
Davies Adam (G)			Rinteln	17 7 92	Scholar
Distin Sylvain (D)	6 3	14 06	Bagnolet	16 12 77	Portsmouth
Duffy Shane (D)	6 4	12 00	County Derry	1 1 92	Scholar
Fellaini Marouane (M)	6 4	13 05	Brussels	22 11 87	Standard Liege
Forshaw Adam (M)	6 1	11 00	Liverpool	8 10 91	Scholar
Gosling Dan (M)	6 0	11 00	Brixham	2 2 90	Plymouth Arg
Hibbert Tony (D)	5 9	11 05	Liverpool	20 2 81	Trainee
Howard Tim (G)	6 3	14 12	North Brunswick	6 3 79	Manchester U
Jagielka Phil (D)	6 0	13 01	Manchester	17 8 82	Sheffield U
Jutkiewicz Lukas (F)	6 1	12 11	Southampton	20 3 89	Swindon T
Kinsella Gerard (M)			Liverpool	13 11 90	Scholar
McAleny Conor (F)			Liverpool	12 8 92	Scholar
Mustafi Shkodran (D)	6 0	11 07	Bad Hersfeld	17 4 92	Hamburg
Neville Phil (M)	5 11	12 00	Bury	21 1 77	Manchester U
Nsiala Aristote (D)			Congo	25 3 92	Scholar
Orenuga Femi (M)			London	18 3 93	Southend U
Osman Leon (F)	5 8	10 09	Billinge	17 5 81	Trainee
Pienaar Steven (M)	5 10	10 06	Westbury	17 3 82	Borussia Dortmund
Roberts Connor (G)			Wrexham	8 12 92	Scholar
Rodwell Jack (D)	6 2	12 08	Birkdale	11 3 91	Scholar
Ruddy John (G)	6 3	12 07	St Ives	24 10 86	Cambridge U
Saha Louis (F)	6 1	12 08	Paris	8 8 78	Manchester U
Turner Iain (G)	6 3	12 10	Stirling	26 1 84	Trainee
Vaughan James (F)	5 11	12 08	Birmingham	14 7 88	Scholar
Wallace James (M)	5 11	13 00	Fazackerly	19 12 91	Scholar
Yakubu Ayegbeni (F)	6 0	14 07	Benin City	22 11 82	Middlesbrough
Yobo Joseph (D)	6 1	13 00	Kano	6 9 80	Marseille

League Appearances: Agard, K. (1); Anichebe, V. 6(5); Arteta, M. 11(2); Baines, L. 37; Baxter, J. (2); Bilyaletdinov, D. 16(7); Cahill, T. 33; Coleman, S. (3); Distin, S. 29; Donovan, L. 7(3); Fellaini, M. 20(3); Gosling, D. 3(8); Heitinga, J. 29(2); Hibbert, T. 17(3); Howard, T. 38; Jagielka, P. 11(1); Jo, 6(9); Lescott, J. 1; Neill, L. 10(2); Neville, P. 22(1); Osman, L. 25(1); Pienaar, S. 30; Rodwell, J. 17(9); Saha, L. 26(7); Senderos, P. 1(1); Vaughan, J. (8); Yakubu, A. 9(16); Yobo, J. 14(3).

Goals – League (60): Saha 13 (2 pens), Cahill 8, Arteta 6 (2 pens), Bilyaletdinov 6, Yakubu 5, Pienaar 4, Donovan 2, Fellaini 2, Gosling 2, Osman 2, Rodwell 2, Anichebe 1, Baines 1 (1 pen), Vaughan 1, Yobo 1, own goals 4.

Carling Cup (4): Gosling 1, Jo 1, Osman 1, Yakubu 1.

FA Cup (4): Baines 1 (pen), Cahill 1, Osman 1, Vaughan 1.

Europa League (14): Pienaar 3, Distin 2, Rodwell 2, Saha 2, Bilyaletdinov 1, Cahill 1, Fellaini 1, Jo 1, Yobo 1.

Ground: Goodison Park, Goodison Road, Liverpool L4 4EL. Telephone (0871) 663 1878.

Record Attendance: 78,299 v Liverpool, Division 1, 18 September 1948. **Capacity:** 40,158.

Manager: David Moyes.

Secretary: David Harrison.

Most League Goals: 121, Division 2, 1930–31.

Highest League Scorer in Season: William Ralph 'Dixie' Dean, 60, Division 1, 1927–28 (All-time League record).

Most League Goals in Total Aggregate: William Ralph 'Dixie' Dean, 349, 1925–37.

Most Capped Player: Neville Southall, 92, Wales.

Most League Appearances: Neville Southall, 578, 1981–98.
Honours – Football League: Division 1 Champions – 1890–91, 1914–15, 1927–28, 1931–32, 1938–39, 1962–63, 1969–70, 1984–85, 1986–87. Division 2 Champions – 1930–31. **FA Cup:** Winners – 1906, 1933, 1966, 1984, 1995. **European Competitions: European Cup-Winners' Cup:** Winners – 1984–85.
Colours: Blue shirts with white trim, white shorts, white stockings.

EXETER CITY   FL CHAMPIONSHIP 1

Archibald-Henville Troy (D)	6 2	13 03	Newham	4 11 88 Tottenham H
Bennett Scott (D)	5 10	12 10	Truro	30 11 90 Scholar
Duffy Richard (D)	5 9	10 03	Swansea	30 8 85 Millwall
Dunne James (M)	5 11	10 12	Farnborough	18 9 89 Arsenal
Frear Elliott (F)			Exeter	11 9 90 Scholar
Golbourne Scott (M)	5 8	11 08	Bristol	29 2 88 Reading
Harley Ryan (D)	5 9	11 00	Bristol	22 1 85 Weston-Super-Mare
Jones Paul (G)	6 3	13 00	Maidstone	28 6 86 Leyton Orient
Logan Richard (F)	6 0	12 05	Bury St Edmunds	4 1 82 Weymouth
Marriott Andy (G)	6 2	13 07	Sutton-in-Ashfield	11 10 70 Boston U
Noble David (M)	6 0	12 04	Hitchin	2 2 82 Bristol C
Norwood James (F)	5 9	11 05	Eastbourne	5 9 90 Eastbourne T
Sercombe Liam (M)	5 10	10 10	Exeter	25 4 90 Youth
Shephard Chris (M)	6 3	13 03	Exeter	2 6 90 Youth
Stansfield Adam (F)	5 11	11 02	Plymouth	10 9 78 Hereford U
Taylor Matt (D)	6 1	12 04	Ormskirk	30 1 82 Team Bath
Tully Steve (D)	5 9	11 00	Paignton	10 2 80 Weymouth
Watson Ben (F)	5 10	10 11	Brighton	06 12 85 Grays Ath

League Appearances: Archibald-Henville, T. 13(2); Burnell, J. 4(4); Corr, B. 17(17); Cozic, B. 21(8); Duffy, R. 41(1); Dunne, J. 18(5); Edwards, R. 17(4); Fleetwood, S. 16(11); Friend, G. 13; Golbourne, S. 30(4); Haber, M. 3(2); Harley, R. 43(1); Jansson, O. 7; Jones, P. 26; Logan, R. 4(30); Marriott, A. 13; McAllister, C. (4); Noone, C. 7; Norwood, J. 2(1); Russell, A. 27(2); Saunders, N. 2(4); Seaborne, D. 17(2); Sercombe, L. 25(3); Stansfield, A. 19(8); Stewart, M. 36(5); Taylor, M. 46; Taylor, R. 3(4); Tully, S. 36(2); Watson, B. (1).
Goals – League (48): Harley 10 (3 pens), Stansfield 7, Taylor M 5, Fleetwood 4, Logan 4, Corr 3, Dunne 3, Cozic 2, Noone 2, Stewart 2 (1 pen), Duffy 1, Friend 1, Russell 1, Sercombe 1, Tully 1, own goal 1.
Carling Cup (0).
FA Cup (7): Corr 3, Taylor M 2, Stansfield 1, own goal 1.
J Paint Trophy (1): Fleetwood 1.
Ground: St James Park, Stadium Way, Exeter EX4 6PX. Telephone: (01392) 411 243.
Record Attendance: 20,984 v Sunderland, FA Cup 6th rd (replay), 4 March 1931.
Ground Capacity: 8,830.
Manager: Paul Tisdale.
Club Secretary: Mike Radford.
Most League Goals: 88, Division 3 (S), 1932–33.
Highest League Scorer in Season: Fred Whitlow, 33, Division 3 (S), 1932–33.
Most League Goals in Total Aggregate: Tony Kellow, 129, 1976–78, 1980–83, 1985–88.
Most Capped Player: Dermot Curtis, 1 (17), Eire.
Most League Appearances: Arnold Mitchell, 495, 1952–66.
Honours – Division 3 (S) Cup: Winners 1934.
Colours: Red and white striped shirts, red sleeves, white shorts, white stockings.

Name				Birthplace				Previous club
Baird Chris (D)	5 10	11 11		Ballymoney	25	2	82	Southampton
Briggs Matthew (D)	6 1	11 12		Wandsworth	6	3	91	Scholar
Buchtmann Christopher (M)	5 8	10 10		Minden	25	4	92	Liverpool
Davies Simon (M)	5 10	11 07		Haverfordwest	23	10	79	Everton
Dempsey Clinton (M)	6 1	12 02		Nacogdoches	9	3	83	New England R
Dikgacoi Kagisho (M)	5 11	12 10		Brandfort	24	11	84	Lamontville GA
Duff Damien (F)	5 9	12 06		Ballyboden	2	3	79	Newcastle U
Elm David (M)	6 4	15 03		Broakulla	10	1	83	Kalmar
Etheridge Neil (G)	6 3	14 00		Enfield	7	2	90	Scholar
Etuhu Dickson (M)	6 2	13 04		Kano	8	6	82	Sunderland
Gera Zoltan (M)	6 0	11 11		Pecs	22	4	79	WBA
Hangeland Brede (D)	6 4	13 05		Houston	20	6	81	FC Copenhagen
Hoesen Danny (F)					15	1	91	Fortuna Sittard
Hughes Aaron (D)	6 0	11 02		Cookstown	8	11	79	Aston Villa
Johnson Andy (F)	5 7	10 09		Bedford	10	2	81	Everton
Johnson Eddie (F)	6 0	12 02		Bunnell	31	3	84	Kansas City Wizards
Kamara Diomansy (F)	6 0	11 05		Paris	8	11	80	WBA
Kelly Stephen (D)	6 0	12 04		Dublin	6	9	83	Birmingham C
Konchesky Paul (D)	5 10	11 07		Barking	15	5	81	West Ham U
Marquez-Sanchez Christian (D)				Barcelona	13	1	93	Scholar
Marsh-Brown Keanu (F)	5 11	12 04		Hammersmith	10	8	92	Scholar
Milsom Robert (D)	5 10	11 05		Redhill	2	1	87	Scholar
Murphy Danny (M)	5 10	11 09		Chester	18	3	77	Tottenham H
Pantsil John (D)	5 10	12 08		Berekum	15	6	81	West Ham U
Payne Stefan (F)				London	10	8	91	Sutton U
Riise Bjorn Helge (M)	5 10	11 11		Alesund	21	6	83	Lillestrom
Saunders Matthew (M)	5 11	11 05		Chertsey	12	9	89	Scholar
Schwarzer Mark (G)	6 4	14 07		Sydney	6	10	72	Middlesbrough
Smalling Chris (D)	6 4	14 02		Greenwich	22	11	89	
Smith Alex (D)	5 9	10 00			31	10	91	Scholar
Stockdale David (G)	6 3	13 04		Leeds	20	9	85	Darlington
Stoor Fredrik (D)	6 0	12 06		Stockholm	28	2	84	Rosenborg
Trotta Marcello (F)				Santa Maria Capua	29	9	92	Napoli
Zamora Bobby (F)	6 1	11 11		Barking	16	1	81	West Ham U

League Appearances: Baird, C. 29(3); Davies, S. 12(5); Dempsey, C. 27(2); Dikgacoi, K. 7(5); Duff, D. 30(2); Elm, D. 3(7); Etuhu, D. 14(6); Gera, Z. 19(8); Greening, J. 15(8); Hangeland, B. 32; Hughes, A. 34; Johnson, A. 7(1); Johnson, E. (2); Kallio, T. (1); Kamara, D. 5(4); Kelly, S. 7(1); Konchesky, P. 27; Murphy, D. 25; Nevland, E. 12(11); Okaka Chuka, S. 3(8); Pantsil, J. 22; Riise, B. 5(7); Schwarzer, M. 37; Seol, K. (2); Shorey, N. 9; Smalling, C. 9(3); Stockdale, D. 1; Stoor, F. (2); Zamora, B. 27.

Goals – League (39): Zamora 8, Dempsey 7 (1 pen), Duff 6, Murphy 5 (3 pens), Nevland 3, Gera 3, Okaka Chuka 2, Elm 1, Greening 1, Hangeland 1, Kamara 1, Konchesky 1, own goal 1.

Carling Cup (1): Gera 1.

FA Cup (9): Zamora 3, Duff 2, Davies 1, Gera 1, Nevland 1, Okaka Chuka 1.

Europa League (31): Zamora 9, Gera 6 (1 pen), Johnson A 3, Davies 2, Dempsey 2, Etuhu 2, Hangeland 2, Murphy 2 (1 pen), Duff 1, Kamara 1 (pen), Seol 1.

Ground: Craven Cottage, Stevenage Road, London SW6 6HH. Telephone: (0870) 442 1222.

Record Attendance: 49,335 v Millwall, Division 2, 8 October 1938. **Capacity:** 26,600.

Manager: Ray Lewington (caretaker).

Secretary: Darren Preston.

Most League Goals: 111, Division 3 (S), 1931–32.
Highest League Scorer in Season: Frank Newton, 43, Division 3 (S), 1931–32.
Most League Goals in Total Aggregate: Gordon Davies, 159, 1978–84, 1986–91.
Most Capped Player: Johnny Haynes, 56, England.
Most League Appearances: Johnny Haynes, 594, 1952–70.
Honours – Football League: Division 1 Champions – 2000–01. Division 2 Champions – 1948–49, 1998–99. Division 3 (S) Champions – 1931–32. **European Competitions: Intertoto Cup:** Winners – 2002.
Colours: White shirts with black trim, black shorts, white stockings.

GILLINGHAM   FL CHAMPIONSHIP 2

Barcham Andy (F)	5 8	10 11	Basildon	16 12 86	Tottenham H
Bentley Mark (M)	6 2	13 07	Hertford	7 1 78	Southend U
Gowling Josh (D)	6 3	12 08	Coventry	29 11 83	Carlisle U
Jackman Danny (D)	5 4	10 00	Worcester	3 1 83	Northampton T
Jackson Simeon (M)	5 10	10 12	Kingston Jam	28 3 87	Rushden & D
Julian Alan (G)	6 2	13 07	Ashford	11 3 83	Brentford
King Simon (D)	6 0	13 00	Oxford	11 4 83	Barnet
Maher Kevin (M)	6 0	12 13	Ilford	17 10 76	Oldham Ath
McCammon Mark (F)	6 2	14 05	Barnet	7 8 78	Doncaster R
Nutter John (D)	6 2	12 10	Taplow	13 6 82	Stevenage B
Palmer Chris (M)	5 7	11 00	Derby	16 10 83	Walsall
Payne Jack (M)	5 9	9 02	Gravesend	5 12 91	Scholar
Rooney Luke (M)	5 8	11 07	Southwark	28 12 90	Scholar
Weston Curtis (M)	5 11	11 09	Greenwich	24 1 87	Leeds U

League Appearances: Barcham, A. 38(4); Bentley, M. 34(2); Brandy, F. 5(2); Dennehy, D. 19; Dickson, C. 4(5); Erskine, J. (4); Fry, M. 11; Fuller, B. 35(1); Gowling, J. 29(1); Howe, R. 18; Jackman, D. 21(1); Jackson, S. 34(8); Julian, A. 30; Lewis, S. 16(4); Maher, K. 21(5); McCammon, M. 3(11); Miller, A. 22(4); Nutter, J. 32(3); Oli, D. 23(13); Palmer, C. 16(4); Payne, J. 14(5); Plummer, T. 2; Richards, G. 16; Rooney, L. 2(11); Royce, S. 16(1); Vernon, S. 1; Walker, J. 2(3); Weston, C. 36(3); Wynter, T. 4(4); Yussuff, R. 2(6).
Goals – League (48): Jackson 14 (3 pens), Barcham 7, Weston 6 (1 pen), Miller 4, Oli 3, Bentley 2, Gowling 2, Howe 2, Rooney 2, Brandy 1, Dickson 1, Lewis 1, Nutter 1, Palmer 1, own goal 1.
Carling Cup (3): Jackson 2 (1 pen), Barcham 1.
FA Cup (4): Weston 2, Bentley 1, Brandy 1.
J Paint Trophy (1): Jackson 1 (pen).
Ground: KRBS Priestfield Stadium, Redfern Avenue, Gillingham, Kent ME7 4DD. Telephone (01634) 300 000.
Record Attendance: 23,002 v QPR, FA Cup 3rd rd, 10 January 1948. **Capacity:** 11,440.
Manager: Andy Hessenthaler.
Secretary: Gwen Poynter.
Most League Goals: 90, Division 4, 1973–74.
Highest League Scorer in Season: Ernie Morgan, 31, Division 3 (S), 1954–55; Brian Yeo, 31, Division 4, 1973–74.
Most League Goals in Total Aggregate: Brian Yeo, 135, 1963–75.
Most Capped Player: Mamady Sidibe, 7 (12), Mali.
Most League Appearances: John Simpson, 571, 1957–72.
Honours – Football League: Division 4 Champions – 1963–64.
Colours: Blue with white sleeves, blue shorts, blue stockings.

Atkinson Rob (D)	6 1	12 00	Beverley	29 4 87	Barnsley
Bird Matthew (M)	6 1	11 00	Grimsby	31 10 90	
Bore Peter (M)	5 11	11 04	Grimsby	4 11 87	Scholar
Colgan Nick (G)	6 1	12 00	Drogheda	19 9 73	Sunderland
Forbes Adrian (F)	5 8	11 10	Greenford	23 1 79	Millwall
Fuller Josh (M)	5 9	11 00	Grimsby	12 12 80	Scholar
Hegarty Nick (M)	5 10	11 00	Hemsworth	25 6 86	Scholar
Hudson Mark (M)	5 10	11 03	Bishop Auckland	24 10 80	Blackpool
Jarman Nathan (F)	5 11	11 03	Scunthorpe	19 9 86	Barnsley
Jones Chris (F)	5 7	10 00	Swansea	12 9 89	Swansea C
Leary Michael (M)	6 0	11 11	Ealing	17 4 83	Barnet
Linwood Paul (D)	6 2	13 03	Birkenhead	24 10 83	Chester C
Overton Leigh (M)	6 0	11 04	Boston	1 12 90	
Peacock Lee (F)	6 0	12 08	Paisley	9 10 76	Swindon T
Rhoades Drew (M)					
Sweeney Peter (M)	6 0	12 11	Glasgow	25 9 84	Leeds U
Widdowson Joe (D)	6 0	12 00	Forest Gate	28 3 89	West Ham U
Wood Bradley (D)	5 9	11 02	Leicester	2 9 91	Scholar
Wright Tommy (F)	6 0	12 02	Leicester	28 9 84	Aberdeen

League Appearances: Akpa Akpro, J. 26(10); Atkinson, R. 37; Bennett, R. 13; Bore, P. 37(3); Boshell, D. 5(1); Chambers, A. 2(2); Clarke, J. 9(4); Colgan, N. 35; Conlon, B. 7(9); Coulson, M. 28(1); Cowan-Hall, P. (3); Devitt, J. 15; Featherstone, N. 7(1); Fletcher, W. 1(5); Forbes, A. 8(5); Forecast, T. 4; Fuller, J. 2(3); Hegarty, N. 5(4); Heywood, M. 1; Hudson, M. 11(5); Jarman, N. 2(5); Jones, C. 6(1); Lancashire, O. 24(1); Leary, M. 19(9); Lillis, J. 4; Linwood, P. 23(5); Magennis, J. 1(1); McCrory, D. 10; Mendy, A. 1; North, D. 9(8); Oxley, M. 3; Peacock, L. 14(3); Proudlock, A. 14(13); Shahin, J. 4(1); Sinclair, D. 16; Stirling, J. 2(2); Stockdale, R. 8; Sweeney, P. 36(4); Widdowson, J. 36(2); Wood, B. 7(1); Wright, B. 1(1); Wright, T. 13(1).
Goals – League (45): Akpa Akpro 5, Conlon 5 (1 pen), Coulson 5, Devitt 5, Sweeney 4, Sinclair 3 (1 pen), Atkinson 2, Chambers 2, Hudson 2, Peacock 2, Fletcher 1, Forbes 1, Jones 1, Lancashire 1, Linwood 1, North 1, Proudlock 1, Wright T 1, own goals 2.
Carling Cup (0).
FA Cup (0).
J Paint Trophy (3): Sweeney 2, Proudlock 1.
Ground: Blundell Park, Cleethorpes, North-East Lincolnshire DN35 7PY. Telephone (01472) 605 050.
Record Attendance: 31,651 v Wolverhampton W, FA Cup 5th rd, 20 February 1937.
Capacity: 9,106.
Manager: Neil Woods.
Chief Executive: Ian Fleming.
Most League Goals: 103, Division 2, 1933–34.
Highest League Scorer in Season: Pat Glover, 42, Division 2, 1933–34.
Most League Goals in Total Aggregate: Pat Glover, 180, 1930–39.
Most Capped Player: Pat Glover, 7, Wales.
Most League Appearances: John McDermott, 647, 1987–2007.
Honours – Football League: Division 2 Champions – 1900–01, 1933–34. Division 3 (N) Champions – 1925–26, 1955–56. Division 3 Champions – 1979–80. Division 4 Champions – 1971–72. **League Group Cup:** Winners – 1981–82. **Auto Windscreens Shield:** Winners – 1997–98.
Colours: Black and white striped shirts, black shorts, white stockings.

Name			Birthplace			Previous Club
Austin Neil (D)	5 10	11 09	Barnsley	26	4 83	Darlington
Behan Denis (M)	6 0	13 05	Abbeyfeale	2	1 84	Cork C
Bjornsson Armann (F)	6 5	14 02	Hofn	7	1 81	Brann
Boyd Adam (F)	5 9	10 12	Hartlepool	25	5 82	Leyton Orient
Brown James (F)	5 11	11 00	Newcastle	3	1 87	Cramlington J
Collins Sam (D)	6 2	14 03	Pontefract	5	6 77	Hull C
Flinders Scott (G)	6 4	13 00	Rotherham	12	6 86	Crystal Palace
Fredriksen Jon-Andre (M)	5 11	12 04	Moss	5	4 82	Sarpsborg
Gamble Joe (M)	5 7	11 00	Cork	14	1 82	Cork C
Greulich Billy (F)	6 3	11 13	London	24	4 91	Brandon U
Hartley Peter (D)	6 0	12 06	Hartlepool	3	4 88	Sunderland
Haslam Steven (M)	5 11	10 10	Sheffield	6	9 79	Bury
Humphreys Richie (M)	5 11	12 07	Sheffield	30	11 77	Cambridge U
Larkin Colin (F)	5 9	11 07	Dundalk	27	4 82	Northampton T
Liddle Gary (D)	6 1	12 06	Middlesbrough	15	6 86	Middlesbrough
Mackay Michael (F)	6 0	11 08	Durham	11	10 82	Consett
McSweeney Leon (F)	5 10	10 11	Cork	19	2 83	Stockport Co
Monkhouse Andrew (M)	6 2	12 06	Leeds	23	10 80	Swindon T
Sweeney Anthony (M)	6 0	11 07	Stockton	5	9 83	Scholar

League Appearances: Austin, N. 36(3); Behan, D. 21(8); Bjornsson, A. 10(8); Boyd, A. 25(15); Brown, J. 19(13); Cherel, J. 1; Clark, B. 6(5); Collins, S. 44; Flinders, S. 46; Foley, D. (2); Fredriksen, J. 4(8); Gamble, J. 22; Greulich, B. (4); Hartley, P. 38; Haslam, S. 15; Humphreys, R. 33(5); Jones, R. 22(11); Larkin, C. 10(12); Liddle, G. 40; Mackay, M. (1); McSweeney, L. 24(7); Monkhouse, A. 43; O'Donovan, R. 15; Power, A. (2); Rowell, J. (6); Sweeney, A. 32(10).

Goals – League (59): Monkhouse 11, O'Donovan 9 (1 pen), Boyd 7, Behan 6 (1 pen), Brown 4, Jones 4, Austin 3, Bjornsson 3, Liddle 3, Gamble 2, Hartley 2, Sweeney 2, Larkin 1, McSweeney 1, own goal 1.

Carling Cup (2): Boyd 2.

FA Cup (0).

J Paint Trophy (0).

Ground: Victoria Park, Clarence Road, Hartlepool TS24 8BZ. Telephone (01429) 272 584.

Record Attendance: 17,426 v Manchester U, FA Cup 3rd rd, 5 January 1957. **Capacity:** 7,630.

Director of Sport: Chris Turner.

Senior Administrator: Maureen Smith.

Most League Goals: 90, Division 3 (N), 1956–57.

Highest League Scorer in Season: William Robinson, 28, Division 3 (N), 1927–28; Joe Allon, 28, Division 4, 1990–91.

Most League Goals in Total Aggregate: Ken Johnson, 98, 1949–64.

Most Capped Player: Ambrose Fogarty, 1 (11), Republic of Ireland.

Most League Appearances: Wattie Moore, 447, 1948–64.

Honours – Nil.

Colours: Broad blue and white striped shirts with blue sleeves, blue shorts, white stockings.

Name			Birthplace			Previous Club
Bartlett Adam (G)	6 0	11 11	Newcastle	27	2 86	Kidderminster H
Lunt Kenny (M)	5 10	10 05	Runcorn	20	11 79	Sheffield W
Manset Mathieu (F)	6 1	13 08	Metz	5	8 89	Le Havre
McCallum Gavin (M)	5 9	12 00	Mississauga	24	8 87	Yeovil T

McQuilkin James (F)	5 8 11 10	Belfast	9 1 89	
Pugh Marc (M)	5 11 11 04	Burnley	2 4 87	Shrewsbury T
Valentine Ryan (D)	5 10 11 05	Wrexham	19 8 82	Darlington
Weir Tyler (M)	5 10 11 08	Gloucester	21 10 90	Scholar

League Appearances: Adamson, C. 1; Ajdarevic, A. (1); Bartlett, A. 45(1); Blanchett, D. 13; Constantine, L. 25(10); Dennehy, D. 6(1); Done, M. 7(13); Downing, P. 6; Elford-Alliyu, L. 1; Godsmark, J. 7(1); Green, R. 31; Gwynne, S. 21(5); Jackson, M. 2(3); Jervis, J. 5(2); Jones, C. 1; Jones, D. 40(1); King, C. 22(4); Lowe, K. 17(2); Lunt, K. 42; Manset, M. 16(13); Marshall, M. 8; McCallum, G. 20(7); McQuilkin, J. 20(2); Morris, L. 5(7); Mutch, J. 3; Plummer, T. 4(1); Preston, D. 4; Pugh, M. 39(1); Rose, R. 22(3); Sonko, E. 5(5); Southam, G. 5(1); Tolley, J. 6(4); Valentine, R. 40; Walker, J. 6; Wedderburn, N. 3; Weir, T. 3; Young, L. 5(1).

Goals – League (54): Pugh 13, McCallum 8, Constantine 6, Valentine 4 (2 pens), Jones D 3, King C 3, Manset 3, Plummer 3 (2 pens), Jervis 2 (1 pen), McQuilkin 2, Godsmark 1, Green 1, Lowe 1, Lunt 1, Walker 1, own goals 2.

Carling Cup (2): Godsmark 1, Plummer 1 (pen).

FA Cup (2): Manset 1, Valentine 1 (pen).

J Paint Trophy (4): Constantine 2, Manset 1, Walker 1.

Ground: Athletic Ground, Edgar Street, Hereford, Herefordshire HR4 9JU. Telephone (08442) 761 939.

Record Attendance: 18,114 v Sheffield Wed., FA Cup 3rd rd, 4 January 1958.

Capacity: 7,149.

Manager: Simon Davey.

Most League Goals: 86, Division 3, 1975–76.

Highest League Scorer in Season: Dixie McNeil, 35, 1975–76.

Most League Goals in Total Aggregate: Stewart Phillips, 93, 1980–88, 1990–91.

Most Capped Player: Trevor Benjamin, 2, Jamaica.

Most League Appearances: Mel Pejic, 412, 1980–92.

Honours – Football League: Division 3 Champions – 1975–76. **Welsh Cup:** Winners – 1990.

Colours: White shirts with black trim, black shorts, white stockings.

HUDDERSFIELD TOWN   FL CHAMPIONSHIP 1

Ainsworth Lionel (F)	5 9 9 10	Nottingham	1 10 87	Watford
Berrett James (M)	5 10 10 13	Halifax	13 1 89	Scholar
Butler Andy (D)	6 0 13 00	Doncaster	4 11 83	Scunthorpe U
Clarke Nathan (D)	6 2 12 00	Halifax	30 11 83	Scholar
Clarke Peter (D)	6 0 12 00	Southport	3 1 82	Southend U
Clarke Tom (D)	5 11 12 02	Halifax	21 12 87	Scholar
Collins Michael (M)	6 0 10 12	Halifax	30 4 86	Scholar
Denton Tom (F)	6 6 14 00	Shepley	24 7 89	Wakefield
Eastwood Simon (G)	6 2 12 09	Luton	26 6 89	Scholar
Franks Lee (D)	5 11 12 00		7 3 91	Scholar
Goodwin Jim (M)	5 9 12 01	Waterford	20 11 81	Scunthorpe U
Hunt Jack (D)	5 9 11 02		6 12 90	Scholar
Kay Antony (D)	5 11 11 08	Barnsley	21 10 82	Tranmere R
Novak Lee (F)	6 0 12 04	Newcastle	28 9 88	Gateshead
Pearce Krystian (D)	6 1 12 00	Birmingham	5 1 90	Birmingham C
Peltier Lee (D)	5 10 12 00	Liverpool	11 12 86	Yeovil T
Pilkington Anthony (M)	5 11 12 00	Manchester	3 11 87	Stockport Co
Rhodes Jordan (F)	6 1 11 03	Oldham	5 2 90	Ipswich T
Ridehalgh Liam (D)	5 10 11 05		20 4 91	Scholar
Roberts Gary (F)	5 10 11 09	Chester	18 3 84	Ipswich T
Robinson Theo (F)	5 9 10 03	Birmingham	22 1 89	Watford
Simpson Robbie (F)	6 1 11 11	Stevenage	15 3 85	Coventry C

| Skarz Joe (D) | 5 11 13 00 | Huddersfield | 13 7 89 | Scholar |
| Smithies Alex (G) | 6 1 10 01 | Huddersfield | 25 3 90 | Scholar |

League Appearances: Ainsworth, L. 2(9); Berrett, J. 2(7); Butler, A. 10(1); Clarke, N. 15(2); Clarke, T. 15(6); Clarke, P. 46; Collins, M. 23(5); Drinkwater, D. 27(6); Eccleston, N. 4(7); Goodwin, J. 3(2); Heffernan, D. 15; Kay, A. 38(2); Novak, L. 24(13); Pearce, K. (1); Peltier, L. 42; Pilkington, A. 42(1); Rhodes, J. 43(2); Roberts, G. 40(3); Robinson, T. 17(20); Simpson, R. 4(9); Skarz, J. 14(1); Smithies, A. 46; Trotman, N. 21; Williams, R. 13(4).

Goals – League (82): Rhodes 19, Robinson 13 (3 pens), Novak 12 (2 pens), Pilkington 7, Roberts 7 (1 pen), Kay 6, Clarke P 5, Collins 3, Drinkwater 2, Trotman 2, Williams 2, Clarke N 1, Eccleston 1, own goals 2.

Carling Cup (6): Rhodes 3, Robinson 3 (1 pen).

FA Cup (7): Novak 2, Roberts 2, Clarke N 1, Rhodes 1, Williams 1.

J Paint Trophy (5): Pilkington 2, Clarke N 1, Clarke P 1, Simpson 1.

Play-Offs (0).

Ground: The Galpharm Stadium, Stadium Way, Leeds Road, Huddersfield HD1 6PX. Telephone 0870 4444 677.

Record Attendance: 67,037 v Arsenal, FA Cup 6th rd, 27 February 1932 (at Leeds Road); 23,678 v Liverpool, FA Cup 3rd rd, 12 December 1999 (at Alfred McAlpine Stadium).

Capacity: 24,554.

Manager: Lee Clark.

Secretary: Ann Hough.

Most League Goals: 101, Division 4, 1979–80.

Highest League Scorer in Season: Sam Taylor, 35, Division 2, 1919–20; George Brown, 35, Division 1, 1925–26.

Most League Goals in Total Aggregate: George Brown, 142, 1921–29.

Most Capped Player: Jimmy Nicholson, 31 (41), Northern Ireland.

Most League Appearances: Billy Smith, 520, 1914–34.

Honours – Football League: Division 1 Champions – 1923–24, 1924–25, 1925–26. Division 2 Champions – 1969–70. Division 4 Champions – 1979–80. **FA Cup:** Winners – 1922.

Colours: Blue and white striped shirts, white shorts, blue stockings.

HULL CITY   FL CHAMPIONSHIP

Ashbee Ian (M)	6 1 13 07	Birmingham	6 9 76	Cambridge U
Atkinson William (M)	5 10 10 07	Beverley	14 10 88	Scholar
Barmby Nick (M)	5 7 11 03	Hull	11 2 74	Leeds U
Bullard Jimmy (M)	5 10 11 05	Newham	23 10 78	Fulham
Cairney Tom (M)	6 0 11 05	Nottingham	20 1 91	Scholar
Cooper Liam (D)	6 2 13 07	Hull	30 8 91	Scholar
Cousin Daniel (F)	6 2 12 13	Libreville	7 2 77	Rangers
Cullen Mark (F)		Ashington	24 4 92	Scholar
Dawson Andy (D)	5 10 11 02	Northallerton	20 10 78	Scunthorpe U
Devitt Jamie (F)	5 10 10 05	Dublin	6 6 90	Scholar
Duke Matt (G)	6 5 13 04	Sheffield	16 7 77	Sheffield U
Fagan Craig (F)	5 11 11 11	Birmingham	11 12 82	Derby Co
Featherstone Nicky (F)	5 7 11 03	Goole	22 9 89	Scholar
Folan Caleb (F)	6 2 14 07	Leeds	26 10 82	Wigan Ath
Garcia Richard (F)	5 11 12 01	Perth	4 9 81	Colchester U
Gardner Anthony (D)	6 3 14 00	Stone	19 9 80	Tottenham H
Gardner Steven (D)	5 9 10 09	Hull	12 5 90	Scholar
Geovanni (F)	5 8 10 08	Acaiaca	11 1 80	Manchester C
Ghilas Kamel (F)	5 10 11 00	Marseille	9 3 84	Celta Vigo

Halmosi Peter (M)	5 10 10 12	Szombathely	25 9 79	Plymouth Arg
Hunt Steve (M)	5 9 10 10	Port Laoise	1 8 80	Reading
Kilbane Kevin (M)	6 1 13 05	Preston	1 2 77	Wigan Ath
McShane Paul (D)	6 0 11 05	Wicklow	6 1 86	Sunderland
Mendy Bernard (D)	5 11 12 02	Evreux	20 8 81	Paris St Germain
Mouyokolo Steven (D)	6 3 13 08	Mellin	24 11 87	Bologne
Myhill Boaz (G)	6 3 14 06	Modesto	9 11 82	Aston Villa
Olofinjana Seyi (M)	6 4 11 10	Lagos	30 6 80	Stoke C
Oxley Mark (G)	5 11 11 05	Sheffield	2 6 90	Rotherham U
Zayatte Kamil (D)	6 2 13 10	Conakry	7 3 85	Lens

League Appearances: Altidore, J. 16(12); Atkinson, W. 2; Barmby, N. 6(14); Boateng, G. 26(3); Bullard, J. 13(1); Cairney, T. 10(1); Cooper, L. 1(1); Cousin, D. 1(2); Cullen, M. 2(1); Dawson, A. 35; Duke, M. 11; Fagan, C. 20(5); Folan, C. 7(1); Garcia, R. 14(4); Gardner, A. 24; Geovanni, 16(10); Ghilas, K. 6(7); Hunt, S. 27; Kilbane, K. 15(6); Marney, D. 15(1); McShane, P. 26(1); Mendy, B. 15(6); Mouyokolo, S. 19(2); Myhill, B. 27; Olofinjana, S. 11(8); Sonko, I. 9; Turner, M. 4; Vennegoor, J. 17(14); Zaki, A. 2(4); Zayatte, K. 21(2).

Goals – League (34): Hunt 6 (1 pen), Bullard 5 (4 pens), Geovanni 3, Vennegoor 3, Fagan 2 (1 pen), Folan 2, Zayatte 2, Altidore 1, Atkinson 1, Boateng 1, Cairney 1, Cullen 1, Dawson 1, Ghilas 1, Kilbane 1, Marney 1, Mouyokolo 1, Olofinjana 1.

Carling Cup (3): Altidore 1, Cairney 1, Geovanni 1.

FA Cup (1): Geovanni 1.

Ground: The Circle, The KC Stadium, Walton St, Hull HU3 6HU. Telephone (01482) 504 600.

Record Attendance: 55,019 v Manchester U, FA Cup 6th rd, 26 February 1949 (Boothferry Park); 25,512 v Sunderland, FL C, 28 October 2007 (KC Stadium).

Capacity: 25,404.

Manager: Nigel Pearson.

Football Secretary: Phil Hough.

Most League Goals: 109, Division 3, 1965–66.

Highest League Scorer in Season: Bill McNaughton, 39, Division 3 (N), 1932–33.

Most League Goals in Total Aggregate: Chris Chilton, 193, 1960–71.

Most Capped Player: Theo Whitmore, 28 (105), Jamaica.

Most League Appearances: Andy Davidson, 520, 1952–67.

Honours – Football League: Division 3 (N) Champions – 1932–33, 1948–49. Division 3 Champions – 1965–66.

Colours: Black and amber striped shirts, black shorts, amber stockings with black hoops.

IPSWICH TOWN   FL CHAMPIONSHIP

Ainsley Jack (D)	5 11 11 00	Ipswich	17 9 90	Scholar
Brown Troy (D)	6 1 12 00	London	17 9 90	Fulham Scholar
Bruce Alex (D)	6 0 11 06	Norwich	28 9 84	Birmingham C
Civelli Luciano (M)	6 2 13 01	Capital Federal	6 10 86	Banfield
Counago Pablo (F)	5 11 11 06	Pontevedra	9 8 79	Malaga
Delaney Damien (D)	6 3 14 00	Cork	20 7 81	QPR
Edwards Carlos (M)	5 8 11 02	Port of Spain	24 10 78	Sunderland
Garvan Owen (M)	6 0 10 07	Dublin	29 1 88	Scholar
Healy Colin (M)	6 1 12 13	Cork	14 3 80	Cork C
Lambe Reggie (M)	5 7 10 09	Bermuda	4 2 91	Scholar
Leadbitter Grant (M)	5 9 11 06	Sunderland	7 1 86	Sunderland
Lee-Barrett Arran (G)	6 2 14 01	Ipswich	28 2 84	Hartlepool U
Lisbie Kevin (F)	5 10 11 06	Hackney	17 10 78	Colchester U
Martin Lee (M)	5 10 10 03	Taunton	9 2 87	Manchester U
McAuley Gareth (D)	6 3 13 00	Larne	5 12 78	Leicester C

McLoughlin Ian (G)	6 3	13 08	Ireland	9	8 91	St Francis
Murphy Brian (G)	6 0	13 00	Waterford	7	5 83	Bohemians
Norris David (M)	5 7	11 06	Stamford	22	2 81	Plymouth Arg
O'Connor Shane (M)	5 9	11 08	Cork	14	4 90	Liverpool
Peters Jaime (M)	5 7	10 12	Toronto	4	5 87	Moor Green
Priskin Tamas (F)	6 2	13 03	Komarno	27	9 86	Watford
Quinn Alan (M)	5 9	10 06	Dublin	13	6 79	Sheffield U
Smith Tommy (D)	6 2	12 02	Macclesfield	31	3 90	Scholar
Stead Jon (F)	6 3	13 03	Huddersfield	7	4 83	Sheffield U
Trotter Liam (M)	6 2	12 02	Ipswich	24	8 88	Scholar
Walters Jon (F)	6 0	12 06	Birkenhead	20	9 83	Chester C
Wickham Connor (F)	6 0	14 01	Ipswich	31	3 93	Ipswich

League Appearances: Balkestein, P. 8(1); Begovic, A. 6; Brown, T. (1); Bruce, A. 12(1); Clark, B. (3); Colback, J. 29(8); Counago, P. 11(16); Delaney, D. 36; Eastman, T. 1; Edwards, C. 21(7); Garvan, O. 14(11); Healy, C. 3; Healy, D. 5(7); John, S. 5(2); Leadbitter, G. 36(2); Lee-Barrett, A. 12(1); Martin, L. 9(7); McAuley, G. 40(1); Murphy, D. 18; Murphy, B. 16; Norris, D. 24; O'Connor, S. 11(1); Peters, J. 22(10); Priskin, T. 9(8); Quinn, A. 8(11); Rosenior, L. 26(3); Smith, T. 11(3); Stead, J. 13(9); Trotter, L. 11(1); Walters, J. 43; Wickham, C. 9(17); Wright, D. 25(1); Wright, R. 12.
Goals – League (50): Walters 8 (1 pen), Murphy D 6, Stead 6, McAuley 5, Colback 4, Wickham 4, Leadbitter 3 (1 pen), Counago 2, Edwards 2, Bruce 1, Healy D 1, John 1, Martin 1, Norris 1, Peters 1, Priskin 1, Rosenior 1, Wright D 1, own goal 1.
Carling Cup (4): Wickham 2, Priskin 1, Quinn 1.
FA Cup (3): Colback 1, Counago 1, Garvan 1.
Ground: Portman Road, Ipswich, Suffolk IP1 2DA. Telephone (01473) 400 500.
Record Attendance: 38,010 v Leeds U, FA Cup 6th rd, 8 March 1975.
Capacity: 30,311.
Manager: Roy Keane.
Secretary: Sally Webb.
Most League Goals: 106, Division 3 (S), 1955–56.
Highest League Scorer in Season: Ted Phillips, 41, Division 3 (S), 1956–57.
Most League Goals in Total Aggregate: Ray Crawford, 204, 1958–63 and 1966–69.
Most Capped Player: Allan Hunter, 47 (53), Northern Ireland.
Most League Appearances: Mick Mills, 591, 1966–82.
Honours – Football League: Division 1 Champions – 1961–62. Division 2 Champions – 1960–61, 1967–68, 1991–92. Division 3 (S) Champions – 1953–54, 1956–57. **FA Cup:** Winners – 1977–78. **European Competitions: UEFA Cup:** Winners – 1980–81.
Colours: Blue shirts with white trim, white shorts, blue stockings.

LEEDS UNITED   FL CHAMPIONSHIP

Becchio Luciano (F)	6 2	13 05	Cordoba	28	12 83	Merida
Bromby Leigh (D)	5 11	11 06	Dewsbury	2	6 80	Watford
Crowe Jason (D)	5 9	10 09	Sidcup	30	9 78	Northampton T
Darville Liam (D)				26	10 90	Scholar
Elliott Tom (F)	5 10	11 02	Leeds	9	9 89	School
Gradel Max (M)	5 9	11 00	Abidjan	30	11 87	Ivory Coast
Grella Mike (F)	5 11	12 02	Glen Cove	23	1 87	Duke Univ
Hatfield Will (M)				10	10 91	Scholar
Higgs Shane (G)	6 3	14 06	Oxford	13	5 77	Cheltenham T
Howson Jonathan (M)	5 11	12 01	Leeds	21	5 88	Scholar
Johnson Brad (M)	6 0	12 10	Hackney	28	4 87	Northampton T
Kandol Tresor (F)	6 1	11 05	Banga	20	8 81	Barnet
Kilkenny Neil (M)	5 8	10 08	Enfield	19	12 85	Birmingham C
Kisnorbo Patrick (D)	6 1	11 11	Melbourne	24	3 81	Leicester C
Lees Tom (M)	6 1	12 02	Warwick	28	11 90	

Martin Alan (G)	6 0	11 11	Glasgow	1	1 89	Motherwell
McCann Joe (M)				11 10 92		Scholar
Michalik Lubomir (D)	6 4	13 00	Cadca	13	8 83	Bolton W
Naylor Richard (D)	6 1	13 07	Leeds	28	2 77	Ipswich T
Parker Ben (D)	5 11	11 06	Pontefract	8 11 87		Scholar
Robinson Andy (M)	5 8	11 04	Birkenhead	3 11 79		Swansea C
Sheehan Alan (D)	5 11	11 02	Athlone	14	9 86	Leicester C
Snodgrass Robert (F)	6 0	12 02	Glasgow	7	9 87	Livingston
Somma Davide (F)	6 1	12 13	Johannesburg	26	3 85	San Jose E
White Aidan (D)	5 7	10 00	Leeds	10 10 91		Scholar

League Appearances: Ankergren, C. 27(2); Becchio, L. 32(5); Beckford, J. 38(4); Bromby, L. 31(1); Capaldi, T. 3; Collins, N. 9; Crowe, J. 16(1); Dickov, P. 1(3); Doyle, M. 42; Ephraim, H. 1(2); Gradel, M. 11(21); Grella, M. 3(14); Higgs, S. 19; Howson, J. 39(6); Hughes, A. 38(1); Johnson, B. 26(10); Kandol, T. (10); Kilkenny, N. 24(11); Kisnorbo, P. 29; Lowry, S. 11; McSheffrey, G. 9(1); Michalik, L. 7(6); Naylor, R. 29; Parker, B. 2(2); Prutton, D. 1(5); Robinson, A. (6); Rui Marques, M. 5; Showunmi, E. (7); Snodgrass, R. 40(4); Vokes, S. 8; Watt, S. 1(5); White, A. 4(4).

Goals – League (77): Beckford 25 (4 pens), Becchio 15, Johnson 7, Snodgrass 7, Gradel 6, Howson 4, Kandol 2, Kilkenny 2, Naylor 2, Bromby 1, Grella 1, Kisnorbo 1, McSheffrey 1, Michalik 1, Vokes 1, own goal 1.

Carling Cup (3): Snodgrass 2, Showunmi 1.

FA Cup (12): Beckford 5 (1 pen), Grella 3, Becchio 2, Howson 1, Kandol 1.

J Paint Trophy (11): Crowe 2, Kilkenny 2, Beckford 1, Ephraim 1, Grella 1, Kandol 1, Robinson 1, Snodgrass 1, own goal 1.

Ground: Elland Road Stadium, Elland Rd, Leeds LS11 0ES. Telephone (0871) 334 1919.

Record Attendance: 57,892 v Sunderland, FA Cup 5th rd (replay), 15 March 1967.

Capacity: 39,457.

Manager: Simon Grayson.

Most League Goals: 98, Division 2, 1927–28.

Highest League Scorer in Season: John Charles, 42, Division 2, 1953–54.

Most League Goals in Total Aggregate: Peter Lorimer, 168, 1965–79 and 1983–86.

Most Capped Player: Lucas Radebe, 58 (70), South Africa.

Most League Appearances: Jack Charlton, 629, 1953–73.

Honours – Football League: Division 1 Champions – 1968–69, 1973–74, 1991–92. Division 2 Champions – 1923–24, 1963–64, 1989–90. **FA Cup:** Winners – 1972. **Football League Cup:** Winners – 1967–68. **European Competitions:** European Fairs Cup: Winners – 1967–68, 1970–71.

Colours: White shirts, white shorts, white stockings with yellow trim.

LEICESTER CITY   FL CHAMPIONSHIP

Adams Nicky (F)	5 10	11 00	Bolton	16 10 86		Bury
Ambrosics Robert (G)			Hungary	22	1 92	
Berner Bruno (M)	6 1	12 13	Zurich	21 11 77		Blackburn R
Bolger Cian (D)						Scholar
Brown Wayne (D)	6 0	12 06	Barking	20	8 77	Hull C
Campbell Dudley (F)	5 10	11 00	London	12 11 81		Birmingham C
Chamberlain Elliott (M)				29	4 92	Scholar
Chambers Ashley (F)	5 10	11 06	Leicester	1	3 90	Scholar
Dyer Lloyd (M)	5 8	10 03	Birmingham	13	9 82	Milton Keynes D
Fryatt Matty (F)	5 10	11 00	Nuneaton	5	3 86	Walsall
Gallagher Paul (F)	6 1	11 00	Glasgow	9	8 84	Blackburn R
Hobbs Jack (D)	6 3	13 05	Portsmouth	18	8 88	Liverpool
Howard Steve (F)	6 3	15 00	Durham	10	5 76	Derby Co
John Jorrin (M)						

Kermorgant Yann (F)	6 0	13 03	Vannes	8 11 81	Reims
King Andy (M)	6 0	11 10	Luton	29 10 88	Scholar
King Craig (F)	5 11	11 12	Chesterfield	6 10 90	Scholar
Logan Conrad (G)	6 0	14 09	Letterkenny	18 4 86	Scholar
Morrison Michael (D)	6 0	12 00	Bury St Edmunds	3 3 88	Cambridge U
N'Guessan Dany (M)	6 0	12 13	Ivry-sur-Seine	11 8 87	Lincoln C
Neilson Robbie (D)	6 0	13 01	Paisley	19 6 80	Hearts
O'Neill Luke (D)			Slough	20 8 91	Scholar
Oakley Matthew (M)	5 10	12 06	Peterborough	17 8 77	Derby Co
Parkes Tom (D)	6 3	12 05	Leicester	15 1 92	Scholar
Pentney Carl (G)	6 0	12 00	Leicester	3 2 89	
Solano Nolberto (M)	5 8	10 07	Callao	12 12 74	Universitario
Tunchev Aleksandar (D)	6 2	13 03	Pazardzhik	10 7 81	CSKA Sofia
Verma Aman (M)			Birmingham	3 1 87	Redditch U
Wellens Richard (M)	5 9	11 06	Manchester	26 3 80	Doncaster R
Wesolowski James (D)	5 8	11 11	Sydney	25 8 87	Scholar
Worley Harry (D)	6 3	13 00	Warrington	25 11 88	Chelsea

League Appearances: Adams, N. 1(17); Berner, B. 34(1); Brown, W. 38(1); Bruce, A. 2(1); Campbell, D. (3); Dickov, P. (1); Dyer, L. 25(8); Fryatt, M. 26(3); Gallagher, P. 31(10); Hobbs, J. 44; Howard, S. 17(19); Kermorgant, Y. 9(11); King, A. 37(6); Logan, C. 1(1); McGivern, R. 9(3); Morrison, M. 30(1); N'Guessan, D. 16(11); Neilson, R. 19; O'Neill, L. (1); Oakley, M. 37(1); Powell, C. 2; Solano, N. 6(5); Spearing, J. 6(1); Tunchev, A. 1(1); Vaughan, J. 2(6); Waghorn, M. 27(16); Weale, C. 45; Wellens, R. 41.

Goals – League (61): Waghorn 12 (2 pens), Fryatt 11 (3 pens), King A 9, Gallagher 7, Howard 5, Berner 4, Dyer 3, N'Guessan 3, Morrison 2, Kermorgant 1, Spearing 1, Vaughan 1, Wellens 1 (1 pen), own goal 1.

Carling Cup (3): Adams 1, Fryatt 1, N'Guessan 1.

FA Cup (4): N'Guessan 2, King A 1, Morrison 1.

Play-Offs (3): Fryatt 1, King A 1, own goal 1.

Ground: Walkers Stadium, Filbert Way, Leicester LE2 7FL. Telephone (0844) 815 6000.

Record Attendance: 47,298 v Tottenham H, FA Cup 5th rd, 18 February 1928. **Capacity:** 32,312.

Manager: Paulo Sousa.

Secretary: Andrew Neville.

Most League Goals: 109, Division 2, 1956–57.

Highest League Scorer in Season: Arthur Rowley, 44, Division 2, 1956–57.

Most League Goals in Total Aggregate: Arthur Chandler, 259, 1923–35.

Most Capped Player: John O'Neill, 39, Northern Ireland.

Most League Appearances: Adam Black, 528, 1920–35.

Honours – Football League: Championship 1 Winners – 2008–09. Division 2 Champions – 1924–25, 1936–37, 1953–54, 1956–57, 1970–71, 1979–80. **Football League Cup:** Winners – 1964, 1997, 2000.

Colours: Blue shirts with white trim, white shorts, blue stockings with white trim.

LEYTON ORIENT   FL CHAMPIONSHIP 1

Ashworth Luke (D)	6 2	12 08	Bolton	4 12 89	Wigan Ath
Chambers Adam (M)	5 10	11 08	Sandwell	20 11 80	Kidderminster H
Chorley Ben (D)	6 3	13 02	Sidcup	30 9 82	Tranmere R
Daniels Charlie (M)	6 1	12 12	Harlow	7 9 86	Tottenham H
Demetriou Jason (M)	5 11	10 08	Newham	18 11 87	Scholar
Jarvis Ryan (F)	6 1	11 11	Fakenham	11 7 86	Norwich C
Jones Jamie (G)	6 2	14 05	Kirkby	18 2 89	Everton
McGleish Scott (F)	5 9	11 09	Barnet	10 2 74	Wycombe W
Mike Cestor (D)			Paris	30 4 92	Youth

Mkandawire Tamika (D)	6 1	12 03	Malawi	28	5 83	Hereford U
Patulea Adrian (F)	5 10	11 04	Targoviste	10 11 84	Lincoln C
Smith Jimmy (M)	6 0	10 03	Newham	7	1 87	Chelsea
Tehoue Jonathan (F)	5 8	11 06	Paris	3	5 84	Alfortville

League Appearances: Adams, N. 6; Ashworth, L. 7(3); Baker, H. (4); Briggs, M. 1; Cave-Brown, A. 12(4); Chambers, A. 26(3); Chorley, B. 42; Daniels, C. 40(1); Demetriou, J. 29(10); Doran, A. 6; Jarvis, R. 34(8); Jones, J. 36; Lichaj, E. 9; McGleish, S. 36(6); Melligan, J. 14(2); Mkandawire, T. 43; Morris, G. 10(1); O'Leary, K. 1(2); Patulea, A. 4(17); Pires, L. (8); Purches, S. 30(1); Scowcroft, J. 13(13); Smith, J. 34(6); Spicer, J. 9; Summerfield, L. 14; Tehoue, J. 5(11); Thornton, S. 28(2); Townsend, A. 17(5).
Goals – League (53): McGleish 12 (1 pen), Jarvis 8, Mkandawire 7, Thornton 7, Smith 2, Tehoue 2, Townsend 2, Chambers 1, Chorley 1, Demetriou 1, Lichaj 1, Melligan 1, Patulea 1, Purches 1, Spicer 1, own goals 5.
Carling Cup (2): Milligan 1, Patulea 1.
FA Cup (1): Ashworth 1.
J Paint Trophy (2): Demetriou 1, Patulea 1.
Ground: Matchroom Stadium, Brisbane Road, Leyton, London E10 5NE. Telephone 0871 310 1881.
Record Attendance: 34,345 v West Ham U, FA Cup 4th rd, 25 January 1964. **Capacity:** 9,300.
Manager: Russell Slade.
Secretary: Lindsey Freeman.
Most League Goals: 106, Division 3 (S), 1955–56.
Highest League Scorer in Season: Tom Johnston, 35, Division 2, 1957–58.
Most League Goals in Total Aggregate: Tom Johnston, 121, 1956–58, 1959–61.
Most Capped Players: Tunji Banjo, 7 (7), Nigeria; John Chiedozie, 7 (9), Nigeria; Tony Grealish, 7 (45), Eire.
Most League Appearances: Peter Allen, 432, 1965–78.
Honours – Football League: Division 3 Champions – 1969–70. Division 3 (S) Champions – 1955–56.
Colours: Red shirts with white insert and striped sleeves, red shorts, red stockings.

LINCOLN CITY   FL CHAMPIONSHIP 2

Anderson Joe (D)	6 0	12 00	Lincoln	13 10 89	Fulham
Clarke Shane (D)	6 1	13 03	Lincoln	7 11 87	Scholar
Fagan Chris (F)	5 8	10 05	Dublin	11 5 89	Manchester U
Gilmour Brian (D)	5 7	10 00	Irvine	8 5 87	Haka
Green Paul (D)	5 8	10 04	Birmingham	15 4 87	Aston Villa
Hone Daniel (D)	6 2	12 00	Croydon	15 9 89	Scholar
Hughton Cian (D)	5 8	10 05	Enfield	25 1 89	Tottenham H
John-Lewis Leneli (M)	5 10 11 10	Hammersmith	17 5 89	Scholar
Keltie Clark (M)	5 11 11 08	Newcastle	31 8 83	Rochdale
Kerr Scott (M)	5 9	10 07	Leeds	11 12 81	Scarborough
Lennon Steven (F)	5 7	10 00	Irvine	20 1 88	Rangers
Musselwhite Paul (G)	6 2	14 00	Portsmouth	22 12 68	Gateshead
Smith Khano (M)	6 3	12 00	Paget	10 1 81	NY Red Bulls
Swaibu Moses (D)	6 2	11 11	Croydon	9 5 89	Crystal Palace
Watts Adam (D)	6 2	12 06	London	4 3 88	Fulham

League Appearances: Adams, N. (2); Anderson, J. 23; Baker, N. 17(1); Bennett, L. (1); Broughton, D. 7; Brown, A. 14(3); Burch, R. 46; Butcher, R. 10(5); Clarke, S. 21(8); Clarke, J. 14(6); Coleman-Carr, L. (1); Connor, P. 8(7); Facey, D. 9(1); Fagan, C. 10(3); Gilmour, B. 14(2); Gordon, M. 4(1); Green, P. 13(2); Heath, J. 3(1); Herd, C. 20; Hone, D. 16(1); Howe, R. 14(3); Hughton, C. 41; Hutchinson, A. (10); John-Lewis, L. 7(17); Keltie, C. 9(2); Kerr, S. 36(3); Kovacs, J. 14; Lennon, S. 15(4); Lichaj, E. 6; Oakes, S. 11(5);

Pearce, I. 5(5); Pulis, A. 7; Saunders, M. 17(1); Smith, K. 4(1); Somma, D. 14; Stephens, D. 3; Swaibu, M. 29(5); Torres, S. 7(1); Uwezu, M. (2); Watts, A. 18.
Goals – League (42): Somma 9, Howe 5 (2 pens), Herd 4, Hughton 4, Fagan 3, Lennon 3, Saunders 3, Gilmour 2, Clarke J 1, Facey 1, Hone 1, John-Lewis 1, Kovacs 1, Swaibu 1, Torres 1, own goals 2.
Carling Cup (0).
FA Cup (6): Clarke J 3, Brown 1, Fagan 1, Torres 1.
J Paint Trophy (0).
Ground: Sincil Bank Stadium, Sincil Bank, Lincoln LN5 8LD. Telephone (01522) 880 011.
Record Attendance: 23,196 v Derby Co, League Cup 4th rd, 15 November 1967.
Capacity: 10,120.
Manager: Chris Sutton.
Football Secretary: Fran Martin.
Most League Goals: 121, Division 3 (N), 1951–52.
Highest League Scorer in Season: Allan Hall, 41, Division 3 (N), 1931–32.
Most League Goals in Total Aggregate: Andy Graver, 144, 1950–55 and 1958–61.
Most Capped Player: Gareth McAuley, 5 (21), Northern Ireland.
Most League Appearances: Grant Brown, 407, 1989–2002.
Honours – Football League: Division 3 (N) Champions – 1931–32, 1947–48, 1951–52. Division 4 Champions – 1975–76. **GM Vauxhall Conference:** Champions – 1987–88.
Colours: Red and white striped shirts, black shorts, red stockings.

LIVERPOOL   FA PREMIERSHIP

Agger Daniel (D)	6 2	12 06	Hvidovre	12 12 84	Brondby
Amoo David (F)			London	23 4 91	Scholar
Aquilani Alberto (M)	6 0	12 03	Rome	7 7 84	Roma
Ayala Daniel (D)	6 3	13 01	Seville	7 11 90	Sevilla
Babel Ryan (F)	6 1	12 04	Amsterdam	19 12 86	Ajax
Benayoun Yossi (M)	5 10	11 00	Beer Sheva	6 6 80	West Ham U
Bouzanis Dean (G)	6 1	13 05	Sydney	2 10 90	Sydney
Brouwer Jordy (F)			Den Haag	26 2 88	Ajax
Bruna Gerardo (M)	5 8	10 02	Mendoza	29 1 91	
Carragher Jamie (D)	5 9	12 01	Liverpool	28 1 78	Trainee
Cavalieri Diego (G)	6 3	13 07	Sao Paulo	1 12 82	Palmeiras
Cooper Alex (M)	5 8	11 08	Birmingham	4 11 91	Scholar
Dalla Valle Lauri (F)	5 9	11 03	Kontiolahti	14 9 91	
Darby Stephen (D)	6 1	11 11	Liverpool	6 10 88	Scholar
Degen Philipp (D)	6 0	12 10	Holstein	15 2 83	Bor Dortmund
Eccleston Nathan (F)	5 10	12 00	Manchester	30 12 90	Scholar
El Zhar Nabil (F)	5 9	11 05	Rabat	27 8 86	St Etienne
Ellison James (F)	5 10	12 08	Liverpool	25 10 91	Scholar
Emilsson Kristjan (M)			Sweden	26 4 93	Scholar
Gerrard Steven (M)	6 0	12 05	Whiston	30 5 80	Trainee
Gulacsi Peter (G)	6 3	13 01	Budapest	6 5 90	MTK Budapest
Hansen Martin (G)	6 2	12 07	Denmark	15 6 90	Scholar
Highdale Sean (M)			Liverpool	4 3 91	
Ince Thomas (F)	5 10	10 05	Liverpool	30 1 92	Scholar
Insua Emiliano (D)	5 10	12 08	Buenos Aires	7 1 89	Boca Juniors
Irwin Steven (D)	5 8	10 06	Liverpool	29 9 90	Scholar
Itandje Charles (G)	6 3	13 01	Bobigny	2 11 82	Lens
Johnson Glen (D)	6 0	13 04	Greenwich	23 8 84	Portsmouth
Kacaniklic Alexander (M)	5 11	10 05	Sweden	13 8 91	Scholar
Kelly Martin (D)	6 3	12 02	Bolton	27 4 90	Scholar
Kohlert Nicolaj (F)	5 10	11 00	Denmark	21 1 93	
Kuyt Dirk (F)	6 0	12 02	Katwijk	22 7 80	Feyenoord

Name			Birthplace			Previous club
Kyrgiakos Sotirios (D)	6 3	14 06	Megalochori	23	7 79	AEK Athens
Lucas (M)	5 10	11 09	Dourados	9	1 87	Gremio
Mascherano Javier (M)	5 10	12 02	San Lorenzo	8	6 84	West Ham U
Mavinga Chrys (D)	5 10	10 03	Meaux	26	5 91	Paris St Germain
Mendy Emmanuel (D)	5 7	11 09	Medina Gounass	30	3 90	Murcia
Mihaylov Nikolay (G)	6 3	14 00	Bulgaria	28	6 88	Levski
N'Gog David (F)	6 3	12 04	Gennevillers	1	4 89	Paris St Germain
N'Goo Michael (F)			London	23	10 92	Southend U
Nemeth Krisztian (M)	5 10	11 07	Gyor	5	1 89	
Pacheco Daniel (F)	5 6	10 07	Malaga	5	1 91	Barcelona
Palsson Victor (M)	6 1	12 00	Iceland	30	4 91	Aarhus
Pepper Adam (M)	5 6	9 04	Liverpool	2	12 91	Scholar
Plessis Damien (M)	6 3	12 02	Neuvy-sous-Bois	5	3 88	Lyon
Reina Jose (G)	6 2	14 06	Madrid	31	8 82	Villarreal
Riera Alberto (M)	6 1	12 01	Manacor	15	4 82	Espanyol
Roberts Michael (M)			Liverpool	5	12 91	
Rodriguez Maxi (M)	5 11	12 06	Rosario	2	1 81	Atletico Madrid
Sama Stephen (D)			Cameroon	5	3 93	Scholar
San Jose Dominguez Mikel (D)	6 0	12 04	Pamplona	30	5 89	Athletic Bilbao
Saric Craig (F)	6 0	10 09	Wirral	7	9 88	Lleida
Shelvey Jonjo (M)	6 1	11 02	Romford	27	2 92	Charlton Ath
Simon Andras (F)	6 0	11 05	Salgotarjan	30	3 90	MTK Budapest
Skrtel Martin (D)	6 3	12 10	Hamdlova	15	12 84	Zenit
Spearing Jay (D)	5 6	11 00	Wirral	25	11 88	Scholar
Torres Fernando (F)	5 9	12 03	Madrid	20	3 84	Atletico Madrid
Weijl Vincent (F)	6 0	12 04	Amsterdam	11	11 90	AZ
Wisdom Andre (D)			Leeds	9	5 93	Scholar

League Appearances: Agger, D. 23; Aquilani, A. 9(9); Ayala, D. 2(3); Babel, R. 9(16); Benayoun, Y. 19(11); Carragher, J. 37; Darby, S. (1); Degen, P. 3(4); Dossena, A. 1(1); Eccleston, N. (1); El Zhar, N. 1(2); Fabio Aurelio, 8(6); Gerrard, S. 32(1); Insua, E. 30(1); Johnson, G. 24(1); Kelly, M. (1); Kuyt, D. 35(2); Kyrgiakos, S. 13(1); Lucas, 32(3); Mascherano, J. 31(3); N'Gog, D. 10(14); Pacheco, D. (4); Reina, J. 38; Riera, A. 9(3); Robinson, J. (1); Rodriguez, M. 14(3); Skrtel, M. 16(3); Spearing, J. 1(2); Torres, F. 20(2); Voronin, A. 1(7).

Goals – League (61): Torres 18, Gerrard 9 (2 pens), Kuyt 9 (1 pen), Benayoun 6, N'Gog 5, Babel 4, Johnson 3, Aquilani 1, Kyrgiakos 1, Rodriguez 1, Skrtel 1, own goals 3.
Carling Cup (2): Insua 1, N'Gog 1.
FA Cup (2): Gerrard 1, own goal 1.
Champions League (5): Benayoun 2, Babel 1, Kuyt 1, N'Gog 1.
Europa League (14): Torres 4, Gerrard 2 (1 pen), Agger 1, Aquilaini 1, Babel 1, Benayoun 1, Kuyt 1, Lucas 1, Mascherano 1, N'Gog 1.
Ground: Anfield Stadium, Anfield Road, Liverpool L4 0TH. Telephone (0151) 260 1433.
Record Attendance: 61,905 v Wolverhampton W, FA Cup 4th rd, 2 February 1952.
Capacity: 45,522.
Manager: Roy Hodgson.
Secretary: Ian Silvester.
Most League Goals: 106, Division 2, 1895–96.
Highest League Scorer in Season: Roger Hunt, 41, Division 2, 1961–62.
Most League Goals in Total Aggregate: Roger Hunt, 245, 1959–69.
Most Capped Player: Steven Gerrard, 84, England.
Most League Appearances: Ian Callaghan, 640, 1960–78.
Honours – Football League: Division 1 – Champions 1900–01, 1905–06, 1921–22, 1922–23, 1946–47, 1963–64, 1965–66, 1972–73, 1975–76, 1976–77, 1978–79, 1979–80, 1981–82, 1982–83, 1983–84, 1985–86, 1987–88, 1989–90 (Liverpool have a record number of 18

League Championship wins). Division 2 Champions – 1893–94, 1895–96, 1904–05, 1961–62. **FA Cup**: Winners – 1965, 1974, 1986, 1989, 1992, 2001, 2006. **League Cup:** Winners – 1981, 1982, 1983, 1984, 1995, 2001, 2003. **League Super Cup:** Winners 1985–86. **European Competitions: European Cup:** Winners – 1976–77, 1977–78, 1980–81, 1983–84. **Champions League:** Winners – 2004–05. **UEFA Cup:** Winners – 1972–73, 1975–76, 2001. **Super Cup:** Winners – 1977, 2005.
Colours: All red with white trim.

MACCLESFIELD TOWN   FL CHAMPIONSHIP 2

Bencherif Hamza (D)	5 9	12 03	Paris	9	2 88	Nottingham F
Brisley Shaun (M)	6 2	12 02	Stockport	6	5 90	Scholar
Brown Nat (D)	6 2	12 05	Sheffield	15	6 81	Lincoln C
Daniel Colin (M)	5 11	11 06	Crewe	15	2 88	Crewe Alex
Draper Ross (M)	6 3	15 05	Wolverhampton	20	10 88	Hednesford T
Lindfield Craig (F)	6 0	10 05	Wirral	7	9 88	Liverpool
Lowe Matt (M)	5 8	10 12	Stoke	20	10 90	Scholar
Morgan Paul (D)	6 0	11 05	Belfast	23	10 78	Bury
Mukendi Vinny (F)	6 2	12 00	Bury	12	3 92	Scholar
Reid Izak (M)	5 5	10 05	Sheffield	08	7 87	Scholar
Rooney John (F)	5 10	12 00	Liverpool	17	12 90	Scholar
Sappleton Ricky (F)	5 10	11 13	Kingston	8	12 89	Leicester C
Sinclair Emile (F)	6 0	11 04	Leeds	20	12 87	Nottingham F
Tremarco Carl (D)	5 8	11 11	Liverpool	11	10 85	Tranmere R
Veiga Jose Manuel (G)	6 2	12 13	Lisbon	18	12 76	Hereford U

League Appearances: Bell, L. 37(5); Bencherif, H. 19; Bolland, P. 17(10); Brain, J. 41; Brisley, S. 29(4); Brown, N. 37(1); Butcher, R. 8; Daniel, C. 34(4); Draper, R. 28(1); Hessey, S. 27; Lindfield, C. 12(6); Lowe, M. 7(3); Mills, G. (1); Morgan, P. 35(1); Mukendi, V. 8(1); Reid, I. 34(3); Rooney, J. 14(11); Sappleton, R. 18(6); Sinclair, E. 33(9); Thomas, M. (4); Tipton, M. 11(20); Tremarco, C. 27(2); Veiga, J. 5; Wilson, K. (4); Wright, B. 25(14).
Goals – League (49): Sappleton 7, Sinclair 7, Wright 6, Bencherif 5, Tipton 5 (3 pens), Brown 4, Daniel 3, Bell 2, Butcher 2, Lindfield 2, Bolland 1, Brisley 1, Draper 1, Mukendi 1, Rooney 1, own goal 1.
Carling Cup (0).
FA Cup (0).
J Paint Trophy (2): Brisley 1, Rooney 1.
Ground: Moss Rose Ground, London Road, Macclesfield, Cheshire SK11 0DQ. Telephone (01625) 264 686.
Record Attendance: 9,008 v Winsford U, Cheshire Senior Cup 2nd rd, 4 February 1948.
Capacity: 6,141.
Manager: Gary Simpson.
Company Secretary: Barrie Darcey.
Most League Goals: 66, Division 3, 1999–2000.
Highest League Scorer in Season: Jon Parkin, 22, League 2, 2004–05.
Most League Goals in Total Aggregate: Matt Tipton, 45, 2002–05; 2006–07.
Most Capped Player: George Abbey, 10(16), Nigeria.
Most League Appearances: Darren Tinson, 263, 1997–2003.
Honours – None.
Colours: Blue shirts with white design, white shorts, blue stockings.

MANCHESTER CITY   FA PREMIERSHIP

Adebayor Emmanuel (F)	6 4	11 08	Lome	26	2 84	Arsenal
Ball David (F)			Whitefield	14	12 89	Scholar

Name			Birthplace	Date			Previous club
Barry Gareth (M)	5 11	12 06	Hastings	23	2	81	Aston Villa
Bellamy Craig (F)	5 9	10 12	Cardiff	13	7	79	West Ham U
Benali Ahmad (M)			Libya	7	2	92	Scholar
Bojinov Valeri (F)	5 10	12 04	Oriahovizca	15	2	86	Juventus
Boyata Anga (M)	6 2	12 00	Uccle	8	9	90	Scholar
Bridge Wayne (D)	5 10	12 13	Southampton	5	8	80	Chelsea
Caicedo Felipe (F)	6 1	12 08	Guayaquil	5	9	88	Basle
Chantler Chris (D)	5 8	11 00	Cheadle Hulme	16	12	90	Scholar
Clayton Adam (M)	5 9	11 11	Manchester	14	1	89	Scholar
Cunningham Greg (D)	6 0	11 00	Cammore	31	1	91	Scholar
De Jong Nigel (M)	5 8	11 05	Amsterdam	30	11	84	Hamburg
Elabdellaoui Omar (M)			Norway	5	12	91	Scholar
Etuhu Calvin (F)	6 0	12 09	Nigeria	30	5	88	Scholar
Garrido Javier (M)	5 10	11 11	Irun	15	3	85	Real Sociedad
Given Shay (G)	6 0	13 03	Lifford	20	4	76	Newcastle U
Gonzalez David (G)	6 4		Medellin	20	7	82	Huracan
Guidetti John (F)			Stockholm	15	4	92	Scholar
Hart Joe (G)	6 5	14 05	Shrewsbury	19	4	87	Shrewsbury T
Helan Jeremy (M)			France	9	5	92	Rennes
Ibrahim Abdisalam (M)	6 0			4	5	91	Scholar
Ireland Stephen (F)	5 8	10 07	Cobh	22	8	86	Scholar
Jo (F)	5 9	11 00	Sao Paulo	20	3	87	CSKA Moscow
Johnson Adam (M)	5 8	10 00	Sunderland	14	7	87	Middlesbrough
Johnson Michael (M)	6 0	12 07	Urmston	3	3	88	Scholar
Kay Scott (M)			Manchester	18	9	89	Scholar
Kompany Vincent (D)	6 3	13 05	Uccle	10	4	86	Hamburg
Lescott Jolean (D)	6 2	13 00	Birmingham	16	8	82	Everton
Logan Shaleum (D)	5 8	10 01	Manchester	29	1	88	Scholar
Mak Robert (M)	5 10	11 00	Slovakia	8	3	91	Scholar
McDermott Donal (M)	6 6	12 00	Dublin	19	10	89	Scholar
McGivern Ryan (D)	5 10	11 07	Newry	8	1	90	Scholar
Mee Ben (D)	5 11	11 09	Manchester	21	9	89	Scholar
Nielsen Gunnar (G)	6 3	14 00	Faeroes	7	10	86	Blackburn R
Nimely-Tchuimeni Alex (F)	5 11	11 03	Monrovia	11	5	91	Cotonsport
Onuoha Nedum (D)	6 2	12 04	Warri	12	11	86	Scholar
Poole James (F)			Stockport	20	3	90	Scholar
Redshaw Jack (F)	5 6	11 00		20	1	90	Scholar
Richards Micah (D)	5 11	13 00	Birmingham	24	6	88	Scholar
Robinho (F)	5 8	10 00	Sao Vicente	25	1	84	Real Madrid
Santa Cruz Roque (F)	6 2	13 12	Asuncion	16	8	81	Blackburn R
Tevez Carlos (F)	5 8	11 11	Cuidadela	5	2	84	Manchester U
Toure Kolo (D)	5 10	13 08	Sokuora Bouake	19	3	81	Arsenal
Trippier Keiran (D)	5 10	11 00	Bury	19	9	90	Scholar
Tutte Andrew (M)	5 9			21	9	90	Scholar
Veseli Frederic (D)			Switzerland	22	11	92	Scholar
Vidal Javan (D)	5 10	10 10	Manchester	10	5	89	Scholar
Wabara Reece (M)				28	12	91	Scholar
Weiss Vladimir (M)	5 8	11 02	Bratislava	30	11	89	Academy
Wood James (G)	6 0	13 01		10	11	91	Scholar
Wright-Phillips Shaun (F)	5 5	10 01	Lewisham	25	10	81	Chelsea
Zabaleta Pablo (D)	5 8	10 12	Buenos Aires	16	1	85	Espanyol

League Appearances: Adebayor, E. 25(1); Barry, G. 34; Bellamy, C. 26(6); Boyata, A. 1(2); Bridge, W. 23; Cunningham, G. (2); De Jong, N. 30(4); Dunne, R. 2; Fulop, M. 3; Garrido, J. 7(2); Given, S. 35; Ibrahim, A. (1); Ireland, S. 16(6); Johnson, M. (1); Johnson, A. 14(2); Kompany, V. 21(4); Lescott, J. 17(1); Mwaruwari, B. 1(1); Nielsen, G. (1); Nimely-Tchuimeni, A. (1); Onuoha, N. 5(5); Petrov, M. 8(8); Richards, M. 19(4);

Robinho, 6(4); Santa Cruz, R. 6(13); Sylvinho, 6(4); Tevez, C. 32(3); Toure, K. 31; Vieira, P. 8(5); Wright-Phillips, S. 19(11); Zabaleta, P. 23(4).
Goals – League (73): Tevez 23 (5 pens), Adebayor 14, Bellamy 10, Petrov 4, Wright-Phillips 4, Richards 3, Santa Cruz 3, Barry 2, Ireland 2, Kompany 2, Garrido 1, Johnson A 1, Lescott 1, Onuoha 1, Toure 1, Vieira 1.
Carling Cup (15): Tevez 6 (1 pen), Wright-Phillips 2, Barry 1, Ireland 1, Johnson M 1, Lescott 1, Santa Cruz R 1, Toure 1, Weiss 1.
FA Cup (7): Bellamy 1, Mwaruwari 1, Onuoha 1, Petrov 1, Robinho 1, Sylvinho 1, Wright-Phillips 1.
Ground: The City of Manchester Stadium, SportCity, Manchester M11 3FF. Telephone (0870) 062 1894.
Record Attendance: (at Maine Road) 84,569 v Stoke C, FA Cup 6th rd, 3 March 1934 (British record for any game outside London or Glasgow) (at City of Manchester Stadium) 47,304 v Chelsea, FA Premier League, 28 February 2004. **Capacity:** 47,726.
Manager: Roberto Mancini.
Secretary: Rebecca Firth.
Most League Goals: 108, Division 2, 1926–27, 108, Division 1, 2001–02.
Highest League Scorer in Season: Tommy Johnson, 38, Division 1, 1928–29.
Most League Goals in Total Aggregate: Tommy Johnson, 158, 1919–30.
Most Capped Player: Colin Bell, 48, England.
Most League Appearances: Alan Oakes, 565, 1959–76.
Honours – Football League: Division 1 Champions – 1936–37, 1967–68, 2001–02. Division 2 Champions – 1898–99, 1902–03, 1909–10, 1927–28, 1946–47, 1965–66. **FA Cup:** Winners – 1904, 1934, 1956, 1969. **Football League Cup:** Winners – 1970, 1976.
European Competitions: European Cup-Winners' Cup: Winners – 1969–70.
Colours: Sky blue shirts with white detail, white shorts with sky blue detail, white stockings with sky blue tops.

MANCHESTER UNITED   FA PREMIERSHIP

Ajose Nicholas (F)	5 8	11 00	Bury	7 10 91	Scholar
Amos Ben (G)	6 2	13 00	Macclesfield	10 4 90	Scholar
Anderson (M)	5 8	10 07	Porto Alegre	13 4 88	Porto
Berbatov Dimitar (F)	6 2	12 06	Blagoevgrad	30 1 81	Tottenham H
Biram Diouf Mame (F)	6 1	11 13	Dakar	16 12 87	Molde
Brady Robert (F)			Belfast	14 1 92	Scholar
Brown Wes (D)	6 1	13 11	Manchester	13 10 79	Scholar
Carrick Michael (M)	6 2	13 03	Wallsend	28 7 81	Tottenham H
Cathcart Craig (D)	6 2	11 06	Belfast	6 2 89	Scholar
Chester James (D)	5 10	11 13	Warrington	23 1 89	Scholar
Cleverley Tom (M)	5 8	10 07	Basingstoke	12 8 89	Scholar
De Laet Ritchie (D)	6 1	12 02	Antwerp	28 11 88	Stoke C
Drinkwater Daniel (M)			Manchester	5 3 90	Scholar
Dudgeon Joe (D)	5 9	11 11	Leeds	26 11 90	Scholar
Eikrem Magnus (M)	5 11	11 00	Molde	8 8 90	Scholar
Evans Corry (M)	5 8	10 12	Belfast	30 7 90	Scholar
Evans Jonny (D)	6 2	12 02	Belfast	3 1 88	Scholar
Evra Patrice (D)	5 8	11 10	Dakar	15 5 81	Monaco
Fabio (D)	5 8	10 03	Rio de Janeiro	9 7 90	Fluminense
Ferdinand Rio (D)	6 2	13 12	Peckham	7 11 78	Leeds U
Fletcher Darren (M)	6 0	13 01	Edinburgh	1 2 84	Scholar
Gibson Darron (M)	6 0	12 04	Londonderry	25 10 87	Scholar
Giggs Ryan (F)	5 11	11 00	Cardiff	29 11 73	School
Gill Oliver (D)	6 2	12 13	Frimley	15 9 90	Scholar
Gray David (F)	5 11	11 02	Edinburgh	4 5 88	Scholar
Hargreaves Owen (M)	5 11	11 07	Calgary	20 1 81	Bayern Munich
Hussain Etzaz (M)	5 9	11 00	Oslo	27 1 93	Scholar

James Matthew (M)			Bacup	22 7 91	Scholar
Johnstone Samuel (G)			Preston	25 3 93	Scholar
Keane William (F)			Stockport	11 11 93	Scholar
King Joshua (F)	6 1	13 03	Oslo	15 1 92	Scholar
Kuszczak Tomasz (G)	6 3	13 03	Krosno Odrzansia	20 3 82	WBA
Macheda Federico (F)	6 0	11 13	Rome	22 8 91	Scholar
Morrison Ravel (M)	5 8	11 01	Wythenshawe	2 2 93	Scholar
Nani (M)	5 9	10 04	Amadora	17 11 86	Sporting Lisbon
Norwood Oliver (M)			Burnley	12 4 91	Scholar
O'Shea John (D)	6 3	12 10	Waterford	30 4 81	Waterford
Obertan Gabriel (F)	6 1	12 06	Pantin	26 2 89	Bordeaux
Owen Michael (F)	5 8	10 12	Chester	14 12 79	Newcastle U
Park Ji-Sung (M)	5 9	11 06	Seoul	25 2 81	PSV Eindhoven
Petrucci Davide (F)	6 0	11 12	Rome	5 10 91	Scholar
Pogba Paul (M)			Lagny-sur-Marne	15 3 93	Scholar
Possebon Rodrigo (M)	6 0	11 13	Sapucaia do Sul	13 2 89	Internacional
Rafael (D)	6 3	12 08	Petropolis	9 7 90	Fluminense
Rooney Wayne (F)	5 10	12 04	Liverpool	24 10 85	Everton
Scholes Paul (M)	5 7	11 00	Salford	16 11 74	Scholar
Stewart Cameron (M)	5 9	11 09	Manchester	8 4 91	Scholar
Tosic Zoran (F)	5 7	10 12	Zrenjanin	28 4 87	Partizan Belgrade
Tunnicliffe Ryan (M)	5 11	12 07	Bury	30 12 92	Scholar
Valencia Luis (M)	5 10	12 04	Lago Agrio	5 8 85	Wigan Ath
Van der Sar Edwin (G)	6 5	14 11	Voorhout	29 10 70	Fulham
Vidic Nemanja (D)	6 1	13 02	Uzice	21 10 81	Spartak Moscow
Welbeck Daniel (F)	6 1	11 07	Manchester	26 11 90	Scholar
Wootton Scott (D)			Birkenhead	12 9 91	Scholar

League Appearances: Anderson, 10(4); Berbatov, D. 24(9); Biram Diouf, M. (5); Brown, W. 18(1); Carrick, M. 22(8); De Laet, R. 2; Evans, J. 18; Evra, P. 37(1); Fabio, 1(4); Ferdinand, R. 12(1); Fletcher, D. 29(1); Foster, B. 9; Gibson, D. 6(9); Giggs, R. 20(5); Hargreaves, O. (1); Kuszczak, T. 8; Macheda, F. 1(4); Nani, 19(4); Neville, G. 15(2); O'Shea, J. 12(3); Obertan, G. 1(6); Owen, M. 5(14); Park, J. 10(7); Rafael, 8; Rooney, W. 32; Scholes, P. 24(4); Valencia, L. 29(5); Van der Sar, E. 21; Vidic, N. 24; Welbeck, D. 1(4).

Goals – League (86): Rooney 26 (4 pens), Berbatov 12, Giggs 5 (2 pens), Valencia 5, Fletcher 4, Nani 4, Carrick 3, Owen 3, Park 3, Scholes 3, Gibson 2, Anderson 1, Biram Diouf 1, Macheda 1, O'Shea 1, Rafael 1, Vidic 1, own goals 10.

Carling Cup (11): Gibson 2, Owen 2, Rooney 2, Welbeck 2, Carrick 1, Giggs 1, Scholes 1.

FA Cup (0).

Champions League (21): Rooney 5, Owen 4, Scholes 3, Nani 2, Valencia 2, Carrick 1, Fletcher 1, Gibson 1, Giggs 1, Park 1.

Community Shield (2): Nani 1, Rooney 1.

Ground: Old Trafford, Sir Matt Busby Way, Manchester M16 0RA. Telephone (0161) 868 8000.

Record Attendance: 76,962 Wolverhampton W v Grimsby T, FA Cup semi-final. 25 March 1939. **Club record:** 76,098 v Blackburn R, Premier League, 31 March 2007.

Capacity: 76,212.

Manager: Sir Alex Ferguson CBE.

Secretary: John Alexander.

Most League Goals: 103, Division 1, 1956–57 and 1958–59.

Highest League Scorer in Season: Dennis Viollet, 32, 1959–60.

Most League Goals in Total Aggregate: Bobby Charlton, 199, 1956–73.

Most Capped Player: Bobby Charlton, 106, England.

Most League Appearances: Bobby Charlton, 606, 1956–73.

Honours – FA Premier League: Champions – 1992–93, 1993–94, 1995–96, 1996–97, 1998–99, 1999–2000, 2000–01, 2002–03, 2006–07, 2007–08, 2008–09. **Football League:**

Division 1 Champions – 1907–8, 1910–11, 1951–52, 1955–56, 1956–57, 1964–65, 1966–67.
Division 2 Champions – 1935–36, 1974–75. **FA Cup:** Winners – 1909, 1948, 1963, 1977,
1983, 1985, 1990, 1994, 1996, 1999, 2004. **Football League Cup:** Winners – 1991–92, 2006,
2009, 2010. **European Competitions: European Cup:** Winners – 1967–68. **Champions
League:** Winners – 1998–99, 2007–08. **European Cup-Winners' Cup:** Winners – 1990–
91. **Super Cup:** Winners – 1991. **Inter-Continental Cup:** Winners – 1999.
Colours: Red shirts with black chevron, white shorts with red side panels, black
stockings.

MIDDLESBROUGH   FL CHAMPIONSHIP

Player			Birthplace				Previous club
Arca Julio (M)	5 9	11 13	Quilmes	31	1 81		Sunderland
Bates Matthew (D)	5 10	12 03	Stockton	10	12 86		Scholar
Bennett Joe (D)	5 10	10 04	Rochdale	28	3 90		Scholar
Coyne Danny (G)	6 0	13 00	Prestatyn	27	8 73		Tranmere R
Digard Didier (M)	6 0	11 13	Gisors	12	7 86		Paris St Germain
Emnes Marvin (M)	5 9	10 06	Rotterdam	27	5 88		Sparta Rotterdam
Flood Willo (M)	5 7	10 05	Dublin	10	4 85		Celtic
Franks Jonathan (M)	5 9	11 03	Stockton	8	4 90		Scholar
Grounds Jonathan (D)	6 1	13 10	Ingleby Barwick	2	2 88		Scholar
Hines Sebastian (M)	6 2	12 04	Wetherby	29	5 88		Scholar
Hoyte Justin (D)	5 11	11 00	Waltham Forest	20	11 84		Arsenal
Johnson John (D)	6 0	12 00	Middlesbrough	16	9 88		Scholar
Jones Brad (G)	6 3	12 01	Armidale	19	3 82		Trainee
Lita Leroy (F)	5 7	11 12	DR Congo	28	12 84		Reading
McDonald Scott (F)	5 7	12 07	Dandenorg	21	8 83		Celtic
McMahon Anthony (D)	5 10	11 04	Bishop Auckland	24	3 86		Scholar
Mido (F)	6 2	14 09	Cairo	23	2 83		Tottenham H
Miller Lee (F)	6 0	11 07	Lanark	18	5 83		Aberdeen
O'Neil Gary (M)	5 10	11 00	Bromley	18	5 83		Portsmouth
Pogatetz Emanuel (D)	6 2	13 05	Steinbock	16	1 83		Graz
Riggott Chris (D)	6 2	13 09	Derby	1	9 80		Derby Co
Robson Barry (M)	5 11	12 00	Aberdeen	7	11 78		Celtic
Smallwood Richard (M)			Redcar	29	12 90		Scholar
Steele Jason (G)	6 2	12 13	Bishop Auckland	18	8 90		Scholar
Taylor Andrew (D)	5 10	11 04	Hartlepool	1	8 86		Trainee
Walker Josh (M)	5 11	11 13	Newcastle	21	2 89		Scholar
Wheater David (D)	6 4	12 12	Redcar	14	2 87		Scholar
Williams Luke (F)	6 1	11 06	Middlesbrough	11	6 93		Scholar
Williams Rhys (D)	6 2	11 05	Perth	14	7 88		Scholar

League Appearances: Aliadiere, J. 16(4); Arca, J. 26(8); Bennett, J. 10(2); Bent, M. 3(4);
Coyne, D. 22(1); Digard, D. 4(5); Emnes, M. 12(4); Flood, W. 11; Folan, C. (1); Franks, J.
9(14); Grounds, J. 16(4); Hines, S. 2; Hoyte, J. 23(7); Huth, R. 4; Johnson, A. 25(1); Jones,
B. 24; Killen, C. 15(2); Kitson, D. 6; Lita, L. 23(17); McDonald, S. 12(1); McMahon, T.
20(1); McManus, S. 16; Miller, L. 6(4); Naughton, K. 12(3); O'Neil, G. 35(1); O'Shea, J.
1(1); Osbourne, I. 9; Pogatetz, E. 13; Riggott, C. 4(2); Robson, B. 18; St Ledger-Hall, S.
14(1); Taylor, A. 8(4); Tuncay, S. (3); Walker, J. 1; Wheater, D. 42; Williams, R. 31(1);
Williams, L. 2(2); Yeates, M. 11(8).
Goals – League (58): Johnson A 11 (4 pens), Lita 8 (1 pen), Robson 5 (2 pens),
Aliadiere 4, McDonald 4, O'Neil 4, Franks 3, Killen 3, Kitson 3, St Ledger-Hall 2, Tun-
cay 2, Williams R 2, Emnes 1, Flood 1, Hoyte 1, McManus 1, Wheater 1, Yeates 1, own
goal 1.
Carling Cup (1): Johnson A 1.
FA Cup (0).
Ground: Riverside Stadium, Middlesbrough TS3 6RS. Telephone (0844) 499 6789.

Record Attendance: Ayresome Park: 53,536 v Newcastle U, Division 1, 27 December 1949. Riverside Stadium: 34,814 v Newcastle U, FA Premier League, 5 March 2003.
Capacity: 35,100.
Manager: Gordon Strachan.
Secretary: Karen Nelson.
Most League Goals: 122, Division 2, 1926–27.
Highest League Scorer in Season: George Camsell, 59, Division 2, 1926–27 (Second Division record).
Most League Goals in Total Aggregate: George Camsell, 325, 1925–39.
Most Capped Player: Wilf Mannion, 26, England.
Most League Appearances: Tim Williamson, 563, 1902–23.
Honours – Football League: Division 1 Champions 1994–95. Division 2 Champions 1926–27, 1928–29, 1973–74. **Football League Cup:** Winners – 2004, 2009. **Amateur Cup:** Winners – 1895, 1898. **Anglo-Scottish Cup:** Winners – 1975–76.
Colours: Red shirts with white design and one white sleeve, white shorts with red trim, white stockings.

MILLWALL   FL CHAMPIONSHIP

Abdou Nadjim (M)	5 10	11 02	Martigues	13 7 84	Plymouth Arg
Alexander Gary (F)	6 0	13 04	Lambeth	15 8 79	Leyton Orient
Barron Scott (D)	5 9	9 08	Preston	2 9 85	Ipswich T
Bolder Adam (M)	5 9	10 08	Hull	25 10 80	QPR
Craig Tony (D)	6 0	10 03	Greenwich	20 4 85	Crystal Palace
Dunne Alan (D)	5 10	10 13	Dublin	23 8 82	Trainee
Forde David (G)	6 3	13 06	Galway	20 12 79	Cardiff C
Frampton Andrew (D)	5 11	10 10	Wimbledon	3 9 79	Brentford
Grabban Lewis (F)	6 0	11 03	Croydon	12 1 88	Crystal Palace
Grimes Ashley (M)	6 0	11 02	Swinton	9 12 86	Manchester C
Hackett Chris (M)	6 0	11 06	Oxford	1 3 83	Hearts
Harris Neil (F)	5 11	12 09	Orsett	12 7 77	Nottingham F
Hughes-Mason Kiernon (F)	5 8	10 05	London	22 10 91	Scholar
Laird Marc (M)	6 1	10 07	Edinburgh	23 1 86	Manchester C
Martin David (M)	5 9	10 10	Erith	3 6 85	Crystal Palace
Morison Steve (F)	6 2	13 07	Enfield	29 8 83	Stevenage B
O'Connor Patrick (M)	6 1	13 00	Croydon	5 9 90	Scholar
Robinson Paul (D)	6 1	11 09	Barnet	7 1 82	Scholar
Schofield Danny (M)	5 10	11 02	Doncaster	10 4 80	Yeovil T
Smith Jack (D)	5 11	11 05	Hemel Hempstead	14 10 83	Swindon T
Sullivan John (G)	5 10	11 04	Brighton	8 3 88	Brighton & HA
Ward Darren (D)	6 3	14 03	Kenton	13 9 78	Wolverhampton W

League Appearances: Abdou, N. 43; Alexander, G. 8(7); Barron, S. 12(11); Batt, S. 10(6); Bolder, A. 5(6); Craig, T. 29(1); Dunne, A. 29(3); Forde, D. 46; Frampton, A. 20(1); Friend, G. 4(2); Fuseini, A. 10(5); Grabban, L. 5(6); Grimes, A. 2(2); Hackett, C. 34(6); Harris, N. 21(11); Henry, J. 6(3); Hughes-Mason, K. (1); Laird, M. 17(3); Marquis, J. (1); Martin, D. 16(4); Morison, S. 42(1); Obika, J. (12); Price, J. 5(10); Robinson, P. 34; Schofield, D. 28(8); Smith, J. 30(1); Trotter, L. 20; Ward, D. 30(1).
Goals – League (76): Morison 20 (2 pens), Harris 13 (1 pen), Schofield 7, Henry 5, Robinson 4, Batt 3, Martin 3 (1 pen), Craig 2, Dunne 2, Frampton 2, Hackett 2, Obika 2, Abdou 1, Alexander 1, Price 1, Trotter 1, Ward 1, own goals 6.
Carling Cup (5): Harris 4, Alexander 1.
FA Cup (11): Morison 2, Price 2, Schofield 2, Dunne 1, Grabban 1, Harris 1, Robinson 1, Smith 1.
J Paint Trophy (0).
Play-Offs (3): Robinson 2, Morison 1.
Ground: The Den, Zampa Road, London SE16 3LN. Telephone (020) 7232 1222.

Record Attendance: 20,093 v Arsenal, FA Cup 3rd rd, 10 January 1994. **Capacity:** 19,734.
Manager: Kenny Jackett.
Secretary: Yvonne Haines.
Most League Goals: 127, Division 3 (S), 1927–28.
Highest League Scorer in Season: Richard Parker, 37, Division 3 (S), 1926–27.
Most League Goals in Total Aggregate: Neil Harris, 114, 1995–2004; 2006–.
Most Capped Player: Eamonn Dunphy, 22 (23), Republic of Ireland.
Most League Appearances: Barry Kitchener, 523, 1967–82.
Honours – Football League: Division 2 Champions – 1987–88, 2000–01. Division 3 (S) Champions – 1927–28, 1937–38. Division 4 Champions – 1961–62. **Football League Trophy:** Winners – 1982–83.
Colours: All blue with white detail on shirts.

MILTON KEYNES DONS   FL CHAMPIONSHIP 1

Baldock George (M)	5 9	10 07			
Baldock Sam (F)	5 7	10 07	Buckingham	15 3 89	Scholar
Carrington Mark (M)	6 0	11 00	Warrington	4 5 87	Crewe Alex
Chadwick Luke (M)	5 11	11 08	Cambridge	18 11 80	Norwich C
Chicksen Adam (M)	5 8	11 09	Coventry	27 9 91	Scholar
Doumbe Stephen (D)	6 1	12 05	Paris	28 10 79	Plymouth Arg
Easter Jermaine (F)	5 9	12 02	Cardiff	15 1 82	Plymouth Arg
Flanagan Tom (D)	6 2	11 05			
Gleeson Stephen (M)	6 2	11 00	Dublin	3 8 88	Wolverhampton W
Gueret Willy (G)	6 1	13 02	Saint Claude	3 8 73	Swansea C
Howell Luke (D)	5 10	10 05	Cuckfield	5 1 87	Gillingham
Ibehre Jabo (F)	6 2	13 13	Islington	28 1 83	Walsall
Johnson Jemal (F)	5 8	11 09	New Jersey	3 5 84	Wolverhampton W
Leven Peter (M)	5 11	12 13	Glasgow	27 9 83	Chesterfield
Lewington Dean (D)	5 11	11 07	Kingston	18 5 84	Scholar
McCracken David (D)	6 2	11 06	Glasgow	16 10 81	Wycombe W
O'Hanlon Sean (D)	6 1	12 05	Southport	2 1 83	Swindon T
Powell Daniel (F)	5 11	13 03	Luton	12 3 91	Scholar
Searle Stuart (G)	6 3	12 04	Wimbledon	27 2 79	Watford
Stirling Jude (D)	6 2	11 12	Enfield	29 6 82	Peterborough U
Wilbraham Aaron (F)	6 3	12 04	Knutsford	21 10 79	Hull C
Woodards Danny (M)	5 11	11 01	Forest Gate	7 10 83	Crewe Alex

League Appearances: Baldock, S. 11(9); Baldock, G. (1); Bridges, M. (1); Carrington, M. 15(5); Chadwick, L. 39(1); Chicksen, A. 4(2); Collins, C. 2; Davis, S. 5(5); Devaney, M. 4(1); Doran, A. 2(2); Doumbe, S. 29(4); Easter, J. 32(4); Flanagan, T. (1); Gleeson, S. 26(3); Gobern, L. 7(13); Gobern, O. (1); Gueret, W. 43; Howell, L. 17(12); Ibehre, J. 3(7); Johnson, J. 12(5); Leven, P. 26(5); Lewington, D. 42; McCracken, D. 41; Morgan, D. 1(8); O'Hanlon, S. 3(3); Partridge, R. 1(3); Powell, Daniel 2; Powell, Darren 19(5); Puncheon, J. 23(1); Quashie, N. 6(1); Rae, A. 2(1); Randall, M. 12(4); Searle, S. 3; Stirling, J. 1(8); Swailes, D. 2; Townsend, A. 8(1); Tunnicliffe, J. 9; Wilbraham, A. 31(4); Woodards, D. 23(6).
Goals – League (60): Easter 14 (2 pens), Wilbraham 10, Puncheon 7, Baldock S 5, Carrington 4, Leven 4 (3 pens), Chadwick 2, Quashie 2, Townsend 2, Doumbe 1, Ibehre 1, Johnson 1, Lewington 1, McCracken 1, Morgan 1, Powell, Daniel 1, Tunnicliffe 1, own goals 2.
Carling Cup (1): Easter 1 (pen).
FA Cup (6): Baldock S 2, Devaney 1, Easter 1, Gobern L 1, Morgan 1.
J Paint Trophy (13): Baldock S 3 (1 pen), Easter 3, Wilbraham 2, Carrington 1, Doran 1, Lewington 1, Puncheon 1, Randall 1.

Ground: Stadium*mk*, Stadium Way West, Milton Keynes, Buckinghamshire MK9 1FA. Telephone (01908) 622 922.
Record Attendance: 30,115 v Manchester U, FA Premier League, 9 May 1993 (at Selhurst Park). **Capacity:** 21,189.
Manager: Karl Robinson.
Head of Football Operations: Kirstine Nicholson.
Most League Goals: 97, Division 3, 1983–84; as Milton Keynes Dons 83, FL 1, 2008–09.
Highest League Scorer in Season: Alan Cork, 29, 1983–84.
Most League Goals in Total Aggregate: Alan Cork, 145, 1977–92.
Most Capped Player: Kenny Cunningham, 40 (72), Republic of Ireland; as MK Dons – Ali Gerba (29), Canada.
Most League Appearances: Alan Cork, 430, 1977–92.
Honours – Football League: Championship 2 Champions – 2007–08. Division 4 Champions – 1982–83. **FA Cup:** Winners – 1987–88. **Johnstone's Paint Trophy:** Winners – 2007–08.
Colours: White shirts with black sleeves, white shorts, white stockings with black tops.

MORECAMBE   FL CHAMPIONSHIP 2

Name	Height	DOB	Birthplace	Signed	Previous Club
Artell Dave (D)	6 3	14 01	Rotherham	22 11 80	Chester C
Bentley Jim (D)	6 1	12 00	Liverpool	11 6 76	Telford U
Drummond Stuart (M)	6 2	13 08	Preston	11 12 75	Shrewsbury T
Duffy Mark (M)	5 9	11 05	Liverpool	7 10 85	Southport
Haining Will (D)	6 0	11 02	Glasgow	2 10 82	St Mirren
Hunter Garry (M)	5 7	10 03	Morecambe	1 1 85	Scholar
Moss Darren (D)	5 10	11 00	Wrexham	24 5 81	Shrewsbury T
Mullin Paul (F)	6 0	12 01	Bury	16 3 74	Accrington S
Parrish Andy (D)	6 0	11 00	Bolton	22 6 88	Bury
Poole Matty (M)	5 11	12 04	Lancaster	22 10 90	Scholar
Roche Barry (G)	6 5	14 08	Dublin	6 4 82	Chesterfield
Stanley Craig (M)	6 0	12 06	Coventry	3 3 83	Hereford U
Wainwright Neil (M)	6 0	12 00	Warrington	4 11 77	Darlington
Wilson Laurence (M)	5 10	10 09	Huyton	10 10 86	Chester C

League Appearances: Adams, D. 15(2); Artell, D. 33(4); Bentley, J. 27(1); Craney, I. 16; Curtis, W. 9(26); Davies, S. 1; Drummond, S. 41(2); Duffy, M. 24(11); Hackney, S. 8; Haining, W. 28(4); Hunter, G. 26(5); Jevons, P. 40; McLachlan, F. 1; McStay, H. (2); Moss, D. 13(3); Mullin, P. 36(2); Panther, M. 14(5); Parrish, A. 34(1); Roche, B. 42; Smith, B. 3; Stanley, C. 31(9); Taylor, A. (3); Twiss, M. 18(8); Wainwright, N. 5(12); Wilson, L. 41.
Goals – League (73): Jevons 18 (6 pens), Mullin 12, Drummond 9, Artell 7, Curtis 4, Duffy 4, Stanley 4, Bentley 3, Wilson 3, Craney 2, Hunter 2, Hackney 1, Haining 1, Moss 1, Twiss 1, own goal 1.
Carling Cup (1): Twiss 1.
FA Cup (2): Duffy 1, Jevons 1.
J Paint Trophy (2): Curtis 1, Hunter 1.
Play-Offs (2): Artell 1, Duffy 1.
Ground: Globe Arena, Christie Way, Westgate, Morecambe LA4 4TB. Telephone (01524) 598 393.
Record Attendance: 9,383 v Weymouth FA Cup 3rd rd, 6 January 1962.
Capacity: 6,402.
Manager: Sammy McIlroy.
Secretary: Neil Marsdin.
Most League Goals: 73, FL 2, 2009–10.
Highest League Scorer in Season: Phil Jevons, 18, 2009–10.
Most League Goals in Total Aggregate: 21, Stuart Drummond 2007–.
Most League Appearances: 88, Jim Bentley, 2007–.

Honours – **Conference:** Promoted to Football League (play-offs) 2006–07. **Presidents Cup:** Winners – 1991–92. **FA Trophy:** Winners 1973–74. **Lancs Senior Cup:** Winners 1967–68. **Lancs Combination:** Champions – 1924–25, 1961–62, 1962–63, 1967–68. **Lancs Combination Cup:** Winners – 1926–27, 1945–46, 1964–65, 1966–67, 1967–68. **Lancs Junior Cup:** Winners – 1927, 1928, 1962, 1963, 1969, 1986, 1987, 1994, 1996, 1999, 2004. **Colours:** Red shirts with black trim, white shorts, red stockings.

NEWCASTLE UNITED   FA PREMIERSHIP

Adjei Samuel (F)	6 1	12 00	Ghana	18	1 92	Jonkoping
Airey Philip (F)			Newcastle	14 11 91		Scholar
Ameobi Foluwashola (F)	6 3	11 13	Zaria	12 10 81		Scholar
Barton Joey (M)	5 11	12 05	Huyton	2	9 82	Manchester C
Best Leon (F)	6 1	13 03	Nottingham	19	9 86	Coventry C
Carroll Andy (F)	6 3	13 08	Newcastle	6	1 89	Scholar
Coloccini Fabricio (D)	6 0	12 04	Cordoba	22	1 82	La Coruna
Donaldson Ryan (F)	5 9	11 00		1	5 91	Scholar
Edmundsson Joan (F)			Faeroes	26	7 91	B68
Ferguson Shane (D)	5 9	10 01	Derry	12	7 91	Scholar
Forster Fraser (G)	6 4	14 00	Newcastle	17	3 88	Scholar
Guthrie Danny (M)	5 9	11 06	Shrewsbury	18	4 87	Liverpool
Gutierrez Jonas (M)	6 0	11 07	Saenz Pena	5	7 82	Mallorca
Harper Steve (G)	6 2	13 10	Easington	14	3 75	Seaham Red Star
Inman Bradden (M)	5 9	11 03	Adelaide	10 12 91		Scholar
Jose Enrique (D)	6 0	12 00	Valencia	23	1 86	Villarreal
Kadar Tamas (D)	6 0	12 10	Veszprem	14	3 90	Zalaegerszegi
Krul Tim (G)	6 2	11 08	Den Haag	3	4 88	Den Haag
Lovenkrands Peter (F)	5 11	11 02	Copenhagen	29	1 80	Schalke
LuaLua Kazenga (F)	5 11	12 00	Kinshasa	10 12 90		Scholar
McLaughlin Patrick (M)			Larne	14	1 91	
Nolan Kevin (M)	6 0	14 00	Liverpool	24	6 82	Bolton W
Ranger Nile (F)	6 2	13 03	London	11	4 91	Southampton
Routledge Wayne (M)	5 6	11 02	Sidcup	7	1 85	QPR
Simpson Danny (D)	5 8	11 10	Salford	4	1 87	Manchester U
Smith Alan (F)	5 10	12 04	Rothwell	28 10 80		Manchester U
Soderberg Ole (G)	6 0	14 03	Norrkoping	20	7 90	BK Hacken
Tavernier James (D)	5 9	11 00	Bradford	31 10 91		Scholar
Taylor Ryan (M)	5 8	10 04	Liverpool	19	8 84	Wigan Ath
Taylor Steven (D)	6 1	13 01	Greenwich	23	1 86	Scholar
Tozer Ben (D)	6 1	13 05	Plymouth	1	3 90	Swindon T
Vuckic Haris (F)	6 2	12 02	Ljubljana	21	8 92	Domzale
Williamson Mike (D)	6 4	13 03	Stoke	8 11 83		Portsmouth
Xisco (F)	6 0	13 03	Palma	26	6 86	La Coruna
Zamblera Fabio (F)	6 3	14 09	Atalanta	7	4 90	Atalanta

League Appearances: Ameobi, S. 11(7); Barton, J. 8(7); Best, L. 6(7); Butt, N. 10(7); Carroll, A. 33(6); Coloccini, F. 37; Donaldson, R. (2); Duff, D. 1; Geremi, 3(4); Guthrie, D. 36(2); Gutierrez, J. 34(3); Hall, F. 7; Harewood, M. 9(6); Harper, S. 45; Jose Enrique, 33(1); Kadar, T. 6(7); Khizanishvili, Z. 6(1); Krul, T. 1(2); Lovenkrands, P. 19(10); LuaLua, K. (1); Nolan, K. 44; Pancrate, F. 5(11); Ranger, N. 4(21); Routledge, W. 15(2); Simpson, D. 39; Smith, A. 31(1); Taylor, R. 19(12); Taylor, S. 21; Tozer, B. (1); Van Aanholt, P. 7; Vuckic, H. (2); Williamson, M. 16; Xisco, (2).
Goals – League (90): Carroll 17, Nolan 17, Lovenkrands 13 (3 pens), Ameobi 10 (2 pens), Harewood 5, Guthrie 4, Gutierrez 4, Taylor R 4, Routledge 3, Coloccini 2, Ranger 2, Barton 1, Duff 1, Jose Enrique 1, Pancrate 1, Simpson 1, Taylor S 1, own goals 3.
Carling Cup (4): Ameobi 1 (pen), Geremi 1, Guthrie 1, Nolan 1.

FA Cup (5): Lovenkrands 3, Carroll 2.
Ground: St James' Park, Newcastle upon Tyne NE1 4ST. Telephone (0191) 201 8400.
Record Attendance: 68,386 v Chelsea, Division 1, 3 Sept 1930. **Capacity:** 52,387.
Manager: Chris Hughton.
Most League Goals: 98, Division 1, 1951–52.
Highest League Scorer in Season: Hughie Gallacher, 36, Division 1, 1926–27.
Most League Goals in Total Aggregate: Jackie Milburn, 177, 1946–57.
Most Capped Player: Shay Given, 82 (103), Republic of Ireland.
Most League Appearances: Jim Lawrence, 432, 1904–22.
Honours – Football League: Division 1 – Champions 1904–05, 1906–07, 1908–09, 1926–27, 1992–93. Division 2 Champions – 1964–65. FL C – Champions 2009–10. **FA Cup:** Winners – 1910, 1924, 1932, 1951, 1952, 1955. **Texaco Cup:** Winners – 1973–74, 1974–75.
European Competitions: European Fairs Cup: Winners – 1968–69. **Anglo-Italian Cup:** Winners – 1973. **Intertoto Cup:** Winners – 2006.
Colours: Black and white striped shirts, black shorts with white trim, black stockings with white trim.

NORTHAMPTON TOWN   FL CHAMPIONSHIP 2

Beckwith Dean (D)	6 3	13 04	Southwark	18 9 83	Hereford U
Davis Liam (M)	5 9	11 07	Wandsworth	23 11 86	Coventry C
Dunn Chris (G)	6 5	13 11	Hammersmith	23 10 87	Scholar
Gilligan Ryan (M)	5 10	11 07	Swindon	18 1 87	Watford
Guinan Stephen (F)	6 1	13 02	Birmingham	24 12 75	Hereford U
Herbert Courtney (F)	6 2	12 08	Northampton	25 10 88	Long Buckby
Hinton Craig (D)	6 0	12 00	Wolverhampton	26 11 77	Bristol R
McCready Chris (D)	6 1	12 05	Ellesmere Port	5 9 81	Crewe Alex
McKay Billy (F)	5 9	10 01	Corby	22 10 88	Leicester C
Osman Abdul (M)	6 0	11 00	Accra	27 2 87	Gretna
Rodgers Paul (D)	5 10	10 10	Edmonton	6 10 89	Arsenal

League Appearances: Akinfenwa, A. 36(4); Beckwith, D. 37(1); Benjamin, J. 2(1); Boden, L. 4; Brown, S. 2; Curtis, J. 18(1); Davis, L. 13(4); Dunn, C. 29; Dyer, A. 4(16); Gilbert, P. 30; Gilligan, R. 41(1); Guinan, S. 19(9); Guttridge, L. 24(7); Harris, S. (9); Herbert, C. 8(15); Hinton, A. 31; Johnson, J. 36; Kanyuka, P. 3; Lumley, B. 2; Marshall, B. 11(4); McCready, C. 13(1); McKay, B. 29(11); Mulligan, G. 2(7); O'Flynn, S. (5); Osman, A. 26(4); Rodgers, P. 24(7); Rose, R. (1); Steele, J. 13; Swailes, D. 3; Thornton, K. 4(7); Threlfall, R. 1(3); Walker, J. 3.
Goals – League (62): Akinfenwa 17 (2 pens), Gilligan 8 (1 pen), McKay 8, Johnson 5, Guinan 4, Guttridge 4, Holt 3, Davis 2, Dyer 2, Herbert 2, Marshall 2, Osman 2, Harris 1, Thornton 1, own goal 1.
Carling Cup (0).
FA Cup (4): Guttridge 2, Gilligan 1 (pen), own goal 1.
J Paint Trophy (5): Guinan 3, Gilligan 2 (2 pens).
Ground: Sixfields Stadium, Upton Way, Northampton NN5 5QA. Telephone 01604 683 700.
Record Attendance: (at County Ground): 24,523 v Fulham, Division 1, 23 April 1966; (at Sixfields Stadium): 7,557 v Manchester C, Division 2, 26 September 1998. **Capacity:** 7,300.
Manager: Ian Sampson.
Secretary: Norman Howells.
Most League Goals: 109, Division 3, 1962–63 and Division 3 (S), 1952–53.
Highest League Scorer in Season: Cliff Holton, 36, Division 3, 1961–62.
Most League Goals in Total Aggregate: Jack English, 135, 1947–60.
Most Capped Player: Edwin Lloyd Davies, 12 (16), Wales.
Most League Appearances: Tommy Fowler, 521, 1946–61.

Honours – Football League: Division 3 Champions – 1962–63. Division 4 Champions – 1986–87.
Colours: Claret shirts, white shorts, white stockings.

NORWICH CITY   FL CHAMPIONSHIP

Adeyemi Thomas (M)	6 1	12 04	Norwich	24 10 91	Scholar
Berthel Askou Jens (D)	6 2	13 00	Videbaek	19 8 82	Kasimpasa
Daley Luke (F)	6 3	12 00	Northampton	10 11 89	Scholar
Drury Adam (D)	5 10 11 08		Cottenham	29 8 78	Peterborough U
Francomb George (D)	5 11 11 07		London	8 9 91	Scholar
Gill Matthew (M)	5 11 11 10		Cambridge	8 11 80	Exeter C
Habergham Sam (D)	6 1	11 07	Rotherham	20 2 92	Scholar
Holt Grant (F)	6 1	14 02	Carlisle	12 4 81	Shrewsbury T
Hoolahan Wes (M)	5 6	10 03	Dublin	10 8 83	Blackpool
Hughes Stephen (M)	5 10 11 04		Motherwell	14 11 82	Motherwell
Johnson Oli (F)	5 11 12 04		Wakefield	6 11 87	Stockport Co
Lappin Simon (M)	5 11 9 06		Glasgow	25 1 83	St Mirren
Martin Chris (F)	6 2	12 06	Norwich	4 11 88	Scholar
Martin Russell (D)	6 0	11 06	Brighton	4 1 86	Peterborough U
McDonald Cody (F)	5 10 11 03		Norwich	30 5 86	Dartford
McNamee Anthony (M)	5 6	10 00	Kensington	13 7 84	Swindon T
Nelson Michael (D)	6 2	13 03	Gateshead	15 3 82	Hartlepool U
Rudd Declan (G)	6 3	12 06	Norwich	16 1 91	Scholar
Russell Darel (M)	5 10 11 09		Mile End	22 10 80	Stoke C
Smith Korey (M)	5 9	11 01	Welwyn	31 1 91	Scholar
Spillane Michael (M)	5 9	11 10	Cambridge	23 3 89	Scholar
Steer Jed (G)	6 2	14 00	Norwich	23 9 92	Scholar
Stephens David (D)	6 3	14 06	Welwyn	8 10 91	Scholar
Tudur-Jones Owain (M)	6 2	12 00	Bangor	15 10 84	Swansea C
Whitbread Zak (D)	6 2	12 07	Houston	4 3 84	Millwall
Wiggins Rhoys (D)	5 8	11 05	Uxbridge	4 11 87	Crystal Palace

League Appearances: Adeyemi, T. 2(9); Alnwick, B. 3; Berthel Askou, J. 21(1); Cureton, J. 3(3); Daley, L. 3(4); Doherty, G. 38; Drury, A. 35; Elliott, S. 4(6); Forster, F. 38; Francomb, G. 2; Gill, M. 5(3); Holt, G. 39; Hoolahan, W. 36(1); Hughes, S. 12(17); Johnson, O. 4(13); Lappin, S. 42(2); Martin, C. 36(6); Martin, R. 26; McDonald, C. 4(13); McNamee, A. 7(10); McVeigh, P. 4(5); Nelson, M. 28(3); Otsemobor, J. 12(1); Rose, M. 11(1); Rudd, D. 4(3); Russell, D. 34(1); Smith, K. 36(1); Spillane, M. 10(3); Theoklitos, M. 1; Tudur-Jones, O. 2(1); Whaley, S. 3; Whitbread, Z. 1(3).
Goals – League (89): Holt 24 (1 pen), Martin C 17, Hoolahan 11 (3 pens), Doherty 5, Johnson 4, Smith 4, Hughes 3, McDonald 3, Nelson 3, Russell 3, Berthel Askou 2, Cureton 2, Elliott 2, McNamee 1, Otsemobor 1, Rose 1, Spillane 1, Tudur-Jones 1, own goal 1.
Carling Cup (5): Holt 3, Hoolahan 2 (1 pen).
FA Cup (8): Martin C 4, Holt 3, Hoolahan 1.
J Paint Trophy (4): Martin C 2, Doherty 1, McDonald 1.
Ground: Carrow Road, Norwich NR1 1JE. Telephone (01603) 760 760.
Record Attendance: 43,984 v Leicester C, FA Cup 6th rd, 30 March 1963. **Capacity:** 26,034.
Manager: Paul Lambert.
Secretary: Kevan Platt.
Most League Goals: 99, Division 3 (S), 1952–53.
Highest League Scorer in Season: Ralph Hunt, 31, Division 3 (S), 1955–56.
Most League Goals in Total Aggregate: Johnny Gavin, 122, 1945–54, 1955–58.
Most Capped Player: Mark Bowen, 35 (41), Wales.
Most League Appearances: Ron Ashman, 592, 1947–64.

Honours – Football League: Division 1 Champions – 2003–04. **Division 2 Champions –** 1971–72, 1985–86. **Division 3 (S) Champions –** 1933–34. **Football League Cup: Winners** – 1962, 1985.
Colours: Yellow shirts with green trim, green shorts, yellow stockings.

NOTTINGHAM FOREST   FL CHAMPIONSHIP

Name	Ht	Wt	Birthplace	D.O.B.	Previous Club
Adebola Dele (F)	6 3	12 08	Lagos	23 6 75	Bristol C
Anderson Paul (M)	5 9	10 04	Leicester	23 7 88	Liverpool
Bennett Julian (D)	6 1	13 00	Nottingham	17 12 84	Walsall
Blackstock Dexter (F)	6 2	13 00	Oxford	20 5 86	QPR
Byrne Mark (M)	5 9	11 00	Dublin	9 11 88	Crumlin
Camp Lee (G)	5 11	11 11	Derby	22 8 84	QPR
Chambers Luke (D)	6 1	11 13	Kettering	28 9 85	Northampton T
Cohen Chris (M)	5 11	10 11	Norwich	5 3 87	Yeovil T
Darlow Karl (G)	6 1	12 05	Northampton	8 10 90	Scholar
Earnshaw Robert (F)	5 8	10 10	Mulfulira	6 4 81	Derby Co
Garner Joe (F)	5 10	11 02	Blackburn	12 4 88	Carlisle U
Gibbons Robert (M)			Dublin	8 10 91	Scholar
Gunter Chris (D)	5 11	11 02	Newport	21 7 89	Tottenham H
Lynch Joel (D)	6 1	12 10	Eastbourne	3 10 87	Brighton & HA
Majewski Radoslaw (M)	5 7	10 06	Pruszkow	15 12 86	Polonia Warsaw
McCleary Garath (F)	5 10	12 06	Oxford	15 5 87	Bromley
McGoldrick David (F)	6 1	11 10	Nottingham	29 11 87	Southampton
McGugan Lewis (M)	5 9	11 06	Long Eaton	25 10 88	Scholar
McKenna Paul (M)	5 7	11 12	Eccleston	20 10 77	Preston NE
Moloney Brendan (M)	6 1	11 02	Enfield	18 1 89	Scholar
Morgan Wes (D)	6 2	14 00	Nottingham	21 1 84	Scholar
Moussi Guy (M)	6 1	12 11	Bondy	23 1 85	Angers
Perch James (D)	5 11	11 05	Mansfield	29 9 85	Scholar
Rodney Nialle (F)			Nottingham	28 2 91	Scholar
Smith Paul (G)	6 3	14 00	Epsom	17 12 79	Southampton
Thornhill Matt (M)	6 1	13 10	Nottingham	11 10 88	Scholar
Tyson Nathan (F)	5 10	10 02	Reading	4 5 82	Wycombe W
Wilson Kelvin (D)	6 2	12 12	Nottingham	3 9 85	Preston NE

League Appearances: Adebola, D. 13(20); Anderson, P. 33(4); Blackstock, D. 30(9); Boyd, G. 5(1); Camp, L. 45; Chambers, L. 17(6); Cohen, C. 44; Earnshaw, R. 20(12); Garner, J. 14(4); Gunter, C. 44; Lynch, J. 9(1); Majewski, R. 31(4); McCleary, G. 1(23); McGoldrick, D. 18(15); McGugan, L. 6(12); McKenna, P. 35; Morgan, W. 44; Moussi, G. 21(6); Perch, J. 14(3); Shorey, N. 9; Smith, P. 1; Tyson, N. 17(16); Wilson, K. 35.
Goals – League (65): Earnshaw 15, Blackstock 12 (3 pens), Anderson 4, Adebola 3, Chambers 3, Cohen 3, Majewski 3, McGoldrick 3, McGugan 3, Morgan 3, Moussi 3, Garner 2, Tyson 2, Boyd 1, Gunter 1, McKenna 1, Perch 1, own goals 2.
Carling Cup (5): Anderson 1, Blackstock 1, Chambers 1, McGugan 1, Majewski 1.
FA Cup (0).
Play-Offs (4): Earnshaw 2, Adebola 1, Cohen 1.
Ground: The City Ground, Nottingham NG2 5FJ. Telephone (0115) 982 4444.
Record Attendance: 49,946 v Manchester U, Division 1, 28 October 1967. **Capacity:** 30,576.
Manager: Billy Davies.
Football Administrator: Jane Carnelly.
Most League Goals: 110, Division 3 (S), 1950–51.
Highest League Scorer in Season: Wally Ardron, 36, Division 3 (S), 1950–51.
Most League Goals in Total Aggregate: Grenville Morris, 199, 1898–1913.
Most Capped Player: Stuart Pearce, 76 (78), England.
Most League Appearances: Bob McKinlay, 614, 1951–70.

Honours – Football League: Division 1 – Champions 1977–78, 1997–98. Division 2 Champions – 1906–07, 1921–22. Division 3 (S) Champions – 1950–51. FA Cup: Winners – 1898, 1959. Football League Cup: Winners – 1977–78, 1978–79, 1988–89, 1989–90. Anglo-Scottish Cup: Winners – 1976–77. Simod Cup: Winners – 1989. Zenith Data Systems Cup: Winners – 1991–92. European Competitions: European Cup: Winners – 1978–79, 1979–80. Super Cup: Winners – 1979–80.
Colours: Red shirt with white trim, white shorts, red stockings.

NOTTS COUNTY   FL CHAMPIONSHIP 1

Bishop Neil (M)	6 1	12 10	Stockton	7 8 81	Barnet
Davies Ben (M)	5 7	12 03	Birmingham	27 5 81	Shrewsbury T
Edwards Mike (D)	6 1	13 01	North Ferriby	25 4 80	Grimsby T
Fox Nathan (M)	5 10	12 02	Nottingham	16 8 93	Scholar
Hawley Karl (F)	5 8	12 02	Walsall	6 12 81	Preston NE
Hughes Lee (F)	5 10	12 00	Smethwick	22 5 76	Oldham Ath
Hunt Steve (D)	6 1	13 05	Southampton	11 11 84	Colchester U
Jackson Johnnie (M)	6 1	12 00	Camden	15 8 82	Colchester U
Lee Graeme (D)	6 2	13 07	Middlesbrough	31 5 78	Bradford C
Ravenhill Ricky (M)	5 10	11 02	Doncaster	16 1 81	Darlington
Rodgers Luke (F)	5 8	11 00	Birmingham	1 1 82	Yeovil T
Thompson John (D)	6 0	12 01	Dublin	12 10 81	Oldham Ath
Westcarr Craig (F)	5 11	11 04	Nottingham	29 1 85	Kettering T

League Appearances: Akinbiyi, A. 1(9); Bishop, N. 39(4); Campbell, S. 1; Canham, S. (1); Clapham, J. 17(13); Davies, B. 45; Edwards, M. 37(3); Facey, D. 7(11); Fox, N. (1); Hamshaw, M. 2(18); Hawley, K. 14(17); Hoult, R. 3(1); Hughes, L. 39; Hunt, S. 32; Jackson, J. 20(4); Jones, D. 7; Lee, G. 31(1); Moloney, B. 18; Ravenhill, R. 40; Ritchie, M. 12(4); Rodgers, L. 27(15); Schmeichel, K. 43; Thompson, J. 38(2); Westcarr, C. 33(9).
Goals – League (96): Hughes 30 (5 pens), Davies 15, Rodgers 13 (1 pen), Westcarr 9 (1 pen), Edwards 5, Lee 4, Hawley 3, Ravenhill 3, Ritchie 3, Facey 2, Jackson 2, Bishop 1, Clapham 1, Hunt 1, Moloney 1, own goals 3.
Carling Cup (0).
FA Cup (10): Hughes 3, Hunt 2, Davies 1, Hawley 1, Jackson 1, Westcarr 1, own goal 1.
J Paint Trophy (2): Facey 1, Westcarr 1.
Ground: Meadow Lane Stadium, Meadow Lane, Nottingham NG2 3HJ. Telephone (0115) 952 9000.
Record Attendance: 47,310 v York C, FA Cup 6th rd, 12 March 1955. Capacity: 20,300.
Manager: Craig Short.
General Manager: Tony Cuthbert.
Most League Goals: 107, Division 4, 1959–60.
Highest League Scorer in Season: Tom Keetley, 39, Division 3 (S), 1930–31.
Most League Goals in Total Aggregate: Les Bradd, 125, 1967–78.
Most Capped Player: Kevin Wilson, 15 (42), Northern Ireland.
Most League Appearances: Albert Iremonger, 564, 1904–26.
Honours – Football League: Division 2 Champions – 1896–97, 1913–14, 1922–23. Division 3 Champions – 1997–98. Division 3 (S) Champions – 1930–31, 1949–50. Division 4 Champions – 1970–71. FA Cup: Winners – 1893–94. Anglo-Italian Cup: Winners – 1995.
Colours: Black and white striped shirts, black shorts, black stockings.

OLDHAM ATHLETIC   FL CHAMPIONSHIP 1

Abbott Pawel (F)	6 2	13 10	York	5 5 82	Darlington
Alessandra Lewis (F)	5 9	11 07	Oldham	8 2 89	Scholar
Bembo Leta Djenny (F)	5 10	11 05	Kinshasa	9 11 91	Scholar

Black Paul (D)	6 0	12 10	Middleton	18 1 90	Scholar
Brill Dean (G)	6 2	14 05	Luton	2 12 85	Luton T
Brooke Ryan (M)	6 1	11 07	Crewe	4 10 90	Scholar
Colbeck Joe (M)	5 10	10 12	Bradford	29 11 86	Bradford C
Dawson Liam (D)				12 1 91	Scholar
Eaves Tom (M)				14 1 92	Liverpool
Fleming Greg (G)	5 11	12 09	Edinburgh	27 9 86	Gretna
Floszmann Tomas (G)					MTK
Fodor Ferenc (D)	5 11				Honved
Furman Dean (M)	6 0	11 08	Cape Town	22 6 88	Bradford C
Gregan Sean (D)	6 2	14 00	Guisborough	29 3 74	Leeds U
Hazell Reuben (D)	5 11	12 05	Birmingham	24 4 79	Chesterfield
Holdsworth Andy (D)	5 9	11 02	Pontefract	29 1 84	Huddersfield T
Jacobson Joe (D)	5 11	12 06	Cardiff	17 11 86	Bristol R
Lee Kieran (D)	6 1	12 00	Tameside	22 6 88	Manchester U
Lomax Kelvin (D)	5 10	12 03	Bury	12 11 86	Scholar
McGrath Phillip (M)	5 9	10 01			Glenavon
Millar Kirk (M)	5 9	10 07	Belfast	7 7 92	
Ojapah Philip (M)	6 2		Liverpool	24 7 89	AFC Liverpool
Ollerenshaw Josh (G)	6 5	12 10	Manchester	5 10 90	Scholar
Purdie Rob (M)	5 9	11 06	Leicester	28 9 82	Darlington
Rowney Chris (M)	5 6	10 01	Oldham	14 2 91	Scholar
Smalley Deane (M)	6 0	11 10	Chadderton	5 9 88	Scholar
Stephens Dale (M)	5 11	11 06	Bolton	12 12 87	Bury
Taylor Chris (M)	5 11	11 00	Oldham	20 12 86	Scholar
Worthington Jon (M)	5 9	11 05	Dewsbury	16 4 83	Huddersfield T

League Appearances: Abbott, P. 38(1); Alessandra, L. (1); Aljofree, H. 1; Black, P. 12(1); Blackman, N. 6(6); Brill, D. 28; Brooke, R. 2(13); Byfield, D. (3); Colbeck, J. 18(9); Eaves, T. (15); Flahavan, D. 18; Furman, D. 32(6); Gilbert, P. 5; Goodwin, J. 8; Gregan, S. 46; Guy, L. 12; Hazell, R. 41; Heffernan, P. 4; Hills, L. 3; Holdsworth, A. 11(1); Jacobson, J. 14(1); Lee, K. 16(8); Lomax, K. 11(4); Marrow, A. 26(6); Millar, K. 2(4); Nardiello, D. 2; Parker, K. 17(10); Price, J. 7; Rowney, C. (1); Sheehan, A. 8; Smalley, D. 23(6); Stephens, D. 24(2); Taylor, C. 27(5); Timar, K. 2; Whitaker, D. 31(10); Worthington, J. 11(5).

Goals – League (39): Abbott 13 (4 pens), Guy 3, Hazell 3, Smalley 3, Parker 2, Stephens 2, Whitaker 2, Black 1, Blackman 1, Brooke 1, Colbeck 1, Gregan 1, Heffernan 1, Lee 1, Marrow 1, Price 1, Sheehan 1, Taylor 1 (1 pen).

Carling Cup (0).

FA Cup (0).

J Paint Trophy (1): Whitaker 1.

Ground: Boundary Park, Furtherwood Road, Oldham OL1 2PA. Telephone (0161) 624 4972.

Record Attendance: 46,471 v Sheffield W, FA Cup 4th rd, 25 January 1930. **Capacity:** 13,624.

Manager: Paul Dickov.

Secretary: Alan Hardy.

Most League Goals: 95, Division 4, 1962–63.

Highest League Scorer in Season: Tom Davis, 33, Division 3 (N), 1936–37.

Most League Goals in Total Aggregate: Roger Palmer, 141, 1980–94.

Most Capped Player: Gunnar Halle, 24 (64), Norway.

Most League Appearances: Ian Wood, 525, 1966–80.

Honours – Football League: Division 2 Champions – 1990–91, Division 3 (N) Champions – 1952–53. Division 3 Champions – 1973–74.

Colours: Blue shirts with white sleeves, white shorts, white stockings.

OXFORD UNITED   FL CHAMPIONSHIP 2

Name	Ht	DoB	Birthplace	Signed	Previous Club
Billy Turley (G)	6 4	15 06	Wolverhampton	15 7 72	Rushden & D
Damien Batt (D)	5 10	11 07	Hoddesdon	16 9 84	Grays Ath
Kevin Sandwith (D)	5 11	12 06	Workington	30 4 78	Weymouth
Dannie Bulman (M)	5 9	11 11	Ashford	24 1 79	Crawley T
Chris Hargreaves (M)	5 11	12 02	Cleethorpes	12 5 72	Torquay U
Mark Creighton (D)	6 4	12 02	Birmingham	8 10 1	Kidderminster H
Adam Chapman (M)	5 10	11 00	Doncaster	29 11 89	Sheffield U
Adam Murray (M)	5 9	10 01	Birmingham	30 9 81	Macclesfield T
James Constable (F)	6 2	12 13	Malmesbury	4 10 84	Shrewsbury T
Jack Midson (F)	5 8	11 07	Stevenage	21 7 83	Histon
Simon Clist (M)	5 9	11 00	Shaftesbury	13 6 81	Forest Green R
Rhys Day (D)	6 2	13 01	Bridgend	31 8 82	Aldershot T
Anthony Tonkin (D)	5 11	12 02	Newlyn	17 1 80	Cambridge U
Francis Green (F)	5 9	11 05	Derby	23 4 80	Kettering T
Sam Deering (M)	5 6	11 00	London	26 2 91	
Ryan Clarke (G)	6 3	12 13	Bristol	30 4 82	Salisbury C
Jamie Cook (M)	5 10	10 10	Oxford	2 9 79	Crawley T
Aaron Woodley (F)			Oxford	13 10 92	

League Appearances: Batt, 31(6); Bulman, 41(1); Cain, (1); Carruthers, 1; Chalmers, 6(2); Chapman, 21(15); Clarke, R. 43; Clist, 40(1); Constable, 35(2); Cook, 14(2); Creighton, 31(3); Day, 15(3); Deering, 15(8); Foster, 20(1); Grant, 4(4); Green, M. 26(15); Green, F. 8(3); Hargreaves, 9(1); Kelly, 2(1); Kinniburgh, 12; Midson, 18(17); Murray, 21; Perry, 4(4); Potter, 12(10); Rhodes, (3); Sandwith, 16(5); Sodje, 1(3); Tonkin, 17; Turley, 1(1); Woodley, A. (3); Wright, 20.

Goals – League (64): Constable 22 (2 pens), Green M 10, Clist 5, Potter 5, Midson 4 (1 pen), Chapman 3 (1 pen), Cook 3, Deering 2, Sandwith 2, Batt 1, Creighton 1, Foster 1, Green F 1, Kinniburgh 1, Murray 1, Sodje 1, own goal 1.

FA Cup (5): Clist 1, Constable 1, Cook 1, Creighton 1, Midson 1.

Play-Offs (6): Constable 3, Green M 2, Potter 1.

Ground: The Kassam Stadium, Grenoble Road, Oxford OX4 4XP. Telephone (01865) 337 500.

Record Attendance: 22,730 (at Manor Ground) v Preston NE, FA Cup 6th rd, 29 February 1964. **Capacity:** 12,500.

Manager: Chris Wilder.

Secretary: Mick Brown.

Most League Goals: 91, Division 3, 1983–84.

Highest League Scorer in Season: John Aldridge, 30, Division 2, 1984–85.

Most League Goals in Total Aggregate: Graham Atkinson, 77, 1962–73.

Most Capped Player: Jim Magilton, 18 (52), Northern Ireland.

Most League Appearances: John Shuker, 478, 1962–77.

Honours – Football League: Division 2 Champions – 1984–85. Division 3 Champions – 1967–68, 1983–84. **Football League Cup:** Winners – 1985–86.

Colours: Yellow shirts, blue shorts, blue stockings.

PETERBOROUGH UNITED   FL CHAMPIONSHIP 1

Name	Ht	DoB	Birthplace	Signed	Previous Club
Appiah Kwesi (F)	5 11	12 06	London	12 8 90	Ebbsfleet U
Batt Shaun (F)	6 3	12 08	Luton	22 2 87	Fisher Ath
Bennett Ryan (D)	6 0	12 05	Orsett	6 3 90	Grimsby T
Boyd George (M)	5 10	11 07	Stevenage	2 10 85	Stevenage B
Diagouraga Toumani (M)	6 2	11 05	Corbeil-Essones	10 6 87	Hereford U
Frecklington Lee (M)	5 8	11 00	Lincoln	8 9 85	Lincoln C

Geohaghon Exodus (D)	6 7	11 11	Birmingham	27 2 85	Kettering T
Green Dominic (F)	5 6	11 02	London	5 7 89	Dagenham & R
Griffiths Scott (D)	5 9	11 09	London	27 11 85	Dagenham & R
Hatch Liam (F)	6 4	13 09	Hitchin	3 4 84	Barnet
Howe Rene (F)	6 0	14 03	Bedford	22 10 86	Kettering T
Koranteng Nathan (M)	6 2	12 07	London	26 5 92	Scholar
Lee Charlie (M)	5 11	11 07	Whitechapel	5 1 87	Tottenham H
Lewis Joe (G)	6 5	12 10	Bury St Edmunds	6 10 87	Norwich C
Mackail-Smith Craig (F)	6 3	12 04	Hertford	25 2 84	Dagenham & R
McCrae Romone (M)	6 2				
McKeown James (G)	6 1	13 07	Birmingham	24 7 89	Scholar
McLean Aaron (F)	5 8	10 03	Hammersmith	25 5 83	Grays Ath
Mills Danny (F)	6 3	13 00	Peterborough	27 11 91	Crawley T
Morgan Craig (D)	6 0	11 00	Asaph	16 6 85	Milton Keynes D
Rendell Scott (F)	6 1	13 00	Ashford	21 10 86	Cambridge U
Rowe Thomas (M)	5 11	12 11	Manchester	1 5 89	Stockport Co
Simpson Josh (M)	5 10	12 00	Cambridge	6 3 87	Histon
Torres Sergio (M)	6 2	12 04	Mar del Plata	8 11 83	Wycombe W
Whelpdale Chris (M)	6 0	12 08	Harold Wood	27 1 87	Billericay T
Wright Ben (F)	6 2	13 05	Basingstoke	10 8 88	Hampton & Richmond B
Zakuani Gaby (D)	6 1	12 13	DR Congo	31 5 86	Fulham

League Appearances: Amos, B. 1; Andrew, D. 2; Batt, S. 5(15); Bennett, R. 20(2); Boyd, G. 32; Coutts, P. 13(3); Day, J. 2(3); Diagouraga, T. 18(1); Dickinson, L. 9; Frecklington, L. 26(9); Geohaghon, E. 17(2); Gilbert, K. 7(3); Green, D. 6(5); Griffiths, S. 20; Keates, D. 2(4); Koranteng, N. 3(1); Lee, C. 28(5); Lewis, J. 43; Little, M. 9; Livermore, J. 9; Mackail-Smith, C. 39(4); Martin, R. 8(2); McCrae, R. (2); McKeown, J. 2(2); McLean, A. 30(5); McLeod, I. 2(2); Mills, D. 1(2); Morgan, C. 33(1); Pearce, K. (2); Reid, R. 5(8); Rose, D. 4(2); Rowe, T. 26(6); Simpson, J. 8(13); Torres, S. 7(2); Whelpdale, C. 27(2); Williams, T. 14(1); Wright, B. (4); Zakuani, G. 28(1).
Goals – League (46): Mackail-Smith 10, Boyd 9 (4 pens), McLean 7, Dickinson 3, Batt 2, Frecklington 2, Lee 2, Rowe 2, Simpson 2, Bennett 1, Geohaghon 1, Green 1, Keates 1, Livermore 1, Morgan 1, Whelpdale 1.
Carling Cup (10): Boyd 3, Frecklington 2, Mackail-Smith 1, McLean 1, Rowe 1, Whelpdale 1, Williams 1.
FA Cup (0).
Ground: London Road Stadium, London Road, Peterborough PE2 8AL. Telephone (01733) 563 947.
Record Attendance: 30,096 v Swansea T, FA Cup 5th rd, 20 February 1965. **Capacity:** 15,460.
Manager: Gary Johnson.
Director of Football and Club Secretary: Barry Fry.
Most League Goals: 134, Division 4, 1960–61.
Highest League Scorer in Season: Terry Bly, 52, Division 4, 1960–61.
Most League Goals in Total Aggregate: Jim Hall, 122, 1967–75.
Most Capped Player: Craig Morgan, 19 (20), Wales.
Most League Appearances: Tommy Robson, 482, 1968–81.
Honours – Football League: Division 4 Champions – 1960–61, 1973–74.
Colours: Blue shirts with white design, white shorts, white stockings.

PLYMOUTH ARGYLE   FL CHAMPIONSHIP 1

Arnason Kari (D)	6 3	13 10	Reykjavik	13 10 82	Aarhus
Barker Chris (D)	6 2	13 08	Sheffield	2 3 80	QPR
Barnes Ashley (F)	6 0	12 00	Bath	30 10 89	Paulton R

Bhasera Onismor (D)	5 9	11 13	Mutare	7 12 86	Kaizer Chiefs
Bolasie Yannick (M)	6 2	13 02	DR Congo	24 5 89	Barnet
Clark Chris (F)	5 7	10 05	Aberdeen	15 9 80	
Donnelly George (F)	6 2	13 03	Plymouth	28 5 88	Skelmersdale U
Duguid Karl (M)	5 11	11 06	Hitchin	21 3 78	Colchester U
Fallon Rory (F)	6 2	11 09	Gisborne	20 3 82	Swansea C
Fletcher Carl (M)	5 10	11 07	Camberley	7 4 80	Crystal Palace
Gow Alan (M)	6 0	11 00	Clydebank	9 10 82	Norwich C
Head Liam (F)	6 1	13 05	Bovey	26 1 92	Scholar
Johnson Damien (M)	5 9	11 09	Lisburn	18 11 78	Birmingham C
Johnson Reda (D)	6 2	13 10	Marseille	21 3 88	Amiens
Larrieu Romain (G)	6 2	13 00	Mont-de-Marsan	31 8 76	ASOA Valence
Mackie Jamie (F)	5 8	11 00	Dorking	22 9 85	Exeter C
MacLean Steve (F)	5 11	12 06	Edinburgh	23 8 82	Cardiff C
Noone Craig (M)	6 3	12 07	Fazackerly	17 11 87	Southport
Paterson Jim (M)	5 11	12 13	Bellshill	25 9 79	
Seip Marcel (D)	6 0	12 04	Wenschoten	5 4 82	Heerenveen
Summerfield Luke (M)	6 0	11 00	Ivybridge	6 12 87	Scholar
Timar Krisztian (D)	6 3	13 08	Budapest	4 10 79	Ferencvaros
Walton Simon (D)	6 1	13 05	Sherburn-in-Elmet	13 9 87	QPR
Wright-Phillps Bradley (M)	5 10	10 07	Lewisham	12 3 85	Southampton

League Appearances: Arnason, K. 32; Barker, C. 10(4); Barnes, A. 3(4); Bhasera, O. 7; Blake, D. 5(2); Bolasie, Y. 8(8); Chester, J. 2(1); Clark, C. 28(9); Cooper, K. (7); Duguid, K. 40(2); Eckersley, R. 7; Fallon, R. 25(8); Fletcher, C. 41; Folly, Y. 4(3); Gow, A. 8(6); Gray, D. 12; Johnson, R. 23(2); Johnson, D. 20; Judge, A. 28(9); Larrieu, R. 25; Leonard, R. (1); Lowry, S. 13; Mackie, J. 42; MacLean, S. 3; Mason, J. 5(14); McNamee, D. 6(3); N'Gala, B. 9; Noone, C. 3(14); Paterson, J. 11(1); Sawyer, G. 28(1); Seip, M. 5; Sheridan, C. 5(8); Stockdale, D. 21; Summerfield, L. 9(3); Timar, K. 6(1); Wright-Phillips, B. 12(3).
Goals – League (43): Mackie 8, Fallon 5, Judge 5 (3 pens), Fletcher 4, Wright-Phillips 4, Mason 3, Arnason 2, Gow 2 (1 pen), Johnson D 2 (1 pen), Barnes 1, Bolasie 1, Clark 1, Duguid 1, Noone 1, Sawyer 1, Timar 1, own goal 1.
Carling Cup (1): Summerfield 1.
FA Cup (0).
Ground: Home Park, Plymouth, Devon PL2 3DQ. Telephone (01752) 562 561.
Record Attendance: 43,596 v Aston Villa, Division 2, 10 October 1936.
Capacity: 21,118.
Manager: Peter Reid.
Secretary: Carole Rowntree.
Most League Goals: 107, Division 3 (S), 1925–26 and 1951–52.
Highest League Scorer in Season: Jack Cock, 32, Division 3 (S), 1926–27.
Most League Goals in Total Aggregate: Sammy Black, 180, 1924–38.
Most Capped Player: Moses Russell, 20 (23), Wales.
Most League Appearances: Kevin Hodges, 530, 1978–92.
Honours – Football League: Division 2 Champions – 2003–04. Division 3 (S) Champions – 1929–30, 1951–52. Division 3 Champions – 1958–59, 2001–02.
Colours: Dark green shirts with white design, white shorts, white stockings with green design.

PORTSMOUTH   FL CHAMPIONSHIP

Belhadj Nadir (D)	5 9	10 07	Saint-Claude	18 6 82	Lens
Ben Haim Tal (D)	5 11	11 09	Rishon Le Zion	31 3 82	Manchester C
Boateng Kevin-Prince (M)	6 0	11 09	Berlin	6 3 87	Tottenham H
Brown Michael (M)	5 9	12 04	Hartlepool	25 1 87	Wigan Ath
Ciftci Nadir (F)	6 1	13 00	Karacan	12 2 92	Scholar
Cowan-Hall Paris (F)			London	5 10 90	Scholar

Cuvelier Florent (M)			Belgium	12	9	92	Scholar
Diop Papa Bouba (M)	6 4	14 12	Dakar	28	1	78	Fulham
Gazet DuChattelier Ryan (M)			Richmond (Aus)	17	2	91	Scholar
Hreidarsson Hermann (D)	6 3	12 12	Reykjavik	11	7	74	Charlton Ath
Hughes Jordan (M)			Belfast	27	8	91	Scholar
Hughes Richard (M)	6 0	13 03	Glasgow	25	6	79	Bournemouth
Hurst James (D)			Sutton Coldfield	31	1	92	Scholar
James David (G)	6 4	14 13	Welwyn	1	8	70	Manchester C
Kanu Nwankwo (F)	6 5	13 00	Owerri	1	8	76	WBA
Kilbey Tom (M)	6 3	13 08	Waltham Forest	19	10	90	Millwall
Mahoto Gautier (M)	5 11	11 05	Paris	21	2	92	Scholar
Mullins Hayden (D)	5 11	11 12	Reading	27	3	79	West Ham U
Nlundulu Gael (F)	6 0	12 04	Paris	29	4	92	Scholar
Nugent Dave (F)	5 11	12 13	Liverpool	2	5	85	Preston NE
O'Brien Liam (G)	6 1	12 06	Brent	30	11	91	Scholar
Pack Marlon (D)	6 0	11 09	Portsmouth	25	3	91	Scholar
Ricardo Rocha (D)	6 0	12 08	Braga	3	10	78	Standard Liege
Ritchie Matt (M)	5 8	11 00	Portsmouth	10	9	89	Scholar
Smith Tommy (F)	5 8	11 04	Hemel Hempstead	22	5	80	Watford
Subotic Danijel (F)	6 1	13 00	Basle	31	1	89	Scholar
Utaka John (F)	5 9	11 02	Enugu	8	1	82	Rennes
Ward Joel (D)	6 2	11 13	Portsmouth	29	10	89	Scholar
Webber Danny (F)	5 10	11 04	Manchester	28	12	81	Sheffield U
Wilson Marc (M)	6 2	12 07	Belfast	17	8	87	Scholar

League Appearances: Ashdown, J. 5(1); Basinas, A. 7(5); Begovic, A. 8(1); Belhadj, N. 16(3); Ben Haim, T. 21(1); Boateng, K. 20(2); Brown, M. 22(2); Dindane, A. 18(1); Diop, P. 9(3); Distin, S. 3; Finnan, S. 20(1); Hreidarsson, H. 17; Hughes, R. 9(1); James, D. 25; Kaboul, Y. 19; Kanu, N. 6(17); Kranjcar, N. 4; Mokoena, A. 21(2); Mullins, H. 15(3); Nugent, D. (3); O'Hara, J. 25(1); Owusu-Abeyie, Q. 3(7); Piquionne, F. 26(8); Ricardo Rocha, 10; Ritchie, M. 1(1); Smith, T. 12(4); Sowah, L. 3(2); Utaka, J. 10(8); Vanden Borre, A. 15(4); Ward, J. 1(2); Webber, D. 4(13); Wilson, M. 28; Yebda, H. 15(3).

Goals – League (34): Dindane 8 (1 pen), Piquionne 5, Belhadj 3, Boateng 3 (1 pen), Kaboul 2, Brown 2, Kanu 2, O'Hara 2, Yebda 2 (1 pen), Hreidarsson 1, Smith 1, Utaka 1, Webber 1.

Carling Cup (13): Piquionne 3, Kanu 2, Webber 2, Dindane 1, Hughes 1, Kranjcar 1, Utaka 1, Vanden Borre 1, own goal 1.

FA Cup (13): Piquionne 3, Boateng 2 (1 pen), Utaka 2, Belhadj 1, Dindane 1, Mokoena 1, O'Hara 1, Owusu-Abeyie 1, own goal 1.

Ground: Fratton Park, Frogmore Road, Portsmouth, Hampshire PO4 8RA. Telephone (02392) 731 204.

Record Attendance: 51,385 v Derby Co, FA Cup 6th rd, 26 February 1949. **Capacity:** 20,688.

Manager: Steve Cotterill.

Secretary: Paul Weld.

Most League Goals: 97, Division 1, 2002–03.

Highest League Scorer in Season: Guy Whittingham, 42, Division 1, 1992–93.

Most League Goals in Total Aggregate: Peter Harris, 194, 1946–60.

Most Capped Player: Jimmy Dickinson, 48, England.

Most League Appearances: Jimmy Dickinson, 764, 1946–65.

Honours – Football League: Division 1 Champions – 1948–49, 1949–50, 2002–03. Division 3 (S) Champions – 1923–24. Division 3 Champions – 1961–62, 1982–83. **FA Cup:** Winners – 1939, 2008.

Colours: Blue shirts with white trim, white shorts, red stockings.

PORT VALE   FL CHAMPIONSHIP 2

Collins Lee (D)	6 1	11 10	Telford	23	9 83	Wolverhampton W
Dodds Louis (F)	5 10	12 04	Leicester	8	10 86	Leicester C
Fraser Tom (M)	5 10	11 00	Brighton	5	12 87	Brighton & HA
Griffith Anthony (M)	6 0	12 00	Huddersfield	28	10 86	Doncaster R
Haldane Lewis (F)	6 0	11 03	Trowbridge	13	3 85	Bristol R
Loft Doug (M)	6 0	12 01	Maidstone	25	12 86	Brighton & HA
Martin Chris (G)	6 0	13 05	Mansfield	21	7 90	Scholar
McCombe John (D)	6 2	13 00	Pontefract	7	5 85	Hereford U
Morsy Sam (M)	5 9	12 06	Wolverhampton	10	9 91	Scholar
Owen Gareth (D)	6 1	11 07	Cheadle	21	9 82	Stockport Co
Richards Marc (F)	6 2	12 06	Wolverhampton	8	7 82	Barnsley
Taylor Kris (M)	5 9	11 05	Stafford	12	1 84	Hereford U
Taylor Rob (F)	5 7	11 05	Nuneaton	16	1 85	Nuneaton B
Yates Adam (D)	5 10	10 07	Stoke	28	5 83	Morecambe

League Appearances: Anyon, J. 7; Collins, L. 45; Davies, C. 22(2); Dodds, L. 33(11); Fraser, T. 33(5); Glover, D. (3); Griffith, A. 38(2); Guy, J. (3); Haldane, L. 29(8); Horsfield, G. 1(8); Howland, D. (4); Jarrett, J. 7(2); Jorgensen, C. (4); Lawrie, J. (3); Loft, D. 21(11); Martin, C. 39; McCombe, J. 37(3); McCrory, D. 2(3); Morsy, S. (1); Owen, G. 40; Prosser, L. 2; Richards, M. 45(1); Richman, S. (5); Rigg, S. 9(17); Stockley, S. 8(1); Taylor, R. 25(14); Taylor, K. 38(3); Yates, A. 25(7).
Goals – League (61): Richards 20 (6 pens), Taylor R 8, Davies 7 (1 pen), Dodds 6, Haldane 3, Loft 3, McCombe 3, Rigg 3, Taylor K 3, Collins 1, Fraser 1, Prosser 1, own goals 2.
Carling Cup (4): Richards 2, Taylor K 1, Taylor R 1.
FA Cup (2): Dodds 1, Yates 1.
J Paint Trophy (5): Dodds 1, Haldane 1, McCombe 1, Richards 1, Taylor R 1.
Ground: Vale Park, Hamil Road, Burslem, Stoke-on-Trent ST6 1AW. Telephone (01782) 655 800.
Record Attendance: 49,768 v Aston Villa, FA Cup 5th rd, 20 February 1960. **Capacity:** 18,982.
Manager: Micky Adams.
Secretary: Bill Lodey.
Most League Goals: 110, Division 4, 1958–59.
Highest League Scorer in Season: Wilf Kirkham 38, Division 2, 1926–27.
Most League Goals in Total Aggregate: Wilf Kirkham, 154, 1923–29, 1931–33.
Most Capped Player: Chris Birchall, 22 (36), Trinidad & Tobago.
Most League Appearances: Roy Sproson, 761, 1950–72.
Honours – Football League: Division 3 (N) Champions – 1929–30, 1953–54. Division 4 Champions – 1958–59. **Autoglass Trophy:** Winners – 1993. **LDV Vans Trophy:** Winners – 2001.
Colours: White shirts with black trim, black shorts with white trim, white stockings.

PRESTON NORTH END   FL CHAMPIONSHIP

Barton Adam (M)	5 11	12 01	Blackburn	7	1 91	Scholar
Brown Chris (F)	6 3	13 01	Doncaster	11	12 84	Norwich C
Carter Darren (M)	6 2	12 11	Solihull	18	12 83	WBA
Chaplow Richard (M)	5 9	9 03	Accrington	2	2 85	WBA
Collins Dominic (D)			Preston	15	4 91	Scholar
Collins Neill (D)	6 3	12 07	Irvine	2	9 83	Wolverhampton W
Coutts Paul (M)	5 9	11 11	Aberdeen	22	7 88	Peterborough U
Davidson Callum (D)	5 10	11 00	Stirling	25	6 76	Leicester C
Dougan Neil (M)	5 6	10 02	Northern Ireland	8	3 92	Scholar

Elliott Stephen (F)	5 8	11 07	Dublin	6 1 84	Wolverhampton W
Hart Michael (M)	5 10	11 06	Bellshill	10 2 80	Aberdeen
Henderson Wayne (G)	5 11	12 02	Dublin	16 9 83	Brighton & HA
Jones Billy (M)	5 11	13 00	Shrewsbury	24 3 87	Crewe Alex
Lonergan Andrew (G)	6 2	13 00	Preston	19 10 83	Scholar
Mawene Youl (D)	6 1	13 00	Caen	16 7 79	Derby Co
Mayor Danny (M)	6 0	11 13	Preston	18 10 90	Scholar
McLaughlin Conor (D)	6 0	11 02	Belfast	26 7 91	Scholar
Mellor Neil (F)	6 0	14 00	Sheffield	4 11 82	Liverpool
Miller George (M)	5 9	12 02	Eccleston	25 11 91	Scholar
Nicholson Barry (M)	5 7	9 01	Dumfries	24 8 78	Aberdeen
Nolan Eddie (D)	6 0	13 05	Waterford	5 8 88	Blackburn R
Parkin Jon (F)	6 4	13 07	Barnsley	30 12 81	Stoke C
Parry Paul (M)	5 11	12 12	Chepstow	19 8 80	Cardiff C
Proctor Jamie (F)	6 2	12 03	Preston	25 3 92	Scholar
St Ledger-Hall Sean (D)	6 0	11 09	Birmingham	28 12 84	Peterborough U
Treacy Keith (M)	6 0	13 02	Dublin	13 9 88	Blackburn R
Trotman Neal (D)	6 3	13 08	Levenshulme	11 3 87	Oldham Ath
Wallace Ross (M)	5 6	9 12	Dundee	23 5 85	Sunderland

League Appearances: Barton, A. 1; Brown, C. 24(19); Carter, D. 11(12); Chaplow, R. 29(2); Chilvers, L. 20(3); Collins, N. 19(2); Coutts, P. 13; Davidson, C. 25(2); Elliott, S. 3(6); Hart, M. 10(1); Henderson, W. 1(1); James, M. 17(1); Jones, B. 42(2); Lonergan, A. 45; Mawene, Y. 18(1); Mayor, D. 4(3); Mellor, N. 29(10); Nicholson, B. 3(1); Nolan, E. 15(4); Parkin, J. 26(17); Parry, P. 12(5); Proctor, J. (1); Sedgwick, C. 25(9); St Ledger-Hall, S. 30; Sumulikoski, V. 9(6); Tonge, M. 7; Treacy, K. 8(9); Wallace, R. 40(1); Ward, E. 4; Welbeck, D. 8; Williams, T. 8(2).

Goals – League (58): Mellor 10, Parkin 10 (2 pens), Wallace 7, Brown 6, Davidson 5 (4 pens), Jones 4, Chaplow 2, James 2, Parry 2, St Ledger-Hall 2, Treacy 2, Welbeck 2, Collins N 1, Coutts 1, Elliott 1, Sedgwick 1.

Carling Cup (8): Brown 4, Elliott 1, Mellor 1, Nicholson 1, Trottman 1.

FA Cup (7): Parkin 3 (1 pen), Brown 1, Carter 1, Sedgwick 1, own goal 1.

Ground: Deepdale, Sir Tom Finney Way, Preston PR1 6RU. Telephone (0844) 856 1964.

Record Attendance: 42,684 v Arsenal, Division 1, 23 April 1938. **Capacity:** 23,408.

Manager: Darren Ferguson.

Secretary: Janet Parr.

Most League Goals: 100, Division 2, 1927–28 and Division 1, 1957–58.

Highest League Scorer in Season: Ted Harper, 37, Division 2, 1932–33.

Most League Goals in Total Aggregate: Tom Finney, 187, 1946–60.

Most Capped Player: Tom Finney, 76, England.

Most League Appearances: Alan Kelly, 447, 1961–75.

Honours – Football League: Division 1 Champions – 1888–89 (first champions), 1889–90. Division 2 Champions – 1903–04, 1912–13, 1950–51, 1999–2000. Division 3 Champions – 1970–71, 1995–96. **FA Cup:** Winners – 1889, 1938.

Colours: White shirts, blue shorts, white stockings.

QUEENS PARK RANGERS   FL CHAMPIONSHIP

Agyemang Patrick (F)	6 1	12 00	Walthamstow	29 9 80	Preston NE
Alberti Matteo (M)	5 10	11 05	Chievo Verona	4 8 88	
Balanta Angelo (F)	5 10	11 11	Colombia	1 7 90	Scholar
Borrowdale Gary (D)	6 0	12 01	Sutton	16 7 85	Coventry C
Brown Lee (M)	6 0	12 06	Farnborough	10 8 90	Scholar
Buzsaky Akos (M)	5 11	11 09	Hungary	7 5 82	Plymouth Arg
Cerny Radek (G)	6 1	14 02	Prague	18 2 74	Tottenham H
Connolly Matthew (D)	6 1	11 03	Barnet	24 9 87	Arsenal
Cook Lee (M)	5 8	11 10	Hammersmith	3 8 82	Fulham

Ehmer Max (M)			Frankfurt	3	2 92	Scholar
Ephraim Hogan (F)	5 9	10 06	Islington	31	3 88	West Ham U
Faurlin Alejandro (M)	6 1	12 06	Argentina	9	8 86	Instituto
German Antonio (F)	5 10	12 03	London	26	12 91	Scholar
Gorkss Kaspars (D)	6 3	13 05	Riga	6	11 81	Blackpool
Hall Fitz (D)	6 3	13 00	Leytonstone	20	12 80	Wigan Ath
Helguson Heidar (F)	5 10	12 09	Akureyri	22	8 77	Bolton W
Leigertwood Mikele (D)	6 1	11 04	Enfield	12	11 82	Sheffield U
Oastler Joe (D)	5 10	11 03	Portsmouth	3	7 90	Scholar
Parker Josh (F)			Slough	1	12 90	
Parmenter Taylor (D)			Bromley	9	9 92	Scholar
Pellicori Alessandro (F)	5 11	11 11	Cosenza	27	2 81	Avellino
Putnins Elvijs (G)			Latvia	12	4 91	FK Auda
Ramage Peter (D)	6 3	11 02	Whitley Bay	22	11 83	Newcastle U
Rose Romone (M)	5 9	11 05	Pennsylvania	19	1 90	Scholar
Rowlands Martin (M)	5 9	10 10	Hammersmith	8	2 79	Brentford
Stewart Damion (D)	6 3	13 08	Kingston	8	8 80	Harbour View
Vine Rowan (F)	5 11	12 10	Basingstoke	21	9 82	Birmingham C

League Appearances: Agyemang, P. 5(12); Ainsworth, G. (1); Balanta, A. 1(3); Bent, M. 2(1); Borrowdale, G. 18(3); Brown, L. (1); Buzsaky, A. 29(10); Cerny, R. 29; Connolly, M. 17(2); Cook, L. 8(8); Ephraim, H. 16(6); Faurlin, A. 36(5); German, A. 5(8); Gorkss, K. 40(1); Hall, F. 12(2); Helguson, H. 3(2); Hill, M. 15(1); Ikeme, C. 17; Leigertwood, M. 39(1); Mahon, G. 5(2); Oastler, J. (1); Parker, J. 1(3); Pellicori, A. 1(7); Priskin, T. 13; Quashie, N. 4; Ramage, P. 29(4); Reid, S. 1(1); Rose, R. (1); Routledge, W. 25; Rowlands, M. 5(1); Simpson, J. 34(5); Stewart, D. 30; Taarabt, A. 32(9); Tosic, D. 5; Vine, R. 8(23); Watson, B. 16; Williams, T. 5.

Goals – League (58): Simpson 12, Buzsaky 10 (4 pens), Taarabt 7 (2 pens), Leigertwood 5, Agyemang 3, Gorkss 3, Connolly 2, German 2, Ramage 2, Routledge 2, Watson 2, Cook 1, Faurlin 1, Helguson 1, Mahon 1, Priskin 1, Stewart 1, Vine 1, own goal 1.

Carling Cup (7): Routledge 4 (1 pen), Ephraim 2, Pellicori 1.

FA Cup (3): Buzsaky 1 (pen), Simpson 1, Stewart 1.

Ground: Loftus Road Stadium, South Africa Road, Shepherds Bush, London W12 7PJ. Telephone (020) 8743 0262.

Record Attendance: 35,353 v Leeds U, Division 1, 27 April 1974. **Capacity:** 18,682.

Manager: Neil Warnock.

Most League Goals: 111, Division 3, 1961–62.

Highest League Scorer in Season: George Goddard, 37, Division 3 (S), 1929–30.

Most League Goals in Total Aggregate: George Goddard, 172, 1926–34.

Most Capped Player: Alan McDonald, 52, Northern Ireland.

Most League Appearances: Tony Ingham, 519, 1950–63.

Honours – Football League: Division 2 Champions – 1982–83. Division 3 (S) Champions – 1947–48. Division 3 Champions – 1966–67. **Football League Cup:** Winners – 1966–67.

Colours: Blue and white hooped shirts, white shorts, white stockings.

READING   FL CHAMPIONSHIP

Andersen Mikkel (G)	6 5	12 08	Herlev	17	12 88	AB Copenhagen
Antonio Michail (M)	6 0	11 11	London	28	3 90	Tooting & M
Armstrong Chris (D)	5 9	11 00	Newcastle	5	8 82	Sheffield U
Bignall Nicholas (F)	5 10	11 12	Reading	11	7 90	Scholar
Church Simon (F)	6 0	13 04	Wycombe	10	12 88	Scholar
Cisse Kalifa (M)	6 2	12 11	Orleans	1	9 84	Boavista
Cummings Shaun (D)	6 0	11 10	Hammersmith	25	2 89	Chelsea
Davies Scott (M)	5 11	12 00	Dublin	10	3 88	Wycombe W
Federici Adam (G)	6 2	14 02	Nowra	31	1 85	

Name			Birthplace		Previous club
Gunnarsson Brynjar (M)	6 1	12 01	Reykjavik	16 10 75	Watford
Hamer Ben (G)	5 11	12 04	Reading	20 11 87	Crawley T
Hector Michael (M)					
Henry James (M)	6 1	11 11	Woodley	10 6 89	Scholar
Howard Brian (M)	5 8	11 00	Winchester	23 1 83	Sheffield U
Hunt Noel (F)	5 8	11 05	Waterford	26 12 82	Dundee U
Ingimarsson Ivar (D)	6 0	12 07	Reykjavik	20 8 77	Wolverhampton W
Joyce Danny (D)				5 6 92	Scholar
Karacan Jem (M)	5 10	11 13	Lewisham	21 2 89	Scholar
Kebe Jimmy (M)	6 2	11 07	Vitry-sur-Seine	19 1 84	Boulogne
Kelly Julian (D)	5 8	11 04	London	6 9 89	Scholar
Long Shane (F)	5 10	11 02	Kilkenny	22 1 87	Cork C
Matejovsky Marek (M)	5 10	11 00	Brandys nad Labem	20 12 81	Mlada Boleslav
McAnuff Jobi (M)	5 11	11 05	Edmonton	9 11 81	Watford
McCarthy Alex (G)	6 1	11 12	Reading	3 12 89	Scholar
Mills Matthew (D)	6 3	12 12	Swindon	14 7 86	Doncaster R
Mooney David (F)	6 0	12 01	Dublin	30 10 84	Cork C
Pearce Alex (D)	6 0	11 10	Reading	9 11 88	Scholar
Rasiak Grzegorz (F)	6 3	13 03	Czczecin	12 1 79	Southampton
Robson-Kanu Hal (F)	5 7	11 08	Hammersmith	21 5 89	
Sigurdsson Gylfi (M)	6 1	12 02	Reykjavik	9 9 89	Scholar
Tabb Jay (M)	5 7	10 00	Tooting	21 2 84	Coventry C
Williams Marcus (D)	5 8	10 07	Doncaster	8 4 86	Scunthorpe U

League Appearances: Antonio, M. (1); Bertrand, R. 44; Bignall, N. (1); Church, S. 22(14); Cisse, K. 14(3); Cummings, S. 8; Davies, S. 3(1); Federici, A. 46; Griffin, A. 21; Gunnarsson, B. 18(8); Harper, J. (3); Henry, J. 1(2); Howard, B. 30(4); Hunt, N. 5(5); Ingimarsson, I. 25; Karacan, J. 19(8); Kebe, J. 30(12); Khizanishvili, Z. 12(3); Long, S. 22(9); Matejovsky, M. 13(2); McAnuff, J. 36; Mills, M. 22(1); O'Dea, D. 7(1); Pearce, A. 24(1); Rasiak, G. 14(15); Robson-Kanu, H. 4(13); Rosenior, L. 5; Sigurdsson, G. 32(6); Tabb, J. 27(1); Thorvaldsson, G. 2(2).

Goals – League (68): Sigurdsson 16 (6 pens), Church 10 (1 pen), Kebe 10, Rasiak 9, Long 6 (1 pen), Pearce 4, McAnuff 3, Howard 2, Hunt N 2 (1 pen), Mills 2, Bertrand 1, Cisse 1, own goals 2.

Carling Cup (6): Bignall 2, Mooney 2, Sigurdsson 1, own goal 1.

FA Cup (11): Long 3, Sigurdsson 3 (1 pen), Church 2, Kebe 2, Howard 1.

Ground: The Madejski Stadium, Junction 11, M4, Reading, Berkshire RG2 0FL. Telephone (0118) 968 1100.

Record Attendance: Elm Park: 33,042 v Brentford, FA Cup 5th rd, 19 February 1927; Madejski Stadium: 24,122 v Aston Villa, Premiership, 10 February 2007. **Capacity:** 24,082.

Manager: Brian McDermott.

Secretary: Sue Hewett.

Most League Goals: 112, Division 3 (S), 1951–52.

Highest League Scorer in Season: Ronnie Blackman, 39, Division 3 (S), 1951–52.

Most League Goals in Total Aggregate: Ronnie Blackman, 158, 1947–54.

Most Capped Player: Kevin Doyle, 26 (35), Republic of Ireland.

Most League Appearances: Martin Hicks, 500, 1978–91.

Honours – Football League: Championship Champions – 2005–06. Division 2 Champions – 1993–94. Division 3 Champions – 1985–86. Division 3 (S) Champions – 1925–26. Division 4 Champions – 1978–79. **Simod Cup:** Winners – 1987–88.

Colours: Blue and white hooped shirts, blue shorts, blue stockings.

ROCHDALE   FL CHAMPIONSHIP 1

Name			Birthplace		Previous club
Arthur Kenny (G)	6 3	13 08	Bellshill	7 12 78	Accrington S
Dagnall Chris (F)	5 8	12 03	Liverpool	15 4 86	Tranmere R

Dawson Craig (D)	6 0	12 04	Rochdale	6	5 90	Radcliffe B
Edwards Matty (G)	6 2	12 11	Liverpool	22	8 90	Leeds U
Flynn Matthew (D)	6 0	11 06	Warrington	10	5 89	Macclesfield T
Gray Reece (F)			Oldham	1	9 92	Scholar
Holness Marcus (D)	6 0	12 02	Oldham	8	12 88	Scholar
Jones Gary (M)	5 11	12 05	Birkenhead	3	6 77	Barnsley
Kennedy Jason (M)	6 1	13 02	Stockton	11	9 86	Darlington
Kennedy Tom (D)	5 10	11 01	Bury	24	6 85	Bury
McArdle Rory (D)	6 1	11 05	Sheffield	1	5 87	Sheffield W
O'Grady Chris (F)	6 3	12 02	Nottingham	25	1 86	Leicester C
Stanton Nathan (D)	5 9	12 06	Nottingham	6	5 81	Scunthorpe U
Thompson Joe (M)	6 0	9 07	Rochdale	5	3 89	Scholar
Wiseman Scott (D)	6 0	11 06	Hull	9	10 85	Darlington

League Appearances: Arthur, K. 15; Atkinson, W. 15; Buckley, W. 12(3); Dagnall, C. 45; Dawson, C. 40(2); Fielding, F. 18; Flynn, M. 7(3); Glover, D. (2); Gray, R. (2); Haworth, A. 3(4); Heaton, T. 12; Higginbotham, K. 6(23); Holness, M. 7(4); Jones, G. 32(2); Kennedy, T. 44; Kennedy, J. 40(2); Le Fondre, A. (1); Lillis, J. 1; Manga, M. (2); McArdle, R. 17(3); O'Grady, C. 43; Obadeyi, T. 5(6); Rundle, A. 6(6); Shaw, J. (1); Spencer, S. (4); Stanton, N. 37(1); Stephens, D. 3(3); Taylor, J. 23; Thompson, J. 27(9); Toner, C. 7(6); Whaley, S. 8(1); Wiseman, S. 33(3).

Goals – League (82): O'Grady 22, Dagnall 20 (1 pen), Dawson 9, Thompson 6, Jones G 4, Atkinson 3, Buckley 3, Higginbotham 3, Kennedy T 3 (3 pens), Whaley 2, Obadeyi 1, Rundle 1, Stephens 1, Taylor 1, Wiseman 1, own goals 2.

Carling Cup (0).

FA Cup (3): Thompson 2, Dawson 1.

J Paint Trophy (1): Dawson 1.

Ground: Spotland Stadium, Willbutts Lane, Rochdale OL11 5DS. Telephone (0844) 826 1907.

Record Attendance: 24,231 v Notts Co, FA Cup 2nd rd, 10 December 1949. **Capacity:** 9,223.

Manager: Keith Hill.

Secretary: Colin Garlick.

Most League Goals: 105, Division 3 (N), 1926–27.

Highest League Scorer in Season: Albert Whitehurst, 44, Division 3 (N), 1926–27.

Most League Goals in Total Aggregate: Reg Jenkins, 119, 1964–73.

Most Capped Player: Leo Bertos, New Zealand, 6 (31).

Most League Appearances: Gary Jones, 379, 1998–2001; 2003–.

Honours – None.

Colours: Black and blue striped shirts, white shorts, blue stockings with black tops.

ROTHERHAM UNITED   FL CHAMPIONSHIP 2

Annerson Jamie (G)	6 2	13 02	Sheffield	21	6 88	Sheffield U
Brogan Stephen (D)	5 7	10 04	Rotherham	12	4 88	Scholar
Ellison Kevin (M)	6 0	12 00	Liverpool	23	2 79	Chester C
Fenton Nick (D)	6 0	10 02	Preston	23	11 79	Grimsby T
Green Jamie (F)	5 7	10 07	Doncaster	18	8 89	Scholar
Harrison Danny (M)	5 11	12 04	Liverpool	4	11 82	Tranmere R
Law Nicky (M)	5 10	11 06	Nottingham	29	3 88	Sheffield U
Le Fondre Adam (F)	5 9	11 04	Stockport	2	12 86	Rochdale
Pope Tom (F)	6 3	11 03	Stoke	27	8 85	Crewe Alex
Sharps Ian (D)	6 3	13 05	Warrington	23	10 80	Tranmere R
Taylor Jason (M)	6 1	11 03	Ashton-under-Lyne	28	1 87	Stockport Co
Taylor Ryan (F)	6 2	10 10	Rotherham	4	5 88	Scholar
Tonge Dale (D)	5 10	10 06	Doncaster	7	5 85	Barnsley

| Warne Paul (M) | 5 10 11 07 | Norwich | 8 5 73 | Yeovil T |
| Warrington Andy (G) | 6 3 12 13 | Sheffield | 10 6 76 | Bury |

League Appearances: Bell-Baggie, A. 2(9); Brogan, S. 1(4); Broughton, D. 6(10); Cummins, M. 6(9); Ellison, K. 36(3); Fenton, N. 34(1); Green, J. 14(5); Gunning, G. 21; Harrison, D. 32(5); Joseph, M. 11(4); Law, N. 41(1); Le Fondre, A. 43(1); Liddell, A. (2); Lynch, M. 21(2); Marshall, M. 13(9); McAllister, C. 7(1); Mills, P. 34(3); Nicholas, A. 7; Pope, T. 26(9); Roberts, R. 11(2); Rundle, A. 4; Sharps, I. 44; Taylor, J. 2; Taylor, R. 3(16); Tonge, D. 18(3); Walker, J. 15; Warne, P. 8(6); Warrington, A. 46.
Goals – League (55): Le Fondre 25 (10 pens), Ellison 8, Harrison 4, Broughton 3, Pope 3, Roberts 3, Walker 3, Law 2, Warne 2, Brogan 1, Cummins 1.
Carling Cup (5): Pope 2, Cummins 1, Ellison 1, Warne 1.
FA Cup (5): Le Fondre 2, Brogan 1, Broughton 1, Ellison 1.
J Paint Trophy (1): Le Fondre 1.
Play-Offs (5): Le Fondre 2, Taylor R 2, Ellison 1.
Ground: Don Valley Stadium, Worksop Road, Sheffield, South Yorkshire S9 3TL. Telephone (08444) 140 737.
Record Attendance: 25,170 v Sheffield U, Division 2, 13 December 1952 (at Millmoor); 7,082 v Aldershot T, FL 2 Play-offs semi-final 2nd leg, 19 May 2010 (at Don Valley).
Capacity: 25,000.
Manager: Ronnie Moore.
Most League Goals: 114, Division 3 (N), 1946–47.
Highest League Scorer in Season: Wally Ardron, 38, Division 3 (N), 1946–47.
Most League Goals in Total Aggregate: Gladstone Guest, 130, 1946–56.
Most Capped Player: Shaun Goater, 14 (36), Bermuda.
Most League Appearances: Danny Williams, 459, 1946–62.
Honours – Football League: Division 3 Champions – 1980–81. Division 3 (N) Champions – 1950–51. Division 4 Champions – 1988–89. **Auto Windscreens Shield:** Winners – 1996.
Colours: Red shirts with white design, white shorts, red stockings.

SCUNTHORPE UNITED   FL CHAMPIONSHIP

Boyes Adam (F)	6 2 11 06	Lingdale	1 11 90	York C
Byrne Cliff (D)	6 0 12 11	Dublin	27 4 82	Sunderland
Canavan Niall (D)	6 3 12 00	Leeds	11 4 91	Scholar
Coleman Rory (D)	6 0 11 09	Rotherham	22 12 90	Scholar
Forte Jonathan (M)	6 0 12 02	Sheffield	25 7 86	Sheffield U
Godden Matthew (F)		Canterbury	29 7 91	Scholar
Hooper Gary (F)	5 10 12 07	Loughton	26 1 88	Southend U
Jones Rob (D)	6 7 12 02	Stockton	30 11 79	Hibernian
Lillis Joshua (G)	6 2 12 09	Scunthorpe	24 6 87	Scholar
McCann Grant (M)	5 10 11 00	Belfast	14 4 80	Barnsley
Mirfin David (D)	6 3 13 00	Sheffield	18 4 85	Huddersfield T
Morris Ian (M)	6 0 11 05	Dublin	27 2 87	Leeds U
Murphy Joe (G)	6 2 13 06	Dublin	21 8 81	Sunderland
O'Connor Michael (M)	6 1 11 08	Belfast	6 10 87	Crewe Alex
Raynes Michael (D)	6 4 12 00	Wythenshawe	15 10 87	Stockport Co
Slocombe Sam (G)	6 0 11 11	Scunthorpe	5 6 88	Bottesford T
Sparrow Matt (M)	5 11 11 06	Wembley	3 10 81	Scholar
Thompson Gary (M)	6 0 14 02	Kendal	24 11 80	Morecambe
Togwell Sam (D)	5 11 12 04	Beaconsfield	14 10 84	Barnsley
Woolford Martyn (M)	6 0 11 09	Pontefract	13 10 85	York C
Wright Andrew (M)	6 1 13 07	Southport	15 1 85	West Virginia Univ
Wright Josh (M)	6 1 11 07	Tower Hamlets	6 11 89	Charlton Ath

League Appearances: Byrne, C. 34(2); Canavan, N. 4(3); Forte, J. 6(22); Friend, G. 2(2); Hayes, P. 45; Hooper, G. 31(4); Jones, R. 28; Lillis, J. 6(2); May, B. (1); McCann, G. 36(6); McDermott, D. 4(5); McNulty, J. 2(1); Milne, K. 4; Mirfin, D. 37; Moloney, B. 1(2); Morris, I. 2(1); Murphy, J. 40; N'Gala, B. (2); O'Connor, M. 23(9); Raynes, M. 12; Slocombe, S. (1); Sparrow, M. 22(8); Spence, J. 9; Thompson, G. 22(14); Togwell, S. 33(8); Williams, M. 37; Woolford, M. 29(11); Wright, A. 13(6); Wright, J. 24(11).

Goals – League (62): Hooper 19 (2 pens), Hayes 9, Thompson 9, McCann 8 (2 pens), Woolford 5, Byrne 2, Forte 2, O'Connor 2, Togwell 2, Canavan 1, Jones 1, Mirfin 1, Sparrow 1.

Carling Cup (7): Hayes 2, Canavan 1, Forte 1, Hooper 1 (pen), McCann 1, Sparrow 1.

FA Cup (3): Hayes 2, own goal 1.

Ground: Glanford Park, Doncaster Road, Scunthorpe DN15 8TD. Telephone (0871) 221 1899.

Record Attendance: Old Showground: 23,935 v Portsmouth, FA Cup 4th rd, 30 January 1954. Glanford Park: 8,906 v Nottingham F, FL 1, 10 March 2007.

Capacity: 9,088.

Manager: Nigel Adkins BSc. (Hons).

General Manager: Jamie Hammond.

Most League Goals: 88, Division 3 (N), 1957–58.

Highest League Scorer in Season: Barrie Thomas, 31, Division 2, 1961–62.

Most League Goals in Total Aggregate: Steve Cammack, 110, 1979–81, 1981–86.

Most Capped Player: Grant McCann, 10 (28), Northern Ireland.

Most League Appearances: Jack Brownsword, 595, 1950–65.

Honours – Football League: FL 1 Champions – 2006–07; Division 3 (N) Champions – 1957–58.

Colours: Claret shirts with light blue sleeves, white shorts, claret stockings.

SHEFFIELD UNITED   FL CHAMPIONSHIP

Aksalu Mihkel (G)	6 3	12 06	Kuressaare	7 11 84	Flora
Cresswell Richard (F)	6 0	13 00	Bridlington	20 9 77	Stoke C
Evans Ched (F)	6 0	12 00	Rhyl	28 12 88	Manchester C
France Ryan (M)	5 11	11 11	Sheffield	13 12 80	Hull C
Henderson Darius (F)	6 3	14 03	Sutton	7 9 81	Watford
Kenny Paddy (G)	6 0	15 10	Halifax	17 5 78	Bury
Lowton Matt (M)	5 11	12 04	Chesterfield	9 6 89	Scholar
Montgomery Nick (M)	5 8	12 08	Leeds	28 10 81	Scholar
Morgan Chris (D)	6 0	13 06	Barnsley	9 11 77	Barnsley
Naysmith Gary (D)	5 9	12 01	Edinburgh	16 11 78	Everton
Pomares Carlos (D)					Scholar
Quinn Stephen (M)	5 6	9 08	Dublin	4 4 86	Scholar
Reid Kyel (M)	5 10	12 05	South London	26 11 87	West Ham U
Sharp Billy (F)	5 9	11 00	Sheffield	5 2 86	Scunthorpe U
Stewart Jordan (D)	6 0	12 09	Birmingham	3 3 82	Derby Co
Taylor Andy (D)	5 11	11 07	Blackburn	14 3 86	Tranmere R
Ward Jamie (M)	5 5	9 04	Birmingham	12 5 86	Chesterfield
Williamson Lee (D)	5 10	10 04	Derby	7 6 82	Watford
Yeates Mark (F)	5 8	13 03	Dublin	11 1 85	Middlesbrough

League Appearances: Bartley, K. 10(4); Bennett, I. 4(1); Bunn, M. 31(1); Camara, H. 9(14); Connolly, P. 7; Cotterill, D. 3(11); Cresswell, R. 28(3); Davies, A. 7(1); Evans, C. 21(12); Fortune, J. 3(2); France, R. 3(6); Geary, D. 5(2); Harper, J. 31(3); Henderson, D. 28(4); Howard, B. 3(1); Ikeme, C. 2; Kallio, T. 2; Kallio, T. 6; Kenny, P. 2; Kilgallon, M. 21; Little, G. 7(9); Lowton, M. 1(1); Montgomery, N. 39; Morgan, C. 37; Naysmith, G. 2; Nosworthy, N. 19; Quinn, S. 38(6); Reid, K. (7); Seip, M. 5(1); Simonsen, S. 7; Stewart, J. 15(8); Taylor, A. 22(4); Treacy, K. 12(4); Walker, K. 26; Ward, J. 25(3); Williamson, L. 14(6); Yeates, M. 11(9).

Goals – League (62): Cresswell 12, Henderson 12 (3 pens), Ward 7, Camara 4, Evans 4, Harper 4, Quinn S 4, Williamson 3, Cotterill 2 (1 pen), Morgan 2, Yeates 2, Fortune 1, Kilgallon 1, Montgomery 1, Treacy 1, own goals 2.
Carling Cup (1): Sharp 1.
FA Cup (4): Cresswell 2, Ward 1, Williamson 1.
Ground: Bramall Lane, Cherry Street, Sheffield S2 4SU. Telephone (0871) 995 1899.
Record Attendance: 68,287 v Leeds U, FA Cup 5th rd, 15 February 1936.
Capacity: 32,500.
Manager: Kevin Blackwell.
Secretary: Donna Fletcher.
Most League Goals: 102, Division 1, 1925–26.
Highest League Scorer in Season: Jimmy Dunne, 41, Division 1, 1930–31.
Most League Goals in Total Aggregate: Harry Johnson, 205, 1919–30.
Most Capped Player: .
Most League Appearances: Joe Shaw, 629, 1948–66.
Honours – Football League: Division 1 Champions – 1897–98. Division 2 Champions – 1952–53. Division 4 Champions – 1981–82. **FA Cup:** Winners – 1899, 1902, 1915, 1925.
Colours: Red and white striped shirts with red sleeves, black shorts, black stockings.

SHEFFIELD WEDNESDAY   FL CHAMPIONSHIP 1

Beevers Mark (D)	6 4	13 00	Barnsley	21 11 89	Scholar
Boden Luke (F)	6 1	12 00	Sheffield	26 11 88	Scholar
Buxton Lewis (D)	6 1	13 11	Newport (IW)	10 12 83	Stoke C
Grant Lee (G)	6 3	13 01	Hemel Hempstead	27 1 83	Derby Co
Hinds Richard (D)	6 2	12 02	Sheffield	22 8 80	Scunthorpe U
Jameson Aaron (G)	6 3	13 00	Sheffield	7 11 89	Scholar
Johnson Jermaine (M)	6 0	12 08	Kingston	25 6 80	Bradford C
Miller Tommy (M)	6 0	11 07	Easington	8 1 79	Ipswich T
O'Connor James (M)	5 8	11 00	Dublin	1 9 79	Burnley
O'Donnell Richard (G)	6 2	13 05	Sheffield	12 9 89	Scholar
Potter Darren (M)	6 0	10 08	Liverpool	21 12 84	Wolverhampton W
Purse Darren (D)	6 2	12 08	Stepney	14 2 77	Cardiff C
Spurr Tommy (D)	6 1	11 05	Leeds	13 9 87	Scholar
Tudgay Marcus (F)	5 10	12 04	Worthing	3 2 83	Derby Co

League Appearances: Beevers, M. 32(3); Buxton, L. 28; Clarke, L. 18(18); Esajas, E. 5(15); Feeney, W. (1); Grant, L. 46; Gray, M. 27(3); Hinds, R. 7(4); Jeffers, F. 1(12); Johnson, J. 29(5); McAllister, S. 5(7); Miller, T. 10(10); Nolan, E. 14; O'Connor, J. 44; Potter, D. 46; Purse, D. 39; Simek, F. 9(3); Soares, T. 17(8); Sodje, A. (11); Spurr, T. 46; Tudgay, M. 41(2); Varney, L. 32(7); Wood, R. 10(1).
Goals – League (49): Tudgay 10 (1 pen), Varney 9, Clarke 6 (1 pen), Johnson 5, O'Connor 3, Potter 3, Esajas 2, Gray 2, Purse 2, Soares 2, Wood R 2, Miller 1, Nolan 1, Spurr 1.
Carling Cup (3): Johnson 2, Esajas 1.
FA Cup (1): own goal 1.
Ground: Hillsborough, Sheffield S6 1SW. Telephone (0871) 995 1867.
Record Attendance: 72,841 v Manchester C, FA Cup 5th rd, 17 February 1934.
Capacity: 39,812.
Manager: Alan Irvine.
Most League Goals: 106, Division 2, 1958–59.
Highest League Scorer in Season: Derek Dooley, 46, Division 2, 1951–52.
Most League Goals in Total Aggregate: Andrew Wilson, 199, 1900–20.
Most Capped Player: Nigel Worthington, 50 (66), Northern Ireland.
Most League Appearances: Andrew Wilson, 501, 1900–20.
Honours – Football League: Division 1 Champions – 1902–03, 1903–04, 1928–29, 1929–30. Division 2 Champions – 1899–1900, 1925–26, 1951–52, 1955–56, 1958–59. **FA Cup:** Winners – 1896, 1907, 1935. **Football League Cup:** Winners – 1990–91.
Colours: Blue and white striped shirts, black shorts, blue stockings.

SHREWSBURY TOWN   FL CHAMPIONSHIP 2

Name	Ht	Wt	Birthplace	D.O.B.	Previous Club
Bradshaw Tom (F)	5 8	11 02	Shrewsbury	27 7 92	Aberystwyth T
Bright Kris (F)	6 2	12 10	Manukau	5 9 86	Panserraikos
Cansdell-Sherriff Shane (D)	5 11	11 08	Sydney	10 11 82	Tranmere R
Disley Craig (M)	5 10	10 13	Worksop	24 8 81	Bristol R
Dunfield Terry (M)	5 11	12 04	Vancouver	20 2 82	Macclesfield T
Elder Nathan (F)	6 1	13 12	Hornchurch	5 4 85	Brentford
Gray Andre (F)	5 10	12 07	Shrewsbury	26 6 91	Scholar
Hibbert Dave (F)	6 2	12 00	Eccleshall	28 1 86	Preston NE
Holden Dean (D)	6 1	12 04	Salford	15 9 79	Falkirk
Hooman Harry (D)	5 11	12 06	Worcester	27 4 91	Scholar
Langmead Kelvin (F)	6 1	12 00	Coventry	23 3 85	Preston NE
Leslie Steve (M)	5 11	12 10	Shrewsbury	5 11 87	Scholar
McIntyre Kevin (M)	6 0	11 10	Liverpool	23 12 77	Macclesfield T
Neal Chris (G)	6 2	12 04	St Albans	23 10 85	Preston NE
Neal Lewis (M)	5 10	11 02	Leicester	14 7 81	Carlisle U
Robinson Jake (F)	5 7	10 10	Brighton	23 10 86	Brighton & HA
Taylor Danny (D)			Chester	5 9 91	
Taylor Jon (M)	5 11	12 04	Liverpool	23 12 89	
Van den Broek Benjamin (M)	6 0	13 03	Geleen	21 9 87	Haarlem

League Appearances: Arestidou, A. 2; Bradshaw, T. 1(5); Bright, K. 4(22); Button, D. 26; Cansdell-Sherriff, S. 41; Coughlan, G. 36; Cureton, J. 10(2); Devitt, J. 8(1); Disley, C. 16(2); Dunfield, T. 28(2); Elder, N. 9(10); Fairhurst, W. 10; Gray, A. (4); Hibbert, D. 37(1); Holden, D. 37; Hooman, H. 1(1); Labadie, J. 11(2); Langmead, K. 44; Leslie, S. 21(13); McIntyre, K. 43(2); Murray, P. 25(2); Neal, C. 7; Neal, L. 21(8); Phillips, S. 11; Riza, O. 1(7); Robinson, J. 15(19); Simpson, J. 14(4); Skarz, J. 20; Taylor, D. 2(1); Taylor, J. (2); Van den Broek, B. 5(6).

Goals – League (55): Hibbert 14 (1 pen), Leslie 6 (1 pen), Labadie 5, Fairhurst 4, Bradshaw 3, Langmead 3, Robinson 3, Bright 2, Coughlan 2, Devitt 2, Dunfield 2, Elder 2, Neal L 2, Cansdell-Sherriff 1, Disley 1, McIntyre 1 (1 pen), Van den Broek 1, own goal 1.

Carling Cup (3): Cansdell-Sherriff 1, Hibbert 1, Robinson 1.

FA Cup (0).

J Paint Trophy (0).

Ground: Greenhous Meadow, Oteley Road, Shrewsbury SY2 6ST. Telephone (01743) 289 177.

Record Attendance: 18,917 v Walsall, Division 3, 26 April 1961; 8,429 v Bury, FL 2, Play-off semi-final, 7 May 2009 (ProStar Stadium). **Capacity:** 10,000.

Manager: Graham Turner.

Secretary/General Manager: Jonathan Harris.

Most League Goals: 101, Division 4, 1958–59.

Highest League Scorer in Season: Arthur Rowley, 38, Division 4, 1958–59.

Most League Goals in Total Aggregate: Arthur Rowley, 152, 1958–65 (completing his League record of 434 goals).

Most Capped Player: Jimmy McLaughlin, 5 (12), Northern Ireland; Bernard McNally, 5, Northern Ireland.

Most League Appearances: Mickey Brown, 418, 1986–91; 1992–94; 1996–2001.

Honours – Football League: Division 3 Champions – 1978–79, 1993–94. **Welsh Cup:** Winners – 1891, 1938, 1977, 1979, 1984, 1985.

Colours: All blue with yellow and red design.

SOUTHAMPTON   FL CHAMPIONSHIP 1

Barnard Lee (F)	5 10	10 10	Romford	18 7 84	Southend U
Bialkowski Bartosz (G)	6 3	12 10	Braniewo	6 7 87	Gornik Zabrze
Davis Kelvin (G)	6 1	14 09	Bedford	29 9 76	Sunderland
Doble Ryan (M)			Wales	1 2 91	Scholar
Fonte Jose (D)	6 2	12 08	Penafiel	22 12 83	Crystal Palace
Forecast Tommy (G)	6 2	12 08	Newham	15 10 86	Tottenham H
Gillett Simon (M)	5 6	11 07	Oxford	6 11 85	Scholar
Gobern Oscar (M)	5 11	10 10	Birmingham	26 1 91	Scholar
Hammond Dean (M)	6 0	11 09	Hastings	7 3 83	Colchester U
Harding Dan (D)	6 0	11 11	Gloucester	23 12 83	Ipswich T
Holmes Lee (M)	5 8	10 06	Mansfield	2 4 87	Derby Co
Jaidi Radhi (D)	6 2	14 00	Tunis	30 8 75	Birmingham C
Lallana Adam (M)			Southampton	10 5 88	Scholar
Lambert Ricky (F)	6 2	14 08	Liverpool	16 2 82	Bristol R
Martin Aaron (D)	6 3	11 13	Newport (IW)	29 9 89	Eastleigh
McNish Callum (M)			Oxford	25 5 92	
Mills Joseph (F)	5 9	11 00	Swindon	30 10 89	Scholar
Molyneux Lee (D)	5 10	11 07	Liverpool	24 2 89	Scholar
Pulis Anthony (M)	5 10	11 13	Bristol	21 7 84	Stoke C
Puncheon Jason (M)	5 9	12 05	Croydon	26 6 86	Plymouth Arg
Racine Aaron (D)			Rustington	30 10 91	Scholar
Reeves Benjamin (D)				19 11 91	Scholar
Saville Jack (D)	6 3	12 00	Frimley	2 4 91	Scholar
Schneiderlin Morgan (M)	5 11	11 11	Zellwiller	8 11 89	Strasbourg
Seaborne Danny (D)	6 0	11 10	Barnstaple	5 3 87	Exeter C
Wotton Paul (D)	5 11	12 00	Plymouth	17 8 77	Plymouth Arg

League Appearances: Antonio, M. 14(14); Barnard, L. 14(6); Bialkowski, B. 6(1); Connolly, D. 9(11); Davis, K. 40; Fonte, J. 21; Gillett, S. (2); Gobern, O. (4); Hammond, D. 40; Harding, D. 42; Holmes, L. 2(3); Jaidi, R. 26(1); James, L. 28(2); Lallana, A. 44; Lambert, R. 44(1); Lancashire, O. 1(1); Martin, A. 2; McNish, C. (1); Mellis, J. 7(5); Mills, J. 8(8); Murty, G. 5(1); Otsemobor, J. 19; Oxlade-Chamberlain, A. (2); Papa Waigo, N. 11(24); Paterson, M. 4(3); Perry, C. 11(1); Puncheon, J. 19; Rasiak, G. 1(2); Saganowski, M. 3(3); Schneiderlin, M. 35(2); Seaborne, D. 11(5); Thomas, W. 10(5); Thomson, J. (4); Trotman, N. 17(1); Wotton, P. 12(14).

Goals – League (85): Lambert 30 (8 pens), Lallana 15, Barnard 9, Connolly 5, Hammond 5, Papa Waigo 5, Antonio 3, Harding 3, Puncheon 3, James 2, Trotman 2, Jaidi 1, Paterson 1, Schneiderlin 1.

Carling Cup (3): Lallana 2, Lambert 1.

FA Cup (10): Antonio 2, Connolly 2, Lambert 2, Hammond 1, Lallana 1, Papa Waigo 1, Thomas 1.

J Paint Trophy (14): Papa Waigo 4, Lambert 3 (1 pen), Antonio 2, Lallana 2, Harding 1, Thomas 1, own goal 1.

Ground: St Mary's Stadium, Britannia Road, Southampton SO14 5FP. Telephone (0845) 688 9448.

Manager: Alan Pardew.

Record Attendance: 32,104 v Liverpool, FA Premier League, 18 January 2003. **Capacity:** 32,689.

Secretary: Liz Coley.

Most League Goals: 112, Division 3 (S), 1957–58.

Highest League Scorer in Season: Derek Reeves, 39, Division 3, 1959–60.

Most League Goals in Total Aggregate: Mike Channon, 185, 1966–77, 1979–82.

Most Capped Player: Peter Shilton, 49 (125), England.

Most League Appearances: Terry Paine, 713, 1956–74.
Honours – Football League: Division 3 (S) Champions – 1921–22. Division 3 Champions – 1959–60. **FA Cup:** Winners – 1975–76. **Johnstone's Paint Trophy:** Winners – 2009–10.
Colours: White shirts with diagonal red stripe, white shorts, black stockings.

SOUTHEND UNITED   FL CHAMPIONSHIP 2

Name	Height		Birthplace	Date of Birth		Previous Club
Barrett Adam (D)	6 1	12 09	Dagenham	29 11 79		Bristol R
Christophe Jean-Francois (M)	6 1	13 01	Creil	13 6 82		Portsmouth
Crawford Harry (F)	6 1	12 04	Saffron Walden	10 12 91		Scholar
Francis Simon (D)	6 3	14 00	Nottingham	16 2 85		Sheffield U
Grant Anthony (M)	5 10	11 01	Lambeth	4 6 87		Chelsea
Herd Johnny (D)	5 9	12 00	Huntingdon	3 10 89		Welling U
Laurent Francis (F)	6 3	14 00	Paris	6 1 86		Mainz
McCormack James (M)	5 9	11 09	Dublin	10 1 84		Preston NE
Mildenhall Steve (G)	6 4	14 01	Swindon	13 5 78		Yeovil T
Milner Marcus (M)			Kingston (Jam)	28 11 91		Scholar
Moussa Franck (M)	5 8	10 08	Brussels	24 9 87		Scholar
O'Keefe Stuart (M)	5 8	10 00	Norwich	4 3 91		Ipswich T
Paterson Matthew (F)	5 10	10 10	Glasgow	18 10 89		Southampton
Scannell Damian (M)	5 10	11 07	Croydon	28 4 85		Eastleigh
Spencer Scott (F)	5 11	12 08	Manchester	1 1 89		Rochdale

League Appearances: Baldwin, P. 18; Barnard, L. 25; Barrett, A. 41; Betsy, K. (2); Christophe, J. 31(5); Crawford, H. 2(5); Francis, S. 45; Freedman, D. 9(11); Friend, G. 5(1); Grant, A. 38; Heath, M. 4; Herd, J. 17(3); Ibehre, J. 4; Joyce, I. 2; Laurent, F. 28(7); M'Voto, J. 15(2); Malone, S. 15(2); McCormack, A. 40(1); Mildenhall, S. 44; Milner, M. (1); Morrison, S. 8; Moussa, F. 41(2); O'Donovan, R. 3(1); O'Keefe, S. 3(4); Paterson, M. 9(7); Revell, A. 1(2); Sankofa, O. 10(2); Sawyer, L. (6); Scannell, D. 15(10); Spencer, S. 5(7); Vernon, S. 17; Walker, J. 2(11); Watt, S. 4; White, J. 5.
Goals – League (51): Barnard 15 (4 pens), Laurent 6, Moussa 5, Spencer 4, Vernon 4 (2 pens), McCormack 3, Barrett 2, Paterson 2, Baldwin 1, Christophe 1, Crawford 1, Francis 1, Freedman 1, Friend 1, M'Voto 1, O'Donovan 1, Scannell 1, own goal 1.
Carling Cup (3): Barnard 2, Moussa 1.
FA Cup (0).
J Paint Trophy (0).
Ground: Roots Hall Stadium, Victoria Avenue, Southend-on-Sea SS2 6NQ. Telephone (01702) 304 050.
Record Attendance: 31,090 v Liverpool FA Cup 3rd rd, 10 January 1979. **Capacity:** 12,260.
Manager: Paul Sturrock.
Secretary: Helen Norbury.
Most League Goals: 92, Division 3 (S), 1950–51.
Highest League Scorer in Season: Jim Shankly, 31, 1928–29; Sammy McCrory, 1957–58, both in Division 3 (S).
Most League Goals in Total Aggregate: Roy Hollis, 122, 1953–60.
Most Capped Player: George Mackenzie, 9, Eire.
Most League Appearances: Sandy Anderson, 452, 1950–63.
Honours – Football League: Championship 1 Champions – 2005–06. Division 4 Champions – 1980–81.
Colours: Navy blue shirts with white collar, navy blue shorts, white stockings.

Player			Birthplace				Previous Club
Ashley Bayes (G)	6 1	13 05	Lincoln	19	4	72	Crawley T
Lawrie Wilson (D)	5 10	11 02	Collier Row	11	9	87	Colchester U
Scott Laird (D)	5 9	11 09	Taunton	15	5	88	Plymouth Arg
Eddie Odhiambo (M)	5 9	11 02	Arusha	31	8	85	Oxford U
Jon Ashton (D)	6 2	13 05	Nuneaton	4	10	82	Grays Ath
Mark Albrighton (D)	6 1	12 08	Nuneaton	6	3	76	Cambridge U
Darren Murphy (M)	6 0	11 11	Cork	28	7	85	Cork C
Stacy Long (M)	5 8	10 01	Bromley	11	1	85	Ebbsfleet U
Charlie Griffin (F)	6 0	12 08	Bath	25	6	79	Salisbury C
Lee Boylan (F)	5 6	11 05	Witham	2	9	78	Cambridge U
Yemi Odubade (F)	5 7	11 07	Lagos	4	7	84	Oxford U
Joel Byrom (M)	6 0	12 04	Oswaldtwistle	14	9	86	Northwich Vic
Mark Roberts (D)	6 1	11 13	Northwich	16	10	83	Northwich Vic
Chris Day (G)	6 2	13 05	Walthamstow	28	7	75	Millwall
Tim Sills (F)	6 2	12 02	Romsey	10	9	79	Torquay U
David Bridges (M)	6 0	11 13	Huntingdon	22	9	82	Kettering T
Chris Beardsley (F)	6 0	12 02	Derby	28	2	84	Kettering T
Mitchell Cole (M)	5 11	11 05	London	6	10	85	Southend U
Andy Drury (M)	5 11	12 06	Sittingbourne	28	11	83	Lewes
Michael Bostwick (D)			London	17	5	88	Ebbsfleet U
Ronnie Henry (D)	5 11	11 11	Hemel Hempstead	2	1	84	
Peter Vincenti (D)	6 2	12 00	Jersey	7	7	86	Millwall

League Appearances: Albrighton, 8(6); Anaclet, (1); Anderson, 1; Ashton, 32(3); Bayes, 4; Beardsley, C. 30(7); Bostwick, 42; Boylan, 14(7); Bridges, 24(3); Brough, 6; Byrom, 28(11); Cole, 19(13); Day, 40; Drury, 21(8); Griffin, 17(9); Henry, 37; Laird, 42; Long, 14(7); Murphy, 20; Odhiambo, 5(10); Odubade, 24(13); Roberts, 38; Sills, 9(8); Vincenti, 2(19); Wilson, 7(5).

Goals – League (79): Odubade 14 (1 pen), Griffin 13 (1 pen), Boylan 7 (2 pens), Beardsley 6, Bostwick 6, Laird 6 (3 pens), Byrom 5, Cole 4 (1 pen), Roberts 4, Ashton 3, Bridges 2, Drury 2, Long 2, Wilson 2, Henry 1, Odhiambo 1, own goal 1.

FA Cup (3): Griffin 2, Vincenti 1.

Ground: Lamex Stadium, Broadhall Way, Stevenage, Herts SG2 8RH. Telephone 01438 223223.

Ground capacity: 6,546.

Record attendance: 6,489 v Kidderminster H, Conference, 25 January 1997.

Manager: Graham Westley.

Secretary: Roger Austin.

Colours: White shirts, red shorts, red stockings with white tops.

Most Appearances: Mike Smith, 466, 1992–2001, 2003–04.

Most Goals: Martin Gittings, 230, 1980–95.

Most Goals in One Season: Martin Gittings, 40, 1991–92.

Colours: White shirts, red shorts, red stockings with white tops.

STOCKPORT COUNTY   FL CHAMPIONSHIP 2

Player			Birthplace				Previous Club
Griffin Adam (D)	5 7	10 04	Salford	26	8	84	Darlington
Halls Andy (D)	6 0	12 02	Altrincham	20	4	92	Scholar
Huntington Paul (D)	6 3	12 08	Carlisle	17	9	87	Leeds U
Mainwaring Matty (M)	5 11	12 02	Salford	28	3	90	Preston NE
Mullins John (D)	5 11	12 07	Hampstead	6	11	85	Mansfield T
Partridge Richie (M)	5 8	11 00	Dublin	12	9	80	Milton Keynes D
Pilkington Danny (F)	5 9	11 10	Blackburn	25	5	90	Myserscough Coll
Poole David (M)	5 8	12 00	Manchester	25	11	84	Darlington

Roberts Craig (M)				Bangor	28 10 91	
Rose Michael (D)	5 11	12 04		Salford	28 7 82	Yeovil T
Rowe Daniel (M)	6 0	11 12		Wythenshawe	9 3 92	Bolton W
Swailes Danny (D)	6 3	12 07		Bolton	1 4 79	Milton Keynes D
Tansey Greg (M)	6 1	12 03		Huyton	21 11 88	Scholar
Thompson Peter (F)	5 9	13 06		Belfast	2 5 84	Linfield
Turnbull Paul (F)	5 10	11 07		Stockport	23 1 89	Scholar
Vincent James (M)	5 11	11 00		Glossop	27 9 89	Scholar
Williams Owain fon (G)	6 1	12 10		Gwynedd	17 3 87	Crewe Alex

League Appearances: Baker, C. 19(1); Barnes, S. 2; Bignall, N. 11; Bridcutt, L. 15; Donnelly, G. 16(3); Edwards, D. (1); Fisher, T. (1); Griffin, A. 9(9); Halls, A. 8(3); Havern, G. 7; Huntington, P. 26; Ibehre, J. 20; Johnson, O. 4(12); Johnson, J. 14(2); McNeil, M. 4(1); Mullins, J. 36; Partridge, R. 20(2); Perkins, D. 22; Pilkington, D. 10(19); Poole, D. 29(7); Raynes, M. 24(1); Ribeiro, C. 7; Rigby, L. 2; Rose, M. 24; Rowe, D. (4); Sadler, M. 20; Swailes, D. 20; Tansey, G. 25(7); Thompson, P. 14(8); Turnbull, P. 24(6); Vincent, J. 30(4); Williams, O. 44.
Goals – League (35): Baker 9 (4 pens), Ibehre 5 (1 pen), Donnelly 4, Bignall 2, Johnson J 2, Rose 2, Tansey 2, Thompson P 2, Johnson O 1, Mullins 1, Partridge 1, Pilkington 1, Raynes 1, own goals 2.
Carling Cup (1): Poole 1.
FA Cup (5): Turnbull 2, Baker 1 (pen), Poole 1, Thompson 1.
J Paint Trophy (5): Baker 3, Bignall 1, Bridcutt 1.
Ground: Edgeley Park, Hardcastle Road, Edgeley, Stockport, Cheshire SK3 9DD. Telephone (0161) 286 8888 (ext. 257).
Record Attendance: 27,833 v Liverpool, FA Cup 5th rd, 11 February 1950. **Capacity:** 10,641.
Manager: Paul Simpson.
Business Operations Manager: Rachael Moss.
Most League Goals: 115, Division 3 (N), 1933–34.
Highest League Scorer in Season: Alf Lythgoe, 46, Division 3 (N), 1933–34.
Most League Goals in Total Aggregate: Jack Connor, 132, 1951–56.
Most Capped Player: Jarkko Wiss, 9 (43), Finland.
Most League Appearances: Andy Thorpe, 489, 1978–86, 1988–92.
Honours – Football League: Division 3 (N) Champions – 1921–22, 1936–37. Division 4 Champions – 1966–67.
Colours: Reflex blue shirts with one broad white band, white shorts, white stockings.

STOKE CITY   FA PREMIERSHIP

Arismendi Diego (M)	6 2	12 13	Montevideo	25 1 88	Nacional
Beattie James (F)	6 1	13 06	Lancaster	27 2 78	Sheffield U
Begovic Asmir (G)	6 5	13 01	Trebinje	20 6 87	Portsmouth
Collins Danny (D)	6 2	11 13	Buckley	6 8 80	Sunderland
Davies Andrew (D)	6 2	12 03	Stockton	17 12 84	Southampton
Delap Rory (M)	6 0	11 10	Sutton Coldfield	6 7 76	Sunderland
Diagne-Faye Aboulaye (D)	6 2	13 10	Dakar	26 2 78	Newcastle U
Dickinson Carl (D)	6 0	12 00	Swadlincote	31 3 87	Scholar
Etherington Matthew (M)	5 10	10 12	Truro	14 8 81	West Ham U
Fuller Ricardo (F)	6 3	13 03	Kingston	31 10 79	Southampton
Griffin Andy (D)	5 9	10 10	Billinge	7 3 79	Derby Co
Higginbotham Danny (D)	6 1	12 03	Manchester	29 12 78	Sunderland
Huth Robert (D)	6 3	14 07	Berlin	18 8 84	Middlesbrough
Kitson David (F)	6 3	12 07	Hitchin	21 1 80	Reading
Lawrence Liam (M)	5 11	11 03	Retford	14 12 81	Sunderland
Lund Matthew (M)	6 0	11 13	Stockport	21 11 90	Crewe Alex
Marshall Ben (F)	5 11	11 13	Salford	29 3 91	Crewe Alex

Moult Louis (F)	6 0	13 05	Stoke	14	5 92	Scholar
Pugh Danny (M)	6 0	12 10	Manchester	19	10 82	Preston NE
Shawcross Ryan (D)	6 3	13 03	Chester	4	10 87	Manchester U
Shotton Ryan (D)	6 3	13 05	Stoke	30	9 88	Scholar
Sidibe Mamady (F)	6 4	12 02	Bamako	18	12 79	Gillingham
Simonsen Steve (G)	6 2	12 00	South Shields	3	4 79	Everton
Soares Tom (M)	6 0	11 04	Reading	10	7 86	Crystal Palace
Sonko Ibrahima (D)	6 3	13 07	Bignola	22	1 81	Reading
Sorensen Thomas (G)	6 5	14 00	Odense	12	6 76	Aston Villa
St Louis-Hamilton Danzelle (G)	6 4	15 00	Stevenage	7	5 90	Scholar
Tonge Michael (M)	6 0	11 10	Manchester	7	4 83	Sheffield U
Tuncay Sanli (F)	5 10	11 00	Sakarya	16	1 82	Middlesbrough
Whelan Glenn (M)	5 11	12 07	Dublin	13	1 84	Sheffield W
Whitehead Dean (M)	5 11	12 06	Abingdon	12	1 82	Sunderland
Wilkinson Andy (D)	5 11	11 00	Stone	6	8 84	Scholar

League Appearances: Beattie, J. 11(11); Begovic, A. 3(1); Collins, D. 22(3); Cresswell, R. 1(1); Delap, R. 34(2); Diagne-Faye, A. 30(1); Diao, S. 11(5); Etherington, M. 33(1); Fuller, R. 22(13); Higginbotham, D. 23(1); Huth, R. 30(2); Kitson, D. 10(8); Lawrence, L. 14(11); Moult, L. (1); Pugh, D. 1(6); Shawcross, R. 27(1); Sidibe, M. 19(5); Simonsen, S. 2(1); Sorensen, T. 33; Tuncay, S. 13(17); Whelan, G. 25(8); Whitehead, D. 33(3); Wilkinson, A. 21(4).

Goals – League (34): Etherington 5 (1 pen), Tuncay 4, Beattie 3 (1 pen), Fuller 3, Huth 3, Kitson 3, Diagne-Faye 2, Shawcross 2, Sidibe 2, Whelan 2, Diao 1, Higginbotham 1, Lawrence 1, Pugh 1, own goal 1.

Carling Cup (5): Etherington 1, Fuller 1, Griffiin 1, Higginbotham 1, Kitson 1.

FA Cup (10): Fuller 4, Etherington 1, Kitson 1, Shawcross 1, Tuncay 1, Whitehead 1, own goal 1.

Ground: Britannia Stadium, Stanley Matthews Way, Stoke-on-Trent ST4 4EG. Telephone (0871) 663 2008.

Record Attendance: 51,380 v Arsenal, Division 1, 29 March 1937 (at Victoria Ground).

Capacity: 28,383.

Manager: Tony Pulis.

Club Secretary: Eddie Harrison.

Most League Goals: 92, Division 3 (N), 1926–27.

Highest League Scorer in Season: Freddie Steele, 33, Division 1, 1936–37.

Most League Goals in Total Aggregate: Freddie Steele, 142, 1934–49.

Most Capped Player: Gordon Banks, 36 (73), England.

Most League Appearances: Eric Skeels, 506, 1958–76.

Honours – Football League: Division 2 Champions – 1932–33, 1962–63, 1992–93. Division 3 (N) Champions – 1926–27. **Football League Cup:** Winners – 1971–72. **Autoglass Trophy:** Winners – 1992. **Auto Windscreens Shield:** Winners – 2000.

Colours: Red and white striped shirts with red sleeves and shoulders, white shorts, white stockings.

SUNDERLAND   FA PREMIERSHIP

Bagnall Liam (D)	5 11	10 04	Newry	17	5 92	Scholar
Bardsley Phillip (D)	5 11	11 13	Salford	28	6 85	Manchester U
Bent Darren (F)	5 11	12 07	Wandsworth	6	2 84	Tottenham H
Campbell Frazier (F)	5 11	12 04	Huddersfield	13	9 87	Manchester U
Cana Lorik (M)	6 1	12 02	Prishtina	27	7 83	Marseille
Carson Trevor (G)	6 0	14 11	Downpatrick	5	3 88	Scholar
Cattermole Lee (M)	5 10	11 13	Stockton	21	3 88	Wigan Ath
Colback Jack (M)	5 9	11 05	Newcastle	24	10 89	Scholar
Cook Jordan (M)	5 10	10 10	Hetton-le-Hole	20	3 90	Scholar

Player	Ht	Wt	Birthplace	Birthdate	Previous Club
Da Silva Paulo (D)	6 0	13 12	Asuncion	1 2 80	Toluca
Egan John (D)	6 1	11 11	Cork		Scholar
Ferdinand Anton (D)	6 2	11 00	Peckham	18 2 85	West Ham U
Fletcher Matthew (F)	6 0		Sydney		Scholar
Fulop Marton (G)	6 6	14 07	Budapest	3 5 83	Tottenham H
Gordon Craig (G)	6 4	12 02	Edinburgh	31 12 82	Hearts
Healy David (F)	5 8	10 09	Downpatrick	5 8 79	Fulham
Henderson Jordan (M)	6 0	10 07	Sunderland	17 6 90	Scholar
Hourihane Conor (M)	6 0	11 05	Cork	2 2 91	Scholar
Jones Kenwyne (F)	6 2	13 06	Trinidad & Tobago	5 10 84	Southampton
Kay Michael (D)	6 0	11 05	Shotley Bridge	12 9 89	Scholar
Kilgallon Matthew (D)	6 1	12 10	York	8 1 84	Sheffield U
Laing Louis (D)	5 11	12 00			Scholar
Liddle Michael (D)	5 6	11 00	London	25 12 89	Scholar
Luscombe Nathan (M)	5 8	11 09	Gateshead	6 11 89	Scholar
Madden Daniel (D)	5 10	14 02	Sunderland	10 9 90	Scholar
Malbranque Steed (M)	5 7	11 07	Mouscron	6 1 80	Tottenham H
McCartney George (D)	5 11	11 02	Belfast	29 4 81	West Ham U
Meyler David (M)	6 3	13 03	Cork	25 5 89	Cork C
Murphy Daryl (F)	6 2	13 12	Waterford	15 3 83	Waterford
Mvoto Jean-Yves (D)	6 4	14 00	Paris	6 9 88	Paris St Germain
Noble Liam (M)	5 9	10 05	Newcastle	8 5 91	Scholar
Noble Ryan (F)	6 0	11 00	Sunderland	11 6 91	Scholar
Nosworthy Nayron (D)	6 0	12 08	Brixton	11 10 80	Gillingham
Reed Adam (M)	5 5	10 03	Hartlepool	8 5 91	Scholar
Reid Andy (M)	5 9	12 08	Dublin	29 7 82	Charlton Ath
Richardson Kieran (M)	5 9	11 13	Greenwich	21 10 84	Manchester U
Tainio Teemu (M)	5 9	11 09	Tornio	27 11 79	Tottenham H
Tounkara Oumare (M)			France		Sedan
Turner Michael (D)	6 4	13 05	Lewisham	9 11 83	Hull C
Waghorn Martyn (F)	5 9	13 01	South Shields	23 1 90	Scholar
Watson Jordan (M)					Scholar
Weir Robbie (M)	5 9	11 07	Belfast	12 12 88	Scholar
Zenden Boudewijn (M)	5 8	11 01	Maastricht	15 8 76	Marseille

League Appearances: Bardsley, P. 18(8); Bent, D. 38; Campbell, F. 19(12); Cana, L. 29(2); Cattermole, L. 19(3); Colback, J. (1); Collins, D. 3; Da Silva, P. 12(4); Ferdinand, A. 19(5); Fulop, M. 12(1); Gordon, C. 26; Healy, D. (3); Henderson, J. 23(10); Hutton, A. 11; Jones, K. 24(8); Kilgallon, M. 6(1); Leadbitter, G. (1); Malbranque, S. 30(1); McCartney, G. 20(5); Mensah, J. 14(2); Meyler, D. 9(1); Murphy, D. 2(1); Mwaruwari, B. 1(7); Nosworthy, N. 7(3); Reid, A. 18(3); Richardson, K. 28(1); Turner, M. 29; Zenden, B. 1(19).

Goals – League (48): Bent 24 (5 pens), Jones 9 (1 pen), Campbell 4, Reid 2, Turner 2, Zenden 2, Henderson 1, Mensah 1, Richardson 1, own goals 2.

Carling Cup (6): Reid 2, Campbell 1, Henderson 1, Tainio 1, own goal 1.

FA Cup (4): Campbell 2, Bent 1, Malbranque 1.

Ground: Stadium of Light, Sunderland, Tyne and Wear SR5 1SU. Telephone (0871) 911 1200.

Record Attendance: 75,118 v Derby Co, FA Cup 6th rd replay, 8 March 1933 (Roker Park). 48,353 v Liverpool, FA Premier League, 13 April 2002 (Stadium of Light).

Capacity: 49,000.

Manager: Steve Bruce.

Club Secretary: Margaret Byrne.

Most League Goals: 109, Division 1, 1935–36.

Highest League Scorer in Season: Dave Halliday, 43, Division 1, 1928–29.

Most League Goals in Total Aggregate: Charlie Buchan, 209, 1911–25.

Most Capped Player: Charlie Hurley, 38 (40), Republic of Ireland.

Most League Appearances: Jim Montgomery, 537, 1962–77.
Honours – Football League: Championship – Winners – 2004–05, 2006–07. Division 1 Champions – 1891–92, 1892–93, 1894–95, 1901–02, 1912–13, 1935–36, 1995–96, 1998–99. Division 2 Champions – 1975–76. Division 3 Champions – 1987–88. **FA Cup:** Winners – 1937, 1973.
Colours: Red and white striped shirts, black shorts, black stockings with red tops.

SWANSEA CITY   FL CHAMPIONSHIP

Allen Joe (M)	5 6	9 10	Carmarthen	14	3 90	Scholar
Beattie Craig (F)	6 0	11 07	Glasgow	16	1 84	WBA
Bessone Fede (D)	5 11	11 13	Cordoba	23	1 84	Gimnastic
Bodde Ferrie (M)	5 10	12 06	Delft	4	5 82	Den Haag
Bond Chad (F)	6 0	11 00	Neath	20	4 87	Scholar
Britton Leon (M)	5 6	10 00	Merton	16	9 82	West Ham U
Burgin James (D)			Derby	6	9 89	Scholar
Butler Thomas (M)	5 7	12 00	Dublin	25	4 81	Hartlepool U
Collins Matthew (M)	5 9	11 07	Merthyr	31	3 86	Fulham
Cornell David (G)	5 11	11 07	Swansea	28	3 91	Scholar
Cotterill David (M)	5 9	11 02	Cardiff	4	12 87	Sheffield U
De Vries Dorus (G)	6 1	12 08	Beverwijk	29	12 80	Dunfermline Ath
Dobbie Stephen (F)	5 10	11 00	Glasgow	5	12 82	Queen of the S
Dyer Nathan (M)	5 5	9 00	Trowbridge	29	11 87	Southampton
Gower Mark (M)	5 11	11 12	Edmonton	5	10 78	Southend U
Grimes Jamie (M)	6 2	12 00	Nottingham	22	12 90	Scholar
Kuqi Shefki (F)	6 2	13 13	Vushtrri	10	11 76	Koblenz
Lopez Jordi (M)	6 0	12 02	Barcelona	28	2 81	QPR
MacDonald Shaun (M)	6 1	11 04	Swansea	17	6 88	Scholar
Monk Garry (D)	6 1	13 00	Bedford	6	3 79	Barnsley
Morgan Kerry (M)	5 10	11 03	Merthyr	31	10 88	Scholar
Orlandi Andrea (M)	6 0	12 01	Barcelona	3	8 84	Alaves
Pintado Gorka (F)	5 11	11 11	San Sebastian	24	3 78	Grenada
Pratley Darren (M)	6 1	11 00	Barking	22	4 85	Fulham
Rangel Angel (D)	5 11	11 09	Tortosa	28	10 82	Terrassa
Richards Jazz (M)	6 1	12 04	Swansea	12	4 91	Scholar
Serran Albert (D)	6 0	12 10	Barcelona	17	7 84	Espanyol
Tate Alan (D)	6 1	13 05	Easington	2	9 82	Manchester U
Thomas Casey (M)	5 9	10 09	Port Talbot	14	11 90	Scholar
Van der Gun Cedric (M)	5 9	11 00	Den Haag	5	7 79	Utrecht
Williams Ashley (D)	6 0	11 02	Wolverhampton	23	8 84	Stockport Co

League Appearances: Allen, J. 13(8); Bauza, G. 3(3); Beattie, C. 12(11); Bessone, F. 21; Bodde, F. 2(2); Bond, C. 1; Britton, L. 35(1); Butler, T. 9(16); Collins, M. 1; Cotterill, D. 14(7); De Vries, D. 46; Dobbie, S. 4(2); Dyer, N. 37(3); Edgar, D. 5; Gower, M. 25(6); Idrizaj, B. 1(3); Kuqi, S. 14(6); Lopez, J. 7(5); Macdonald, S. 2(1); Monk, G. 22(1); Morgan, K. 1(2); Orlandi, A. 22(8); Painter, M. 4; Pintado, G. 16(16); Pratley, D. 33(3); Rangel, A. 37(1); Richards, J. 10(5); Serran, A. 3(3); Tate, A. 39; Thomas, C. (1); Trundle, L. 2(17); Van der Gun, C. 20(5); Williams, A. 45(1).
Goals – League (40): Pratley 7, Kuqi 5, Trundle 5 (1 pen), Williams 5, Beattie 3, Cotterill 3 (1 pen), Dyer 2, Pintado 2, Van der Gun 2, Bessone 1, Butler 1, Edgar 1, Gower 1, Orlandi 1, Tate 1.
Carling Cup (4): Dobbie 3, Monk 1.
FA Cup (1): Cotterill 1.
Ground: Liberty Stadium, Morfa, Landore, Swansea SA1 2FA. Telephone (01792) 616 600.
Record Attendance: 32,796 v Arsenal, FA Cup 4th rd, 17 February 1968 (at Vetch Field). **Capacity:** 20,520.

Manager: TBC.
Secretary: Jackie Rockey.
Most League Goals: 90, Division 2, 1956–57.
Highest League Scorer in Season: Cyril Pearce, 35, Division 2, 1931–32.
Most League Goals in Total Aggregate: Ivor Allchurch, 166, 1949–58, 1965–68.
Most Capped Player: Ivor Allchurch, 42 (68), Wales.
Most League Appearances: Wilfred Milne, 585, 1919–37.
Honours – Football League: Championship 1 – Winners – 2007–08, Division 3 Champions – 1999–2000. Division 3 (S) Champions – 1924–25, 1948–49. **Autoglass Trophy:** Winners – 1994, 2006. **Football League Trophy:** Winners – 2006. **Welsh Cup:** Winners – 11 times.
Colours: All white.

SWINDON TOWN   FL CHAMPIONSHIP 1

Amankwaah Kevin (D)	6 1	12 12	Harrow	19	5 82	Swansea C
Austin Charlie (F)	6 2	13 03	Hungerford	5	7 89	Poole T
Cuthbert Scott (D)	6 2	14 00	Alexandria	15	6 87	Celtic
Douglas Jonathan (M)	5 11	11 11	Monaghan	22 11 81		Leeds U
Easton Craig (M)	5 11	11 03	Bellshill	26	2 79	Leyton Orient
Ferry Simon (M)	5 9	11 00	Dundee	11	1 88	Celtic
Greer Gordon (D)	6 2	12 05	Glasgow	14 12 80		Doncaster R
Jesionkowski Jakub (G)	6 3	13 01	Poznan	7	3 89	Zaglebie
Kennedy Callum (M)	6 1	12 10	Cheltenham	6	1 89	Scholar
Lescinel Jean-Francois (M)	6 2	12 04	Cayenne	2 10 86		Guingamp
Lucas David (G)	6 1	13 07	Preston	23 11 77		Leeds U
McGovern John-Paul (M)	5 10	12 02	Glasgow	3 10 80		Milton Keynes D
Morrison Sean (D)	6 4	14 00	Plymouth	8	1 91	Plymouth Arg
O'Brien Alan (M)	5 10	10 10	Dublin	20	2 85	Hibernian
Paynter Billy (F)	6 1	14 01	Liverpool	13	7 84	Southend U
Pericard Vincent de Paul (F)	6 1	13 08	Efok	3 10 82		Carlisle U
Scott Mark (M)	5 9	12 04	Cheltenham	14	3 86	
Smith Phil (G)	6 0	15 02	Harrow	14 12 79		Crawley T
Timlin Michael (M)	5 8	11 08	Lambeth	19	3 85	Fulham

League Appearances: Amankwaah, K. 33(3); Austin, C. 29(4); Cuthbert, S. 39; Darby, S. 12; Douglas, J. 43; Easton, C. 2(10); Ferry, S. 40; Greer, G. 43(1); Hutchinson, B. 6(4); Kennedy, C. 4(4); Lescinel, J. 27(6); Lucas, D. 41; Macklin, L. 1(8); Marshall, M. 1(6); McGovern, J. 45; McNamee, A. 14(3); Morrison, S. 8(1); Nouble, F. 3(5); O'Brien, A. 3(6); Obadeyi, T. 9(3); Paynter, B. 37(5); Peacock, L. (4); Pericard, V. 2(12); Revell, A. 7(3); Ritchie, M. (4); Sheehan, A. 22; Smith, P. 5(1); Timlin, M. 6(15); Ward, D. 24(4).
Goals – League (73): Paynter 26 (8 pens), Austin 19, Ward 7, Amankwaah 3, Cuthbert 3, Ferry 2, Obadeyi 2, Revell 2, Greer 1, Hutchinson 1, McGovern 1, McNamee 1, Morrison 1, Sheehan 1, own goals 3.
Carling Cup (4): Paynter 2, McGovern 1, own goal 1.
FA Cup (2): Greer 1, Paynter 1.
J Paint Trophy (1): McNamee 1.
Play-Offs (3): Ward 2, Austin 1.
Ground: The County Ground, County Road, Swindon, Wiltshire SN1 2ED. Telephone (0871) 423 6433.
Record Attendance: 32,000 v Arsenal, FA Cup 3rd rd, 15 January 1972. **Capacity:** 14,700.
Manager: Danny Wilson.
Secretary: Louise Fletcher.
Most League Goals: 100, Division 3 (S), 1926–27.
Highest League Scorer in Season: Harry Morris, 47, Division 3 (S), 1926–27.

Most League Goals in Total Aggregate: Harry Morris, 216, 1926–33.
Most Capped Player: Rod Thomas, 30 (50), Wales.
Most League Appearances: John Trollope, 770, 1960–80.
Honours – Football League: Division 2 Champions – 1995–96. Division 4 Champions – 1985–86. Football League Cup: Winners – 1968–69, 2007–08. Anglo-Italian Cup: Winners – 1970.
Colours: Red shirts with white inserts, red shorts with white inserts, red stockings with white inserts.

TORQUAY UNITED   FL CHAMPIONSHIP 2

Benyon Elliot (F)	5 9	10 01	High Wycombe	29	8 87	Bristol C
Bevan Scott (G)	6 6	15 04	Southampton	19	9 79	Shrewsbury T
Carayol Mustapha (M)	5 9	11 11	Banjul	10	6 89	Milton Keynes D
Carlisle Wayne (M)	5 7	11 00	Lisburn	9	9 79	Exeter C
Charnock Kieran (D)	6 1	13 07	Preston	3	8 84	Peterborough U
Ellis Mark (D)	6 2	12 04	Plymouth	30	9 88	Bolton W
Green Matthew (F)	5 8	10 05	Bath	13	5 87	Cardiff C
Mansell Lee (M)	5 9	10 10	Gloucester	23	9 82	Oxford U
Nicholson Kevin (M)	5 8	11 05	Derby	2	10 80	Forest Green R
Robertson Chris (D)	6 3	11 09	Dundee	11	10 86	Sheffield U
Rowe-Turner Lathaniel (D)	6 1	13 00	Leicester	12	11 89	Leicester C
Stevens Danny (F)	5 10	11 07	Enfield	26	11 86	Luton T
Wroe Nicky (M)	5 11	10 01	Sheffield	28	9 85	York C
Zebroski Chris (F)	6 1	11 07	Swindon	29	10 86	Wycombe W

League Appearances: Barnes, A. 6; Benyon, E. 31(14); Bevan, S. 17(1); Branston, G. 16; Brough, M. 1(1); Camara, M. 2; Carayol, M. 11(9); Carlisle, W. 20(4); Charnock, K. 22(2); Collis, S. 1; Cox, S. 1(2); Ellis, M. 25(2); Hargreaves, C. 21(2); Hodges, L. 2(3); Macklin, L. 3(1); Mansell, L. 35(4); Mills, D. 2(2); Nicholson, K. 23(4); O'Kane, E. 5(11); Poke, M. 28(1); Rendell, S. 28(7); Robertson, C. 45; Rowe-Turner, L. 5(1); Sills, T. 12(6); Smith, A. 16; Stevens, D. 16(11); Thompson, T. 17(7); Thomson, J. 13(2); Todd, C. 9; Williams, M. 1(3); Wroe, N. 45; Zebroski, C. 30.
Goals – League (64): Rendell 12, Benyon 11, Wroe 9 (6 pens), Carayol 6, Zebroski 6, Ellis 3, Hargreaves 3, Carlisle 2, Mansell 2, Robertson 2, Sills 2, O'Kane 1, Stevens 1, Thomson 1, Todd 1, own goals 2.
Carling Cup (1): Sills 1.
FA Cup (7): Benyon 3, Wroe 3 (2 pens), Rendell 1.
J Paint Trophy (5): Stevens 2, Benyon 1, Sills 1, Wroe 1 (pen).
Ground: Plainmoor Ground, Torquay, Devon TQ1 3PS. Telephone (01803) 328 666.
Record Attendance: 21,908 v Huddersfield T, FA Cup 4th rd, 29 January 1955.
Capacity: 6,117.
Manager: Paul Buckle.
Secretary: Ann Sandford.
Most League Goals: 89, Division 3 (S), 1956–57.
Highest League Scorer in Season: Sammy Collins, 40, Division 3 (S), 1955–56.
Most League Goals in Total Aggregate: Sammy Collins, 204, 1948–58.
Most Capped Player: Tony Bedeau, 4, Grenada.
Most League Appearances: Dennis Lewis, 443, 1947–59.
Honours – None.
Colours: All yelow with blue inserts.

TOTTENHAM HOTSPUR   FA PREMIERSHIP

Alnwick Ben (G)	6 0	12 09	Prudhoe	1	1 87	Sunderland
Assou-Ekotto Benoit (D)	5 10	11 00	Douala	24	3 84	Lens

Name	Ht	Born	Birthplace	Previous Club
Bale Gareth (D)	6 0	11 10	Cardiff	16 7 89 Southampton
Bassong Sebastien (D)	6 2	11 07	Paris	9 7 86 Newcastle U
Bentley David (F)	5 10	11 03	Peterborough	27 8 84 Blackburn R
Blackwood Anton (D)			Edmonton	18 8 91 Arsenal
Bostock John (M)	5 10	11 11	Romford	13 10 91 Crystal Palace
Butcher Callum (D)			Rochford	26 2 91 Scholar
Button David (G)	6 3	13 00	Stevenage	27 2 89 Scholar
Caulker Steven (D)	6 3	12 00	Feltham	29 12 91 Scholar
Corluka Vedran (D)	6 3	13 03	Zagreb	9 2 86 Manchester C
Crouch Peter (F)	6 7	13 03	Macclesfield	30 1 81 Portsmouth
Cudicini Carlo (G)	6 1	12 08	Milan	6 9 73 Chelsea
Dawson Michael (D)	6 2	12 02	Northallerton	18 11 83 Nottingham F
Defoe Jermain (F)	5 7	10 04	Beckton	7 10 82 Portsmouth
Dervite Dorian (D)	6 3	13 06	Lille	25 7 88 Lille
Giovani (F)	5 8	12 03	Monterrey	11 5 89 Barcelona
Gomes Heurelho (G)	6 3	12 13	Joao Pinheiro	15 2 81 PSV Eindhoven
Huddlestone Tom (M)	6 2	11 02	Nottingham	28 12 86 Derby Co
Hutton Alan (D)	6 1	11 05	Glasgow	30 11 84 Rangers
Jansson Oscar (G)	6 0	12 13	Orebro	23 12 90 Karlslund
Jenas Jermaine (M)	5 11	11 00	Nottingham	18 2 83 Newcastle U
Kaboul Younes (D)	6 2	13 07	St-Julien-en-Genevois	4 1 86 Portsmouth
Keane Robbie (F)	5 9	12 06	Dublin	8 7 80 Leeds U
King Ledley (D)	6 2	14 05	Bow	12 10 80 Trainee
Kranjcar Niko (M)	6 1	12 13	Zagreb	13 8 84 Portsmouth
Lennon Aaron (M)	5 6	10 03	Leeds	16 4 87 Leeds U
Livermore Jake (M)			Enfield	14 11 89 Scholar
Mason Ryan (M)	5 9	10 00	Enfield	13 6 91 Scholar
Modric Luka (M)	5 8	10 03	Zadar	9 9 85 Dinamo Zagreb
Mpuku Paul-Jose (M)			Kinshasa	19 4 92 Scholar
Naughton Kyle (D)	5 11	11 07	Sheffield	11 11 88 Sheffield U
O'Hara Jamie (M)	5 11	12 04	Dartford	25 9 86 Scholar
Obika Jonathan (F)	6 0	12 00	Enfield	12 9 90 Scholar
Palacios Wilson (D)	5 10	11 11	La Ceiba	29 7 84 Wigan Ath
Parrett Dean (M)	5 10	11 04	Hampstead	16 11 91 Scholar
Pavlyuchenko Roman (F)	6 2	12 04	Mostovskoy	15 12 81 Spartak Moscow
Ranieri Mirko (G)			Italy	8 2 92 Perugia
Rose Danny (M)	5 8	11 11	Doncaster	2 7 90 Scholar
Smith Adam (D)	5 8	10 05	Leytonstone	29 4 91 Scholar
Taarabt Adel (M)	5 9	10 12	Berre-l'Etang	24 5 89 Lens
Townsend Andros (M)	6 0	12 00	Whipps Cross	16 7 91 Scholar
Walker Kyle (D)	5 10	11 07	Sheffield	28 5 90 Sheffield U
Woodgate Jonathan (D)	6 2	12 06	Middlesbrough	22 1 80 Middlesbrough

League Appearances: Alnwick, B. 1; Assou-Ekotto, B. 29(1); Bale, G. 18(5); Bassong, S. 25(3); Bentley, D. 11(4); Corluka, V. 29; Crouch, P. 21(17); Cudicini, C. 6(1); Dawson, M. 25(4); Defoe, J. 31(3); Giovani, (1); Gomes, H. 31; Gudjohnsen, E. 3(8); Huddlestone, T. 33; Hutton, A. 1(7); Jenas, J. 9(10); Kaboul, Y. 8(2); Keane, R. 15(5); King, L. 19(1); Kranjcar, N. 19(5); Lennon, A. 20(2); Livermore, J. (1); Modric, L. 21(4); Naughton, K. (1); O'Hara, J. (2); Palacios, W. 29(4); Pavlyuchenko, R. 8(8); Rose, D. 1; Walker, K. 2; Woodgate, J. 3.

Goals – League (67): Defoe 18 (1 pen), Crouch 8, Keane 6 (1 pen), Kranjcar 6, Pavlyuchenko 5, Bale 3, Lennon 3, Modric 3, Bentley 2, Dawson 2, Huddlestone 2, King 2, Assou-Ekotto 1, Bassong 1, Corluka 1, Gudjohnsen 1, Jenas 1, Palacios 1, Rose 1.

Carling Cup (12): Crouch 4, Huddlestone 2, Keane 2, Bentley 1, Defoe 1, O'Hara 1, Pavlyuchenko 1.

FA Cup (17): Defoe 5, Pavlyuchenko 4, Kranjcar 2, Bentley 1, Crouch 1, Gudjohnsen 1, Keane 1 (pen), own goals 2.
Ground: White Hart Lane, Bill Nicholson Way, 748 High Road, Tottenham, London N17 0AP. Telephone (0844) 499 5000.
Record Attendance: 75,038 v Sunderland, FA Cup 6th rd, 5 March 1938.
Capacity: 36,534.
Manager: Harry Redknapp.
Secretary: Darren Eales.
Most League Goals: 115, Division 1, 1960–61.
Highest League Scorer in Season: Jimmy Greaves, 37, Division 1, 1962–63.
Most League Goals in Total Aggregate: Jimmy Greaves, 220, 1961–70.
Most Capped Player: Pat Jennings, 74 (119), Northern Ireland.
Most League Appearances: Steve Perryman, 655, 1969–86.
Honours – Football League: Division 1 Champions – 1950–51, 1960–61. Division 2 Champions – 1919–20, 1949–50. **FA Cup:** Winners – 1901 (as non-League club), 1921, 1961, 1962, 1967, 1981, 1982, 1991. **Football League Cup:** Winners – 1970–71, 1972–73, 1998–99, 2007–08. **European Competitions: European Cup-Winners' Cup:** Winners – 1962–63. **UEFA Cup:** Winners – 1971–72, 1983–84.
Colours: White shirts with black and yellow trim, black shorts, white stockings.

TRANMERE ROVERS   FL CHAMPIONSHIP 1

Bakayogo Zaoumana (D)	5 9	10 08	Paris	11	8 86	Millwall
Broomes Marlon (D)	6 0	12 12	Birmingham	28 11 77		Blackpool
Collister Joe (G)	6 0	13 10	Wirral	15 12 91		Schoalr
Cresswell Aaron (D)	5 7	10 05	Liverpool	15 12 89		Scholar
Curran Craig (F)	5 11	11 11	Liverpool	23	8 89	Scholar
Fraughan Ryan (M)	5 7	11 02	Liverpool	11	2 91	Scholar
Goodison Ian (D)	6 1	12 06	St James, Jam	21 11 72		Seba U
Gornell Terry (F)	5 11	12 04	Liverpool	16 12 89		Scholar
Mahon Alan (M)	5 8	12 03	Dublin	4	4 78	Burnley
McLaren Paul (M)	6 0	13 04	High Wycombe	17 11 76		Bradford C
Taylor Ash (M)	6 0	12 00	Chester	2	9 89	Scholar
Thomas-Moore Ian (F)	5 11	12 00	Birkenhead	26	8 76	Hartlepool U
Welsh John (M)	5 7	12 02	Liverpool	10	1 84	Hull C

League Appearances: Bain, K. (10); Bakayogo, Z. 29; Barnett, C. 1(6); Broomes, M. 31; Carole, S. 4; Collister, J. 1(2); Cresswell, A. 13(1); Curran, C. 38(5); Daniels, L. 37; Edds, G. 24(11); Fraughan, R. 1(5); Goodison, I. 44; Gordon, B. 4; Gornell, T. 18(9); Gulacsi, P. 5; Gunning, G. 6; Labadie, J. 5(4); Logan, S. 32(1); Mahon, A. 8(8); Martin, D. 3; McCready, C. 8; McLaren, P. 36(2); O'Neill, L. 4; Ricketts, M. 7(5); Robinson, A. 3(2); Savage, B. 10(3); Shuker, C. 16(10); Sordell, M. 6(2); Taylor, A. 27(6); Thomas-Moore, I. 41(2); Welsh, J. 44(1).
Goals – League (45): Thomas-Moore 13 (4 pens), Curran 5, Welsh 4, Edds 3, Goodison 3, Labadie 3, Gornell 2, Ricketts 2, Shuker 2, Barnett 1, Broomes 1, Mahon 1, Robinson 1, Sordell 1, Taylor 1, own goals 2.
Carling Cup (4): Curran 1, Edds 1, McLaren 1, Thomas-Moore 1 (pen).
FA Cup (4): Gornell 1, Shuker 1, Taylor 1, Thomas-Moore 1.
J Paint Trophy (1): Curran 1.
Ground: Prenton Park, Prenton Road West, Birkenhead, Merseyside CH42 9PY. Telephone (0871) 221 2001.
Record Attendance: 24,424 v Stoke C, FA Cup 4th rd, 5 February 1972.
Capacity: 16,587.
Manager: Les Parry.
Chief Executive/Secretary: Mick Horton.
Most League Goals: 111, Division 3 (N), 1930–31.

Highest League Scorer in Season: Bunny Bell, 35, Division 3 (N), 1933–34.
Most League Goals in Total Aggregate: Ian Muir, 142, 1985–95.
Most Capped Player: John Aldridge, 30 (69), Republic of Ireland.
Most League Appearances: Harold Bell, 595, 1946–64 (incl. League record 401 consecutive appearances).
Honours – Football League: Division 3 (N) Champions – 1937–38. **Welsh Cup:** Winners – 1935. **Leyland Daf Cup:** Winners – 1990.
Colours: White shirts, white shorts, blue and white hooped stockings.

WALSALL   FL CHAMPIONSHIP 1

Byfield Darren (F)	5 11 12 07	Sutton Coldfield	29 9 76	Oldham Ath
Deeney Troy (F)	5 11 12 00	Birmingham	29 6 88	Chelmsley T
Geddes Sean (M)	5 6 10 02	West Bromwich	13 2 92	Scholar
Gilmartin Rene (G)	6 5 13 06	Islington	31 5 87	St Patrick's BC
Grigg Will (M)	5 11 11 00	Solihull	3 7 91	Stratford T
Hughes Mark (D)	6 1 13 03	Liverpool	9 12 86	Northampton T
Jones Steve (F)	5 10 10 05	Derry	25 10 76	Burnley
McDonald Clayton (D)	6 6 11 00	Liverpool	26 12 88	Manchester C
Nicholls Alex (F)	5 10 11 00	Stourbridge	19 12 87	Scholar
Richards Matt (D)	5 8 11 00	Harlow	26 12 84	Ipswich T
Smith Manny (D)	6 2 12 03	Birmingham	8 11 88	Scholar
Taundry Richard (D)	5 9 12 10	Walsall	15 2 89	Scholar
Vincent Jamie (D)	5 10 11 08	Wimbledon	18 6 75	Swindon T
Westlake Darryl (D)	5 9 11 00	Sutton Coldfield	1 3 91	Scholar

League Appearances: Adkins, S. (1); Bradley, M. 19(9); Byfield, D. 31(6); Deeney, T. 42; Gilmartin, R. 22; Gray, J. 17(1); Hughes, M. 24(2); Ince, C. 24(1); Jones, S. 25(5); Mattis, D. 34; McDonald, C. 24(2); Nicholls, A. 20(17); O'Keefe, J. 8(5); Parkin, S. 7(17); Richards, M. 39(1); Roberts, S. 1; Sansara, N. 17; Smith, M. 30(3); Taundry, R. 24(6); Till, P. 18(10); Vincent, J. 37(1); Westlake, D. 20(2); Weston, R. 23(4).
Goals – League (60): Deeney 14, Byfield 10 (1 pen), Jones 9, Gray 4, Nicholls 4, Richards 4, Smith 4, Parkin 3 (2 pens), Taundry 3, Mattis 2, Hughes M 1, McDonald 1, own goal 1.
Carling Cup (1): Nicholls 1.
FA Cup (1): Jones 1.
J Paint Trophy (0).
Ground: Banks's Stadium, Bescot Crescent, Walsall WS1 4SA. Telephone (01922) 622 791.
Record Attendance: 11,037 v Wolverhampton W, Division 1, 11 January 2003. **Capacity:** 11,300.
Manager: Chris Hutchings.
Secretary: Roy Whalley.
Most League Goals: 102, Division 4, 1959–60.
Highest League Scorer in Season: Gilbert Alsop, 40, Division 3 (N), 1933–34 and 1934–35.
Most League Goals in Total Aggregate: Tony Richards, 184, 1954–63; Colin Taylor, 184, 1958–63, 1964–68, 1969–73.
Most Capped Player: Mick Kearns, 15 (18), Republic of Ireland.
Most League Appearances: Colin Harrison, 467, 1964–82.
Honours – Football League: FL 2 Champions – 2006–07. Division 4 Champions – 1959–60.
Colours: Red shirts with black trim, red shorts, red stockings with black tops.

Bennett Dale (D)				6 1 90	Scholar
Bryan Michael (M)	5 8	10 00	Wexford	21 2 90	Scholar
Buckley Will (F)	6 0	13 00	Burnley	12 8 88	Rochdale
Cowie Don (M)	5 5	8 05	Inverness	15 2 83	Inverness CT
Doyley Lloyd (D)	5 10	12 05	Whitechapel	1 12 82	Scholar
Ellington Nathan (F)	5 10	13 01	Bradford	2 7 81	WBA
Eustace John (M)	5 11	11 12	Solihull	3 11 79	Stoke C
Graham Danny (F)	5 11	12 05	Gateshead	12 8 85	Carlisle U
Henderson Liam (F)	5 11	12 02	Gateshead	28 12 89	Hartlepool U
Hodson Lee (D)			Watford	2 10 91	Scholar
Jenkins Ross (M)	5 11	12 06	Watford	9 11 90	Scholar
Kiernan Robert (D)	6 1	11 13	Watford	13 1 91	Scholar
Lee Richard (G)	6 0	13 03	Oxford	5 10 82	Scholar
Loach Scott (G)	6 1	13 01	Nottingham	27 5 88	Lincoln C
Mariappa Adrian (D)	5 10	11 12	Harrow	3 10 86	Scholar
Massey Gavin (F)			Watford	14 10 92	Scholar
McGinn Stephen (M)	5 9	10 00	Glasgow	2 12 88	St Mirren
Oshodi Eddie (D)	6 3	12 07	Brentford	14 1 92	Scholar
Parkes Jordan (D)	6 0	12 00	Watford	26 7 89	Scholar
Sadler Matthew (D)	5 11	11 08	Birmingham	26 2 85	Birmingham C
Severin Scott (D)	5 11	12 13	Stirling	15 2 79	Aberdeen
Sordell Marvin (F)	5 9	12 06	Brent	17 2 91	Scholar
Taylor Martin (D)	6 4	15 00	Ashington	9 11 79	Birmingham C
Travner Jure (D)	5 11	12 08	Celje	28 9 85	Celje

League Appearances: Bennett, D. 8(2); Bryan, M. 1(6); Buckley, W. 4(2); Cathcart, C. 12; Cleverley, T. 33; Cowie, D. 40(1); DeMerit, J. 25(2); Doyley, L. 43(1); Ellington, N. 2(15); Eustace, J. 39(3); Graham, D. 37(9); Harley, J. 20(18); Helguson, H. 26(3); Henderson, L. (13); Hodson, L. 29(2); Hoskins, W. 5(13); Jenkins, R. 21(3); Lansbury, H. 34(3); Loach, S. 46; Mariappa, A. 46; Massey, G. (1); McAnuff, J. 3; McGinn, S. 2(7); Oshodi, Eddie (1); Severin, S. 4(5); Smith, T. 4; Sordell, M. 1(5); Taylor, M. 17(2); Williamson, M. 4.

Goals – League (61): Graham 14 (1 pen), Cleveriey 11, Helguson 11 (1 pen), Lansbury 5, Eustace 4, Hoskins 3, Cowie 2, Smith 2, Taylor 2, Buckley 1, Doyley 1, Ellington 1, Harley 1, Mariappa 1, Sordell 1, Williamson 1.

Carling Cup (3): Severin 1, Sordell 1, Williamson M 1.

FA Cup (0).

Ground: Vicarage Road Stadium, Vicarage Road, Watford, Hertfordshire WD18 0ER. Telephone 0844 856 1881.

Record Attendance: 34,099 v Manchester U, FA Cup 4th rd (replay), 3 February 1969.

Capacity: 19,920.

Manager: Malky Mackay.

Secretary: Michelle Ives.

Most League Goals: 92, Division 4, 1959–60.

Highest League Scorer in Season: Cliff Holton, 42, Division 4, 1959–60.

Most League Goals in Total Aggregate: Luther Blissett, 148, 1976–83, 1984–88, 1991–92.

Most Capped Player: John Barnes, 31 (79), England and Kenny Jackett, 31, Wales.

Most League Appearances: Luther Blissett, 415, 1976–83, 1984–88, 1991–92.

Honours – Football League: Division 2 Champions – 1997–98. Division 3 Champions – 1968–69. Division 4 Champions – 1977–78.

Colours: Yellow shirts with red and black trim, black shorts, yellow stockings.

Barnes Giles (M)	6 0	12 10	Barking	5 8 88	Derby Co
Barnett Leon (D)	6 0	12 04	Stevenage	30 11 85	Luton T
Bednar Roman (F)	6 3	13 03	Prague	26 3 83	Hearts
Borja Valero (M)	5 9	11 07	Madrid	12 1 85	Mallorca
Brunt Chris (M)	6 1	13 04	Belfast	14 12 84	Sheffield W
Carson Scott (G)	6 3	14 00	Whitehaven	3 9 85	Liverpool
Cech Marek (D)	6 0	11 09	Trebisov	26 1 83	Porto
Cox Simon (F)	5 10	10 12	Reading	28 4 87	Swindon T
Daniels Luke (G)	6 1	12 10	Bolton	5 1 88	Manchester U
Dorrans Graham (F)	5 9	11 07	Glasgow	5 5 87	Livingston
Elford-Alliyu Lateef (F)	5 8	11 00	Ibadan	1 6 92	Hereford U
Greening Jonathan (M)	5 11	11 00	Scarborough	2 1 79	Middlesbrough
Haber Marcus (F)	6 3	13 05	Vancouver	11 1 89	Vancouver W
Jara Gonzalo (D)	5 10	12 02	Santiago	29 8 85	Colo Colo
Kiely Dean (G)	6 1	12 05	Salford	10 10 70	Portsmouth
Mattock Joe (D)	5 11	12 05	Leicester	15 5 90	Leicester C
Meite Abdoulaye (D)	6 1	12 13	Paris	6 10 80	Bolton W
Miller Ishmael (F)	6 3	14 00	Manchester	5 3 87	Manchester C
Moore Luke (F)	5 11	11 13	Birmingham	13 2 86	Aston Villa
Morrison James (M)	5 10	10 06	Darlington	25 5 86	Middlesbrough
Mulumbu Youssef (M)	5 9	10 03	Kinshasa	25 1 87	Paris St Germain
Olsson Jonas (D)	6 4	12 08	Landskrona	10 3 83	NEC Nijmegen
Reid Reuben (F)	6 0	12 02	Bristol	26 7 88	Rotherham U
Sawyers Romaine (M)	5 9	11 00	Birmingham	11 10 90	Scholar
Tamas Gabriel (D)	6 2	12 02	Brasov	9 11 83	Dinamo Bucharest
Thomas Jerome (M)	5 9	11 09	Wembley	23 3 83	Portsmouth
Thorne George (M)	6 2	13 01	Chatham	4 1 93	Scholar
Wood Chris (F)	6 3	12 10	Auckland	7 12 91	Waikato
Zuiverloon Gianni (D)	5 10	11 00	Rotterdam	30 12 86	Heerenveen

League Appearances: Barnes, G. 1(8); Barnett, L. (2); Beattie, C. (3); Bednar, R. 21(6); Borja Valero, (1); Brunt, C. 39(1); Carson, S. 43; Cech, M. 29(4); Cox, S. 17(11); Cummings, S. 3; Dorrans, G. 42(3); Greening, J. 2; Jara, G. 20(2); Kiely, D. 3(2); Koren, R. 26(8); Martis, S. 10(3); Mattock, J. 26(3); Meite, A. 16(4); Miller, I. 4(11); Moore, L. 23(3); Morrison, J. 5(6); Mulumbu, Y. 35(5); Nouble, F. 3; Olsson, J. 43; Reid, R. (4); Reid, S. 10; Slory, A. 1(5); Tamas, G. 23; Teixeira, F. 1(8); Thomas, J. 22(5); Thorne, G. (1); Watson, B. 6(1); Wood, C. 6(12); Zuiverloon, G. 26(4).

Goals – League (89): Brunt 13, Dorrans 13 (6 pens), Bednar 11, Cox 9, Thomas 7, Koren 5, Moore 4, Olsson 4, Zuiverloon 4, Mulumbu 3, Cech 2, Martis 2, Miller 2, Tamas 2, Jara 1, Morrison 1, Reid S 1, Watson 1, Wood 1, own goals 3.

Carling Cup (6): Beattie 2, Dorrans 2, Cox 1, own goal 1.

FA Cup (10): Dorrans 3 (2 pens), Koren 3, Mattock 1, Olsson 1, Thomas 1, Wood 1.

Ground: The Hawthorns, West Bromwich, West Midlands B71 4LF. Telephone (0871) 271 1100.

Record Attendance: 64,815 v Arsenal, FA Cup 6th rd, 6 March 1937. **Capacity:** 28,003.

Head Coach: Roberto Di Matteo.

Legal Counsel/Secretary: Richard Garlick.

Most League Goals: 105, Division 2, 1929–30.

Highest League Scorer in Season: William 'Ginger' Richardson, 39, Division 1, 1935–36.

Most League Goals in Total Aggregate: Tony Brown, 218, 1963–79.

Most Capped Player: Stuart Williams, 33 (43), Wales.

Most League Appearances: Tony Brown, 574, 1963–80.

Honours – Football League: Division 1 Champions – 1919–20. Championship winners – 2007–08. Division 2 Champions – 1901–02, 1910–11. **FA Cup:** Winners – 1888, 1892, 1931, 1954, 1968. **Football League Cup:** Winners – 1965–66.
Colours: Navy blue and white striped shirts, white shorts, white stockings.

WEST HAM UNITED   FA PREMIERSHIP

Abdullah Ahmed (F)		Saudi Arabia	12 11 91	Scholar
Behrami Valon (M)	6 0 11 02	Kosovka Mitrovika	19 4 85	Lazio
Boa Morte Luis (F)	5 9 12 06	Lisbon	4 8 77	Fulham
Cole Carlton (F)	6 3 14 02	Croydon	12 11 83	Chelsea
Collison Jack (M)	6 0 13 10	Watford	2 10 88	Scholar
Da Costa Manuel (D)	6 1 12 12	Saint-Max	6 5 86	Sampdoria
Daprela Fabio (D)	5 11 10 03	Ticino	19 2 91	Grasshoppers
Diamanti Alessandro (F)	5 9 11 09	Prato	2 5 83	Livorno
Dyer Kieron (M)	5 8 10 01	Ipswich	29 12 78	Newcastle U
Edgar Anthony (M)	5 8 11 00	London	30 9 90	Scholar
Eyjolfsson Holmar (D)	6 2 11 08	Iceland	6 8 90	
Faubert Julien (M)	5 10 11 08	Le Havre	1 8 83	Bordeaux
Fry Matt (D)	6 1 12 02	Ebbsfleet	26 9 90	Scholar
Gabbidon Daniel (D)	6 0 13 05	Cwmbran	8 8 79	Cardiff C
Green Robert (G)	6 3 14 09	Chertsey	18 1 80	Norwich C
Hines Zavon (F)	5 10 10 07	Jamaica	27 12 88	Scholar
Ilunga Herita (D)	5 11 11 09	Kinshasa	25 2 82	Toulouse
Kovac Radoslav (D)	6 2 12 04	Sumperk	27 11 79	Spartak Moscow
Kurucz Peter (G)	6 2 13 09	Budapest	30 5 88	Ujpest
McCarthy Benni (F)	6 0 12 08	Ciudad de Cabo	11 12 77	Blackburn R
Modelski Filip (D)		Poland	28 9 92	Scholar
Noble Mark (M)	5 11 12 00	West Ham	8 5 87	Scholar
Nouble Frank (F)	6 3 12 08	Marseille	24 9 91	Chelsea
Parker Scott (M)	5 9 11 10	Lambeth	13 10 80	Newcastle U
Sears Freddie (F)	5 8 10 01	Hornchurch	27 11 89	Scholar
Spector Jonathan (D)	6 0 12 08	Arlington	1 3 86	Manchester U
Spence Jordan (M)	5 11 11 13	Woodford	24 5 90	Scholar
Stanislas Junior (M)	6 0 12 00	Kidbrooke	26 11 89	Scholar
Stech Marek (G)	6 3 14 00	Prague	28 1 90	Scholar
Street Adam (G)		Canada	7 7 91	Scholar
Tomkins James (D)	6 3 11 10	Basildon	29 3 89	Scholar
Upson Matthew (D)	6 1 11 04	Stowmarket	18 4 79	Birmingham C

League Appearances: Behrami, V. 24(3); Boa Morte, L. 1; Cole, C. 26(4); Collins, J. 3; Collison, J. 19(3); Da Costa, M. 12(3); Daprela, F. 4(3); Diamanti, A. 18(9); Dyer, K. 4(6); Faubert, J. 32(1); Franco, G. 16(7); Gabbidon, D. 8(2); Green, R. 38; Hines, Z. 5(8); Ilan, 6(5); Ilunga, H. 16; Jimenez, L. 6(5); Kovac, R. 27(4); Kurucz, P. (1); McCarthy, B. 2(3); Mido, 5(4); Noble, M. 25(2); Nouble, F. 3(5); Parker, S. 30(1); Sears, F. (1); Spector, J. 22(5); Spence, J. (1); Stanislas, J. 11(15); Tomkins, J. 22(1); Upson, M. 33.
Goals – League (47): Cole 10 (1 pen), Diamanti 7 (4 pens), Franco 5, Ilan 4, Stanislas 3, Upson 3, Collison 2, Da Costa 2, Kovac 2, Noble 2 (1 pen), Parker 2, Behrami 1, Boa Morte 1, Faubert 1, Hines 1, Jimenez 1 (1 pen).
Carling Cup (4): Stanislaus 2 (1 pen), Hines 1, Ilunga 1.
FA Cup (1): Diamanti 1.
Ground: The Boleyn Ground, Upton Park, Green Street, London E13 9AZ. Telephone (020) 8548 2748.
Record Attendance: 42,322 v Tottenham H, Division 1, 17 October 1970. **Capacity:** 35,303.
Manager: Avram Grant.
Secretary: Peter Barnes.

Most League Goals: 101, Division 2, 1957–58.
Highest League Scorer in Season: Vic Watson, 42, Division 1, 1929–30.
Most League Goals in Total Aggregate: Vic Watson, 298, 1920–35.
Most Capped Player: Bobby Moore, 108, England.
Most League Appearances: Billy Bonds, 663, 1967–88.
Honours – Football League: Division 2 Champions – 1957–58, 1980–81. **FA Cup:** Winners – 1964, 1975, 1980. **European Competitions: European Cup-Winners' Cup:** Winners – 1964–65. **Intertoto Cup:** Winners – 1999.
Colours: Claret shirts with blue trim, white shorts, claret stockings.

WIGAN ATHLETIC   FA PREMIERSHIP

Amaya Antonion (D)	6 3	13 07	Madrid	31	5 83	Rayo Vallecano
Boyce Emmerson (D)	6 0	12 06	Aylesbury	24	9 79	Crystal Palace
Bramble Titus (D)	6 2	13 10	Ipswich	31	7 81	Newcastle U
Caldwell Gary (D)	5 11	11 10	Stirling	12	4 82	Celtic
Cho Won-Hee (M)	5 10	11 07	Seoul	17	4 83	Suwon Blue Wings
Cywka Tomasz (M)	5 10	11 09	Gliwice	27	6 88	Gwarek Zabrze
De Ridder Daniel (M)	5 11	10 12	Amsterdam	6	3 84	Birmingham C
Diame Mohamed (M)	6 1	11 02	Creteil	14	6 87	Rayo Vallecano
Figueroa Maynor (D)	5 11	12 02	Jutiapa	2	5 83	Victoria La Ceiba
Gohouri Steve (D)	6 2	13 01	Treichville	8	2 81	Mgladbach
Gomez Jordi (M)	5 10	11 09	Barcelona	24	5 85	Swansea C
Holt Joe (F)	5 8	11 07	Liverpool	1	2 90	Scholar
Kapo Olivier (M)	6 1	12 06	Abidjan	27	9 80	Birmingham C
Kirkland Chris (G)	6 5	14 05	Leicester	2	5 81	Liverpool
Koumas Jason (M)	5 10	11 02	Wrexham	25	9 79	WBA
McCarthy James (M)	5 11	11 05	Glasgow	12	11 90	Hamilton A
McManaman Callum (F)	5 9	11 03	Huyton	25	4 91	Everton
Moses Victor (F)	5 10	11 07	Lagos	12	12 90	Crystal Palace
N'Zogbia Charles (M)	5 9	11 00	Le Havre	28	5 86	Newcastle U
Pollitt Mike (G)	6 4	15 03	Farnworth	29	2 72	Rotherham U
Rodallega Hugo (F)	5 11	11 05	El Carmelo	25	7 85	Necaxa
Routledge Jon (M)	5 7	11 05	Liverpool	23	11 89	Liverpool
Scotland Jason (F)	5 8	11 10	Morvant	18	2 79	Swansea C
Thomas Hendry (M)	5 11	12 08	La Ceiba	23	2 85	Olimpija
Watson Ben (M)	5 10	10 11	Camberwell	9	7 85	Crystal Palace

League Appearances: Boyce, E. 23(1); Bramble, T. 35; Brown, M. 2; Caldwell, G. 16; Cho, W. 1(3); Diame, M. 34; Edman, E. 2(1); Figueroa, M. 35; Gohouri, S. 4(1); Gomez, J. 11(12); Kapo, O. (1); King, M. (3); Kirkland, C. 32; Koumas, J. 6(2); McCarthy, J. 19(1); Melchiot, M. 32; Moreno, M. 9(3); Moses, V. 2(12); N'Zogbia, C. 35(1); Pollitt, M. 2(2); Rodallega, H. 38; Scharner, P. 30(8); Scotland, J. 14(18); Sinclair, S. 1(17); Stojkovic, V. 4; Thomas, H. 27(4); Watson, B. 4(1).
Goals – League (37): Rodallega 10 (1 pen), N'Zogbia 5, Scharner 4, Boyce 3, Bramble 2, Caldwell 2, Diame 1, Figueroa 1, Gohouri 1, Gomez 1, Koumas 1, McCarthy 1, Moses 1, Scotland 1, Sinclair 1, Watson 1, own goal 1.
Carling Cup (1): Amaya 1.
FA Cup (6): N'Zogbia 2, McCarthy 1, Scotland 1, Sinclair 1, Watson 1.
Ground: The DW Stadium, Robin Park Complex, Newtown, Wigan, Lancashire WN5 0UZ. Telephone (01942) 774 000.
Record Attendance: 27,526 v Hereford U, FA Cup 2nd rd, 12 December 1953 (at Springfield Park). **Capacity:** 25,138.
Manager: Roberto Martinez.
Secretary: Stuart Hayton.
Most League Goals: 84, Division 3, 1996–97.
Highest League Scorer in Season: Graeme Jones, 31, Division 3, 1996–97.

Most League Goals in Total Aggregate: Andy Liddell, 70, 1998–2004.
Most Capped Player: Kevin Kilbane, 22 (103), Republic of Ireland; Henri Camara, 22 (89), Senegal.
Most League Appearances: Kevin Langley, 317, 1981–86, 1990–94.
Honours – Football League: Division 2 Champions – 2002–03. Division 3 Champions – 1996–97. **Freight Rover Trophy:** Winners – 1984–85. **Auto Windscreens Shield:** Winners – 1998–99.
Colours: Blue and white striped shirts with blue sleeves, blue shorts, white stockings.

WOLVERHAMPTON WANDERERS   FA PREMIERSHIP

Player	Height	Weight	Birthplace	Born	From
Batth Danny (D)	6 3	13 05	Brierley Hill	21 9 90	Scholar
Berra Christophe (D)	6 1	12 10	Edinburgh	31 1 85	Hearts
Davis David (M)	5 8	12 03	Smethwick	20 2 91	Scholar
Doyle Kevin (F)	5 11	12 06	Adamstown	18 9 83	Reading
Dunleavy Johnny (D)	6 0	11 02	Donegal	3 7 91	Scholar
Ebanks-Blake Sylvan (F)	5 10	13 04	Cambridge	29 3 86	Plymouth Arg
Edwards Dave (M)	5 11	11 04	Shrewsbury	3 2 86	Luton T
Elokobi George (D)	5 10	13 02	Cameroon	31 1 86	Colchester U
Foley Kevin (D)	5 9	11 11	Luton	1 11 84	Luton T
Hahnemann Marcus (G)	6 3	13 03	Seattle	15 6 72	Reading
Halford Greg (D)	6 4	12 10	Chelmsford	8 12 84	Sunderland
Hemmings Ashley (M)	5 8	11 06	Wolverhampton	3 3 91	Scholar
Hennessey Wayne (G)	6 0	11 06	Anglesey	24 1 87	Scholar
Henry Karl (M)	6 0	11 02	Wolverhampton	26 11 82	Stoke C
Hill Matt (D)	5 7	12 06	Bristol	26 3 81	Preston NE
Ikeme Carl (G)	6 2	13 09	Sutton Coldfield	8 6 86	Scholar
Iwelumo Chris (F)	6 3	15 03	Coatbridge	1 8 78	Charlton Ath
Jarvis Matthew (M)	5 8	11 10	Middlesbrough	22 5 86	Gillingham
Jones David (M)	5 11	10 10	Southport	4 11 84	Derby Co
Keogh Andy (F)	6 0	11 00	Dublin	16 5 86	Scunthorpe U
Kightly Michael (F)	5 9	11 09	Basildon	24 1 86	Grays Ath
Maierhofer Stefan (F)	6 8	14 11	Gablitz	16 8 82	Rapid Vienna
Malone Scott (D)	6 2	11 11	Rowley Regis	25 3 91	Scholar
Mendez-Laing Nathaniel (M)	5 10	11 12	Birmingham	15 4 92	Scholar
Milijas Nenad (M)	6 2	13 09	Belgrade	30 4 83	Red Star Belgrade
Murray Matt (G)	6 4	13 10	Solihull	2 5 81	Trainee
Shackell Jason (D)	6 4	13 06	Stevenage	27 9 83	Norwich C
Spray James (F)	6 0	12 01	Birmingham	2 12 92	Scholar
Stearman Richard (D)	6 2	10 08	Wolverhampton	19 8 87	Leicester C
Surman Andrew (M)	5 10	11 06	Johannesburg	20 8 86	Southampton
Vokes Sam (F)	6 1	13 10	Southampton	21 10 89	Bournemouth
Ward Stephen (F)	5 11	12 01	Dublin	20 8 85	Bohemians
Winnall Sam (F)	5 9	11 04	Wolverhampton	19 1 91	Scholar
Zubar Ronald (D)	6 1	12 08	Guadeloupe	20 9 85	Marseille

League Appearances: Berra, C. 32; Castillo, S. 7(1); Craddock, J. 33; Doyle, K. 33(1); Ebanks-Blake, S. 12(11); Edwards, D. 16(4); Elokobi, G. 17(5); Foley, K. 23(2); Friend, G. 1; Guedioura, A. 7(7); Hahnemann, M. 25; Halford, G. 12(3); Hennessey, W. 13; Henry, K. 34; Hill, M. 2; Iwelumo, C. 2(13); Jarvis, M. 30(4); Jones, David 16(4); Keogh, A. 8(5); Kightly, M. 3(6); Maierhofer, S. 1(7); Mancienne, M. 22(8); Milijas, N. 12(7); Mujangi Bia, G. 1(2); Stearman, R. 12(4); Surman, A. 3(4); Vokes, S. (5); Ward, S. 18(4); Zubar, R. 23.
Goals – League (32): Doyle 9 (1 pen), Craddock 5, Jarvis 3, Ebanks-Blake 2 (1 pen), Milijas 2, Edwards 1, Guedioura 1, Jones, David 1, Keogh 1, Maierhofer 1, Stearman 1, Zubar 1, own goals 4.

Carling Cup (0).
FA Cup (4): Henry 1, Jarvis 1, Jones 1, Zubar 1.
Ground: Molineux Stadium, Waterloo Road, Wolverhampton WV1 4QR. Telephone (0871) 222 2220.
Record Attendance: 61,315 v Liverpool, FA Cup 5th rd, 11 February 1939. **Capacity:** 28,565.
Manager: Mick McCarthy.
Secretary: Richard Skirrow.
Most League Goals: 115, Division 2, 1931–32.
Highest League Scorer in Season: Dennis Westcott, 38, Division 1, 1946–47.
Most League Goals in Total Aggregate: Steve Bull, 250, 1986–99.
Most Capped Player: Billy Wright, 105, England (70 consecutive).
Most League Appearances: Derek Parkin, 501, 1967–82.
Honours – Football League: Championship Winners – 2008–09. Division 1 Champions – 1953–54, 1957–58, 1958–59. Division 2 Champions – 1931–32, 1976–77. Division 3 (N) Champions – 1923–24. Division 3 Champions – 1988–89. Division 4 Champions – 1987–88. **FA Cup:** Winners – 1893, 1908, 1949, 1960. **Football League Cup:** Winners – 1973–74, 1979–80. **Texaco Cup:** Winners – 1971. **Sherpa Van Trophy:** Winners – 1988.
Colours: Gold shirts with black trim, black shorts, gold stockings.

WYCOMBE WANDERERS   FL CHAMPIONSHIP 2

Name			Birthplace			
Ainsworth Gareth (M)	5 10	12 06	Blackburn	10 5 73	QPR
Arnold Steven (G)	6 1	13 02	Welham Green	22 8 89	Grays Ath
Beavon Stuart (F)	5 7	10 10	Reading	5 5 84	Weymouth
Betsy Kevin (M)	6 1	11 02	Woking	20 3 78	Southend U
Bloomfield Matt (M)	5 9	11 00	Ipswich	8 2 84	Ipswich T
Green Stuart (M)	5 10	11 01	Whitehaven	15 6 81	Blackpool
Hinshelwood Adam (D)	5 10	12 10	Oxford	8 1 84	Aldershot T
Johnson Leon (D)	6 1	13 05	Shoreditch	10 5 81	Gillingham
McLeod Kevin (M)	5 11	11 00	Liverpool	12 9 80	Brighton & HA
Montrose Lewis (M)	6 0	12 00	Manchester	17 11 88	Wigan Ath
Mousinho John (D)	6 1	12 07	Buckingham	30 4 86	Brentford
Phillips Matthew (M)	6 0	12 10	Aylesbury	13 3 91	Scholar
Pittman Jon-Paul (F)	5 9	11 00	Oklahoma City	24 10 86	Crawley T
Westlake Ian (M)	5 10	11 06	Clacton	10 7 83	Cheltenham T
Westwood Chris (D)	5 11	12 10	Dudley	13 2 77	Peterborough U
Woodman Craig (D)	5 9	10 11	Tiverton	22 12 82	Bristol C

League Appearances: Ainsworth, G. 12(2); Akinde, J. 4(2); Beavon, S. 14(11); Bennett, A. 5; Bennett, A. 1; Betsy, K. 35(4); Bloomfield, M. 8(6); Chambers, A. (3); Davies, S. 14(1); Doherty, T. 11(1); Duberry, M. 18; Green, S. 10(3); Harris, D. (2); Harrold, M. 29(7); Heaton, T. 16; Hinshelwood, A. 13; Hunt, L. 26(1); Johnson, L. 5; Keates, D. 13; Kelly, J. 9; McLeod, K. 8(3); Moncur, T. 4; Montrose, L. 11(3); Mousinho, J. 37(2); Oliver, L. 19(4); Pack, M. 7(1); Payne, J. 3; Phillips, M. 18(18); Pittman, J. 21(20); Revell, A. 11(4); Shearer, S. 29; Smith, A. 3; Westlake, I. 7(2); Westwood, C. 28; Woodman, C. 44; Young, J. 1; Zebroski, C. 12(3).
Goals – League (56): Harrold 8 (5 pens), Pittman 7, Revell 6 (1 pen), Betsy 5, Phillips 5, Beavon 3, Davies 3, Ainsworth 2, Bloomfield 2, Westwood 2, Zebroski 2, Akinde 1, Bennett 1, Chambers 1, Hinshelwood 1, Keates 1, Kelly 1, Mousinho 1, Payne 1, Woodman 1, own goals 2.
Carling Cup (0).
FA Cup (4): Harrold 2 (1 pen), Davies 1, Pittman 1.
J Paint Trophy (2): Pittman 2 (1 pen).
Ground: Adams Park, Hillbottom Road, Sands, High Wycombe HP12 4HJ. Telephone (01494) 472 100.
Record Attendance: 9,921 v Fulham, FA Cup 3rd rd, 9 January 2002.

Capacity: 10,000.
Manager: Gary Waddock.
Secretary: Keith Allen.
Most League Goals: 72, Championship 2, 2005–06.
Highest League Goalscorer in Season: Scott McGleish, 25, 2007–08.
Most League Goals in Total Aggregate: Nathan Tyson, 42, 2005–06.
Most Capped Player: Mark Rogers, 7, Canada.
Most League Appearances: Steve Brown, 371, 1994–2004.
Honours – GM Vauxhall Conference: Winners – 1993. **FA Trophy:** Winners – 1991, 1993.
Colours: Light blue and dark blue quartered shirts, dark blue shorts, light blue stockings.

YEOVIL TOWN   FL CHAMPIONSHIP 1

Alcock Craig (D)	5 8	11 00	Truro	8	12 87	Scholar
Bowditch Dean (F)	5 11	11 05	Bishop's Stortford	15	6 86	Ipswich T
Forbes Terrell (D)	5 11	12 07	Southwark	17	8 81	Oldham Ath
Hutchins Daniel (D)	6 0	12 00	London	23	9 89	Tottenham H
Kalala Jean-Paul (M)	5 10	12 02	Lubumbashi	16	2 82	Oldham Ath
Murtagh Kieran (M)	6 0	12 00	Wapping	29	10 88	Fisher Ath
Smith Nathan (D)	5 11	12 00	Enfield	11	1 87	Potters Bar T
Stam Stefan (D)	6 2	13 02	Amersfoort	14	9 79	Oldham Ath
Tomlin Gavin (F)	6 0	12 02	Brentford	21	8 83	Yeading
Welsh Andy (M)	5 8	10 03	Manchester	24	1 83	Blackpool
Williams Sam (F)	5 11	10 08	London	9	6 87	Aston Villa

League Appearances: Alcock, C. 39(3); Ayling, L. 1(3); Bowditch, D. 26(4); Caulker, S. 44; Davies, C. 2(2); Davies, A. 4(6); Davies, S. 4; Downes, A. 2(3); Forbes, T. 35(3); Hutchins, D. 4(3); Jones, N. 18; Kalala, J. 32(2); Lindegaard, A. 2(3); Macdonald, S. 31; Martin, R. 2(1); Mason, R. 26(2); McCarthy, A. 44; McCollin, A. (2); Murray, S. 10(10); Murtagh, K. 13(14); O'Callaghan, G. 7(5); Obika, J. 13(9); Schofield, D. 4; Smith, N. 27(7); Stam, S. 18; Tomlin, G. 29(6); Tudur-Jones, O. 6; Welsh, A. 28(14); Williams, S. 28(6); Williams, G. 7(1).
Goals – League (55): Bowditch 10, Tomlin 7 (4 pens), Mason 6 (1 pen), Obika 6, Williams G 5, Williams S 4, Macdonald 3, Murtagh 3, Murray 2 (1 pen), Welsh 2, Alcock 1, Forbes 1, Kalala 1, Schofield 1, Stam 1, Tudur-Jones 1, own goal 1.
Carling Cup (0).
FA Cup (0).
J Paint Trophy (1): Obika 1.
Ground: Huish Park, Lufton Way, Yeovil, Somerset BA22 8YF. Telephone (01935) 423 662.
Record Attendance: 9,527 v Leeds U, FL 1, 25 April 2008 (16,318 v Sunderland at Huish). **Capacity:** 9,665.
Manager: Terry Skiverton.
Secretary: Jean Cotton.
Most League Goals: 90, FL 2, 2004–05.
Highest League Goalscorer in Season: Phil Jevons, 27, 2004–05.
Most League Goals in Total Aggregate: Phil Jevons, 42, 2004–06.
Most Capped Player: Andrejs Stolcers, 1 (81), Latvia and Arron Davies, 1, Wales.
Most League Appearances: Terry Skiverton, 195, 2003–09.
Honours – Football League: Championship 2 – Winners 2004–05. **Football Conference:** Champions – 2002–03. **FA Trophy:** Winners 2001–02.
Colours: Green and white hooped shirts with green sleeves and black trim, white shorts, white stockings.

LEAGUE POSITIONS: FA PREMIER from 1992–93 and DIVISION 1 1984–85 to 1991–92

	2008-09	2007-08	2006-07	2005-06	2004-05	2003-04	2002-03	2001-02	2000-01	1999-2000	1998-99	1997-98	1996-97
Arsenal	4	3	4	4	2	1	2	1	2	2	2	1	3
Aston Villa	6	6	11	16	10	6	16	8	8	6	6	7	5
Barnsley	–	–	–	–	–	–	–	–	–	–	–	19	–
Birmingham C	–	19	–	18	12	10	13	–	–	–	–	–	–
Blackburn R	15	7	10	6	15	15	6	10	–	–	19	6	13
Bolton W	13	16	7	8	6	8	17	16	–	–	–	18	–
Bradford C	–	–	–	–	–	–	–	–	20	17	–	–	–
Charlton Ath	–	–	19	13	11	7	12	14	9	–	18	–	–
Chelsea	3	2	2	1	1	2	4	6	6	5	3	4	6
Coventry C	–	–	–	–	–	–	–	–	19	14	15	11	17
Crystal Palace	–	–	–	–	18	–	–	–	–	–	–	20	–
Derby Co	–	20	–	–	–	–	–	19	17	16	8	9	12
Everton	5	5	6	11	4	17	7	15	16	13	14	17	15
Fulham	7	17	16	12	13	9	14	13	–	–	–	–	–
Hull C	17	–	–	–	–	–	–	–	–	–	–	–	–
Ipswich T	–	–	–	–	–	–	–	18	5	–	–	–	–
Leeds U	–	–	–	–	–	19	15	5	4	3	4	5	11
Leicester C	–	–	–	–	–	18	–	20	13	8	10	10	9
Liverpool	2	4	3	3	5	4	5	2	3	4	7	3	4
Luton T	–	–	–	–	–	–	–	–	–	–	–	–	–
Manchester C	10	9	14	15	8	16	9	–	18	–	–	–	–
Manchester U	1	1	1	2	3	3	1	3	1	1	1	2	1
Middlesbrough	19	13	12	14	7	11	11	12	14	12	9	–	19
Millwall	–	–	–	–	–	–	–	–	–	–	–	–	–
Newcastle U	18	12	13	7	14	5	3	4	11	11	13	13	2
Norwich C	–	–	–	–	19	–	–	–	–	–	–	–	–
Nottingham F	–	–	–	–	–	–	–	–	–	–	20	–	20
Notts Co	–	–	–	–	–	–	–	–	–	–	–	–	–
Oldham Ath	–	–	–	–	–	–	–	–	–	–	–	–	–
Oxford U	–	–	–	–	–	–	–	–	–	–	–	–	–
Portsmouth	14	8	9	17	16	13	–	–	–	–	–	–	–
QPR	–	–	–	–	–	–	–	–	–	–	–	–	–
Reading	–	18	8	–	–	–	–	–	–	–	–	–	–
Sheffield U	–	–	18	–	–	–	–	–	–	–	–	–	–
Sheffield W	–	–	–	–	–	–	–	–	–	19	12	16	7
Southampton	–	–	–	–	20	12	8	11	10	15	17	12	16
Stoke C	12	–	–	–	–	–	–	–	–	–	–	–	–
Sunderland	16	15	–	20	–	–	20	17	7	7	–	–	18
Swindon T	–	–	–	–	–	–	–	–	–	–	–	–	–
Tottenham H	8	11	5	5	9	14	10	9	12	10	11	14	10
Watford	–	–	20	–	–	–	–	–	–	20	–	–	–
WBA	20	–	–	19	17	–	19	–	–	–	–	–	–
West Ham U	9	10	15	9	–	–	18	7	15	9	5	8	14
Wigan Ath	11	14	17	10	–	–	–	–	–	–	–	–	–
Wimbledon	–	–	–	–	–	–	–	–	–	18	16	15	8
Wolverhampton W	–	–	–	–	–	20	–	–	–	–	–	–	–

1995-96	1994-95	1993-94	1992-93	1991-92	1990-91	1989-90	1988-89	1987-88	1986-87	1985-86	1984-85	
5	12	4	10	4	1	4	1	6	4	7	7	Arsenal
4	18	10	2	7	17	2	17	–	22	16	10	Aston Villa
–	–	–	–	–	–	–	–	–	–	–	–	Barnsley
–	–	–	–	–	–	–	–	–	–	21	–	Birmingham C
7	1	2	4	–	–	–	–	–	–	–	–	Blackburn R
20	–	–	–	–	–	–	–	–	–	–	–	Bolton W
–	–	–	–	–	–	–	–	–	–	–	–	Bradford C
–	–	–	–	–	19	14	17	19	–	–	–	Charlton Ath
11	11	14	11	14	11	5	–	18	14	6	6	Chelsea
16	16	11	15	19	16	12	7	10	10	17	18	Coventry C
–	19	–	20	10	3	15	–	–	–	–	–	Crystal Palace
–	–	–	–	–	20	16	5	15	–	–	–	Derby Co
6	15	17	13	12	9	6	8	4	1	2	1	Everton
–	–	–	–	–	–	–	–	–	–	–	–	Fulham
–	–	–	–	–	–	–	–	–	–	–	–	Hull C
–	22	19	16	–	–	–	–	–	–	20	17	Ipswich T
13	5	5	17	1	4	–	–	–	–	–	–	Leeds U
–	21	–	–	–	–	–	–	–	20	19	15	Leicester C
3	4	8	6	6	2	1	2	1	2	1	2	Liverpool
–	–	–	–	20	18	17	16	9	7	9	13	Luton T
18	17	16	9	5	5	14	–	–	21	15	–	Manchester C
1	2	1	1	2	6	13	11	2	11	4	4	Manchester U
12	–	–	21	–	–	–	18	–	–	–	–	Middlesbrough
–	–	–	–	–	20	10	–	–	–	–	–	Millwall
2	6	3	–	–	–	–	20	8	17	11	14	Newcastle U
–	20	12	3	18	15	10	4	14	5	–	20	Norwich C
9	3	–	22	8	8	9	3	3	8	8	9	Nottingham F
–	–	–	–	21	–	–	–	–	–	–	–	Notts Co
–	–	21	19	17	–	–	–	–	–	–	–	Oldham Ath
–	–	–	–	–	–	–	21	18	18	–	–	Oxford U
–	–	–	–	–	–	–	19	–	–	–	–	Portsmouth
19	8	9	5	11	12	11	9	5	16	13	19	QPR
–	–	–	–	–	–	–	–	–	–	–	–	Reading
–	–	20	14	9	13	–	–	–	–	–	–	Sheffield U
15	13	7	7	3	–	18	15	11	13	5	8	Sheffield W
17	10	18	18	16	14	7	13	12	12	14	5	Southampton
–	–	–	–	–	–	–	–	–	–	–	22	Stoke C
–	–	–	–	19	–	–	–	–	–	–	21	Sunderland
–	–	22	–	–	–	–	–	–	–	–	–	Swindon T
8	7	15	8	15	10	3	6	13	3	10	3	Tottenham H
–	–	–	–	–	–	–	20	9	12	11	–	Watford
–	–	–	–	–	–	–	–	–	–	22	12	WBA
10	14	13	–	22	–	–	19	16	15	3	16	West Ham U
–	–	–	–	–	–	–	–	–	–	–	–	Wigan Ath
14	9	6	12	13	7	8	12	7	6	–	–	Wimbledon
–	–	–	–	–	–	–	–	–	–	–	–	Wolverhampton W

LEAGUE POSITIONS: DIVISION 1 from 1992–93, CHAMPIONSHIP from 2004–05 and DIVISION 2 1984–85 to 1991–92

	2008–09	2007–08	2006–07	2005–06	2004–05	2003–04	2002–03	2001–02	2000–01	1999–2000	1998–99	1997–98	1996–97
Aston Villa	–	–	–	–	–	–	–	–	–	–	–	–	–
Barnsley	20	18	20	–	–	–	–	23	16	4	13	–	2
Birmingham C	2	–	2	–	–	–	–	5	5	5	4	7	10
Blackburn R	–	–	–	–	–	–	–	2	11	–	–	–	–
Blackpool	16	19	–	–	–	–	–	–	–	–	–	–	–
Bolton W	–	–	–	–	–	–	–	–	3	6	6	–	1
Bournemouth	–	–	–	–	–	–	–	–	–	–	–	–	–
Bradford C	–	–	–	–	23	19	15	–	–	–	2	13	21
Brentford	–	–	–	–	–	–	–	–	–	–	–	–	–
Brighton & HA	–	–	–	24	20	–	23	–	–	–	–	–	–
Bristol C	10	4	–	–	–	–	–	–	–	–	24	–	–
Bristol R	–	–	–	–	–	–	–	–	–	–	–	–	–
Burnley	5	13	15	17	13	19	16	7	7	–	–	–	–
Bury	–	–	–	–	–	–	–	–	–	–	22	17	–
Cambridge U	–	–	–	–	–	–	–	–	–	–	–	–	–
Cardiff C	7	12	13	11	16	13	–	–	–	–	–	–	–
Carlisle U	–	–	–	–	–	–	–	–	–	–	–	–	–
Charlton Ath	24	11	–	–	–	–	–	–	–	1	–	4	15
Chelsea	–	–	–	–	–	–	–	–	–	–	–	–	–
Colchester U	–	24	10	–	–	–	–	–	–	–	–	–	–
Coventry C	17	21	17	8	19	12	20	11	–	–	–	–	–
Crewe Alex	–	–	–	22	21	18	–	22	14	19	18	11	–
Crystal Palace	15	5	12	6	–	6	14	10	21	15	14	–	6
Derby Co	18	–	3	20	4	20	18	–	–	–	–	–	–
Doncaster R	14	–	–	–	–	–	–	–	–	–	–	–	–
Fulham	–	–	–	–	–	–	–	–	1	9	–	–	–
Gillingham	–	–	–	–	22	21	11	12	13	–	–	–	–
Grimsby T	–	–	–	–	–	–	24	19	18	20	11	–	22
Huddersfield T	–	–	–	–	–	–	–	–	22	8	10	16	20
Hull C	–	3	21	18	–	–	–	–	–	–	–	–	–
Ipswich T	9	8	14	15	3	5	7	–	–	3	3	5	4
Leeds U	–	–	24	5	14	–	–	–	–	–	–	–	–
Leicester C	–	22	19	16	15	–	2	–	–	–	–	–	–
Luton T	–	–	23	10	–	–	–	–	–	–	–	–	–
Manchester C	–	–	–	–	–	–	–	1	–	2	–	22	14
Middlesbrough	–	–	–	–	–	–	–	–	–	–	–	2	–
Millwall	–	–	–	23	10	10	9	4	–	–	–	–	–
Newcastle U	–	–	–	–	–	–	–	–	–	–	–	–	–
Norwich C	22	17	16	9	–	1	8	6	15	12	9	15	13
Nottingham F	19	–	–	–	23	14	6	16	11	14	–	1	–
Notts Co	–	–	–	–	–	–	–	–	–	–	–	–	–
Oldham Ath	–	–	–	–	–	–	–	–	–	–	–	–	23
Oxford U	–	–	–	–	–	–	–	–	–	–	23	12	17
Peterborough U	–	–	–	–	–	–	–	–	–	–	–	–	–
Plymouth Arg	21	10	11	14	17	–	–	–	–	–	–	–	–
Port Vale	–	–	–	–	–	–	–	–	–	23	21	19	8
Portsmouth	–	–	–	–	–	–	1	17	20	18	19	20	7
Preston NE	6	15	7	4	5	15	12	8	4	–	–	–	–
QPR	11	14	18	21	11	–	–	–	23	10	20	21	9

1995–96	1994–95	1993–94	1992–93	1991–92	1990–91	1989–90	1988–89	1987–88	1986–87	1985–86	1984–85	
–	–	–	–	–	–	–	–	2	–	–	–	Aston Villa
10	6	18	13	16	8	19	7	14	11	12	11	Barnsley
15	–	22	19	–	–	–	23	19	19	–	2	Birmingham C
–	–	–	–	6	19	5	5	5	12	19	5	Blackburn R
–	–	–	–	–	–	–	–	–	–	–	–	Blackpool
–	3	14	–	–	–	–	–	–	–	–	–	Bolton W
–	–	–	–	–	–	22	12	17	–	–	–	Bournemouth
–	–	–	–	–	–	23	14	4	10	13	–	Bradford C
–	–	–	22	–	–	–	–	–	–	–	–	Brentford
–	–	–	–	23	6	18	19	–	22	11	6	Brighton & HA
–	23	13	15	17	9	–	–	–	–	–	–	Bristol C
–	–	–	24	13	13	–	–	–	–	–	–	Bristol R
–	22	–	–	–	–	–	–	–	–	–	–	Burnley
–	–	–	–	–	–	–	–	–	–	–	–	Bury
–	–	–	23	5	–	–	–	–	–	–	–	Cambridge U
–	–	–	–	–	–	–	–	–	–	–	21	Cardiff C
–	–	–	–	–	–	–	–	–	–	20	16	Carlisle U
6	15	11	12	7	16	–	–	–	–	2	17	Charlton Ath
–	–	–	–	–	–	–	1	–	–	–	–	Chelsea
–	–	–	–	–	–	–	–	–	–	–	–	Colchester U
–	–	–	–	–	–	–	–	–	–	–	–	Coventry C
–	–	–	–	–	–	–	–	–	–	–	–	Crewe Alex
3	–	1	–	–	–	–	3	6	6	5	15	Crystal Palace
2	9	6	8	3	–	–	–	–	1	–	–	Derby Co
–	–	–	–	–	–	–	–	–	–	–	–	Doncaster R
–	–	–	–	–	–	–	–	–	–	22	9	Fulham
–	–	–	–	–	–	–	–	–	–	–	–	Gillingham
17	10	16	9	19	–	–	–	–	21	15	10	Grimsby T
8	–	–	–	–	–	–	–	23	17	16	13	Huddersfield T
–	–	–	–	–	24	14	21	15	14	6	–	Hull C
7	–	–	–	1	14	9	8	8	5	–	–	Ipswich T
–	–	–	–	–	–	1	10	7	4	14	7	Leeds U
5	–	4	6	4	22	13	15	13	–	–	–	Leicester C
24	16	20	20	–	–	–	–	–	–	–	3	Luton T
–	–	–	–	–	–	–	2	9	–	–	3	Manchester C
–	1	9	–	2	7	21	–	3	–	21	19	Middlesbrough
22	12	3	7	15	5	–	–	1	16	9	–	Millwall
–	–	–	1	20	11	3	–	–	–	–	–	Newcastle U
16	–	–	–	–	–	–	–	–	–	1	–	Norwich C
–	–	2	–	–	–	–	–	–	–	–	–	Nottingham F
–	24	7	17	–	4	–	–	–	–	–	20	Notts Co
18	14	–	–	–	1	8	16	10	3	8	14	Oldham Ath
–	–	23	14	21	10	17	17	–	–	–	1	Oxford U
–	–	24	10	–	–	–	–	–	–	–	–	Peterborough U
–	–	–	–	22	18	16	18	16	7	–	–	Plymouth Arg
12	17	–	–	24	15	11	–	–	–	–	–	Port Vale
21	18	17	3	9	17	12	20	–	2	4	4	Portsmouth
–	–	–	–	–	–	–	–	–	–	–	–	Preston NE
–	–	–	–	–	–	–	–	–	–	–	–	QPR

LEAGUE POSITIONS: DIVISION 1 from 1992–93, CHAMPIONSHIP from 2004–05 and DIVISION 2 1984–85 to 1991–92 (cont.)

	2008-09	2007-08	2006-07	2005-06	2004-05	2003-04	2002-03	2001-02	2000-01	1999-2000	1998-99	1997-98	1996-97
Reading	4	–	–	1	7	9	4	–	–	–	–	24	18
Rotherham U	–	–	–	–	24	17	15	21	–	–	–	–	–
Scunthorpe U	–	23	–	–	–	–	–	–	–	–	–	–	–
Sheffield U	3	9	–	2	8	8	3	13	10	16	8	6	5
Sheffield W	12	16	9	19	–	–	22	20	17	–	–	–	–
Shrewsbury T	–	–	–	–	–	–	–	–	–	–	–	–	–
Southampton	23	20	6	12	–	–	–	–	–	–	–	–	–
Southend U	–	–	22	–	–	–	–	–	–	–	–	–	24
Stockport Co	–	–	–	–	–	–	–	24	19	17	16	8	–
Stoke C	–	2	8	13	12	11	21	–	–	–	–	23	12
Sunderland	–	–	1	–	1	3	–	–	–	–	1	3	–
Swansea C	8	–	–	–	–	–	–	–	–	–	–	–	–
Swindon T	–	–	–	–	–	–	–	–	–	24	17	18	19
Tranmere R	–	–	–	–	–	–	–	–	24	13	15	14	11
Walsall	–	–	–	–	–	22	17	18	–	22	–	–	–
Watford	13	6	–	3	18	16	13	14	9	–	5	–	–
WBA	–	1	4	–	–	2	–	2	6	21	12	10	16
West Ham U	–	–	–	–	6	4	–	–	–	–	–	–	–
Wigan Ath	–	–	–	–	2	7	–	–	–	–	–	–	–
Wimbledon	–	–	–	–	–	24	10	9	8	–	–	–	–
Wolverhampton W	1	7	5	7	9	–	5	3	12	7	7	9	3

LEAGUE POSITIONS: DIVISION 2 from 1992–93, LEAGUE 1 from 2004–05 and DIVISION 3 1984–85 to 1991–92

	2008-09	2007-08	2006-07	2005-06	2004-05	2003-04	2002-03	2001-02	2000-01	1999-2000	1998-99	1997-98	1996-97
Aldershot	–	–	–	–	–	–	–	–	–	–	–	–	–
Barnet	–	–	–	–	–	–	–	–	–	–	–	–	–
Barnsley	–	–	–	5	13	12	19	–	–	–	–	–	–
Birmingham C	–	–	–	–	–	–	–	–	–	–	–	–	–
Blackpool	–	–	3	19	16	14	13	16	–	22	14	12	7
Bolton W	–	–	–	–	–	–	–	–	–	–	–	–	–
Bournemouth	–	21	19	17	8	9	–	21	7	16	7	9	16
Bradford C	–	–	22	11	11	–	–	–	–	–	–	–	–
Brentford	–	–	24	3	4	17	16	3	14	17	–	21	4
Brighton & HA	16	7	18	–	–	4	–	1	–	–	–	–	–
Bristol C	–	–	2	9	7	3	3	7	9	9	–	2	5
Bristol R	11	16	–	–	–	–	–	–	21	7	13	5	17
Burnley	–	–	–	–	–	–	–	–	–	2	15	20	9
Bury	–	–	–	–	–	–	–	22	16	15	–	–	1
Cambridge U	–	–	–	–	–	–	–	24	19	19	–	–	–
Cardiff C	–	–	–	–	–	–	6	4	–	21	–	–	–
Carlisle U	20	4	8	–	–	–	–	–	–	–	–	23	–
Cheltenham T	23	19	17	–	–	–	21	–	–	–	–	–	–

1995-96	1994-95	1993-94	1992-93	1991-92	1990-91	1989-90	1988-89	1987-88	1986-87	1985-86	1984-85	
19	2	–	–	–	–	–	–	22	13	–	–	Reading
–	–	–	–	–	–	–	–	–	–	–	–	Rotherham U
–	–	–	–	–	–	–	–	–	–	–	–	Scunthorpe U
9	8	–	–	–	–	2	–	21	9	7	18	Sheffield U
–	–	–	–	–	3	–	–	–	–	–	–	Sheffield W
–	–	–	–	–	–	–	22	18	18	17	8	Shrewsbury T
–	–	–	–	–	–	–	–	–	–	–	–	Southampton
14	13	15	18	12	–	–	–	–	–	–	–	Southend U
–	–	–	–	–	–	–	–	–	–	–	–	Stockport Co
4	11	10	–	–	–	24	13	11	8	10	–	Stoke C
1	20	12	21	18	–	6	11	–	20	18	–	Sunderland
–	–	–	–	–	–	–	–	–	–	–	–	Swansea C
–	21	–	5	8	21	4	6	12	–	–	–	Swindon T
13	5	5	4	14	–	–	–	–	–	–	–	Tranmere R
–	–	–	–	–	–	–	24	–	–	–	–	Walsall
23	7	19	16	10	20	15	4	–	–	–	–	Watford
11	19	21	–	–	23	20	9	20	15	–	–	WBA
–	–	–	2	–	2	7	–	–	–	–	–	West Ham U
–	–	–	–	–	–	–	–	–	–	–	–	Wigan Ath
–	–	–	–	–	–	–	–	–	–	3	12	Wimbledon
20	4	8	11	11	12	10	–	–	–	–	22	Wolverhampton W

1995-96	1994-95	1993-94	1992-93	1991-92	1990-91	1989-90	1988-89	1987-88	1986-87	1985-86	1984-85	
–	–	–	–	–	–	–	24	20	–	–	–	Aldershot
–	–	24	–	–	–	–	–	–	–	–	–	Barnet
–	1	–	–	2	12	7	–	–	–	–	–	Barnsley
3	12	20	18	–	–	23	19	10	9	12	–	Birmingham C
–	–	–	2	13	4	6	10	–	21	18	17	Blackpool
14	19	17	17	8	9	–	–	–	1	15	10	Bolton W
6	14	7	10	16	8	–	–	–	–	–	1	Bradford C
15	2	16	–	1	6	13	7	12	11	10	13	Brentford
23	16	14	9	–	–	–	–	2	–	–	–	Brighton & HA
13	–	–	–	–	2	11	5	6	9	5	–	Bristol C
10	4	8	–	–	1	5	8	19	16	6	–	Bristol R
17	–	6	13	–	–	–	–	–	–	–	21	Burnley
–	–	–	–	21	7	5	13	14	16	20	–	Bury
–	20	10	–	–	1	–	–	–	–	–	24	Cambridge U
–	22	19	–	–	–	21	16	–	–	22	–	Cardiff C
21	–	–	–	–	–	–	–	–	22	–	–	Carlisle U
–	–	–	–	–	–	–	–	–	–	–	–	Cheltenham T

LEAGUE POSITIONS: DIVISION 2 from 1992–93, LEAGUE 1 from 2004–05 and DIVISION 3 1984–85 to 1991–92 (cont.)

	2008-09	2007-08	2006-07	2005-06	2004-05	2003-04	2002-03	2001-02	2000-01	1999-2000	1998-99	1997-98	1996-97
Chester C	–	–	–	–	–	–	–	–	–	–	–	–	–
Chesterfield	–	–	21	16	17	20	20	18	–	24	9	10	10
Colchester U	12	–	–	2	15	11	12	15	17	18	18	–	–
Crewe Alex	22	20	13	–	–	–	2	–	–	–	–	–	6
Darlington	–	–	–	–	–	–	–	–	–	–	–	–	–
Derby Co	–	–	–	–	–	–	–	–	–	–	–	–	–
Doncaster R	–	3	11	8	10	–	–	–	–	–	–	–	–
Exeter C	–	–	–	–	–	–	–	–	–	–	–	–	–
Fulham	–	–	–	–	–	–	–	–	–	–	1	6	–
Gillingham	–	22	16	14	–	–	–	–	–	3	4	8	11
Grimsby T	–	–	–	–	–	21	–	–	–	–	–	3	–
Hartlepool U	19	15	–	21	6	6	–	–	–	–	–	–	–
Hereford U	24	–	–	–	–	–	–	–	–	–	–	–	–
Huddersfield T	9	10	15	4	9	–	22	6	–	–	–	–	–
Hull C	–	–	–	–	2	–	–	–	–	–	–	–	–
Leeds U	4	5	–	–	–	–	–	–	–	–	–	–	–
Leiceser C	1	–	–	–	–	–	–	–	–	–	–	–	–
Leyton Orient	14	14	20	–	–	–	–	–	–	–	–	–	–
Lincoln C	–	–	–	–	–	–	–	–	–	–	23	–	–
Luton T	–	24	–	–	1	10	9	–	22	13	12	17	3
Macclesfield T	–	–	–	–	–	–	–	–	–	–	24	–	–
Manchester C	–	–	–	–	–	–	–	–	–	–	3	–	–
Mansfield T	–	–	–	–	–	–	23	–	–	–	–	–	–
Middlesbrough	–	–	–	–	–	–	–	–	–	–	–	–	–
Millwall	5	17	10	–	–	–	–	–	1	5	10	18	14
Newport Co	–	–	–	–	–	–	–	–	–	–	–	–	–
Northampton T	21	9	14	–	–	–	24	20	18	–	22	4	–
Nottingham F	–	2	4	7	–	–	–	–	–	–	–	–	–
Notts Co	–	–	–	–	–	23	15	19	8	8	16	–	24
Oldham Ath	10	8	6	10	19	15	5	9	15	14	20	13	–
Oxford U	–	–	–	–	–	–	–	–	24	20	–	–	–
Peterborough U	2	–	–	–	23	18	11	17	12	–	–	–	21
Plymouth Arg	–	–	–	–	–	1	8	–	–	–	–	22	19
Port Vale	–	23	12	13	18	7	17	14	11	–	–	–	–
Preston NE	–	–	–	–	–	–	–	–	–	1	5	15	15
QPR	–	–	–	–	–	2	4	8	–	–	–	–	–
Reading	–	–	–	–	–	–	–	2	3	10	11	–	–
Rotherham U	–	–	23	20	–	–	–	–	2	–	–	–	23
Rushden & D	–	–	–	–	22	–	–	–	–	–	–	–	–
Scunthorpe U	6	–	1	12	–	–	–	–	–	23	–	–	–
Sheffield U	–	–	–	–	–	–	–	–	–	–	–	–	–
Sheffield W	–	–	–	–	5	16	–	–	–	–	–	–	–
Shrewsbury T	–	–	–	–	–	–	–	–	–	–	–	–	22
Southend U	8	6	–	1	–	–	–	–	–	–	–	24	–
Stockport Co	18	–	–	–	24	19	14	–	–	–	–	–	2
Stoke C	–	–	–	–	–	–	–	5	5	6	8	–	–
Sunderland	–	–	–	–	–	–	–	–	–	–	–	–	–
Swansea C	–	1	7	6	–	–	–	–	23	–	–	–	–
Swindon T	15	13	–	23	12	5	10	13	20	–	–	–	–

1995-96	1994-95	1993-94	1992-93	1991-92	1990-91	1989-90	1988-89	1987-88	1986-87	1985-86	1984-85	
–	23	–	24	18	19	16	8	15	15	–	–	Chester C
7	–	–	–	–	–	–	22	18	17	17	–	Chesterfield
–	–	–	–	–	–	–	–	–	–	–	–	Colchester U
5	3	–	–	–	22	12	–	–	–	–	–	Crewe Alex
–	–	–	–	24	–	–	–	–	23	13	–	Darlington
–	–	–	–	–	–	–	–	–	–	3	7	Derby Co
–	–	–	–	–	–	–	–	24	13	11	14	Doncaster R
–	–	22	19	20	16	–	–	–	–	–	–	Exeter C
–	–	21	12	9	21	20	4	9	18	–	–	Fulham
–	–	–	–	–	–	–	23	13	5	5	4	Gillingham
–	–	–	–	3	–	–	22	–	–	–	–	Grimsby T
–	–	23	16	11	–	–	–	–	–	–	–	Hartlepool U
–	–	–	–	–	–	–	–	–	–	–	–	Hereford U
–	5	11	15	3	11	8	14	–	–	–	–	Huddersfield T
24	8	9	20	14	–	–	–	–	–	–	3	Hull C
–	–	–	–	–	–	–	–	–	–	–	–	Leeds U
–	–	–	–	–	–	–	–	–	–	–	–	Leicester C
–	24	18	7	10	13	14	–	–	–	–	22	Leyton Orient
–	–	–	–	–	–	–	–	–	–	21	19	Lincoln C
–	–	–	–	–	–	–	–	–	–	–	–	Luton T
–	–	–	–	–	–	–	–	–	–	–	–	Macclesfield T
–	–	–	–	–	–	–	–	–	–	–	–	Manchester C
–	–	–	22	–	24	15	15	19	10	–	–	Mansfield T
–	–	–	–	–	–	–	–	–	2	–	–	Middlesbrough
–	–	–	–	–	–	–	–	–	–	–	2	Millwall
–	–	–	–	–	–	–	–	–	23	19	18	Newport Co
–	–	–	–	–	–	22	20	6	–	–	–	Northampton T
–	–	–	–	–	–	–	–	–	–	–	–	Nottingham F
4	–	–	–	–	3	9	4	7	8	–	–	Notts Co
–	–	–	–	–	–	–	–	–	–	–	–	Oldham Ath
2	7	–	–	–	–	–	–	–	–	–	–	Oxford U
19	15	–	–	6	–	–	–	–	–	–	–	Peterborough U
–	21	3	14	–	–	–	–	–	–	2	15	Plymouth Arg
–	–	2	3	–	–	–	3	11	12	–	–	Port Vale
–	–	–	21	17	17	19	6	16	–	–	23	Preston NE
–	–	–	–	–	–	–	–	–	–	–	–	QPR
–	–	1	8	12	15	10	18	–	–	1	9	Reading
16	17	15	11	–	23	9	–	21	14	14	12	Rotherham U
–	–	–	–	–	–	–	–	–	–	–	–	Rushden & D
–	–	–	–	–	–	–	–	–	–	–	–	Scunthorpe U
–	–	–	–	–	–	–	2	–	–	–	–	Sheffield U
–	–	–	–	–	–	–	–	–	–	–	–	Sheffield W
18	18	–	–	22	18	11	–	–	–	–	–	Shrewsbury T
–	–	–	–	–	2	–	21	17	–	–	–	Southend U
9	11	4	6	5	–	–	–	–	–	–	–	Stockport Co
–	–	–	1	4	14	–	–	–	–	–	–	Stoke C
–	–	–	–	–	–	–	–	1	–	–	–	Sunderland
22	10	13	5	19	20	17	12	–	–	24	20	Swansea C
1	–	–	–	–	–	–	–	–	3	–	–	Swindon T

119

LEAGUE POSITIONS: DIVISION 2 from 1992–93, LEAGUE 1 from 2004–05 and DIVISION 3 1984–85 to 1991–92 (cont.)

	2008-09	2007-08	2006-07	2005-06	2004-05	2003-04	2002-03	2001-02	2000-01	1999-2000	1998-99	1997-98	1996-97
Torquay U	–	–	–	–	21	–	–	–	–	–	–	–	–
Tranmere R	7	11	9	18	3	8	7	12	–	–	–	–	–
Walsall	13	12	–	24	14	–	–	–	4	–	2	19	12
Watford	–	–	–	–	–	–	–	–	–	–	–	1	13
WBA	–	–	–	–	–	–	–	–	–	–	–	–	–
Wigan Ath	–	–	–	–	–	–	1	10	6	4	6	11	–
Wimbledon	3†	–	–	22†	20†	–	–	–	–	–	–	–	–
Wolverhampton W	–	–	–	–	–	–	–	–	–	–	–	–	–
Wrexham	–	–	–	–	22	13	–	23	10	11	17	7	8
Wycombe W	–	–	–	–	–	24	18	11	13	12	19	14	18
Yeovil T	17	18	5	15	–	–	–	–	–	–	–	–	–
York C	–	–	–	–	–	–	–	–	–	–	21	16	20

†As Milton Keynes D

LEAGUE POSITIONS: DIVISION 3 from 1992–93, LEAGUE 2 from 2004–05 and DIVISION 4 1984–85 to 1991–92

	2008-09	2007-08	2006-07	2005-06	2004-05	2003-04	2002-03	2001-02	2000-01	1999-2000	1998-99	1997-98	1996-97
Accrington S	16	17	20	–	–	–	–	–	–	–	–	–	–
Aldershot T	15	–	–	–	–	–	–	–	–	–	–	–	–
Barnet	17	12	14	18	–	–	–	–	24	6	16	7	15
Blackpool	–	–	–	–	–	–	–	–	7	–	–	–	–
Bolton W	–	–	–	–	–	–	–	–	–	–	–	–	–
Boston U	–	–	23	11	16	11	15	–	–	–	–	–	–
Bournemouth	21	–	–	–	–	–	4	–	–	–	–	–	–
Bradford C	9	10	–	–	–	–	–	–	–	–	–	–	–
Brentford	1	14	–	–	–	–	–	–	–	–	1	–	–
Brighton & HA	–	–	–	–	–	–	–	–	1	11	17	23	23
Bristol R	–	–	6	12	12	15	20	23	–	–	–	–	–
Burnley	–	–	–	–	–	–	–	–	–	–	–	–	–
Bury	4	13	21	19	17	12	7	–	–	–	–	–	–
Cambridge U	–	–	–	–	24	13	12	–	–	–	2	16	10
Cardiff C	–	–	–	–	–	–	–	–	2	–	3	21	7
Carlisle U	–	–	–	1	–	23	22	17	22	23	23	–	3
Cheltenham T	–	–	–	5	14	14	–	4	9	8	–	–	–
Chester C	23	22	18	15	20	–	–	–	–	24	14	14	6
Chesterfield	10	8	–	–	–	–	–	–	3	–	–	–	–
Colchester U	–	–	–	–	–	–	–	–	–	–	–	4	8
Crewe Alex	–	–	–	–	–	–	–	–	–	–	–	–	–
Dagenham & R	8	20	–	–	–	–	–	–	–	–	–	–	–

*Record expunged

1995-96	1994-95	1993-94	1992-93	1991-92	1990-91	1989-90	1988-89	1987-88	1986-87	1985-86	1984-85	
–	–	–	–	23	–	–	–	–	–	–	–	Torquay U
–	–	–	–	–	5	4	–	–	–	–	–	Tranmere R
11	–	–	–	–	–	24	–	3	8	6	11	Walsall
–	–	–	–	–	–	–	–	–	–	–	–	Watford
–	–	–	4	7	–	–	–	–	–	–	–	WBA
–	–	–	23	15	10	18	17	7	4	4	16	Wigan Ath
–	–	–	–	–	–	–	–	–	–	–	–	Wimbledon
–	–	–	–	–	–	–	1	–	–	23	–	Wolverhampton W
8	13	12	–	–	–	–	–	–	–	–	–	Wrexham
12	6	–	–	–	–	–	–	–	–	–	–	Wycombe W
–	–	–	–	–	–	–	–	–	–	–	–	Yeovil T
20	9	5	–	–	–	–	–	23	20	7	8	York C

1995-96	1994-95	1993-94	1992-93	1991-92	1990-91	1989-90	1988-89	1987-88	1986-87	1985-86	1984-85	
–	–	–	–	–	–	–	–	–	–	–	–	Accrington S
–	–	–	–	*	23	22	–	–	6	16	13	Aldershot T
9	11	–	3	7	–	–	–	–	–	–	–	Barnet
–	–	–	4	5	–	–	–	–	–	–	2	Blackpool
–	–	–	–	–	–	–	3	–	–	–	–	Bolton W
–	–	–	–	–	–	–	–	–	–	–	–	Boston U
–	–	–	–	–	–	–	–	–	–	–	–	Bradford C
–	–	–	–	–	–	–	–	–	–	–	–	Leeds U
–	–	–	–	–	–	–	–	–	–	–	–	Brentford
–	–	–	–	–	–	–	–	–	–	–	–	Brighton & HA
–	–	–	–	–	–	–	–	–	–	–	–	Bristol R
–	–	–	1	6	16	16	10	22	14	–	–	Burnley
3	4	13	7	–	–	–	–	–	–	–	4	Bury
16	–	–	–	–	–	6	8	15	11	22	–	Cambridge U
22	–	–	1	9	13	–	–	2	13	–	–	Cardiff C
–	1	7	18	22	20	8	12	23	–	–	–	Carlisle U
–	–	–	–	–	–	–	–	–	–	–	–	Cheltenham T
8	–	2	–	–	–	–	–	–	–	2	16	Chester C
–	3	8	12	13	18	7	–	–	–	–	1	Chesterfield
7	10	17	10	–	–	24	22	9	5	6	7	Colchester U
–	–	3	6	6	–	–	3	17	17	12	10	Crewe Alex
–	–	–	–	–	–	–	–	–	–	–	–	Dagenham & R

LEAGUE POSITIONS: DIVISION 3 from 1992–93, LEAGUE 2 from 2004–05 and DIVISION 4 1984–85 to 1991–92 (cont.)

	2008-09	2007-08	2006-07	2005-06	2004-05	2003-04	2002-03	2001-02	2000-01	1999-2000	1998-99	1997-98	1996-97
Darlington	12	6	11	8	8	18	14	15	20	4	11	19	18
Doncaster R	–	–	–	–	–	1	–	–	–	–	–	24	19
Exeter C	2	–	–	–	–	–	23	16	19	21	12	15	22
Fulham	–	–	–	–	–	–	–	–	–	–	–	–	2
Gillingham	5	–	–	–	–	–	–	–	–	–	–	–	–
Grimsby T	22	16	15	4	18	–	–	–	–	–	–	–	–
Halifax T	–	–	–	–	–	–	–	24	23	18	10	–	–
Hartlepool U	–	–	2	–	–	–	2	7	4	7	22	17	20
Hereford U	–	3	16	–	–	–	–	–	–	–	–	–	24
Huddersfield T	–	–	–	–	–	4	–	–	–	–	–	–	–
Hull C	–	–	–	–	–	2	13	11	6	14	21	22	17
Kidderminster H	–	–	–	–	23	16	11	10	16	–	–	–	–
Leyton Orient	–	–	–	3	11	19	18	18	5	19	6	11	16
Lincoln C	13	15	5	7	6	7	6	22	18	15	–	3	9
Luton T	24	–	–	–	–	–	–	2	–	–	–	–	–
Macclesfield T	20	19	22	17	5	20	16	13	14	13	–	2	–
Maidstone U	–	–	–	–	–	–	–	–	–	–	–	–	–
Mansfield T	–	23	17	16	13	5	–	3	13	17	8	12	11
Morecambe	11	11	–	–	–	–	–	–	–	–	–	–	–
Newport Co	–	–	–	–	–	–	–	–	–	–	–	–	–
Northampton T	–	–	–	2	7	6	–	–	–	3	–	–	4
Notts Co	19	21	13	21	19	–	–	–	–	–	–	1	–
Oxford U	–	–	–	23	15	9	8	21	–	–	–	–	–
Peterborough U	–	2	10	9	–	–	–	–	–	5	9	10	–
Plymouth Arg	–	–	–	–	–	–	–	1	12	12	13	–	–
Port Vale	18	–	–	–	–	–	–	–	–	–	–	–	–
Preston NE	–	–	–	–	–	–	–	–	–	–	–	–	–
Rochdale	6	5	9	14	9	21	19	5	8	10	19	18	14
Rotherham U	14	9	–	–	–	–	–	–	–	2	5	9	–
Rushden & D	–	–	–	24	22	–	1	6	–	–	–	–	–
Scarborough	–	–	–	–	–	–	–	–	–	–	24	6	12
Scunthorpe U	–	–	–	–	2	22	5	8	10	–	4	8	13
Shrewsbury T	7	18	7	10	21	–	24	9	15	22	15	13	–
Southend U	–	–	–	–	4	17	17	12	11	16	18	–	–
Stockport Co	–	4	8	22	–	–	–	–	–	–	–	–	–
Swansea C	–	–	–	–	3	10	21	20	–	1	7	20	5
Swindon T	–	–	3	–	–	–	–	–	–	–	–	–	–
Torquay U	–	–	24	20	–	3	9	19	21	9	20	5	21
Tranmere R	–	–	–	–	–	–	–	–	–	–	–	–	–
Walsall	–	–	1	–	–	–	–	–	–	–	–	–	–
Wigan Ath	–	–	–	–	–	–	–	–	–	–	–	–	1
Wimbledon	–	1†	4†	–	–	–	–	–	–	–	–	–	–
Wolverhampton W	–	–	–	–	–	–	–	–	–	–	–	–	–
Wrexham	–	24	19	13	–	–	3	–	–	–	–	–	–
Wycombe W	3	7	12	6	10	–	–	–	–	–	–	–	–
Yeovil T	–	–	–	–	1	8	–	–	–	–	–	–	–
York C	–	–	–	–	–	24	10	14	17	20	–	–	–

†As Milton Keynes D

1995–96	1994–95	1993–94	1992–93	1991–92	1990–91	1989–90	1988–89	1987–88	1986–87	1985–86	1984–85	
5	20	21	15	–	1	–	24	13	–	–	3	Darlington
13	9	15	16	21	11	20	23	–	–	–	–	Doncaster R
14	22	–	–	–	–	1	13	22	14	21	18	Exeter C
17	8	–	–	–	–	–	–	–	–	–	–	Fulham
2	19	16	21	11	15	14	–	–	–	–	–	Gillingham
–	–	–	–	–	–	2	9	–	–	–	–	Grimsby T
–	–	–	22	20	22	23	21	18	15	20	21	Halifax T
20	18	–	–	–	3	19	19	16	18	7	19	Hartlepool U
6	16	20	17	17	17	17	15	19	16	10	5	Hereford U
–	–	–	–	–	–	–	–	–	–	–	–	Huddersfield T
–	–	–	–	–	–	–	–	–	–	–	–	Hull C
–	–	–	–	–	–	–	–	–	–	–	–	Kidderminster H
21	–	–	–	–	–	–	6	8	7	5	–	Leyton Orient
18	12	18	8	10	14	10	10	–	24	–	–	Lincoln C
–	–	–	–	–	–	–	–	–	–	–	–	Luton T
–	–	–	–	–	–	–	–	–	–	–	–	Macclesfield T
–	–	–	–	18	19	5	–	–	–	–	–	Maidstone U
19	6	12	–	3	–	–	–	–	–	3	14	Mansfield T
–	–	–	–	–	–	–	–	–	–	–	–	Morecambe
–	–	–	–	–	–	–	–	24	–	–	–	Newport Co
11	17	22	20	16	10	–	–	–	1	8	23	Northampton T
–	–	–	–	–	–	–	–	–	–	–	–	Notts Co
–	–	–	–	–	–	–	–	–	–	–	–	Oxford U
–	–	–	–	–	4	9	17	7	10	17	11	Peterborough U
4	–	–	–	–	–	–	–	–	–	–	–	Plymouth Arg
–	–	–	–	–	–	–	–	–	–	4	12	Port Vale
1	5	5	–	–	–	–	–	–	2	23	–	Preston NE
15	15	9	11	8	12	12	18	21	21	18	17	Rochdale
–	–	–	2	–	–	1	–	–	–	–	–	Rotherham U
–	–	–	–	–	–	–	–	–	–	–	–	Rushden & D
23	21	14	13	12	9	18	5	12	–	–	–	Scarborough
12	7	11	14	5	8	11	4	4	8	15	9	Scunthorpe U
–	–	1	9	–	–	–	–	–	–	–	–	Shrewsbury T
–	–	–	–	–	–	3	–	–	3	9	20	Southend U
–	–	–	–	–	2	4	20	20	19	11	22	Stockport Co
–	–	–	–	–	–	–	6	12	–	–	–	Swansea C
–	–	–	–	–	–	–	–	–	–	1	8	Swindon T
24	13	6	19	–	7	15	14	5	23	24	24	Torquay U
–	–	–	–	–	–	2	14	20	19	6	–	Tranmere R
–	2	10	5	15	16	–	–	–	–	–	–	Walsall
10	14	19	–	–	–	–	–	–	–	–	–	Wigan Ath
–	–	–	–	–	–	–	–	–	–	–	–	Wimbledon
–	–	–	–	–	–	–	–	1	4	–	–	Wolverhampton W
–	–	–	2	14	24	21	7	11	9	13	15	Wrexham
–	–	4	–	–	–	–	–	–	–	–	–	Wycombe W
–	–	–	–	–	–	–	–	–	–	–	–	Yeovil T
–	–	–	4	19	21	13	11	–	–	–	–	York C

LEAGUE CHAMPIONSHIP HONOURS

FA PREMIER LEAGUE

Maximum points: 126

	First	Pts	Second	Pts	Third	Pts
1992–93	Manchester U	84	Aston Villa	74	Norwich C	72
1993–94	Manchester U	92	Blackburn R	84	Newcastle U	77
1994–95	Blackburn R	89	Manchester U	88	Nottingham F	77

Maximum points: 114

1995–96	Manchester U	82	Newcastle U	78	Liverpool	71
1996–97	Manchester U	75	Newcastle U*	68	Arsenal*	68
1997–98	Arsenal	78	Manchester U	77	Liverpool	65
1998–99	Manchester U	79	Arsenal	78	Chelsea	75
1999–00	Manchester U	91	Arsenal	73	Leeds U	69
2000–01	Manchester U	80	Arsenal	70	Liverpool	69
2001–02	Arsenal	87	Liverpool	80	Manchester U	77
2002–03	Manchester U	83	Arsenal	78	Newcastle U	69
2003–04	Arsenal	90	Chelsea	79	Manchester U	75
2004–05	Chelsea	95	Arsenal	83	Manchester U	77
2005–06	Chelsea	91	Manchester U	83	Liverpool	82
2006–07	Manchester U	89	Chelsea	83	Liverpool*	68
2007–08	Manchester U	87	Chelsea	85	Arsenal	83
2008–09	Manchester U	90	Liverpool	86	Chelsea	83
2009–10	Chelsea	86	Manchester U	85	Arsenal	75

FOOTBALL LEAGUE CHAMPIONSHIP

Maximum points: 138

2004–05	Sunderland	94	Wigan Ath	87	Ipswich T††	85
2005–06	Reading	106	Sheffield U	90	Watford	81
2006–07	Sunderland	88	Birmingham C	86	Derby Co	84
2007–08	WBA	81	Stoke C	79	Hull C	75
2008–09	Wolverhampton W	90	Birmingham C	83	Sheffield U††	80
2009–10	Newcastle U	102	WBA	91	Nottingham F††	79

DIVISION 1

Maximum points: 138

1992–93	Newcastle U	96	West Ham U*	88	Portsmouth††	88
1993–94	Crystal Palace	90	Nottingham F	83	Millwall††	74
1994–95	Middlesbrough	82	Reading††	79	Bolton W	77
1995–96	Sunderland	83	Derby Co	79	Crystal Palace††	75
1996–97	Bolton W	98	Barnsley	80	Wolverhampton W††	76
1997–98	Nottingham F	94	Middlesbrough	91	Sunderland††	90
1998–99	Sunderland	105	Bradford C	87	Ipswich T††	86
1999–00	Charlton Ath	91	Manchester C	89	Ipswich T	87
2000–01	Fulham	101	Blackburn R	91	Bolton W	87
2001–02	Manchester C	99	WBA	89	Wolverhampton W††	86
2002–03	Portsmouth	98	Leicester C	92	Sheffield U††	80
2003–04	Norwich C	94	WBA	86	Sunderland††	79

FOOTBALL LEAGUE CHAMPIONSHIP 1

Maximum points: 138

2004–05	Luton T	98	Hull C	86	Tranmere R††	79
2005–06	Southend U	82	Colchester U	79	Brentford††	76
2006–07	Scunthorpe U	91	Bristol C	85	Blackpool	83

	First	Pts	Second	Pts	Third	Pts
2007–08	Swansea C	92	Nottingham F	82	Doncaster R	80
2008–09	Leicester C	96	Peterborough U	89	Milton Keynes D††	87
2009–10	Norwich C	95	Leeds U	86	Millwall	85

DIVISION 2

Maximum points: 138

	First	Pts	Second	Pts	Third	Pts
1992–93	Stoke C	93	Bolton W	90	Port Vale††	89
1993–94	Reading	89	Port Vale	88	Plymouth Arg††	85
1994–95	Birmingham C	89	Brentford††	85	Crewe Alex††	83
1995–96	Swindon T	92	Oxford U	83	Blackpool††	82
1996–97	Bury	84	Stockport Co	82	Luton T††	78
1997–98	Watford	88	Bristol C	85	Grimsby T	72
1998–99	Fulham	101	Walsall	87	Manchester C	82
1999–00	Preston NE	95	Burnley	88	Gillingham	85
2000–01	Millwall	93	Rotherham U	91	Reading††	86
2001–02	Brighton & HA	90	Reading	84	Brentford*††	83
2002–03	Wigan Ath	100	Crewe Alex	86	Bristol C††	83
2003–04	Plymouth Arg	90	QPR	83	Bristol C††	82

FOOTBALL LEAGUE CHAMPIONSHIP 2

Maximum points: 138

2004–05	Yeovil T	83	Scunthorpe U*	80	Swansea C	80
2005–06	Carlisle U	86	Northampton T	83	Leyton Orient	81
2006–07	Walsall	89	Hartlepool U	88	Swindon T	85
2007–08	Milton Keynes D	97	Peterborough U	92	Hereford U	88
2008–09	Brentford	85	Exeter C	79	Wycombe W*	78
2009–10	Notts Co	93	Bournemouth	83	Rochdale	82

DIVISION 3

Maximum points: 126

1992–93	Cardiff C	83	Wrexham	80	Barnet	79
1993–94	Shrewsbury T	79	Chester C	74	Crewe Alex	73
1994–95	Carlisle U	91	Walsall	83	Chesterfield	81

Maximum points: 138

1995–96	Preston NE	86	Gillingham	83	Bury	79
1996–97	Wigan Ath*	87	Fulham	87	Carlisle U	84
1997–98	Notts Co	99	Macclesfield T	82	Lincoln C	75
1998–99	Brentford	85	Cambridge U	81	Cardiff C	80
1999–00	Swansea C	85	Rotherham U	84	Northampton T	82
2000–01	Brighton & HA	92	Cardiff C	82	Chesterfield¶	80
2001–02	Plymouth Arg	102	Luton T	97	Mansfield T	79
2002–03	Rushden & D	87	Hartlepool U	85	Wrexham	84
2003–04	Doncaster R	92	Hull C	88	Torquay U*	81

* *Won or placed on goal average (ratio)/goal difference.*
†† *Not promoted after play-offs.* ¶ *9 pts deducted for irregularities.*

FOOTBALL LEAGUE

Maximum points: a 44; *b* 60

1888–89*a*	Preston NE	40	Aston Villa	29	Wolverhampton W	28
1889–90*a*	Preston NE	33	Everton	31	Blackburn R	27
1890–91*a*	Everton	29	Preston NE	27	Notts Co	26
1891–92*b*	Sunderland	42	Preston NE	37	Bolton W	36

Maximum points: a 44; b 52; c 60; d 68; e 76; f 84; g 126; h 120; k 114.

	First	Pts	Second	Pts	Third	Pts
1892–93c	Sunderland	48	Preston NE	37	Everton	36
1893–94c	Aston Villa	44	Sunderland	38	Derby Co	36
1894–95c	Sunderland	47	Everton	42	Aston Villa	39
1895–96c	Aston Villa	45	Derby Co	41	Everton	39
1896–97c	Aston Villa	47	Sheffield U*	36	Derby Co	36
1897–98c	Sheffield U	42	Sunderland	37	Wolverhampton W*	35
1898–99d	Aston Villa	45	Liverpool	43	Burnley	39
1899–1900d	Aston Villa	50	Sheffield U	48	Sunderland	41
1900–01d	Liverpool	45	Sunderland	43	Notts Co	40
1901–02d	Sunderland	44	Everton	41	Newcastle U	37
1902–03d	The Wednesday	42	Aston Villa*	41	Sunderland	41
1903–04d	The Wednesday	47	Manchester C	44	Everton	43
1904–05d	Newcastle U	48	Everton	47	Manchester C	46
1905–06e	Liverpool	51	Preston NE	47	The Wednesday	44
1906–07e	Newcastle U	51	Bristol C	48	Everton*	45
1907–08e	Manchester U	52	Aston Villa*	43	Manchester C	43
1908–09e	Newcastle U	53	Everton	46	Sunderland	44
1909–10e	Aston Villa	53	Liverpool	48	Blackburn R*	45
1910–11e	Manchester U	52	Aston Villa	51	Sunderland*	45
1911–12e	Blackburn R	49	Everton	46	Newcastle U	44
1912–13e	Sunderland	54	Aston Villa	50	Sheffield W	49
1913–14e	Blackburn R	51	Aston Villa	44	Middlesbrough*	43
1914–15e	Everton	46	Oldham Ath	45	Blackburn R*	43
1919–20f	WBA	60	Burnley	51	Chelsea	49
1920–21f	Burnley	59	Manchester C	54	Bolton W	52
1921–22f	Liverpool	57	Tottenham H	51	Burnley	49
1922–23f	Liverpool	60	Sunderland	54	Huddersfield T	53
1923–24f	Huddersfield T*	57	Cardiff C	57	Sunderland	53
1924–25f	Huddersfield T	58	WBA	56	Bolton W	55
1925–26f	Huddersfield T	57	Arsenal	52	Sunderland	48
1926–27f	Newcastle U	56	Huddersfield T	51	Sunderland	49
1927–28f	Everton	53	Huddersfield T	51	Leicester C	48
1928–29f	Sheffield W	52	Leicester C	51	Aston Villa	50
1929–30f	Sheffield W	60	Derby Co	50	Manchester C*	47
1930–31f	Arsenal	66	Aston Villa	59	Sheffield W	52
1931–32f	Everton	56	Arsenal	54	Sheffield W	50
1932–33f	Arsenal	58	Aston Villa	54	Sheffield W	51
1933–34f	Arsenal	59	Huddersfield T	56	Tottenham H	49
1934–35f	Arsenal	58	Sunderland	54	Sheffield W	49
1935–36f	Sunderland	56	Derby Co*	48	Huddersfield T	48
1936–37f	Manchester C	57	Charlton Ath	54	Arsenal	52
1937–38f	Arsenal	52	Wolverhampton W	51	Preston NE	49
1938–39f	Everton	59	Wolverhampton W	55	Charlton Ath	50
1946–47f	Liverpool	57	Manchester U*	56	Wolverhampton W	56
1947–48f	Arsenal	59	Manchester U*	52	Burnley	52
1948–49f	Portsmouth	58	Manchester U*	53	Derby Co	53
1949–50f	Portsmouth*	53	Wolverhampton W	53	Sunderland	52
1950–51f	Tottenham H	60	Manchester U	56	Blackpool	50
1951–52f	Manchester U	57	Tottenham H*	53	Arsenal	53
1952–53f	Arsenal*	54	Preston NE	54	Wolverhampton W	51
1953–54f	Wolverhampton W	57	WBA	53	Huddersfield T	51
1954–55f	Chelsea	52	Wolverhampton W*	48	Portsmouth*	48

	First	*Pts*	*Second*	*Pts*	*Third*	*Pts*
1955–56*f*	Manchester U	60	Blackpool*	49	Wolverhampton W	49
1956–57*f*	Manchester U	64	Tottenham H*	56	Preston NE	56
1957–58*f*	Wolverhampton W	64	Preston NE	59	Tottenham H	51
1958–59*f*	Wolverhampton W	61	Manchester U	55	Arsenal*	50
1959–60*f*	Burnley	55	Wolverhampton W	54	Tottenham H	53
1960–61*f*	Tottenham H	66	Sheffield W	58	Wolverhampton W	57
1961–62*f*	Ipswich T	56	Burnley	53	Tottenham H	52
1962–63*f*	Everton	61	Tottenham H	55	Burnley	54
1963–64*f*	Liverpool	57	Manchester U	53	Everton	52
1964–65*f*	Manchester U*	61	Leeds U	61	Chelsea	56
1965–66*f*	Liverpool	61	Leeds U*	55	Burnley	55
1966–67*f*	Manchester U	60	Nottingham F*	56	Tottenham H	56
1967–68*f*	Manchester C	58	Manchester U	56	Liverpool	55
1968–69*f*	Leeds U	67	Liverpool	61	Everton	57
1969–70*f*	Everton	66	Leeds U	57	Chelsea	55
1970–71*f*	Arsenal	65	Leeds U	64	Tottenham H*	52
1971–72*f*	Derby Co	58	Leeds U*	57	Liverpool*	57
1972–73*f*	Liverpool	60	Arsenal	57	Leeds U	53
1973–74*f*	Leeds U	62	Liverpool	57	Derby Co	48
1974–75*f*	Derby Co	53	Liverpool*	51	Ipswich T	51
1975–76*f*	Liverpool	60	QPR	59	Manchester U	56
1976–77*f*	Liverpool	57	Manchester C	56	Ipswich T	52
1977–78*f*	Nottingham F	64	Liverpool	57	Everton	55
1978–79*f*	Liverpool	68	Nottingham F	60	WBA	59
1979–80*f*	Liverpool	60	Manchester U	58	Ipswich T	53
1980–81*f*	Aston Villa	60	Ipswich T	56	Arsenal	53
1981–82*g*	Liverpool	87	Ipswich T	83	Manchester U	78
1982–83*g*	Liverpool	82	Watford	71	Manchester U	70
1983–84*g*	Liverpool	80	Southampton	77	Nottingham F*	74
1984–85*g*	Everton	90	Liverpool*	77	Tottenham H	77
1985–86*g*	Liverpool	88	Everton	86	West Ham U	84
1986–87*g*	Everton	86	Liverpool	77	Tottenham H	71
1987–88*h*	Liverpool	90	Manchester U	81	Nottingham F	73
1988–89*k*	Arsenal*	76	Liverpool	76	Nottingham F	64
1989–90*k*	Liverpool	79	Aston Villa	70	Tottenham H	63
1990–91*k*	Arsenal†	83	Liverpool	76	Crystal Palace	69
1991–92*k*	Leeds U	82	Manchester U	78	Sheffield W	75

No official competition during 1915–19 and 1939–46; Regional Leagues operating.
* *Won or placed on goal average (ratio)/goal difference.*
† *2 pts deducted*

DIVISION 2 to 1991–92

Maximum points: a 44; b 56; c 60; d 68; e 76; f 84; g 126; h 132; k 138.

1892–93*a*	Small Heath	36	Sheffield U	35	Darwen	30
1893–94*b*	Liverpool	50	Small Heath	42	Notts Co	39
1894–95*c*	Bury	48	Notts Co	39	Newton Heath*	38
1895–96*c*	Liverpool*	46	Manchester C	46	Grimsby T*	42
1896–97*c*	Notts Co	42	Newton Heath	39	Grimsby T	38
1897–98*c*	Burnley	48	Newcastle U	45	Manchester C	39
1898–99*d*	Manchester C	52	Glossop NE	46	Leicester Fosse	45
1899–1900*d*	The Wednesday	54	Bolton W	52	Small Heath	46
1900–01*d*	Grimsby T	49	Small Heath	48	Burnley	44
1901–02*d*	WBA	55	Middlesbrough	51	Preston NE*	42
1902–03*d*	Manchester C	54	Small Heath	51	Woolwich A	48

	First	Pts	*Second*	Pts	*Third*	Pts
1903–04d	Preston NE	50	Woolwich A	49	Manchester U	48
1904–05d	Liverpool	58	Bolton W	56	Manchester U	53
1905–06e	Bristol C	66	Manchester U	62	Chelsea	53
1906–07e	Nottingham F	60	Chelsea	57	Leicester Fosse	48
1907–08e	Bradford C	54	Leicester Fosse	52	Oldham Ath	50
1908–09e	Bolton W	52	Tottenham H*	51	WBA	51
1909–10e	Manchester C	54	Oldham Ath*	53	Hull C*	53
1910–11e	WBA	53	Bolton W	51	Chelsea	49
1911–12e	Derby Co*	54	Chelsea	54	Burnley	52
1912–13e	Preston NE	53	Burnley	50	Birmingham	46
1913–14e	Notts Co	53	Bradford PA*	49	Woolwich A	49
1914–15e	Derby Co	53	Preston NE	50	Barnsley	47
1919–20f	Tottenham H	70	Huddersfield T	64	Birmingham	56
1920–21f	Birmingham*	58	Cardiff C	58	Bristol C	51
1921–22f	Nottingham F	56	Stoke C*	52	Barnsley	52
1922–23f	Notts Co	53	West Ham U*	51	Leicester C	51
1923–24f	Leeds U	54	Bury*	51	Derby Co	51
1924–25f	Leicester C	59	Manchester U	57	Derby Co	55
1925–26f	Sheffield W	60	Derby Co	57	Chelsea	52
1926–27f	Middlesbrough	62	Portsmouth*	54	Manchester C	54
1927–28f	Manchester C	59	Leeds U	57	Chelsea	54
1928–29f	Middlesbrough	55	Grimsby T	53	Bradford PA*	48
1929–30f	Blackpool	58	Chelsea	55	Oldham Ath	53
1930–31f	Everton	61	WBA	54	Tottenham H	51
1931–32f	Wolverhampton W	56	Leeds U	54	Stoke C	52
1932–33f	Stoke C	56	Tottenham H	55	Fulham	50
1933–34f	Grimsby T	59	Preston NE	52	Bolton W*	51
1934–35f	Brentford	61	Bolton W*	56	West Ham U	56
1935–36f	Manchester U	56	Charlton Ath	55	Sheffield U*	52
1936–37f	Leicester C	56	Blackpool	55	Bury	52
1937–38f	Aston Villa	57	Manchester U*	53	Sheffield U	53
1938–39f	Blackburn R	55	Sheffield U	54	Sheffield W	53
1946–47f	Manchester C	62	Burnley	58	Birmingham C	55
1947–48f	Birmingham C	59	Newcastle U	56	Southampton	52
1948–49f	Fulham	57	WBA	56	Southampton	55
1949–50f	Tottenham H	61	Sheffield W*	52	Sheffield U*	52
1950–51f	Preston NE	57	Manchester C	52	Cardiff C	50
1951–52f	Sheffield W	53	Cardiff C*	51	Birmingham C	51
1952–53f	Sheffield U	60	Huddersfield T	58	Luton T	52
1953–54f	Leicester C*	56	Everton	56	Blackburn R	55
1954–55f	Birmingham C*	54	Luton T*	54	Rotherham U	54
1955–56f	Sheffield W	55	Leeds U	52	Liverpool*	48
1956–57f	Leicester C	61	Nottingham F	54	Liverpool	53
1957–58f	West Ham U	57	Blackburn R	56	Charlton Ath	55
1958–59f	Sheffield W	62	Fulham	60	Sheffield U*	53
1959–60f	Aston Villa	59	Cardiff C	58	Liverpool*	50
1960–61f	Ipswich T	59	Sheffield U	58	Liverpool	52
1961–62f	Liverpool	62	Leyton Orient	54	Sunderland	53
1962–63f	Stoke C	53	Chelsea*	52	Sunderland	52
1963–64f	Leeds U	63	Sunderland	61	Preston NE	56
1964–65f	Newcastle U	57	Northampton T	56	Bolton W	50
1965–66f	Manchester C	59	Southampton	54	Coventry C	53
1966–67f	Coventry C	59	Wolverhampton W	58	Carlisle U	52
1967–68f	Ipswich T	59	QPR*	58	Blackpool	58

	First	Pts	Second	Pts	Third	Pts
1968–69f	Derby Co	63	Crystal Palace	56	Charlton Ath	50
1969–70f	Huddersfield T	60	Blackpool	53	Leicester C	51
1970–71f	Leicester C	59	Sheffield U	56	Cardiff C*	53
1971–72f	Norwich C	57	Birmingham C	56	Millwall	55
1972–73f	Burnley	62	QPR	61	Aston Villa	50
1973–74f	Middlesbrough	65	Luton T	50	Carlisle U	49
1974–75f	Manchester U	61	Aston Villa	58	Norwich C	53
1975–76f	Sunderland	56	Bristol C*	53	WBA	53
1976–77f	Wolverhampton W	57	Chelsea	55	Nottingham F	52
1977–78f	Bolton W	58	Southampton	57	Tottenham H*	56
1978–79f	Crystal Palace	57	Brighton & HA*	56	Stoke C	56
1979–80f	Leicester C	55	Sunderland	54	Birmingham C*	53
1980–81f	West Ham U	66	Notts Co	53	Swansea C*	50
1981–82g	Luton T	88	Watford	80	Norwich C	71
1982–83g	QPR	85	Wolverhampton W	75	Leicester C	70
1983–84g	Chelsea*	88	Sheffield W	88	Newcastle U	80
1984–85g	Oxford U	84	Birmingham C	82	Manchester C	74
1985–86g	Norwich C	84	Charlton Ath	77	Wimbledon	76
1986–87g	Derby Co	84	Portsmouth	78	Oldham Ath††	75
1987–88h	Millwall	82	Aston Villa*	78	Middlesbrough	78
1988–89k	Chelsea	99	Manchester C	82	Crystal Palace	81
1989–90k	Leeds U*	85	Sheffield U	85	Newcastle U††	80
1990–91k	Oldham Ath	88	West Ham U	87	Sheffield W	82
1991–92k	Ipswich T	84	Middlesbrough	80	Derby Co	78

No official competition during 1915–19 and 1939–46; Regional Leagues operating.
* Won or placed on goal average (ratio)/goal difference.
†† Not promoted after play-offs.

DIVISION 3 to 1991–92

Maximum points: 92; 138 from 1981–82.

1958–59	Plymouth Arg	62	Hull C	61	Brentford*	57
1959–60	Southampton	61	Norwich C	59	Shrewsbury T*	52
1960–61	Bury	68	Walsall	62	QPR	60
1961–62	Portsmouth	65	Grimsby T	62	Bournemouth*	59
1962–63	Northampton T	62	Swindon T	58	Port Vale	54
1963–64	Coventry C*	60	Crystal Palace	60	Watford	58
1964–65	Carlisle U	60	Bristol C*	59	Mansfield T	59
1965–66	Hull C	69	Millwall	65	QPR	57
1966–67	QPR	67	Middlesbrough	55	Watford	54
1967–68	Oxford U	57	Bury	56	Shrewsbury T	55
1968–69	Watford*	64	Swindon T	64	Luton T	61
1969–70	Orient	62	Luton T	60	Bristol R	56
1970–71	Preston NE	61	Fulham	60	Halifax T	56
1971–72	Aston Villa	70	Brighton & HA	65	Bournemouth*	62
1972–73	Bolton W	61	Notts Co	57	Blackburn R	55
1973–74	Oldham Ath	62	Bristol R*	61	York C	61
1974–75	Blackburn R	60	Plymouth Arg	59	Charlton Ath	55
1975–76	Hereford U	63	Cardiff C	57	Millwall	56
1976–77	Mansfield T	64	Brighton & HA	61	Crystal Palace*	59
1977–78	Wrexham	61	Cambridge U	58	Preston NE*	56
1978–79	Shrewsbury T	61	Watford*	60	Swansea C	60
1979–80	Grimsby T	62	Blackburn R	59	Sheffield W	58
1980–81	Rotherham U	61	Barnsley*	59	Charlton Ath	59
1981–82	Burnley*	80	Carlisle U	80	Fulham	78

129

	First	Pts	Second	Pts	Third	Pts
1982–83	Portsmouth	91	Cardiff C	86	Huddersfield T	82
1983–84	Oxford U	95	Wimbledon	87	Sheffield U*	83
1984–85	Bradford C	94	Millwall	90	Hull C	87
1985–86	Reading	94	Plymouth Arg	87	Derby Co	84
1986–87	Bournemouth	97	Middlesbrough	94	Swindon T	87
1987–88	Sunderland	93	Brighton & HA	84	Walsall	82
1988–89	Wolverhampton W	92	Sheffield U*	84	Port Vale	84
1989–90	Bristol R	93	Bristol C	91	Notts Co	87
1990–91	Cambridge U	86	Southend U	85	Grimsby T*	83
1991–92	Brentford	82	Birmingham C	81	Huddersfield T	78

Won or placed on goal average (ratio)/goal difference.

DIVISION 4 (1958–1992)

Maximum points: 92; 138 from 1981–82.

	First	Pts	Second	Pts	Third	Pts
1958–59	Port Vale	64	Coventry C*	60	York C	60
1959–60	Walsall	65	Notts Co*	60	Torquay U	60
1960–61	Peterborough U	66	Crystal Palace	64	Northampton T*	60
1961–62†	Millwall	56	Colchester U	55	Wrexham	53
1962–63	Brentford	62	Oldham Ath*	59	Crewe Alex	59
1963–64	Gillingham*	60	Carlisle U	60	Workington	59
1964–65	Brighton & HA	63	Millwall*	62	York C	62
1965–66	Doncaster R*	59	Darlington	59	Torquay U	58
1966–67	Stockport Co	64	Southport*	59	Barrow	59
1967–68	Luton T	66	Barnsley	61	Hartlepools U	60
1968–69	Doncaster R	59	Halifax T	57	Rochdale*	56
1969–70	Chesterfield	64	Wrexham	61	Swansea C	60
1970–71	Notts Co	69	Bournemouth	60	Oldham Ath	59
1971–72	Grimsby T	63	Southend U	60	Brentford	59
1972–73	Southport	62	Hereford U	58	Cambridge U	57
1973–74	Peterborough U	65	Gillingham	62	Colchester U	60
1974–75	Mansfield T	68	Shrewsbury T	62	Rotherham U	59
1975–76	Lincoln C	74	Northampton T	68	Reading	60
1976–77	Cambridge U	65	Exeter C	62	Colchester U*	59
1977–78	Watford	71	Southend U	60	Swansea C*	56
1978–79	Reading	65	Grimsby T*	61	Wimbledon*	61
1979–80	Huddersfield T	66	Walsall	64	Newport Co	61
1980–81	Southend U	67	Lincoln C	65	Doncaster R	56
1981–82	Sheffield U	96	Bradford C*	91	Wigan Ath	91
1982–83	Wimbledon	98	Hull C	90	Port Vale	88
1983–84	York C	101	Doncaster R	85	Reading*	82
1984–85	Chesterfield	91	Blackpool	86	Darlington	85
1985–86	Swindon T	102	Chester C	84	Mansfield T	81
1986–87	Northampton T	99	Preston NE	90	Southend U	80
1987–88	Wolverhampton W	90	Cardiff C	85	Bolton W	78
1988–89	Rotherham U	82	Tranmere R	80	Crewe Alex	78
1989–90	Exeter C	89	Grimsby T	79	Southend U	75
1990–91	Darlington	83	Stockport Co*	82	Hartlepool U	82
1991–92§	Burnley	83	Rotherham U*	77	Mansfield T	77

Won or placed on goal average (ratio)/goal difference.
† *Maximum points: 88 owing to Accrington Stanley's resignation.* †† *Not promoted after play-offs.*
§ *Maximum points: 126 owing to Aldershot being expelled.*

DIVISION 3—SOUTH (1920–1958)

1920–21 Season as Division 3.

Maximum points: a 84; b 92.

	First	Pts	Second	Pts	Third	Pts
1920–21a	Crystal Palace	59	Southampton	54	QPR	53
1921–22a	Southampton*	61	Plymouth Arg	61	Portsmouth	53
1922–23a	Bristol C	59	Plymouth Arg*	53	Swansea T	53
1923–24a	Portsmouth	59	Plymouth Arg	55	Millwall	54
1924–25a	Swansea T	57	Plymouth Arg	56	Bristol C	53
1925–26a	Reading	57	Plymouth Arg	56	Millwall	53
1926–27a	Bristol C	62	Plymouth Arg	60	Millwall	56
1927–28a	Millwall	65	Northampton T	55	Plymouth Arg	53
1928–29a	Charlton Ath*	54	Crystal Palace	54	Northampton T*	52
1929–30a	Plymouth Arg	68	Brentford	61	QPR	51
1930–31a	Notts Co	59	Crystal Palace	51	Brentford	50
1931–32a	Fulham	57	Reading	55	Southend U	53
1932–33a	Brentford	62	Exeter C	58	Norwich C	57
1933–34a	Norwich C	61	Coventry C*	54	Reading*	54
1934–35a	Charlton Ath	61	Reading	53	Coventry C	51
1935–36a	Coventry C	57	Luton T	56	Reading	54
1936–37a	Luton T	58	Notts Co	56	Brighton & HA	53
1937–38a	Millwall	56	Bristol C	55	QPR*	53
1938–39a	Newport Co	55	Crystal Palace	52	Brighton & HA	49
1939–46	*Competition cancelled owing to war.*					
1946–47a	Cardiff C	66	QPR	57	Bristol C	51
1947–48a	QPR	61	Bournemouth	57	Walsall	51
1948–49a	Swansea T	62	Reading	55	Bournemouth	52
1949–50a	Notts Co	58	Northampton T*	51	Southend U	51
1950–51b	Nottingham F	70	Norwich C	64	Reading*	57
1951–52b	Plymouth Arg	66	Reading*	61	Norwich C	61
1952–53b	Bristol R	64	Millwall*	62	Northampton T	62
1953–54b	Ipswich T	64	Brighton & HA	61	Bristol C	56
1954–55b	Bristol C	70	Leyton Orient	61	Southampton	59
1955–56b	Leyton Orient	66	Brighton & HA	65	Ipswich T	64
1956–57b	Ipswich T*	59	Torquay U	59	Colchester U	58
1957–58b	Brighton & HA	60	Brentford*	58	Plymouth Arg	58

* Won or placed on goal average (ratio).

DIVISION 3—NORTH (1921–1958)

Maximum points: a 76; b 84; c 80; d 92.

1921–22a	Stockport Co	56	Darlington*	50	Grimsby T	50
1922–23a	Nelson	51	Bradford PA	47	Walsall	46
1923–24b	Wolverhampton W	63	Rochdale	62	Chesterfield	54
1924–25b	Darlington	58	Nelson*	53	New Brighton	53
1925–26b	Grimsby T	61	Bradford PA	60	Rochdale	59
1926–27b	Stoke C	63	Rochdale	58	Bradford PA	55
1927–28b	Bradford PA	63	Lincoln C	55	Stockport Co	54
1928–29g	Bradford C	63	Stockport Co	62	Wrexham	52
1929–30b	Port Vale	67	Stockport Co	63	Darlington*	50
1930–31b	Chesterfield	58	Lincoln C	57	Wrexham*	54
1931–32c	Lincoln C*	57	Gateshead	57	Chester	50
1932–33b	Hull C	59	Wrexham	57	Stockport Co	54
1933–34b	Barnsley	62	Chesterfield	61	Stockport Co	59
1934–35b	Doncaster R	57	Halifax T	55	Chester	54

	First	*Pts*	*Second*	*Pts*	*Third*	*Pts*
1935–36*b*	Chesterfield	60	Chester*	55	Tranmere R	55
1936–37*b*	Stockport Co	60	Lincoln C	57	Chester	53
1937–38*b*	Tranmere R	56	Doncaster R	54	Hull C	53
1938–39*b*	Barnsley	67	Doncaster R	56	Bradford C	52
1939–46	*Competition cancelled owing to war.*					
1946–47*b*	Doncaster R	72	Rotherham U	64	Chester	56
1947–48*b*	Lincoln C	60	Rotherham U	59	Wrexham	50
1948–49*b*	Hull C	65	Rotherham U	62	Doncaster R	50
1949–50*b*	Doncaster R	55	Gateshead	53	Rochdale*	51
1950–51*d*	Rotherham U	71	Mansfield T	64	Carlisle U	62
1951–52*d*	Lincoln C	69	Grimsby T	66	Stockport Co	59
1952–53*d*	Oldham Ath	59	Port Vale	58	Wrexham	56
1953–54*d*	Port Vale	69	Barnsley	58	Scunthorpe U	57
1954–55d	Barnsley	65	Accrington S	61	Scunthorpe U*	58
1955–56*d*	Grimsby T	68	Derby Co	63	Accrington S	59
1956–57*d*	Derby Co	63	Hartlepools U	59	Accrington S*	58
1957–58*d*	Scunthorpe U	66	Accrington S	59	Bradford C	57

* *Won or placed on goal average (ratio).*

PROMOTED AFTER PLAY-OFFS

(Not accounted for in previous section)
1986–87   Aldershot to Division 3.
1987–88   Swansea C to Division 3.
1988–89   Leyton Orient to Division 3.
1989–90   Cambridge U to Division 3; Notts Co to Division 2; Sunderland to Division 1.
1990–91   Notts Co to Division 1; Tranmere R to Division 2; Torquay U to Division 3.
1991–92   Blackburn R to Premier League; Peterborough U to Division 1.
1992–93   Swindon T to Premier League; WBA to Division 1; York C to Division 2.
1993–94   Leicester C to Premier League; Burnley to Division 1; Wycombe W to Division 2.
1994–95   Huddersfield T to Division 1.
1995–96   Leicester C to Premier League; Bradford C to Division 1; Plymouth Arg to Division 2.
1996–97   Crystal Palace to Premier League; Crewe Alex to Division 1; Northampton T to Division 2.
1997–98   Charlton Ath to Premier League; Colchester U to Division 2.
1998–99   Watford to Premier League; Scunthorpe to Division 2.
1999–00   Peterborough U to Division 2.
2000–01   Walsall to Division 1; Blackpool to Division 2.
2001–02   Birmingham C to Premier League; Stoke C to Division 1; Cheltenham T to Division 2.
2002–03   Wolverhampton W to Premier League; Cardiff C to Division 1; Bournemouth to Division 2.
2003–04   Crystal Palace to Premier League; Brighton & HA to Division 1; Huddersfield T to Division 2.
2004–05   West Ham U to Premier League; Sheffield W to Football League Championship, Southend U to Football League Championship 1.
2005–06   Watford to Premier League; Barnsley to Football League Championship; Cheltenham T to Football League Championship 1.
2006–07   Derby Co to Premier League; Blackpool to Football League Championship; Bristol R to Football League Championship 1.
2007–08   Hull C to Premier League; Doncaster R to Football League Championship; Stockport Co to Football League Championship 1.
2008–09   Burnley to Premier League; Scunthorpe U to Championship; Gillingham to Championship 1.
2009–10   Blackpool to Premier League; Millwall to Championship; Dagenham & R to Championship 1.

RELEGATED CLUBS

FA PREMIER LEAGUE TO DIVISION 1

1992–93   Crystal Palace, Middlesbrough, Nottingham F
1993–94   Sheffield U, Oldham Ath, Swindon T
1994–95   Crystal Palace, Norwich C, Leicester C, Ipswich T
1995–96   Manchester C, QPR, Bolton W
1996–97   Sunderland, Middlesbrough, Nottingham F
1997–98   Bolton W, Barnsley, Crystal Palace
1998–99   Charlton Ath, Blackburn R, Nottingham F
1999–90   Wimbledon, Sheffield W, Watford
2000–01   Manchester C, Coventry C, Bradford C
2001–02   Ipswich T, Derby Co, Leicester C
2002–03   West Ham U, WBA, Sunderland
2003–04   Leicester C, Leeds U, Wolverhampton W

FA PREMIER LEAGUE TO FOOTBALL LEAGUE CHAMPIONSHIP

2004–05   Crystal Palace, Norwich C, Southampton
2005–06   Birmingham C, WBA, Sunderland
2006–07   Sheffield U, Charlton Ath, Watford
2007–08   Reading, Birmingham C, Derby Co
2008–09   Newcastle U, Middlesbrough, WBA
2009–10   Burnley, Hull C, Portsmouth

DIVISION 1 TO DIVISION 2

1898–99 Bolton W and Sheffield W
1899–1900 Burnley and Glossop
1900–01 Preston NE and WBA
1901–02 Small Heath and Manchester C
1902–03 Grimsby T and Bolton W
1903–04 Liverpool and WBA
1904–05 League extended. Bury and Notts Co, two bottom clubs in First Division, re-elected.
1905–06 Nottingham F and Wolverhampton W
1906–07 Derby Co and Stoke C
1907–08 Bolton W and Birmingham C
1908–09 Manchester C and Leicester Fosse
1909–10 Bolton W and Chelsea
1910–11 Bristol C and Nottingham F
1911–12 Preston NE and Bury
1912–13 Notts Co and Woolwich Arsenal
1913–14 Preston NE and Derby Co
1914–15 Tottenham H and Chelsea*
1919–20 Notts Co and Sheffield W
1920–21 Derby Co and Bradford PA
1921–22 Bradford C and Manchester U
1922–23 Stoke C and Oldham Ath
1923–24 Chelsea and Middlesbrough
1924–25 Preston NE and Nottingham F
1925–26 Manchester C and Notts Co
1926–27 Leeds U and WBA
1927–28 Tottenham H and Middlesbrough

1928–29 Bury and Cardiff C
1929–30 Burnley and Everton
1930–31 Leeds U and Manchester U
1931–32 Grimsby T and West Ham U
1932–33 Bolton W and Blackpool
1933–34 Newcastle U and Sheffield U
1934–35 Leicester C and Tottenham H
1935–36 Aston Villa and Blackburn R
1936–37 Manchester U and Sheffield W
1937–38 Manchester C and WBA
1938–39 Birmingham C and Leicester C
1946–47 Brentford and Leeds U
1947–48 Blackburn R and Grimsby T
1948–49 Preston NE and Sheffield U
1949–50 Manchester C and Birmingham C
1950–51 Sheffield W and Everton
1951–52 Huddersfield T and Fulham
1952–53 Stoke C and Derby Co
1953–54 Middlesbrough and Liverpool
1954–55 Leicester C and Sheffield W
1955–56 Huddersfield T and Sheffield U
1956–57 Charlton Ath and Cardiff C
1957–58 Sheffield W and Sunderland
1958–59 Portsmouth and Aston Villa
1959–60 Luton T and Leeds U
1960–61 Preston NE and Newcastle U
1961–62 Chelsea and Cardiff C
1962–63 Manchester C and Leyton Orient
1963–64 Bolton W and Ipswich T

1964–65 Wolverhampton W and Birmingham C	1985–86 Ipswich T, Birmingham C, WBA
1965–66 Northampton T and Blackburn R	1986–87 Leicester C, Manchester C, Aston Villa
1966–67 Aston Villa and Blackpool	1987–88 Chelsea**, Portsmouth, Watford, Oxford U
1967–68 Fulham and Sheffield U	
1968–69 Leicester C and QPR	1988–89 Middlesbrough, West Ham U, Newcastle U
1969–70 Sunderland and Sheffield W	
1970–71 Burnley and Blackpool	1989–90 Sheffield W, Charlton Ath, Millwall
1971–72 Huddersfield T and Nottingham F	
	1990–91 Sunderland and Derby Co
1972–73 Crystal Palace and WBA	1991–92 Luton T, Notts Co, West Ham U
1973–74 Southampton, Manchester U, Norwich C	1992–93 Brentford, Cambridge U, Bristol R
1974–75 Luton T, Chelsea, Carlisle U	1993–94 Birmingham C, Oxford U, Peterborough U
1975–76 Wolverhampton W, Burnley, Sheffield U	
	1994–95 Swindon T, Burnley, Bristol C, Notts Co
1976–77 Sunderland, Stoke C, Tottenham H	
	1995–96 Millwall, Watford, Luton T
1977–78 West Ham U, Newcastle U, Leicester C	1996–97 Grimsby T, Oldham Ath, Southend U
1978–79 QPR, Birmingham C, Chelsea	1997–98 Manchester C, Stoke C, Reading
1979–80 Bristol C, Derby Co, Bolton W	1998–99 Bury, Oxford U, Bristol C
1980–81 Norwich C, Leicester C, Crystal Palace	1999–00 Walsall, Port Vale, Swindon T
	2000–01 Huddersfield T, QPR, Tranmere R
1981–82 Leeds U, Wolverhampton W, Middlesbrough	
	2001–02 Crewe Alex, Barnsley, Stockport Co
1982–83 Manchester C, Swansea C, Brighton & HA	
	2002–03 Sheffield W, Brighton & HA, Grimsby T
1983–84 Birmingham C, Notts Co, Wolverhampton W	
	2003–04 Walsall, Bradford C, Wimbledon
1984–85 Norwich C, Sunderland, Stoke C	

** Relegated after play-offs.
* Subsequently re-elected to Division 1 when League was extended after the War.

FOOTBALL LEAGUE CHAMPIONSHIP
TO FOOTBALL LEAGUE CHAMPIONSHIP 1

2004–05 Gillingham, Nottingham F, Rotherham U
2005–06 Crewe Alex, Millwall, Brighton & HA
2006–07 Southend U, Luton T, Leeds U
2007–08 Leicester C, Scunthorpe U, Colchester U
2008–09 Norwich C, Southampton, Charlton Ath
2009–10 Sheffield W, Plymouth Arg, Peterborough U

DIVISION 2 TO DIVISION 3

1920–21 Stockport Co	1931–32 Barnsley and Bristol C
1921–22 Bradford PA and Bristol C	1932–33 Chesterfield and Charlton Ath
1922–23 Rotherham Co and Wolverhampton W	1933–34 Millwall and Lincoln C
	1934–35 Oldham Ath and Notts Co
1923–24 Nelson and Bristol C	1935–36 Port Vale and Hull C
1924–25 Crystal Palace and Coventry C	1936–37 Doncaster R and Bradford C
1925–26 Stoke C and Stockport Co	1937–38 Barnsley and Stockport Co
1926–27 Darlington and Bradford C	1938–39 Norwich C and Tranmere R
1927–28 Fulham and South Shields	1946–47 Swansea T and Newport Co
1928–29 Port Vale and Clapton Orient	1947–48 Doncaster R and Millwall
1929–30 Hull C and Notts Co	1948–49 Nottingham F and Lincoln C
1930–31 Reading and Cardiff C	1949–50 Plymouth Arg and Bradford PA

1950–51 Grimsby T and Chesterfield	1985–86 Carlisle U, Middlesbrough, Fulham
1951–52 Coventry C and QPR	1986–87 Sunderland**, Grimsby T,
1952–53 Southampton and Barnsley	Brighton & HA
1953–54 Brentford and Oldham Ath	1987–88 Huddersfield T, Reading, Sheffield
1954–55 Ipswich T and Derby Co	U**
1955–56 Plymouth Arg and Hull C	1988–89 Shrewsbury T, Birmingham C,
1956–57 Port Vale and Bury	Walsall
1957–58 Doncaster R and Notts Co	1989–90 Bournemouth, Bradford C,
1958–59 Barnsley and Grimsby T	Stoke C
1959–60 Bristol C and Hull C	1990–91 WBA and Hull C
1960–61 Lincoln C and Portsmouth	1991–92 Plymouth Arg, Brighton & HA,
1961–62 Brighton & HA and Bristol R	Port Vale
1962–63 Walsall and Luton T	1992–93 Preston NE, Mansfield T,
1963–64 Grimsby T and Scunthorpe U	Wigan Ath, Chester C
1964–65 Swindon T and Swansea T	1993–94 Fulham, Exeter C, Hartlepool U,
1965–66 Middlesbrough and Leyton Orient	Barnet
1966–67 Northampton T and Bury	1994–95 Cambridge U, Plymouth Arg,
1967–68 Plymouth Arg and Rotherham U	Cardiff C, Chester C, Leyton
1968–69 Fulham and Bury	Orient
1969–70 Preston NE and Aston Villa	1995–96 Carlisle U, Swansea C, Brighton &
1970–71 Blackburn R and Bolton W	HA, Hull C
1971–72 Charlton Ath and Watford	1996–97 Peterborough U, Shrewsbury T,
1972–73 Huddersfield T and Brighton & HA	Rotherham U, Notts Co
1973–74 Crystal Palace, Preston NE,	1997–98 Brentford, Plymouth Arg, Carlisle
Swindon T	U, Southend U
1974–75 Millwall, Cardiff C, Sheffield W	1998–99 York C, Northampton T, Lincoln
1975–76 Oxford U, York C, Portsmouth	C, Macclesfield T
1976–77 Carlisle U, Plymouth Arg,	1999–00 Cardiff C, Blackpool, Scunthorpe
Hereford U	U, Chesterfield
1977–78 Blackpool, Mansfield T, Hull C	2000–01 Bristol R, Luton T, Swansea C,
1978–79 Sheffield U, Millwall, Blackburn R	Oxford U
1979–80 Fulham, Burnley, Charlton Ath	2001–02 Bournemouth, Bury, Wrexham,
1980–81 Preston NE, Bristol C, Bristol R	Cambridge U
1981–82 Cardiff C, Wrexham, Orient	2002–03 Cheltenham T, Huddersfield T,
1982–83 Rotherham U, Burnley, Bolton W	Mansfield T, Northampton T
1983–84 Derby Co, Swansea C, Cambridge U	2003–04 Grimsby T, Rushden & D, Notts
1984–85 Notts Co, Cardiff C,	Co, Wycombe W
Wolverhampton W	

FOOTBALL LEAGUE CHAMPIONSHIP 1
TO FOOTBALL LEAGUE CHAMPIONSHIP 2

2004–05 Torquay U, Wrexham, Peterborough U, Stockport Co
2005–06 Hartlepool U, Milton Keynes D, Swindon T, Walsall
2006–07 Chesterfield, Bradford C, Rotherham U, Brentford
2007–08 Bournemouth, Gillingham, Port Vale, Luton T
2008–09 Northampton T, Crewe Alex, Cheltenham T, Hereford U
2009–10 Gillingham, Wycombe W, Southend U, Stockport Co

DIVISION 3 TO DIVISION 4

1958–59 Rochdale, Notts Co,	1961–62 Newport Co, Brentford,
Doncaster R, Stockport Co	Lincoln C, Torquay U
1959–60 Accrington S, Wrexham,	1962–63 Bradford PA, Brighton & HA,
Mansfield T, York C	Carlisle U, Halifax T
1960–61 Chesterfield, Colchester U,	1963–64 Millwall, Crewe Alex, Wrexham,
Bradford C, Tranmere R	Notts Co

1964–65	Luton T, Port Vale, Colchester U, Barnsley
1965–66	Southend U, Exeter C, Brentford, York C
1966–67	Doncaster R, Workington, Darlington, Swansea T
1967–68	Scunthorpe U, Colchester U, Grimsby T, Peterborough U (demoted)
1968–69	Oldham Ath, Crewe Alex, Hartlepool, Northampton T
1969–70	Bournemouth, Southport, Barrow, Stockport Co
1970–71	Reading, Bury, Doncaster R, Gillingham
1971–72	Mansfield T, Barnsley, Torquay U, Bradford C
1972–73	Rotherham U, Brentford, Swansea C, Scunthorpe U
1973–74	Cambridge U, Shrewsbury T, Southport, Rochdale
1974–75	Bournemouth, Tranmere R, Watford, Huddersfield T
1975–76	Aldershot, Colchester U, Southend U, Halifax T
1976–77	Reading, Northampton T, Grimsby T, York C
1977–78	Port Vale, Bradford C, Hereford U, Portsmouth
1978–79	Peterborough U, Walsall, Tranmere R, Lincoln C
1979–80	Bury, Southend U, Mansfield T, Wimbledon
1980–81	Sheffield U, Colchester U, Blackpool, Hull C
1981–82	Wimbledon, Swindon T, Bristol C, Chester
1982–83	Reading, Wrexham, Doncaster R, Chesterfield
1983–84	Scunthorpe U, Southend U, Port Vale, Exeter C
1984–85	Burnley, Orient, Preston NE, Cambridge U
1985–86	Lincoln C, Cardiff C, Wolverhampton W, Swansea C
1986–87	Bolton W**, Carlisle U, Darlington, Newport Co
1987–88	Doncaster R, York C, Grimsby T, Rotherham U**
1988–89	Southend U, Chesterfield, Gillingham, Aldershot
1989–90	Cardiff C, Northampton T, Blackpool, Walsall
1990–91	Crewe Alex, Rotherham U, Mansfield T
1991–92	Bury, Shrewsbury T, Torquay U, Darlington

** Relegated after play-offs.

LEAGUE STATUS FROM 1986–1987

	RELEGATED FROM LEAGUE	PROMOTED TO LEAGUE
1986–87	Lincoln C	Scarborough
1987–88	Newport Co	Lincoln C
1988–89	Darlington	Maidstone U
1989–90	Colchester U	Darlington
1990–91	—	Barnet
1991–92	—	Colchester U
1992–93	Halifax T	Wycombe W
1993–94	—	—
1994–95	—	—
1995–96	—	—
1996–97	Hereford U	Macclesfield T
1997–98	Doncaster R	Halifax T
1998–99	Scarborough	Cheltenham T
1999–2000	Chester C	Kidderminster H
2000–01	Barnet	Rushden & D
2001–02	Halifax T	Boston U
2002–03	Shrewsbury T, Exeter C	Yeovil T, Doncaster R
2003–04	Carlisle U, York C	Chester C, Shrewsbury T
2004–05	Kidderminster H, Cambridge U	Barnet, Carlisle U
2005–06	Oxford U, Rushden & D	Accrington S, Hereford U
2006–07	Boston U, Torquay U	Dagenham & R, Morecambe
2007–08	Mansfield T, Wrexham	Aldershot T, Exeter C
2008–09	Chester C, Luton T	Burton Alb, Torquay U
2009–10	Grimsby T, Darlington	Stevenage B, Oxford U

LEAGUE TITLE WINS

FA PREMIER LEAGUE – Manchester U 11, Arsenal 3, Chelsea 3, Blackburn R 1.

FOOTBALL LEAGUE CHAMPIONSHIP – Sunderland 2, Newcastle U 1,
Reading 1, WBA 1, Wolverhampton W 1.

LEAGUE DIVISION 1 – Liverpool 18, Arsenal 10, Everton 9, Sunderland 8, Aston
Villa 7, Manchester U 7, Newcastle U 5, Sheffield W 4, Huddersfield T 3, Leeds U 3,
Manchester C 3, Portsmouth 3, Wolverhampton W 3, Blackburn R 2, Burnley 2,
Derby Co 2, Nottingham F 2, Preston NE 2, Tottenham H 2; Bolton W,
Charlton Ath, Chelsea, Crystal Palace, Fulham, Ipswich T, Middlesbrough, Norwich
C, Sheffield U, WBA 1 each.

FOOTBALL LEAGUE CHAMPIONSHIP 1 – Leicester C 1, Luton T 1, Norwich C 1,
Scunthorpe U 1, Southend U 1, Swansea C 1.

LEAGUE DIVISION 2 – Leicester C 6, Manchester C 6, Birmingham C (one as Small
Heath) 5, Sheffield W 5, Derby Co 4, Liverpool 4, Preston NE 4, Ipswich T 3,
Leeds U 3, Middlesbrough 3, Notts Co 3, Stoke C 3, Aston Villa 2, Bolton W 2,
Burnley 2, Bury 2, Chelsea 2, Fulham 2, Grimsby T 2, Manchester U 2, Millwall 2,
Norwich C 2, Nottingham F 2, Tottenham H 2, WBA 2, West Ham U 2,
Wolverhampton W 2; Blackburn R, Blackpool, Bradford C, Brentford, Brighton &
HA, Bristol C, Coventry C, Crystal Palace, Everton, Huddersfield T, Luton T,
Newcastle U, Plymouth Arg, QPR, Oldham Ath, Oxford U, Reading, Sheffield U,
Sunderland, Swindon T, Watford, Wigan Ath 1 each.

FOOTBALL LEAGUE CHAMPIONSHIP 2 – Brentford 1, Carlisle U 1,
Milton Keynes D 1, Notts Co 1, Walsall 1, Yeovil T 1.

LEAGUE DIVISION 3 – Brentford 2, Carlisle U 2, Oxford U 2, Plymouth Arg 2,
Portsmouth 2, Preston NE 2, Shrewsbury T 2; Aston Villa, Blackburn R, Bolton W,
Bournemouth, Bradford C, Brighton & HA, Bristol R, Burnley, Bury, Cambridge
U, Cardiff C, Coventry C, Doncaster R, Grimsby T, Hereford U, Hull C, Leyton
Orient, Mansfield T, Northampton T, Notts Co, Oldham Ath, QPR, Reading,
Rotherham U, Rushden & D, Southampton, Sunderland, Swansea C, Watford,
Wigan Ath, Wolverhampton W, Wrexham 1 each.

LEAGUE DIVISION 4 – Chesterfield 2, Doncaster R 2, Peterborough U 2; Brentford,
Brighton & HA, Burnley, Cambridge U, Darlington, Exeter C, Gillingham,
Grimsby T, Huddersfield T, Lincoln C, Luton T, Mansfield T, Millwall, Northampton
T, Notts Co, Port Vale, Reading, Rotherham U, Sheffield U, Southend U, Southport,
Stockport Co, Swindon T, Walsall, Watford, Wimbledon, Wolverhampton W, York C
1 each.

DIVISION 3 (South) – Bristol C 3, Charlton Ath 2, Ipswich T 2, Millwall 2, Notts Co 2,
Plymouth Arg 2, Swansea T 2; Brentford, Brighton & HA, Bristol R, Cardiff C,
Coventry C, Crystal Palace, Fulham, Leyton Orient, Luton T, Newport Co,
Norwich C, Nottingham F, Portsmouth, QPR, Reading, Southampton 1 each.

DIVISION 3 (North) – Barnsley 3, Doncaster R 3, Lincoln C 3, Chesterfield 2,
Grimsby T 2, Hull C 2, Port Vale 2, Stockport Co 2; Bradford C, Bradford PA,
Darlington, Derby Co, Nelson, Oldham Ath, Rotherham U, Scunthorpe U, Stoke C,
Tranmere R, Wolverhampton W 1 each.

FOOTBALL LEAGUE PLAY-OFFS 2009–2010

■ *Denotes player sent off.*

CHAMPIONSHIP FIRST LEG

Blackpool	(1) 2	Nottingham F	(1) 1
Leicester C	(0) 0	Cardiff C	(0) 1

CHAMPIONSHIP SECOND LEG

Nottingham F	(1) 3	Blackpool	(0) 4
Cardiff C	(1) 2	Leicester C	(2) 3

(aet; Cardiff C won 4-3 on penalties.)

CHAMPIONSHIP FINAL (at Wembley) Saturday, 22 May 2010

Blackpool (3) 3 *(Adam 13, Taylor-Fletcher 41, Ormerod 45)*

Cardiff C (2) 2 *(Chopra 9, Ledley 37)* 82,244

Blackpool: Gilks; Coleman, Crainey, Southern, John-Baptiste, Evatt, Adam, Taylor-Fletcher (Burgess), Ormerod (Dobbie), Campbell, Vaughan (Bannan).
Cardiff C: Marshall; McNaughton (Gerrard), Kennedy, Whittingham, Hudson, Blake, Burke (McCormack), McPhail, Bothroyd (Etuhu), Chopra, Ledley.
Referee: A. Marriner (West Midlands).

LEAGUE 1 FIRST LEG

Swindon T	(0) 2	Charlton Ath	(0) 1
Huddersfield T	(0) 0	Millwall	(0) 0

LEAGUE 1 SECOND LEG

Charlton Ath	(2) 2	Swindon T	(0) 1

(aet; Swindon T won 5-4 on penalties.)

Millwall	(1) 2	Huddersfield T	(0) 0

LEAGUE 1 FINAL (at Wembley) Saturday, 29 May 2010

Millwall (1) 1 *(Robinson 39)*

Swindon T (0) 0 73,108

Millwall: Forde; Barron, Craig (Frampton), Trotter, Robinson, Ward, Batt (Hackett), Abdou, Morison, Harris, Schofield.
Swindon T: Lucas; Amankwaah, Lescinel, Douglas, Cuthbert, Sheehan (Darby), McGovern (O'Brien), Ward, Paynter (Pericard), Austin, Ferry.
Referee: C. Webster (Tyne & Wear).

LEAGUE 2 FIRST LEG

Aldershot T	(0) 0	Rotherham U	(0) 1
Dagenham & R	(2) 6	Morecambe	(0) 0

LEAGUE 2 SECOND LEG

Rotherham U	(1) 2	Aldershot T	(0) 0
Morecambe	(0) 2	Dagenham & R	(0) 1

LEAGUE 2 FINAL (at Wembley) Sunday, 30 May 2010

Dagenham & R (1) 3 *(Benson 38, Green 56, Nurse 70)*

Rotherham U (1) 2 *(Taylor R 39, 61)* 32,054

Dagenham & R: Roberts; Ogogo, McCrory, Arber, Doe, Vincelot, Green, Nurse (Montgomery), Benson, Scott (Walsh), Gain.
Rotherham U: Warrington; Lynch, Gunning, Mills (Marshall), Sharps, Fenton, Law, Harrison, Taylor R, Le Fondre, Ellison (Bell-Baggie).
Referee: J. Linington (Isle of Wight).

LEAGUE ATTENDANCES 2009–2010

FA BARCLAYCARD PREMIERSHIP ATTENDANCES

	Average Gate			Season 2009–10	
	2008–09	2009–10	+/–%	Highest	Lowest
Arsenal	60,040	59,927	–0.19	60,103	59,084
Aston Villa	39,812	38,573	–3.11	42,788	32,917
Birmingham City	19,090	25,246	+32.25	28,958	19,922
Blackburn Rovers	23,479	25,428	+8.30	29,912	21,287
Bolton Wanderers	22,486	21,880	–2.70	25,370	17,849
Burnley	13,082	20,653	+57.87	21,761	18,397
Chelsea	41,589	41,422	–0.40	41,836	40,137
Everton	35,667	36,725	+2.97	39,652	32,163
Fulham	24,344	23,909	–1.79	25,700	20,831
Hull City	24,816	24,389	–1.72	25,030	22,822
Liverpool	43,611	42,863	–1.72	44,392	37,697
Manchester City	42,899	45,512	+6.09	47,370	40,292
Manchester United	75,304	74,864	–0.58	75,316	73,709
Portsmouth	19,830	18,249	–7.97	20,821	16,207
Stoke City	26,960	27,162	+0.75	27,604	25,104
Sunderland	40,168	40,355	+0.47	47,641	34,821
Tottenham Hotspur	35,929	35,794	–0.38	36,041	35,318
West Ham United	33,701	33,683	–0.05	34,989	30,024
Wigan Athletic	18,350	18,006	–1.87	22,113	14,323
Wolverhampton Wanderers	24,153	28,365	+17.44	29,023	26,668

FOOTBALL LEAGUE CHAMPIONSHIP ATTENDANCES

	Average Gate			Season 2009–10	
	2008–09	2009–10	+/–%	Highest	Lowest
Barnsley	13,189	12,964	–1.71	20,079	11,116
Blackpool	7,843	8,611	+9.79	12,296	6,855
Bristol City	16,816	14,600	–13.18	19,144	13,009
Cardiff City	18,044	20,717	+14.81	25,630	17,686
Coventry City	17,451	17,305	–0.84	22,209	14,426
Crystal Palace	15,220	14,770	–2.96	20,643	12,328
Derby County	29,440	29,230	–0.71	33,010	26,186
Doncaster Rovers	11,964	10,991	–8.13	14,850	8,827
Ipswich Town	20,961	20,840	–0.58	27,059	19,283
Leicester City	20,253	23,942	+18.21	31,759	18,928
Middlesbrough	28,429	19,948	–29.83	27,721	16,847
Newcastle United	48,750	43,387	–11.00	52,181	36,944
Nottingham Forest	22,299	23,831	+6.87	29,155	18,332
Peterborough United	7,599	8,913	+17.29	12,877	6,445
Plymouth Argyle	11,533	10,316	–10.55	14,792	7,243
Preston North End	13,426	12,934	–3.66	19,840	10,270
Queens Park Rangers	14,090	13,348	–5.27	17,082	10,940
Reading	19,942	17,495	–12.27	23,163	14,096
Scunthorpe United	4,998	6,463	+29.31	8,921	4,995
Sheffield United	26,023	25,120	–3.47	29,210	22,555
Sheffield Wednesday	21,542	23,179	+7.60	37,121	18,329
Swansea City	15,195	15,407	+1.40	18,794	12,775
Watford	14,858	14,344	–3.46	17,120	12,179
West Bromwich Albion	25,828	22,199	–14.05	25,297	19,390

Premiership and Football League attendance averages and highest crowd figures for 2009–10 are unofficial.

FOOTBALL LEAGUE CHAMPIONSHIP 1 ATTENDANCES

	Average Gate			Season 2009–10	
	2008–09	2009–10	+/–%	Highest	Lowest
Brentford	5,707	6,017	+5.43	9,031	4,200
Brighton & Hove Albion	6,092	6,466	+6.14	7,784	4,711
Bristol Rovers	7,171	7,042	–1.80	11,448	5,322
Carlisle United	6,268	5,210	–16.88	8,728	3,731
Charlton Athletic	20,894	17,407	–16.69	23,198	14,636
Colchester United	5,084	5,529	+8.75	10,064	3,601
Exeter City	4,939	5,832	+18.08	8,549	4,106
Gillingham	5,307	6,335	+19.37	10,304	3,840
Hartlepool United	3,835	3,443	–10.22	5,115	2,465
Huddersfield Town	13,298	14,381	+8.14	21,764	11,269
Leeds United	23,813	24,817	+4.22	38,234	17,635
Leyton Orient	4,692	4,937	+5.22	8,013	2,669
Millwall	8,940	10,834	+21.19	17,632	6,617
Milton Keynes Dons FC	10,551	10,289	–2.48	16,713	8,528
Norwich City	24,543	24,671	+0.52	25,506	23,041
Oldham Athletic	5,636	4,630	–17.85	8,569	2,833
Southampton	17,858	20,982	+17.49	30,890	16,402
Southend United	7,850	7,718	–1.68	10,329	6,382
Stockport County	6,130	4,420	–27.90	7,768	3,281
Swindon Town	7,499	8,389	+11.87	14,508	6,183
Tranmere Rovers	5,820	5,670	–2.58	8,694	4,317
Walsall	4,572	4,028	–11.90	8,483	2,929
Wycombe Wanderers	5,109	5,544	+8.51	8,400	3,899
Yeovil Town	4,423	4,664	+5.45	7,484	3,469

FOOTBALL LEAGUE CHAMPIONSHIP 2 ATTENDANCES

	Average Gate			Season 2009–10	
	2008–09	2009–10	+/–%	Highest	Lowest
Accrington Stanley	1,414	1,980	+40.03	3,396	1,210
Aldershot Town	3,276	3,085	–5.83	4,506	2,053
Barnet	2,153	2,059	–4.37	4,638	1,298
AFC Bournemouth	4,931	5,719	+15.98	9,055	4,019
Bradford City	12,704	11,422	–10.09	12,403	10,831
Burton Albion	2,401	3,195	+33.07	5,801	2,027
Bury	3,342	3,028	–9.40	6,528	2,123
Cheltenham Town	3,854	3,185	–17.36	4,134	2,331
Chesterfield	3,449	3,849	+11.60	6,196	3,104
Crewe Alexandra	4,537	4,075	–10.18	6,943	3,272
Dagenham & Redbridge	2,048	2,097	+2.39	3,721	1,683
Darlington	2,932	1,943	–33.73	2,744	1,296
Grimsby Town	4,475	4,458	–0.38	7,033	3,090
Hereford United	3,270	2,138	–34.62	3,280	1,208
Lincoln City	3,940	3,670	–6.85	6,012	2,457
Macclesfield Town	1,898	1,928	+1.58	3,449	1,035
Morecambe	2,153	2,262	+5.06	5,268	1,537
Northampton Town	5,200	4,375	–15.87	5,647	3,206
Notts County	4,446	7,352	+65.36	11,331	4,606
Port Vale	5,522	5,079	–8.02	8,467	3,231
Rochdale	3,222	3,443	+6.86	5,371	2,311
Rotherham United	3,587	3,817	+6.41	10,254	2,604
Shrewsbury Town	5,664	5,481	–3.23	7,096	4,328
Torquay United	2,243	2,855	+27.28	5,124	2,122

TRANSFERS 2009–2010

JUNE 2009

	From	To
11 Barry, Gareth	Aston Villa	Manchester City
15 Chapman, Adam	Sheffield United	Oxford United
16 Dann, Scott	Coventry City	Birmingham City
17 Diagouraga, Toumani	Hereford United	Peterborough United
30 Doyle, Kevin E.	Reading	Wolverhampton Wanderers
26 Johnson, Glen M.C.	Portsmouth	Liverpool
25 Johnson, Roger	Cardiff City	Birmingham City
30 Kane, Anthony M.	Blackburn Rovers	Carlisle United
29 McGoldrick, David J.	Southampton	Nottingham Forest
5 Morison, Steve	Stevenage Borough	Millwall
30 Peltier, Lee A.	Yeovil Town	Huddersfield Town
5 Pope, Thomas J.	Crewe Alexandra	Rotherham United
24 Santa Cruz, Roque	Blackburn Rovers	Manchester City
30 Simpson, Robert	Coventry City	Huddersfield Town
30 Surman, Andrew R.E.	Southampton	Wolverhampton Wanderers
17 Tudur-Jones, Owain	Swansea City	Norwich City
16 Williamson, Lee	Watford	Sheffield United

TEMPORARY TRANSFERS

9 Hatch, Liam M.A. – Peterborough United – Luton Town; 27 Heath, Joseph – Nottingham Forest – Lincoln City; 26 Sears, Fred – West Ham United – Crystal Palace

JULY 2009

24 Adebayor, Emmanuel	Arsenal	Manchester City
27 Allott, Mark S.	Tranmere Rovers	Chesterfield
1 Anderson, Paul	Liverpool	Nottingham Forest
15 Barker, Shaun	Blackpool	Derby County
22 Blackstock, Dexter A.	Queens Park Rangers	Nottingham Forest
2 Boyd, Adam	Leyton Orient	Hartlepool United
30 Boyes, Adam J.	York City	Scunthorpe United
22 Bromby, Leigh	Watford	Sheffield United
1 Brown, Wayne L.	Hull City	Leicester City
3 Camp, Lee M.J.	Queens Park Rangers	Nottingham Forest
20 Campbell, Fraizer L.	Manchester United	Sunderland
14 Chopra, Rocky M.	Sunderland	Cardiff City
24 Clingan, Samuel G.	Norwich City	Coventry City
8 Cox, Simon	Swindon Town	West Bromwich Albion
28 Crouch, Peter J.	Portsmouth	Tottenham Hotspur
9 Delaney, Damien	Queens Park Rangers	Ipswich Town
15 Dickinson, Liam M.	Derby County	Brighton & Hove Albion
16 Downing, Stewart	Middlesbrough	Aston Villa
8 Draper, Ross	Hednesford Town	Macclesfield Town
1 Dyer, Nathan A.J.	Southampton	Swansea City
17 Easter, Jermaine M.	Plymouth Argyle	Milton Keynes Dons
23 Evans, Chedwyn M.	Manchester City	Sheffield United
10 Evans, Gareth C.	Macclesfield Town	Bradford City
4 Gerken, Dean J.	Colchester United	Bristol City
24 Gerrard, Anthony	Walsall	Cardiff City
1 Gleeson, Stephen M.	Wolverhampton Wanderers	Milton Keynes Dons
21 Gunter, Christopher R.	Tottenham Hotspur	Nottingham Forest
3 Halford, Gregory	Sunderland	Wolverhampton Wanderers

14 Haynes, Danny L.	Ipswich Town	Bristol City
24 Holt, Grant	Shrewsbury Town	Norwich City
2 Hudson, Mark A.	Charlton Athletic	Cardiff City
6 Law, Nicholas	Sheffield United	Rotherham United
3 Legge, Leon	Tonbridge Angels	Brentford
22 Lynch, Joel J.	Brighton & Hove Albion	Nottingham Forest
7 Martin, Lee R.	Manchester United	Ipswich Town
28 McCrae, Romone	Crawley Town	Peterborough United
20 McKenna, Paul S.	Preston North End	Nottingham Forest
7 Mears, Tyrone	Derby County	Burnley
23 Mills, Daniel P.	Crawley Town	Peterborough United
1 Moxey, Dean	Exeter City	Derby County
24 Naughton, Kyle	Sheffield United	Tottenham Hotspur
14 Neal, Christopher M.	Preston North End	Shrewsbury Town
15 Nyatanga, Lewin J.	Derby County	Bristol City
8 O'Connor, Michael J.	Crewe Alexandra	Scunthorpe United
9 Penn, Russell	Kidderminster Harriers	Burton Albion
2 Robinson, Theo L.R.	Watford	Huddersfield Town
9 Smith, James D.	Chelsea	Leyton Orient
1 Surman, Andrew R.	Southampton	Wolverhampton Wanderers
31 Talbot, Andrew	Luton Town	Chesterfield
15 Taylor, Andrew	Tranmere Rovers	Sheffield United
27 Tipton, Matthew J.	Droylsden	Macclesfield Town
31 Toure, Kolo A.	Arsenal	Manchester City
14 Tunnicliffe, James M.	Stockport County	Brighton & Hove Albion
1 Valencia, Luis Antonio	Wigan Athletic	Manchester United
30 Walker, Kyle	Sheffield United	Tottenham Hotspur
14 Wellens, Richard P.	Doncaster Rovers	Leicester City
24 Whaley, Simon	Preston North End	Norwich City
24 Whitehead, Dean	Sunderland	Stoke City
24 Wiggins, Rhoys	Crystal Palace	Norwich City
10 Williams, Benjamin P.	Carlisle United	Colchester United
31 Wright, Jake M.	Crawley Town	Brighton & Hove Albion
9 Yeates, Mark	Colchester United	Middlesbrough

TEMPORARY TRANSFERS

24 Akurang, Cliff C. – Barnet – Rushden & Diamonds; 24 Alnwick, Ben – Tottenham Hotspur – Norwich City; 24 Archibald-Henville, Troy – Tottenham Hotspur – Exeter City; 14 Bolasie, Yannick – Plymouth Argyle – Barnet; 30 Bunn, Mark – Blackburn Rovers – Sheffield United; 24 Button, David R.E. – Tottenham Hotspur – Crewe Alexandra; 20 Byrne, Mark – Nottingham Forest – Rushden & Diamonds; 16 Caulker, Steven R. – Tottenham Hotspur – Yeovil Town; 29 Craney, Ian T.W. – Accrington Stanley – Morecambe; 21 Daniels, Luke M. – West Bromwich Albion – Tranmere Rovers; 14 Dennehy, Darren J. – Cardiff City – Hereford United; 27 Eastwood, Simon C. – Huddersfield Town – Bradford City; 31 Forster, Fraser G. – Newcastle United – Bristol Rovers; 29 Gazet Du Chattelier, Ryan – Portsmouth – Weymouth; 20 Gowling, Joshua A.I. – Carlisle United – Gillingham; 23 Green, Matthew J. – Torquay United – Oxford United; 1 Hart, Charles J.J. – Manchester City – Birmingham City; 1 Heath, Joseph – Nottingham Forest – Lincoln City; 30 Heath, Matthew P. – Leeds United – Southend United; 29 Jevons, Phillip – Huddersfield Town – Morecambe; 24 Logan, Shaleum – Manchester City – Tranmere Rovers; 23 McCarthy, Alex S. – Reading – Yeovil Town; 19 Mason, Ryan G. – Tottenham Hotspur – Yeovil Town; Moloney, Brendon A. – Nottingham Forest – Notts County; 20 Medley, Luke A.C. – Barnet – Woking; 20 Pearce, Krystian M.V. – Birmingham City – Peterborough United; 3 Potter, Alfie J. – Peterborough United – Oxford United; 10 Price, Lewis P. – Derby County –

Brentford; 29 Puddy, Willem J.S. – Cheltenham Town – Bath City; 14 Redmond, Shane P. – Nottingham Forest – Burton Albion; 6 Reid, James A. – Nottingham Forest – Rushden & Diamonds; 28 Rendell, Scott D. – Peterborough United – Torquay United; 27 Reynolds, Callum F. – Portsmouth – Luton Town; 22 Robinson, Paul P. – West Bromwich Albion – Bolton Wanderers; 24 Sawyer, Lee T. – Chelsea – Southend United; 6 Shroot, Robin – Birmingham City – Burton Albion; 27 Taarabt, Adel – Tottenham Hotspur – Queens Park Rangers; 13 Taiwo, Thomas J.W. – Chelsea – Carlisle United; 21 Thornhill, Matthew – Nottingham Forest – Brighton & Hove Albion; 24 Treacy, Keith – Blackburn Rovers – Sheffield United; 30 White, John A. – Colchester United – Southend United

AUGUST 2009

8 Bassong, Sebastian A.	Newcastle United	Tottenham Hotspur
28 Beattie, Craig	West Bromwich Albion	Swansea City
20 Bennett, Elliott	Wolverhampton Wanderers	Brighton & Hove Albion
6 Bent, Darren	Tottenham Hotspur	Sunderland
7 Beye, Habib	Newcastle United	Aston Villa
18 Bikey, Andre S.	Reading	Burnley
31 Boateng, Kevin P.	Tottenham Hotspur	Portsmouth
28 Brown, Michael R.	Wigan Athletic	Portsmouth
12 Cattermole, Lee B.	Wigan Athletic	Sunderland
6 Charnock, Kieran J.	Peterborough United	Torquay United
27 Chimbonda, Pascal	Tottenham Hotspur	Blackburn Rovers
13 Cranie, Martin J.	Portsmouth	Coventry City
4 Delph, Fabian	Leeds United	Aston Villa
28 Distin, Sylvain	Portsmouth	Everton
18 Duff, Damien A.	Newcastle United	Fulham
12 Eardley, Neal	Oldham Athletic	Blackpool
7 Elder, Nathan	Brentford	Shrewsbury Town
3 Evans, Chedwyn M.	Manchester City	Sheffield United
27 Flynn, Matthew E.	Macclesfield Town	Rochdale
21 Gallagher, Paul	Blackburn Rovers	Leicester City
27 Gowling, Joshua A.I.	Carlisle United	Gillingham
24 Gray, Andrew D.	Charlton Athletic	Barnsley
10 Hammill, Adam	Liverpool	Barnsley
18 Hammond, Dean J.	Colchester United	Southampton
11 Hunt, Stephen P.	Reading	Hull City
17 Hurst, Kevan	Scunthorpe United	Carlisle United
28 Huth, Robert	Middlesbrough	Stoke City
14 Knight, Zatyiah	Aston Villa	Bolton Wanderers
10 Lambert, Rickie L.	Bristol Rovers	Southampton
12 Le Fondre, Adam J.	Rochdale	Rotherham United
26 Lescott, Joleon P.	Everton	Manchester City
10 Mattock, Joseph W.	Leicester City	West Bromwich Albion
27 McAnuff, Joel J.F.M.	Watford	Reading
5 McIndoe, Michael	Bristol City	Coventry City
28 McShane, Paul D.	Sunderland	Hull City
6 Mills, Matthew C.	Doncaster Rovers	Reading
31 Mullin, Paul B.	Accrington Stanley	Morecambe
3 N'Guessen, Diombo	Lincoln City	Leicester City
6 Olofinjana, Seyi G.	Stoke City	Hull City
6 Parry, Paul I.	Cardiff City	Preston North End
7 Priskin, Tamas	Watford	Ipswich Town
27 Rasiak, Grzegorz	Southampton	Reading
7 Reid, Reuben J.	Rotherham United	West Bromwich Albion

14 Ricketts, Sam D.	Hull City	Bolton Wanderers
21 Schmeichel, Kaspar P.	Manchester City	Notts County
29 Shumulikoski, Veliche	Ipswich Town	Preston North End
27 Smith, Thomas W.	Watford	Portsmouth
27 Taiwo, Soloman O.	Dagenham & Redbridge	Cardiff City
14 Taylor, Cleveland K.W.	Carlisle United	Brentford
28 Warnock, Stephen	Blackburn Rovers	Aston Villa

TEMPORARY TRANSFERS

26 Adams, Stephen M. – Torquay United – Forest Green Rovers; 5 Ademola, Moses – Brentford – Woking; 20 Alessandra, Lewis P. – Oldham Athletic – Chester City; 28 Artus, Frankie – Bristol City – Cheltenham Town; 4 Bertrand, Ryan – Chelsea – Reading; 7 Bevan, David – Aston Villa – Ilkeston Town; 31 Bignall, Nicholas C. – Reading – Stockport County; 20 Blackman, Nicholas A. – Blackburn Rovers – Oldham Athletic; 28 Blake, Darcy J. – Cardiff City – Plymouth Argyle; 7 Blanchett, Daniel W. – Peterborough United – Stevenage Borough; 28 Boden, Luke – Sheffield Wednesday – Northampton Town; 6 Bozanic, Oliver J. – Reading – Cheltenham Town; 21 Bridcutt, Liam R. – Chelsea – Stockport County; 28 Calver, Craig T. – Southend United – St Albans City; 21 Chambers, Ashley R. – Leicester City – Wycombe Wanderers; 7 Chandler, Jamie – Sunderland – Darlington; 17 Cleverley, Thomas W. – Manchester United – Watford; 19 Clough, Charlie – Bristol Rovers – Chippenham Town; 7 Colback, Jack R. – Sunderland – Ipswich Town; 27 Coleman, Rory C. – Scunthorpe United – Harrogate Town; 28 Cook, Andrew E. – Carlisle United – Workington; 18 Cook, Jordan A. – Sunderland – Darlington; 21 Cork, Jack F.P. – Chelsea – Coventry City; 17 Cummings, Shaun – Chelsea – West Bromwich Albion; 11 Daly, George J. – Wycombe Wanderers – Hayes & Yeading United; 10 Davidson, Ross – Port Vale – Stafford Rangers; 17 Dean, Harlee J. – Dagenham & Redbridge – Braintree Town; 6 Denton, Tom – Huddersfield Town – Cheltenham Town; 28 Dickov, Paul – Leicester City – Derby County; 14 Di Santo, Franco – Chelsea – Blackburn Rovers; 29 Donnelly, Georgie J. – Plymouth Argyle – Luton Town; 7 Dowson, David – Sunderland – Darlington; 6 Doyle, Michael P. – Coventry City – Leeds United; 14 Drinkwater, Daniel N. – Manchester United – Huddersfield Town; 7 Eardley, Neal – Oldham Athletic – Blackpool; 7 Eastham, Ashley – Blackpool – Hyde United; 30 Edward, Daniel G. – Port Vale – Altrincham; 26 Ellis, Marc – Torquay United – Forest Green Rovers; 17 Emmanuel-Thomas, Jay-Aston – Arsenal – Blackpool; 22 Etuhu, Kelvin – Manchester City – Cardiff City; 28 Fairclough, Benjamin M.S. – Notts County – Ilkeston Town; 13 Flynn, Matthew E. – Macclesfield Town – Rochdale; 21 Foley, David J. – Hartlepool United – Barrow; 14 Forecast, Tommy S. – Southampton – Grimsby Town; 28 Forster, Fraser G. – Newcastle United – Norwich City; 14 Friend, George A.J. – Wolverhampton Wanderers – Millwall; 28 Gaughran, Samuel D. – Peterborough United – Grays Athletic; 15 Glover, Daniel – Port Vale – Salisbury City; 6 Godsmark, Jonathan – Newcastle United – Hereford United; 22 Gray, Andrew D. – Charlton Athletic – Barnsley; 21 Green, Michael J. – Bristol Rovers – Gloucester City; 21 Greening, Jonathan – West Bromwich Albion – Fulham; 19 Grimes, Jamie N. – Swansea City – Haverfordwest County; 6 Gunning, Gavin – Blackburn Rovers – Tranmere Rovers; 18 Halstead, Mark J. – Blackpool – Burscough; 15 Heaton, Thomas D. – Manchester United – Queens Park Rangers; 6 Howe, Jermaine R. – Peterborough United – Lincoln City; 25 Jackman, Daniel J. – Northampton Town – Gillingham; 21 Jackson, Marlon M. – Bristol City – Hereford United; 14 Jo – Manchester City – Everton; 6 Judge, Alan – Blackburn Rovers – Plymouth Argyle; 21 Kay, Adam B. – Burnley – Chester City; 4 Kee, Billy R. – Leicester City – Accrington Stanley; 6 Kite, Alexandros – Bristol Rovers – Gloucester City; 14 Krysiak, Artur L. – Birmingham City – Burton Albion; 7 Labadie, Josh C. – West Bromwich Albion – Shrewsbury Town; 21 Lansbury, Henri G. – Arsenal – Watford; 27 Levet, Ciaran A. – Plymouth Argyle – Yeovil Town; 4 Lisbie, Kevin A. – Ipswich Town – Colchester United; 7 Livermore, Jake C. – Tottenham Hotspur – Derby

County; 21 Lynch, Christopher M. – Burnley – Chester City; 24 McCrory, Damien P. –
Plymouth Argyle – Port Vale; 7 McDermott, Donal – Manchester City – Chesterfield;
31 McGivern, Ryan – Manchester City – Leicester City; 5 Mackay, Michael –
Hartlepool United – Gateshead; 14 Mancienne, Michael I. – Chelsea – Wolverhampton
Wanderers; 7 Marrow, Alexander J. – Blackburn Rovers – Oldham Athletic; 7 Marshall,
Ben – Stoke City – Northampton Town; 4 Martin, Alan – Leeds United – Accrington
Stanley; 14 Mellis, Jacob A. – Chelsea – Southampton; 21 Mitchley, Daniel J. –
Blackpool – Burscough; 31 Moffatt, Scott L. – Manchester United – Altrincham; 7
Mvoto, Jean – Sunderland – Southend United; 14 Obadeyi, Temitope – Bolton
Wanderers – Swindon Town; 11 Obika, Jonathan – Tottenham Hotspur – Yeovil Town;
28 Ojapah, Philip – Oldham Athletic – Stalybridge Celtic; 21 O'Grady, Christopher J. –
Oldham Athletic – Rochdale; 31 O'Hara, Jamie – Tottenham Hotspur – Portsmouth; 31
O'Leary, Kristian D. – Swansea City – Leyton Orient; 28 Pack, Marlon – Portsmouth –
Wycombe Wanderers; 17 Panther, Emmanuel – Exeter City – Morecambe; 26 Phillips,
Steven J. – Bristol Rovers – Shrewsbury Town; 6 Picton, Jake M. – Scunthorpe United –
Gainsborough Trinity; 21 Plummer, Tristan D. – Bristol City – Hereford United; 18
Porritt, Nathan J. – Middlesbrough – Darlington; 18 Powell, Darren D. – Brentford –
Crawley Town; 15 Prosser, Luke B. – Port Vale – Salisbury City; 7 Puncheon, Jason D.I.
– Barnet – Milton Keynes Dons; 22 Rigg, Sean M. – Bristol Rovers – Forest Green
Rovers; 14 Robertson, Jordan – Sheffield United – Bury; 7 Rose, Romone A.A. –
Queens Park Rangers – Northampton Town; 28 Sappleton, Reneil S.A. – Leicester City
– Macclesfield Town; 14 Shackell, Jason – Wolverhampton Wanderers – Doncaster
Rovers; 28 Shaw, Jon S. – Rochdale – Barrow; 7 Shumulikoski, Veliche – Ipswich Town
– Preston North End; 14 Simpson, Daniel P. – Manchester United – Newcastle United;
27 Simpson, Jay-Alistaire F. – Arsenal – Queens Park Rangers; 6 Sinclair, Scott A. –
Chelsea – Wigan Athletic; 7 Smith, Adam J. – Tottenham Hotspur – Wycombe
Wanderers; 18 Spence, Jordan – West Ham United – Scunthorpe United; 14 Stephens,
Dale C. – Oldham Athletic – Rochdale; 5 St Louis-Hamilton, Danzelle D. – Stoke City
– Vauxhall Motors; 7 Taylor, Aaron M. – Morecambe – Barrow; 7 Tejan-Sie, Thomas M.
– Dagenham & Redbridge – Braintree Town; 22 Thomas, Simon V. – Crystal Palace –
Ebbsfleet United; 21 Threlfall, Robert R. – Liverpool – Northampton Town; 7
Townsend, Andros – Tottenham Hotspur – Leyton Orient; 20 Trotman, Neal A. –
Preston North End – Southampton; 28 Trundle, Lee C. – Bristol City – Swansea City;
27 Tuncay – Sanli – Middlesbrough – Stoke City; 14 Tymon, Matthew R. – Hartlepool
United – Whitby Town; 21 Tyrrell, James R. – Bristol Rovers – Paulton Rovers; 7 Van
Aanholt, Patrick J.M. – Chelsea – Coventry City; 21 Varney, Luke I. – Derby County –
Sheffield Wednesday; 10 Verma, Aman – Leicester City – Crewe Alexandra; 7
Waghorn, Martyn T. – Sunderland – Leicester City; 5 Walker, Kyle A. – Tottenham
Hotspur – Sheffield United; 31 Walton, Simon W. – Plymouth Argyle – Crewe
Alexandra; 21 White, Joseph S. – Bristol Rovers – Yate Town; 21 Wilson, James S. –
Bristol City – Brentford; 14 Worley, Harry J. – Leicester City – Crewe Alexandra; 6
Worrall, David R. – West Bromwhich Albion – Bury

SEPTEMBER 2009

1 Ben Haim, Tal	Manchester City	Portsmouth
1 Bromby, Leigh	Sheffield United	Leeds United
1 Colbeck, Philip J.	Bradford City	Oldham Athletic
1 Colins, Daniel L.	Sunderland	Stoke City
1 Cummings, Shaun M.	Chelsea	Reading
3 Diop, Papa B.	Fulham	Portsmouth
1 Dunne, Richard P.	Manchester City	Aston Villa
1 Edwards, Carlos A.	Sunderland	Ipswich Town
1 Howard, Brian R.W.	Sheffield United	Reading
10 Jackman, Daniel J.	Northampton Town	Gillingham
1 Kranjcar, Nico	Portsmouth	Tottenham Hotspur

1 Leadbitter, Grant	Sunderland	Ipswich Town
21 McCombe, Jamie	Lincoln City	Bristol City
10 Myhill, Boaz G.O.	Aston Villa	Hull City
1 Schofield, Daniel J.	Yeovil Town	Millwall
1 Turner, Michael T.	Hull City	Sunderland
22 Whelan, Glenn D.	Sheffield Wednesday	Stoke City
1 Williamson, Michael J.	Watford	Portsmouth
8 Wilson, Brian	Cheltenham Town	Bristol City
1 Wright, Mark A.	Brighton & Hove Albion	Bristol Rovers

TEMPORARY TRANSFERS

8 Aldred, Thomas M. – Carlisle United – Workington; 3 Allen-Djilali, Kieran S.L. – Crystal Palace – Crawley Town; 1 Andersen, Mikkel – Reading – Bristol Rovers; 19 Andrew,Daniel K. – Peterborough United – Tamworth; 25 Appiah, Kwesi – Peterborough United – Kings Lynn; 1 Barton, Adam J. – Preston North End – Crawley Town; 17 Batth, Daniel T. – Wolverhampton Wanderers – Colchester United; 29 Bialkowski, Bartosz M. – Southampton – Barnsley; 1 Betsy, Kevin – Southend United – Wycombe Wanderers; 17 Blanchett, Daniel W. – Wigan Athletic – Hereford United; 29 Bogdan, Adam – Bolton Wanderers – Crewe Alexandra; 25 Brough, Michael – Torquay United – Stevenage Borough; 25 Brown, Lee J. – Queens Park Rangers – Salisbury City; 1 Button, David R.E. – Tottenham Hotspur – Crewe Alexandra; 4 Canham, Sean – Notts County – Hayes & Yeading United; 25 Carayol, Mustapha L. – Torquay United – Kettering Town; 14 Cathcart, Craig G. – Manchester United – Watford; 18 Cayford, Daniel – Bristol Rovers – Chippenham Town; 18 Chester, James G. – Manchester United – Plymouth Argyle; 21 Clark, Robert J. – Doncaster Rovers – Boston United; 1 Collins, Dominic – Preston North End – Crawley Town; 1 Collins, Neill – Wolverhampton Wanderers – Preston North End; 11 Convey, Matthew T. – Bradford City – Hyde United; 29 Cresswell, Richard P.W. – Leeds United – Sheffield United; 29 Crook, Billy T. – Peterborough United – Histon; 18 Cumbers, Luis C. – Gillingham – Ebbsfleet United; 1 Cox, Samuel P. – Tottenham Hotspur – Cheltenham Town; 18 Davies, Andrew D. – Stoke City – Sheffield United; 1 Davies, Aaron R. – Nottingham Forest – Brighton & Hove Albion; 25 Davies, Craig M. – Brighton & Hove Albion – Yeovil Town; 17 Devitt, Jamie M. – Hull City – Darlington; 25 Dickinson, Carl M. – Stoke City – Barnsley; 18 Dickson, Christopher A.K. – Charlton Athletic – Bristol Rovers; 19 Doyle, Nathan L.R. – Hull City – Barnsley; 14 Edwards, Declan A. – Stockport County – Northwich Victoria; 18 Elliott, Thomas J. – Leeds United – Bury; 29 Fielding, Francis D. – Blackburn Rovers – Leeds United; 1 Fleetwood, Stuart K.W. – Charlton Athletic – Exeter City; 19 Folan, Caleb C. – Hull City – Middlesbrough; 8 Franks, Oliver C. – Doncaster Rovers – Brigg Town; 19 Francis, Fraser G. – Brentford – Basingstoke Town; 18 Friend, George A.J. – Wolverhampton Wanderers – Southend United; 17 Gobern, Oscar L. – Southampton – Milton Keynes Dons; 18 Gray, David P. – Manchester United – Plymouth Argyle; 1 Haldane, Lewis O. – Bristol Rovers – Port Vale; 25 Harewood, Marlon A. – Aston Villa – Newcastle United; 1 Harper, James A.J. – Reading – Sheffield United; 15 Helguson, Heidar – Queens Park Rangers – Watford; 10 Henry, James – Reading – Millwall; 17 Hoult, Russell – Notts County – Darlington; 3 Howard, Kieran C. – Swansea City – Neath; 11 Huntington, Paul D. – Leeds United – Stockport County; 1 Jansson, Oscar – Tottenham Hotspur – Exeter City; 15 Johnson, Jermaine J. – Derby County – Stafford Rangers; 25 Johnson, John J. – Middlesbrough – Northampton Town; 25 Jones, Daniel J. – Wolverhampton Wanderers – Notts County; 18 Kane, Anthony M. – Carlisle United – Darlington; 25 Keltie, Clark S.B. – Rochdale – Chester City; 18 Khizanishvili, Zurab – Blackburn Rovers – Newcastle United; 1 Kilbey, Thomas C. – Portsmouth – Dagenham & Redbridge; 17 King, Craig S. – Leicester City – Hereford United; 24 Knowles, James – Burton Albion – Harrogate Town; 1 Lees, Thomas J. – Leeds United – Accrington Stanley; 1 Lillis, Joshua M. – Scunthorpe United – Grimsby Town; 18 Lowry, Shane T. – Aston Villa – Plymouth

Argyle; 25 MacAuley, Joshua – Tranmere Rovers – Colwyn Bay; 21 MacDonald, Shaun B. – Swansea City – Yeovil Town; 28 McManus, Scott H. – Crewe Alexandra – Curzon Ashton; 18 Marshall, Mark A. – Swindon Town – Hereford United; 1 McDonald, Clayton – Manchester City – Walsall; 18 Mills, Daniel P. – Peterborough United – Torquay United; 23 Mills, Gregory A. – Derby County – Solihull Moors; 11 Noone, Craig – Plymouth Argyle – Exeter City; 25 Oastler, Joseph J. – Queens Park Rangers – Salisbury City; 18 Odejayi, Olukayode – Barnsley – Colchester United; 17 O'Donovan, Roy S. – Sunderland – Southend United; 1 O'Toole, John J. – Watford – Colchester United; 18 Parrett, Dean G. – Tottenham Hotspur – Aldershot Town; 4 Plummer, Neikell – Bristol Rovers – Paulton Rovers; 1 Poke, Michael H. – Southampton – Torquay United; 10 Porter, Levi R. – Leicester City – Mansfield Town; 10 Pugh, Andrew J. – Gillingham – Dover Athletic; 1 Revell, Alexander D. – Southend United – Swindon Town; 1 Ritchie, Matthew T. – Portsmouth – Notts County; 1 Rosenior, Liam J. – Reading – Ipswich Town; 1 Rice, Martin – Torquay United – Truro City; 29 Rose, Daniel L. – Tottenham Hotspur – Peterborough United; 28 Rothwell, Josh – Bury – Chorley; 18 Rowe-Turner, Lathaniel A. – Leicester City – Kings Lynn; 15 Scott, Mark J. – Swindon Town – Hungerford Town; 28 Seip, Marcel – Plymouth Argyle – Blackpool; 1 Sharp, Billy L. – Sheffield United – Doncaster Rovers; 1 Sheehan, Alan – Leicester City – Oldham Athletic; 25 Shotton, Ryan C. – Stoke City – Barnsley; 1 Sonko, Ibrahima – Stoke City – Hull City; 11 Spence, Lewwis G. – Crystal Palace – Forest Green Rovers; 15 St Ledger-Hall, Sean P. – Preston North End – Middlesbrough; 26 Stoor, Frederick – Fulham – Derby County; 24 Summerfield, Luke J. – Plymouth Argyle – Leyton Orient; 1 Tainio, Teemu – Sunderland – Birmingham City; 5 Thompson, Stephen – Port Vale – Stafford Rangers; 17 Torres, Sergio R. – Peterborough United – Lincoln City; 1 Uddin, Anwar – Dagenham & Redbridge – Grays Athletic; 18 Vaughan, James O. – Everton – Derby County; 25 Wainwright, Neil – Morecambe – Barrow; 22 Walker, James L.N. – Southend United – Hereford United; 11 Ward, Darren P. – Wolverhampton Wanderers – Millwall; 1 Watson, Ben – Wigan Athletic – Queens Park Rangers; 18 Whaley, Simon – Norwich City – Rochdale; 1 Wilson, James S. – Bristol City – Brentford; 29 Wright, Benjamin M. – Peterborough United – Luton Town; 23 Wright, Matthew J. – Crystal Palace – Maidstone United

OCTOBER 2009

1 Tuncay, Sanli	Middlesbrough	Stoke City

TEMPORARY TRANSFERS
12 Adams, Stephen M. – Torquay United – Truro City; 29 Amos, Benjamin P. – Manchester United – Peterborough United; 30 Andrew, Daniel K. – Peterborough United – Kidderminster Harriers; 5 Antonio, Michail G. – Reading – Southampton; 16 Artus, Frankie – Bristol City – Cheltenham Town; 22 Baker, Nathan – Aston Villa – Lincoln City; 9 Barnett, Moses – Everton – Darlington; 16 Begovic, Asmir – Portsmouth – Ipswich Town; 23 Bennett, Ryan – Grimsby Town – Peterborough United; 30 Bent, Marcus N. – Birmingham City – Middlesbrough; 23 Blanchett, Daniel W. – Peterborough United – Hereford United; 16 Boyes, Adam J. – Scunthorpe United – York City; 14 Butcher, Lee A. – Tottenham Hotspur – Leyton Orient; 30 Bryant, Mitchell J. – Reading – Woking; 16 Charles, Elliott G. – Barnet – Ebbsfleet United; 22 Collins, James S. – Aston Villa – Darlington; 9 Cook, Andrew E. – Carlisle United – Barrow; 16 Coulson, Michael J. – Barnsley – Chester City; 16 Dawson, Liam – Oldham Athletic – Nantwich Town; 16 Davies, Scott M.E. – Reading – Wycombe Wanderers; 22 Davis, David L. – Wolverhampton Wanderers – Darlington; 29 Devaney, Martin T. – Barnsley – Milton Keynes Dons; 22 Devitt, Jamie M. – Hull City – Shrewsbury Town; 5 Doran, Aaron B. – Blackburn Rovers – Milton Keynes Dons; 2 Dudley, Mark – Derby County – Alfreton Town; 2 Edgar, Anthony J. – West Ham United – AFC Bournemouth; 6 Eley, Edward D.M. – Grimsby Town – Mansfield Town; 16 Erskine, Emmanuel J. – Gillingham – Bromley; 2 Eyjolfsson, Holmar O. – West Ham United –

Cheltenham Town; 23 Fairhurst, Waide S. – Doncaster Rovers – Shrewsbury Town; 24 Frear, Elliott – Exeter City – Tiverton Town; 30 Friend, George A.J. – Wolverhampton Wanderers – Scunthorpe United; 15 Fry, Matthew – West Ham United – Gillingham; 17 Gaughran, Samuel D. – Peterborough United – Tamworth; 5 German, Antonio T. – Queens Park Rangers – Aldershot Town; 12 Gillett, Simon J. – Southampton – Doncaster Rovers; 19 Gradel, Max A. – Leicester City – Leeds United; 23 Griffiths, Scott R. – Dagenham & Redbridge – Peterborough United; 6 Guy, Jamie L. – Colchester United – Port Vale; 13 Hall, Matthew – Leyton Orient – Billericay Town; 9 Hector, Michael – Millwall – Bracknell Town; 9 Hodges, Lee L. – Torquay United – Truro City; 9 Hoyte, Gavin A. – Arsenal – Brighton & Hove Albion; 23 Hughes, Bryan – Hull City – Derby County; 19 Hussey, Christopher I. – AFC Wimbledon – Coventry City; 16 Ide, Lewis B. – Brighton & Hove Albion – Bognor Regis Town; 29 Ikeme, Carl – Wolverhampton Wanderers – Charlton Athletic; 9 Jameson, Arron T. – Sheffield Wednesday – Harrogate Town; 1 Joyce, Ben P. – Swindon Town – Weston-Super-Mare; 2 King, David P. – Milton Keynes Dons – Forest Green Rovers; 24 Lancashire, Oliver J. – Southampton – Grimsby Town; 30 Lavers, Louis J. – Yeovil Town – Dorchester Town; 22 Lichaj, Eric J. – Aston Villa – Lincoln City; 30 Lillis, Joshua M. – Scunthorpe United – Rochdale; 6 Little, Mark D. – Wolverhampton Wanderers – Chesterfield; 30 Lockwood, Matthew D. – Colchester United – Dagenham & Redbridge; 30 McCollin, Andre – Yeovil Town – Dorchester Town; 20 Madine, Gary L. – Carlisle United – Coventry City; 16 Magennis, Joshua B.D. – Cardiff City – Grimsby Town; 2 Makofo, Serge – Grays Athletic – Burton Albion; 16 Martin, David E. – Liverpool – Tranmere Rovers; 2 Mellor, Kelvin – Crewe Alexandra – Nantwich Town; 16 Mendy, Arnaud – Derby County – Grimsby Town; 22 Mills, Daniel P. – Peterborough United – Rushden & Diamonds; 31 Mitchell, Aaron – Nottingham Forest – Ilkeston Town; 16 Mooney, David – Reading – Charlton Athletic; 17 Morgan, Kerry D. – Swansea City – Newport County; 30 Ngala, Bondz – West Ham United – Scunthorpe United; 26 Normington, Grant – Grimsby Town – Frickley Athletic; 30 Omozusi, Elliott – Fulham – Charlton Athletic; 23 Oxley, Mark T. – Hull City – Walsall; 22 Payne, Joshua J. – West Ham United – Colchester United; 2 Perkins, David P. – Colchester United – Chesterfield; 16 Powell, Daniel – Milton Keynes Dons – Forest Green Rovers; 8 Pulis, Anthony J. – Stoke City – Lincoln City; 8 Rose, Romone A.A. – Queens Park Rangers – Cheltenham Town; 16 Smith, Benjamin J. – Doncaster Rovers – Morecambe; 16 Thomas, Casey E. – Swansea City – Newport County; 16 Thomas, Simon V. – Crystal Palace – Darlington; 16 Thompson, David A.R. – Bury – Hyde United; 27 Thomson, Jake S. – Southampton – Torquay United; 16 Titchiner, Alexander – Crewe Alexandra – Chasetown; 15 Vernon, Scott M. – Colchester United – Gillingham; 17 Vokes, Samuel M. – Wolverhampton Wanderers – Leeds United; 2 Watts, Adam – Fulham – Lincoln City; 7 White, Jamie A. – Southampton – Eastleigh; 16 Winn, Peter H. – Scunthorpe United – Gateshead; 7 Winters, Ruairidh T.P. – Morecambe – Kendal Town; 30 Wynter, Thomas L. – Gillingham – Dover Athletic

NOVEMBER 2009 TEMPORARY TRANSFERS

6 Ainsley, Jack W. – Ipswich Town – Rushden & Diamonds; 20 Ainsworth, Gareth – Queens Park Rangers – Wycombe Wanderers; 13 Akinde, John J.A. – Bristol City – Wycombe Wanderers; 13 Allen-Djilali, Kieran S.L. – Crystal Palace – Chesterfield; 19 Atkinson, William H. – Hull City – Rochdale; 6 Bains, Rikki – Darlington – Blyth Spartans; 20 Baldwin, Patrick M. – Colchester United – Bristol Rovers; 20 Balkestein, Pim – Ipswich Town – Brentford; 26 Bannan, Barry – Aston Villa – Blackpool; 4 Barnett, Leon P. – West Bromwich Albion – Coventry City; 9 Benjamin, Joseph J. – Northampton Town – Eastbourne Borough; 27 Bentley, Alexander A. – Dagenham & Redbridge – Aveley; 20 Bingham, Billy C. – Dagenham & Redbridge – Grays Athletic; 5 Bird, Matthew – Grimsby Town – Frickley Athletic; 13 Bostock, John – Tottenham Hotspur – Brentford; 26 Bouzanis, Dean A. – Liverpool – Accrington Stanley; 27 Bozanic, Oliver J. – Reading – Aldershot Town; 18 Bowery, Jordan – Chesterfield – Barrow; 5 Brandy, Febian E. – Manchester United – Gillingham; 23 Brough, Michael –

Torquay United – Mansfield Town; 26 Butcher, Callum J. – Tottenham Hotspur – Barnet; 20 Button, David R.E. – Tottenham Hotspur – Shrewsbury Town; 20 Cadogan, Kieron J.N. – Crystal Palace – Burton Albion; 26 Cain, Ashley T. – Coventry City – Luton Town; 26 Campbell, Dudley J. – Leicester City – Derby County; 10 Clark, Jack A. – Charlton Athletic – Bognor Regis Town; 26 Capaldi, Anthony C. – Cardiff City – Leeds United; 2 Clayton, Adam S. – Manchester City – Carlisle United; 20 Cook, Steve A. – Brighton & Hove Albion – Eastleigh; 24 Cotterill, David R.G.B. – Sheffield United – Swansea City; 19 Coulson, Michael J. – Barnsley – Grimsby Town; 16 Cresswell, Richard P.W. – Leeds United – Sheffield United; 18 Cumbers, Luis C. – Gillingham – AFC Wimbledon; 23 Currie, Darren P. – Chesterfield – Dagenham & Redbridge; 26 Davis, Sol S. – Milton Keynes Dons – Kettering Town; 26 Day, Jamie R. – Peterborough United – Dagenham & Redbridge; 20 Dean, Harlee J. – Dagenham & Redbridge – Grays Athletic; 12 Dennis, Kristian – Macclesfield Town – Woodley Sports; 12 Dudley, Mark – Derby County – Hinckley United; 26 Eastham, Ashley – Blackpool – Cheltenham Town; 3 Elding, Anthony L. – Crew Alexandra – Kettering Town; 26 Ephraim, Hogan – Queens Park Rangers – Leeds United; 26 Facey, Delroy M. – Gillingham – Lincoln City; 19 Featherstone, Nicky L. – Hull City – Grimsby Town; 26 Feeney, Warren J. – Cardiff City – Sheffield Wednesday; 5 Flahavan, Darryl J. – Southend United – Oldham Athletic; 26 Flynn, Jonathan J. – Blackburn Rovers – Accrington Stanley; 26 Franks, Fraser G. – Brentford – Basingstoke Town; 10 Gall, Kevin A. – Darlington – York City; 25 Geohagan, Exodus – Kettering Town – Peterborough United; 26 Glover, Daniel – Port Vale – Rochdale; 26 Goodfellow, Marc D. – Burton Albion – Barrow; 26 Hall, Daniel A. – Chesterfield – Darlington; 26 Harsley, Paul – Chesterfield – Darlington; 13 Heaton, Thomas D. – Manchester United – Rochdale; 9 Hector, Michael A.J. – Reading – Didcot Town; 26 Heffernan, Paul – Doncaster Rovers – Oldham Athletic; 20 Helguson, Heidar – Queens Park Rangers – Watford; 26 Herd, Christopher – Aston Villa – Lincoln City; 5 Hills, Lee M. – Crystal Palace – Oldham Athletic; 20 Hogg, Jonathan – Aston Villa – Darlington; 26 Ibehre, Jabo O. – Milton Keynes Dons – Southend United; 26 Ikeme, Carl – Wolverhampton Wanderers – Sheffield United; 14 Jackson, Ben – Morecambe – Rossendale United; 26 Jackson, Marlon M. – Bristol City – Aldershot Town; 26 Jameson, Arron T. – Sheffield Wednesday – Matlock Town; 26 John, Stern – Crystal Palace – Ipswich Town; 19 Johnson, Jermaine J. – Derby County – Stafford Rangers; 26 Kabba, Steven – Brentford – Burton Albion; 26 Kallio, Toni – Fulham – Sheffield United; 25 Keltie, Clark S.B. – Rochdale – Gateshead; 10 Kerry, Lloyd – Sheffield United – Alfreton Town; 27 Kite, Alexandrous – Bristol Rovers – Paulton Rovers; 19 Kitson, David B. – Stoke City – Middlesbrough; 20 Labadie, Joss C. – West Bromwich Albion – Cheltenham Town; 26 Lathrope, Damon L. – Norwich City – Bishop Stortford; 26 McAllister, Craig – Exeter City – Barnet; 9 McCrory, Damian P. – Plymouth Argyle – Grimsby Town; 13 McDonald, Clayton – Manchester City – Walsall; 12 McLaggon, Kayne S. – Southampton – Eastbourne Borough; 26 McNamee, Anthony – Swindon Town – Norwich City; 24 Malone, Scott L. – Wolverhampton Wanderers – Southend United; 7 Malton, Russell J. – Colchester United – Heybridge Swifts; 26 Martin, David E. – Liverpool – Leeds United; 26 Martin, Russell K.A. – Peterborough United – Norwich City; 13 Marshall, Ben – Stoke City – Cheltenham Town; 13 Miller, Adam E. – Gillingham – Dagenham & Redbridge; 26 Milne, Andrew A. – Leeds United – Darlington; 23 Mills, Gregory A. – Derby County – Solihull Moors; 26 Morris, Ian – Scunthorpe United – Chesterfield; 24 Morris, Lee – Hereford United – Mansfield Town; 14 Morrison, Sean J. – Swindon Town – Southend United; 24 Murphy, Rhys P.E. – Arsenal – Brentford; 26 Mutch, Jordon J.E.S. – Birmingham City – Hereford United; 13 Nardiello, Daniel A. – Blackpool – Bury; 20 Norwood, James T. – Exeter City – Sutton United; 13 Nwokeji, Mark O. – Dagenham & Redbridge – Luton Town; 13 Ofori-Twumasi, Seth N. – Chelsea – Dagenham & Redbridge; 5 Osbourne, Isaiah G. – Aston Villa – Middlesbrough; 26 Partridge, Richard J. – Milton Keynes Dons – Kettering Town; 13 Pelling, Joshua R.A. – Brighton & Hove Albion – Horsham; 2

Phillips, Steven J. – Bristol Rovers – Crewe Alexandra; 13 Pilkington, Kevin W. – Notts County – Luton Town; 26 Pinney, Nathaniel B. – Crystal Palace – Woking; 26 Pipe, David R. – Bristol Rovers – Cheltenham Town; 19 Puddy, Willem J.S. – Cheltenham Town – Oxford City; 20 Pugh, Andrew J. – Gillingham – Welling United; 24 Quashie, Nigel F. – West Ham United – Milton Keynes Dons; 13 Ranieri, Mirko – Tottenham Hotspur – Ipswich Town; 13 Reed, Stephen L. – Macclesfield Town – Grays Athletic; 19 Reid, Steven J. – Blackburn Rovers – Queens Park Rangers; 20 Ribeiro, Christian M. – Bristol City – Stockport County; 24 Rigg, Sean M. – Bristol Rovers – Port Vale; 26 Rothery, Gavin M. – Carlisle United – Barrow; 3 Rothwell, Josh C. – Bury – Watford; 23 Rundle, Adam – Rochdale – Rotherham United; 13 Scott, Mark J. – Swindon Town – Chippenham Town; 25 Shaw, Jon S. – Rochdale – Gateshead; 26 Sheehan, Alan – Leeds United – Swindon Town; 25 Shephard, Christopher J. – Exeter City – Weston-Super-Mare; 26 Shorey, Nicholas – Aston Villa – Nottingham Forest; 5 Simpson, Joshua R. – Histon – Peterborough United; 26 Sinclair, Dean M. – Charlton Athletic – Barnet; 20 Smith, Adam J. – Tottenham Hotspur – Torquay United; 26 Soares, Thomas J. – Stoke City – Sheffield Wednesday; 14 Sodje, Akpo – Sheffield Wednesday – Charlton Athletic; 24 Sodje, Onome S. – Barnsley – Oxford United; 26 Somma, Davide E. – Leeds United – Chesterfield; 26 Stavrinou, Alexander M. – Charlton Athletic – Ebbsfleet United; 26 Swailes, Daniel – Milton Keynes Dons – Northampton Town; 20 Szczesny, Wojciech T. – Arsenal – Brentford; 13 Tabiri, Joseph O. – Barnet – Havant & Waterlooville; 19 Taylor, Jason J.F. – Rotherham United – Rochdale; 20 Taylor, Rhys F. – Chelsea – Queens Park Rangers; 28 Todd, Christopher R. – Torquay United – Salisbury City; 19 Tonge, Michael W.E. – Stoke City – Preston North End; 20 Walker, Joshua – Middlesbrough – Northampton Town; 26 Ward, Daniel C. – Bolton Wanderers – Swindon Town; 26 Wedderburn, Nathaniel C. – Stoke City – Hereford United; 20 Whaley, Simon – Norwich City – Bradford City; 9 Williams, Thomas A. – Peterborough United – Queens Park Rangers; 19 Wood, Richard M. – Sheffield Wednesday – Coventry City; 26 Wright, Benjamin M. – Peterborough United – Grimsby Town; 26 Wright, Matthew J. – Crystal Palace – Woking; 20 Zebroski, Christopher M. – Millwall – Torquay United

DECEMBER 2009 TEMPORARY TRANSFERS

4 Bryant, Mitchell J. – Reading – Basingstoke Town; 11 Charles, Elliott G. – Barnet – Havant & Waterlooville; 4 Corcoran, Samuel J. – Colchester United – Wealdstone; 4 Davies, Richard P. – Walsall – Solihull Moors; 15 Dean, Luke A. – Bradford City – Halifax Town; 14 Gibson, William M.H. – Watford – Wealdstone; 24 Hall, Grant T. – Brighton & Hove Albion – Bognor Regis Town; 14 Harris, Spencer J. – Huddersfield Town – Curzon Ashton; 10 Harrison, Callum J. – Sheffield Wednesday – Sheffield; 19 Hunt, Ben – Bristol Rovers – Gloucester City; 15 Locke, Simon J. – Reading – Gillingham; 24 Malak, Matthew E. – Chesterfield – Loughborough University; 21 Morris, Aaron J. – Cardiff City – Newport County; 18 Normington, Grant – Grimsby Town – Frickley Athletic; 17 Reed, Stephen L. – Torquay United – Weymouth; 11 Stech, Marek – West Ham United – Bournemouth; 10 Wood, Nicholas J. – Sheffield Wednesday – Sheffield

JANUARY 2010

29 Ademola, Moses	Brentford	Woking
1 Anderson, Joe	Fulham	Lincoln City
8 Baker, Carl P.	Stockport County	Coventry City
22 Barnard, Lee J.	Southend United	Southampton
15 Bennett, Ryan	Grimsby Town	Peterborough United
27 Buckley, William E.	Rochdale	Watford
21 Campbell-Ryce, Jamal J.	Barnsley	Bristol City
6 Collins, Neill	Wolverhampton Wanderers	Preston North End
28 Conlon, Barry J.	Grimsby Town	Chesterfield

28 Cort, Leon T.A.	Stoke City	Burnley
8 Cotterill, David R.G.B.	Sheffield United	Swansea City
8 Cresswell, Richard P.W.	Stoke City	Sheffield United
13 Doyle, Nathan L.R.	Hull City	Barnsley
12 Fonte, Jose M.	Crystal Palace	Southampton
27 Gardner, Craig	Aston Villa	Birmingham City
25 Gradel, Max A.	Leicester City	Leeds United
22 Griffiths, Scott R.	Dagenham & Redbridge	Peterborough United
25 Harper, James A.J.	Reading	Sheffield United
1 Hinshelwood, Adam	Aldershot Town	Wycombe Wanderers
8 Johnson, Oliver T.	Stockport County	Norwich City
30 Kaboul, Younes	Portsmouth	Tottenham Hotspur
21 Kilgallon, Matthew	Sheffield United	Sunderland
4 Martin, Russell K.A.	Peterborough United	Norwich City
1 McDonald, Clayton	Manchester City	Walsall
4 McNamee, Anthony	Swindon Town	Norwich City
1 Odejayi, Olukayode	Barnsley	Colchester United
15 O'Grady, Christopher J.	Oldham Athletic	Rochdale
4 O'Toole, John J.	Watford	Colchester United
14 Otsemobor, Jon	Norwich City	Southampton
22 Paterson, Matthew	Southampton	Southend United
25 Pearce, Krystian M.V.	Birmingham City	Huddersfield Town
28 Robinson, Paul P.	West Bromwich Albion	Bolton Wanderers
26 Routledge, Wayne N.A.	Queens Park Rangers	Newcastle United
13 Seaborne, Daniel A.	Exeter City	Southampton
21 Simpson, Daniel P.	Manchester United	Newcastle United
14 Taiwo, Thomas J.W.	Chelsea	Carlisle United
1 Ward, Darren P.	Wolverhampton Wanderers	Millwall
4 Watts, Adam	Fulham	Lincoln City
8 Whitbread, Zak B.	Millwall	Norwich City
28 Williamson, Michael J.	Portsmouth	Newcastle United
4 Wood, Richard M.	Sheffield Wednesday	Coventry City
8 Worrall, David R.	West Bromwich Albion	Bury
20 Yeates, Mark S.	Middlesbrough	Sheffield United
8 Zebroski, Christopher M.	Wycombe Wanderers	Torquay United

TEMPORARY TRANSFERS

15 Adams, Nicholas W. – Leicester City – Leyton Orient; 15 Adams, Stephen M. – Torquay United – Truro City; 8 Adelakun, Hakeem A.D. – Crystal Palace – Dover Athletic; 11 Adkins, Sam – Walsall – Hednesford Town; 25 Agyemang, Patrick – Queens Park Rangers – Bristol City; 28 Ainsworth, Lionel G.R. – Huddersfield Town – Brentford; 2 Andersen, Mikkel – Reading – Bristol Rovers; 12 Andrew, Daniel K. – Peterborough United – Cheltenham Town; 5 Antonio, Michail G. – Reading – Southampton; 19 Appiah, Kwesi – Peterborough United – Kettering Town; 21 Artus, Frankie – Bristol City – Chesterfield; 22 Atkins, Ross M. – Derby County – Burton Albion; 21 Bains, Rikki – Darlington – Gateshead; 29 Baldwin, Patrick M. – Colchester United – Southend United; 25 Batt, Shaun A.S.P. – Peterborough United – Millwall; 15 Benjamin, Joseph J. – Northampton Town – Eastbourne Borough; 14 Bentley, Alexander A. – Dagenham & Redbridge – Bishop's Stortford; 5 Bozanic, Oliver J. – Reading – Aldershot Town; 29 Branston, Guy P.B. – Burton Albion – Torquay United; 15 Briggs, Matthew – Fulham – Leyton Orient; 2 Bunn, Mark J. – Blackburn Rovers – Sheffield United; 22 Burns, Michael – Carlisle United – Stafford Rangers; 7 Butler, Andrew P. – Huddersfield Town – Blackpool; 7 Byrne, Mark – Nottingham Forest – Rushden & Diamonds; 22 Chambers, Ashley R. – Leicester City – Grimsby Town; 19 Clayton, Adam S. – Manchester City – Carlisle United; 5 Cleverley, Thomas W. –

Manchester United – Watford; 16 Conlon, Barry J. – Grimsby Town & – Chesterfield; 22 Coulson, Michael J. – Barnsley – Grimsby Town; 1 Cowan-Hall, Paris – Portsmouth – Grimsby Town; 22 Cox, Samuel P. – Tottenham Hotspur – Torquay United; 23 Davidson, Ross – Port Vale – Nantwich Town; 15 Davies, Craig M. – Brighton & Hove Albion – Port Vale; 22 Dean, Harlee J. – Dagenham & Redbridge – Grays Athletic; 21 Dennehy, Darren J. – Cardiff City – Gillingham; 21 Diagouraga, Toumani – Peterborough United – Brentford; 1 Dickinson, Carl M. – Stoke City – Barnsley; 29 Donnelly, Georgie J. – Plymouth Argyle – Stockport County; 26 Downing, Paul – West Bromwich Albion – Hereford United; 28 Eccleston, Nathan – Liverpool – Huddersfield Town; 28 Elford-Alliyu, Lateef – West Bromwich Albion – Hereford United; 1 Elliott, Thomas J. – Leeds United – Bury; 12 Facey, Delroy M. – Notts County – Lincoln City; 15 Featherstone, Nicky L. – Hull City – Grimsby Town; 29 Fielding, Francis D. – Blackburn Rovers – Rochdale; 27 Fisher, Oliver C. – Doncaster Rovers – Frickley Athletic; 15 Fletcher, Wesleigh J. – Burnley – Grimsby Town; 5 Forster, Fraser G. – Newcastle United – Norwich City; 22 Franks, Leigh D. – Huddersfield Town – Fleetwood Town; 25 Frear, Elliott – Exeter City – Tiverton Town; 16 Gilbert, Kerrea K. – Arsenal – Peterborough United; 2 Goodwin, James M. – Huddersfield Town – Oldham Athletic; 15 Green, Dominic A. – Peterborough United – Chesterfield; 11 Griffin, Andrew – Stoke City – Reading; 15 Grimes, Jamie N. – Swansea City – Haverfordwest County; 22 Gunning, Gavin – Blackburn Rovers – Rotherham United; 1 Haldane, Lewis O. – Bristol Rovers – Port Vale; 29 Hall, Fitz – Queens Park Rangers – Newcastle United; 29 Hart, Danny – Barnet – Hemel Hempstead Town; 23 Haworth, Andrew A.D. – Blackburn Rovers – Rochdale; 22 Hector, Michael A.J. – Reading – Havant & Waterlooville; 11 Helguson, Heidar – Queens Park Rangers – Watford; 4 Herd, Christopher – Aston Villa – Lincoln City; 25 Hill, Matthew C. – Wolverhampton Wanderers – Queens Park Rangers; 15 Hodges, Lee L. – Torquay United – Truro City; 29 Holroyd, Christopher – Cambridge United – Brighton & Hove Albion; 26 Howard, Kieran C. – Swansea City – Neath; 21 Howe, Jermaine R. – Peterborough United – Gillingham; 12 Hoyte, Gavin A. – Arsenal – Brighton & Hove Albion; 22 Hunt, Jack P. – Huddersfield Town – Grays Athletic; 7 Hunt, Nicholas B. – Bolton Wanderers – Derby County; 19 Ibehre, Jabo O. – Milton Keynes Dons – Stockport County; 7 Ikeme, Carl – Wolverhampton Wanderers – Queens Park Rangers; 25 Jackson, Marlon M. – Bristol City – Aldershot Town; 19 Johnson, Jemal P. – Milton Keynes Dons – Stockport County; 1 Johnson, John J. – Middlesbrough – Northampton Town; 1 Johnson, Lee D. – Bristol City – Derby County; 15 Joyce, Ben P. – Torquay United – Weston-Super-Mare; 15 Kabba, Steven – Brentford – Burton Albion; 19 Kee, Billy R. – Leicester City – Accrington Stanley; 25 Khizanishvili, Zurab – Blackburn Rovers – Reading; 26 King, David P. – Milton Keynes Dons – Wealdstone; 5 Kite, Alexandrous – Bristol Rovers – Chippenham Town; 4 Krysiak, Artur L. – Birmingham City – Burton Albion; 1 Lansbury, Henri G. – Arsenal – Watford; 12 Livermore, Jake C. – Tottenham Hotspur – Peterborough United; 22 Lockwood, Matthew D. – Colchester United – Barnet; 29 Lowry, Shane T. – Aston Villa – Leeds United; 1 MacDonald, Shaun B. – Swansea City – Yeovil Town; 25 Malone, Scott L. – Wolverhampton Wanderers – Southend United; 19 Malton, Russell J. – Colchester United – Billericay Town; 6 Marrow, Alexander J. – Blackburn Rovers – Oldham Athletic; 22 Marshall, Marcus – Blackburn Rovers – Rotherham United; 14 Martin, Richard W. – Yeovil Town – Grays Athletic; 21 McCready, Christopher J. – Northampton Town – Tranmere Rovers; 27 McDermott, Donal – Manchester City – Scunthorpe United; 11 McLeod, Izale M. – Charlton Athletic – Peterborough United; 29 McSheffrey, Gary – Birmingham City – Leeds United; 29 Mills, Gregory A. – Derby County – Macclesfield Town; 27 Moloney, Brendon A. – Nottingham Forest – Scunthorpe United; 13 Mooney, David – Reading – Charlton Athletic; 15 Morgan, Kerry D. – Swansea City – Newport County; 25 Mutch, Jordon J.E.S. – Birmingham City – Doncaster Rovers; 12 Mvoto, Yves O.J. – Sunderland – Southend United; 12 Nwokeji, Mark O. – Dagenham & Redbridge – Luton Town; 29 Obadeyi, Temitope – Bolton Wanderers – Rochdale; 29 O'Hara, Jamie

– Tottenham Hotspur – Portsmouth; 6 Pack, Marlon – Portsmouth – Dagenham & Redbridge; 14 Painter, Marcos – Swansea City – Brighton & Hove Albion; 22 Parkes, Thomas P.W. – Leicester City – Burton Albion; 22 Payne, Joshua J. – West Ham United – Wycombe Wanderers; 19 Pearce, Krystian M.V. – Birmingham City – Huddersfield Town; 19 Perkins, David P. – Colchester United – Stockport County; 6 Phillips, Steven J. – Bristol Rovers – Crewe Alexandra; 21 Plummer, Tristan D. – Bristol City – Gillingham; 3 Poke, Michael H. – Southampton – Torquay United; 17 Powell, Daniel – Milton Keynes Dons – Forest Green Rovers; 26 Prutton, David T. – Leeds United – Colchester United; 13 Puddy, Willem J.S. – Cheltenham Town – Oxford City; 15 Randall, Mark – Arsenal – Milton Keynes Dons; 26 Redmond, Shane P. – Nottingham Forest – Darlington; 15 Reed, Stephen L. – Macclesfield Town – Weymouth; 29 Reid, Kyel R. – Sheffield United – Charlton Athletic; 5 Reid, Reuben J. – West Bromwich Albion – Peterborough United; 29 Revell, Alexander D. – Southend United – Wycombe Wanderers; 22 Ribeiro, Christian M. – Bristol City – Colchester United; 12 Rigg, Sean M. – Bristol Rovers – Port Vale; 29 Riley, Daniel – Darlington – Billingham Town; 29 Rose, Michael – Stockport County – Norwich City; 29 Sadler, Matthew – Watford – Stockport County; 2 Sappleton, Reneil St. A – Leicester City – Macclesfield Town; 1 Saunders, Matthew – Fulham – Lincoln City; 1 Seip, Marcel – Plymouth Argyle – Sheffield United; 25 Senderos, Philippe – Arsenal – Everton; 1 Shackell, Jason – Wolverhampton Wanderers – Doncaster Rovers; 7 Sheehan, Alan – Leeds United – Swindon Town; 1 Shotton, Ryan C. – Stoke City – Barnsley; 28 Sinclair, Dean M. – Charlton Athletic – Grimsby Town; 21 Skarz, Joseph P. – Huddersfield Town – Shrewsbury Town; 8 Smith, Thomas J. – Ipswich Town – Brentford; 26 Soares, Thomas J. – Stoke City – Sheffield Wednesday; 15 Spencer, James C. – Huddersfield Town – Northwich Victoria; 8 Stavrinou, Alexander M. – Charlton Athletic – Ebbsfleet United; 22 Stockdale, David A. – Fulham – Plymouth Argyle; 15 Taylor, Cleveland K.W. – Brentford – Burton Albion; 14 Taylor, Jason J.F. – Rotherham United – Rochdale; 29 Taylor, Martin – Birmingham City – Watford; 29 Thomson, Jake S. – Southampton – Torquay United; 19 Thompson, O'Neil A.M.T. – Barnsley – Burton Albion; 21 Thornhill, Matthew – Nottingham Forest – Cheltenham Town; 1 Timar, Krisztian – Plymouth Argyle – Oldham Athletic; 12 Todd, Christopher R. – Torquay United – Newport County; 14 Townsend, Andros – Tottenham Hotspur – Milton Keynes Dons; 7 Trotter, Liam A. – Ipswich Town – Millwall; 21 Trottman, Neal A. – Preston North End – Huddersfield Town; 1 Trundle, Lee C. – Bristol City – Swansea City; 12 Titchiner, Alexander – Crewe Alexandra – Colwyn Bay; 26 Tudur-Jones, Owain – Norwich City – Yeovil Town; 1 Uwezu, Michael – Fulham – Lincoln City; 29 Van Aanholt, Patrick J.M. – Chelsea – Newcastle United; 21 Varney, Luke I. – Derby County – Sheffield Wednesday; 29 Vernon, Scott M. – Colchester United – Southend United; 25 Weiss, Vladimir – Manchester City – Bolton Wanderers; 25 Welbeck, Daniel – Manchester United – Preston North End; 15 White, Alan – Luton Town – Darlington; 1 White, Joseph S. – Bristol Rovers – Paulton Rovers; 29 Wiggins, Rhoys B. – Norwich City – AFC Bournemouth; 5 Wilkinson, Luke A. – Portsmouth – Northampton Town; 27 Williamson, Michael J. – Portsmouth – Newcastle United; 29 Wilshere, Jack A. – Arsenal – Bolton Wanderers; 26 Wilson, Kyle P. – Macclesfield Town – FC United of Manchester; 4 Worley, Harry J. – Leicester City – Crewe Alexandra; 1 Wright, Jake M. – Brighton & Hove Albion – Oxford United; 23 Wright, Matthew J. – Crystal Palace – Woking

FEBRUARY 2010

1 Archibald-Henville, Troy	Tottenham Hotspur	Exeter City
2 Austin, Charles	Poole Town	Swindon Town
1 Begovic, Asmir	Portsmouth	Stoke City
1 Best, Leon J.	Coventry City	Newcastle United
1 Buchtmann, Christopher	Liverpool	Fulham
2 Coutts, Paul	Peterborough United	Preston North End

1 Johnson, Adam	Middlesbrough	Manchester City
1 McCarthy, Benedict S.	Blackburn Rovers	West Ham United
5 Johnson, Damien M.	Birmingham City	Plymouth Argyle
1 Martis, Shelton	West Bromwich Albion	Doncaster Rovers
1 McCrory, Damien P.	Plymouth Argyle	Dagenham & Redbridge
1 Moses, Victor	Crystal Palace	Wigan Athletic
1 Puncheon, Jason D.I.	Plymouth Argyle	Southampton
1 Raynes, Michael	Stockport County	Scunthorpe United
1 Rowe-Turner, Lathaniel A.	Leicester City	Torquay United
1 Treacy, Keith	Blackburn Rovers	Preston North End

TEMPORARY TRANSFERS

5 Abnett, Michael M. – Crystal Palace – Dover Athletic; 1 Ainsworth, Lionel G.R. – Huddersfield Town – Brentford; 1 Akinde, John J.A. – Bristol City – Brentford; 1 Atkinson, William H. – Hull City – Rochdale; 19 Bannan, Barry – Aston Villa – Blackpool; 9 Barnes, Ashley L. – Plymouth Argyle – Torquay United; 1 Barnett, Leon P. – West Bromwich Albion – Coventry City; 9 Bartley, Kyle – Arsenal – Sheffield United; 16 Bennett, Alan J. – Brentford – Wycombe Wanderers; 1 Bent, Marcus N. – Birmingham City – Queens Park Rangers; 5 Brough, Michael – Torquay United – Mansfield Town; 16 Broughton, Drewe O. – Rotherham United – Lincoln City; 1 Brown, Wayne J. – Fulham – Bristol Rovers; 1 Bruce, Alex S. – Ipswich Town – Leicester City; 9 Butcher, Richard T. – Lincoln City – Macclesfield Town; 19 Cain, Ashley T. – Coventry City – Oxford United; 9 Calver, Craig T. – Sheffield United – Braintree Town; 1 Campbell, Dudley J. – Leicester City – Blackpool; 1 Clark, Robert J. – Doncaster Rovers – Brigg Town; 1 Cork, Jack F.P. – Chelsea – Burnley; 12 Cumbers, Luis C. – Gillingham – Dover Athletic; 17 Cureton, Jamie – Norwich City – Shrewsbury Town; 11 Davies, Arron R. – Brighton & Hove Albion – Yeovil Town; 17 Devitt, Jamie M. – Hull City – Grimsby Town; 15 Dickinson, Liam M. – Brighton & Hove Albion – Peterborough United; 15 Dickson, Christopher A.K. – Charlton Athletic – Gillingham; 1 Dobbie, Stephen – Swansea City – Blackpool; 22 Doran Cogan, Aaron B. – Bristol Rovers – Leyton Orient; 5 Dudley, Mark – Derby County – Hinckley United; 1 Duffy, Darryl A. – Bristol Rovers – Carlisle United; 12 Durrant, Jack W. – Cheltenham Town – Worcester City; 25 Emmanuel-Thomas, Jay-Aston – Arsenal – Doncaster Rovers; 23 Erskine, Emmanuel J.K. – Dagenham & Redbridge-Bishop's Stortford; 1 Flahavan, Darryl J. – Crystal Palace – Oldham Athletic; 1 Flynn, Jonathan J. – Blackburn Rovers – Accrington Stanley; 27 Folly, Yoann – Plymouth Argyle – Dagenham & Redbridge; 1 Goodfellow, Marc D. – Burton Albion – Kidderminster Harriers; 18 Haber, Marcus – West Bromwich Albion – Exeter City; 1 Harris, Edward G. – Queens Park Rangers – Hayes & Yeading United; 1 Healy, David J. – Sunderland – Ipswich Town; 12 Heaton, Thomas D. – Manchester United – Wycombe Wanderers; 9 Heffernan, Paul – Doncaster Rovers – Bristol Rovers; 1 Henderson, Stephen – Bristol City – Aldershot Town; 1 Hewson, Sam – Manchester United – Bury; 1 Holden, Luke – Charlton Athletic – Wrexham; 1 Hutton, Alan – Tottenham Hotspur – Sunderland; 12 Ireland, Daniel A. – Coventry City – Forest Green Rovers; 12 Iwelumo, Christopher R. – Wolverhampton Wanderers – Bristol City; 18 Jackson, Johnnie A. – Notts County – Charlton Athletic; 9 James, Matthew – Manchester United – Preston North End; 15 Jones, Daniel J. – Wolverhampton Wanderers – Bristol Rovers; 5 Joyce, Daniel D. – Reading – Bognor Regis Town; 1 Kallio, Toni – Fulham – Sheffield United; 16 Kelly, Julian J. – Reading – Wycombe Wanderers; 15 Knight, Joshua – West Bromwich Albion – Torquay United; 1 Lancashire, Oliver J. – Southampton – Grimsby Town; 12 Leach, Daniel J. – Barnet – Dover Athletic; 16 Lloyd-Weston, Daniel – Port Vale – Nantwich Town; 9 LuaLua, Kazenga – Newcastle United – Brighton & Hove Albion; 1 Lund, Jonathan – Burnley – Rotherham United; 19 Macklin, Lloyd J. – Swindon Town – Torquay United; 12 Madine, Gary L. – Carlisle United – Chesterfield; 12 MacAuley, Joshua L. – Tranmere Rovers – Vauxhall Motors; 1 Marshall, Ben – Stoke City –

Carlisle United; 9 Martin, David J. – Millwall – Derby County; 26 McCammon, Mark J. – Gillingham – Bradford City; 19 McCollin, Andre S. – Yeovil Town – Farnborough Town; 5 Medley, Luke A.C. – Barnet – Havant & Waterlooville; 1 Murphy, Daryl – Sunderland – Ipswich Town; 1 Mwaruwari, Benjani – Manchester City – Sunderland; 1 Naughton, Kyle – Tottenham Hotspur – Middlesbrough; 9 Nicholas, Andrew P. – Rotherham United – Mansfield Town; 19 Nolan, Edward W. – Preston North End – Sheffield Wednesday; 2 North, Jonathan P. – Watford – Oxford City; 1 Nosworthy, Nyron – Sunderland – Sheffield United; 9 Nouble, Franck H. – West Ham United – West Bromwich Albion; 1 Nugent, David J. – Portsmouth – Burnley; 12 Obika, Jonathan – Tottenham Hotspur – Millwall; 23 O'Donovan, Roy S. – Sunderland – Hartlepool United; 18 O'Neill, Luke M. – Leicester City – Tranmere Rovers; 26 Oxley, Mark T. – Hull City – Grimsby Town; 9 Pelling, Joshua R.A. – Brighton & Hove Albion – Horsham; 13 Pinney, Nathaniel B. – Crystal Palace – Woking; 26 Preston, Daniel S. – Birmingham City – Hereford United; 1 Price, Jason J. – Millwall – Oldham Athletic; 1 Priskin, Tamas – Ipswich Town – Queens Park Rangers; 19 Putnins, Elvijs – Queens Park Rangers – Hemel Hempstead Town; 12 Ritchie, Matthew T. – Portsmouth – Swindon Town; 1 Rodriguez, Jay E. – Burnley – Barnsley; 26 Scott, Mark J. – Swindon Town – Banbury United; 12 Sears, Fred – West Ham United – Coventry City; 1 Shorey, Nicholas – Aston Villa – Fulham; 8 Smith, Thomas J. – Ipswich Town – Brentford; 1 Sodje, Akpo – Sheffield Wednesday – Charlton Athletic; 25 Somma, Davide E. – Leeds United – Lincoln City; 1 Sordell, Marvin A. – Watford – Tranmere Rovers; 26 Spencer, Damian – Kettering Town – Aldershot Town; 16 Stead, Jonthan G. – Ipswich Town – Coventry City; 26 Steele, Jason – Middlesbrough – Northampton Town; 19 Sunu, Gilles – Arsenal – Derby County; 1 Szczesny, Wojciech T. – Arsenal – Brentford; 5 Tabiri, Joseph O. – Barnet – Havant & Waterlooville; 1 Teixeira, Filipe – West Bromwich Albion – Barnsley; 23 Threlfall, Robert R. – Liverpool – Bradford City; 1 Tonge, Michael W.E. – Stoke City – Derby County; 1 Treacy, Keith – Blackburn Rovers – Preston North End; 9 Trippier, Kieran J. – Manchester City – Barnsley; 11 Tunnicliffe, James – Brighton & Hove Albion – Milton Keynes Dons; 16 Tymon, Matthew R. – Hartlepool United – Spennymoor United; 1 Vidal, Javan – Manchester City – Derby County; 27 Walker, Joshua – Middlesbrough – Rotherham United; 16 Walker, Mitchell C.A. – Brighton & Hove Albion – Eastbourne Borough; 1 Ward, Daniel C. – Bolton Wanderers – Swindon Town; 15 Ward, Elliott L. – Coventry City – Doncaster Rovers; 22 Watson, Ben – Wigan Athletic – West Bromwich Albion; 1 Watt, Herschel O.S. – Arsenal – Southend United; 15 Williams, Thomas A. – Peterborough United – Preston North End; 26 Winters, Ruairidh T.P. – Morecambe – Vauxhall Motors

MARCH 2010 TEMPORARY TRANSFERS

25 Ajdarevic, Astrit – Leicester City – Hereford United; 19 Almond, Louis J. – Blackpool – Cheltenham Town; 2 Arismendi, Hugo D. – Stoke City – Brighton & Hove Albion; 17 Ayling, Luke D. – Arsenal – Yeovil Town; 25 Balkestein, Pim – Ipswich Town – Brentford; 25 Barnes, Ashley L. – Plymouth Argyle – Brighton & Hove Albion; 12 Bell-Baggie, Abdulai H. – Reading – Rotherham United; 25 Bennett, Alan J. – Reading – Wycombe Wanderers; 5 Bolder, Adam P. – Millwall – Bradford City; 18 Borrowdale, Gary I. – Queens Park Rangers – Charlton Athletic; 4 Boyd, George J. – Peterborough United – Nottingham Forest; 1 Boyes, Adam J. – Scunthorpe United – Kidderminster Harriers; 19 Brinkhurst, Steven W. – Brighton & Hove Albion – Lewes; 25 Butcher, Callum J. – Tottenham Hotspur – Exeter City; 2 Button, David R.E. – Tottenham Hotspur – Shrewsbury Town; 19 Chalmers, Lewis J. – Aldershot Town – Oxford United; 16 Clark, Jack A. – Charlton Athletic – Cray Wanderers; 25 Clements, Christopher L. – Crewe Alexandra – Hednesford Town; 19 Coleman, Seamus – Everton – Blackpool; 24 Collins, Neill – Preston North End – Leeds United; 19 Connerton, Jordan – Crewe Alexandra – Lancaster City; 16 Connolly, Paul – Derby County – Sheffield United; 25 Cywka, Tomasz – Wigan Athletic – Derby County; 12 Darby, Stephen – Liverpool – Swindon Town; 25 Darville, Liam T. – Leeds United – Rotherham United; 25 Davidson,

Ross – Port Vale – Stafford Rangers; 15 Davies, Scott M.E. – Reading – Yeovil Town; 24 Dawson, Liam – Oldham Athletic – Ashton United; 1 Demetriou, Stephen – Dagenham & RedbridgeT – Aveley; 19 Demontagnac, Ishmel – Blackpool – Chesterfield; 5 Dennehy, Darren J. – Cardiff City – Gillingham; 2 Dennis, Kristian – Macclesfield Town – Woodley Sports; 3 Dickov, Paul – Derby County – Leeds United; 5 Eckersley, Richard J. – Manchester United – Plymouth Argyle; 23 Edgar, David E. – Burnley – Swansea City; 5 Elito, Medy E. – Colchester United – Cheltenham Town; 5 Elliott, Stephen W. – Preston North End – Norwich City; 25 Erskine, Emmanuel J.K. – Gillingham – Croydon Athletic; 25 Forster, Nicholas M. – Brighton & Hove Albion – Charlton Athletic; 4 Friend, George A.J. – Wolverhampton Wanderers – Exeter City; 25 Fry, Matthew – West Ham United – Charlton Athletic; 31 Gaughran, Samuel D. – Peterborough United – Halesowen Town; 25 Glover, Daniel – Port Vale – Stafford Rangers; 25 Gordon, Benjamin C. – Chelsea – Tranmere Rovers; 25 Grabban, Lewis J. – Millwall – Brentford; 19 Grant, John A.C. – Aldershot Town – Oxford United; 4 Grey, Andre A. – Shrewsbury Town – Hinckley United; 16 Guy, Lewis B. – Doncaster Rovers – Oldham Athletic; 8 Hackney, Simon J. – Colchester United – Morecambe; 12 Hall, Grant T. – Brighton & Hove Albion – Lewes; 9 Halstead, Mark J. – Blackpool – Hyde United; 13 Harsley, Paul – Chesterfield – York City; 15 Head, Liam T. – Plymouth Argyle – Tiverton Town; 23 Hendrie, Lee A. – Derby County – Brighton & Hove Albion; 12 Heslop, Simon J. – Barnsley – Luton Town; 25 Hughes-Mason, Kiernan P. – Millwall – Cheltenham Town; 3 Hunt, Ben – Bristol Rovers – Gloucester City; 30 Hunt, Ben – Bristol Rovers – Newport County; 19 Jervis, Jake M. – Birmingham City – Hereford United; 17 Kendall, Ryan P. – Hull City – Bradford City; 25 Kerry, Lloyd – Chesterfield – Kidderminster Harriers; 24 Labadie, Josh C. – West Bromwich Albion – Tranmere Rovers; 18 Leitch-Smith, A-Jay – Crewe Alexandra – Curzon Ashton; 5 Lescott, Aaron A. – Bristol Rovers – Cheltenham Town; 25 Lichaj, Eric J. – Aston Villa – Leyton Orient; 2 Little, Mark D. – Wolverhampton Wanderers – Peterborough United; 24 Lowry, Shane T. – Aston Villa – Leeds United; 13 Lund, Jonathan – Burnley – Barnsley; 16 Maierhofer, Stefan – Wolverhampton Wanderers – Bristol City; 6 Malton, Russell J. – Colchester United – Heybridge Swifts; 2 Marshall, Ben – Stoke City – Carlisle United; 2 Martin, Aaron – Southampton – Salisbury City; 12 Martin, David E. – Liverpool – Derby County; 11 McAllister, Craig – Exeter City – Rotherham United; 9 McCarten, James – Everton – Accrington Stanley; 17 McDermott, Donal – Manchester City – Scunthorpe United; 23 McNulty, Jimmy – Brighton & Hove Albion – Scunthorpe United; 15 Mellor, Kevin – Crewe Alexandra – Newcastle Town; 5 Milne, Andrew A. – Leeds United – Darlington; 25 Mitchley, Daniel J. – Blackpool – Wrexham; 25 Molyneux, Lee R. – Southampton – Port Vale; 25 Morgan, Dean L. – Milton Keynes Dons – Aldershot Town; 19 Morris, Lee – Hereford United – Forest Green Rovers; 25 Naisbitt, Daniel J. – Histon – Brighton & Hove Albion; 4 Nardiello, Daniel A. – Blackpool – Oldham Athletic; 16 N'Gala, Bondz – West Ham United – Plymouth Argyle; 11 Nightingale, Lewis J. – Huddersfield Town – Salford City; 25 Noble, Ryan – Sunderland – Watford; 19 Nouble, Frank H. – West Ham United – Swindon Town; 3 Oliver, Luke J. – Wycombe Wanderers – Bradford City; 25 O'Shea, James – Birmingham City – Middlesbrough; 18 Parker, Keigan – Oldham Athletic – Bury; 26 Plummer, Neikell – Bristol Rovers – Gloucester City; 25 Poole, James A. – Manchester City – Bury; 10 Price, Jason J. – Millwall – Carlisle United; 25 Prosser, Luke B. – Port Vale – Kidderminster Harriers; 2 Pugh, Andrew J. – Gillingham – Histon; 25 Queudrue, Franck – Birmingham City – Colchester United; 5 Reid, Steven J. – Blackburn Rovers – West Bromwich Albion; 12 Riley, Daniel – Darlington – Billingham Town; 25 Robinson, Andrew M. – Leeds United – Tranmere Rovers; 23 Rodney, Nialle – Nottingham Forest – Ilkeston Town; 16 Rooney, Luke W. – Gillingham – Eastbourne Borough; 17 Saunders, Matthew – Fulham – Lincoln City; 25 Sawyer, Gary D. – Plymouth Argyle – Bristol City; 25 Shephard, Christopher J. – Exeter City – Salisbury City; 19 Simonsen, Steven P.A. – Stoke City – Sheffield United; 23 Spearing, Jay F. – Liverpool – Leicester City; 25 Spicer, John W. – Doncaster Rovers

– Leyton Orient; 19 Stephens, David R.R. – Norwich City – Lincoln City; 20 Stirling, Jude B. – Milton Keynes Dons – Grimsby Town; 12 Stokes, Christopher M.T. – Bolton Wanderers – Crewe Alexandra; 13 Tabiri, Joseph O. – Barnet – Dover Athletic; 25 Taylor, Ryan P. – Rotherham United – Exeter City; 25 Thomas, Wesley A.N. – Dagenham & Redbridge – Rushden & Diamonds; 25 Titchiner, Alexander – Crewe Alexandra – Colwyn Bay; 25 Tosic, Dusko – Portsmouth – Queens Park Rangers; 12 Upson, Edward J. – Ipswich Town – Barnet; 12 Vaughan, James O. – Everton – Leicester City; 23 Ward, Elliott L. – Coventry City – Preston North End; 25 Watt, Herschel O.S. – Arsenal – Leeds United; 5 Whing, Andrew J. – Brighton & Hove Albion – Chesterfield; 11 Williams, Gavin J. – Bristol City – Yeovil Town; 11 Wright, Benjamin M. – Peterborough United – Barnet; 19 Young, Lewis J. – Watford – Hereford United

APRIL 2010 TEMPORARY TRANSFERS

7 Bird, Matthew – Grimsby Town – Boston United; 13 Cayford, Daniel – Bristol Rovers – Clevedon Town; 28 Fulop, Marton – Sunderland – Manchester City; 16 Gulacsi, Peter – Liverpool – Tranmere Rovers; 26 Mellor, Kelvin – Newcastle Town – Crewe Alexandra; 2 Oxley, Mark T. – Hull City – Grimsby Town; 13 Tyrrell, James R. – Bristol Rovers – Clevedon Town

MAY 2010

22 Crofts, Andrew L.	Brighton & Hove Albion	Norwich City
18 Mackie, James	Plymouth Argyle	Queens Park Rangers
28 Marney, Dean E.	Hull City	Burnley
13 Sarcevic, Antoni C.	Woodley Sports	Crewe Alexandra
17 Shackell, Jason	Wolverhampton Wanderers	Barnsley
17 Sodje, Akpo	Sheffield Wednesday	Charlton Athletic

TEMPORARY TRANSFERS

6 Bannan, Barry – Aston Villa – Blackpool; 11 Batt, Shaun – Peterborough United – Millwall; 7 Collis, Stephen P. – Bristol City – Torquay United; 10 Trotter, Liam A. – Ipswich Town – Millwall

FOREIGN TRANSFERS 2009–2010

JUNE 2009	From	To
Altidore, Jozy	Villareal	Hull City
Amaya, Antonio	Rayo Vallecano	Wigan Athletic
Aquilani, Alberto	Roma	Liverpool
Benitez, Christian	Santos Laguna	Birmingham City
Bilyaletdinov, Diniyar	Lokomotiv Moscow	Everton
Cana, Lorik	Marseille	Sunderland
Da Silva, Paulo	Toluca	Sunderland
Diamanti, Alessandro	Livorno	West Ham United
Diame, Mohamed	Rayo Vallecano	Wigan Athletic
Dikgacoi, KIagisho	Golden Arrows	Fulham
Dindane, Aruna	Lens	Portsmouth
Diouf, Mame Biram	Molde	Manchester United
Elm, David	Kalmar	Fulham
Franco, Guillermo	Villarreal	West Ham United
Ghilas, Kamel	Celta Viga	Hull City
Guerrero, Fernando	Indep del Valle	Burnley
Heitinga, Johnny	Atletico Madrid	Everton
Jimenez, Luis	Internazionale	West Ham United

Kakuta, Gael	Lens	Chelsea
Kalinic, Nikola	Hajduk Split	Blackburn Rovers
Klasnic, Ivan	Nantes	Bolton Wanderers
Kovac, Radoslav	Spartak Moscow	West Ham United
Kyrgiakos, Sotirios	AEK Athens	Liverpool
Lee Chung-Yong	FC Seoul	Bolton Wanderers
Maierhofer, Stefan	Rapid Vienna	Wolverhampton Wanderers
Matic, Nemanja	Kosice	Chelsea
Mensah, John	Lyon	Sunderland
Milijas, Nenad	Red Star Belgrade	Wolverhampton Wanderers
Mouyokolo, Steven	Bologne	Hull City
N'Zonzi, Steven	Amiens	Blackburn Rovers
Obertan, Gabriel	Bordeaux	Manchester United
Penny, Diego	Coronel Bolognesi	Burnley
Piquionne, Frederic	Lyon	Portsmouth
Riise, Bjorn Helge	Lillestrom	Fulham
Salgado, Michel	Real Madrid	Blackburn Rovers
Thomas, Hendry	Dep Olimpia	Wigan Athletic
Vanden Borre, Anthony	Genoa	Portsmouth
Van Heerden, Elrio	Club Brugge	Blackburn Rovers
Vennegoor of Hesselink, Jan	Celtic	Hull City
Vermaelen, Thomas	Ajax	Arsenal
Yebda, Hassan	Benfica	Portsmouth
Zhirkov, Yuri	CSKA Moscow	Chelsea
Zubar, Ronald	Marseille	Wolverhampton Wanderers

JANUARY/FEBRUARY 2010

Basturk, Yildiray	Stuttgart	Blackburn Rovers
Donovan, Landon	LA Galaxy	Everton
Gohouri, Steve	Moenchengladbach	Wigan Athletic
Guedioura, Adlene	Charleroi	Wolverhampton Wanderers
Holden, Stuart	Houston Dynamo	Bolton Wanderers
Ilan	St Etienne	West Ham United
Michel	Gijon	Birmingham City
Moreno, Marcelo	Shakhtar Donetsk	Wigan Athletic
Mujangi Bia, Geoffrey	Charleroi	Wolverhampton Wanderers
Okaka Chuka, Stefano	Roma	Fulham
Rodriguez, Maxi	Atletico Madrid	Liverpool
Stojkovic, Vladimir	Sporting Lisbon	Wigan Athletic

PLAYERS WHO WERE PREVIOUSLY SIGNED BUT DID NOT APPEAR UNTIL 2009–10

Ayala, Daniel	Liverpool
Begovic, Asmir	Stoke City
Borini, Fabio	Chelsea
Bruma, Jeffrey	Chelsea
Degn, Philipp	Liverpool
Fabio	Manchester United
Hines, Zavon	West Ham United
Hoilett, David	Blackburn Rovers
Pacheco, Dani	Liverpool
Nielsen, Gunnar	Manchester City
Weiss, Vladimir	Manchester City

NB: Jordi Gomez and Jason Scotland at Wigan Athletic previously played for Swansea City.

THE FA CUP 2009–2010

FIRST ROUND

Bristol R	(0) 2	Southampton	(0) 3
Huddersfield T	(4) 6	Dagenham & R	(0) 1
Notts Co	(1) 2	Bradford C	(0) 1
Accrington S	(2) 2	Salisbury C	(0) 1
AFC Telford U	(0) 1	Lincoln C	(1) 3
Aldershot T	(2) 2	Bury	(0) 0
Barnet	(1) 3	Darlington	(0) 1
Barrow	(1) 2	Eastleigh	(0) 1
Bromley	(0) 0	Colchester U	(2) 4
Cambridge U	(1) 4	Ilkeston T	(0) 0
Carlisle U	(1) 2	Morecambe	(0) 2
Chesterfield	(1) 1	Bournemouth	(2) 3
Forest Green R	(1) 1	Mansfield T	(0) 1
Gateshead	(0) 2	Brentford	(0) 2
Gillingham	(2) 3	Southend U	(0) 0
Grimsby T	(0) 0	Bath C	(1) 2
Hartlepool U	(0) 0	Kettering T	(1) 1
Hereford U	(1) 2	Sutton U	(0) 0
Luton T	(3) 3	Rochdale	(0) 3
Milton Keynes D	(1) 1	Macclesfield T	(0) 0
Northampton T	(1) 2	Fleetwood T	(1) 1
Nuneaton T	(0) 0	Exeter C	(4) 4
Oldham Ath	(0) 0	Leeds U	(1) 2
Oxford U	(0) 1	Yeovil T	(0) 0
Paulton R	(0) 0	Norwich C	(3) 7
Port Vale	(1) 1	Stevenage B	(0) 1
Rushden & D	(1) 3	Hinckley U	(0) 1
Shrewsbury T	(0) 0	Staines T	(1) 1
Stockport Co	(3) 5	Tooting & M	(0) 0
Stourbridge	(0) 0	Walsall	(1) 1
Swindon T	(1) 1	Woking	(0) 0
Torquay U	(2) 3	Cheltenham T	(1) 1
Tranmere R	(0) 1	Leyton Orient	(1) 1
Wrexham	(0) 1	Lowestoft T	(0) 0
Wycombe W	(2) 4	Brighton & HA	(2) 4
York C	(1) 3	Crewe Alex	(2) 2
Burton Alb	(2) 3	Oxford C	(1) 2
Northwich Vic	(0) 1	Charlton Ath	(0) 0
Wealdstone	(0) 2	Rotherham U	(2) 3
Millwall	(0) 4	AFC Wimbledon	(0) 1

FIRST ROUND REPLAYS

Rochdale	(0) 0	Luton T	(0) 2
Brentford	(2) 5	Gateshead	(0) 2
Leyton Orient	(0) 0	Tranmere R	(0) 1
Mansfield T	(0) 1	Forest Green R	(1) 2
Morecambe	(0) 0	Carlisle U	(1) 1
Stevenage B	(0) 0	Port Vale	(1) 1
Brighton & HA	(1) 2	Wycombe W	(0) 0

SECOND ROUND

Accrington S	(1) 2	Barnet	(0) 2
Bath C	(1) 1	Forest Green R	(1) 2
Bournemouth	(1) 1	Notts Co	(0) 2

Brentford	(1) 1	Walsall	(0) 0
Brighton & HA	(2) 3	Rushden & D	(2) 2
Cambridge U	(0) 1	York C	(2) 2
Carlisle U	(1) 3	Norwich C	(1) 1
Gillingham	(0) 1	Burton Alb	(0) 0
Hereford U	(0) 0	Colchester U	(0) 1
Milton Keynes D	(1) 4	Exeter C	(0) 3
Northampton T	(0) 2	Southampton	(2) 3
Northwich Vic	(0) 1	Lincoln C	(1) 3
Oxford U	(1) 1	Barrow	(1) 1
Port Vale	(0) 0	Huddersfield T	(1) 1
Rotherham U	(1) 2	Luton T	(1) 2
Staines T	(0) 1	Millwall	(0) 1
Tranmere R	(0) 0	Aldershot T	(0) 0
Wrexham	(0) 0	Swindon T	(0) 1
Kettering T	(0) 1	Leeds U	(0) 1
Stockport Co	(0) 0	Torquay U	(3) 4

SECOND ROUND REPLAYS

Aldershot T	(0) 1	Tranmere R	(1) 2
Barnet	(0) 0	Accrington S	(1) 1
Barrow	(1) 3	Oxford U	(0) 1
Leeds U	(1) 5	Kettering T	(0) 1
(aet.)			
Luton T	(2) 3	Rotherham U	(0) 0
Millwall	(1) 4	Staines T	(0) 0

THIRD ROUND

Aston Villa	(2) 3	Blackburn R	(0) 1
Blackpool	(0) 1	Ipswich T	(1) 2
Bolton W	(0) 4	Lincoln C	(0) 0
Everton	(1) 3	Carlisle U	(1) 1
Fulham	(1) 1	Swindon T	(0) 0
Huddersfield T	(0) 0	WBA	(0) 2
Leicester C	(1) 2	Swansea C	(1) 1
Middlesbrough	(0) 0	Manchester C	(1) 1
Millwall	(0) 1	Derby Co	(0) 1
Milton Keynes D	(0) 1	Burnley	(2) 2
Nottingham F	(0) 0	Birmingham C	(0) 0
Plymouth Arg	(0) 0	Newcastle U	(0) 0
Portsmouth	(1) 1	Coventry C	(1) 1
Preston NE	(2) 7	Colchester U	(0) 0
Reading	(1) 1	Liverpool	(1) 1
Scunthorpe U	(0) 1	Barnsley	(0) 0
Sheffield W	(1) 1	Crystal Palace	(1) 2
Southampton	(1) 1	Luton T	(0) 0
Stoke C	(2) 3	York C	(1) 1
Sunderland	(1) 3	Barrow	(0) 0
Torquay U	(0) 0	Brighton & HA	(0) 1
Tottenham H	(1) 4	Peterborough U	(0) 0
Wigan Ath	(0) 4	Hull C	(1) 1
Chelsea	(3) 5	Watford	(0) 0
Manchester U	(0) 0	Leeds U	(1) 1
Sheffield U	(1) 1	QPR	(1) 1
Tranmere R	(0) 0	Wolverhampton W	(0) 1
West Ham U	(1) 1	Arsenal	(0) 2
Bristol C	(0) 1	Cardiff C	(0) 1
Accrington S	(0) 1	Gillingham	(0) 0

| Brentford | (0) 0 | Doncaster R | (0) 1 |
| Notts Co | (0) 2 | Forest Green R | (0) 1 |

THIRD ROUND REPLAYS

Birmingham C	(0) 1	Nottingham F	(0) 0
Coventry C	(1) 1	Portsmouth	(0) 2
(aet.)			
Derby Co	(0) 1	Millwall	(0) 1
(aet; Derby Co won 5-3 on penalties.)			
QPR	(0) 2	Sheffield U	(1) 3
Liverpool	(1) 1	Reading	(0) 2
(aet.)			
Newcastle U	(2) 3	Plymouth Arg	(0) 0
Cardiff C	(0) 1	Bristol C	(0) 0

FOURTH ROUND

Accrington S	(1) 1	Fulham	(1) 3
Aston Villa	(1) 3	Brighton & HA	(1) 2
Bolton W	(0) 2	Sheffield U	(0) 0
Cardiff C	(1) 4	Leicester C	(2) 2
Derby Co	(0) 1	Doncaster R	(0) 0
Everton	(0) 1	Birmingham C	(2) 2
Notts Co	(2) 2	Wigan Ath	(0) 2
Portsmouth	(1) 2	Sunderland	(1) 1
Preston NE	(0) 0	Chelsea	(1) 2
Reading	(0) 1	Burnley	(0) 0
Southampton	(1) 2	Ipswich T	(0) 1
Tottenham H	(1) 2	Leeds U	(0) 2
WBA	(2) 4	Newcastle U	(0) 2
Wolverhampton W	(1) 2	Crystal Palace	(1) 2
Scunthorpe U	(1) 2	Manchester C	(2) 4
Stoke C	(1) 3	Arsenal	(1) 1

FOURTH ROUND REPLAYS

Crystal Palace	(0) 3	Wolverhampton W	(0) 1
Wigan Ath	(0) 0	Notts Co	(0) 2
Leeds U	(1) 1	Tottenham H	(1) 3

FIFTH ROUND

Chelsea	(1) 4	Cardiff C	(1) 1
Derby Co	(0) 1	Birmingham C	(0) 2
Manchester C	(1) 1	Stoke C	(0) 1
Reading	(1) 2	WBA	(1) 2
Southampton	(0) 1	Portsmouth	(0) 4
Bolton W	(1) 1	Tottenham H	(0) 1
Crystal Palace	(1) 2	Aston Villa	(1) 2
Fulham	(2) 4	Notts Co	(0) 0

FIFTH ROUND REPLAYS

Aston Villa	(1) 3	Crystal Palace	(0) 1
Stoke C	(0) 3	Manchester C	(0) 1
(aet.)			
Tottenham H	(2) 4	Bolton W	(0) 0
WBA	(1) 2	Reading	(1) 3
(aet.)			

SIXTH ROUND

Fulham	(0) 0	Tottenham H	(0) 0
Portsmouth	(0) 2	Birmingham C	(0) 0
Chelsea	(1) 2	Stoke C	(0) 0
Reading	(2) 2	Aston Villa	(0) 4

SIXTH ROUND REPLAY

Tottenham H	(0) 3	Fulham	(1) 1

SEMI-FINALS

Aston Villa	(0) 0	Chelsea	(0) 3
Tottenham H	(0) 0	Portsmouth	(0) 2

(aet.)

THE FA CUP FINAL

(Saturday, 15 May 2010 at Wembley Stadium, attendance 88,335)

Chelsea (0) 1   Portsmouth (0) 0

Chelsea: Cech; Ivanovic, Cole A, Ballack (Belletti), Terry, Alex, Kalou (Cole J), Lampard, Anelka (Sturridge), Drogba, Malouda.
Scorer: Drogba 59.

Portsmouth: James; Finnan, Mullins (Belhadj), Boateng (Utaka), Ricardo Rocha, Mokoena, Brown, Diop (Kanu), Piquionne, Dindane, O'Hara.
Referee: C. Foy (Merseyside).

Did You Know?

Since Queen's Park was already a member of the Football Association, Scottish clubs were allowed to apply for entry to the FA Challenge Cup in the early days of the competition. This is why it is never referred to as the English Cup. But after Rangers reached the semi-final in 1887 where they were beaten 3-1 by Aston Villa, the Scottish FA made a ruling thus barring their clubs from entering any other nation's competition. Actually Gretna, then playing in England, was allowed until briefly joining the Scottish League. Several Irish clubs also competed until 1890 but Welsh clubs continue to play in the FA Cup, though they have to apply earlier each year than their English colleagues. Druids were their first in 1876.

PAST FA CUP FINALS

Details of one goalscorer is not available in 1878.

1872	The Wanderers.............................1 Betts	Royal Engineers 0
1873	The Wanderers.............................2 Kinnaird, Wollaston	Oxford University 0
1874	Oxford University ....2 Mackarness, Patton	Royal Engineers 0
1875	Royal Engineers...........................1 Renny-Tailyour	Old Etonians...1* Bonsor
Replay	Royal Engineers...........................2 Renny-Tailyour, Stafford	Old Etonians...0
1876	The Wanderers.............................1 Edwards	Old Etonians...1* Bonsor
Replay	The Wanderers.............................3 Wollaston, Hughes 2	Old Etonians...0
1877	The Wanderers.............................2 Lindsay, Kenrick	Oxford University ....1* Kinnaird (og)
1878	The Wanderers.............................3 Kenrick 2, Kinnaird	Royal Engineers ....1 Unknown
1879	Old Etonians................................1 Clerke	Clapham Rovers..0
1880	Clapham Rovers...........................1 Lloyd-Jones	Oxford University 0
1881	Old Carthusians...........................3 Wyngard, Parry, Todd	Old Etonians...0
1882	Old Etonians................................1 Anderson	Blackburn Rovers 0
1883	Blackburn Olympic.......................2 Costley, Matthews	Old Etonians...1* Goodhart
1884	Blackburn Rovers ....2 Sowerbutts, Forrest	Queen's Park, Glasgow ....1 Christie
1885	Blackburn Rovers ....2 Forrest, Brown	Queen's Park, Glasgow 0
1886	Blackburn Rovers 0	West Bromwich Albion 0
Replay	Blackburn Rovers ....2 Brown, Sowerbutts	West Bromwich Albion 0
1887	Aston Villa ....2 Hunter, Hodgetts	West Bromwich Albion 0
1888	West Bromwich Albion ....2 Woodhall, Bayliss	Preston NE..1 Dewhurst
1889	Preston NE....................................3 Dewhurst, J. Ross, Thompson	Wolverhampton W 0
1890	Blackburn Rovers ....6 Walton, John Southworth, Lofthouse, Townley 3	Sheffield W...1 Bennett
1891	Blackburn Rovers ....3 Dewar, John Southworth, Townley	Notts Co ....1 Oswald
1892	West Bromwich Albion ....3 Geddes, Nicholls, Reynolds	Aston Villa 0
1893	Wolverhampton W ....1 Allen	Everton..0

1894	Notts Co	4	Bolton W	1
	Watson, Logan 3		*Cassidy*	
1895	Aston Villa	1	West Bromwich Albion	0
	J. Devey			
1896	Sheffield W	2	Wolverhampton W	1
	Spiksley 2		*Black*	
1897	Aston Villa	3	Everton	2
	Campbell, Wheldon,		*Boyle, Bell*	
	Crabtree			
1898	Nottingham F	3	Derby Co	1
	Cape 2, McPherson		*Bloomer*	
1899	Sheffield U	4	Derby Co	1
	Bennett, Beers, Almond,		*Boag*	
	Priest			
1900	Bury	4	Southampton	0
	McLuckie 2, Wood, Plant			
1901	Tottenham H	2	Sheffield U	2
	Brown 2		*Bennett, Priest*	
Replay	Tottenham H	3	Sheffield U	1
	Cameron, Smith, Brown		*Priest*	
1902	Sheffield U	1	Southampton	1
	Common		*Wood*	
Replay	Sheffield U	2	Southampton	1
	Hedley, Barnes		*Brown*	
1903	Bury	6	Derby Co	0
	Ross, Sagar, Leeming 2,			
	Wood, Plant			
1904	Manchester C	1	Bolton W	0
	Meredith			
1905	Aston Villa	2	Newcastle U	0
	Hampton 2			
1906	Everton	1	Newcastle U	0
	Young			
1907	Sheffield W	2	Everton	1
	Stewart, Simpson		*Sharp*	
1908	Wolverhampton W	3	Newcastle U	1
	Hunt, Hedley, Harrison		*Howey*	
1909	Manchester U	1	Bristol C	0
	A. Turnbull			
1910	Newcastle U	1	Barnsley	1
	Rutherford		*Tufnell*	
Replay	Newcastle U	2	Barnsley	0
	Shepherd 2 (1 pen)			
1911	Bradford C	0	Newcastle U	0
Replay	Bradford C	1	Newcastle U	0
	Speirs			
1912	Barnsley	0	West Bromwich Albion	0
Replay	Barnsley	1	West Bromwich Albion	0*
	Tufnell			
1913	Aston Villa	1	Sunderland	0
	Barber			
1914	Burnley	1	Liverpool	0
	Freeman			
1915	Sheffield U	3	Chelsea	0
	Simmons, Masterman, Kitchen			

1920	Aston Villa 1	Huddersfield T.................................0*
	Kirton	
1921	Tottenham H....................................1	Wolverhampton W 0
	Dimmock	
1922	Huddersfield T...............................1	Preston NE.......................................0
	Smith (pen)	
1923	Bolton W 2	West Ham U 0
	Jack, J.R. Smith	
1924	Newcastle U....................................2	Aston Villa 0
	Harris, Seymour	
1925	Sheffield U 1	Cardiff C...0
	Tunstall	
1926	Bolton W 1	Manchester C....................................0
	Jack	
1927	Cardiff C..1	Arsenal 0
	Ferguson	
1928	Blackburn Rovers 3	Huddersfield T.................................1
	Roscamp 2, McLean	*A. Jackson*
1929	Bolton W 2	Portsmouth.......................................0
	Butler, Blackmore	
1930	Arsenal..2	Huddersfield T.................................0
	James, Lambert	
1931	West Bromwich Albion 2	Birmingham 1
	W.G. Richardson 2	*Bradford*
1932	Newcastle U....................................2	Arsenal 1
	Allen 2	*John*
1933	Everton...3	Manchester C....................................0
	Stein, Dean, Dunn	
1934	Manchester C.................................2	Portsmouth.......................................1
	Tilson 2	*Rutherford*
1935	Sheffield W 4	West Bromwich Albion 2
	Rimmer 2, Palethorpe, Hooper	*Boyes, Sandford*
1936	Arsenal..1	Sheffield U 0
	Drake	
1937	Sunderland.....................................3	Preston NE.......................................1
	Gurney, Carter, Burbanks	*F. O'Donnell*
1938	Preston NE.....................................1	Huddersfield T.................................0*
	Mutch (pen)	
1939	Portsmouth.....................................4	Wolverhampton W 1
	Parker 2, Barlow, Anderson	*Dorsett*
1946	Derby Co...4	Charlton Ath......................................1*
	H. Turner (og), Doherty, Stamps 2	*H. Turner*
1947	Charlton Ath...................................1	Burnley...0*
	Duffy	
1948	Manchester U 4	Blackpool 2
	Rowley 2, Pearson, Anderson	*Shimwell (pen), Mortensen*
1949	Wolverhampton W 3	Leicester C..1
	Pye 2, Smyth,	*Griffiths*
1950	Arsenal..2	Liverpool..0
	Lewis 2	
1951	Newcastle U....................................2	Blackpool 0
	Milburn 2	

1952	Newcastle U ....1 *G. Robledo*	Arsenal 0
1953	Blackpool..4 *Mortensen 3, Perry*	Bolton W ....3 *Lofthouse, Moir, Bell*
1954	West Bromwich Albion ....3 *Allen 2 (1 pen), Griffin*	Preston NE..2 *Morrison, Wayman*
1955	Newcastle U ....3 *Milburn, Mitchell,* *Hannah*	Manchester C....................................1 *Johnstone*
1956	Manchester C...................................3 *Hayes, Dyson, Johnstone*	Birmingham C ....1 *Kinsey*
1957	Aston Villa ....2 *McParland 2*	Manchester U ....1 *T. Taylor*
1958	Bolton W ....2 *Lofthouse 2*	Manchester U 0
1959	Nottingham F....................................2 *Dwight, Wilson*	Luton T..1 *Pacey*
1960	Wolverhampton W ....3 *McGrath (og), Deeley 2*	Blackburn Rovers 0
1961	Tottenham H.....................................2 *Smith, Dyson*	Leicester C 0
1962	Tottenham H.....................................3 *Greaves, Smith,* *Blanchflower (pen)*	Burnley..1 *Robson*
1963	Manchester U ....3 *Herd 2, Law*	Leicester C ....1 *Keyworth*
1964	West Ham U ....3 *Sissons, Hurst, Boyce*	Preston NE..2 *Holden, Dawson*
1965	Liverpool...2 *Hunt, St John*	Leeds U ....1* *Bremner*
1966	Everton...3 *Trebilcock 2, Temple*	Sheffield W ....2 *McCalliog, Ford*
1967	Tottenham H.....................................2 *Robertson, Saul*	Chelsea ....1 *Tambling*
1968	West Browmwich Albion ....1 *Astle*	Everton...0*
1969	Manchester C...................................1 *Young*	Leicester C 0
1970	Chelsea ....2 *Houseman, Hutchinson*	Leeds U ....2* *Charlton, Jones*
Replay	Chelsea ....2 *Osgood, Webb*	Leeds U ....1* *Jones*
1971	Arsenal ....2 *Kelly, George*	Liverpool..1* *Heighway*
1972	Leeds U ....1 *Clarke*	Arsenal 0
1973	Sunderland ....1 *Porterfield*	Leeds U 0
1974	Liverpool...3 *Keegan 2, Heighway*	Newcastle 0
1975	West Ham U ....2 *A. Taylor 2*	Fulham...0
1976	Southampton ....1 *Stokes*	Manchester U 0

Year	Winner	Score	Runner-up	Score
1977	Manchester U *Pearson, J. Greenhoff*	2	Liverpool *Case*	1
1978	Ipswich T *Osborne*	1	Arsenal	0
1979	Arsenal *Talbot, Stapleton, Sunderland*	3	Manchester U *McQueen, McIlroy*	2
1980	West Ham U *Brooking*	1	Arsenal	0
1981	Tottenham H *Hutchison (og)*	1	Manchester C *Hutchison*	1*
Replay	Tottenham H *Villa 2, Crooks*	3	Manchester C *MacKenzie, Reeves (pen)*	2
1982	Tottenham H *Hoddle*	1	QPR *Fenwick*	1*
Replay	Tottenham H *Hoddle (pen)*	1	QPR	0
1983	Manchester U *Stapleton, Wilkins*	2	Brighton & HA *Smith, Stevens*	2*
Replay	Manchester U *Robson 2, Whiteside, Muhren (pen)*	4	Brighton & HA	0
1984	Everton *Sharp, Gray*	2	Watford	0
1985	Manchester U *Whiteside*	1	Everton	0*
1986	Liverpool *Rush 2, Johnston*	3	Everton *Lineker*	1
1987	Coventry C *Bennett, Houchen, Mabbutt (og)*	3	Tottenham H *C. Allen, Kilcline (og)*	2*
1988	Wimbledon *Sanchez*	1	Liverpool	0
1989	Liverpool *Aldridge, Rush 2*	3	Everton *McCall 2*	2*
1990	Manchester U *Robson, Hughes 2*	3	Crystal Palace *O'Reilly, Wright 2*	3*
Replay	Manchester U *Martin*	1	Crystal Palace	0
1991	Tottenham H *Stewart, Walker (og)*	2	Nottingham F *Pearce*	1*
1992	Liverpool *Thomas, Rush*	2	Sunderland	0
1993	Arsenal *Wright*	1	Sheffield W *Hirst*	1*
Replay	Arsenal *Wright, Linighan*	2	Sheffield W *Waddle*	1*
1994	Manchester U *Cantona 2 (2 pens), Hughes, McClair*	4	Chelsea	0
1995	Everton *Rideout*	1	Manchester U	0
1996	Manchester U *Cantona*	1	Liverpool	0
1997	Chelsea *Di Matteo, Newton*	2	Middlesbrough	0

1998	Arsenal 2	Newcastle U 0
	Overmars, Anelka	
1999	Manchester U 2	Newcastle U 0
	Sheringham, Scholes	
2000	Chelsea 1	Aston Villa 0
	Di Matteo	
2001	Liverpool......................2	Arsenal..1
	Owen 2	*Ljungberg*
2002	Arsenal 2	Chelsea 0
	Parlour, Ljungberg	
2003	Arsenal 1	Southampton 0
	Pires	
2004	Manchester U 3	Millwall...0
	Ronaldo, Van Nistelrooy 2 (1 pen)	
2005	Arsenal 0	Manchester U 0*
	Arsenal won 5-4 on penalties	
2006	Liverpool......................3	West Ham U 3*
	Cisse, Gerrard 2	*Carragher (og), Ashton, Konchesky*
	Liverpool won 3-1 on penalties	
2007	Chelsea 1	Manchester U 0*
	Drogba	
2008	Portsmouth....................1	Cardiff C...0
	Kanu	
2009	Chelsea 2	Everton..1
	Drogba, Lampard	*Saha*
	*After extra time	
2010	Chelsea 1	Portsmouth..0
	Drogba	

FA CUP ATTENDANCES 1969–2010

	Total	No. of matches	Average per match		Total	No. of matches	Average per match
2009–10	1,884,421	151	12,480	1988–89	1,966,318	164	12,173
2008–09	2,131,669	163	13,078	1987–88	2,050,585	155	13,229
2007–08	2,011,320	152	13,232	1986–87	1,877,400	165	11,378
2006–07	2,218,846	158	14,043	1985–86	1,971,951	168	11,738
2005–06	1,966,638	160	12,291	1984–85	1,909,359	157	12,162
2004–05	1,999,752	146	13,697	1983–84	1,941,400	166	11,695
2003–04	1,870,103	149	12,551	1982–83	2,209,625	154	14,348
2002–03	1,850,326	150	12,336	1981–82	1,840,955	160	11,506
2001–02	1,809,093	148	12,224	1980–81	2,756,800	169	16,312
2000–01	1,804,535	151	11,951	1979–80	2,661,416	163	16,328
1999–2000	1,700,913	158	10,765	1978–79	2,604,002	166	15,687
1998–99	2,107,947	155	13,599	1977–78	2,594,578	160	16,216
1997–98	2,125,696	165	12,883	1976–77	2,982,102	174	17,139
1996–97	1,843,998	151	12,211	1975–76	2,759,941	161	17,142
1995–96	2,046,199	167	12,252	1974–75	2,968,903	172	17,261
1994–95	2,015,249	161	12,517	1973–74	2,779,952	167	16,646
1993–94	1,965,146	159	12,359	1972–73	2,928,975	160	18,306
1992–93	2,047,670	161	12,718	1971–72	3,158,562	160	19,741
1991–92	1,935,340	160	12,095	1970–71	3,220,432	162	19,879
1990–91	2,038,518	162	12,583	1969–70	3,026,765	170	17,805
1989–90	2,190,463	170	12,885				

SUMMARY OF FA CUP WINNERS SINCE 1872

Manchester United	11	Preston North End	2
Arsenal	10	Sunderland	2
Tottenham Hotspur	8	Barnsley	1
Aston Villa	7	Blackburn Olympic	1
Liverpool	7	Blackpool	1
Blackburn Rovers	6	Bradford City	1
Chelsea	6	Burnley	1
Newcastle United	6	Cardiff City	1
Everton	5	Charlton Athletic	1
The Wanderers	5	Clapham Rovers	1
West Bromwich Albion	5	Coventry City	1
Bolton Wanderers	4	Derby County	1
Manchester City	4	Huddersfield Town	1
Sheffield United	4	Ipswich Town	1
Wolverhampton Wanderers	4	Leeds United	1
Sheffield Wednesday	3	Notts County	1
West Ham United	3	Old Carthusians	1
Bury	2	Oxford University	1
Nottingham Forest	2	Royal Engineers	1
Old Etonians	2	Southampton	1
Portsmouth	2	Wimbledon	1

APPEARANCES IN FA CUP FINAL

Manchester United	18	Sunderland	4
Arsenal	17	Blackpool	3
Everton	13	Burnley	3
Liverpool	13	Cardiff City	3
Newcastle United	13	Nottingham Forest	3
Aston Villa	10	Barnsley	2
Chelsea	10	Birmingham City	2
West Bromwich Albion	10	Bury	2
Tottenham Hotspur	9	Charlton Athletic	2
Blackburn Rovers	8	Clapham Rovers	2
Manchester City	8	Notts County	2
Wolverhampton Wanderers	8	Queen's Park (Glasgow)	2
Bolton Wanderers	7	Blackburn Olympic	1
Preston North End	7	Bradford City	1
Old Etonians	6	Brighton & Hove Albion	1
Sheffield United	6	Bristol City	1
Sheffield Wednesday	6	Coventry City	1
Huddersfield Town	5	Crystal Palace	1
Portsmouth	5	Fulham	1
The Wanderers	5	Ipswich Town	1
West Ham United	5	Luton Town	1
Derby County	4	Middlesbrough	1
Leeds United	4	Millwall	1
Leicester City	4	Old Carthusians	1
Oxford University	4	Queen's Park Rangers	1
Royal Engineers	4	Watford	1
Southampton	4	Wimbledon	1

CARLING CUP 2009–2010

FIRST ROUND

Darlington	(0) 0	Leeds U	(0) 1
Accrington S	(0) 2	Walsall	(1) 1
Barnet	(0) 0	Watford	(0) 2
(aet.)			
Brentford	(0) 0	Bristol C	(0) 1
Bristol R	(1) 2	Aldershot T	(0) 1
Bury	(0) 0	WBA	(2) 2
Cardiff C	(2) 3	Dagenham & R	(0) 1
Carlisle U	(0) 1	Oldham Ath	(0) 0
Cheltenham T	(1) 1	Southend U	(0) 2
Colchester U	(0) 1	Leyton Orient	(1) 2
Crewe Alex	(0) 1	Blackpool	(0) 2
Crystal Palace	(0) 2	Torquay U	(0) 1
Exeter C	(0) 0	QPR	(0) 5
Gillingham	(2) 2	Plymouth Arg	(0) 1
Hereford U	(0) 1	Charlton Ath	(0) 0
(aet.)			
Huddersfield T	(1) 3	Stockport Co	(0) 1
Lincoln C	(0) 0	Barnsley	(0) 1
Millwall	(2) 4	Bournemouth	(0) 0
Milton Keynes D	(0) 1	Swindon T	(1) 4
Notts Co	(0) 0	Doncaster R	(0) 1
Preston NE	(2) 5	Morecambe	(0) 1
Reading	(4) 5	Burton Alb	(0) 1
Rotherham U	(1) 2	Derby Co	(1) 1
Scunthorpe U	(1) 2	Chesterfield	(0) 1
Sheffield U	(1) 1	Port Vale	(2) 2
Sheffield W	(2) 3	Rochdale	(0) 0
Shrewsbury T	(2) 3	Ipswich T	(2) 3
(aet; Ipswich T won 4-2 on penalties.)			
Southampton	(1) 2	Northampton T	(0) 0
Swansea C	(1) 3	Brighton & HA	(0) 0
Tranmere R	(3) 4	Grimsby T	(0) 0
Wycombe W	(0) 0	Peterborough U	(2) 4
Yeovil T	(0) 0	Norwich C	(0) 4
Coventry C	(0) 0	Hartlepool U	(0) 1
(aet.)			
Macclesfield T	(0) 0	Leicester C	(0) 2
Nottingham F	(0) 3	Bradford C	(0) 0

SECOND ROUND

Norwich C	(0) 1	Sunderland	(3) 4
Gillingham	(0) 1	Blackburn R	(1) 3
Hartlepool U	(1) 1	Burnley	(0) 2
(aet.)			
Hull C	(2) 3	Southend U	(1) 1
Leeds U	(1) 2	Watford	(0) 1
(aet.)			
Nottingham F	(0) 2	Middlesbrough	(1) 1
Peterborough U	(1) 2	Ipswich T	(1) 1
Port Vale	(0) 2	Sheffield W	(0) 0
Portsmouth	(3) 4	Hereford U	(0) 1
Preston NE	(1) 2	Leicester C	(1) 1
QPR	(0) 2	Accrington S	(0) 1

Reading	(0) 1	Barnsley	(0) 2
Southampton	(0) 1	Birmingham C	(0) 2
Swansea C	(0) 1	Scunthorpe U	(1) 2
Tranmere R	(0) 0	Bolton W	(1) 1
West Ham U	(0) 3	Millwall	(1) 1
(aet.)			
Wolverhampton W	(0) 0	Swindon T	(0) 0
(aet; Wolverhampton W won 6-5 on penalties.)			
Blackpool	(3) 4	Wigan Ath	(0) 1
Bristol C	(0) 0	Carlisle U	(0) 2
Cardiff C	(1) 3	Bristol R	(0) 1
Doncaster R	(0) 1	Tottenham H	(3) 5
Leyton Orient	(0) 0	Stoke C	(0) 1
(aet.)			
Newcastle U	(1) 4	Huddersfield T	(2) 3
WBA	(1) 4	Rotherham U	(1) 3
(aet.)			
Crystal Palace	(0) 0	Manchester C	(0) 2

THIRD ROUND

Arsenal	(0) 2	WBA	(0) 0
Barnsley	(2) 3	Burnley	(1) 2
Bolton W	(0) 3	West Ham U	(0) 1
(aet.)			
Carlisle U	(1) 1	Portsmouth	(2) 3
Leeds U	(0) 0	Liverpool	(0) 1
Nottingham F	(0) 0	Blackburn R	(1) 1
Peterborough U	(2) 2	Newcastle U	(0) 0
Scunthorpe U	(0) 2	Port Vale	(0) 0
(aet.)			
Stoke C	(0) 4	Blackpool	(1) 3
Sunderland	(2) 2	Birmingham C	(0) 0
Aston Villa	(1) 1	Cardiff C	(0) 0
Chelsea	(0) 1	QPR	(0) 0
Hull C	(0) 0	Everton	(3) 4
Manchester C	(0) 2	Fulham	(1) 1
(aet.)			
Manchester U	(0) 1	Wolverhampton W	(0) 0
Preston NE	(0) 1	Tottenham H	(2) 5

FOURTH ROUND

Barnsley	(0) 0	Manchester U	(1) 2
Blackburn R	(2) 5	Peterborough U	(1) 2
Portsmouth	(1) 4	Stoke C	(0) 0
Sunderland	(0) 0	Aston Villa	(0) 0
(aet; Aston Villa won 3-1 on penalties.)			
Tottenham H	(1) 2	Everton	(0) 0
Arsenal	(1) 2	Liverpool	(1) 1
Chelsea	(2) 4	Bolton W	(0) 0
Manchester C	(2) 5	Scunthorpe U	(1) 1

QUARTER-FINALS

Manchester U	(2) 2	Tottenham H	(0) 0
Portsmouth	(1) 2	Aston Villa	(2) 4
Blackburn R	(1) 3	Chelsea	(0) 3
(aet; Blackburn R won 4-3 on penalties.)			
Manchester C	(0) 3	Arsenal	(0) 0

SEMI-FINALS FIRST LEG

Blackburn R	(0) 0	Aston Villa	(1) 1
Manchester C	(1) 2	Manchester U	(1) 1

SEMI-FINALS SECOND LEG

Aston Villa	(2) 6	Blackburn R	(2) 4
Manchester U	(0) 3	Manchester C	(0) 1

FINAL

Aston Villa	(1) 1	Manchester U	(1) 2

THE CARLING CUP FINAL

(Sunday, 28 February 2010 at Wembley Stadium, attendance 88,596)

Aston Villa (1) 1   Manchester U (1) 2

Aston Villa: Friedel; Cuellar (Carew), Warnock, Collins JM, Dunne, Downing, Milner, Petrov, Agbonlahor, Heskey, Young A.
Scorer: Milner 5 (pen).

Manchester U: Kuszczak; Rafael (Neville), Evra, Carrick, Evans J, Vidic, Valencia, Fletcher, Berbatov, Owen (Rooney), Park (Gibson).
Scorers: Owen 12, Rooney 74.

Referee: P. Dowd (Staffordshire).

Did You Know?

The first Football League Cup tournament was held in the 1960–61 season and it was not compulsory for clubs in membership to enter. Some bigger clubs declined on the grounds that they did not wish to risk losing to a lower division team. However once it became eligible to enter Europe and the UEFA Cup it was much more popular. Teams competing in European competitions are given byes to later rounds, too. Since 1981 there have been a number of sponsors who have used their name to promote the tournament. Originally the Milk Cup, in subsequent years it became the Littlewoods Challenge Cup, Rumbelows Cup, Coca-Cola Cup, Worthington Cup and since 2003 the Carling Cup.

PAST LEAGUE CUP FINALS

Played as two legs up to 1966

1961	Rotherham U.....................2 Webster, Kirkman	Aston Villa.....................0		
	Aston Villa.....................3 O'Neill, Burrows, McParland	Rotherham U.....................0*		
1962	Rochdale.....................0 Lythgoe 2, Punton	Norwich C.....................3		
	Norwich C.....................1 Hill	Rochdale.....................0		
1963	Birmingham C.....................3 Leek 2, Bloomfield	Aston Villa.....................1 Thomson		
	Aston Villa.....................0	Birmingham C.....................0		
1964	Stoke C.....................1 Bebbington	Leicester C.....................1 Gibson		
	Leicester C.....................3 Stringfellow, Gibson, Riley	Stoke C.....................2 Viollet, Kinnell		
1965	Chelsea.....................3 Tambling, Venables (pen), McCreadie	Leicester C.....................2 Appleton, Goodfellow		
	Leicester C.....................0	Chelsea.....................0		
1966	West Ham U.....................2 Moore, Byrne	WBA.....................1 Astle		
	WBA.....................4 Kaye, Brown, Clark, Williams	West Ham U.....................1 Peters		
1967	QPR.....................3 Morgan R, Marsh, Lazarus	WBA.....................2 Clark C 2		
1968	Leeds U.....................1 Cooper	Arsenal.....................0		
1969	Swindon T.....................3 Smart, Rogers 2	Arsenal.....................1* Gould		
1970	Manchester C.....................2 Doyle, Pardoe	WBA.....................1* Astle		
1971	Tottenham H.....................2 Chivers 2	Aston Villa.....................0		
1972	Chelsea.....................1 Osgood	Stoke C.....................2 Conroy, Eastham		
1973	Tottenham H.....................1 Coates	Norwich C.....................0		
1974	Wolverhampton W.....................2 Hibbitt, Richards	Manchester C.....................1 Bell		
1975	Aston Villa.....................1 Graydon	Norwich C.....................0		
1976	Manchester C.....................2 Barnes, Tueart	Newcastle U.....................1 Gowling		
1977	Aston Villa.....................0	Everton.....................0		
Replay	Aston Villa.....................1 Kenyon (og)	Everton.....................1* Latchford		
Replay	Aston Villa.....................3 Little 2, Nicholl	Everton.....................2* Latchford, Lyons		
1978	Nottingham F.....................0	Liverpool.....................0*		
Replay	Nottingham F.....................1 Robertson (pen)	Liverpool.....................0		

Year	Winner	Score	Runner-up	Score
1979	Nottingham F 3		Southampton 2	
	Birtles 2, Woodcock		*Peach, Holmes*	
1980	Wolverhampton W 1		Nottingham F 0	
	Gray			
1981	Liverpool 1		West Ham U 1*	
	Kennedy A		*Stewart (pen)*	
Replay	Liverpool 2		West Ham U 1	
	Dalglish, Hansen		*Goddard*	
1982	Liverpool 3		Tottenham H 1*	
	Whelan 2, Rush		*Archibald*	
1983	Liverpool 2		Manchester U 1*	
	Kennedy A, Whelan		*Whiteside*	
1984	Liverpool 0		Everton 0*	
Replay	Liverpool 1		Everton 0	
	Souness			
1985	Norwich C 1		Sunderland 0	
	Chisholm (og)			
1986	Oxford U 3		QPR 0	
	Hebberd, Houghton, Charles			
1987	Arsenal 2		Liverpool 1	
	Nicholas 2		*Rush*	
1988	Luton T 3		Arsenal 2	
	Stein B 2, Wilson		*Hayes, Smith*	
1989	Nottingham F 3		Luton T 1	
	Clough 2, Webb		*Harford*	
1990	Nottingham F 1		Oldham Ath 0	
	Jemson			
1991	Sheffield W 1		Manchester U 0	
	Sheridan			
1992	Manchester U 1		Nottingham F 0	
	McClair			
1993	Arsenal 2		Sheffield W 1	
	Merson, Morrow		*Harkes*	
1994	Aston Villa 3		Manchester U 1	
	Atkinson, Saunders 2 (1 pen)		*Hughes*	
1995	Liverpool 2		Bolton W 1	
	McManaman 2		*Thompson*	
1996	Aston Villa 3		Leeds U 0	
	Milosevic, Taylor, Yorke			
1997	Leicester C 1		Middlesbrough 1*	
	Heskey		*Ravanelli*	
Replay	Leicester C 1		Middlesbrough 0*	
	Claridge			
1998	Chelsea 2		Middlesbrough 0*	
	Sinclair, Di Matteo			
1999	Tottenham H 1		Leicester C 0	
	Nielsen			
2000	Leicester C 2		Tranmere R 1	
	Elliott 2		*Kelly*	
2001	Liverpool 1		Birmingham C 1	
	Fowler		*Purse (pen)*	
	Liverpool won 5-4 on penalties.			
2002	Blackburn 2		Tottenham H 1	
	Jansen, Cole		*Ziege*	

2003	Liverpool 2	Manchester U 0
	Gerrard, Owen	
2004	Middlesbrough 2	Bolton W 1
	Job, Zenden (pen)	*Davies*
2005	Chelsea 3	Liverpool...2*
	Gerrard (og), Drogba, Kezman	*Riise, Nunez*
2006	Manchester U 4	Wigan Ath 0
	Rooney 2, Saha, Ronaldo	
2007	Chelsea 2	Arsenal 1
	Drogba 2	*Walcott*
2008	Tottenham H...................................2	Chelsea 1*
	Berbatov, Woodgate	*Drogba*
2009	Manchester U 0	Tottenham H...0*

Manchester U won 4-1 on penalties.

2010	Manchester U 2	Aston Villa 1
	Owen, Rooney	*Milner (pen)*

*After extra time

LEAGUE CUP ATTENDANCES 1960–2010

	Total	No. of matches	Average per match		Total	No. of matches	Average per match
2009–10	1,376,405	93	14,800	1984–85	1,876,429	167	11,236
2008–09	1,329,753	93	14,298	1983–84	1,900,491	168	11,312
2007–08	1,332,841	94	14,179	1982–83	1,679,756	160	10,498
2006–07	1,098,403	93	11,811	1981–82	1,880,682	161	11,681
2005–06	1,072,362	93	11,531	1980–81	2,051,576	161	12,743
2004–05	1,313,693	93	14,216	1979–80	2,322,866	169	13,745
2003–04	1,267,729	93	13,631	1978–79	1,825,643	139	13,134
2002–03	1,242,478	92	13,505	1977–78	2,038,295	148	13,772
2001–02	1,076,390	93	11,574	1976–77	2,236,636	147	15,215
2000–01	1,501,304	154	9,749	1975–76	1,841,735	140	13,155
1999–2000	1,354,233	153	8,851	1974–75	1,901,094	127	14,969
1998–99	1,555,856	153	10,169	1973–74	1,722,629	132	13,050
1997–98	1,484,297	153	9,701	1972–73	1,935,474	120	16,129
1996–97	1,529,321	163	9,382	1971–72	2,397,154	123	19,489
1995–96	1,776,060	162	10,963	1970–71	2,035,315	116	17,546
1994–95	1,530,478	157	9,748	1969–70	2,299,819	122	18,851
1993–94	1,744,120	163	10,700	1968–69	2,064,647	118	17,497
1992–93	1,558,031	161	9,677	1967–68	1,671,326	110	15,194
1991–92	1,622,337	164	9,892	1966–67	1,394,553	118	11,818
1990–91	1,675,496	159	10,538	1965–66	1,205,876	106	11,376
1989–90	1,836,916	168	10,934	1964–65	962,802	98	9,825
1988–89	1,552,780	162	9,585	1963–64	945,265	104	9,089
1987–88	1,539,253	158	9,742	1962–63	1,029,893	102	10,097
1986–87	1,531,498	157	9,755	1961–62	1,030,534	104	9,909
1985–86	1,579,916	163	9,693	1960–61	1,204,580	112	10,755

JOHNSTONE'S PAINT TROPHY 2009–2010

NORTHERN SECTION FIRST ROUND

Burton Alb	(0) 1	Chesterfield	(1) 5
Crewe Alex	(0) 1	Stockport Co	(3) 4
Darlington	(1) 1	Lincoln C	(0) 0
Morecambe	(1) 2	Carlisle U	(0) 2

(Carlisle U won 4-2 on penalties.)

Oldham Ath	(1) 1	Accrington S	(0) 2
Rochdale	(0) 1	Bradford C	(0) 2
Rotherham U	(1) 1	Huddersfield T	(2) 2
Walsall	(0) 0	Bury	(0) 0

(Bury won 5-4 on penalties.)

SOUTHERN SECTION FIRST ROUND

Barnet	(1) 2	Millwall	(0) 0
Bournemouth	(1) 2	Yeovil T	(0) 1
Cheltenham T	(0) 1	Torquay U	(3) 3
Gillingham	(0) 1	Colchester U	(0) 1

(Gillingham won 4-3 on penalties.)

Hereford U	(0) 0	Bristol R	(0) 0

(Hereford U won 4-2 on penalties.)

Milton Keynes D	(0) 3	Dagenham & R	(0) 1
Norwich C	(1) 1	Brentford	(0) 0
Wycombe W	(0) 2	Northampton T	(1) 2

(Northampton T won 3-0 on penalties.)

NORTHERN SECTION SECOND ROUND

Bradford C	(1) 2	Notts Co	(1) 2

(Bradford C won 3-2 on penalties.)

Bury	(0) 2	Tranmere R	(1) 1
Carlisle U	(0) 4	Macclesfield T	(1) 2
Chesterfield	(0) 3	Huddersfield T	(0) 3

(Chesterfield won 4-2 on penalties.)

Hartlepool U	(0) 0	Grimsby T	(2) 2
Leeds U	(2) 2	Darlington	(1) 1
Port Vale	(3) 3	Stockport Co	(1) 1
Accrington S	(0) 2	Shrewsbury T	(0) 0

SOUTHERN SECTION SECOND ROUND

Charlton Ath	(2) 4	Barnet	(1) 1
Exeter C	(0) 1	Swindon T	(1) 1

(Swindon T won 4-3 on penalties.)

Gillingham	(0) 0	Norwich C	(0) 1
Hereford U	(1) 2	Aldershot T	(1) 2

(Hereford U won 4-3 on penalties.)

Leyton Orient	(0) 1	Brighton & HA	(0) 0
Milton Keynes D	(2) 2	Southend U	(0) 0
Northampton T	(0) 2	Bournemouth	(1) 1
Southampton	(0) 2	Torquay U	(2) 2

(Southampton won 5-3 on penalties.)

NORTHERN SECTION QUARTER-FINALS

Accrington S	(2) 3	Bury	(1) 2
Bradford C	(0) 2	Port Vale	(1) 2

(Bradford C won 5-4 on penalties.)

Chesterfield	(1) 1	Carlisle U	(0) 3
Leeds U	(2) 3	Grimsby T	(0) 1

SOUTHERN SECTION QUARTER-FINALS

Leyton Orient	(0) 1	Hereford U	(1) 1

(Hereford U won 3-2 on penalties.)

Milton Keynes D	(3) 3	Northampton T	(0) 1
Swindon T	(0) 0	Norwich C	(0) 0

(Norwich C won 5-3 on penalties.)

Southampton	(1) 2	Charlton Ath	(0) 1

NORTHERN SECTION SEMI-FINALS

Carlisle U	(1) 3	Bradford C	(0) 0
Leeds U	(1) 2	Accrington S	(0) 0

SOUTHERN SECTION SEMI-FINALS

Hereford U	(0) 1	Milton Keynes D	(1) 4
Southampton	(1) 2	Norwich C	(1) 2

(Southampton won 6-5 on penalties.)

NORTHERN FINAL FIRST LEG

Leeds U	(0) 1	Carlisle U	(1) 2

SOUTHERN FINAL FIRST LEG

Milton Keynes D	(0) 0	Southampton	(1) 1

NORTHERN FINAL SECOND LEG

Carlisle U	(1) 2	Leeds U	(0) 3

(Carlisle U won 6-5 on penalties.)

SOUTHERN FINAL SECOND LEG

Southampton	(2) 3	Milton Keynes D	(1) 1

JOHNSTONE'S PAINT TROPHY FINAL

(Sunday, 28 March 2010 at Wembley Stadium, attendance 73,476)

Carlisle U (0) 1   Southampton (2) 4

Carlisle U: Collin; Keogh, Horwood, Thirlwell (Taiwo), Harte, Murphy, Bridge-Wilkinson (Anyinsah), Kavanagh (Madine), Clayton, Dobie, Robson.
Scorer: Madine 84.

Southampton: Davis; Mills, Harding, Hammond, Jaidi (Perry), Fonte, Lallana, Wotton (Connolly), Lambert, Papa Waigo (Gillett), Antonio.
Scorers: Lambert 15 (pen), Lallana 44, Papa Waigo 50, Antonio 60.

Referee: S. Mathieson (Cheshire).

THE FA COMMUNITY SHIELD 2009

Chelsea (0) 2, Manchester United (1) 2

Chelsea won 4-1 on penalties.

At Wembley Stadium, 9 August 2009, attendance 85,896

Chelsea: Cech; Ivanovic (Bosingwa 46), Cole A, Mikel (Ballack 65), Terry, Ricardo Carvalho, Essien, Lampard, Anelka (Kalou 83), Drogba, Malouda (Deco 77).
Scorers: Ricardo Carvalho 52, Lampard 71.

Manchester United: Foster; O'Shea (Fabio 76), Evra, Carrick, Ferdinand, Evans J, Park (Giggs 75), Fletcher (Scholes 75), Berbatov (Owen 75), Rooney, Nani (Valencia 62).
Scorers: Nani 10, Rooney 90.

Chelsea won 4-1 on penalties: Lampard scored; Giggs saved; Ballack scored; Carrick scored; Drogba scored; Evra saved; Kalou scored.

Referee: C. Foy (Merseyside).

SCOTTISH LEAGUE TABLES 2009–2010

			Home				Away				Total					
Premier League	P	W	D	L	F	A	W	D	L	F	A	W	D	L	F	A	GD	Pts
1 Rangers	38	15	4	0	52	13	11	5	3	30	15	26	9	3	82	28	54	87
2 Celtic	38	14	4	1	42	14	11	2	6	33	25	25	6	7	75	39	36	81
3 Dundee U	38	8	4	7	22	21	9	8	2	33	26	17	12	9	55	47	8	63
4 Hibernian	38	9	4	6	29	21	6	5	8	29	34	15	9	14	58	55	3	54
5 Motherwell	38	8	5	5	29	25	5	9	6	23	29	13	14	11	52	54	–2	53
6 Hearts	38	9	4	6	19	20	4	5	10	16	26	13	9	16	35	46	–11	48
7 Hamilton A	38	6	7	6	19	17	7	3	9	20	29	13	10	15	39	46	–7	49
8 St Johnstone (P)	38	6	6	7	31	28	6	5	8	26	33	12	11	15	57	61	–4	47
9 Aberdeen	38	6	4	10	20	31	4	7	7	16	21	10	11	17	36	52	–16	41
10 St Mirren	38	5	9	5	18	18	2	4	13	18	31	7	13	18	36	49	–13	34
11 Kilmarnock	38	5	6	8	23	27	3	3	13	6	24	8	9	21	29	51	–22	33
12 Falkirk	38	3	6	10	17	29	3	7	9	14	28	6	13	19	31	57	–26	31

			Home				Away				Total					
First Division	P	W	D	L	F	A	W	D	L	F	A	W	D	L	F	A	GD	Pts
1 Inverness CT (R)	36	11	4	3	36	20	10	6	2	36	12	21	10	5	72	32	40	73
2 Dundee	36	12	4	2	30	13	4	9	5	18	21	16	13	7	48	34	14	61
3 Dunfermline Ath	36	9	3	6	31	23	8	4	6	23	21	17	7	12	54	44	10	58
4 Queen of the S	36	10	4	4	30	15	5	7	6	23	25	15	11	10	53	40	13	56
5 Ross Co	36	9	6	3	28	20	6	5	7	18	24	15	11	10	46	44	2	56
6 Partick Th	36	9	3	6	23	15	5	3	10	20	25	14	6	16	43	40	3	48
7 Raith R (P)	36	6	6	6	20	19	5	3	10	16	28	11	9	16	36	47	–11	42
8 Morton	36	6	4	8	21	24	5	0	13	19	41	11	4	21	40	65	–25	37
9 Airdrie U	36	5	6	7	25	22	3	3	12	16	34	8	9	19	41	56	–15	33
10 Ayr U (P)	36	5	5	8	17	30	2	5	11	12	30	7	10	19	29	60	–31	31

			Home				Away				Total					
Second Division	P	W	D	L	F	A	W	D	L	F	A	W	D	L	F	A	GD	Pts
1 Stirling Alb	36	7	8	3	30	22	11	3	4	38	26	18	11	7	68	48	20	65
2 Alloa Ath	36	11	2	5	27	21	8	6	4	22	14	19	8	9	49	35	14	65
3 Cowdenbeath (P)¶	36	10	5	3	36	19	6	6	6	24	22	16	11	9	60	41	19	59
4 Brechin C	36	9	6	3	30	20	6	3	9	20	25	15	9	12	50	45	5	54
5 Peterhead	36	8	5	5	23	18	7	1	10	22	31	15	6	15	45	49	–4	51
6 Dumbarton (P)	36	5	4	9	21	32	9	2	7	28	26	14	6	16	49	58	–9	48
7 East Fife	36	6	5	7	23	22	4	6	8	23	31	10	11	15	46	53	–7	41
8 Stenhousemuir	36	5	6	7	16	22	4	7	7	22	20	9	13	14	38	42	–4	40
9 Arbroath	36	4	5	9	22	33	6	5	7	19	22	10	10	16	41	55	–14	40
10 Clyde (R)	36	6	0	12	17	29	2	7	9	20	28	8	7	21	37	57	–20	31

¶*Cowdenbeath promoted via play-offs.*

			Home				Away				Total					
Third Division	P	W	D	L	F	A	W	D	L	F	A	W	D	L	F	A	GD	Pts
1 Livingston (R)	36	14	2	2	32	12	10	4	4	31	13	24	6	6	63	25	38	78
2 Forfar Ath¶	36	9	6	3	34	21	9	3	6	25	23	18	9	9	59	44	15	63
3 East Stirling	36	12	2	4	32	19	7	2	9	18	27	19	4	13	50	46	4	61
4 Queen's Park (R)	36	7	2	9	24	27	8	4	6	18	15	15	6	15	42	42	0	51
5 Albion R	36	9	5	4	21	12	4	6	8	14	23	13	11	12	35	35	0	50
6 Berwick R	36	9	3	6	19	18	5	5	8	27	32	14	8	14	46	50	–4	50
7 Stranraer (R)	36	8	5	5	25	23	5	3	10	23	31	13	8	15	48	54	–6	47
8 Annan Ath	36	7	6	5	19	16	4	4	10	22	26	11	10	15	41	42	–1	43
9 Elgin C	36	3	2	13	19	36	6	5	7	27	23	9	7	20	46	59	–13	34
10 Montrose	36	1	6	11	16	35	4	3	11	14	28	5	9	22	30	63	–33	24

¶*Forfar Ath promoted via play-offs.*
At the end of the 2008–09 season, Livingston were relegated to the Third Division, Airdrie U reinstated in the First Division and Cowdenbeath promoted to the Second Division.

CLYDESDALE BANK SCOTTISH PREMIER LEAGUE RESULTS 2009–2010

	Aberdeen	Celtic	Dundee U	Falkirk	Hamilton A	Hearts	Hibernian	Kilmarnock	Motherwell	Rangers	St Johnstone	St Mirren
Aberdeen	—	1-3 4-4	0-2 2-2	0-1 *1-0*	1-2 1-3	1-1 0-1	0-2	1-0 *1-2*	0-0 0-3	1-0	2-1 1-3	1-0 2-1
Celtic	3-0	—	1-1 1-0	1-1	2-0	2-1 2-0	1-2 *3-2*	3-0 3-1	0-0 2-1	1-1 *2-1*	5-2 3-0	3-1
Dundee U	0-1	2-1 *0-2*	—	2-1 3-0	1-1 0-2	2-0 1-0	1-0 *0-2*	0-0	0-1 3-0	0-3 0-0	3-3	3-2
Falkirk	0-0 3-1	3-3 0-2	1-4	—	2-0 *0-1*	0-1	1-3 1-3	0-0 0-1	0-0	1-3	1-2 *0-0*	1-1
Hamilton A	0-3 1-1	1-2 0-1	0-1	0-0 2-2	—	2-1	2-1 2-0	0-0 *3-0*	2-2 0-0	0-1	0-2 1-0	1-3 2-1
Hearts	0-3	2-1 *1-2*	0-0 *0-0*	0-0 3-2	2-1	—	1-1 *1-2*	1-2	1-0 *0-2*	1-2 1-4	1-2	2-1 1-1
Hibernian	2-0 2-2	0-1 0-1	1-1 2-4	2-0	2-1 2-0	0-0 2-1	—	1-1	2-0	1-1 3-0	3-0 1-1	1-1
Kilmarnock	1-1 2-0	1-0	0-2 4-4	1-2 *0-0*	5-1	1-0 1-0	1-0 1-0	—	0-3	0-0 0-2	2-1 3-2 *1-2*	2-1 2-1
Motherwell	1-1	2-3	2-2 *2-3*	1-0 0-1	3-0 1-2	1-0 3-1	1-3 1-0 *6-6*	3-1 1-0	—	6-1 *3-3*	1-3	1-2 1-1
Rangers	0-0 3-1	2-1 1-0	7-1	4-1 3-0	4-1 1-0	1-1 *2-0*	1-1 3-0	3-0	0-0 1-1	—	1-2 4-1	2-0
St Johnstone	1-0 *1-1*	1-4	2-3 0-1	3-1	1-1 *2-3*	1-2	5-1	0-1	2-2 1-2	3-0	—	1-0 *2-2*
St Mirren	1-0 *0-1*	0-2 4-0	0-0 1-2	1-1	0-2 0-0	2-1 1-1	1-0	1-0 *1-0*	3-3 0-0	0-2	1-1 1-1	—

IRN BRU SCOTTISH LEAGUE—DIVISION ONE RESULTS 2009–2010

	Airdrie	Ayr U	Dundee	Dunfermline Ath	Inverness CT	Morton	Partick Th	Queen of the S	Raith R	Ross Co
Airdrie	— —	3-1 1-1	1-1 3-0	1-1 0-1	1-1 0-1	2-4 3-0	2-5 2-0	1-1 0-1	1-2 3-0	0-1 1-1
Ayr U	1-1 1-4	— —	2-2 1-1	1-0 1-2	1-5 0-7	0-2 2-0	1-1 1-0	0-1 3-0	1-0 0-2	1-1 0-1
Dundee	2-1 0-1	3-1 3-0	— —	1-0 3-2	2-2 2-2	1-0 3-1	2-0 1-0	0-0 1-1	2-1 2-0	2-0 0-1
Dunfermline Ath	2-0 2-0	3-1 0-1	1-1 2-1	— —	0-1 0-0	3-1 4-1	3-1 1-2	1-4 3-1	0-2 2-1	3-3 1-2
Inverness CT	2-0 4-0	0-0 3-3	1-1 1-0	1-1 2-0	— —	4-1 1-0	2-3 2-1	1-3 3-1	1-0 4-3	1-3 3-0
Morton	1-0 2-1	1-0 2-1	0-1 2-2	0-2 1-2	0-3 0-2	— —	0-2 1-0	1-2 3-3	5-0 1-1	0-1 1-1
Partick Th	2-0 2-0	2-0 0-1	0-2 0-1	2-0 1-4	2-1 0-1	5-0 1-0	— —	2-2 1-0	1-2 0-0	0-0 2-1
Queen of the S	3-0 2-2	2-0 3-0	2-0 1-1	1-2 2-0	1-1 1-3	2-3 1-2	1-0 1-0	— —	1-1 3-0	2-0 1-0
Raith R	1-1 0-1	0-0 1-1	2-2 1-0	1-2 1-2	0-1 0-4	3-0 1-2	1-1 1-0	1-0 0-0	— —	2-1 4-1
Ross Co	2-1 5-3	2-1 1-0	0-1 1-1	0-0 2-2	2-1 0-0	3-1 2-1	2-2 1-2	3-2 1-1	0-1 1-0	— —

IRN BRU SCOTTISH LEAGUE—DIVISION TWO RESULTS 2009–2010

	Alloa Ath	Arbroath	Brechin C	Clyde	Cowdenbeath	Dumbarton	East Fife	Peterhead	Stenhousemuir	Stirling Alb
Alloa Ath	— —	0-1 1-0	2-1 2-3	2-0 2-2	2-1 3-1	1-3 1-2	0-0 2-0	1-0 2-1	1-4 2-1	1-0 2-1
Arbroath	2-2 0-0	— —	1-4 1-0	0-3 2-0	0-1 1-1	3-1 3-1	0-1 2-2	0-1 1-4	0-3 1-1	3-4 2-4
Brechin C	2-1 1-1	0-0 0-2	— —	2-2 3-1	3-1 3-3	3-1 0-1	3-2 1-0	3-0 1-2	1-0 2-2	1-0 1-1
Clyde	0-1 0-2	1-0 0-2	1-0 0-3	— —	0-1 1-2	0-2 4-2	1-3 2-1	1-3 3-1	2-1 0-2	0-1 1-2
Cowdenbeath	1-1 1-1	1-2 2-1	0-0 4-0	1-0 3-1	— —	2-1 0-0	2-1 6-2	5-0 1-3	2-1 1-0	1-2 3-3
Dumbarton	1-3 3-1	1-0 0-2	0-0 0-1	3-3 3-3	0-3 2-1	— —	0-3 0-1	1-0 1-3	0-0 2-1	2-3 2-4
East Fife	0-2 0-1	1-1 3-1	2-0 2-0	1-0 1-1	1-1 2-2	0-1 2-3	— —	1-2 3-0	2-1 1-1	1-2 0-3
Peterhead	0-0 2-0	1-2 3-0	1-0 0-3	2-0 0-0	0-2 1-0	1-2 2-1	1-1 3-1	— —	2-2 0-1	3-2 1-1
Stenhousemuir	1-0 0-2	3-0 1-1	1-1 1-2	1-0 0-3	0-2 0-0	0-3 1-0	1-1 1-1	2-0 1-1	— —	1-2 1-3
Stirling Alb	0-1 0-3	2-2 2-2	1-0 6-2	1-1 1-0	2-2 1-0	2-2 1-2	3-0 3-3	2-1 2-0	0-0 1-1	— —

IRN BRU SCOTTISH LEAGUE—DIVISION THREE RESULTS 2009–2010

	Albion R	Annan Ath	Berwick R	East Stirling	Elgin C	Forfar Ath	Livingston	Montrose	Queen's Park	Stranraer
Albion R	— / —	0-0 / 1-0	2-1 / 4-1	3-0 / 2-1	1-1 / 1-2	1-1 / 0-1	1-0 / 0-2	0-0 / 1-0	0-1 / 1-0	3-1 / 0-0
Annan Ath	0-0 / 1-2	— / —	1-1 / 0-1	0-1 / 1-0	0-2 / 3-3	1-0 / 1-1	0-0 / 2-0	2-0 / 0-0	3-1 / 0-2	1-0 / 3-2
Berwick R	2-0 / 1-2	2-1 / 0-2	— / —	0-1 / 2-2	2-0 / 2-1	0-1 / 0-4	1-0 / 1-1	2-0 / 0-2	1-0 / 1-1	1-0 / 1-0
East Stirling	2-0 / 3-1	1-3 / 3-1	1-0 / 3-2	— / —	1-1 / 2-0	2-1 / 4-0	3-1 / 0-2	1-0 / 2-3	1-0 / 0-3	1-1 / 2-0
Elgin C	0-2 / 3-1	1-1 / 1-0	3-3 / 1-5	1-2 / 0-1	— / —	0-2 / 0-2	1-6 / 0-1	0-1 / 5-2	1-0 / 0-3	1-2 / 2-3
Forfar Ath	2-2 / 1-1	2-1 / 1-5	3-0 / 2-0	5-1 / 4-1	3-3 / 1-0	— / —	0-1 / 2-2	2-2 / 2-0	0-1 / 1-1	1-0 / 2-0
Livingston	2-0 / 2-0	2-0 / 3-2	1-1 / 0-0	2-0 / 1-0	3-2 / 1-0	1-2 / 2-3	— / —	2-0 / 1-0	2-1 / 2-0	3-0 / 2-1
Montrose	0-0 / 0-0	0-0 / 1-2	1-3 / 1-1	0-3 / 0-1	1-1 / 0-4	1-2 / 4-0	0-3 / 0-5	— / —	1-2 / 1-2	1-1 / 4-5
Queen's Park	0-1 / 1-0	0-0 / 3-2	2-0 / 2-3	1-0 / 2-0	0-3 / 0-1	2-2 / 1-3	1-2 / 0-1	3-2 / 3-0	— / —	1-2 / 2-5
Stranraer	1-1 / 2-1	2-0 / 3-2	2-4 / 3-1	1-2 / 2-2	0-2 / 2-1	1-0 / 2-0	0-3 / 1-1	2-0 / 0-2	1-1 / 0-0	— / —

ABERDEEN   PREMIER LEAGUE

Ground: Pittodrie Stadium, Aberdeen AB24 5QH (01224) 650400
Ground capacity: 21,421 (all seated). **Colours:** All red.
Manager: Mark McGhee.
League Appearances: Aluko, S. 15(7); Considine, A. 15(1); Crawford, J. 2; Diamond, Z. 15(1); Duff, S. 11(6); Foster, R. 37; Fyvie, F. 17(9); Gibson, D. 1; Grassi, D. 16(7); Grimmer, J. (2); Ifil, J. 25(2); Kerr, M. 37; Langfield, J. 35; Low, N. (1); Mackie, D. 21(11); MacLean, S. 15(1); Maguire, C. 5(12); Marshall, P. 6(3); McDonald, G. 24; Megginson, M. (2); Miller, L. 18; Mulgrew, C. 37; Nelson, S. 3; Paterson, J. 7; Paton, M. 22(13); Pawlett, P. 11(3); Robertson, C. 1(2); Ross, S. 6; Wright, T. (3); Young, D. 16(4).
Goals – League (36): MacLean 5 (1 pen), Mackie 4, Mulgrew 4, Aluko 3, Diamond 3, McDonald 3, Miller, L. 3 (1 pen), Paton 3 (1 pen), Young 3, Considine 1, Fyvie 1, Kerr 1, Maguire 1, own goal 1.
Scottish Cup (3): McDonald 1, Mackie 1, Miller 1.
CIS Cup (2): Paton 2.
Europa League (1): Mulgrew 1.
Honours – Division 1: Champions – 1954–55, **Premier Division:** Champions – 1979–80, 1983–84, 1984–85. **Scottish Cup winners** 1947, 1970, 1982, 1983, 1984, 1986, 1990. **League Cup winners** 1956, 1977, 1986, 1990, 1996. **European Cup-Winners' Cup winners** 1983.

AIRDRIE UNITED   DIV. 2

Ground: Shyberry Excelsior Stadium, Airdrie ML6 8QZ (01236) 622000
Postal address: 60 St Enoch Square, Glasgow G1 4AG.
Ground capacity: 10,171. **Colours:** White shirts with red diamond, red shorts, red stockings.
Manager: Kenny Black.
League Appearances: Bain, J. 1; Baird, J. 26(5); Donnelly, B. 28(2); Gemmill, S. 16(8); Hollis, L. 2(1); Keast, F. (1); Keegan, P. 4(24); Lagana, F. 14(5); Lovering, P. 21(3); McCann, R. 30(2); McDonald, K. 21(9); McLaughlin, S. 33; Nixon, D. 6; Nolan, T. (2); O'Carroll, D. 28; O'darll, D. 1(1); Parratt, T. 12(1); Robertson, S. 34; Smith, Darren 11(6); Smyth, M. 24; Storey, S. 32; Trouten, A. 23(3); Waddell, R. 27(2); Watt, K. 2(18).
Goals – League (41): Baird 11 (1 pen), Gemmill 5, O'Carroll 5, Waddell 4, Lovering 3 (3 pens), McDonald 3 (3 pens), McLaughlin 3, Trouten 2, Donnelly 1, Keegan 1, Nixon 1, own goals 2.
Scottish Cup (7): Baird 2, Donnelly 2, Trouten 2, O'Carroll 1.
CIS Cup (0).
Challenge Cup (0).
Play-Offs (1): Gemmill 1.
Honours – Second Division: Champions – 2003–04. **League Challenge Cup winners** 2008–09.

ALBION ROVERS   DIV. 3

Ground: Cliftonhill Stadium, Main Street, Coatbridge ML5 3RB (01236) 606334
Ground capacity: 1249 (seated: 489). **Colours:** Red and yellow striped shirts, red shorts with yellow flashes, yellow stockings.
Manager: Paul Martin.
League Appearances: Bannantyne, L. 1; Barr, B. 11; Benton, A. 31(1); Boyle, C. 21(1); Canning, M. 20(2); Crozier, B. (2); Donnelly, C. 23(2); Ewings, J 15(1); Ferry, D. 5(5); Gaston, D. 21; Gilmartin, J. 2(7); Gormley, D. 4; Hoolickin, L. 2(2); Lumsden, T 8; McCusker, M. 12(10); McFarlane, D. 18(6); McGowan, M. 36; McGrath, P. 1; McKeown, S. 17(8); McLauchlin, D. 7(7); McLeod, P. 9(8); O'Boyle, J. 1(2); O'Byrne, M. 30; Pollock, M. 10(3); Reid, A. 33; Stewart, P. 2(7); Strachan, A. 4; Thomson, R. 11(4); Tyrrell, P. 26; Walker, P. 15(16).
Goals – League (35): McCusker 6 (2 pens), McLeod 5 (2 pens), Boyle 3, McFarlane 3,

Walker 3, Donnelly 2, McKeown 2, O'Byrne 2, Pollock 2, Barr 1 (1 pen), Canning M 1, Ferry 1, Thomson 1, Tyrrell 1, own goals 2.
Scottish Cup (4): Walker 2, Barr 1, Pollock 1.
CIS Cup (3): Barr 1, McCusker 1, own goal 1.
Challenge Cup (2): Barr 1, McFarlane 1.
Honours – Division II: Champions – 1933–34. **Second Division:** Champions 1988–89.

ALLOA ATHLETIC   DIV. 2

Ground: Recreation Park, Alloa FK10 1RY (01259) 722695
Ground capacity: 3100. **Colours:** Black shirts with gold hoops on front, black shorts, black stockings.
Manager: Allan Maitland.
League Appearances: Agnew, S. 11(4); Bloom, J. 5; Brown, M. 31(1); Buist, S. 23(1); Carrigan, B. 11(2); Carroll, G. 19(10); Craig, C. 1(3); Crawford, D. 36; Ferguson, B. 25(2); Gilhaney, M. 16(3); Gormley, D. 7(10); Grant, J. 29(2); Hay, J (5); Kerr, H. 2(11); Main, D. 1(1); McAvoy, D. 7(1); McCafferty, M. 16(2); McClune, D. 26; Noble, S. 24(5); Phelps, R. (2); Philp, R. (3); Prunty, B. 18; Russell, I. 4(2); Scott, A. 27(6); Spence, G. (1); Stevenson, A. 5(1); Thomson, J. (3); Townsley, C. 18(3); Walker, S. 31; Welsh, K. 3; Wilson, D (4).
Goals – League (49): Noble 10, Prunty 8, Scott 7 (3 pens), Carrigan 4 (1 pen), Ferguson B 3, Agnew 2, Carroll 2, Gormley 2, Grant 2, Walker 2, Gilhaney 1, McAvoy 1, McClune 1, Russell 1, own goals 3.
Scottish Cup (2): Brown 1, Gilhaney 1.
CIS Cup (0).
Challenge Cup (2): Spence 1, own goal 1.
Play-Offs (1): Gormley 1.
Honours – Division II: Champions – 1921–22. **Third Division:** Champions – 1997–98.
League Challenge Cup winners 1999–2000.

ANNAN ATHLETIC   DIV. 3

Ground: Galabank, North Street, Annan DG12 5DQ (01461) 204108
Ground capacity: 3000 (426 seated). **Colours:** Black and gold striped shirts, black shorts, black stockings.
Manager: Harry Cairney.
League Appearances: Adamson, R. 1; Anson, S. 6(12); Bell, G. 29(4); Clarke, T. (1); Cox, D. 29(1); Gilfillan, B. 33; Hoolickin, L. (1); Inglis, A. 3(3); Jack, M. 20(6); Jamieson, J. 1(1); Jardine, C. 31; Kelly, G. 15; McBeth, J. 30(4); Muir, N. 2; Muirhead, A. 22(1); Neilson, K. 30(1); O'Connor, S. 2; Phillips, J. (1); Redpath, G. (4); Sloan, S. 16(12); Sloan, L. 27(4); Steele, J. 27(4); Storey, P. 11(23); Summersgill, C. 20; Townsley, D. 9; Watson, J. 32(1).
Goals – League (41): Bell 9, Cox 5, Gilfillan 5, Anson 4, Sloan L 4 (1 pen), Jack 3, Jardine 2, McBeth 2, Storey 2, Watson 2, Neilson 1, O'Connor 1, Steele 1.
Scottish Cup (1): Watson 1.
CIS Cup (0).
Challenge Cup (7): Jack 2 (1 pen), Bell 1, Gilfillan 1, Inglis 1, Storey 1, Watson 1.
Honours – East of Scotland Premier League: Winners (4). **East of Scotland League Cup:** Winners (1). **East of Scotland Div 1:** Winners (1). **South of Scotland League:** Winners (2). **South of Scotland League Cup:** Winners (4). **Scottish Challenge Cup South:** Winners (1). **Scottish Qualifying Cup South:** Winners (1).

ARBROATH   DIV. 3

Ground: Gayfield Park, Arbroath DD11 1QB (01241) 872157
Ground capacity: 4165 (860 seated; 3305 standing). **Colours:** Maroon shirts with white trim, maroon shorts, maroon stockings.
Manager: Paul Sheerin.

League Appearances: Bishop, J. 12(1); Booth, C. 15; Dobbins, I. 11; Dorris, S. 27(3); Faulds, K. 3; Gates, S. (2); Gibson, K. 29(3); Hill, D. 36; Hislop, S. 24(5); Jackson, A. 6(2); Lunan, P. 19(7); McCaffrey, D. 6; McCulloch, M. 27(1); McGuire, P. 7; McIlravey, M. (3); McKay, D. 1; McLaughlin, J. 11; McLean, K. 15(5); McMullan, K. 12(7); Megginson, M. 5; Milne, K. (10); Moffat, K. (1); Morrison, S (1); Moyes, E. 16; Nimmo, I. 4(5); Raeside, R. 6(1); Rattray, A. 30; Redman, J. 20(4); Rennie, S. 17(5); Ross, R. 9(16); Scott, B. 11(9); Sellars, B. 12; Watson, P. 3(1); Weir, J. (1); Winters, D. 2.

Goals – League (41): Hislop 8 (1 pen), Dorris 6, Scott 6 (1 pen), Redman 4, Ross 4, Megginson 3, Sellars 3, Booth 1, Gibson 1, Lunan 1, McLean 1 (1 pen), Raeside 1, Rattray 1, Winters 1.

Scottish Cup (0).

CIS Cup (3): Bishop 1, Raeside 1, Sellars 1.

Challenge Cup (1): Redman 1.

Play-Offs (6): McCulloch 1, Megginson 1, Moyes 1, Nimmo 1, Redman 1, Ross 1.

Honours – Nil.

AYR UNITED   DIV. 2

Ground: Somerset Park, Ayr KA8 9NB (01292) 263435

Ground capacity: 10,185 (1597 seated). **Colours:** White shirts with black hoops, white shorts, white stockings.

Manager: Brian Reid.

League Appearances: Aitken, C. 12(2); Aitken, A. 22; Borris, R. 21(7); Bowey, S. 17(1); Campbell, M. 24; Cawley, K. 3(8); Connelly, A. 1(3); Connolly, K. 17(14); Easton, W. 19(3); Gibson, B. 19(6); Gormley, D. 1(8); Grindlay, S. 4(1); James, K. 13(1); Keenan, D. 31(3); Lafferty, D. 12(2); McGowan, N. 10(3); McGowan, R. 28; McKay, D. 5(8); McManus, T. 17; Mendes, J. 8(13); Mitchell, C. 14; Prunty, B. 6(4); Reynolds, S. 2(2); Roberts, M. 31(2); Samson, C. 32; Stevenson, R. 17; Visconte, R. 2(1); Winters, R. 1; Woodburn, A. 7(8).

Goals – League (29): Roberts 8 (2 pens), McManus 5 (1 pen), McKay 4, Stevenson 2, Aitken C 1 (1 pen), Aitken A 1, Bowey 1, Connolly 1, Keenan 1, Lafferty 1, McGowan R 1, Mitchell 1, Reynolds 1, own goal 1.

Scottish Cup (3): McManus 1, Roberts 1, Stevenson 1.

CIS Cup (2): Aitken A 1, Easton 1.

Challenge Cup (0).

Honours – Division II: Champions – 1911–12, 1912–13, 1927–28, 1936–37, 1958–59, 1965–66. **Second Division:** Champions – 1987–88, 1996–97.

BERWICK RANGERS   DIV. 3

Ground: Shielfield Park, Berwick-on-Tweed TD15 2EF (01289) 307424

Ground capacity: 4131. **Colours:** Black shirt with broad gold vertical stripes, black shorts, gold stockings.

Manager: Jimmy Crease.

League Appearances: Brazil, A. 26(1); Callaghan, S. 30(2); Cropley, J. (2); Currie, P. 29(2); Ewart, J. 25(1); Gair, S. 5; Gray, D. 22(9); Greenhill, D. 25(8); Guy, G. 13(5); Horn, R. 2(1); Kerr, G. 10; Little, I. 22(9); McCaldon, I. 2; McGregor, H. 1(2); McLaren, F. 25(1); McLean, A. 21(3); McMenamin, C. 1(4); McMullan, P. 15(7); Notman, S. 29; Peat, M. 34; Radznski, S. 6(8); Russell, O. 11(6); Savage, J. (2); Shields, J. 10(3); Smith, E. 32(1).

Goals – League (46): Gray 11 (1 pen), Brazil 5, Currie 5, Greenhill D 4, McLaren 4, McLean 4, Little 3, Callaghan 2 (1 pen), Radznski 2, Ewart 1, Guy 1, McMullan 1, Russell 1, own goals 2.

Scottish Cup (3): Brazil 2, Little 1.

CIS Cup (1): Little 1.

Challenge Cup (2): Ewart 1, Little 1.

Honours – Second Division: Champions – 1978–79. **Third Division:** Champions – 2006–07.

BRECHIN CITY   DIV. 2

Ground: Glebe Park, Brechin DD9 6BJ (01356) 622856
Ground capacity: 3960. **Colours:** Red with white trim.
Manager: Jim Weir.
League Appearances: Archdeacon, M. 8(1); Barr, B. 4; Byers, K. 19(8); Canning, S. 8(14); Cowan, M. 2(15); Docherty, M. 30(5); Dyer, W. 25; Fusco, G. 36; Harty, I. 4(3); Janczyk, N. 27(1); King, C. 34(2); Kurakins, A. 2; Masson, T. 1(6); McAllister, R. 34; McGroarty, C. (2); McKenna, S. (4); McLean, P. 33; Murie, D. 1; Nelson, C. 36; Nimmo, I. 1(5); Renton, K. 2(9); Scott, D. (1); Seeley, J. 13(2); Smith, B. 31; Tulloch, B. (2); Vallers, K. 7; Walker, R. 35; Walker, A. 3.
Goals – League (50): McAllister 21 (1 pen), King 11 (4 pens), Docherty 4, Archdeacon 3, Byers 3, McLean 3, Canning 1, Fusco 1, Harty 1 (1 pen), Janczyk 1, Vallers 1.
Scottish Cup (8): McAllister 3, King 2, Byers 1, Doherty 1, Fusco 1.
CIS Cup (4): McAllister 2, Byers 1, McKenna 1.
Challenge Cup (1): McAllister 1.
Play-Offs (3): McAllister 2, King 1 (pen).
Honours – Second Division: Champions – 1982–83, 1989–90, 2004–05. **Third Division:** Champions – 2001–02. **C Division:** Champions – 1953–54.

CELTIC   PREMIER LEAGUE

Ground: Celtic Park, Glasgow G40 3RE (0871) 226 1888
Ground capacity: 60,355 (all seated). **Colours:** Emerald green and white hooped shirts, white shorts with emerald green trim, whie stockings with emerald green trim.
Manager: Neil Lennon.
League Appearances: Boruc, A. 28; Braafheid, E. 9(1); Brown, S. 19(2); Caddis, P. 3(7); Caldwell, G. 14; Crosas, M. 14(3); Donati, M. 2; Flood, Willo ; Flood, W (1); Forrest, J. (2); Fortune, M. 22(8); Fox, D. 15; Hinkel, A. 30(1); Hooiveld, J. 2; Kamara, D. 8(1); Keane, R. 15(1); Ki, S. 5(5); Killen, C. 2(3); Loovens, G. 20; Maloney, S. 8(1); McCourt, P. 3(6); McDonald, S. 16(2); McGeady, A. 35; McGinn, N. 6(11); McGowan, P. 2(3); McManus, S. 6(2); Mizuno, K. (1); N'Guemo, L. 30; Naylor, L. 11(1); O'Dea, D. 16(3); Rasmussen, M. 2(8); Robson, B. 9(1); Rogne, T. 3(1); Samaras, G. 20(12); Thompson, J. 16(2); Wilson, M. 8(2); Zaluska, L. 10(1); Zheng-Zhi, 9(7).
Goals – League (75): Keane 12 (3 pens), Fortune 10, McDonald, S 10, Samaras 10, McGeady 7 (1 pen), Maloney 4, Loovens 3, Thompson 3, Kamara 2, McCourt 2, McGinn 2, Rasmussen 2, Brown S 1, Caldwell 1, Forrest 1, Killen 1, Naylor 1, O'Dea 1, Robson 1 (1 pen), Zheng-Zhi 1.
Scottish Cup (8): Keane 4 (1 pen), Kamara 1, McGinn 1, Rasmussen 1, own goal 1.
CIS Cup (4): McDonald 2, Killen 1, McCourt 1.
Champions League (3): Donati 1, McDonald 1, Samaras 1.
Europa League (7): Fortune 2, Samaras 2, McDonald 1, McGowan 1, Robson 1.
Honours – Division I: Champions – 1892–93, 1893–94, 1895–96, 1897–98, 1904–05, 1905–06, 1906–07, 1907–08, 1908–09, 1909–10, 1913–14, 1914–15, 1915–16, 1916–17, 1918–19, 1921–22, 1925–26, 1935–36, 1937–38, 1953–54, 1965–66, 1966–67, 1967–68, 1968–69, 1969–70, 1970–71, 1971–72, 1972–73, 1973–74. **Premier Division:** Champions – 1976–77, 1978–79, 1980–81, 1981–82, 1985–86, 1987–88, 1997–98. **Premier League:** 2000–01, 2001–02, 2003–04, 2005–06, 2006–07, 2007–08. **Scottish Cup winners** 1892, 1899, 1900, 1904, 1907, 1908, 1911, 1912, 1914, 1923, 1925, 1927, 1931, 1933, 1937, 1951, 1954, 1965, 1967, 1969, 1971, 1972, 1974, 1975, 1977, 1980, 1985, 1988, 1989, 1995, 2001, 2004, 2005, 2007. **League Cup winners** 1957, 1958, 1966, 1967, 1968, 1969, 1970, 1975, 1983, 1998, 2000, 2001, 2004, 2006, 2009. **European Cup winners** 1967.

CLYDE   DIV. 3

Ground: Broadwood Stadium, Cumbernauld G68 9NE (01236) 451511
Ground capacity: 8006. **Colours:** White shirts with red flashes, black shorts, red stockings.
Head Coach: Stuart Millar.

League Appearances: Allan, J. 2(1); Bark, A. 2; Borisovs, D. 3(7); Boyle, C. 8(1); Casey, M. 16(1); Cassidy, C. 9(2); Coakley, A. 2(3); Davidson, B. 2; Doolan, K. 9; Doyle, J. 4; Findlay, S. 1(1); Gair, S. 3(1); Graham, L. 4(2); Gramovics, A. 14(3); Halliday, R. 11(1); Higgins, C. 4(5); Howarth, S. 5(6); Kinniburgh, W. 14; Lang, J. 4(4); Lithgow, A. 32; McCulloch, W. 6; McFadden, A. 2(7); McGowan, N. 17; McKay, D 4(3); McLauchlan, W. 27(2); McLeod, P. 10(5); McNeil, A. 1; Muir, G. 4(3); Odunewu, S. 1(5); Park, A. 31; Reidford, C. 32; Sawyers, W. 24(8); Stevenson, C. 15(6); Stewart, P. 24(7); Strachan, A. 18; Walker, D. 1(2); White, J. 17(3); Wilson, M. 13(1).
Goals – League (37): Sawyers 10 (1 pen), Lithgow 4, Stewart 4, Strachan 4 (2 pens), White 4, McLeod 3, McLauchlan 2, Park 2, Borisovs 1, Gramovics 1, Howarth 1, McGowan N 1.
Scottish Cup (2): Lithgow 2.
CIS Cup (1): own goal 1.
Challenge Cup (0).
Honours – Division II: Champions – 1904–05, 1951–52, 1956–57, 1961–62, 1972–73. **Second Division:** Champions – 1977–78, 1981–82, 1992–93, 1999–2000. **Scottish Cup winners** 1939, 1955, 1958. **League Challenge Cup winners** 2006–07.

COWDENBEATH   DIV. 1

Ground: Central Park, Cowdenbeath KY4 9QQ (01383) 610166
Ground capacity: 4370 (1431 seated). **Colours:** Royal blue shirts, royal blue shorts, royal blue stockings.
Manager: Jimmy Nicholl.
League Appearances: Adamson, K. 20(5); Armstrong, J. 28; Baxter, M. 14(9); Bower, K. (1); Bradley, P. 1; Brett, D. 1; Dempster, J. 5(12); Droudge, D. 25(1); Fairbairn, B. 24(7); Ferguson, J. (8); Hay, D. 34; Linton, S. 24(2); MacKay, D (2); Mbu, J. 32; McBride, S. 16(9); McCabe, N. (4); McGregor, D. 16(1); McKay, C. 1; McQuade, P. 27(4); Ramsay, M. 18(13); Robertson, J. 29(2); Robinson, M. 1; Shields, J. 3; Stein, J. 19(13); Tomana, M. (1); Veiculis, A. 1; Wallace, D (1); Wardlaw, G. 31; Winter, C. 26(3).
Goals – League (60): Wardlaw 16, McQuade 12 (1 pen), McBride 6 (2 pens), McGregor 5, Robertson 5, Stein 5, Dempster 4, Fairbairn 2, Baxter 1, Ferguson 1, Linton 1, Mbu 1, Ramsay 1.
Scottish Cup (0).
CIS Cup (1): McQuade 1 (pen).
Challenge Cup (2): McBride 1, McQuade 1.
Play-Offs (6): Wardlaw 3, Dempster 1, McQuade 1, Mbu 1.
Honours – Division II: Champions – 1913–14, 1914–15, 1938–39. **Third Division:** Champions – 2005–06.

DUMBARTON   DIV. 2

Ground: Strathclyde Homes Stadium, Castle Road, Dumbarton G82 1JJ (01389) 762569/767864
Ground capacity: 2025. **Colours:** Amber shirts with thin black stripe, black shorts, black stockings.
Manager: Jim Chapman.
League Appearances: Brannan, K. 5(8); Carcary, D. 9(22); Chaplain, S. 29(5); Chisholm, I. 27(4); Clark, R. 14(8); Cook, A. 10; Craig, C. 16(1); Dunlop, M. 34; Geggan, A. 27; Gordon, B. 34; Harvey, R. 1; Hunter, R. 14(6); Lynch, S. (1); McEwan, D. 2; McGeown, M. 1; McLaughlin, D. 10(4); McNiff, M. 13(2); McStay, R. 19(4); Murray, S. 17(15); O'Donoghue, R. 15(4); Smith, C. 34; Strachan, A. 1(2); Vosachek, I. 24; White, M. 9(2); Winters, D. 15; Wyness, D. 16(1).
Goals – League (49): Chaplain 10 (2 pens), Carcary 5, Hunter 5, Winters 5, Wyness 5, Cook 3, Gordon 3, Clark 2 (1 pen), Dunlop 2, Geggan 2, Chisholm 1, Craig C 1, McLaughlin 1, McStay 1, Murray 1, O'Donoghue 1, own goal 1.
Scottish Cup (0).
CIS Cup (0).

Challenge Cup (0).
Honours – Division I: Champions – 1890–91 (Shared), 1891–92. **Division II:** Champions – 1910–11, 1971–72. **Second Division:** Champions – 1991–92. **Third Division:** Champions – 2008–09. **Scottish Cup winners** 1883.

DUNDEE   DIV. 1

Ground: Dens Park, Dundee DD3 7JY (01382) 889966
Ground capacity: 11,760 (all seated). **Colours:** Navy blue shirts, white shorts, navy blue stockings.
Manager: Gordon Chisholm.
League Appearances: Benedictus, K. 4(1); Bullock, T 19; Cameron, C. 5(9); Casement, C. (1); Clarke, P. 4(13); Cowan, D. 5(1); Douglas, R. 15(1); Forsyth, C. 21(3); Geddes, R. (1); Griffiths, L. 24(5); Harkins, G. 32(2); Hart, R. 20(6); Higgins, S. 15(11); Hutchinson, B. 5(4); Kerr, B. 29(4); Klimpl, M. 16(2); Lauchlan, J. 25; MacKenzie, G. 25; Malcolm, R. 2(1); Malone, E. 33; McHale, P. 11(3); McKeown, C 9(2); McMenamin, C. 24(7); O'Leary, R. 8; Paton, E. 32; Shinnie, A. 9(3); Soutar, D. 2; Young, D. 2(3).
Goals – League (48): Harkins 14 (2 pens), Griffiths 13 (2 pens), McMenamin 7, Higgins 6 (1 pen), Forsyth 2, Clarke 1, Hutchinson 1, Kerr 1, MacKenzie 1, Malone 1, Paton 1.
Scottish Cup (4): Forsyth 1, Griffiths 1, Harkins 1, Hutchinson 1.
CIS Cup (13): Griffiths 4, Antoine-Curier 2, Cameron 1, Forsyth 1, Harkins 1, Higgins 1, McMenamin 1, Malone 1, own goal 1.
Challenge Cup (11): Griffiths 3, Forsyth 2, Harkins 2, Antoine-Curier 1, Clarke 1, Higgins 1, own goal 1.
Honours – Division I: Champions – 1961–62. **First Division:** Champions – 1978–79, 1991–92, 1997–98. **Division II:** Champions – 1946–47. **Scottish Cup winners** 1910. **League Cup winners** 1952, 1953, 1974. **League Challenge Cup winners** 2009-10, **B&Q (Centenary) Cup winners** 1991.

DUNDEE UNITED   PREMIER LEAGUE

Ground: Tannadice Park, Dundee DD3 7JW (01382) 833166
Ground capacity: 14,223. **Colours:** Tangerine shirts, black shorts, tangerine stockings.
Manager: Peter Houston.
League Appearances: Banks, S. 1; Buaben, P. 33(1); Cadamarteri, D. 15(6); Cameron, G. (1); Casalinuovo, D. 16(9); Conway, C. 29(4); Daly, J. 16(7); Dillon, S. 25(8); Dixon, P. 25; Dods, D. 23(4); Dow, R. (2); Fotheringham, M. 2(1); Gomis, M. 31; Goodwillie, D. 23(10); Hill, C. 1; Hilson, D. (2); Kenneth, G. 26(2); Kovacevic, M. 24(1); Mihadjuks, P. 3; Myrie-Williams, J. 11(13); Pernis, D. 19; Robertson, S. 8(5); Robertson, D. 8(6); Sandaza, F 1(6); Shala, A. 2(10); Smith, K. 2(1); Swanson, D. 22(9); Watson, K. 7(1); Weaver, N. 18; Webster, A. 26; Wilkie, L. 1.
Goals – League (55): Daly 13 (2 pens), Goodwillie 9 (1 pen), Casalinuovo 6 (1 pen), Swanson 5, Cadamarteri 4 (2 pens), Conway 4, Gomis 4, Webster 3, Buaben 2, Dods 1, Kenneth 1, Myrie-Williams 1, Sandaza, F 1, own goal 1.
Scottish Cup (12): Goodwillie 4, Conway 2, Casalinuovo 1, Kovacevic 1, Robertson D 1, Shala 1, Weaver 1, own goal 1.
CIS Cup (5): Buaben 1, Goodwillie 1, Russell 1, Shala 1, Wilkie 1.
Honours – Premier Division: Champions – 1982–83. **Division II:** Champions – 1924–25, 1928–29. **Scottish Cup winners** 1994, 2010. **League Cup winners** 1980, 1981.

DUNFERMLINE ATHLETIC   DIV. 1

Ground: East End Park, Dunfermline KY12 7RB (01383) 724295
Ground capacity: 12,509. **Colours:** Black and white striped shirts, white shorts, black stockings.
Manager: Jim McIntyre.

League Appearances: Bayne, G. 15(1); Bell, S. 29(2); Burke, A. 25(2); Campbell, R 3(10); Cardle, J. 16(9); Dowie, A. 32; Fleming, G. 25(1); Gibson, W. 30(4); Glass, S. 1; Graham, D. 28(1); Higgins, C. 13(4); Holmes, G. 6(11); Kirk, A. 17(4); Mason, G. 11(2); McCann, A. 28(2); McDougall, S. 17(5); McGregor, N. 24; McIntyre, J. (2); Muirhead, S. 2(5); Paterson, G. 3; Phinn, N. 16(17); Ross, G. 22(2); Smith, C. 8; Willis, P (2); Woods, C. 25(4).

Goals – League (54): Gibson 9 (2 pens), Bell 8 (2 pens), Kirk 8 (1 pen), Cardle 5, McDougall 5, Phinn 5, Bayne 3, Graham 3, Mason 2, Woods 2, Campbell, R 1, McGregor 1, own goals 2.

Scottish Cup (11): Kirk 4 (1 pen), Cardle 2, Graham 2, Gibson 1, McDougall 1, Phinn 1.

CIS Cup (9): Kirk 4, Bayne 1, Bell 1, Burke 1, Graham 1, own goal 1.

Challenge Cup (3): Bell 1, Cardle 1, Kirk 1.

Honours – First Division: Champions – 1988–89, 1995–96. **Division II:** Champions – 1925–26. **Second Division:** Champions – 1985–86. **Scottish Cup winners** 1961, 1968.

EAST FIFE   DIV. 2

Ground: Bayview Park, Methil, Fife KY8 3RW (01333) 426323

Ground capacity: 1992. **Colours:** Gold shirts with black stripes, black shorts, gold stockings.

Manager: Stevie Crawford.

League Appearances: Baillie, S. 6(1); Brown, M. 26; Campbell, R. 12(8); Campbell, S. 3; Cargill, S. 7(15); Conway, A. 10(15); Cook, A. 6(3); Crawford, S. 28(6); Fagan, S. 9(6); Gourlay, D. 4(4); Kerr, G. 7(4); Linn, B. 23(10); Lowing, A. 7; McCunnie, J. 28; McManus, P. 28(4); McRae, J. 1; Muir, D. 36; Murdock, S. 13(1); Nugent, P. 23; Ovenstone, J. 33; Ridgers, M. 4; Sheerin, J. 4(5); Sludden, P. 4(2); Smart, J. 27(1); Staunton, M. 5(6); Thomson, D. (1); Thomson, S. 3; Watson, K. 6; Young, L. 33(2).

Goals – League (46): McManus 15 (2 pens), Crawford 6, Linn 6 (1 pen), Muir 5, Young 4, McCunnie 2, Cargill 1, Conway 1, Cook 1, Kerr 1, Murdock 1, Ovenstone 1, Smart 1, Thomson S 1.

Scottish Cup (1): McManus 1.

CIS Cup (2): Linn 1, Muir 1.

Challenge Cup (0).

Honours – Division II: Champions – 1947–48. **Third Division:** Champions – 2007–08. **Scottish Cup winners** 1938. **League Cup winners** 1948, 1950, 1954.

EAST STIRLINGSHIRE   DIV. 3

Ground: Ochilview Park, Gladstone Road, Stenhousemuir FK5 4QL (01324) 562992 (match day only).

Ground capacity: 3776 (626 seated). **Colours:** All black with white chevrons.

Head Coach: Jim McInally.

League Appearances: Barclay, J. 33; Bolochoweckyj, M. 29(1); Brady, C. (4); Donaldson, C. 24(2); Dunn, D. 14(12); Elliot, J. (3); Forrest, E. 24; Harding, R. 20(2); Hay, P. 28(4); Johnston, S. 2(11); King, D. 12; Lynch, S. 31(2); Maquire, S. 23(13); McKenzie, M. 2(27); Richardson, D. 31(2); Rodgers, A. 29(4); Sorley, G. 3; Stevenson, J. 32; Tully, C. 15(2); Ure, D. 17(11); Weaver, P. 27(1).

Goals – League (50): Lynch 13, Rodgers 9 (1 pen), Stevenson 9 (1 pen), Maquire 8, Bolochoweckyj 3, Dunn 2, Richardson 2, Donaldson 1, Tully 1, Ure 1, Weaver 1.

Scottish Cup (2): Dunn 1, Rodgers 1.

CIS Cup (3): Rodgers 2, McGuire 1.

Challenge Cup (0).

Play-Offs (2): Rodgers 2.

Honours – Division II: Champions – 1931–32. **C Division:** Champions – 1947–48.

ELGIN CITY   DIV. 3

Ground: Borough Briggs, Elgin IV30 1AP (01343) 551114
Ground capacity: 3927 (478 seated). **Colours:** Black and white striped shirts, black shorts, red stockings.
Manager: Ross Jack.
League Appearances: Calder, D. 1(11); Cameron, B. 9(15); Craig, DA 15(7); Craig, DW 27; Crooks, J. 15(12); Dempsie, A. 20; Dunne, M. 4; Edwards, S. 19(8); Fraser, S. (1); Frizzel, C. 33(1); Gibson, J. 36; Gunn, C. 31(5); Inglis, J. 9(5); Jack, A. 1(2); Kaczan, P. 28; MacAulay, K. 27(6); MacLeod, D. (3); McConachie, M. (1); McDonald, N. 21(2); Morrison, G. 15; Nicolson, M. 32; Niven, D. 25; Smith, D. 2(10); Sutherland, S. 17; Tatters, G. 9; Trialist, E. (1).
Goals – League (46): Gunn 17 (1 pen), Sutherland 5, MacAulay 4, Nicolson 4, Crooks 3 (1 pen), Frizzel 3, Morrison 2, Smith 2, Cameron 1, Dunne 1, Jack A 1, Niven 1, Tatters 1, own goal 1.
Scottish Cup (4): Frizzel 3 (1 pen), Crooks 1 (pen).
CIS Cup (0).
Challenge Cup (8): Crooks 2 (1 pen), Gunn 2, Cameron 1, Edwards 1, Frizzel 1, own goal 1.
Honours – Nil.

FALKIRK   DIV. 1

Ground: Brockville Park, Falkirk FK1 5AX (01324) 624121
Ground capacity: 8000. **Colours:** Navy blue shirts with white seams, white shorts, white stockings.
Manager: Steven Pressley.
League Appearances: Allison, B. 4; Arfield, S. 35(1); Barr, D. 38; Bullen, L. (9); Compton, J. 3(10); Duffy, K. 5(1); Finnbogason, K. 7; Finnigan, C. 20(7); Flynn, R. 36; Healy, C. 17(2); Lima, V. 22(4); Lynch, S. 3(5); MacDonald, A. 4(7); Marceta, D. 8(7); McLean, B. 36; McNamara, J. 13; Mitchell, C. 5(3); Moutinho, P. 20(5); Murdoch, S. (3); O'Brien, B. 23(4); Olejnik, R. 38; Pele, P. 7(2); Robertson, D. (1); Scobbie, T. 19(1); Showunmi, E. 15(6); Stewart, M. 7(12); Twaddle, M. 30(3); Zerara, T. 3.
Goals – League (31): Finnigan 5, Flynn 5, Moutinho 5, Arfield 3 (2 pens), Barr 2, Stewart M 2, Bullen 1, Finnbogason 1, Healy 1, MacDonald 1, Mitchell 1, Pele 1, Showunmi 1, Twaddle 1, own goal 1.
Scottish Cup (0).
CIS Cup (0).
Europa League (1): Flynn 1.
Honours – Division II: Champions – 1935–36, 1969–70, 1974–75. **First Division:** Champions – 1990–91, 1993–94, 2002–03, 2004–05. **Second Division:** Champions – 1979–80. **Scottish Cup winners** 1913, 1957. **B&Q Cup winners** 1994. **League Challenge Cup winners** 1998, 2005.

FORFAR ATHLETIC   DIV. 2

Ground: Station Park, Carseview Road, Forfar DD8 3BT. (01307) 463576
Ground capacity: 5177 (739 seated). **Colours:** Sky and navy blue hooped shirts, navy blue shorts, navy blue stockings.
Manager: Dick Campbell.
League Appearances: Andreoni, M. 1; Bishop, J. 17(1); Brady, D. 4(1); Brown, A. 28; Campbell, R. 29(6); Campbell, I. 32; Deasley, B. 9(13); Divine, A. 3(1); Fotheringham, M. 19(8); Fotheringham, K. 26(3); Fusco, S. (1); Gibson, G. 9(17); Gordon, K. 8(10); Grant, C. 2; Harty, I. 21(5); Malcolm, S. 5; McCulloch, M. 23; McGroarty, C. 1; McLean, E. 6; McNally, S. (5); Mowat, D. 31(1); Sellars, B. 15(3); Smith, C. 3(10); Smith, N. 3(3); Templeman, C. 25(7); Tod, A. 33; Tulloch, S. 31(1); Watson, P. 12(5); Winter, C. (1).
Goals – League (59): Campbell R 16 (3 pens), Harty 10, Sellars 5, Templeman 5,

Fotheringham M 4, Watson 4, Fotheringham K 3 (1 pen), Tulloch 3, Campbell I 2, Deasley 2, Gibson 2, Bishop 1, Gordon 1, Mowat 1.
Scottish Cup (5): Campbell R 2, Harty 1 (pen), Templeman 1, Tod 1.
CIS Cup (5): Campbell R 2, Deasley 1, Fotheringham M 1, Tulloch 1.
Challenge Cup (3): Fotheringham M 1, Fotheringham K 1, Templeman 1.
Play-Offs (5): Bishop 1, Campbell R 1 (pen), Deasley 1, Fotheringham M 1, Tulloch 1.
Honours – Second Division: Champions – 1983–84. **Third Division:** Champions – 1994–95.

HAMILTON ACADEMICAL   PREMIER LEAGUE

Ground: New Douglas Park, Cadzow Avenue, Hamilton ML3 0FT (01698) 368650
Ground capacity: 6078. **Colours:** Red and white hooped shirts, white shorts.
Manager: Billy Reid.
League Appearances: Andrews, M. 2; Antoine-Curier, M. 25(1); Beuzelin, G. 3(4); Canning, M. 37; Cerny, T. 34; Crawford, A. (7); Easton, B. 12; Elebert, D. 15(10); Elliott, S. 2(3); Evans, G. 5(4); Gillespie, G. (1); Hastings, R. 17; Imrie, D. 16; Iriekpen, I. 2; Kirkpatrick, J. 1(4); Kissock, J. 2; Knight, L. (6); Louhoungu, D. (6); Lyle, D. 4(1); Mason, G. 5; McArthur, J. 35; McClenahan, T. 23(4); McLaughlin, M. 32; McQueen, B. (1); Mensing, S. 37; Mills, S. (2); Murdoch, S. 4(2); Neil, A. 22; Offiong, R. 1; Paixao, F. 18(7); Paixao, M. 23(10); Rubiales, L. 3; Sullivan, S. 1(1); Taylor, S. (1); Thomas, J. 2(9); Van Zanten, D. 4(2); Welsh, K. 1; Wesolowski, J. 27(2); Wilkie, K. 3(9).
Goals – League (39): Mensing 8 (5 pens), Antoine-Curier 7, Paixao F 6, Paixao M 5, Wesolowski 4, Thomas 3, Imrie 2, McLaughlin 2, Canning 1, McArthur 1.
Scottish Cup (3): Antoine-Curier 1, Mensing 1 (pen), Paixao M 1.
CIS Cup (1): Mensing 1.
Honours – First Division: Champions – 1985–86, 1987–88, 2007–08. **Division II:** Champions – 1903–04. **Division III:** Champions – 2000–01. **B&Q Cup winners** 1992, 1993.

HEART OF MIDLOTHIAN   PREMIER LEAGUE

Ground: Tynecastle Park, McLeod Street, Edinburgh EH11 2NL (0871) 663 1874
Ground capacity: 17,402. **Colours:** Maroon shirts with white trim, white shorts, white stockings.
Manager: Jim Jefferies.
League Appearances: Balogh, J. 16; Black, I. 17(9); Bouzid, I. 26; Cinikas, M. 1(1); Driver, A. 11(1); Elliot, C. 6(7); Glen, G. 10(8); Goncalves, J. 19; Jonsson, E. 27(1); Kello, M. 14; Kingston, L. 10(4); Kucharski, D. 10(4); MacDonald, J. 8(1); Mole, J. 5(2); Mulrooney, P. 3(3); Nade, C. 15(8); Novikovas, A. 5(8); Obua, D. 30(2); Palazuelos, R. 26(1); Robinson, S. 7(6); Santana, S. 21(6); Smith, G. 2(6); Stevenson, R. 9(2); Stewart, M. 24(1); Stewart, J. (1); Templeton, D. 7(9); Thomson, J. 15(1); Thomson, C. 15(5); Visconte, R. 1(1); Wallace, L. 32; Wallace, R. (2); Witteveen, D. 5(5); Zaliukas, M. 21(1).
Goals – League (35): Santana 6, Stewart M 5 (4 pens), Driver 3, Jonsson 3, Obua 3, Goncalves 2, Nade 2, Templeton 2, Zaliukas 2, Black 1, Bouzid 1, Glen 1, Robinson 1, Smith 1, Wallace L 1, Witteveen 1.
Scottish Cup (0).
CIS Cup (3): Stewart 2 (2 pens), Glen 1.
Europa League (2): Stewart 1, Zaliukas 1.
Honours – Division I: Champions – 1894–95, 1896–97, 1957–58, 1959–60. **First Division:** Champions – 1979–80. **Scottish Cup winners** 1891, 1896, 1901, 1906, 1956, 1998, 2006. **League Cup winners** 1955, 1959, 1960, 1963.

HIBERNIAN   PREMIER LEAGUE

Ground: Easter Road Stadium, 12 Albion Place, Edinburgh EH7 5QG (0131) 661 2159
Ground capacity: 17,400. **Colours:** Green shirts with white sleeves, white shorts, white stockings.
Manager: John Hughes.

League Appearances: Bamba, S. 30; Benjelloun, A. 8(20); Byrne, K. (4); Cregg, P. 10(5); Galbraith, D. (14); Gow, A. 3(4); Hanlon, P. 16(2); Hogg, C. 33; Ma-Kalambay, Y. 6(1); McBride, K. 21(5); McCann, K. 1; McCormack, D. 7(2); Miller, L. 32(1); Murray, I. 34; Nish, C. 23(9); Rankin, J. 30(3); Riordan, D. 35(2); Smith, G. 12; Stack, G. 20; Stevenson, L. 7(3); Stokes, A. 36(1); Thicot, S. 8(2); Van Zanten, D. 1; Wotherspoon, D. 30(3); Zemmama, M. 15(6).

Goals – League (58): Stokes 22 (3 pens), Riordan 13, Nish 9, Benjelloun 3 (2 pens), Bamba 2, Miller 2, Zemmama 2, Cregg 1, Galbraith 1, Wotherspoon 1, own goals 2.

Scottish Cup (11): Nish 3, Riordan 3, Benjelloun 1, Gow 1, Hanlon 1, Stokes 1, Zemmama 1.

CIS Cup (4): Hanlon 1, Riordan 1, Stokes 1, own goal 1.

Honours – Division I: Champions – 1902–03, 1947–48, 1950–51, 1951–52. **First Division:** Champions – 1980–81, 1998–99. **Division II:** Champions – 1893–94, 1894–95, 1932–33. **Scottish Cup winners** 1887, 1902. **League Cup winners** 1973, 1992, 2007.

INVERNESS CALEDONIAN THISTLE
PREMIER LEAGUE

Ground: Tulloch Caledonian Stadium, East Longman, Inverness IV1 1FF (01463) 715816
Ground capacity: 7780. **Colours:** All blue.
Manager: Terry Butcher.

League Appearances: Allison, K. (1); Barrowman, A. 1(4); Bulvitis, N. 27(5); Cox, L. 27(6); Djebi-Zadi, L. 10(1); Duff, J. 3; Duncan, R. 23(3); Eagle, R. 7(12); Esson, R. 36; Foran, R. 31; Golabek, S. 24; Hayes, J. 29(6); Imrie, D. 8(5); McBain, R. 2(5); Morrison, G. 1(2); Munro, G. 35; Odhiambo, E. 16(7); Proctor, D. 31(3); Rooney, A. 27(8); Ross, N. 3(3); Sanchez, D. 19(13); Shinnie, G. 1; Stratford, D. 8(6); Tokely, R. 27.

Goals – League (72): Rooney 24 (6 pens), Foran 14, Hayes 10, Odhiambo 5, Sanchez 4, Proctor 3, Bulvitis 2, Cox 2, Munro 2, Eagle 1, Imrie 1, Morrison 1, Ross 1, Stratford 1, Tokely 1.

Scottish Cup (2): Bulvitis 1, Imrie 1.

CIS Cup (10): Eagle 2, Munro 2, Rooney 2, Barrowman 1, Bulvitis 1, Imrie 1, Sanchez 1.

Challenge Cup (8): Foran 2, Sanchez 2, Bulvitis 1, Eagle 1, Rooney 1, own goal 1.

Honours – First Division: Champions – 2003–04, 2009-10. **Third Division:** Champions – 1996–97. **League Challenge Cup winners** 2004.

KILMARNOCK
PREMIER LEAGUE

Ground: Rugby Park, Kilmarnock KA1 2DP (01563) 525184
Ground capacity: 18,128. **Colours:** Blue and white striped shirts, white shorts, white stockings.
Manager: Maxu Paatelainen.

League Appearances: Adams, J. (1); Bell, C. 21; Brown, M. 14; Bryson, C. 33; Burchill, M. 9(6); Clancy, T. 19(1); Combe, A. 3; Fernandez, D. 9(4); Flannigan, I. 3(4); Ford, S. 22(1); Fowler, J. 19(9); Hamill, J. 31(4); Hay, G. 27(1); Invincibile, D. 16(9); Kelly, L. 13(2); Kiernan, R. 2(2); Kyle, K. 29(3); Maguire, C. 12(2); O'Leary, R. 10(1); Old, S. 8(2); Owens, G. 1(5); Pascali, M. 20(2); Robinson, L. (1); Russell, A. 6(8); Sammon, C. 14(9); Severin, S. 13(1); Skelton, G. 16(4); Taouil, M. 21(6); Wright, F. 27.

Goals – League (29): Kyle 8, Bryson 4, Maguire 4, Hamill 2, Invincibile 2, Burchill 1, Ford 1, Hay 1, Kelly 1, Pascali 1, Russell 1, Sammon 1, Wright 1, own goal 1.

Scottish Cup (4): Kelly 2, Pascali 1, Sammon 1.

CIS Cup (4): Kyle 2, Sammon 2 (1 pen).

Honours – Division I: Champions – 1964–65. **Division II:** Champions – 1897–98, 1898–99. **Scottish Cup winners** 1920, 1929, 1997.

LIVINGSTON   DIV. 2

Ground: The Braidwood Motor Company Stadium, Almondvale Stadium Road, Livingston EH54 7DN (01506) 417 000
Ground capacity: 10,005. **Colours:** Yellow shirts, black shorts, yellow stockings.
Manager: Gary Bollan.
League Appearances: Barr, B. 13(7); Brown, J. 16; De Vita, R. 23(6); Fox, L. 30(1); Griffin, D. 23(2); Halliday, A. 23(9); Hamill, J. 7(3); Hamilton, J. 6(5); Hastings, N. 1; Husband, S. 4(3); Jacobs, Kyle 6(8); Jacobs, Keaghan 28(6); Jacobs, D. 5; Jacobs, S. (1); Jamieson, D. 1; MacDonald, C. 21(2); Malone, C. 6(3); McDonald, C. 3; McDowall, C. 2; McKee, J. (1); McKenzie, R. 32; McNeil, A. 1; McNulty, M. 2(7); McPartland, A. 3(1); Moyes, E. 6(1); One, A. 1(1); Sinclair, D. 20(10); Talbot, J. 32; Tosh, S. 12(3); Watson, P. 25(1); Winters, D. 10(5); Winters, R. 34(1).
Goals – League (63): Halliday 14, Winters R 11, De Vita 9, Fox 6 (1 pen), Keaghan Jacobs 6, Hamilton 2 (1 pen), Talbot 2, Tosh 2 (1 pen), Winters D 2, Brown 1, Griffin 1, McNulty 1, Moyes 1, Sinclair 1, Watson 1, own goals 3.
Scottish Cup (11): De Vita 2, Fox 3 (1 pen), Halliday 2, Winters R 2, Hamill 1, Keaghan Jacobs 1.
CIS Cup (0).
Challenge Cup (0).
Honours – First Division: Champions – 2000–01. **Second Division:** Champions – 1986–87, 1998–99. **Third Division:** Champions – 1995–96, 2009-10. **League Cup winners** 2004.

MONTROSE   DIV. 3

Ground: Links Park, Montrose DD10 8QD (01674) 673200
Ground capacity: 3292. **Colours:** Royal blue shirts, royal blue shorts, royal blue stockings.
Player Manager: Steven Tweed.
League Appearances: Adams, K. 1; Anderson, S. 12(2); Boyle, M. 1(4); Campbell, A. 29; Collier, J. 2(2); Coutts, S. 7(1); Crighton, S. 29; Davidson, H. 31(1); Deane, P. 1; Fleming, S. 7(3); Gemmell, J. 19(3); Gray, N. (6); Hall, S. (1); Hegarty, C. 28; Leyden, J. (6); Maitland, J. 15(7); McGowan, D. 2(1); McNalley, S. 19; McNeil, A. 29; Milligan, F. 25(3); Nicholas, S. 14(1); Nicol, D. 15(18); Pope, G. 2(2); Presly, J. (2); Russell, M. (1); Sinclair, A. 29(1); Stewart, R. 4(4); Tomana, M. 15(5); Tosh, P. 18; Tresly, J. (1); Tweed, S. 31; Voigt, J. 3; Watson, P. 8.
Goals – League (30): Tosh 9 (2 pens), Gemmell 4, Nicol 3, Anderson 2, Hegarty 2 (1 pen), Sinclair 2, Campbell 1, Maitland 1, McNalley 1, Milligan 1, Tomana 1, Tweed 1, Watson 1, own goal 1.
Scottish Cup (9): Milligan 2, Watson 2, Gemmell 1, Hegarty 1, Maitland 1, Nicholas 1, Nicoll 1.
CIS Cup (0).
Challenge Cup (1): Leyden 1.
Honours – Second Division: Champions – 1984–85.

MORTON   DIV. 1

Ground: Cappielow Park, Sinclair St, Greenock PA15 2TY (01475) 723571
Ground capacity: 11,612. **Colours:** Blue and white hooped shirts, blue shorts, blue stockings.
Manager: Allan Moore.
League Appearances: Cuthbert, K 5; Finlayson, K. 27(4); Grady, J. 1(4); Graham, B. 10(12); Greacen, S. 30; Halliwell, B. 1; Harding, R. 2; Jenkins, A. 18(6); Kane, R. (4); MacFarlane, N. 16; MacGregor, D. 21(5); Masterton, S. 11(5); McAlister, J. 30; McGuffie, R. 30(2); McKinlay, K. 7(1); McManus, A. 12; McWilliams, R. 3; Monti, C. 16(4); Paartalu, E. 16(10); Reid, A 16; Russell, I. 4(1); Shimmin, D. 17; Simmons, D. 7(7); Stewart, C. 27(1); Tidser, M. 13; Van Zanten, D. 7; Wake, B. 6(6); Walker, A. 3; Weatherson, P. 31(2); Witteveen, D. 9.
Goals – League (40): Weatherson 10, Witteveen 5, Monti 4 (3 pens), Wake 4, Masterton 3 (1 pen), Paartalu 3, Graham 2, MacGregor 2, McGuffie 2, Greacen 1, Jenkins 1, McAlister 1, Simmons 1, Van Zanten 1.

Scottish Cup (1): Graham 1.
CIS Cup (4): Weatherson 2, McFarlane 1, McGuffie 1 (pen).
Challenge Cup (2): Jenkins 1, Masterton 1.
Honours – First Division: Champions – 1977–78, 1983–84, 1986–87. **Division II:** Champions – 1949–50, 1963–64, 1966–67. **Second Division:** Champions – 1994–95, 2006–07. **Third Division:** Champions 2002–03. **Scottish Cup winners** 1922.

MOTHERWELL   PREMIER LEAGUE

Ground: Fir Park, Motherwell ML1 2QN (01698) 333333
Ground capacity: 13,742. **Colours:** Amber shirts with claret hoop and trim, amber shorts, amber stockings.
Manager: Craig Brown.
League Appearances: Coke, G. 25(7); Craigan, S. 28; Fitzpatrick, M. 1(2); Forbes, R. 22(6); Fraser, M. 4(1); Halsman, J. (1); Hammell, S. 33; Hateley, T. 38; Humphrey, C. 6(22); Hutchinson, S. 4(1); Jennings, S. 21(8); Jutkiewicz, L. 27(6); Lasley, K. 15(5); McGarry, S. (1); McGlinchey, M. 1(7); McHugh, R. 2(8); Meechan, S. 1(1); Moutaouakil, Y. 13; Murphy, J. 24(11); O'Brien, J. 29(6); Pollock, J. (1); Reynolds, M. 37; Ruddy, J. 34; Saunders, S. 22(3); Slane, P. (2); Sutton, J. 31(4).
Goals – League (52): Jutkiewicz 12 (1 pen), Sutton 12, Murphy 6, Forbes 5 (3 pens), Reynolds 4, Hutchinson 3, O'Brien 3, Coke 2, Hateley 2, Jennings 2, Saunders 1.
Scottish Cup (0).
CIS Cup (3): Forbes 1, McHugh 1, own goal 1.
Europa League (12): Murphy 4, Forbes 3 (1 pen), Sutton 2, Hutchinson 1, McHugh 1, Slane 1.
Honours – Division I: Champions – 1931–32. **First Division:** Champions – 1981–82, 1984–85. **Division II:** Champions – 1953–54, 1968–69. **Scottish Cup winners** 1952, 1991. **League Cup winners** 1951.

PARTICK THISTLE   DIV. 1

Ground: Firhill Stadium, Glasgow G20 7AL (0141) 579 1971
Ground capacity: 13,141. **Colours:** Red and yellow hooped shirts, black shorts, black stockings.
Manager: Ian McCall.
League Appearances: Adams, J. 6(1); Archibald, A. 27; Boyle, P. 5(1); Buchanan, L. 23(3); Burns, K. (5); Cairney, P. 30(2); Conroy, R. 15; Corcoran, M. 25(6); Corrigan, M. 9(2); Donnelly, S. 27(8); Doohlan, K. 4(13); Erskine, C. 11(23); Grehan, M. 2(3); Halliwell, B. 2; Hamilton, J. 2(7); Hinchcliffe, C. 1; Hodge, B. 20(9); Kinniburgh, W. 1(1); Lovell, S. 10(6); MacBeth, R. 1(2); Maxwell, I. 27; McGeough, R. 1(1); McKeown, S. 9(6); McNamara, M. 4; Paton, P. 28(1); Robertson, J. 34(1); Rowson, D. 35; Shields, G. 4; Tuffey, J. 33.
Goals – League (43): Buchanan 10, Donnelly 8, Cairney 7, Corcoran 4, Lovell 3, Adams 2, Doohlan 2, Hodge 2, Archibald 1, Erskine 1, Grehan 1, McKeown 1, Paton 1.
Scottish Cup (0).
CIS Cup (6): Buchanan 2 (1 pen), Erskine 2, Donnelly 1, Hodge 1.
Challenge Cup (8): Buchanan 2, Hamilton 2, Cairney 1, Donnelly 1, Doolan 1, Rowson 1.
Honours – First Division: Champions – 1975–76, 2001–02. **Division II:** Champions – 1896–97, 1899–1900, 1970–71. **Second Division:** Champions 2000–01. **Scottish Cup winners** 1921. **League Cup winners** 1972.

PETERHEAD   DIV. 2

Ground: Balmoor Stadium, Balmoor Terrace, Peterhead AB42 1EU (01779) 478256
Ground capacity: 3250 (1000 seated). **Colours:** Royal blue shirts with navy sleeves, royal blue shorts, royal blue stockings.
Manager: Neale Cooper.
League Appearances: Bateman, J. 17(1); Bavidge, M. 31; Bowden, C. (2); Bruce, P. 8(19); Cameron, D. 10(4); Clark, N. 18(5); Crawford, J. 14; Donald, D. 27; Emslie, P. 12(3); Gethans, C. 4(9); Jarvie, P. 19(1); MacDonald, C. 21(1); Mann, B. 27; McVitie, N.

27(2); Michie, S. 2(2); Moore, D 10; Ross, D. 33(1); Sharp, G. 24(5); Smith, S. 35; Smith, J. 1(9); Stewart, J. 9(1); Strachan, R. 30(4); Sutherland, Z. 2; Wilson, B. 15(1); Young, P. (2).
Goals – League (45): Bavidge 11, Ross 7, Wilson 5 (2 pens), Clark 4, Stewart 4 (1 pen), Bruce 2, Emslie 2, Gethans 2, Mann 2, Sharp 2, Cameron 1, MacDonald 1, McVitie 1, Michie 1.
Scottish Cup (1): Stewart 1.
CIS Cup (0).
Challenge Cup (1): Bavidge 1.
Honours – None.

QUEEN OF THE SOUTH   DIV. 1

Ground: Palmerston Park, Dumfries DG2 9BA (01387) 254853
Ground capacity: 6412. **Colours:** Royal blue shirts with white flashes, white shorts, royal blue stockings.
Manager: Kenny Brannigan.
League Appearances: Adams, J 7; Andrews, M. 5(1); Burns, P. 35; Fox, S. 5(1); Hamill, J. 5(6); Harris, R. 32; Holmes, D. 35(1); Hutton, D. 27(1); Kean, S. 14(15); Knight, L. 3(3); Lilley, D. 30; McAusland, M. 21(4); McKenna, S. 27(1); McLaren, W. 28(6); McLaughlan, G. 4(2); McMillan, J. 16; McParland, A. (4); McQuilken, J. 1(5); O'Connor, S 4(7); Quinn, R. 29(2); Reid, C. 32; Roy, L. 4; Scally, N. 9(1); Tosh, S. 3(2); Weatherston, D. 12(18); Wilson, B. 5(7); Wyness, D. 3(4).
Goals – League (53): Holmes 12 (2 pens), Weatherston 8, Kean 7 (2 pens), Burns 6, McLaren 6, Harris 4, Quinn 4, Wyness 2, Lilley 1, McKenna 1, Tosh 1 (1 pen), Wilson 1.
Scottish Cup (0).
CIS Cup (7): Weatherston 2, Wilson 2, Burns 1, Harris 1, Quinn 1.
Challenge Cup (3): Kean 1, Tosh 1, Wilson 1.
Honours – Division II: Champions – 1950–51. **Second Division:** Champions – 2001–02.
League Challenge Cup winners 2003.

QUEEN'S PARK   DIV. 3

Ground: Hampden Park, Glasgow G42 9BA (0141) 632 1275
Ground capacity: 52,000. **Colours:** Black and white shirts, white shorts, white stockings with black tops.
Coach: Gardner Spiers.
League Appearances: Black, S. 11; Brough, J. 29(1); Burns, P. 1; Capuano, G. 32(1); Carrol, F. 9(6); Daly, M. 22(5); Douglas, B. 35; Dunlop, R. 7(4); Gallagher, P. 13(1); Green, D. (1); Hamilton, C. 16(13); Hamilton, P. 10(1); Harkins, P. 1; Henry, J 6(6); Holmes, R. 14(8); Lauchlan, G. 4; Little, R. 24; Martin, R. (1); McBride, M. 33(1); McGeown, M. 15; McGinn, P. 4(2); Murray, D. 15(8); O'Hara, M. 5(3); Quinn, T. 24(3); Quinn, P. 9; Reilly, S. 3; Sinclair, R. 9; Stewart, P. 15; Tiernan, F. (1); Ure, M. 7(1); Walker, R. 17; Watt, I. 6(13).
Goals – League (42): Douglas 8 (2 pens), McBride 6, Daly 5, Murray 5, Carrol 2, Hamilton C 2, Henry, J 2, Quinn P 2, Stewart 2, Watt 2, Capuano 1, Holmes 1, O'Hara 1, Quinn T 1, own goals 2.
Scottish Cup (1): Quinn T 1.
CIS Cup (1): Douglas 1.
Challenge Cup (0).
Play-Offs (2): Daly 1, own goal 1.
Honours – Second Division: Champions – 1980–81. **Third Division:** Champions – 1999–2000. **Scottish Cup winners** 1874, 1875, 1876, 1880, 1881, 1882, 1884, 1886, 1890, 1893.

RAITH ROVERS   DIV. 1

Ground: Stark's Park, Pratt Street, Kirkcaldy KY1 1SA (01592) 263514
Ground capacity: 10,104 (all seated). **Colours:** Navy with white shirts, navy shorts, navy stockings with white tops.
Manager: John McGlynn.

League Appearances: Amaya, J. 1(4); Armstrong, D 7(1); Brown, K. 1; Bryce, L. (8); Cameron, G. 2; Campbell, M. 15(1); Casalinuovo, D. 3; Corredera, J. 1; Davidson, I. 18(2); Ellis, L. 29; Ferry, M. 11(17); Gatheussi, T. 10(4); Hill, D. 26(3); Mackie, J. (3); McGurn, D. 35; Mole , J. 6(2); Murray, G. 34; O'Connor, G 1; Russell, J. 18(5); Shields, D. 3(6); Simmons, S. 17(2); Sloan, R. 10(17); Smith, K. 4(1); Smith, D. 17(10); Tade, G. 31(1); Walker, A. 34(1); Wallas, B. 3(1); Wedderburn, C. (4); Weir, G. 13(10); Williamson, I. 25(2); Wilson, C. 21.
Goals – League (36): Tade 5, Russell 4, Williamson 4, Murray 3, Walker 3, Casalinuovo 2, Hill 2, Smith K 2 (1 pen), Armstrong, D 1, Campbell 1, Corredera 1, Davidson 1, Ellis 1, Ferry 1, Mole 1, Simmons 1, Sloan 1, Smith D 1, Wallas 1.
Scottish Cup (14): Smith K 3, Tade 3, Simmons 2, Smith D 2, Ellis 1, Russell 1 (pen), Williamson 1, own goal 1.
CIS Cup (4): Williamson 2 (1 pen), Tade 1, Walker 1.
Challenge Cup (1): Walker 1.
Honours – First Division: Champions – 1992–93, 1994–95. **Second Division:** Champions – 2002–03, 2008–09. **Division II:** Champions – 1907–08, 1909–10 (Shared), 1937–38, 1948–49.
League Cup winners 1995.

RANGERS   PREMIER LEAGUE

Ground: Ibrox Stadium, Glasgow G51 2XD 0871 7021972
Ground capacity: 51,082. **Colours:** Royal blue shirts with red and white trim, white shorts with red and blue trim, black stockings with red tops.
Manager: Walter Smith.
League Appearances: Alexander, N. 4(1); Beasley, D. 6(3); Bougherra, M. 16(1); Boyd, K. 28(3); Broadfoot, K. 12; Davis, S. 36; Edu, M. 8(7); Fleck, J. 8(7); Lafferty, K. 17(11); Little, A. 2(4); McCulloch, L. 32(2); McGregor, A. 34; Miller, K. 29(4); Naismith, S. 20(8); Novo, N. 14(21); Papac, S. 34; Pedro Mendes, 4; Rothen, J. 3(1); Smith, S. 7(5); Thomson, K. 20(5); Weir, D. 38; Whittaker, S. 32(3); Wilson, D. 14; Wylde, G. (2).
Goals – League (82): Boyd 23 (4 pens), Miller 18 (2 pens), Lafferty 7, Whittaker 7, Novo 6, McCulloch 5, Davis 3, Naismith 3, Beasley 2, Edu 2, Papac 2, Bougherra 1, Fleck 1, Little 1, Wilson 1.
Scottish Cup (9): Boyd 3 (2 pens), Whittaker 3, Miller 2 (1 pen), Novo 1.
CIS Cup (8): Davis 1, Fleck 1, McCulloch 1, Miller 1, Naismith 1, Novo 1, Whittaker 1, own goal 1.
Champions League (4): Bougherra 1, McCulloch 1, Novo 1, own goal 1.
Honours – Division I: Champions – 1890–91 (Shared), 1898–99, 1899–1900, 1900–01, 1901–02, 1910–11, 1911–12, 1912–13, 1917–18, 1919–20, 1920–21, 1922–23, 1923–24, 1924–25, 1926–27, 1927–28, 1928–29, 1929–30, 1930–31, 1932–33, 1933–34, 1934–35, 1936–37, 1938–39, 1946–47, 1948–49, 1949–50, 1952–53, 1955–56, 1956–57, 1958–59, 1960–61, 1962–63, 1963–64, 1974–75. **Premier Division:** Champions – 1975–76, 1977–78, 1986–87, 1988–89, 1989–90, 1990–91, 1991–92, 1992–93, 1993–94, 1994–95, 1995–96, 1996–97. **Premier League:** Champions – 1998–99, 1999–2000, 2002–03, 2004–05, 2008–09, 2009–10. **Scottish Cup winners** 1894, 1897, 1898, 1903, 1928, 1930, 1932, 1934, 1935, 1936, 1948, 1949, 1950, 1953, 1960, 1962, 1963, 1964, 1966, 1973, 1976, 1978, 1979, 1981, 1992, 1993, 1996, 1999, 2000, 2002, 2003, 2008, 2009. **League Cup winners** 1947, 1949, 1961, 1962, 1964, 1965, 1971, 1976, 1978, 1979, 1982, 1984, 1985, 1987, 1988, 1989, 1991, 1993, 1994, 1997, 1999, 2002, 2003, 2005, 2008, 2010. **European Cup-Winners' Cup winners** 1972.

ROSS COUNTY   DIV. 1

Ground: Victoria Park Stadium, Jubilee Road, Dingwall IV15 9QW (01349) 860860
Ground capacity: 6700. **Colours:** Navy blue with white flashes, navy shorts with white flashes, white stockings.
Manager: Derek Adam.
League Appearances: Barrowman, A. 12(2); Boyd, S. 29(2); Brittain, R. 34; Craig, S. 12(12); Di Giacomo, P. 20(11); Gardyne, M. 30(4); Girvan, G. 3(1); Grant, R. (1); Keddie, A. 30; Kettlewell, S. 22(9); Lawson, P. 25(3); Malin, J 1; McGovern, M. 35; Miller, G.

31(1); Moore, D. (3); Morrison, S. 35; Scott, M. 20(10); Smith, G. 1(3); Stephen, R. 1; Stewart, J. (2); Vigurs, I. 25(10); Watt, S. 16(3); Wood, G. 14(16).
Goals – League (46): Brittain 9 (5 pens), Barrowman 5 (1 pen), Craig 5, Gardyne 5, Boyd 4, Lawson 4, Wood 4, Di Giacomo 3, Vigurs 3, Scott 2, Morrison 1, Watt 1.
Scottish Cup (24): Wood 5, Craig 4, Gardyne 3, Di Giacomo 2, Morrison 2, Boyd 1, Brittain 1 (pen), Keddie 1, Kettlewell 1, Lawson 1, Miller 1, Scott 1, own goal 1.
CIS Cup (7): Gardyne 2, Brittain 1, Craig 1, Di Giacomo 1, Morrison 1, Stewart 1.
Challenge Cup (7): Gardyne 3, Craig 1, Di Giacomo 1, Lawson 1, Wood 1.
Honours – Second Division: Champions – 2007–08. **Third Division:** Champions – 1998–99. **League Challenge Cup winners** 2007.

ST JOHNSTONE   PREMIER LEAGUE

Ground: McDiarmid Park, Crieff Road, Perth PH1 2SJ (01738) 459090
Ground capacity: 10,673. **Colours:** Royal blue shirts, royal blue shorts, royal blue stockings.
Manager: Derek Adams.
League Appearances: Anderson, S. 14(3); Connolly, M. 1; Craig, L. 22(9); Davidson, M. 30(3); Deuchar, K. 25(10); Duberry, M. 17; Falkingham, J. (1); Gartland, G. 20(1); Grainger, D. 35(1); Hardie, M. 4(6); Irvine, G. 13(4); Jackson, A. (2); Johansson, J. 2(4); MacDonald, P. 5(2); MacKay, D. 36; Main, A. 9; McCaffrey, S. 9(1); Millar, C. 33(3); Milne, S. 10(6); Moon, K. 10(4); Morais, F. 20(10); Morris, J. 33(1); Reynolds, S. (4); Rutkiewicz, K. 7; Samuel, C. 16(11); Sheerin, P. 3(8); Sheridan, C. 12(4); Smith, G. 29; Swankie, G. 3(7).
Goals – League (57): Craig 9 (4 pens), MacDonald 6, Sheridan 6, Davidson 5, Deuchar 5, Samuel 5, Millar 3, Gartland 2, Hardie 2, Morais 2, Morris 2, Anderson 1, Duberry 1, Grainger 1, Johansson 1, MacKay 1, Milne 1, Sheerin 1 (1 pen), own goals 3.
Scottish Cup (3): Craig 2, Milne 1.
CIS Cup (16): Deuchar 4, Milne 3, Samuel 3, Anderson 1, Millar 1, Morais 1, Morris 1, Swankie 1, own goal 1.
Honours – First Division: Champions – 1982–83, 1989–90, 1996–97, 2008–09. **Division II:** Champions – 1923–24, 1959–60, 1962–63. **League Challenge Cup winners** 2008.

ST MIRREN   PREMIER LEAGUE

Ground: St Mirren Park, Greenhill Road, Paisley PA3 1RU (0141) 889 2558
Ground capacity: 10,476 (all seated). **Colours:** Black and white striped shirts, black shorts, white stockings.
Manager: Danny Lennon.
League Appearances: Barron, D. 34; Brady, G. 19(3); Brighton, T. 1(7); Carey, G. 10(5); Dargo, C. 13(16); Dorman, A. 29(5); Gallacher, P. 36; Higdon, M. 22(11); Howard, M 2; Innes, C. 18(3); Johnston, A. 1(9); Loy, R. (8); Mair, L. 30(1); McGinn, S. 18; Mehmet, B. 35(2); Murray, H. 35; O'Donnell, S. 10(12); Potter, J. 35; Ramsey, C. (5); Robb, S. 12(8); Ross, J. 28; Thomson, S. 30.
Goals – League (36): Dorman 6, Higdon 4, Carey 3, Innes 3, McGinn 3, Mehmet 3 (1 pen), O'Donnell 3, Thomson 3, Dargo 2, Murray 2, Brighton 1, Robb 1, own goals 2.
Scottish Cup (3): Mehmet 2, own goal 1.
CIS Cup (14): Mehmet 7, Higdon 2, Dorman 1, McGinn 1, O'Donnell 1, Ross 1, own goal 1.
Honours – First Division: Champions – 1976–77, 1999–2000, 2005–06. **Division II:** Champions – 1967–68. **Scottish Cup winners** 1926, 1959, 1987.
League Challenge Cup winners 2005–06.

STENHOUSEMUIR   DIV. 2

Ground: Ochilview Park, Stenhousemuir FK5 4QL (01324) 562992
Ground capacity: 3776 (626 seated). **Colours:** All maroon.
Head Coach: John O'Neill.

League Appearances: Anderson, G. (1); Bennett, S 2; Bradley, K. 10(10); Brand, A. 5(5); Currie, L. 2; Dalziel, S. 31(4); Diack, I. 17(9); Dickson, S. (2); Gair, S. 2; Gibb, S. 12(1); Hunter, M. 1(1); Lawson, A. (1); Love, R. 13(10); Lyle, W. 24(2); McCluskey, C. 34; McLeod, C. 29(1); Molloy, C. 26(3); Motion, K. 32(1); O'Reilly, C. 4(7); Quinn, P. 2(10); Reid, A. 2; Scullion, P. 27(2); Smith, J. 30; Smith, D. 2; Stirling, A. 5(10); Thom, G. 28; Thomson, I. 27(3); Thomson, S. 27; Welsh, S. 2.

Goals – League (38): Motion 7 (3 pens), Dalziel 6, Diack 4, Love 4, Molloy 4, Scullion 3, Quinn 2, Smith J 2, Thom 2, Gibb 1, Lyle 1, McLeod 1, Thomson I 1.

Scottish Cup (6): Bradley 2 (1 pen), Motion 2, Molloy 1, Thompson I 1.

CIS Cup (0).

Challenge Cup (3): Dalziel 2, O'Reilly 1.

Honours – Second Division: Champions – 2009–10. **League Challenge Cup winners** 1996.

STIRLING ALBION   DIV. 1

Ground: Forthbank Stadium, Springkerse Industrial Estate, Stirling FK7 7UJ (01786) 450399

Ground capacity: 3808. **Colours:** All red.

Head Coach: John O'Neill.

League Appearances: Aitken, C. 18(1); Allison, B. 16(1); Byrne, K. 2(1); Christie, S. 26; Colqhoen, D. 4(4); Corr, L. 1(10); Devine, S. 12(3); Elliott, S. 5(2); Feaks, K. 9(1); Forsyth, R. 32; Gibson, A. 30(5); Graham, A. 36; Grehan, M. 14(2); Hogarth, M. 10; McCord, R. 4(7); McKenna, D. 19(15); McKeown, C. 2; Mullen, M. 14(14); Murphy, P. 18(10); O'Brian, D. 34(2); O'Neil, J. 10(6); Page, J. 16; Prunty, B. 3; Robertson, S. 27(6); Roycroft, S. 10; Russell, I. 10; Taggart, N. 11(10); Young , C. 3(2).

Goals – League (68): Grehan 8, Russell 7, Graham 6, McKenna 6, Mullen 6, O'Brian 6, Robertson 6, Aitken 5 (2 pens), Devine 3, Forsyth 3 (1 pen), Murphy 2, Page 2, Colqhoen 1, Corr 1, Elliott 1, Gibson 1, McCord 1, Taggart 1, own goals 2.

Scottish Cup (5): Mullen 2, Corr 1, Forsyth 1, Murphy 1.

CIS Cup (1): Devine 1.

Challenge Cup (6): McKenna 2, Devine 1 (pen), Graham 1, Mullen 1, Robertson 1.

Honours – Division II: Champions – 1952–53, 1957–58, 1960–61, 1964–65. **Second Division:** Champions – 1976–77, 1990–91, 1995–96, 2009–10.

STRANRAER   DIV. 3

Ground: Stair Park, Stranraer DG9 8BS (01776) 703271

Ground capacity: 5600. **Colours:** Royal blue shirts with white design, white shorts, royal blue stockings.

Manager: Keith Knox.

League Appearances: Agnew, S. 20; Agostini, D. 21(2); Aitken, S. 3(5); Bouadii, R. 21; Carnaghan, A. (1); Cawley, K. 14(1); Donald, B. (1); Henderson, M. 26(3); Jack, M. 8(8); Jones, R. 2(4); Marshall, R. 1; McColm, S. 15(6); McGeouch, D. 13(5); McGrath, P. (2); McInnes, P. 12(4); McKillop, R. (1); McMahon, D. (1); McManus, S. 5(6); Danny Mitchel, 34; Mitchell, David 35; Mitchell, G. 24(2); Montgomerie, R. 13(19); Moore, M. 25(6); Nicoll, K. 26(1); Noble, S. 34; One, A. 15(4); Sharp, L. 25; Wright, K. 4(3).

Goals – League (48): Moore 8 (1 pen), One 8, Agnew 6 (1 pen), McColm 6, Danny Mitchel, 4, Montgomerie 3, Bouadii 2, Cawley 2, McInnes 2, Nicoll 2, Noble 2, Henderson 1, Jack 1, McGeouch 1.

Scottish Cup (1): Moore 1.

CIS Cup (0).

Challenge Cup (4): Danny Mitchell 2 (1 pen), Jack 1, Montgomerie 1.

Honours – Second Division: Champions – 1993–94, 1997–98. **Third Division:** Champions – 2003–04. **League Challenge Cup winners** 1997.

SCOTTISH LEAGUE HONOURS

*On goal average (ratio)/difference. †Held jointly after indecisive play-off.
‡Won on deciding match. ††Held jointly. ¶Two points deducted for fielding ineligible
player. Competition suspended 1940–45 during war; Regional Leagues operating.
‡‡Two points deducted for registration irregularities. §Not promoted after play-offs.

PREMIER LEAGUE
Maximum points: 108

	First	Pts	Second	Pts	Third	Pts
1998–99	Rangers	77	Celtic	71	St Johnstone	57
1999–00	Rangers	90	Celtic	69	Hearts	54

Maximum points: 114

2000–01	Celtic	97	Rangers	82	Hibernian	66
2001–02	Celtic	103	Rangers	85	Livingston	58
2002–03	Rangers*	97	Celtic	97	Hearts	63
2003–04	Celtic	98	Rangers	81	Hearts	68
2004–05	Rangers	93	Celtic	92	Hibernian*	61
2005–06	Celtic	91	Hearts	74	Rangers	73
2006–07	Celtic	84	Rangers	72	Aberdeen	65
2007–08	Celtic	89	Rangers	86	Motherwell	60
2008–09	Rangers	86	Celtic	82	Hearts	59
2009–10	Rangers	87	Celtic	81	Dundee U	63

PREMIER DIVISION
Maximum points: 72

1975–76	Rangers	54	Celtic	48	Hibernian	43
1976–77	Celtic	55	Rangers	46	Aberdeen	43
1977–78	Rangers	55	Aberdeen	53	Dundee U	40
1978–79	Celtic	48	Rangers	45	Dundee U	44
1979–80	Aberdeen	48	Celtic	47	St Mirren	42
1980–81	Celtic	56	Aberdeen	49	Rangers*	44
1981–82	Celtic	55	Aberdeen	53	Rangers	43
1982–83	Dundee U	56	Celtic*	55	Aberdeen	55
1983–84	Aberdeen	57	Celtic	50	Dundee U	47
1984–85	Aberdeen	59	Celtic	52	Dundee U	47
1985–86	Celtic*	50	Hearts	50	Dundee U	47

Maximum points: 88

1986–87	Rangers	69	Celtic	63	Dundee U	60
1987–88	Celtic	72	Hearts	62	Rangers	60

Maximum points: 72

1988–89	Rangers	56	Aberdeen	50	Celtic	46
1989–90	Rangers	51	Aberdeen*	44	Hearts	44
1990–91	Rangers	55	Aberdeen	53	Celtic*	41

Maximum points: 88

1991–92	Rangers	72	Hearts	63	Celtic	62
1992–93	Rangers	73	Aberdeen	64	Celtic	60
1993–94	Rangers	58	Aberdeen	55	Motherwell	54

Maximum points: 108

1994–95	Rangers	69	Motherwell	54	Hibernian	53
1995–96	Rangers	87	Celtic	83	Aberdeen*	55
1996–97	Rangers	80	Celtic	75	Dundee U	60
1997–98	Celtic	74	Rangers	72	Hearts	67

DIVISION 1
Maximum points: 52

	First	Pts	Second	Pts	Third	Pts
1975–76	Partick Th	41	Kilmarnock	35	Montrose	30

	First	*Pts*	*Second*	*Pts*	*Third*	*Pts*
			Maximum points: 78			
1976–77	St Mirren	62	Clydebank	58	Dundee	51
1977–78	Morton*	58	Hearts	58	Dundee	57
1978–79	Dundee	55	Kilmarnock*	54	Clydebank	54
1979–80	Hearts	53	Airdrieonians	51	Ayr U*	44
1980–81	Hibernian	57	Dundee	52	St Johnstone	51
1981–82	Motherwell	61	Kilmarnock	51	Hearts	50
1982–83	St Johnstone	55	Hearts	54	Clydebank	50
1983–84	Morton	54	Dumbarton	51	Partick Th	46
1984–85	Motherwell	50	Clydebank	48	Falkirk	45
1985–86	Hamilton A	56	Falkirk	45	Kilmarnock	44
			Maximum points: 88			
1986–87	Morton	57	Dunfermline Ath	56	Dumbarton	53
1987–88	Hamilton A	56	Meadowbank Th	52	Clydebank	49
			Maximum points: 78			
1988–89	Dunfermline Ath	54	Falkirk	52	Clydebank	48
1989–90	St Johnstone	58	Airdrieonians	54	Clydebank	44
1990–91	Falkirk	54	Airdrieonians	53	Dundee	52
			Maximum points: 88			
1991–92	Dundee	58	Partick Th*	57	Hamilton A	57
1992–93	Raith R	65	Kilmarnock	54	Dunfermline Ath	52
1993–94	Falkirk	66	Dunfermline Ath	65	Airdrieonians	54
			Maximum points: 108			
1994–95	Raith R	69	Dunfermline Ath*	68	Dundee	68
1995–96	Dunfermline Ath	71	Dundee U*	67	Morton	67
1996–97	St Johnstone	80	Airdrieonians	60	Dundee*	58
1997–98	Dundee	70	Falkirk	65	Raith R*	60
1998–99	Hibernian	89	Falkirk	66	Ayr U	62
1999–00	St Mirren	76	Dunfermline Ath	71	Falkirk	68
2000–01	Livingston	76	Ayr U	69	Falkirk	56
2001–02	Partick Th	66	Airdrieonians	56	Ayr U	52
2002–03	Falkirk	81	Clyde	72	St Johnstone	67
2003–04	Inverness CT	70	Clyde	69	St Johnstone	57
2004–05	Falkirk	75	St Mirren*	60	Clyde	60
2005–06	St Mirren	76	St Johnstone	66	Hamilton A	59
2006–07	Gretna	66	St Johnstone	65	Dundee*	53
2007–08	Hamilton A	76	Dundee	69	St Johnstone	58
2008–09	St Johnstone	65	Partick Th	55	Dunfermline Ath	51
2009–10	Inverness CT	73	Dundee	61	Dunfermline Ath	58

DIVISION 2

			Maximum points: 52			
1975–76	Clydebank*	40	Raith R	40	Alloa Ath	35
			Maximum points: 78			
1976–77	Stirling Alb	55	Alloa Ath	51	Dunfermline Ath	50
1977–78	Clyde*	53	Raith R	53	Dunfermline Ath	48
1978–79	Berwick R	54	Dunfermline Ath	52	Falkirk	50
1979–80	Falkirk	50	East Stirling	49	Forfar Ath	46
1980–81	Queen's Park	50	Queen of the S	46	Cowdenbeath	45
1981–82	Clyde	59	Alloa Ath*	50	Arbroath	50
1982–83	Brechin C	55	Meadowbank Th	54	Arbroath	49
1983–84	Forfar Ath	63	East Fife	47	Berwick R	43
1984–85	Montrose	53	Alloa Ath	50	Dunfermline Ath	49
1985–86	Dunfermline Ath	57	Queen of the S	55	Meadowbank Th	49
1986–87	Meadowbank Th	55	Raith R*	52	Stirling Alb*	52
1987–88	Ayr U	61	St Johnstone	59	Queen's Park	51

	First	Pts	*Second*	Pts	*Third*	Pts
1988–89	Albion R	50	Alloa Ath	45	Brechin C	43
1989–90	Brechin C	49	Kilmarnock	48	Stirling Alb	47
1990–91	Stirling Alb	54	Montrose	46	Cowdenbeath	45
1991–92	Dumbarton	52	Cowdenbeath	51	Alloa Ath	50
1992–93	Clyde	54	Brechin C*	53	Stranraer	53
1993–94	Stranraer	56	Berwick R	48	Stenhousemuir*	47

Maximum points: 108

	First	Pts	*Second*	Pts	*Third*	Pts
1994–95	Morton	64	Dumbarton	60	Stirling Alb	58
1995–96	Stirling Alb	81	East Fife	67	Berwick R	60
1996–97	Ayr U	77	Hamilton A	74	Livingston	64
1997–98	Stranraer	61	Clydebank	60	Livingston	59
1998–99	Livingston	77	Inverness CT	72	Clyde	53
1999–00	Clyde	65	Alloa Ath	64	Ross County	62
2000–01	Partick Th	75	Arbroath	58	Berwick R*	54
2001–02	Queen of the S	67	Alloa Ath	59	Forfar Ath	53
2002–03	Raith R	59	Brechin C	55	Airdrie U	54
2003–04	Airdrie U	70	Hamilton A	62	Dumbarton	60
2004–05	Brechin C	72	Stranraer	63	Morton	62
2005–06	Gretna	88	Morton§	70	Peterhead*§	57
2006–07	Morton	77	Stirling Alb	69	Raith R§	62
2007–08	Ross Co	73	Airdrie U	66	Raith R§	60
2008–09	Raith R	76	Ayr U	74	Brechin C§	62
2009–10	Stirling Alb*	65	Alloa Ath§	65	Cowdenbeath	59

DIVISION 3
Maximum points: 108

	First	Pts	*Second*	Pts	*Third*	Pts
1994–95	Forfar Ath	80	Montrose	67	Ross Co	60
1995–96	Livingston	72	Brechin C	63	Caledonian Th	57
1996–97	Inverness CT	76	Forfar Ath*	67	Ross Co	67
1997–98	Alloa Ath	76	Arbroath	68	Ross Co*	67
1998–99	Ross Co	77	Stenhousemuir	64	Brechin C	59
1999–00	Queen's Park	69	Berwick R	66	Forfar Ath	61
2000–01	Hamilton A*	76	Cowdenbeath	76	Brechin C	72
2001–02	Brechin C	73	Dumbarton	61	Albion R	59
2002–03	Morton	72	East Fife	71	Albion R	70
2003–04	Stranraer	79	Stirling Alb	77	Gretna	68
2004–05	Gretna	98	Peterhead	78	Cowdenbeath	51
2005–06	Cowdenbeath*	76	Berwick R§	76	Stenhousemuir§	73
2006–07	Berwick R	76	Arbroath§	75	Queen's Park	68
2007–08	East Fife	88	Stranraer	75	Montrose§	59
2008–09	Dumbarton	67	Cowdenbeath§	63	East Stirling§	61
2009–10	Livingston	78	Forfar Ath	63	East Stirling§	61

DIVISION 1 to 1974–75
Maximum points: a 36; b 44; c 40; d 52; e 60; f 68; g 76; h 84.

	First	Pts	*Second*	Pts	*Third*	Pts
1890–91*a*	Dumbarton††	29	Rangers††	29	Celtic	21
1891–92*b*	Dumbarton	37	Celtic	35	Hearts	34
1892–93*a*	Celtic	29	Rangers	28	St Mirren	20
1893–94*a*	Celtic	29	Hearts	26	St Bernard's	23
1894–95*a*	Hearts	31	Celtic	26	Rangers	22
1895–96*a*	Celtic	30	Rangers	26	Hibernian	24
1896–97*a*	Hearts	28	Hibernian	26	Rangers	25
1897–98*a*	Celtic	33	Rangers	29	Hibernian	22
	First	Pts	*Second*	Pts	*Third*	Pts
1898–99*a*	Rangers	36	Hearts	26	Celtic	24
1899–1900*a*	Rangers	32	Celtic	25	Hibernian	24
1900–01*c*	Rangers	35	Celtic	29	Hibernian	25
1901–02*a*	Rangers	28	Celtic	26	Hearts	22
1902–03*b*	Hibernian	37	Dundee	31	Rangers	29

201

First	Pts	Second	Pts	Third	Pts
1903–04d Third Lanark	43	Hearts	39	Celtic*	38
1904–05d Celtic‡	41	Rangers	41	Third Lanark	35
1905–06e Celtic	49	Hearts	43	Airdrieonians	38
1906–07f Celtic	55	Dundee	48	Rangers	45
1907–08f Celtic	55	Falkirk	51	Rangers	50
1908–09f Celtic	51	Dundee	50	Clyde	48
1909–10f Celtic	54	Falkirk	52	Rangers	46
1910–11f Rangers	52	Aberdeen	48	Falkirk	44
1911–12f Rangers	51	Celtic	45	Clyde	42
1912–13f Rangers	53	Celtic	49	Hearts*	41
1913–14g Celtic	65	Rangers	59	Hearts*	54
1914–15g Celtic	65	Hearts	61	Rangers	50
1915–16g Celtic	67	Rangers	56	Morton	51
1916–17g Celtic	64	Morton	54	Rangers	53
1917–18f Rangers	56	Celtic	55	Kilmarnock*	43
1918–19f Celtic	58	Rangers	57	Morton	47
1919–20h Rangers	71	Celtic	68	Motherwell	57
1920–21h Rangers	76	Celtic	66	Hearts	50
1921–22h Celtic	67	Rangers	66	Raith R	51
1922–23g Rangers	55	Airdrieonians	50	Celtic	46
1923–24g Rangers	59	Airdrieonians	50	Celtic	46
1924–25g Rangers	60	Airdrieonians	57	Hibernian	52
1925–26g Celtic	58	Airdrieonians*	50	Hearts	50
1926–27g Rangers	56	Motherwell	51	Celtic	49
1927–28g Rangers	60	Celtic*	55	Motherwell	55
1928–29g Rangers	67	Celtic	51	Motherwell	50
1929–30g Rangers	60	Motherwell	55	Aberdeen	53
1930–31g Rangers	60	Celtic	58	Motherwell	56
1931–32g Motherwell	66	Rangers	61	Celtic	48
1932–33g Rangers	62	Motherwell	59	Hearts	50
1933–34g Rangers	66	Motherwell	62	Celtic	47
1934–35g Rangers	55	Celtic	52	Hearts	50
1935–36g Celtic	66	Rangers*	61	Aberdeen	61
1936–37g Rangers	61	Aberdeen	54	Celtic	52
1937–38g Celtic	61	Hearts	58	Rangers	49
1938–39g Rangers	59	Celtic	48	Aberdeen	46
1946–47e Rangers	46	Hibernian	44	Aberdeen	39
1947–48e Hibernian	48	Rangers	46	Partick Th	36
1948–49e Rangers	46	Dundee	45	Hibernian	39
1949–50e Rangers	50	Hibernian	49	Hearts	43
1950–51e Hibernian	48	Rangers*	38	Dundee	38
1951–52e Hibernian	45	Rangers	41	East Fife	37
1952–53e Rangers*	43	Hibernian	43	East Fife	39
1953–54e Celtic	43	Hearts	38	Partick Th	35
1954–55e Aberdeen	49	Celtic	46	Rangers	41
1955–56e Rangers	52	Aberdeen	46	Hearts*	45
1956–57f Rangers	55	Hearts	53	Kilmarnock	42
1957–58f Hearts	62	Rangers	49	Celtic	46
1958–59f Rangers	50	Hearts	48	Motherwell	44
1959–60f Hearts	54	Kilmarnock	50	Rangers*	42
1960–61f Rangers	51	Kilmarnock	50	Third Lanark	42
1961–62f Dundee	54	Rangers	51	Celtic	46
1962–63f Rangers	57	Kilmarnock	48	Partick Th	46
1963–64f Rangers	55	Kilmarnock	49	Celtic*	47
1964–65f Kilmarnock*	50	Hearts	50	Dunfermline Ath	49
1965–66f Celtic	57	Rangers	55	Kilmarnock	45
1966–67f Celtic	58	Rangers	55	Clyde	46
1967–68f Celtic	63	Rangers	61	Hibernian	45
1968–69f Celtic	54	Rangers	49	DunfermlineAth	45
1969–70f Celtic	57	Rangers	45	Hibernian	44

	First	*Pts*	*Second*	*Pts*	*Third*	*Pts*
1970–71f	Celtic	56	Aberdeen	54	St Johnstone	44
1971–72f	Celtic	60	Aberdeen	50	Rangers	44
1972–73f	Celtic	57	Rangers	56	Hibernian	45
1973–74f	Celtic	53	Hibernian	49	Rangers	48
1974–75f	Rangers	56	Hibernian	49	Celtic	45

DIVISION 2 to 1974–75

Maximum points: a 76; b 72; c 68; d 52; e 60; f 36; g 44.

	First	*Pts*	*Second*	*Pts*	*Third*	*Pts*
1893–94f	Hibernian	29	Cowlairs	27	Clyde	24
1894–95f	Hibernian	30	Motherwell	22	Port Glasgow	20
1895–96f	Abercorn	27	Leith Ath	23	Renton	21
1896–97f	Partick Th	31	Leith Ath	27	Kilmarnock*	21
1897–98f	Kilmarnock	29	Port Glasgow	25	Morton	22
1898–99f	Kilmarnock	32	Leith Ath	27	Port Glasgow	25
1899–1900f	Partick Th	29	Morton	28	Port Glasgow	20
1900–01f	St Bernard's	25	Airdrieonians	23	Abercorn	21
1901–02g	Port Glasgow	32	Partick Th	31	Motherwell	26
1902–03g	Airdrieonians	35	Motherwell	28	Ayr U*	27
1903–04g	Hamilton A	37	Clyde	29	Ayr U	28
1904–05g	Clyde	32	Falkirk	28	Hamilton A	27
1905–06g	Leith Ath	34	Clyde	31	Albion R	27
1906–07g	St Bernard's	32	Vale of Leven*	27	Arthurlie	27
1907–08g	Raith R	30	Dumbarton‡‡	27	Ayr U	27
1908–09g	Abercorn	31	Raith R*	28	Vale of Leven	28
1909–10g	Leith Ath‡	33	Raith R	33	St Bernard's	27
1910–11g	Dumbarton	31	Ayr U	27	Albion R	25
1911–12g	Ayr U	35	Abercorn	30	Dumbarton	27
1912–13d	Ayr U	34	Dunfermline Ath	33	East Stirling	32
1913–14g	Cowdenbeath	31	Albion R	27	Dunfermline Ath*	26
1914–15d	Cowdenbeath*	37	St Bernard's*	37	Leith Ath	37
1921–22a	Alloa Ath	60	Cowdenbeath	47	Armadale	45
1922–23a	Queen's Park	57	Clydebank ¶	50	St Johnstone ¶	45
1923–24a	St Johnstone	56	Cowdenbeath	55	Bathgate	44
1924–25a	Dundee U	50	Clydebank	48	Clyde	47
1925–26a	Dunfermline Ath	59	Clyde	53	Ayr U	52
1926–27a	Bo'ness	56	Raith R	49	Clydebank	45
1927–28a	Ayr U	54	Third Lanark	45	King's Park	44
1928–29b	Dundee U	51	Morton	50	Arbroath	47
1929–30a	Leith Ath*	57	East Fife	57	Albion R	54
1930–31a	Third Lanark	61	Dundee U	50	Dunfermline Ath	47
1931–32a	East Stirling*	55	St Johnstone	55	Raith R*	46
1932–33c	Hibernian	54	Queen of the S	49	Dunfermline Ath	47
1933–34c	Albion R	45	Dunfermline Ath*	44	Arbroath	44
1934–35c	Third Lanark	52	Arbroath	50	St Bernard's	47
1935–36c	Falkirk	59	St Mirren	52	Morton	48
1936–37c	Ayr U	54	Morton	51	St Bernard's	48
1937–38c	Raith R	59	Albion R	48	Airdrieonians	47
1938–39c	Cowdenbeath	60	Alloa Ath*	48	East Fife	48
1946–47d	Dundee	45	Airdrieonians	42	East Fife	31
1947–48e	East Fife	53	Albion R	42	Hamilton A	40
1948–49e	Raith R*	42	Stirling Alb	42	Airdrieonians*	41
1949–50e	Morton	47	Airdrieonians	44	Dunfermline Ath*	36
1950–51e	Queen of the S*	45	Stirling Alb	45	Ayr U*	36
1951–52e	Clyde	44	Falkirk	43	Ayr U	39
1952–53e	Stirling Alb	44	Hamilton A	43	Queen's Park	37
1953–54e	Motherwell	45	Kilmarnock	42	Third Lanark*	36
1954–55e	Airdrieonians	46	Dunfermline Ath	42	Hamilton A	39
1955–56b	Queen's Park	54	Ayr U	51	St Johnstone	49
1956–57b	Clyde	64	Third Lanark	51	Cowdenbeath	45
1957–58b	Stirling Alb	55	Dunfermline Ath	53	Arbroath	47

203

	First	Pts	*Second*	Pts	*Third*	Pts
1958–59*b*	Ayr U	60	Arbroath	51	Stenhousemuir	46
1959–60*b*	St Johnstone	53	Dundee U	50	Queen of the S	49
1960–61*b*	Stirling Alb	55	Falkirk	54	Stenhousemuir	50
1961–62*b*	Clyde	54	Queen of the S	53	Morton	44
1962–63*b*	St Johnstone	55	East Stirling	49	Morton	48
1963–64*b*	Morton	67	Clyde	53	Arbroath	46
1964–65*b*	Stirling Alb	59	Hamilton A	50	Queen of the S	45
1965–66*b*	Ayr U	53	Airdrieonians	50	Queen of the S	47
1966–67*a*	Morton	69	Raith R	58	Arbroath	57
1967–68*b*	St Mirren	62	Arbroath	53	East Fife	49
1968–69*b*	Motherwell	64	Ayr U	53	East Fife*	48
1969–70*b*	Falkirk	56	Cowdenbeath	55	Queen of the S	50
1970–71*b*	Partick Th	56	East Fife	51	Arbroath	46
1971–72*b*	Dumbarton*	52	Arbroath	52	Stirling Alb	50
1972–73*b*	Clyde	56	Dumferline Ath	52	Raith R*	47
1973–74*b*	Airdrieonians	60	Kilmarnock	58	Hamilton A	55
1974–75*a*	Falkirk	54	Queen of the S*	53	Montrose	53

Elected to Division 1: 1894 Clyde; 1895 Hibernian; 1896 Abercorn; 1897 Partick Th; 1899 Kilmarnock; 1900 Morton and Partick Th; 1902 Port Glasgow and Partick Th; 1903 Airdrieonians and Motherwell; 1905 Falkirk and Aberdeen; 1906 Clyde and Hamilton A; 1910 Raith R; 1913 Ayr U and Dumbarton.

SCOTTISH LEAGUE PLAY-OFFS 2009–2010

DIVISION 1 SEMI-FINALS FIRST LEG

Brechin C	(2) 2	Airdrie U	(1) 1
Cowdenbeath	(0) 1	Alloa Ath	(1) 1

DIVISION 1 SEMI-FINALS SECOND LEG

Airdrie U	(0) 0	Brechin C	(0) 1
Alloa Ath	(0) 0	Cowdenbeath	(0) 2

DIVISION 1 FINAL FIRST LEG

Cowdenbeath	(0) 0	Brechin C	(0) 0

DIVISION 1 FINAL SECOND LEG

Brechin C	(0) 0	Cowdenbeath	(3) 3

DIVISION 2 SEMI-FINALS FIRST LEG

East Stirling	(0) 0	Forfar Ath	(0) 1
Queen's Park	(0) 0	Arbroath	(2) 4

DIVISION 2 SEMI-FINALS SECOND LEG

Arbroath	(2) 2	Queen's Park	(0) 2
Forfar Ath	(1) 2	East Stirling	(0) 2

DIVISION 2 FINAL FIRST LEG

Arbroath	(0) 0	Forfar Ath	(0) 0

DIVISION 2 FINAL SECOND LEG

Forfar Ath	(1) 2	Arbroath	(0) 0

RELEGATED CLUBS

From Premier League

1998–99 Dunfermline Ath
1999–00 *No relegated team*
2000–01 St Mirren
2001–02 St Johnstone
2002–03 *No relegated team*
2003–04 Partick Th

2004–05 Dundee
2005–06 Livingston
2006–07 Dunfermline Ath
2007–08 Gretna
2008–09 Inverness CT
2009–10 Falkirk

From Premier Division

1974–75 *No relegation due to League reorganisation*
1975–76 Dundee, St Johnstone
1976–77 Hearts, Kilmarnock
1977–78 Ayr U, Clydebank
1978–79 Hearts, Motherwell
1979–80 Dundee, Hibernian
1980–81 Kilmarnock, Hearts
1981–82 Partick Th, Airdrieonians
1982–83 Morton, Kilmarnock
1983–84 St Johnstone, Motherwell
1984–85 Dumbarton, Morton
1985–86 *No relegation due to League reorganisation*

1986–87 Clydebank, Hamilton A
1987–88 Falkirk, Dunfermline Ath, Morton
1988–89 Hamilton A
1989–90 Dundee
1990–91 None
1991–92 St Mirren, Dunfermline Ath
1992–93 Falkirk, Airdrieonians
1993–94 *See footnote, page 210*
1994–95 Dundee U
1995–96 Partick Th, Falkirk
1996–97 Raith R
1997–98 Hibernian

From Division 1

1974–75 *No relegation due to League reorganisation*
1975–76 Dunfermline Ath, Clyde
1976–77 Raith R, Falkirk
1977–78 Alloa Ath, East Fife
1978–79 Montrose, Queen of the S
1979–80 Arbroath, Clyde
1980–81 Stirling Alb, Berwick R
1981–82 East Stirling, Queen of the S
1982–83 Dunfermline Ath, Queen's Park
1983–84 Raith R, Alloa Ath
1984–85 Meadowbank Th, St Johnstone
1985–86 Ayr U, Alloa Ath
1986–87 Brechin C, Montrose
1987–88 East Fife, Dumbarton
1988–89 Kilmarnock, Queen of the S
1989–90 Albion R, Alloa Ath
1990–91 Clyde, Brechin C
1991–92 Montrose, Forfar Ath

1992–93 Meadowbank Th, Cowdenbeath
1993–94 *See footnote*
1994–95 Ayr U, Stranraer
1995–96 Hamilton A, Dumbarton
1996–97 Clydebank, East Fife
1997–98 Partick Th, Stirling Alb
1998–99 Hamilton A, Stranraer
1999–00 Clydebank
2000–01 Morton, Alloa Ath
2001–02 Raith R
2002–03 Alloa Ath, Arbroath
2003–04 Ayr U, Brechin C
2004–05 Partick Th, Raith R
2005–06 Stranraer, Brechin C
2006–07 Airdrie U, Ross Co
2007–08 Stirling Alb
2008–09 Clyde
2009–10 Airdrie U, Ayr U

From Division 2

1994–95 Meadowbank Th, Brechin C
1995–96 Forfar Ath, Montrose
1996–97 Dumbarton, Berwick R
1997–98 Stenhousemuir, Brechin C
1998–99 East Fife, Forfar Ath
1999–00 Hamilton A**
2000–01 Queen's Park, Stirling Alb
2001–02 Morton

2002–03 Stranraer, Cowdenbeath
2003–04 East Fife, Stenhousemuir
2004–05 Arbroath, Berwick R
2005–06 Dumbarton
2006–07 Stranraer, Forfar Ath
2007–08 Cowdenbeath, Berwick R
2008–09 Stranraer, Queen's Park
2009–10 Arbroath, Clyde

From Division 1 1973–74

1921–22 *Queen's Park, Dumbarton, Clydebank
1922–23 Albion R, Alloa Ath
1923–24 Clyde, Clydebank
1924–25 Third Lanark, Ayr U
1925–26 Raith R, Clydebank
1926–27 Morton, Dundee U
1927–28 Dunfermline Ath, Bo'ness
1928–29 Third Lanark, Raith R
1929–30 St Johnstone, Dundee U
1930–31 Hibernian, East Fife
1931–32 Dundee U, Leith Ath
1932–33 Morton, East Stirling
1933–34 Third Lanark, Cowdenbeath
1934–35 St Mirren, Falkirk
1935–36 Airdrieonians, Ayr U
1936–37 Dunfermline Ath, Albion R
1937–38 Dundee, Morton
1938–39 Queen's Park, Raith R
1946–47 Kilmarnock, Hamilton A
1947–48 Airdrieonians, Queen's Park
1948–49 Morton, Albion R
1949–50 Queen of the S, Stirling Alb
1950–51 Clyde, Falkirk

1951–52 Morton, Stirling Alb
1952–53 Motherwell, Third Lanark
1953–54 Airdrieonians, Hamilton A
1954–55 *No clubs relegated*
1955–56 Stirling Alb, Clyde
1956–57 Dunfermline Ath, Ayr U
1957–58 East Fife, Queen's Park
1958–59 Queen of the S, Falkirk
1959–60 Arbroath, Stirling Alb
1960–61 Ayr U, Clyde
1961–62 St Johnstone, Stirling Alb
1962–63 Clyde, Raith R
1963–64 Queen of the S, East Stirling
1964–65 Airdrieonians, Third Lanark
1965–66 Morton, Hamilton A
1966–67 St Mirren, Ayr U
1967–68 Motherwell, Stirling Alb
1968–69 Falkirk, Arbroath
1969–70 Raith R, Partick Th
1970–71 St Mirren, Cowdenbeath
1971–72 Clyde, Dunfermline Ath
1972–73 Kilmarnock, Airdrieonians
1973–74 East Fife, Falkirk

*Season 1921–22 – only 1 club promoted, 3 clubs relegated.
**15 pts deducted for failing to field a team.

Scottish League championship wins: Rangers 53, Celtic 41, Aberdeen 4, Hearts 4, Hibernian 4, Dumbarton 2, Dundee 1, Dundee U 1, Kilmarnock 1, Motherwell 1, Third Lanark 1.

The Scottish Football League was reconstructed into three divisions at the end of the 1974–75 season, so the usual relegation statistics do not apply. Further reorganization took place at the end of the 1985–86 season. From 1986–87, the Premier and First Division had 12 teams each. The Second Division remained at 14. From 1988–89, the Premier Division reverted to 10 teams, and the First Division to 14 teams but in 1991–92 the Premier and First Division reverted to 12. At the end of the 1997–98 season, the top nine clubs in Premier Division broke away from the Scottish League to form a new competition, the Scottish Premier League, with the club promoted from Division One. At the end of the 1999–2000 season two teams were added to the Scottish League. There was no relegation from the Premier League but two promoted from the First Division and three from each of the Second and Third Divisions. One team was relegated from the First Division and one from the Second Division, leaving 12 teams in each division. In season 2002–03, Falkirk were not promoted to the Premier League due to the failure of their ground to meet League standards. Inverness CT were promoted after a previous refusal in 2003–04 because of ground sharing. At the end of 2005–06 the Scottish League introduced play-offs for the team finishing second from the bottom of Division 1 against the winners of the second, third and fourth finishing teams in Division 2 and with a similar procedure for Division 2 and Division 3.

PAST SCOTTISH LEAGUE CUP FINALS

1946–47	Rangers	4	Aberdeen	0
1947–48	East Fife	0 4	Falkirk	0* 1
1948–49	Rangers	2	Raith Rovers	0
1949–50	East Fife	3	Dunfermline	0
1950–51	Motherwell	3	Hibernian	0
1951–52	Dundee	3	Rangers	2
1952–53	Dundee	2	Kilmarnock	0
1953–54	East Fife	3	Partick Th	2
1954–55	Hearts	4	Motherwell	2
1955–56	Aberdeen	2	St Mirren	1
1956–57	Celtic	0 3	Partick Th	0 0
1957–58	Celtic	7	Rangers	1
1958–59	Hearts	5	Partick Th	1
1959–60	Hearts	2	Third Lanark	1
1960–61	Rangers	2	Kilmarnock	0
1961–62	Rangers	1 3	Hearts	1 1
1962–63	Hearts	1	Kilmarnock	0
1963–64	Rangers	5	Morton	0
1964–65	Rangers	2	Celtic	1
1965–66	Celtic	2	Rangers	1
1966–67	Celtic	1	Rangers	0
1967–68	Celtic	5	Dundee	3
1968–69	Celtic	6	Hibernian	2
1969–70	Celtic	1	St Johnstone	0
1970–71	Rangers	1	Celtic	0
1971–72	Partick Th	4	Celtic	1
1972–73	Hibernian	2	Celtic	1
1973–74	Dundee	1	Celtic	0
1974–75	Celtic	6	Hibernian	3
1975–76	Rangers	1	Celtic	0
1976–77	Aberdeen	2	Celtic	1
1977–78	Rangers	2	Celtic	1*
1978–79	Rangers	2	Aberdeen	1
1979–80	Aberdeen	0 0	Dundee U	0* 3
1980–81	Dundee	0	Dundee U	3
1981–82	Rangers	2	Dundee U	1
1982–83	Celtic	2	Rangers	1
1983–84	Rangers	3	Celtic	2
1984–85	Rangers	1	Dundee U	0
1985–86	Aberdeen	3	Hibernian	0
1986–87	Rangers	2	Celtic	1
1987–88	Rangers†	3	Aberdeen	3*
1988–89	Aberdeen	2	Rangers	3*
1989–90	Aberdeen	2	Rangers	1
1990–91	Rangers	2	Celtic	1
1991–92	Hibernian	2	Dunfermline Ath	0
1992–93	Rangers	2	Aberdeen	1*
1993–94	Rangers	2	Hibernian	1
1994–95	Raith R†	2	Celtic	2*
1995–96	Aberdeen	2	Dundee	0
1996–97	Rangers	4	Hearts	3
1997–98	Celtic	3	Dundee U	0
1998–99	Rangers	2	St Johnstone	1

1999–2000	Celtic	2	Aberdeen	0
2000–01	Celtic	3	Kilmarnock	0
2001–02	Rangers	4	Ayr U	0
2002–03	Rangers	2	Celtic	1
2003–04	Livingston	2	Hibernian	0
2004–05	Rangers	5	Motherwell	1
2005–06	Celtic	3	Dunfermline Ath	0
2006–07	Hibernian	5	Kilmarnock	1
2007–08	Rangers†	2	Dundee U	2*
2008–09	Celtic	2	Rangers	0*
2009–10	Rangers	1	St Mirren	0

†Won on penalties *After extra time

PAST LEAGUE CHALLENGE FINALS

1990–91	Dundee	3	Ayr U	2
1991–92	Hamilton A	1	Ayr U	0
1992–93	Hamilton A	3	Morton	2
1993–94	St Mirren	9	Falkirk	3
1994–95	Airdrieonians	3	Dundee	2
1995–96	Stenhousemuir	0	Dundee U	0
	(aet; Stenhousemuir won 5-4 on penalties.)			
1996–97	Stranraer	1	St Johnstone	0
1997–98	Falkirk	1	Qeeen of the South	0
1998–99	no competition			
1999–2000	Alloa Ath	4	Inverness CT	4
	(aet; Alloa Ath won 5-4 on penalties.)			
2000–01	Airdrieonians	2	Livingston	2
	(aet; Airdrieonians won 3-2 on penalties.)			
2001–02	Airdrieonians	2	Alloa Ath	1
2002–03	Queen of the S	2	Brechin C	0
2003–04	Inverness CT	2	Airdrie U	0
2004–05	Falkirk	2	Ross Co	1
2005–06	St Mirren	2	Hamilton A	1
2006–07	Ross Co	1	Clyde	1
	(aet; Ross Co won 5-4 on penalties.)			
2007–08	St Johnstone	3	Dunfermline Ath	2
2008–09	Airdrie	2	Ross Co	2
	(aet; Airdrie U won 3-2 on penalties.)			
2009–10	Dundee	3	Inverness CT	2

CIS SCOTTISH LEAGUE CUP 2009–2010

FIRST ROUND

Airdrie U	(0) 0	Alloa Ath	(0) 0
(aet; Alloa Ath won 4-3 on penalties.)			
Albion R	(1) 3	Livingston	(0) 0
Brechin C	(1) 4	Elgin C	(0) 0
Clyde	(1) 1	Forfar Ath	(0) 3
Cowdenbeath	(1) 1	Morton	(2) 3
Dumbarton	(0) 0	Dunfermline Ath	(3) 5
Dundee	(3) 5	Stranraer	(0) 0
East Fife	(2) 2	Raith R	(0) 3
Inverness CT	(1) 4	Annan Ath	(0) 0
Partick Th	(1) 5	Berwick R	(0) 1
Peterhead	(0) 0	Arbroath	(1) 3
Queen's Park	(0) 1	Queen of the S	(3) 4
Ross Co	(1) 5	Montrose	(0) 0
Stenhousemuir	(0) 0	St Johnstone	(2) 5
Stirling Alb	(1) 1	Ayr U	(0) 2
(aet.)			
East Stirling	(3) 3	St Mirren	(4) 6

SECOND ROUND

Alloa Ath	(0) 0	Dundee U	(2) 2
Fofar Ath	(0) 2	Dundee	(3) 4
Inverness CT	(3) 4	Albion R	(0) 0
Kilmarnock	(1) 3	Morton	(1) 1
Partick Th	(1) 1	Queen of the S	(0) 2
Ross Co	(1) 2	Hamilton A	(0) 1
Arbroath	(0) 0	St Johnstone	(4) 6
Ayr U	(0) 0	St Mirren	(1) 2
Dunfermline Ath	(1) 3	Raith R	(0) 1
Hibernian	(2) 3	Brechin C	(0) 0

THIRD ROUND

Dundee	(1) 3	Aberdeen	(0) 2
(aet.)			
Hibernian	(1) 1	St Johnstone	(1) 3
Kilmarnock	(0) 1	St Mirren	(0) 2
Motherwell	(1) 3	Inverness CT	(0) 2
(aet.)			
Ross Co	(0) 0	Dundee U	(1) 2
Falkirk	(0) 0	Celtic	(1) 4
Hearts	(0) 2	Dunfermline Ath	(1) 1
Queen of the S	(0) 1	Rangers	(1) 2

QUARTER-FINALS

Dundee	(1) 1	Rangers	(1) 3
St Johnstone	(0) 2	Dundee U	(0) 1
St Mirren	(1) 3	Motherwell	(0) 0
Celtic	(0) 0	Hearts	(0) 1

SEMI-FINALS

Hearts	(0) 0	St Mirren	(0) 1
(at Fir Park.)			
Rangers	(2) 2	St Johnstone	(0) 0
(at Hampden Park.)			

FINAL

St Mirren	(0) 0	Rangers	(0) 1

ALBA LEAGUE CHALLENGE CUP 2009–2010

FIRST ROUND NORTH-EAST

Dunfermline Ath	(0) 2	Arbroath	(0) 1
East Fife	(0) 0	Forfar Ath	(1) 2
Elgin C	(1) 3	Brechin C	(0) 1
Inverness CT	(1) 1	Montrose	(0) 1
(aet; Inverness CT won 5-3 on penalties.)			
Peterhead	(1) 1	Cowdenbeath	(0) 2
Ross Co	(0) 3	Alloa Ath	(1) 2
(aet.)			
Stirling Alb	(1) 2	Raith R	(0) 1

FIRST ROUND SOUTH-WEST

Airdrie U	(0) 0	Partick Th	(0) 1
Annan Ath	(1) 2	Queen's Park	(0) 0
Ayr U	(0) 0	Albion R	(0) 2
Queen of the S	(1) 1	Livingston	(0) 0
Stenhousemuir	(0) 2	Clyde	(0) 0
Stranraer	(2) 4	Berwick R	(1) 2
Dumbarton	(0) 0	Morton	(1) 1

SECOND ROUND

Annan Ath	(0) 1	East Stirling	(0) 0
Cowdenbeath	(0) 0	Dundee	(1) 3
Dunfermline Ath	(0) 1	Queen of the S	(1) 2
Elgin C	(0) 3	Albion R	(0) 0
Forfar Ath	(0) 1	Partick Th	(1) 6
Inverness CT	(3) 3	Stranraer R	(0) 0
Ross Co	(0) 2	Morton	(0) 1
Stirling Alb	(1) 3	Stenhousemuir	(0) 1

QUARTER-FINALS

Annan Ath	(0) 4	Elgin C	(2) 2
Partick Th	(0) 1	Inverness CT	(1) 1
(aet; Inverness CT won 4-3 on penalties.)			
Ross Co	(1) 2	Queen of the S	(0) 0
Stirling Alb	(0) 1	Dundee	(2) 2

SEMI-FINALS

Dundee	(1) 3	Annan Ath	(0) 0
Inverness CT	(1) 1	Ross Co	(0) 0

FINAL

Dundee	(0) 3	Inverness CT	(2) 2

ACTIVE NATION SCOTTISH CUP 2009–2010

THIRD ROUND

Airdrie U	(3) 4	Queen of the S	(0) 0
Albion R	(0) 1	Elgin C	(0) 0
Cowdenbeath	(0) 0	Alloa Ath	(0) 0
Deveronvale	(0) 0	Ayr U	(0) 1
Edinburgh C	(2) 3	Keith	(0) 1
Irvine Meadow	(1) 1	Arbroath	(0) 0
Montrose	(0) 2	East Fife	(0) 1
Morton	(0) 0	Dumbarton	(0) 0
Raith R	(0) 0	Peterhead	(0) 0
Ross Co	(3) 5	Berwick R	(0) 1
Spartans	(0) 0	Forfar Ath	(0) 1
Stirling Alb	(1) 2	Auchinleck Talbot	(1) 1
Threave R	(0) 1	Inverurie Locos	(1) 2
Wick Academy	(3) 4	Brechin C	(2) 4
Stenhousemuir	(5) 5	Cove Rangers	(0) 0
Clyde	(0) 1	Livingston	(0) 1

THIRD ROUND REPLAYS

Peterhead	(0) 1	Raith R	(0) 4
Dumbarton	(0) 0	Morton	(0) 1
Alloa Ath	(0) 1	Cowdenbeath	(0) 0
Brechin C	(2) 4	Wick Academy	(1) 2
Livingston	(2) 7	Clyde	(1) 1

FOURTH ROUND

Aberdeen	(0) 2	Hearts	(0) 0
Dunfermline Ath	(4) 7	Stenhousemuir	(0) 1

(Dunfermline Ath originally disqualified for fielding an ineligible player; reinstated on appeal, but forced to replay at Stenhousemuir.)

Hibernian	(2) 3	Irvine Meadow	(0) 0
Partick Th	(0) 0	Dundee U	(1) 2
St Mirren	(2) 3	Alloa Ath	(1) 1
Hamilton A	(3) 3	Rangers	(2) 3
Albion R	(0) 0	Stirling Alb	(0) 0
Ayr U	(1) 1	Brechin C	(0) 0
Edinburgh C	(1) 1	Montrose	(1) 3
Forfar Ath	(0) 0	St Johnstone	(2) 3
Inverness CT	(1) 2	Motherwell	(0) 0
Kilmarnock	(0) 1	Falkirk	(0) 0
Ross Co	(1) 4	Inverurie Locos	(0) 0
Morton	(0) 0	Celtic	(1) 1
Livingston	(0) 0	Dundee	(1) 1
Raith R	(0) 1	Airdrie U	(1) 1

FOURTH ROUND REPLAYS

Rangers	(0) 2	Hamilton A	(0) 0
(aet.)			
Stirling Alb	(3) 3	Albion R	(1) 1
Stenhousemuir	(0) 1	Dunfermline Ath	(1) 2
(aet.)			
Airdrie U	(1) 1	Raith R	(2) 3

FIFTH ROUND

Dundee	(1) 2	Ayr U	(1) 1
Hibernian	(2) 5	Montrose	(0) 1
Kilmarnock	(2) 3	Inverness CT	(0) 0
Raith R	(0) 1	Aberdeen	(0) 1
Ross Co	(3) 9	Stirling Alb	(0) 0
St Johnstone	(0) 0	Dundee U	(1) 1
St Mirren	(0) 0	Rangers	(0) 0
Dunfermline Ath	(2) 2	Celtic	(2) 4

FIFTH ROUND REPLAYS

Aberdeen	(0) 0	Raith R	(0) 1
Rangers	(0) 1	St Mirren	(0) 0

SIXTH ROUND

Dundee	(0) 1	Raith R	(2) 2
Hibernian	(2) 2	Ross Co	(1) 2
Kilmarnock	(0) 0	Celtic	(0) 3
Rangers	(2) 3	Dundee U	(1) 3

SIXTH ROUND REPLAYS

Ross Co	(0) 2	Hibernian	(0) 1
Dundee U	(0) 1	Rangers	(0) 0

SEMI-FINALS

Celtic	(0) 0	Ross Co	(0) 2
Dundee U	(1) 2	Raith R	(0) 0

FINAL

Dundee U	(0) 3	Ross Co	(0) 0

Did You Know?

The Scottish Cup changed its format in recent years to eliminate the need for a qualifying competition. From 2007–08 for the first time in the history of the competition, four Junior clubs were allowed to enter. Three were winners of the Super League, the fourth the successful winner of the Junior Cup. In 2009–10 the new formula produced a first with Junior club Irvine Meadow defeating Arbroath 1-0 in the third round to become the first so to do against a senior team. In previous years there had been other shocks in the competition, notably in 1967 when Glasgow Rangers was beaten by Berwick Rangers and in 1959 the Highland League club Fraserburgh overcame Dundee by the same 1-0 margin.

PAST SCOTTISH CUP FINALS

1874	Queen's Park	2	Clydesdale	0
1875	Queen's Park	3	Renton	0
1876	Queen's Park	1 2	Third Lanark	1 0
1877	Vale of Leven	0 1 3	Rangers	0 1 2
1878	Vale of Leven	1	Third Lanark	0
1879	Vale of Leven	1	Rangers	1
	Vale of Leven awarded cup, Rangers did not appear for replay			
1880	Queen's Park	3	Thornlibank	0
1881	Queen's Park	2 3	Dumbarton	1 1
	Replayed because of protest			
1882	Queen's Park	2 4	Dumbarton	2 1
1883	Dumbarton	2 2	Vale of Leven	2 1
1884	*Queen's Park awarded cup when Vale of Leven did not appear for the final*			
1885	Renton	0 3	Vale of Leven	0 1
1886	Queen's Park	3	Renton	1
1887	Hibernian	2	Dumbarton	1
1888	Renton	6	Cambuslang	1
1889	Third Lanark	3 2	Celtic	0 1
	Replayed because of protest			
1890	Queen's Park	1 2	Vale of Leven	1 1
1891	Hearts	1	Dumbarton	0
1892	Celtic	1 5	Queen's Park	0 1
	Replayed because of protest			
1893	Queen's Park	2	Celtic	1
1894	Rangers	3	Celtic	1
1895	St Bernards	3	Renton	1
1896	Hearts	3	Hibernian	1
1897	Rangers	5	Dumbarton	1
1898	Rangers	2	Kilmarnock	0
1899	Celtic	2	Rangers	0
1900	Celtic	4	Queen's Park	3
1901	Hearts	4	Celtic	3
1902	Hibernian	1	Celtic	0
1903	Rangers	1 0 2	Hearts	1 0 0
1904	Celtic	3	Rangers	2
1905	Third Lanark	0 3	Rangers	0 1
1906	Hearts	1	Third Lanark	0
1907	Celtic	3	Hearts	0
1908	Celtic	5	St Mirren	1
1909	*After two drawn games between Celtic and Rangers, 2-2, 1-1, there was a riot and the cup was withheld*			
1910	Dundee	2 0 2	Clyde	2 0 1
1911	Celtic	0 2	Hamilton Acad	0 0
1912	Celtic	2	Clyde	0
1913	Falkirk	2	Raith R	0
1914	Celtic	0 4	Hibernian	0 1
1920	Kilmarnock	3	Albion R	2
1921	Partick Th	1	Rangers	0
1922	Morton	1	Rangers	0
1923	Celtic	1	Hibernian	0
1924	Airdrieonians	2	Hibernian	0
1925	Celtic	2	Dundee	1
1926	St Mirren	2	Celtic	0
1927	Celtic	3	East Fife	1
1928	Rangers	4	Celtic	0
1929	Kilmarnock	2	Rangers	0
1930	Rangers	0 2	Partick Th	0 1

1931	Celtic	2 4	Motherwell	2 2
1932	Rangers	1 3	Kilmarnock	1 0
1933	Celtic	1	Motherwell	0
1934	Rangers	5	St Mirren	0
1935	Rangers	2	Hamilton A	1
1936	Rangers	1	Third Lanark	0
1937	Celtic	2	Aberdeen	1
1938	East Fife	1 4	Kilmarnock	1 2
1939	Clyde	4	Motherwell	0
1947	Aberdeen	2	Hibernian	1
1948	Rangers	1 1	Morton	1 0
1949	Rangers	4	Clyde	1
1950	Rangers	3	East Fife	0
1951	Celtic	1	Motherwell	0
1952	Motherwell	4	Dundee	0
1953	Rangers	1 1	Aberdeen	1 0
1954	Celtic	2	Aberdeen	1
1955	Clyde	1 1	Celtic	1 0
1956	Hearts	3	Celtic	1
1957	Falkirk	1 2	Kilmarnock	1 1
1958	Clyde	1	Hibernian	0
1959	St Mirren	3	Aberdeen	1
1960	Rangers	2	Kilmarnock	0
1961	Dunfermline Ath	0 2	Celtic	0 0
1962	Rangers	2	St Mirren	0
1963	Rangers	1 3	Celtic	1 0
1964	Rangers	3	Dundee	1
1965	Celtic	3	Dunfermline Ath	2
1966	Rangers	0 1	Celtic	0 0
1967	Celtic	2	Aberdeen	0
1968	Dunfermline Ath	3	Hearts	1
1969	Celtic	4	Rangers	0
1970	Aberdeen	3	Celtic	1
1971	Celtic	1 2	Rangers	1 1
1972	Celtic	6	Hibernian	1
1973	Rangers	3	Celtic	2
1974	Celtic	3	Dundee U	0
1975	Celtic	3	Airdrieonians	1
1976	Rangers	3	Hearts	1
1977	Celtic	1	Rangers	0
1978	Rangers	2	Aberdeen	1
1979	Rangers	0 0 3	Hibernian	0 0 2
1980	Celtic	1	Rangers	0
1981	Rangers	0 4	Dundee U	0 1
1982	Aberdeen	4	Rangers	1 (aet)
1983	Aberdeen	1	Rangers	0 (aet)
1984	Aberdeen	2	Celtic	1 (aet)
1985	Celtic	2	Dundee U	1
1986	Aberdeen	3	Hearts	0
1987	St Mirren	1	Dundee U	0 (aet)
1988	Celtic	2	Dundee U	1
1989	Celtic	1	Rangers	0
1990	Aberdeen	0	Celtic	0
	(aet; Aberdeen won 9-8 on penalties)			
1991	Motherwell	4	Dundee U	3
	(aet.)			
1992	Rangers	2	Airdrieonians	1
1993	Rangers	2	Aberdeen	1
1994	Dundee U	1	Rangers	0

1995	Celtic	1	Airdrieonians	0
1996	Rangers	5	Hearts	1
1997	Kilmarnock	1	Falkirk	0
1998	Hearts	2	Rangers	1
1999	Rangers	1	Celtic	0
2000	Rangers	4	Aberdeen	0
2001	Celtic	3	Hibernian	0
2002	Rangers	3	Celtic	2
2003	Rangers	1	Dundee	0
2004	Celtic	3	Dunfermline Ath	1
2005	Celtic	1	Dundee U	0
2006	Hearts	1	Gretna	1
	(aet; Hearts won 4-2 on penalties)			
2007	Celtic	1	Dunfermline Ath	0
2008	Rangers	3	Queen of the S	2
2009	Rangers	1	Falkirk	0
2010	Dundee U	3	Ross Co	0

SCOTS-ADS HIGHLAND LEAGUE 2009–2010

			Home				Away				Total					
	P	W	D	L	F	A	W	D	L	F	A	W	D	L	F	A	GD	Pts
1 Buckie Thistle	34	14	2	1	46	12	12	3	2	37	14	26	5	3	83	26	57	83
2 Cove Rangers	34	14	3	0	54	16	9	3	5	43	26	23	6	5	97	42	55	75
3 Deveronvale	34	11	1	5	48	21	10	4	3	43	26	21	5	8	91	47	44	68
4 Fraserburgh	34	11	3	3	47	29	10	2	5	28	19	21	5	8	75	48	27	68
5 Forres Mechanics	34	14	1	2	44	16	6	4	7	28	26	20	5	9	72	42	30	65
6 Formartine United	34	9	3	5	38	22	9	3	5	37	25	18	6	10	75	47	28	60
7 Huntly	34	10	1	6	31	26	9	2	6	35	23	19	3	12	66	49	17	60
8 Keith	34	10	2	5	43	21	7	4	6	34	33	17	6	11	77	54	23	57
9 Wick Academy	34	9	3	5	43	29	7	3	7	36	35	16	6	12	79	64	15	54
10 Inverurie Loco Works	34	8	4	5	28	25	7	2	8	32	22	15	6	13	60	47	13	51
11 Nairn County	34	7	3	7	30	34	8	2	7	31	25	15	5	14	61	59	2	50
12 Clachnacuddin	34	8	3	6	42	33	4	4	9	31	40	12	7	15	73	73	0	43
13 Turriff United	34	5	2	10	31	39	4	2	11	29	47	9	4	21	60	86	–26	31
14 Lossiemouth	34	5	4	8	36	33	2	2	13	16	41	7	6	21	52	74	–22	27
15 Brora Rangers	34	4	3	10	18	36	2	3	12	14	45	6	6	22	32	81	–49	24
16 Rothes	34	6	2	9	23	42	1	1	15	16	60	7	3	24	39	102	–63	24
17 Fort William	34	3	2	12	22	41	3	0	14	15	57	6	2	26	37	98	–61	20
18 Strathspey Thistle	34	3	3	11	15	45	0	1	16	15	75	3	4	27	30	120	–90	13

CENTRAL TAXIS EAST OF SCOTLAND LEAGUE PREMIER DIVISION 2009–2010

	P	W	D	L	F	A	GD	Pts
1 Spartans	20	17	1	2	63	18	45	52
2 Whitehill Welfare	20	12	1	7	30	22	8	37
3 Lothian Thistle	20	11	3	6	46	25	21	36
4 Tynecastle	20	9	6	5	40	32	8	33
5 Civil Service Strollers	20	9	6	5	27	26	1	33
6 Heriot-Watt University	20	10	0	10	42	45	–3	30
7 Edinburgh City	20	9	1	10	37	39	–2	28
8 Edinburgh University	20	6	5	9	21	25	–4	23
9 Preston Athletic	20	5	2	13	27	39	–12	17
10 Selkirk	20	4	3	13	28	56	–28	15
11 Coldstream	20	3	2	15	28	62	–34	11

PRINCIPALITY BUILDING SOCIETY
WELSH PREMIER LEAGUE 2009–10

		Home					Away					Total					
	P	W	D	L	F	A	W	D	L	F	A	W	D	L	F	A	GD	Pts
1 The New Saints	34	14	3	0	49	6	11	4	2	20	7	25	7	2	69	13	56	82
2 Llanelli	34	14	2	1	49	14	11	3	3	30	12	25	5	4	79	26	53	80
3 Port Talbot Town	34	12	3	2	35	8	7	5	5	21	15	19	8	7	56	23	33	65
4 Aberystwyth Town	34	8	4	5	27	25	11	3	3	27	16	19	7	8	54	41	13	64
5 Bangor City	34	11	3	3	43	19	8	3	6	32	26	19	6	9	75	45	30	63
6 Rhyl	34	11	3	3	45	17	7	5	5	29	26	18	8	8	74	43	31	62
7 Airbus UK Br.	34	6	6	5	25	18	6	7	4	24	19	12	13	9	49	37	12	49
8 Prestatyn Town	34	6	7	4	19	20	6	5	6	34	33	12	12	10	53	53	0	48
9 Neath Athletic	34	6	6	5	25	21	6	5	6	16	17	12	11	11	41	38	3	47
10 Carmarthen Town	34	5	4	8	21	21	7	5	5	24	17	12	9	13	45	38	7	45
11 Bala Town	34	5	6	6	18	23	7	3	7	21	24	12	9	13	39	47	–8	45
12 Haverfordwest Co.	34	6	6	5	22	20	5	5	7	21	27	11	11	12	43	47	–4	44
13 Newtown	34	6	4	7	29	31	4	7	6	25	26	10	11	13	54	57	–3	41
14 Connah's Quay	34	7	4	6	20	15	4	4	9	11	27	11	8	15	31	42	–11	41
15 CPD Porthmadog	34	2	4	11	10	28	4	2	11	13	38	6	6	22	23	66	–43	24
16 Welshpool Town	34	3	2	12	15	33	3	3	11	15	37	6	5	23	30	70	–40	23
17 Caersws	34	3	2	12	13	37	0	2	15	13	57	3	4	27	26	94	–68	13
18 Cefn Druids	34	1	4	12	8	28	0	2	15	8	49	1	6	27	16	77	–61	9

NORTHERN IRELAND
CARLING PREMIERSHIP 2009–10

		Home					Away					Total					
	P	W	D	L	F	A	W	D	L	F	A	W	D	L	F	A	GD	Pts
1 Linfield	38	13	2	4	41	16	9	6	4	37	21	22	8	8	78	37	41	74
2 Cliftonville	38	13	1	6	40	19	8	5	5	29	23	21	6	11	69	42	27	69
3 Glentoran	38	9	5	5	22	20	10	3	6	36	26	19	8	11	58	46	12	65
4 Crusaders	38	8	4	7	35	31	9	5	5	22	21	17	9	12	57	52	5	60
5 Dungannon Swifts	38	7	7	4	28	27	9	2	9	28	31	16	9	13	56	58	–2	57
6 Portadown	38	10	4	5	35	21	5	6	8	35	34	15	10	13	70	55	15	55
7 Coleraine	38	10	4	4	41	29	6	5	9	35	33	16	9	13	76	62	14	57
8 Glenavon	38	6	6	8	28	34	6	1	11	19	33	12	7	19	47	67	–20	43
9 Newry City	38	6	5	9	22	33	4	7	7	16	30	10	12	16	38	63	–25	42
10 Ballymena United	38	7	2	10	23	25	4	5	10	23	31	11	7	20	46	56	–10	40
11 Lisburn Distillery	38	4	5	9	22	38	7	1	12	23	38	11	6	21	45	76	–31	39
12 Institute	38	3	7	9	18	28	3	6	10	18	34	6	13	19	36	62	–26	31

REPUBLIC OF IRELAND LEAGUE 2009

		Home					Away					Total					
	P	W	D	L	F	A	W	D	L	F	A	W	D	L	F	A	GD	Pts
1 Bohemians	36	14	2	2	39	8	10	3	5	23	13	24	5	7	62	21	41	77
2 Shamrock Rovers	36	11	4	3	29	16	10	6	2	22	11	21	10	5	51	27	24	73
3 Cork City	36	9	4	5	16	11	8	5	5	26	17	17	9	10	42	28	14	60
4 Derry City	36	8	3	7	21	16	10	2	6	28	15	18	5	13	49	31	18	59
5 Dundalk	36	7	3	8	22	19	5	5	8	24	32	12	8	16	46	51	–5	44
6 Sligo Rovers	36	7	3	8	21	26	4	7	7	20	25	11	10	15	41	51	–10	43
7 St Patrick's Ath	36	7	3	8	18	25	6	1	11	11	21	13	4	19	29	46	–17	43
8 Galway United	36	7	3	8	19	25	5	3	10	17	32	12	6	18	36	57	–21	42
9 Drogheda United	36	3	7	8	18	23	4	4	10	14	27	7	11	18	32	50	–18	32
10 Bray Wanderers	36	3	7	8	20	26	3	3	12	10	30	6	10	20	30	56	–26	28

UEFA CHAMPIONS LEAGUE 2009–2010

■ *Denotes player sent off. * Winner after extra time.*

FIRST QUALIFYING ROUND FIRST LEG

Hibernians	(0) 0	Mogren	(1) 2
Tre Fiori	(0) 1	Sant Julia	(1) 1

FIRST QUALIFYING ROUND SECOND LEG

Sant Julia	(1) 1	Tre Fiori	(0) 1
Mogren	(2) 4	Hibernians	(0) 0

SECOND QUALIFYING ROUND FIRST LEG

EB/Streymur	(0) 0	Apoel	(1) 2
Ekranas	(0) 2	Baku	(0) 2
Makedonija	(0) 0	BATE Borisov	(1) 2
Pyunik	(0) 0	Dinamo Zagreb	(0) 0
Rhyl	(0) 0	Partizan Belgrade	(3) 4
Debrecen	(0) 2	Kalmar	(0) 0
FC Copenhagen	(3) 6	Mogren	(0) 0
Hafnarfjordur	(0) 0	Aktobe	(0) 4
Inter Turku	(0) 0	Sheriff	(1) 1
Levski	(0) 4	Sant Julia	(0) 0
Maccabi Haifa	(1) 6	Glentoran	(0) 0
Salzburg	(1) 1	Bohemians	(0) 1
SK Tirana	(0) 1	Stabaek	(1) 1
Ventspils	(0) 3	F91 Dudelange	(0) 0
Wisla	(0) 1	Levadia	(1) 1
WIT Georgia	(0) 0	Maribor	(0) 0
Zrinjski	(0) 1	Slovan Bratislava	(0) 0

Tuesday, 14 July 2009

Rhyl (0) 0

Partizan Belgrade (3) 4 *(Krstajic 17, Cleo 18, Diarra 45, Dordevic 69)*   1726

Rhyl: Kendall; Naylor, Strong, Horan, Stones, Leah, Owen, Sherbon (Connolly 70), Holden, Roberts, Williams (Hunt 55).
Partizan Belgrade: Bozovic M; Stevanovic (Knezevic 72), Dordevic, Krstajic, Gavrancic, Tomic (Vujovic 72), Petrovic, Almani Moreira, Cleo (Bogunovic 83), Ilic, Diarra.

Wednesday, 15 July 2009

Maccabi Haifa (1) 6 *(Rafaelov 36, Katan 52, Dvalishvili 57, 81, Arbeitman 83, Ghadir 89)*

Glentoran (0) 0   11,500

Maccabi Haifa: Davidovitch; Teixeira, Culma (Golasa 55), Masilela, Keinan, Meshumar, Kayal, Rafaelov (Boccoli 61), Dvalishvili, Ghadir, Katan (Arbeitman 72).
Glentoran: Morris; Nixon, Neill, Leeman, Ward, Taylor, Clarke (Fitzgerald 68), Fordyce (Hall 79), Black, Waterworth (Halliday 68), Hamilton.

Salzburg (1) 1 *(Dudic 25)*

Bohemians (0) 1 *(N'Do 60)*   12,300

Salzburg: Gustafsson; Dudic, Schwegler, Opdam (Jezek 66), Sekagya, Svento, Cziommer (Ilic 64), Leitgeb, Aufhauser, Janko (Nelisse 73), N'Gwat-Mahop.
Bohemians: Murphy B; Powell, Oman, Shelley, Rossiter, Brennan, Deegan, Keegan, N'Do, Crowe, Byrne (Murphy A 73).

SECOND QUALIFYING ROUND SECOND LEG

Apoel	(1) 3	EB/Streymur	(0) 0
Baku	(0) 4	Ekranas	(0) 2
BATE Borisov	(0) 2	Makedonija	(0) 0
Dinamo Zagreb	(1) 3	Pyunik	(0) 0
Partizan Belgrade	(4) 8	Rhyl	(0) 0
Sant Julia	(0) 0	Levski	(3) 5
Sheriff	(0) 1	Inter Turku	(0) 0
Slovan Bratislava	(2) 4	Zrinjski	(0) 0
Stabaek	(3) 4	SK Tirana	(0) 0
Aktobe	(1) 2	Hafnarfjordur	(0) 0
Bohemians	(0) 0	Salzburg	(0) 1
F91 Dudelange	(1) 1	Ventspils	(1) 3
Glentoran	(0) 0	Maccabi Haifa	(1) 4
Kalmar	(2) 3	Debrecen	(1) 1
Levadia	(0) 1	Wisla	(0) 0
Maribor	(2) 3	WIT Georgia	(1) 1
Mogren	(0) 0	FC Copenhagen	(4) 6

Tuesday, 21 July 2009

Partizan Belgrade (4) 8 *(Diarra 4, Cleo 17, 53, 72 (pen), Dordevic 20, Ilic 38, 65, Petrovic 67)*

Rhyl (0) 0   9321

Partizan Belgrade: Bozovic M; Stevanovic, Dordevic (Jovanovic B 60), Krstajic, Gavrancic, Tomic (Bogunovic 70), Petrovic, Almani Moreira (Brezancic 60), Cleo, Ilic, Diarra.
Rhyl: Kendall (Pritchard 86); Naylor, Strong, Horan, Stones, Connolly, Leah, Owen, Sherbon (Williams 65), Holden, Roberts.

Wednesday, 22 July 2009

Bohemians (0) 0

Salzburg (0) 1 *(Jezek 86)*   6000

Bohemians: Murphy B; Powell, Oman, Shelley, Rossiter (McGuinness 87), Brennan (Murphy A 65), Deegan, Keegan, N'Do, Crowe, Byrne (Cronin 84).
Salzburg: Gustafsson; Dudic, Schwegler, Schiemer, Ulmer (Jezek 58), Augustinussen, Tchoyi, Svento, Ilic (Vladavic 62), Leitgeb (Nelisse 72), Janko.

Glentoran (0) 0

Maccabi Haifa (1) 4 *(Bello 9, 53, Masilela 62, Arbeitman 90)*   872

Glentoran: Morris; Neill, Leeman (Nixon 32), Ward, Taylor, Clarke, McCabe, Fordyce, Black (Gardiner 61), Waterworth (Halliday 67), Hamilton.
Maccabi Haifa: Davidovitch; Teixeira, Culma (Boccoli 46), Masilela, Keinan, Meshumar, Golasa (Ghadir 57), Kayal, Rafaelov, Dvalishvili, Bello (Arbeitman 64).

THIRD QUALIFYING ROUND FIRST LEG

Aktobe	(0) 0	Maccabi Haifa	(0) 0
Anderlecht	(3) 5	Sivas	(0) 0
Baku	(0) 0	Levski	(0) 0
Sparta Prague	(2) 3	Panathinaikos	(0) 1
Apoel	(0) 2	Partizan Belgrade	(0) 0
Celtic	(0) 0	Dynamo Moscow	(1) 1
FC Copenhagen	(2) 3	Stabaek	(0) 1
Levadia	(0) 0	Debrecen	(0) 1
Salzburg	(1) 1	Dinamo Zagreb	(0) 1
Shakhtar Donetsk	(0) 2	Timisoara	(1) 2
Sheriff	(0) 0	Slavia Prague	(0) 0

Slovan Bratislava	(0) 0	Olympiakos	(2) 2
Sporting Lisbon	(0) 0	Twente	(0) 0
Ventspils	(0) 1	BATE Borisov	(0) 0
Zurich	(2) 2	Maribor	(2) 3

Wednesday, 29 July 2009

Celtic (0) 0

Dynamo Moscow (1) 1 *(Kokorin 7)*   54,184

Celtic: Boruc; Hinkel, Naylor, Caldwell, Loovens, N'Guemo, Maloney, Donati (Fox 67), McDonald (Killen 61), Fortune (Samaras 60), McGeady.
Dynamo Moscow: Gabulov; Kowalczyk, Fernandez, Granat, Kolodin, Kombarov K, Kombarov D, Wilkshire, Svezhov, Kerzhakov, Kokorin (Smolov 74).

THIRD QUALIFYING ROUND SECOND LEG

Dinamo Zagreb	(0) 1	Salzburg	(1) 2
Maccabi Haifa	(2) 4	Aktobe	(3) 3
Panathinaikos	(1) 3	Sparta Prague	(0) 0
Sivas	(2) 3	Anderlecht	(1) 1
Twente	(1) 1	Sporting Lisbon	(0) 1
BATE Borisov	(1) 2	Ventspils	(1) 1
Debrecen	(0) 1	Levadia	(0) 0
Dynamo Moscow	(0) 0	Celtic	(1) 2
Levski	(0) 2	Baku	(0) 0
Maribor	(0) 0	Zurich	(2) 3
Olympiakos	(1) 2	Slovan Bratislava	(0) 0
Partizan Belgrade	(1) 1	Apoel	(0) 0
Slavia Prague	(1) 1	Sheriff	(0) 1
Stabaek	(0) 0	FC Copenhagen	(0) 0
Timisoara	(0) 0	Shakhtar Donetsk	(0) 0

Wednesday, 5 August 2009

Dynamo Moscow (0) 0

Celtic (1) 2 *(McDonald 44, Samaras 90)*   13,753

Dynamo Moscow: Gabulov; Kowalczyk, Fernandez (Ropotan 90), Granat, Kolodin, Kombarov K, Khokhlov, Kombarov D, Wilkshire, Svezhov (Kokorin 84), Kerzhakov.
Celtic: Boruc; Hinkel, Fox, Donati, Caldwell, Loovens, N'Guemo, Maloney, McDonald (Samaras 79), Fortune (Brown S 69), McGeady.

PLAY-OFF ROUND FIRST LEG

Celtic	(0) 0	Arsenal	(1) 2
FC Copenhagen	(0) 1	Apoel	(0) 0
Sheriff	(0) 0	Olympiakos	(0) 2
Sporting Lisbon	(0) 2	Fiorentina	(1) 2
Timisoara	(0) 0	Stuttgart	(2) 2
Levski	(0) 1	Debrecen	(1) 2
Lyon	(4) 5	Anderlecht	(0) 1
Panathinaikos	(0) 2	Atletico Madrid	(1) 3
Salzburg	(0) 1	Maccabi Haifa	(1) 2
Ventspils	(0) 0	Zurich	(1) 3

Tuesday, 18 August 2009

Celtic (0) 0

Arsenal (1) 2 *(Gallas 43, Caldwell 71 (og))*   58,165

Celtic: Boruc; Hinkel, Fox, Donati (McDonald 56), Caldwell, Loovens, N'Guemo (McCourt 76), Brown S, Samaras (Fortune 56), Maloney, McGeady.
Arsenal: Almunia; Sagna, Clichy, Denilson, Vermaelen, Gallas, Song Billong, Fabregas, Bendtner, Van Persie, Arshavin (Diaby 70).

PLAY-OFF ROUND SECOND LEG

Anderlecht	(0) 1	Lyon	(3) 3
Atletico Madrid	(1) 2	Panathinaikos	(0) 0
Debrecen	(2) 2	Levski	(0) 0
Maccabi Haifa	(1) 3	Salzburg	(0) 0
Zurich	(1) 2	Ventspils	(1) 1
Apoel	(3) 3	FC Copenhagen	(1) 1
Arsenal	(1) 3	Celtic	(0) 1
Fiorentina	(0) 1	Sporting Lisbon	(1) 1
Olympiakos	(0) 1	Sheriff	(0) 0
Stuttgart	(0) 0	Timisoara	(0) 0

Wednesday, 26 August 2009

Arsenal (1) 3 *(Eduardo 28 (pen), Eboue 53, Arshavin 74)*

Celtic (0) 1 *(Donati 90)*   59,962

Arsenal: Almunia; Sagna, Clichy, Denilson, Vermaelen, Gallas, Eboue (Wilshere 72), Diaby (Ramsey 61), Eduardo (Arshavin 72), Bendtner, Song Billong.
Celtic: Boruc; Hinkel, Fox, Donati, Caldwell (O'Dea 46), Loovens, Maloney (Flood 61), Brown S, McDonald, Fortune, McGeady (Naylor 61).

GROUP A

Juventus	(0) 1	Bordeaux	(0) 1
Maccabi Haifa	(0) 0	Bayern Munich	(0) 3
Bayern Munich	(0) 0	Juventus	(0) 0
Bordeaux	(0) 1	Maccabi Haifa	(0) 0
Bordeaux	(2) 2	Bayern Munich	(1) 1
Juventus	(0) 1	Maccabi Haifa	(0) 0
Bayern Munich	(0) 0	Bordeaux	(1) 2
Maccabi Haifa	(0) 0	Juventus	(1) 1
Bayern Munich	(0) 1	Maccabi Haifa	(0) 0
Bordeaux	(0) 2	Juventus	(0) 0
Juventus	(1) 1	Bayern Munich	(1) 4
Maccabi Haifa	(0) 0	Bordeaux	(1) 1

Group A Table	P	W	D	L	F	A	Pts
Bordeaux	6	5	1	0	9	2	16
Bayern Munich	6	3	1	2	9	5	10
Juventus	6	2	2	2	4	7	8
Maccabi Haifa	6	0	0	6	0	8	0

GROUP B

Besiktas	(0) 0	Manchester U	(0) 1
Wolfsburg	(2) 3	CSKA Moscow	(0) 1
CSKA Moscow	(1) 2	Besiktas	(0) 1
Manchester U	(0) 2	Wolfsburg	(0) 1
CSKA Moscow	(0) 0	Manchester U	(0) 1
Wolfsburg	(0) 0	Besiktas	(0) 0
Besiktas	(0) 0	Wolfsburg	(1) 3
Manchester U	(1) 3	CSKA Moscow	(2) 3
CSKA Moscow	(0) 2	Wolfsburg	(1) 1
Manchester U	(0) 0	Besiktas	(1) 1
Besiktas	(0) 1	CSKA Moscow	(1) 2
Wolfsburg	(0) 1	Manchester U	(1) 3

Tuesday, 15 September 2009

Besiktas (0) 0

Manchester U (0) 1 *(Scholes 77)* 26,448

Besiktas: Hakan; Ibrahim K, Ibrahim U, Ferrari, Sivok, Tabata (Tello 69), Dag, Serdar (Yusuf 59), Ernst, Mert, Holosko (Nihat 86).
Manchester U: Foster; Neville, Evra, Carrick (Berbatov 63), Evans J, Vidic, Valencia (Park 86), Scholes, Rooney (Owen 64), Anderson, Nani.

Wednesday, 30 September 2009

Manchester U (0) 2 *(Giggs 59, Carrick 78)*

Wolfsburg (0) 1 *(Dzeko 56)* 74,037

Manchester U: Kuszczak; O'Shea, Evra, Carrick, Ferdinand, Vidic, Valencia (Fletcher 82), Anderson, Owen (Berbatov 20), Rooney, Giggs.
Wolfsburg: Benaglio; Schafer, Ricardo Costa, Madlung, Riether, Josue, Misimovic, Hasebe (Ziani 73), Gentner, Dzeko, Grafite (Martins 82).

Wednesday, 21 October 2009

CSKA Moscow (0) 0

Manchester U (0) 1 *(Valencia 86)* 45,000

CSKA Moscow: Akinfeev; Semberas, Ignashevich, Berezutski A, Odiah, Berezutski V, Shchennikov (Mamaev 61), Dzagoev, Krasic, Rahimic (Daniel Carvalho 89), Necid (Piliev 73).
Manchester U: Van der Sar; Neville, Fabio (Carrick 88), O'Shea, Ferdinand (Brown 56), Vidic, Valencia, Anderson, Berbatov, Scholes (Owen 70), Nani.

Tuesday, 3 November 2009

Manchester U (1) 3 *(Owen 29, Scholes 84, Valencia 90)*

CSKA Moscow (2) 3 *(Dzagoev 25, Krasic 31, Berezutski V 47)* 73,718

Manchester U: Van der Sar; Neville, Fabio (Evra 59), Fletcher, Brown, Evans J, Valencia, Scholes, Macheda (Obertan 82), Owen, Nani (Rooney 58).
CSKA Moscow: Akinfeev; Semberas■, Ignashevich, Berezutski A, Berezutski V, Shchennikov, Dzagoev (Daniel Carvalho 72), Mamaev (Rahimic 70), Krasic, Aldonin, Necid (Piliev 85).

Wednesday, 25 November 2009

Manchester U (0) 0

Besiktas (1) 1 *(Tello 20)* 74,242

Manchester U: Foster; Neville, Rafael (Evra 74), Anderson, Brown, Vidic, Park (Owen 69), Welbeck, Obertan, Macheda, Gibson (Carrick 74).
Besiktas: Rustu; Ismail, Ibrahim K, Ibrahim U, Ibrahim T (Erhan 67), Ferrari, Fink, Tello (Ugur 75), Dag, Ernst, Bobo (Batuhan 84).

Tuesday, 8 December 2009

Wolfsburg (0) 1 *(Dzeko 56)*

Manchester U (1) 3 *(Owen 44, 83, 90)* 26,490

Wolfsburg: Benaglio; Schafer, Ricardo Costa, Riether, Barzagli, Josue, Misimovic, Hasebe (Ziani 72), Gentner, Dzeko, Grafite (Dejagah 72).
Manchester U: Kuszczak; Park, Evra, Carrick, Fletcher, Anderson, Gibson, Scholes, Welbeck (Valencia 74), Owen, Nani (Obertan 74).

Group B Table	P	W	D	L	F	A	Pts
Manchester U	6	4	1	1	10	6	13
CSKA Moscow	6	3	1	2	10	10	10
Wolfsburg	6	2	1	3	9	8	7
Besiktas	6	1	1	4	3	8	4

GROUP C

Marseille	(0) 1	AC Milan	(1) 2
Zurich	(0) 2	Real Madrid	(3) 5
AC Milan	(0) 0	Zurich	(1) 1
Real Madrid	(0) 3	Marseille	(0) 0
Real Madrid	(1) 2	AC Milan	(0) 3
Zurich	(0) 0	Marseille	(0) 1
AC Milan	(1) 1	Real Madrid	(1) 1
Marseille	(2) 6	Zurich	(1) 1
AC Milan	(1) 1	Marseille	(1) 1
Real Madrid	(1) 1	Zurich	(0) 0
Marseille	(1) 1	Real Madrid	(1) 3
Zurich	(1) 1	AC Milan	(0) 1

Group C Table	P	W	D	L	F	A	Pts
Real Madrid	6	4	1	1	15	7	13
AC Milan	6	2	3	1	8	7	9
Marseille	6	2	1	3	10	10	7
Zurich	6	1	1	4	5	14	4

GROUP D

Atletico Madrid	(0) 0	Apoel	(0) 0
Chelsea	(0) 1	Porto	(0) 0
Apoel	(0) 0	Chelsea	(1) 1
Porto	(0) 2	Atletico Madrid	(0) 0
Chelsea	(1) 4	Atletico Madrid	(0) 0
Porto	(1) 2	Apoel	(1) 1
Apoel	(0) 0	Porto	(0) 1
Atletico Madrid	(0) 2	Chelsea	(0) 2
Apoel	(1) 1	Atletico Madrid	(0) 1
Porto	(0) 0	Chelsea	(0) 1
Atletico Madrid	(0) 0	Porto	(2) 3
Chelsea	(2) 2	Apoel	(1) 2

Tuesday, 15 September 2009

Chelsea (0) 1 *(Anelka 48)*

Porto (0) 0   39,436

Chelsea: Cech; Ivanovic, Cole A, Essien, Terry, Ricardo Carvalho, Ballack, Lampard, Anelka, Kalou (Belletti 77), Malouda.
Porto: Helton; Bruno Alves, Fucile, Rolando, Raul Meireles, Guarin, Cristian Rodriguez (Varela 64), Mariano Gonzalez (Falcao 53), Alvaro Pereira, Fernando■, Hulk.

Wednesday, 30 September 2009

Apoel (0) 0

Chelsea (1) 1 *(Anelka 18)*   21,657

Apoel: Chiotis; Grncarov, Nuno Morais, Poursaitidis, Charalambides (Paulista 85), Helio Pinto, Kontis, Haxhi, Michael (Breska 80), Alexandrou (Kosowski 58), Mirosavl-jevic.
Chelsea: Cech; Belletti (Deco 68), Cole A, Ivanovic, Terry, Ricardo Carvalho, Essien, Lampard, Anelka, Kalou (Cole J 80), Malouda.

Wednesday, 21 October 2009

Chelsea (1) 4 *(Kalou 41, 52, Lampard 69, Perea 90 (og))*

Atletico Madrid (0) 0   39,000

Chelsea: Cech; Belletti, Cole A (Malouda 75), Essien, Terry, Ivanovic, Ballack, Lampard, Anelka (Sturridge 78), Kalou (Zhirkov 73), Deco.
Atletico Madrid: Sergio Asenjo; Antonio Lopez, Ujfalusi, Alvaro Dominguez, Perea, Raul Garcia, Paulo Assuncao (Jurado 54), Simao (Reyes 77), Cleber Santana (Maxi Rodriguez 66), Forlan, Aguero.

Tuesday, 3 November 2009

Atletico Madrid (0) 2 *(Aguero 66, 90)*

Chelsea (0) 2 *(Drogba 82, 88)*   36,284

Atletico Madrid: Sergio Asenjo; Antonio Lopez, Juanito, Perea, Ibanez, Paulo Assuncao, Simao (Jurado 83), Cleber Santana, Forlan, Sinama-Pongolle (Aguero 53), Reyes (Maxi Rodriguez 73).
Chelsea: Cech; Belletti, Cole A, Essien (Ballack 59), Terry, Alex, Cole J (Deco 70), Lampard, Drogba, Kalou (Anelka 70), Malouda.

Wednesday, 25 November 2009

Porto (0) 0

Chelsea (0) 1 *(Anelka 69)*   38,410

Porto: Beto; Bruno Alves, Rolando, Sapunaru (Farias 80), Raul Meireles, Belluschi (Guarin 72), Cristian Rodriguez, Alvaro Pereira, Fernando, Falcao, Varela (Hulk 59).
Chelsea: Cech; Ivanovic, Zhirkov, Mikel, Terry, Ricardo Carvalho, Ballack (Essien 68), Deco (Cole J 76), Anelka, Drogba, Malouda.

Tuesday, 8 December 2009

Chelsea (2) 2 *(Essien 19, Drogba 26)*

Apoel (1) 2 *(Zewlakow 6, Mirosavljevic 87)*   40,917

Chelsea: Turnbull; Belletti, Zhirkov, Mikel, Terry, Ricardo Carvalho, Essien (Lampard 27), Cole J, Kakuta (Borini 73), Drogba, Malouda.
Apoel: Chiotis; Paulo Jorge, Nuno Morais, Poursaitidis, Charalambides, Kosowski (Mirosavljevic 71), Broerse, Helio Pinto, Haxhi (Elia 34), Michael, Zewlakow (Breska 83).

Group D Table	P	W	D	L	F	A	Pts
Chelsea	6	4	2	0	11	4	14
Porto	6	4	0	2	8	3	12
Atletico Madrid	6	0	3	3	3	12	3
Apoel	6	0	3	3	4	7	3

GROUP E

Liverpool	(1) 1	Debrecen	(0) 0
Lyon	(0) 1	Fiorentina	(0) 0
Debrecen	(0) 0	Lyon	(3) 4
Fiorentina	(2) 2	Liverpool	(0) 0
Debrecen	(2) 3	Fiorentina	(4) 4
Liverpool	(1) 1	Lyon	(0) 2
Fiorentina	(1) 5	Debrecen	(1) 2
Lyon	(0) 1	Liverpool	(0) 1
Debrecen	(0) 0	Liverpool	(1) 1
Fiorentina	(1) 1	Lyon	(0) 0
Liverpool	(1) 1	Fiorentina	(0) 2
Lyon	(2) 4	Debrecen	(0) 0

Wednesday, 16 September 2009

Liverpool (1) 1 *(Kuyt 45)*

Debrecen (0) 0   41,591

Liverpool: Reina; Johnson, Insua, Lucas, Carragher, Skrtel, Benayoun (Mascherano 88), Gerrard, Torres, Kuyt (Fabio Aurelio 90), Riera (Babel 80).
Debrecen: Poleksic; Bodnar, Komlosi, Fodor, Leandro, Ramos (Laczko 67), Meszaros, Kiss, Szakaly (Feczesin 78), Czvitkovics, Coulibaly.

Tuesday, 29 September 2009

Fiorentina (2) 2 *(Jovetic 28, 37)*

Liverpool (0) 0   33,426

Fiorentina: Frey; Dainelli, Gamberini, Vargas (Jorgensen 75), Comotto, Zanetti, Montolivo, Gobbi, Marchionni (De Silvestri 90), Jovetic, Mutu (Donadel 82).
Liverpool: Reina; Johnson, Inusa (Babel 72), Fabio Aurelio, Carragher, Skrtel, Benayoun, Gerrard, Torres, Kuyt (Voronin 80), Lucas.

Tuesday, 20 October 2009

Liverpool (1) 1 *(Benayoun 41)*

Lyon (0) 2 *(Gonalons 72, Delgado 90)*   41,562

Liverpool: Reina; Agger, Insua, Mascherano, Carragher, Kelly (Skrtel 74), Benayoun (Voronin 85), Gerrard (Fabio Aurelio 25), N'Gog, Kuyt, Lucas.
Lyon: Lloris; Cris (Gonalons 43), Reveillere, Cissokho, Kallstrom, Pjanic, Ederson (Gomis 61), Makoun, Toulalan, Lisandro Lopez (Delgado 86), Govou.

Wednesday, 4 November 2009

Lyon (0) 1 *(Lisandro Lopez 90)*

Liverpool (0) 1 *(Babel 83)*   39,180

Lyon: Lloris; Cris, Reveillere (Gassama 18), Cissokho, Kallstrom, Bastos, Pjanic (Ederson 40), Makoun, Toulalan, Lisandro Lopez, Gomis (Govou 73).
Liverpool: Reina; Kyrgiakos, Insua, Mascherano, Carragher, Agger, Benayoun, Lucas, Torres (N'Gog 87), Voronin (Babel 67), Kuyt.

Tuesday, 24 November 2009

Debrecen (0) 0

Liverpool (1) 1 *(N'Gog 4)*   41,500

Debrecen: Poleksic; Bodnar, Fodor (Dombi 78), Mijadinoski, Szelesi, Meszaros, Kiss, Szakaly (Coulibaly 62), Czvitkovics, Laczko, Rudolf.
Liverpool: Reina; Johnson, Insua, Agger, Carragher, Fabio Aurelio (Dossena 89), Mascherano, Gerrard (Aquilani 90), N'Gog (Benayoun 77), Kuyt, Lucas.

Wednesday, 9 December 2009

Liverpool (1) 1 *(Benayoun 43)*

Fiorentina (0) 2 *(Jorgensen 63, Gilardino 90)*   40,863

Liverpool: Diego; Dossena, Insua, Darby, Agger, Skrtel, Benayoun, Gerrard, Aquilani (Pacheco 76), Kuyt (Torres 65), Mascherano (Fabio Aurelio 86).
Fiorentina: Frey; Kroldrup, Natali, Pasqual, Comotto, De Silvestri (Castillo 83), Donadel, Montolivo, Jorgensen (Marchionni 71), Santana (Vargas 71), Gilardino.

Group E Table	P	W	D	L	F	A	Pts
Fiorentina	6	5	0	1	14	7	15
Lyon	6	4	1	1	12	3	13
Liverpool	6	2	1	3	5	7	7
Debrecen	6	0	0	6	5	19	0

GROUP F

Dynamo Kiev	(0) 3	Rubin	(1) 1
Internazionale	(0) 0	Barcelona	(0) 0
Barcelona	(1) 2	Dynamo Kiev	(0) 0
Rubin	(1) 1	Internazionale	(1) 1
Barcelona	(0) 1	Rubin	(1) 2
Internazionale	(1) 2	Dynamo Kiev	(2) 2
Dynamo Kiev	(1) 1	Internazionale	(0) 2
Rubin	(0) 0	Barcelona	(0) 0
Barcelona	(2) 2	Internazionale	(0) 0
Rubin	(0) 0	Dynamo Kiev	(0) 0
Dynamo Kiev	(1) 1	Barcelona	(1) 2
Internazionale	(1) 2	Rubin	(0) 0

Group F Table	P	W	D	L	F	A	Pts
Barcelona	6	3	2	1	7	3	11
Internazionale	6	2	3	1	7	6	9
Rubin	6	1	3	2	4	7	6
Dynamo Kiev	6	1	2	3	7	9	5

GROUP G

Sevilla	(1) 2	Unirea	(0) 0
Stuttgart	(1) 1	Rangers	(0) 1
Rangers	(0) 1	Sevilla	(0) 4
Unirea	(0) 1	Stuttgart	(1) 1
Rangers	(1) 1	Unirea	(1) 4
Stuttgart	(0) 1	Sevilla	(1) 3
Sevilla	(1) 1	Stuttgart	(0) 1
Unirea	(0) 1	Rangers	(0) 1
Rangers	(0) 0	Stuttgart	(1) 2
Unirea	(1) 1	Sevilla	(0) 0
Sevilla	(1) 1	Rangers	(0) 0
Stuttgart	(3) 3	Unirea	(0) 1

Wednesday, 16 September 2009

Stuttgart (1) 1 *(Pogrebnyak 18)*

Rangers (0) 1 *(Bougherra 77)* 39,000

Stuttgart: Lehmann; Tasci, Boka, Delpierre, Trasch, Hitzlsperger, Hilbert, Hleb (Gebhart 67), Khedira, Cacau (Schieber 88), Pogrebnyak.
Rangers: McGregor; Whittaker, Papac, Thomson, Bougherra, McCulloch, Pedro Mendes, Davis, Miller (Novo 90), Rothen, Naismith.

Tuesday, 29 September 2009

Rangers (0) 1 *(Novo 88)*

Sevilla (0) 4 *(Konko 50, Adriano 64, Luis Fabiano 72, Kanoute 74)* 40,572

Rangers: McGregor; Whittaker, Papac, Thomson, Weir, Bougherra, Pedro Mendes, Davis, McCulloch (Boyd 73), Naismith, Rothen (Novo 73).
Sevilla: Palop; Squillaci, Escude, Fernando Navarro, Lolo, Adriano (Diego Capel 66), Jesus Navas, Zokora, Konko, Luis Fabiano (Romaric 79), Kanoute (Negredo 75).

Tuesday, 20 October 2009

Rangers (1) 1 *(Ricardo Vilana 2 (og))*

Unirea (1) 4 *(Bilasco 32, Lafferty 49 (og), McCulloch 59 (og), Brandan 65)* 39,476

Rangers: McGregor; Whittaker, Papac, Thomson, Weir, Pedro Mendes (Lafferty 46), Davis, McCulloch, Naismith, Miller, Rothen (Novo 67).
Unirea: Tudor; Galamaz, Nicu (Onofras 19), Brandan, Bruno Fernandes, Maftei, Ricardo Vilana, Balan (Frunza 75), Apostol, Bilasco, Varga (Paduretu 89).

Wednesday, 4 November 2009

Unirea (0) 1 *(Onofras 88)*

Rangers (0) 1 *(McCulloch 79)*   9923

Unirea: Arlauskis; Galamaz, Brandan, Bordeanu, Maftei, Ricardo Vilana (Paduretu 81), Balan (Onofras 28), Frunza, Apostol, Bilasco, Varga (Semedo 81).
Rangers: McGregor; Whittaker, Papac, Thomson (Fleck 85), Weir, Wilson, Davis, McCulloch, Lafferty, Miller (Novo 82), Naismith.

Tuesday, 24 November 2009

Rangers (0) 0

Stuttgart (1) 2 *(Rudy 16, Kuzmanovic 59)*   41,468

Rangers: McGregor; Whittaker, Papac, McCulloch, Weir, Wilson, Davis, Thomson (Fleck 76), Boyd, Miller (Novo 68), Lafferty (Beasley 85).
Stuttgart: Lehmann; Osorio, Niedermeier, Boka, Delpierre, Trasch, Rudy (Gebhart 90), Hleb, Kuzmanovic (Hitzlsperger 75), Cacau (Schieber 83), Pogrebnyak.

Wednesday, 9 December 2009

Sevilla (1) 1 *(Kanoute 8 (pen))*

Rangers (0) 0   31,560

Sevilla: Palop; Dragutinovic, Fernando Navarro, Konko, Cala, Jesus Navas (Kone 81), Zokora, Renato, Diego Capel, Romaric (Duscher 74), Kanoute (Negredo 60).
Rangers: McGregor; Whittaker, Papac, Thomson, Weir, Bougherra, Davis, Smith (Fleck 84), Beasley (Lafferty 46), Miller (Novo 46), McCulloch.

Group G Table	P	W	D	L	F	A	Pts
Sevilla	6	4	1	1	11	4	13
Stuttgart	6	2	3	1	9	7	9
Unirea	6	2	2	2	8	8	8
Rangers	6	0	2	4	4	13	2

GROUP H

Olympiakos	(0) 1	AZ	(0) 0
Standard Liege	(2) 2	Arsenal	(1) 3
Arsenal	(0) 2	Olympiakos	(0) 0
AZ	(0) 1	Standard Liege	(0) 1
AZ	(0) 1	Arsenal	(1) 1
Olympiakos	(1) 2	Standard Liege	(1) 1
Arsenal	(2) 4	AZ	(0) 1
Standard Liege	(1) 2	Olympiakos	(0) 0
Arsenal	(2) 2	Standard Liege	(0) 0
AZ	(0) 0	Olympiakos	(0) 0
Olympiakos	(0) 1	Arsenal	(0) 0
Standard Liege	(0) 1	AZ	(1) 1

Wednesday, 16 September 2009

Standard Liege (2) 2 *(Mangala 2, Jovanovic 5 (pen))*

Arsenal (1) 3 *(Bendtner 45, Vermaelen 78, Eduardo 81)*   23,022

Standard Liege: Bolat; Ricardo Rocha, Camozzato, Sarr, Dalmat (Goreux 80), Mangala, Witsel (Traore 84), Carcela-Gonzalez, Mbokani, De Camargo, Jovanovic (Nicaise 59).
Arsenal: Mannone; Eboue (Sagna 78), Clichy, Song Billong, Vermaelen, Gallas, Diaby, Fabregas, Eduardo (Wilshere 86), Bendtner, Rosicky (Ramsey 70).

Tuesday, 29 September 2009

Arsenal (0) 2 *(Van Persie 78, Arshavin 86)*

Olympiakos (0) 0   59,884

Arsenal: Mannone; Eboue, Clichy, Song Billong, Vermaelen, Gallas, Diaby (Vela 77), Fabregas, Arshavin, Van Persie (Ramsey 85), Rosicky (Eduardo 66).
Olympiakos: Nikopolidis; Mellberg, Zewlakow, Raul Bravo, Leonardo (Oscar 83), Torosidis, Dudu Cearense, Papadopoulos A, Ledesma (Mitroglou 79), Diogo, Zairi (Stoltidis 46).

Tuesday, 20 October 2009

AZ (0) 1 *(Mendes da Silva 90)*

Arsenal (1) 1 *(Fabregas 35)*   16,666

AZ: Romero; Jaliens, Moreno, Moisander (Wernbloom 85), Mendes da Silva, Schaars, Martens (Lens 69), Poulsen, Holman (Pelle 73), El Hamdaoui, Dembele.
Arsenal: Mannone; Sagna, Clichy, Song Billong, Vermaelen, Gallas, Eboue (Ramsey 83), Fabregas, Arshavin, Van Persie (Vela 74), Diaby.

Wednesday, 4 November 2009

Arsenal (2) 4 *(Fabregas 25, 52, Nasri 43, Diaby 72)*

AZ (0) 1 *(Lens 82)*   59,345

Arsenal: Almunia; Eboue, Gibbs, Song Billong, Vermaelen, Gallas, Diaby, Fabregas (Ramsey 67), Arshavin (Rosicky 75), Van Persie (Eduardo 67), Nasri.
AZ: Romero; Jaliens, Moreno, Moisander, Mendes da Silva (Wernbloom 70), Schaars, Martens, Poulsen (Pocognoli 64), Holman, Dembele (Lens 58), Pelle.

Tuesday, 24 November 2009

Arsenal (2) 2 *(Nasri 35, Denilson 45)*

Standard Liege (0) 0   59,941

Arsenal: Almunia; Eboue, Gibbs, Denilson (Rosicky 67), Vermaelen, Gallas (Silvestre 46), Song Billong, Fabregas, Vela, Arshavin, Nasri (Walcott 60).
Standard Liege: Bolat; Goreux, Felipe, Mulemo, Camozzato, Sarr, Dalmat (Traore 64), Mangala, Witsel, Carcela-Gonzalez■, Mbokani (Cyriac 68).

Wednesday, 9 December 2009

Olympiakos (0) 1 *(Leonardo 47)*

Arsenal (0) 0   30,277

Olympiakos: Nikopolidis; Mellberg, Raul Bravo, Leonardo, Galitsios, Galletti, Oscar (Pantos 90), Dudu Cearense (Domi 85), Papadopoulos A, Maresca, Mitroglou.
Arsenal: Fabianski; Gilbert, Cruise, Song Billong, Bartley, Silvestre, Ramsey, Merida, Vela, Walcott, Wilshere (Sunu 75).

Group H Table	P	W	D	L	F	A	Pts
Arsenal	6	4	1	1	12	5	13
Olympiakos	6	3	1	2	4	5	10
Standard Liege	6	1	2	3	7	9	5
AZ	6	0	4	2	4	8	4

KNOCK-OUT ROUND FIRST LEG

AC Milan	(1) 2	Manchester U	(1) 3
Lyon	(0) 1	Real Madrid	(0) 0
Bayern Munich	(1) 2	Fiorentina	(0) 1
Porto	(1) 2	Arsenal	(1) 1
Olympiakos	(0) 0	Bordeaux	(1) 1
Stuttgart	(1) 1	Barcelona	(0) 1
CSKA Moscow	(0) 1	Sevilla	(1) 1
Internazionale	(1) 2	Chelsea	(0) 1

Tuesday, 16 February 2010

AC Milan (1) 2 *(Ronaldinho 3, Seedorf 85)*

Manchester U (1) 3 *(Scholes 36, Rooney 66, 74)*   78,587

AC Milan: Dida; Nesta, Bonera, Thiago Silva, Pirlo, Ambrosini, Beckham (Seedorf 72), Antonini (Favalli 38), Ronaldinho, Pato, Huntelaar (Inzaghi 77).
Manchester U: Van der Sar; Rafael (Brown), Evra, Carrick■, Ferdinand, Evans J, Park, Scholes, Fletcher, Rooney, Nani (Valencia 65).

Wednesday, 17 February 2010

Porto (1) 2 *(Varela 11, Falcao 51)*

Arsenal (1) 1 *(Campbell 18)*   45,600

Porto: Helton; Bruno Alves, Fucile, Rolando, Raul Meireles (Tomas Costa 68), Alvaro Pereira, Fernando, Ruben Micael (Belluschi 85), Falcao, Hulk (Mariano Gonzalez 81), Varela.
Arsenal: Fabianski; Sagna, Clichy, Denilson, Vermaelen, Campbell, Rosicky (Walcott 68), Fabregas, Bendtner (Vela 83), Diaby, Nasri (Eboue 88).

Wednesday, 24 February 2010

Internazionale (1) 2 *(Milito 3, Cambiasso 55)*

Chelsea (0) 1 *(Kalou 51)*   78,971

Internazionale: Julio Cesar; Zanetti, Lucio, Maicon, Samuel, Stankovic (Ali Muntari 84), Thiago Motta (Balotelli 58), Sneijder, Cambiasso, Eto'o (Pandev 68), Milito.
Chelsea: Cech (Hilario 61); Ivanovic, Malouda, Mikel, Terry, Ricardo Carvalho, Ballack, Lampard, Anelka, Drogba, Kalou (Sturridge 78).

KNOCK-OUT ROUND SECOND LEG

Arsenal	(2) 5	Porto	(0) 0
Fiorentina	(1) 3	Bayern Munich	(0) 2
Manchester U	(1) 4	AC Milan	(0) 0
Real Madrid	(1) 1	Lyon	(0) 1
Chelsea	(0) 0	Internazionale	(0) 1
Sevilla	(1) 1	CSKA Moscow	(1) 2
Barcelona	(2) 4	Stuttgart	(0) 0
Bordeaux	(1) 2	Olympiakos	(0) 1

Tuesday, 9 March 2010

Arsenal (2) 5 *(Bendtner 9, 25, 90 (pen), Nasri 63, Eboue 66)*

Porto (0) 0   59,661

Arsenal: Almunia; Sagna, Clichy, Song Billong, Vermaelen, Campbell, Diaby, Rosicky (Eboue 57), Arshavin (Walcott 76), Bendtner, Nasri (Denilson 73).
Porto: Helton; Bruno Alves, Fucile, Rolando, Nuno Andre (Cristian Rodriguez 46), Raul Meireles, Alvaro Pereira, Ruben Micael (Guarin 76), Falcao, Hulk, Varela (Mariano Gonzalez 76).

Wednesday, 10 March 2010

Manchester U (1) 4 *(Rooney 13, 46, Park 60, Fletcher 88)*

AC Milan (0) 0   74,595

Manchester U: Van der Sar; Neville (Rafael 66), Evra, Fletcher, Ferdinand, Vidic, Valencia, Scholes (Gibson 73), Rooney (Berbatov 66), Park, Nani.
AC Milan: Abbiati; Jankulovski, Bonera (Seedorf 46), Thiago Silva, Flamini, Abate (Beckham 64), Pirlo, Ambrosini, Ronaldinho, Huntelaar, Borriello (Inzaghi 69).

Tuesday, 16 March 2010

Chelsea (0) 0

Internazionale (0) 1 *(Eto'o 78)*   38,107

Chelsea: Turnbull; Ivanovic, Zhirkov (Kalou 73), Mikel, Terry, Alex, Ballack (Cole J 63), Lampard, Anelka, Drogba■, Malouda.
Internazionale: Julio Cesar; Zanetti, Lucio, Maicon, Samuel, Thiago Motta (Materazzi 90), Sneijder (Mariga 84), Cambiasso, Eto'o, Milito, Pandev (Stankovic 75).

QUARTER-FINALS FIRST LEG

Bayern Munich	(0) 2	Manchester U	(1) 1
Lyon	(2) 3	Bordeaux	(1) 1
Arsenal	(0) 2	Barcelona	(0) 2
Internazionale	(0) 1	CSKA Moscow	(0) 0

Tuesday, 30 March 2010

Bayern Munich (0) 2 *(Ribery 76, Olic 90)*

Manchester U (1) 1 *(Rooney 2)*   66,000

Bayern Munich: Butt; Van Buyten, Demichelis, Lahm, Badstuber, Ribery, Hamit Altintop (Klose 86), Van Bommel, Pranjic (Tymoshchuk 89), Muller (Gomez 73), Olic.
Manchester U: Van der Sar; Neville, Evra, Carrick (Valencia 70), Ferdinand, Vidic, Park (Berbatov 70), Scholes, Fletcher, Rooney, Nani (Giggs 82).

Wednesday, 31 March 2010

Arsenal (0) 2 *(Walcott 69, Fabregas 85 (pen))*

Barcelona (0) 2 *(Ibrahimovic 46, 59)*   59,572

Arsenal: Almunia; Sagna (Walcott 66), Clichy, Song Billong, Vermaelen, Gallas (Denilson 46), Diaby, Fabregas, Bendtner, Arshavin (Eboue 27), Nasri.
Barcelona: Victor Valdes; Dani Alves, Pique, Puyol■, Maxwell, Xavi, Keita, Busquets, Ibrahimovic (Henry 77), Messi (Milito 86), Pedro.

QUARTER-FINALS SECOND LEG

Barcelona	(3) 4	Arsenal	(1) 1
CSKA Moscow	(0) 0	Internazionale	(1) 1
Bordeaux	(1) 1	Lyon	(0) 0
Manchester U	(3) 3	Bayern Munich	(1) 2

Tuesday, 6 April 2010

Barcelona (3) 4 *(Messi 21, 37, 42, 88)*

Arsenal (1) 1 *(Bendtner 18)*   93,330

Barcelona: Victor Valdes; Dani Alves, Marquez, Milito, Abidal (Maxwell 53), Xavi, Keita, Busquets, Messi, Bojan (Yaya Toure 56), Pedro (Iniesta 85).
Arsenal: Almunia; Sagna, Clichy, Denilson, Vermaelen, Silvestre (Eboue 63), Walcott, Diaby, Bendtner, Rosicky (Eduardo 73), Nasri.

Wednesday, 7 April 2010

Manchester U (3) 3 *(Gibson 3, Nani 7, 41)*

Bayern Munich (1) 2 *(Olic 43, Robben 74)* 74,482

Manchester U: Van der Sar; Rafael■, Evra, Carrick (Berbatov 80), Ferdinand, Vidic, Valencia, Fletcher, Gibson (Giggs 81), Rooney (O'Shea 55), Nani.

Bayern Munich: Butt; Van Buyten, Demichelis, Lahm, Badstuber, Ribery, Van Bommel, Muller (Gomez 46), Schweinsteiger, Robben (Hamit Altintop 76), Olic (Pranjic 84).

SEMI-FINALS FIRST LEG

Internazionale	(1) 3	Barcelona	(1) 1
Bayern Munich	(0) 1	Lyon	(0) 0

SEMI-FINALS SECOND LEG

Lyon	(0) 0	Bayern Munich	(1) 3
Barcelona	(0) 1	Internazionale	(0) 0

UEFA CHAMPIONS LEAGUE FINAL 2010

Saturday, 22 May 2010

Bayern Munich (0) 0   Internazionale (1) 2 *(Milito 35, 70)*

(in Madrid, 74,954)

Bayern Munich: Butt; Van Buyten, Demichelis, Lahm, Badstuber, Hamit Altintop (Klose 63), Van Bommel, Muller, Schweinsteiger, Robben, Olic (Gomez 74).

Internazionale: Julio Cesar; Zanetti, Lucio, Maicon, Samuel, Chivu (Stankovic 68), Sneijder, Cambiasso, Eto'o, Milito (Materazzi 90), Pandev (Ali Muntari 79).

Referee: H. Webb (England).

Did You Know?

Sir Alex Ferguson has a unique record in the Champions League. In 2009–10 he led Manchester United to their 15th season in it. England manager Fabio Capello was in charge of AC Milan for three seasons, two each with Roma and Juventus and once at the head of Real Madrid. However, Arsene Wenger at Arsenal made it his 12th season with the Gunners in the Champions League having originally been in charge of Monaco in 1993–94. Jose Mourinho as manager of the 2009–10 winners Internazionale had been in his second season with the Italian club after four years at Chelsea and two earlier on at Porto. Mourinho then moved to take on the challenge of Real Madrid the first European Cup winners in 1956.

UEFA CHAMPIONS LEAGUE 2010–2011

PARTICIPATING CLUBS
This list is provisional and subject to final confirmation from UEFA.

GROUP STAGE
FC Internazionale Milano (ITA)
FC Barcelona (ESP)
Manchester United FC (ENG)
Chelsea FC (ENG)
Arsenal FC (ENG)
FC Bayern München (GER)
AC Milan (ITA)
Olympique Lyonnais (FRA)
Real Madrid CF (ITA)
AS Roma (ITA)
FC Shakhtar Donetsk (UKR)
SL Benfica (POR)
Valencia CF (ESP)
Olympique de Marseille (FRA)
Panathinaikos FC (GRE)
Rangers FC (SCO)
FC Schalke 04 (GER)
FC Spartak Moskva (RUS)
FC Twente (NED)
FC Rubin Kazan (RUS)
CFR 1907 Cluj (ROU)
Bursaspor (TUR)

PLAY-OFF – NON-CHAMPIONS
Sevilla FC (ESP)
Werder Bremen (GER)
Tottenham Hotspur FC (ENG)
UC Sampdoria (ITA)
AJ Auxerre (FRA)

THIRD QUALIFYING ROUND – NON-CHAMPIONS
FC Zenit St. Petersburg (RUS)
AFC Ajax (NED)
Fenerbahçe SK (TUR)
FC Dynamo Kyiv (UKR)
SC Braga (POR)
Celtic FC (SCO)
FC Unirea Urziceni (ROU)
PAOK FC (GRE)
BSC Young Boys (SUI)
KAA Gent (BEL)

THIRD QUALIFYING ROUND – CHAMPIONS
FC Basel 1893 (SUI)
RSC Anderlecht (BEL)
FC København (DEN)

SECOND QUALIFYING ROUND
Hapoel Tel-Aviv FC (ISR)
AC Sparta Praha (CZE)
Rosenborg BK (NOR)
FC Salzburg (AUT)
PFC Litex Lovech (BUL)
NK Dinamo Zagreb (CRO)
FK Partizan (SRB)
FC BATE Borisov (BLR)
KKS Lech Poznań (POL)
MŠK Žilina (SVK)
FC Sheriff (MDA)
Debreceni VSC (HUN)
AC Omonia (CYP)
AIK Solna (SWE)
Bohemians FC (IRL)
FK Ekranas (LTU)
HJK Helsinki (FIN)
FK Aktobe (KAZ)
FC Levadia Tallinn (EST)
SK Liepājas Metalurgs (LVA)
FH Hafnarfjördur (ISL)
FK Željezničar (BIH)
FC Olimpi Rustavi (GEO)
FC Pyunik (ARM)
FC Koper (SVN)
FC Inter Bakı (AZE)
FK Renova (MKD)
KS Dinamo Tirana (ALB)
HB Tórshavn (FRO)
The New Saints FC (WAL)
Linfield FC (NIR)
AS Jeunesse Esch (LUX)

FIRST QUALIFYING ROUND
FC Santa Coloma (AND)
SP Tre Fiori (SMR)
Birkirkara FC (MLT)
FK Rudar Pljevlja (MNE)

UEFA EUROPA LEAGUE 2009–2010

■ *Denotes player sent off.* * *Winner after extra time.*

FIRST QUALIFYING ROUND FIRST LEG

Anorthosis	(2) 5	Kaerjeng	(0) 0
Banants	(0) 0	Siroki	(1) 2
Buducnost	(0) 0	Polonia	(0) 2
Dinaburg	(0) 2	Kalju	(0) 1
Dynamo Minsk	(0) 2	Renova	(1) 1
Fram	(1) 2	The New Saints	(1) 1
Grevenmacher	(0) 0	Vetra	(2) 3
Haladas	(0) 1	Irtysh	(0) 0
Helsingborg	(0) 3	Mika	(0) 1
Lahti	(2) 4	Dinamo Tirana	(1) 1
Lisburn Distillery	(0) 1	Zestafoni	(4) 5
Motherwell	(0) 0	Llanelli	(1) 1
NSI Runavik	(0) 0	Rosenborg	(1) 3
Olimpi	(1) 2	B36	(0) 0
Randers	(1) 4	Linfield	(0) 0
Simurq	(0) 0	Bnei Yehuda	(0) 1
Slaven	(1) 1	Birkirkara	(0) 0
Sligo Rovers	(0) 1	Vllaznia	(0) 2
Spartak Trnava	(2) 2	Inter Baku	(0) 1
Sutjeska	(0) 1	MTZ-Ripo	(0) 1
Trans	(0) 0	Rudar	(1) 3
Valletta	(1) 3	Keflavik	(0) 0
Zimbru	(0) 1	Okzhetpes	(0) 2

Thursday, 2 July 2009

Fram (1) 2 *(Tillen S 33 (pen), Juliusson 48)*

The New Saints (1) 1 *(Evans 24)* 592

Fram: Halldorsson; Hauksson, Tillen S, Fjoluson, McShane, Olason (Magnusson 87), Jonsson, Gudmundsson, Juliusson (Tillen J 70), Thorarinsson, Ormarsson (Bjornsson 70).
The New Saints: Harrison; Holmes T, Evans, Baker (McKenna 89), Holmes D (Marriott 83), Hogan, Ruscoe, Jones C, Murtagh (Darlington 73), Berkeley, Wood.

Lisburn Distillery (0) 1 *(Whelan 88)*

Zestafoni (4) 5 *(Gelashvili 11, 34, Grigalashvili 22, 38, Aphtsiarui 52)* 600

Lisburn Distillery: Murphy; McShane, Thompson S, Simpson, Callaghan, Melaugh, Gilmartin, Whelan, Shaw (Browne 56), Armour (Kingsberry 69), Thompson G (Corey 55).
Zestafoni: Mamaladze; Oniani, Todua, Khidesheli, Eliava, Daushvili, Dzaria (Benashvili 58), Aphtsiarui, Grigalashvili (Gorgiashvili 74), Gelashvili, Dvali (Kvakhvadze 88).

Motherwell (0) 0

Llanelli (1) 1 *(Jones S 28)* 4307

Motherwell: Fraser; Hammell, Reynolds, Craigan, Saunders, Lasley (Slane 46), Forbes, Sutton, Murphy, O'Brien (McHugh 74), McGarry.
Llanelli: Morris; Jones S, Corbisiero, Venables, Jarman (Thomas 16), Legg (Warlow 51), Phillips, Howard, Mumford, Jones C (Follows 65), Griffiths.

Randers (1) 4 *(Berg 36, Sane 47, Nygaard 80, Lorentzen 81)*

Linfield (0) 0   5114

Randers: Stuhr-Ellegaard; Ahmed, Addy, Fenger, Lorentzen, Pedersen S, Grahn (Beck-mann 73), Pedersen K (Damborg 82), Sane (Olsen 73), Berg, Nygaard.
Linfield: Blayney; Douglas, Bailie, Burns (Curran 69), Ervin, Lowry (Allen 62), O'Kane, Garrett, Mulgrew, Carvill, McAllister (McHugh 74).

Sligo Rovers (0) 1 *(Cretaro 89 (pen))*

Vllaznia (0) 2 *(Smajlaj 69, Keane 75 (og))*   2700

Sligo Rovers: Brush; Ventre, Keane, Holmes, Ryan, O'Grady, Feeney (Noctor 64), Cre-taro, Boco, Morrison, Cash (Doherty 73).
Vllaznia: Grima■; Mrvaljevic, Osja, Belisha, Hallaci, Beqiri, Smajlaj, Shtubina, Ksapi (Olsi 88), Nallbani, Sinani (Balaj 85).

FIRST QUALIFYING ROUND SECOND LEG

B36	(0) 0	Olimpi	(2) 2
Birkirkara	(0) 0	Slaven	(0) 0
Bnei Yehuda	(1) 3	Simurq	(0) 0
Dinamo Tirana	(1) 2	Lahti	(0) 0
Inter Baku	(1) 1	Spartak Trnava	(2) 3
Irtysh	(2) 2	Haladas	(1) 1
Kaerjeng	(0) 1	Anorthosis	(1) 2
Kalju	(0) 0	Dinaburg	(0) 0
Keflavik	(0) 2	Valletta	(1) 2
Linfield	(0) 0	Randers	(1) 3
Llanelli	(0) 0	Motherwell	(2) 3
Mika	(0) 1	Helsingborg	(0) 1
MTZ-Ripo	(0) 2	Sutjeska	(0) 1
(aet.)			
Okzhetpes	(0) 0	Zimbru	(2) 2
Polonia	(0) 0	Buducnost	(0) 1
Renova	(1) 1	Dynamo Minsk	(1) 1
Rosenborg	(1) 3	NSI Runavik	(1) 1
Rudar	(1) 3	Trans	(0) 1
Siroki	(0) 0	Banants	(0) 1
The New Saints	(1) 1	Fram	(1) 2
Vetra	(3) 3	Grevenmacher	(0) 0
Vllaznia	(1) 1	Sligo Rovers	(0) 1
Zestafoni	(4) 6	Lisburn Distillery	(0) 0

Thursday, 9 July 2009

Linfield (0) 0

Randers (1) 3 *(Olsen 21, Lorentzen 51, Berg 82)*   1000

Linfield: Blayney; Douglas, Bailie, Burns, Ervin, Lowry, O'Kane, Garrett, Mulgrew (Gault 67), Carvill (Allen 59), McAllister (Miskimmin 78).
Randers: Stuhr-Ellegaard; Olesen (Fischer 73), Da Cruz, Jepsen, Damborg, Fenger, Lorentzen, Beckmann (Byskov 77), Berg, Olsen, Nygaard (Konig 63).

Llanelli (0) 0

Motherwell (2) 3 *(Sutton 8, 25, Murphy 71)*   3025

Llanelli: Morris; Jones S (Jenkins 67), Corbisiero, Venables, Legg (Warlow 76), Phillips (Moses 80), Howard, Mumford, Thomas, Griffiths, Follows.
Motherwell: Fraser; Hammell, Reynolds, Craigan, Saunders (Page 78), Lasley, Forbes, Sutton (Archdeacon 76), O'Brien, McGarry (Murphy 69), Slane.

The New Saints (1) 1 *(Evans 11)*

Fram (1) 2 *(Ormarsson 16, Tillen S 66 (pen))*   933

The New Saints: Harrison; Marriott, Holmes T, Evans, Baker, Holmes D, Hogan, Ruscoe, Williams (Berkeley 74), Jones C (Sergeant 70), Darlington (Wood 70).
Fram: Halldorsson; Hauksson, Tillen S, Fjoluson, McShane, Olason, Jonsson (Olafsson 90), Gudmundsson, Juliusson (Tillen J 87), Thorarinsson, Ormarsson (Bjornsson 82).

Vllaznia (1) 1 *(Shtubina 43)*

Sligo Rovers (0) 1 *(Keane 87)*   5000

Vllaznia: Olsi; Mrvaljevic, Belisha, Hallaci, Beqiri (Basic 61), Smajlaj, Shtubina, Kasapi (Sykaj 90), Nallbani, Sinani■, Balaj (Nika 64).
Sligo Rovers: Brush; Holmes, Ventre, Keane, Feeney, Doherty (Morrison 66), Cretaro, Boco, Ryan, O'Grady■, Cash (Kelly 57).

Zestafoni (4) 6 *(Dvali 5, 39, 42, Gelashvili 44, Benashvili 86, 90)*

Lisburn Distillery (0) 0   3100

Zestafoni: Mamaladze; Lobjanidze, Oniani, Khidesheli, Eliava (Benashvili 46), Daushvili (Makaryan 46), Dzaria (Gorgiashvili 60), Aphtsiauri, Grigalashvili, Gelashvili, Dvali.
Lisburn Distillery: Murphy; McShane, Thompson S, Simpson, Callaghan, Melaugh, Gilmartin, Whelan, Kingsberry (Shaw 46), Browne (Corey 46), Armour (Thompson G 73).

SECOND QUALIFYING ROUND FIRST LEG

Crusaders	(0) 1	Rabotnicki	(0) 1
Sliema Wanderers	(0) 0	Maccabi Netanya	(0) 0
Aalborg	(0) 0	Slavija	(0) 0
Anorthosis	(2) 2	Petrovac	(0) 1
Basle	(1) 3	Santa Coloma	(0) 0
Bnei Yehuda	(2) 4	Dinaburg	(0) 0
Brondby	(0) 0	Flora	(0) 1
Cherno More	(1) 1	Iskra-Stal	(0) 0
Differdange	(0) 1	Rijeka	(0) 0
Dynamo Minsk	(0) 0	Tromso	(0) 0
Elfsborg	(0) 3	Szombathelyi	(0) 0
Falkirk	(0) 1	Vaduz	(0) 0
Flamurtari	(0) 1	Motherwell	(0) 0
Gorica	(1) 1	Lahti	(0) 0
Honka	(1) 2	Bangor City	(0) 0
Juvenes/Dogana	(0) 0	Polonia	(1) 1
KR Reykjavik	(0) 2	Larissa	(0) 0
Legia	(1) 3	Olimpi	(0) 0
Metalurg Donetsk	(2) 3	MTZ-Ripo	(0) 0
Metalurgs Liepajas	(1) 2	Dinamo Tbilisi	(0) 1
Milano	(0) 0	Slaven	(4) 4
NAC Breda	(1) 6	Gandzasar	(0) 0
Naftan	(1) 2	Gent	(0) 1
Omonia	(3) 4	HB Torshavn	(0) 0
Rapid Vienna	(1) 5	Vllaznia	(0) 0
Rosenborg	(0) 0	Karabakh	(0) 0
Rudar	(0) 0	Red Star Belgrade	(0) 1
Sarajevo	(1) 1	Spartak Trnava	(0) 0
Sevojno	(0) 0	Kaunas	(0) 0
Sigma Olomouc	(0) 1	Fram	(1) 1
Skonto Riga	(1) 1	Derry City	(1) 1
St Patrick's Ath	(1) 1	Valletta	(0) 1
Steaua	(0) 2	Ujpest	(0) 0

Sturm Graz	(2) 2	Siroki	(0) 1
Suduva	(0) 0	Randers	(1) 1
Tobol	(1) 1	Galatasaray	(0) 1
Vetra	(0) 0	HJK Helsinki	(1) 1
Zestafoni	(0) 1	Helsingborg	(0) 2
Zilina	(0) 2	Dacia	(0) 0
Zimbru	(0) 0	Pacos de Ferreira	(0) 0

Tuesday, 14 July 2009

Crusaders (0) 1 *(Rainey 90)*

Rabotnicki (0) 1 *(Bozinovski B 47)* 950

Crusaders: Keenan; McKeown, Magowan, Coates■, McBride, McCann, Doherty (Black 74), Donnelly, Morrow (Owens 63), Dickson, Rainey.
Rabotnicki: Naumovski■; Bojovic, Bozinovski V, Ristov, Sekulovski, Bozinovski B, Savic, Todorovski, Muarem (Carlos 70), Gligorov, Wandeir.

Thursday, 16 July 2009

Falkirk (0) 1 *(Flynn 50)*

Vaduz (0) 0 5763

Falkirk: Olejnik; Barr, Scobbie, Twaddle, McNamara, McLean, O'Brien, Arfield, Flynn (Mitchell 75), Finnigan (Robertson 77), McDonald (Sludden 89).
Vaduz: Jehle; Steil, Stuckmann (Sutter 84), Cerrone, Stegmayer, Bellon, Koitka (Franjic 79), Burgmeier, Noll, Colocci, Proschwitz.

Flamurtari (0) 1 *(Strati 66)*

Motherwell (0) 0 4012

Flamurtari: Mocka; Guga, Begaj, Veliu, Strati, Beqiri, Alviz, Mema (Galica 78), Ngjele (Beck 46), Zeqiri, Shehaj (Roshi 37).
Motherwell: Fraser; Hammell, Reynolds, Craigan, Saunders (Page 40), Lasley, Forbes (Murphy 75), Sutton, O'Brien, McGarry (Fitzpatrick 65), Slane.

Honka (1) 2 *(Perovuo 15, Schuller 74)*

Bangor City (0) 0 1668

Honka: Henriksson; Koskinen, Aalto, Koskimaa, Hakanpaa, Perovuo, Lepola (Vasara 46), Schuller, Vuorinen, Kokko (Puustinen 77), Savage (Otaru 89).
Bangor City: Smith; Johnston, Brewerton, Morley, Roberts, Hoy, Killackey, Limbert (Beattie 87), Stott, Sharp, Smyth (Edwards 77).

Skonto Riga (1) 1 *(Kozlovs 17)*

Derry City (1) 1 *(McManus 44)* 1950

Skonto Riga: Malins; Hscanovics, Laizans (Agafonovs 77), Juniors, Smirnovs, Golubevs, Gamezardashvili, Kozlovs, Fertovs, Semjonovs (Cauna 62), Tarasovs.
Derry City: Doherty; Hutton, Gray (McCallion 81), O'Brien, Delaney, Higgins, Martyn, McGlynn, Molloy, Farren (Stewart 87), McManus (Morrow 81).

St Patrick's Ath (1) 1 *(O'Brien 38)*

Valletta (0) 1 *(Agius G 65)* 2000

St Patrick's Ath: Rogers; Partridge, Harris, Stevens, Maher, Byrne, Cawley, Ryan B (Fitzpatrick 70), O'Connor, Guy, O'Brien.
Valletta: Hogg; Dimech, Bezzina, Scicluna, Briffa, Pace, Falzon (Sammit 77), Cruyff, Agius G, Den Ouden (Agius E 90), Priso.

SECOND QUALIFYING ROUND SECOND LEG

Bangor City	(0) 0	Honka	(1) 1
(at Wrexham.)			
Dacia	(0) 0	Zilina	(0) 1
Derry City	(0) 1	Skonto Riga	(0) 0
Dinaburg	(0) 0	Bnei Yehuda	(1) 1
Dinamo Tbilisi	(1) 3	Metalurgs Liepajas	(0) 1
Flora	(0) 1	Brondby	(3) 4
Fram	(0) 0	Sigma Olomouc	(0) 2
Galatasaray	(0) 2	Tobol	(0) 0
Gandzasar	(0) 0	NAC Breda	(2) 2
Gent	(0) 1	Naftan	(0) 0
Haladas	(0) 0	Elfsborg	(0) 0
HB Torshavn	(0) 1	Omonia	(1) 4
Helsingborg	(0) 2	Zestafoni	(2) 2
(aet.)			
HJK Helsinki	(1) 1	Vetra	(2) 3
Iskra-Stal	(0) 0	Cherno More	(1) 3
Karabakh	(1) 1	Rosenborg	(0) 0
Kaunas	(0) 1	Sevojno	(0) 1
Lahti	(0) 2	Gorica	(0) 0
Larissa	(1) 1	KR Reykjavik	(0) 1
Maccabi Netanya	(0) 3	Sliema Wanderers	(0) 0
Motherwell	(6) 8	Flamurtari	(0) 1
MTZ-Ripo	(1) 1	Metalurg Donetsk	(1) 2
Olimpi	(0) 0	Legia	(1) 1
Pacos de Ferreira	(0) 1	Zimbru	(0) 0
Petrovac	(1) 3	Anorthosis	(1) 1
(aet.)			
Polonia	(2) 4	Juvenes/Dogana	(0) 0
Rabotnicki	(2) 4	Crusaders	(0) 2
Randers	(1) 1	Suduva	(0) 1
Red Star Belgrade	(1) 4	Rudar	(0) 0
Rijeka	(2) 3	Differdange	(0) 0
Santa Coloma	(1) 1	Basle	(3) 4
Siroki	(0) 1	Sturm Graz	(1) 1
Slaven	(2) 8	Milano	(0) 2
Slavija	(1) 3	Aalborg	(0) 1
Spartak Trnava	(1) 1	Sarajevo	(0) 1
Tromso	(1) 4	Dynamo Minsk	(0) 1
Ujpest	(0) 1	Steaua	(0) 2
Vaduz	(1) 2	Falkirk	(0) 0
(aet.)			
Valletta	(0) 0	St Patrick's Ath	(0) 1
Vllaznia	(0) 0	Rapid Vienna	(0) 3

Thursday, 23 July 2009

Bangor City (0) 0

Honka (1) 1 *(Puustinen 39)*   602

Bangor City: Smith; Johnston, Brewerton (Williams 78), Morley, Roberts, Hoy, Kil-lackey, Limbert (Edwards 59), Stott, Sharp (Davies 60), Smyth.
Honka: Henriksson; Koskinen (Haarala 69), Aalto, Koskimaa, Hakanpaa, Perovuo, Schuller, Vuorinen (Kokko 77), Puustinen, Vasara, Savage (Otaru 61).
at Wrexham.

Derry City (0) 1 *(Deery 57)*

Skonto Riga (0) 0 2500

Derry City: Doherty; McCallion, Hutton, O'Brien, Delaney, McGlynn (Scullion 89), Deery, Molloy, Morrow (Higgins 50), Stewart (Farren 75), McManus.
Skonto Riga: Malins; Hscanovics, Juniors (Agafonovs 84), Smirnovs, Golubevs, Gamezardashvili, Kozlovs, Fertovs (Mingazovs 66), Tarasovs (Laizans 69), Cauna, Blanks.

Motherwell (6) 8 *(Murphy 16, 19, 34, Slane 25, Forbes 28 (pen), 50, Hutchinson 38, McHugh 72)*

Flamurtari (0) 1 *(Roshi 65)* 4641

Motherwell: Fraser; Reynolds, Craigan, Humphrey (McHugh 67), Jennings (Lasley 68), Forbes, Hutchinson, Sutton, Murphy, O'Brien, Slane (Page 77).
Flamurtari: Mocka; Sakaj, Guga, Begaj, Veliu, Strati, Beqiri (Roshi 38), Alviz, Mema (Galica 46), Ngjele (Shehaj 46), Zeqiri.

Rabotnicki (2) 4 *(Bozinovski B 20, Ze Carlos 35, 79, Petkovski 84)*

Crusaders (0) 2 *(Owens 69, Donnelly 90)* 1900

Rabotnicki: Bogatinov; Bojovic, Bozinovski V, Ristov, Sekulovski, Bozinovski B, Savic (Petkovski■ 67), Ze Carlos (Muarem 79), Todorovski, Gligorov, Wandeir (Carlos 84).
Crusaders: Keenan; McKeown, Black (Caddell 67), Magowan, Magee (Rainey 46), McBride, McCann, Doherty, Donnelly, Morrow (Owens 46), Dickson.

Vaduz (1) 2 *(Noll 24, Burgmeier 105)*

Falkirk (0) 0 1810

Vaduz: Jehle; Steil, Stuckmann, Cerrone, Stegmayer, Bellon, Koitka (Kempe 73), Burgmeier, Noll, Colocci (Bader 119), Proschwitz (Franjic 110).
Falkirk: Olejnik; Barr, Scobbie, Twaddle, McNamara, McLean, Mitchell (Sludden 106), O'Brien (Lynch 90), Arfield, Finnigan, McDonald (Flynn 59).
aet.

Valletta (0) 0

St Patrick's Ath (0) 1 *(O'Brien 80)* 1800

Valletta: Hogg; Grioli (Agius E 70), Dimech, Bezzina, Scicluna, Briffa, Pace, Falzon (Sammit 81), Cruyff, Agius G, Den Ouden.
St Patrick's Ath: Rogers; Partridge, Harris, Gavin, Stevens, Maher (Lynch 80), Byrne (Cawley 58), Ryan B (Ryan D■ 73), O'Connor, Guy, O'Brien.

THIRD QUALIFYING ROUND FIRST LEG

Bnei Yehuda	(0) 1	Pacos de Ferreira	(0) 0
Aberdeen	(1) 1	Sigma Olomouc	(1) 5
Athletic Bilbao	(0) 0	Young Boys	(1) 1
Braga	(0) 1	Elfsborg	(1) 2
Brondby	(0) 1	Legia	(1) 1
Club Brugge	(2) 3	Lahti	(1) 2
CSKA Sofia	(0) 1	Derry City	(0) 0
Dinamo Tbilisi	(1) 2	Red Star Belgrade	(0) 0
Fenerbahce	(3) 5	Honved	(0) 1
Fredrikstad	(0) 1	Lech	(3) 6
Helsingborg	(1) 2	Sarajevo	(1) 1
Honka	(0) 0	Karabakh	(0) 1
IFK Gothenburg	(1) 1	Hapoel Tel Aviv	(0) 3
KR Reykjavik	(2) 2	Basle	(0) 2
Maccabi Netanya	(1) 1	Galatasaray	(1) 4
Metalurg Donetsk	(1) 2	Interblock	(0) 0
Petrovac	(1) 1	Sturm Graz	(0) 2

Polonia	(0) 0	NAC Breda	(1) 1
PSV Eindhoven	(0) 1	Cherno More	(0) 0
Rabotnicki	(2) 3	Odense	(2) 4
Randers	(0) 0	Hamburg	(2) 4
Rapid Vienna	(1) 2	APOP	(0) 1
Rijeka	(0) 1	Metalist Kharkiv	(1) 2
Roma	(0) 3	Gent	(1) 1
Sevojno	(0) 0	Lille	(2) 2
Slavija	(0) 0	Kosice	(1) 2
St Patrick's Ath	(0) 1	Krylia	(0) 0
Steaua	(2) 3	Motherwell	(0) 0
Tromso	(0) 2	Slaven	(1) 1
Vaduz	(0) 0	Slovan Liberec	(1) 1
Valerenga	(1) 1	PAOK Salonika	(2) 2
Vaslui	(1) 2	Omonia	(0) 0
Vetra	(0) 0	Fulham	(1) 3
Vojvodina	(1) 1	FK Austria	(1) 1
Zilina	(0) 1	Hajduk Split	(0) 1

Thursday, 30 July 2009

Aberdeen (1) 1 *(Mulgrew 23)*

Sigma Olomouc (1) 5 *(Hubnik 18, Bajer 65, Petr 69, Ordos 83, Horava 90)*   13,973

Aberdeen: Langfield; Foster, Mulgrew, Duff, McDonald, Considine, Miller, Kerr, Mackie (Maguire 60), Young, Aluko (Paton 72).
Sigma Olomouc: Drobisz; Dreksa, Skerle, Horava, Onofrej, Rossi, Otepka (Kascak 57), Bajer, Hubnik (Heidenreich 85), Petr (Ordos 74), Janotka.

CSKA Sofia (0) 1 *(Stoyanov I 74)*

Derry City (0) 0   10,500

CSKA Sofia: Chavdarov; Vidanov, Kotev, Ivanov, Yanev, Minev, Timonov (Saidhodzha 66), Petrov (Orlinov 58), Marquinhos, Stoyanov I, Rui Miguel (Todorov 80).
Derry City: Doherty; Hutton, Gray, O'Brien, Delaney, Higgins (Martyn 81), McGlynn (McCallion 73), Deery, Molloy, Stewart, McManus (Farren 71).

St Patrick's Ath (0) 1 *(O'Brien 71)*

Krylia (0) 0   3500

St Patrick's Ath: Rogers; Partridge, Harris, Lynch, Gavin, Stevens, Byrne (Dempsey 72), O'Connor, Fitzpatrick (Ryan B 46), Guy, O'Brien.
Krylia: Lobos; Leilton, Shishkin, Belozerov, Kalachev, Bober, Jarosik, Adzhindzhal, Ignatiev, Ivanov O (Kulik 78), Savin.

Steaua (2) 3 *(Craigan 31 (og), Nicolita 45, Stancu 60)*

Motherwell (0) 0   22,000

Steaua: Tatarusanu; Goian, Golanski, Baciu, Ninu, Szekely (Grzelak 26), Nicolita (Ochirosii 87), Ionescu, Onicas, Surdu (Bibishkov 72), Stancu.
Motherwell: Ruddy; Reynolds, Craigan, Saunders, Coke, Humphrey (O'Brien 55), Jennings (Murphy 77), Forbes (Hammell 37), Hutchinson, Sutton, Slane.

Vetra (0) 0

Fulham (1) 3 *(Zamora 45, Murphy 57 (pen), Seol 85)*   12,000

Vetra: Valinicius; Borovskij, Kijanskas, Jankauskas, Ngapounou (Stanaitis 46), Paulauskas, Masitsev, Vezevicius, Razanauskas, Grigaitis (Eliosius 76), Vasiliauskas (Moroz 58).
Fulham: Schwarzer; Pantsil, Konchesky, Murphy (Riise 87), Hughes, Hangeland, Baird, Dempsey (Seol 81), Johnson A (Nevland 69), Zamora, Gera.

THIRD QUALIFYING ROUND SECOND LEG

Omonia	(0) 1	Vaslui	(0) 1
APOP	(1) 2	Rapid Vienna	(1) 2
(aet.)			
Basle	(1) 3	KR Reykjavik	(1) 1
Cherno More	(0) 0	PSV Eindhoven	(1) 1
Derry City	(0) 1	CSKA Sofia	(0) 1
Elfsborg	(2) 2	Braga	(0) 0
FK Austria	(1) 4	Vojvodina	(1) 2
Fulham	(0) 3	Vetra	(0) 0
Galatasaray	(2) 6	Maccabi Netanya	(0) 0
Gent	(0) 1	Roma	(1) 7
Hajduk Split	(0) 0	Zilina	(0) 1
Hamburg	(0) 0	Randers	(1) 1
Hapoel Tel Aviv	(1) 1	IFK Gothenburg	(0) 1
Honved	(0) 1	Fenerbahce	(1) 1
(Behind closed doors.)			
Interblock	(0) 0	Metalurg Donetsk	(0) 3
Karabakh	(1) 2	Honka	(1) 1
Kosice	(1) 3	Slavija	(1) 1
Krylia	(1) 3	St Patrick's Ath	(0) 2
Lahti	(0) 1	Club Brugge	(0) 1
Lech	(0) 1	Fredrikstad	(2) 2
Legia	(1) 2	Brondby	(1) 2
Lille	(0) 2	Sevojno	(0) 0
Metalist Kharkiv	(1) 2	Rijeka	(0) 0
Motherwell	(1) 1	Steaua	(0) 3
NAC Breda	(2) 3	Polonia	(0) 1
Odense	(0) 3	Rabotnicki	(0) 0
Pacos de Ferreira	(0) 0	Bnei Yehuda	(1) 1
PAOK Salonika	(0) 0	Valerenga	(0) 1
Red Star Belgrade	(3) 5	Dinamo Tbilisi	(2) 2
Sarajevo	(1) 2	Helsingborg	(1) 1
(aet; Sarajevo won 5-4 on penalties.)			
Sigma Olomouc	(3) 3	Aberdeen	(0) 0
Slaven	(0) 0	Tromso	(1) 2
Slovan Liberec	(2) 2	Vaduz	(0) 0
Sturm Graz	(2) 5	Petrovac	(0) 0
Young Boys	(0) 1	Athletic Bilbao	(1) 2

Thursday, 6 August 2009

Derry City (0) 1 *(Scullion 82)*

CSKA Sofia (0) 1 *(Marquinhos 70)*   2700

Derry City: Doherty; Hutton, Gray, O'Brien, Delaney, Higgins, Deery, Molloy (Scullion 74), Stewart, Farren (McGlynn■ 53), McManus (Nash 90).
CSKA Sofia: Chavdarov (Karadzhov 30); Vidanov, Kotev, Ivanov, Yanev, Todorov, Minev, Timonov (Rui Miguel 66), Petrov, Marquinhos (Orlinov 83), Stoyanov I.

Fulham (0) 3 *(Etuhu 57, Johnson A 80, 84)*

Vetra (0) 0   15,016

Fulham: Schwarzer; Pantsil (Kelly 78), Konchesky, Murphy, Hughes, Hangeland, Gera (Riise 78), Etuhu, Johnson A, Zamora (Johnson E 84), Dempsey.
Vetra: Valinicius; Borovskij, Kijanskas, Jankauskas, Paulauskas, Stanaitis, Vezevicius (Eliosius 46), Razanauskas, Grigaitis, Vasiliauskas (Zulpa 80), Grigalevicius (Moroz 57).

Krylia (1) 3 *(Bober 43, Savin 54, 57)*

St Patrick's Ath (0) 2 *(Bober 73 (og), O'Brien 79)* 17,000

Krylia: Lobos; Shishkin, Taranov, Belozerov, Kalachev, Bober, Adzhindzhal, Ignatiev (Kulik 39), Budylin (Leilton 68), Ivanov O, Savin.
St Patrick's Ath: Rogers; Partridge, Harris, Lynch, Gavin (Maher 66), Stevens (Ryan D 76), Byrne, Ryan B (Cawley 63), O'Connor, Guy, O'Brien.

Motherwell (1) 1 *(Forbes 17)*

Steaua (0) 3 *(Marin 55 (pen), Stancu 67, 84)* 4975

Motherwell: Ruddy; Coke (Jennings 71), Hammell, Hutchinson, Reynolds (Humphrey 60), Craigan, Forbes, Murphy (McHugh 60), Sutton, Slane, O'Brien.
Steaua: Zapata; Baciu, Marin, Ghionea (Tudose 76), Ninu, Nicolita, Ionescu, Onicas (Iacob 81), Grzelak, Stancu, Bibishkov (Ochirosii 62).

Sigma Olomouc (3) 3 *(Janotka 5, Kascak 12 (pen), Hubnik 45)*

Aberdeen (0) 0 7405

Sigma Olomouc: Drobisz; Dreksa, Skerle, Horava (Ordos 46), Kascak, Onofrej, Rossi, Bajer, Hubnik (Otepka 66), Petr (Sultes 58), Janotka.
Aberdeen: Langfield; Foster, Mulgrew, Duff, Considine, Kerr, McDonald, Maguire (Megginson 85), Miller, Mackie, Aluko.

PLAY-OFF ROUND FIRST LEG

Ajax	(1) 5	Slovan Bratislava	(0) 0
Athletic Bilbao	(0) 3	Tromso	(1) 2
Baku	(0) 1	Basle	(0) 3
BATE Borisov	(0) 0	Litex	(0) 1
Benfica	(1) 4	Vorskla	(0) 0
Bnei Yehuda	(0) 0	PSV Eindhoven	(1) 1
Brondby	(0) 2	Hertha Berlin	(0) 1
CSKA Sofia	(0) 0	Dynamo Moscow	(0) 0
Dinamo Bucharest	(0) 0	Slovan Liberec	(1) 2
(Abandoned 84 minutes; match forfeited and awarded 3-0 to Slovan Liberec.)			
Dinamo Zagreb	(2) 4	Hearts	(0) 0
Everton	(2) 4	Sigma Olomouc	(0) 0
Fulham	(1) 3	Amkar	(0) 1
Galatasaray	(2) 5	Levadia	(0) 0
Genk	(0) 1	Lille	(1) 2
Genoa	(1) 3	Odense	(0) 1
Guingamp	(0) 1	Hamburg	(3) 5
Kosice	(1) 3	Roma	(1) 3
Lazio	(2) 3	Elfsborg	(0) 0
Lech	(0) 1	Club Brugge	(0) 0
Maribor	(0) 0	Sparta Prague	(1) 2
Metalurg Donetsk	(1) 2	FK Austria	(1) 2
NAC Breda	(1) 1	Villarreal	(1) 3
Nacional	(2) 4	Zenit	(1) 3
PAOK Salonika	(0) 1	Heerenveen	(1) 1
Partizan Belgrade	(1) 1	Zilina	(1) 1
Rapid Vienna	(1) 1	Aston Villa	(0) 0
Sarajevo	(0) 1	Cluj	(1) 1
Sion	(0) 0	Fenerbahce	(1) 2
Sivas	(0) 0	Shakhtar Donetsk	(1) 3
Slavia Prague	(1) 3	Red Star Belgrade	(0) 0
Stabaek	(0) 0	Valencia	(2) 3
Steaua	(0) 3	St Patrick's Ath	(0) 0
(Behind closed doors.)			
Sturm Graz	(1) 1	Metalist Kharkiv	(0) 1

Teplice	(0) 1	Hapoel Tel Aviv	(0) 2
Trabzonspor	(1) 1	Toulouse	(1) 3
Twente	(1) 3	Karabakh	(1) 1
Vaslui	(1) 2	AEK Athens	(0) 1
Werder Bremen	(3) 6	Aktobe	(2) 3

Thursday, 20 August 2009

Dinamo Zagreb (2) 4 *(Mandzukic 5, Papadopoulos D 35, Vrdoljak 56, Biscan 60)*

Hearts (0) 0 22,000

Dinamo Zagreb: Butina; Carlos, Barbaric, Vrdoljak, Etto (Tomecak 20), Sammir (Kramaric 61), Badelj, Biscan, Morales (Calello 76), Mandzukic, Papadopoulos D.
Hearts: Kello; Jonsson, Wallace, Bouzid (Black 46), Goncalves, Palazuelos, Suso (Novikovas 81), Stewart, Zaliukas, Nade (Glen 58), Obua.

Everton (2) 4 *(Saha 34, 73, Rodwell 40, 54)*

Sigma Olomouc (0) 0 27,433

Everton: Howard; Hibbert, Baines, Yobo, Neville, Rodwell (Gosling 76), Osman, Fellaini, Saha (Jo 78), Cahill, Pienaar (Vaughan 82).
Sigma Olomouc: Drobisz; Dreksa, Skerle, Horava, Kascak, Onofrej, Rossi, Otepka (Bajer 61), Ordos (Sultes 46), Hubnik, Petr (Janotka 74).

Fulham (1) 3 *(Johnson A 4, Dempsey 51, Zamora 75)*

Amkar (0) 1 *(Grishin 77)* 13,000

Fulham: Schwarzer; Pantsil, Konchesky, Murphy, Hughes, Hangeland, Gera (Duff 75), Etuhu (Baird 78), Johnson A (Nevland 68), Zamora, Dempsey.
Amkar: Narubin; Sirakov, Gaal, Belorukov, Peev, Novakovic (Telkiyski 68), Drincic, Cherenchikov, Jean Carlos (Junuzovic 85), Zhilyaev (Grishin 60), Kushev.

Rapid Vienna (1) 1 *(Jelavic 1)*

Aston Villa (0) 0 17,800

Rapid Vienna: Payer; Patocka, Jovanovic, Katzer, Dober, Heikkinen, Hofmann, Drazan (Boskovic 83), Pehlivan, Jelavic, Konrad (Trimmel 62).
Aston Villa: Guzan; Beye, Shorey, Sidwell, Davies (Lowry 81), Cuellar, Milner, Reo-Coker, Heskey, Gardner (Agbonlahor 55), Young A.

Steaua (0) 3 *(Nicolita 55, Stancu 65, 80)*

St Patrick's Ath (0) 0

Steaua: Tatarusanu; Golanski (Tininho 86), Tudose, Baciu, Marin, Nicolita, Ionescu, Ochirosii (Stancu 53), Onicas, Kapetanos (Grzelak 81), Surdu.
St Patrick's Ath: Rogers; Partridge, Harris, Lynch (Cawley 86), Gavin, Stevens, Byrne (Dempsey 70), O'Connor, Fitzpatrick (Quigley 61), Guy, O'Brien.
Behind closed doors.

PLAY-OFF ROUND SECOND LEG

Shakhtar Donetsk	(1) 2	Sivas	(0) 0
AEK Athens	(0) 3	Vaslui	(0) 0
Aktobe	(0) 0	Werder Bremen	(2) 2
Amkar	(0) 1	Fulham	(0) 0
Aston Villa	(1) 2	Rapid Vienna	(0) 1
Basle	(3) 5	Baku	(0) 1
Club Brugge	(0) 1	Lech	(0) 0
(aet; Club Brugge won 4-3 on penalties.)			
Cluj	(1) 2	Sarajevo	(0) 1

Dynamo Moscow	(1) 1	CSKA Sofia	(1) 2
Elfsborg	(0) 1	Lazio	(0) 0
Fenerbahce	(2) 2	Sion	(2) 2
FK Austria	(1) 3	Metalurg Donetsk	(1) 2
(aet.)			
Hamburg	(1) 3	Guingamp	(0) 1
Hapoel Tel Aviv	(0) 1	Teplice	(0) 1
Hearts	(1) 2	Dinamo Zagreb	(0) 0
Heerenveen	(0) 0	PAOK Salonika	(0) 0
Hertha Berlin	(0) 3	Brondby	(0) 1
Karabakh	(0) 0	Twente	(0) 0
Levadia	(0) 1	Galatasaray	(0) 1
Lille	(1) 4	Genk	(1) 2
Litex	(0) 0	BATE Borisov	(0) 4
(aet.)			
Metalist Kharkiv	(0) 0	Sturm Graz	(1) 1
Odense	(1) 1	Genoa	(0) 1
PSV Eindhoven	(1) 1	Bnei Yehuda	(0) 0
Red Star Belgrade	(2) 2	Slavia Prague	(0) 1
Roma	(5) 7	Kosice	(1) 1
Sigma Olomouc	(0) 1	Everton	(1) 1
Slovan Bratislava	(1) 1	Ajax	(1) 2
Slovan Liberec	(0) 0	Dinamo Bucharest	(1) 3
(aet; Dinamo Bucharest won 9-8 on penalties.)			
Sparta Prague	(1) 1	Maribor	(0) 0
St Patrick's Ath	(0) 1	Steaua	(0) 2
Toulouse	(0) 0	Trabzonspor	(0) 1
Tromso	(0) 1	Athletic Bilbao	(0) 1
Valencia	(2) 4	Stabaek	(1) 1
Villarreal	(3) 6	NAC Breda	(0) 1
Vorskla	(0) 2	Benfica	(0) 1
Zenit	(1) 1	Nacional	(0) 1
Zilina	(0) 0	Partizan Belgrade	(0) 2

Thursday, 27 August 2009

Amkar (0) 1 *(Kushev 90)*

Fulham (0) 0 20,000

Amkar: Narubin; Sirakov, Gaal, Belorukov, Grishin (Junuzovic 76), Telkiyski (Novakovic 60), Peev, Drincic, Cherenchikov, Jean Carlos (Zhilyaev 64), Kushev.
Fulham: Schwarzer; Pantsil, Kelly, Riise (Seol 76), Hughes, Hangeland, Baird, Etuhu, Gera, Nevland (Kamara 68), Duff.

Aston Villa (1) 2 *(Milner 38 (pen), Carew 53)*

Rapid Vienna (0) 1 *(Jelavic 76)* 23,563

Aston Villa: Guzan; Beye, Shorey, Delph (Albrighton 86), Davies (Lowry 83), Cuellar, Milner, Petrov, Heskey (Agbonlahor 82), Carew, Young A.
Rapid Vienna: Payer; Patocka, Katzer, Soma, Dober, Heikkinen, Hofmann, Drazan, Pehlivan, Jelavic (Boskovic 87), Trimmel (Maierhofer 56).

Hearts (1) 2 *(Stewart 17, Zaliukas 55)*

Dinamo Zagreb (0) 0 11,769

Hearts: Balogh; Thomson, Bouzid, Stewart, Goncalves, Palazuelos (Black 82), Suso, Zaliukas, Glen (Driver 60), Nade (Smith 55), Obua.
Dinamo Zagreb: Butina; Lovren, Carlos, Barbaric, Vrdoljak, Sammir (Tomecak 68), Badelj, Biscan, Morales (Calello 87), Mandzukic, Papadopoulos D (Slepicka 89).

Sigma Olomouc (0) 1 *(Sultes 80)*

Everton (1) 1 *(Pienaar 44)*   10,212

Sigma Olomouc: Lovasik; Dreksa, Skerle, Horava, Kascak, Onofrej, Rossi, Bajer (Otepka 73), Ordos, Petr (Stepan 84), Janotka (Sultes 73).
Everton: Howard; Hibbert■, Baines, Yobo, Neville, Rodwell, Gosling, Osman (Baxter 66), Jo (Yakubu 76), Fellaini, Pienaar (Wallace 66).

St Patrick's Ath (0) 1 *(O'Connor 49)*

Steaua (0) 2 *(Nicolita 80, Ochirosil 89)*   15,000

St Patrick's Ath: Rogers; Partridge, Harris (Gavin 86), Lynch, Stevens (Ryan B 46), Byrne (Dempsey 79), Cawley, O'Connor, Quigley, Guy, O'Brien.
Steaua: Zapata; Golanski, Tudose, Ghionea, Ninu, Szekely (Ochirosil 86), Ionescu, Onicas, Grzelak (Nicolita 57), Stancu (Surdu 79), Bibishkov.

GROUP A

Ajax	(0) 0	Timisoara	(0) 0
Dinamo Zagreb	(0) 0	Anderlecht	(0) 2
Anderlecht	(0) 1	Ajax	(0) 1
Timisoara	(0) 0	Dinamo Zagreb	(1) 3
Ajax	(1) 2	Dinamo Zagreb	(0) 1
Timosoara	(0) 0	Anderlecht	(0) 0
Anderlecht	(1) 3	Timisoara	(0) 1
Dinamo Zagreb	(0) 0	Ajax	(2) 2

(Behind closed doors.)

Anderlecht	(0) 0	Dinamo Zagreb	(0) 1
Timisoara	(1) 1	Ajax	(1) 2
Ajax	(0) 1	Anderlecht	(3) 3
Dinamo Zagreb	(0) 1	Timisoara	(0) 2

(Behind closed doors.)

Group A Table	P	W	D	L	F	A	Pts
Anderlecht	6	3	2	1	9	4	11
Ajax	6	3	2	1	8	6	11
Dinamo Zagreb	6	2	0	4	6	8	6
Timisoara	6	1	2	3	4	9	5

GROUP B

Genoa	(2) 2	Slavia Prague	(0) 0
Lille	(0) 1	Valencia	(0) 1
Slavia Prague	(1) 1	Lille	(0) 5
Valencia	(0) 3	Genoa	(1) 2
Lille	(1) 3	Genoa	(0) 0
Valencia	(0) 1	Slavia Prague	(1) 1
Genoa	(1) 3	Lille	(0) 2
Slavia Prague	(0) 2	Valencia	(1) 2
Slavia Prague	(0) 0	Genoa	(0) 0
Valencia	(2) 3	Lille	(0) 1
Genoa	(0) 1	Valencia	(1) 2
Lille	(2) 3	Slavia Prague	(0) 1

Group B Table	P	W	D	L	F	A	Pts
Valencia	6	3	3	0	12	8	12
Lille	6	3	1	2	15	9	10
Genoa	6	2	1	3	8	10	7
Slavia Prague	6	0	3	3	5	13	3

GROUP C

Hapoel Tel Aviv	(0) 2	Celtic	(1) 1
Rapid Vienna	(2) 3	Hamburg	(0) 0
Celtic	(1) 1	Rapid Vienna	(1) 1
Hamburg	(3) 4	Hapoel Tel Aviv	(1) 2
Celtic	(0) 0	Hamburg	(0) 1
Hapoel Tel Aviv	(1) 5	Rapid Vienna	(1) 1
Hamburg	(0) 0	Celtic	(0) 0
Rapid Vienna	(0) 0	Hapoel Tel Aviv	(1) 3
Celtic	(1) 2	Hapoel Tel Aviv	(0) 0
Hamburg	(0) 2	Rapid Vienna	(0) 0
Hapoel Tel Aviv	(1) 1	Hamburg	(0) 0
Rapid Vienna	(3) 3	Celtic	(1) 3

Thursday, 17 September 2009

CSKA Sofia (0) 1 *(Michel 61)*

Fulham (0) 1 *(Kamara 65)*   28,000

CSKA Sofia: Karadzhov; Stoyanov K, Kotev, Ivanov, Yanev (Manchev V 78), Todorov, Minev, Yanchev, Morozs (Marquinhos 46), Stoyanov I (Michel 54), Delev.
Fulham: Stockdale; Kelly, Baird, Riise, Pantsil, Smalling, Greening, Davies, Nevland, Kamara, Gera.

Thursday, 1 October 2009

Fulham (0) 1 *(Murphy 57)*

Basle (0) 0   16,100

Fulham: Schwarzer; Kelly, Konchesky, Murphy, Baird, Smalling, Riise, Greening, Johnson A, Zamora, Dempsey.
Basle: Costanzo; Cagdas, Abraham (Da Silva 69), Safari, Sahin, Gelabert (Chipperfield 86), Huggel, Stocker, Carlitos (Almerares 82), Streller, Frei.

Thursday, 22 October 2009

Fulham (1) 1 *(Hangeland 24)*

Roma (0) 1 *(Andreolli 90)*   23,561

Fulham: Schwarzer; Kelly■, Konchesky (Pantsil 46), Riise (Duff 75), Hughes, Hangeland, Baird, Greening, Kamara, Zamora (Nevland 62), Gera.
Roma: Doni; Andreolli, Mexes, Riise, Burdisso, Taddei (Vucinic 63), De Rossi, Guberti, Brighi (Perrotta 46), Okaka Chuka (Pizarro 46), Menez.

Thursday, 5 November 2009

Roma (0) 2 *(Riise 69, Okaka Chuka 76)*

Fulham (1) 1 *(Kamara 19 (pen))*   20,000

Roma: Doni (Julio Sergio 46); Cicinho (Taddei 46), Andreolli, Mexes, Riise, Cassetti, Pizarro, De Rossi, Baptista, Guberti (Menez 66), Okaka Chuka.
Fulham: Schwarzer; Pantsil, Konchesky■, Riise (Zamora 70), Hughes, Hangeland, Gera, Greening, Kamara (Nevland■ 46), Etuhu (Baird 77), Dempsey.

Thursday, 3 December 2009

Fulham (1) 1 *(Gera 15)*

CSKA Sofia (0) 0   23,604

Fulham: Schwarzer; Pantsil, Kelly, Murphy (Duff 79), Baird, Hangeland (Hughes 46), Smalling, Riise, Gera, Zamora, Davies (Dempsey 70).
CSKA Sofia: Chavdarov; Vidanov, Stoyanov K, Ivanov (Yanev 64), Popov, Todorov (Rui Miguel 72), Minev, Yanchev, Timonov (Michel 54), Morozs, Delev.

Wednesday, 16 December 2009

Basle (0) 2 *(Frei 64 (pen), Streller 87)*

Fulham (2) 3 *(Zamora 41, 44, Gera 76)* 20,063

Basle: Colomba; Cagdas, Abraham, Safari (Shaqiri 46), Inkoom, Huggel, Stocker, Cabral (Almerares 46), Carlitos (Schurpf 79), Streller, Frei.
Fulham: Schwarzer; Pantsil, Kelly, Murphy, Hughes, Smalling, Riise, Greening (Dempsey 70), Gera, Zamora (Duff 80), Etuhu.

Thursday, 17 September 2009

Hapoel Tel Aviv (0) 2 *(Vucicevic 75, Lala 88)*

Celtic (1) 1 *(Samaras 25)* 15,500

Hapoel Tel Aviv: Enyeama; Da Silva, Ben Dayan, Kanada, Yadin, Natcho (Zahavy 68), Badir, Vermouth, Menteshashvili (Lala 54), Vucicevic (Mare 80), Yeboah.
Celtic: Boruc; Hinkel, Fox, Loovens, Caldwell (McDonald 89), McManus, N'Guemo (McGinn 66), Brown S, Maloney, Samaras (Killen 70), McGeady.

Thursday, 1 October 2009

Celtic (1) 1 *(McDonald 21)*

Rapid Vienna (1) 1 *(Jelavic 3)* 40,577

Celtic: Boruc; Wilson, Fox, N'Guemo (Robson 81), Caldwell, McManus, Maloney (Killen 81), Brown S, McDonald, Samaras, McGeady (McGinn 82).
Rapid Vienna: Payer; Patocka, Katzer, Soma, Dober, Heikkinen, Hofmann, Kavlak, Boskovic (Drazan 63), Pehlivan, Jelavic.

Thursday, 22 October 2009

Celtic (0) 0

Hamburg (0) 1 *(Berg 63)* 38,821

Celtic: Boruc; Wilson, Naylor, N'Guemo, Caldwell, McManus, Maloney (McGinn 76), Brown S (McCourt 76), McDonald (Samaras 61), Robson, McGeady.
Hamburg: Rost; Rozehnal, Mathijsen, Aogo, Jansen (Trochowski 77), Ze Roberto, Jarolim, Demel, Pitroipa (Tesche 89), Elia, Berg.

Thursday, 5 November 2009

Hamburg (0) 0

Celtic (0) 0 45,037

Hamburg: Rost; Rozehnal, Mathijsen, Aogo, Jansen (Trochowski 83), Ze Roberto, Jarolim, Pitroipa (Torun 88), Rincon, Elia, Berg.
Celtic: Zaluska; Hinkel, Fox, Crosas, Caldwell, Loovens, N'Guemo, Robson (McGinn 75), McDonald (Fortune 59), Samaras, McGeady (Naylor 59).

Wednesday, 2 December 2009

Celtic (1) 2 *(Samaras 22, Robson 68)*

Hapoel Tel Aviv (0) 0 32,000

Celtic: Zaluska; Hinkel, Fox, Crosas, Caldwell, Loovens, Robson, N'Guemo, McDonald, Samaras (Fortune 63), McGeady (Naylor 74).
Hapoel Tel Aviv: Enyeama; Da Silva, Bondarv, Ben Dayan, Yadin (Zahavy 79), Natcho, Badir, Vermouth, Menteshashvili (Vucicevic 46), Shechter, Yeboah (Lala 46).

Thursday, 17 December 2009

Rapid Vienna (3) 3 *(Jelavic 1, 8, Salihi 19)*

Celtic (1) 3 *(Fortune 23, 67, McGowan 90)* 45,000

Rapid Vienna: Hedl; Patocka, Katzer, Soma, Dober (Trimmel 30), Kulovits, Hofmann, Kavlak (Drazan 59), Boskovic, Salihi (Ildiz 78), Jelavic.
Celtic: Boruc; Caddis, Wilson, Crosas, Loovens, McManus, Flood, N'Guemo, Fortune (Killen 90), McGowan, McGinn (Carey 78).

Group C Table	P	W	D	L	F	A	Pts
Hapoel Tel Aviv	6	4	0	2	13	8	12
Hamburg	6	3	1	2	7	6	10
Celtic	6	1	3	2	7	7	6
Rapid Vienna	6	1	2	3	8	14	5

GROUP D

Heerenveen	(1) 2	Sporting Lisbon	(2) 3
Hertha Berlin	(1) 1	Ventspils	(0) 1
Sporting Lisbon	(1) 1	Hertha Berlin	(0) 0
Ventspils	(0) 0	Heerenveen	(0) 0
Hertha Berlin	(0) 0	Heerenveen	(1) 1
Ventspils	(0) 1	Sporting Lisbon	(1) 2
Heerenveen	(2) 2	Hertha Berlin	(1) 3
Sporting Lisbon	(1) 1	Ventspils	(1) 1
Sporting Lisbon	(0) 1	Heerenveen	(0) 1
Ventspils	(0) 0	Hertha Berlin	(1) 1
Heerenveen	(0) 5	Ventspils	(0) 0
Hertha Berlin	(0) 1	Sporting Lisbon	(0) 0

Group D Table	P	W	D	L	F	A	Pts
Sporting Lisbon	6	3	2	1	8	6	11
Hertha Berlin	6	3	1	2	6	5	10
Heerenveen	6	2	2	2	11	7	8
Ventspils	6	0	3	3	3	10	3

GROUP E

Basle	(1) 2	Roma	(0) 0
CSKA Sofia	(0) 1	Fulham	(0) 1
Fulham	(0) 1	Basle	(0) 0
Roma	(2) 2	CSKA Sofia	(0) 0
CSKA Sofia	(0) 0	Basle	(1) 2
Fulham	(1) 1	Roma	(0) 1
Basle	(2) 3	CSKA Sofia	(0) 1
Roma	(0) 2	Fulham	(1) 1
Fulham	(1) 1	CSKA Sofia	(0) 0
Roma	(1) 2	Basle	(0) 1
Basle	(0) 2	Fulham	(2) 3
CSKA Sofia	(0) 0	Roma	(1) 3

Group E Table	P	W	D	L	F	A	Pts
Roma	6	4	1	1	10	5	13
Fulham	6	3	2	1	8	6	11
Basle	6	3	0	3	10	7	9
CSKA Sofia	6	0	1	5	2	12	1

GROUP F

Panathinaikos	(0) 1	Galatasaray	(1) 3
Sturm Graz	(0) 0	Dinamo Bucharest	(0) 1
Dinamo Bucharest	(0) 0	Panathinaikos	(0) 1
(Behind closed doors.)			
Galatasaray	(0) 1	Sturm Graz	(1) 1
Galatasaray	(2) 4	Dinamo Bucharest	(0) 1
Panathinaikos	(0) 1	Sturm Graz	(0) 0
Dinamo Bucharest	(0) 0	Galatasaray	(2) 3
(Behind closed doors.)			

Sturm Graz	(0) 0	Panathinaikos	(0) 1
Dinamo Bucharest	(1) 2	Sturm Graz	(1) 1
Galatasaray	(0) 1	Panathinaikos	(0) 0
Panathinaikos	(0) 3	Dinamo Bucharest	(0) 0
Sturm Graz	(1) 1	Galatasaray	(0) 0

Group F Table	P	W	D	L	F	A	Pts
Galatasaray	6	4	1	1	12	4	13
Panathinaikos	6	4	0	2	7	4	12
Dinamo Bucharest	6	2	0	4	4	12	6
Sturm Graz	6	1	1	4	3	6	4

GROUP G

Lazio	(0) 1	Salzburg	(0) 2
Villarreal	(0) 1	Levski	(0) 0
Levski	(0) 0	Lazio	(2) 4
Salzburg	(1) 2	Villarreal	(0) 0
Lazio	(1) 2	Villarreal	(1) 1
Salzburg	(1) 1	Levski	(0) 0
Levski	(0) 0	Salzburg	(0) 1
Villarreal	(3) 4	Lazio	(0) 1
Levski	(0) 0	Villarreal	(1) 2
Salzburg	(0) 2	Lazio	(0) 1
Lazio	(0) 0	Levski	(0) 1
Villarreal	(0) 0	Salzburg	(1) 1

Group G Table	P	W	D	L	F	A	Pts
Salzburg	6	6	0	0	9	2	18
Villarreal	6	3	0	3	8	6	9
Lazio	6	2	0	4	9	10	6
Levski	6	1	0	5	1	9	3

Group H Table	P	W	D	L	F	A	Pts
Fenerbahce	6	5	0	1	8	3	15
Twente	6	2	2	2	5	6	8
Serif	6	1	2	3	4	5	5
Steaua	6	0	4	2	3	6	4

GROUP H

Fenerbahce	(0) 1	Twente	(0) 2
Steaua	(0) 0	Sheriff	(0) 0
(Behind closed doors.)			
Sheriff	(0) 0	Fenerbahce	(0) 1
Twente	(0) 0	Steaua	(0) 0
Sheriff	(1) 2	Twente	(0) 0
Steaua	(0) 0	Fenerbahce	(0) 1
Fenerbahce	(1) 3	Steaua	(1) 1
Twente	(1) 2	Sheriff	(0) 1
Sheriff	(0) 1	Steaua	(0) 1
Twente	(0) 0	Fenerbahce	(0) 1
Fenerbahce	(1) 1	Sheriff	(0) 0
Steaua	(1) 1	Twente	(1) 1

GROUP I

| Benfica | (2) 2 | BATE Borisov | (0) 0 |
| Everton | (3) 4 | AEK Athens | (0) 0 |

AEK Athens	(1) 1	Benfica	(0) 0
BATE Borisov	(1) 1	Everton	(0) 2
BATE Borisov	(0) 2	AEK Athens	(1) 1
Benfica	(1) 5	Everton	(0) 0
AEK Athens	(2) 2	BATE Borisov	(2) 2
Everton	(0) 0	Benfica	(0) 2
AEK Athens	(0) 0	Everton	(1) 1
BATE Borisov	(0) 1	Benfica	(0) 2
Benfica	(1) 2	AEK Athens	(0) 1
Everton	(0) 0	BATE Borisov	(0) 1

Thursday, 17 September 2009

Everton (3) 4 *(Yobo 10, Distin 17, Pienaar 37, Jo 82)*

AEK Athens (0) 0   26,747

Everton: Howard; Bilyaletdinov (Yakubu 52), Baines, Yobo, Distin, Rodwell, Gosling, Fellaini, Jo, Cahill (Osman 46), Pienaar (Saha■ 67).
AEK Athens: Saja; Araujo■, Alves (Nsaliwa 13) (Manduca 48), Juanfran, Jahic, Bianchi, Kafes, Leonardo (Yahaya 71), Makos, Blanco, Scocco.

Thursday, 1 October 2009

BATE Borisov (1) 1 *(Likhtarovich 16)*

Everton (0) 2 *(Fellaini 68, Cahill 76)*   21,200

BATE Borisov: Veremko; Sosnovskiy, Shitov, Yurevich, Bordachev, Likhtarovich (Goaryan 81), Krivets, Nekhaichik, Pavlov (Volodzo 78), Skavysh (Stasevich 28), Rodionov.
Everton: Howard; Hibbert, Baines, Gosling, Distin, Bilyaletdinov (Baxter 90), Osman, Fellaini, Jo, Yakubu (Agard 78), Cahill.

Thursday, 22 October 2009

Benfica (1) 5 *(Saviola 14, 83, Cardozo 47, 48, Luisao 52)*

Everton (0) 0   44,534

Benfica: Julio Cesar; Luisao, David Luiz, Ruben Amorim, Javier Garcia, Ramires, Aimar (Carlos Martins 69), Di Maria, Cesar Peixoto, Cardozo (Fabio Coentrao 77), Saviola (Weldon 84).
Everton: Howard; Hibbert, Coleman, Rodwell, Distin, Cahill, Bilyaletdinov (Saha 61), Gosling, Jo, Yakubu (Baxter 71), Fellaini.

Thursday, 5 November 2009

Everton (0) 0

Benfica (0) 2 *(Saviola 63, Cardozo 76)*   30,790

Everton: Howard; Hibbert, Baines, Yobo, Distin, Rodwell, Bilyaletdinov, Gosling (Jo 69), Yakubu (Agard 81), Fellaini, Cahill.
Benfica: Julio Cesar; Luisao, David Luiz, Sidnei, Ruben Amorim, Javier Garcia, Ramires (Maxi Pereira 46), Fabio Coentrao (Aimar 61), Di Maria, Cardozo, Saviola (Felipe Menezes 87).

Wednesday, 2 December 2009

AEK Athens (0) 0

Everton (1) 1 *(Bilyaletdinov 6)*   15,000

AEK Athens: Saja; Alves, Majstorovic, Juanfran, Georgeas, Kafes, Hersi, Leonardo (Scocco 46), Makos (Manduca 30), Tachtsidis, Pavlis (Blanco 62).
Everton: Howard; Hibbert, Baines, Gosling (Baxter 11), Coleman, Distin (Duffy 18), Bilyaletdinov, Fellaini, Jo (Yakubu 73), Cahill, Pienaar.

Thursday, 17 December 2009

Everton (0) 0

BATE Borisov (0) 1 *(Yurevich 75)*   18,242

Everton: Nash; Hibbert (Mustafi 75), Bidwell, Rodwell (Akpan 9), Coleman, Duffy, Osman (Craig 82), Forshaw, Yakubu, Agard, Baxter.
BATE Borisov: Veremko; Sosnovskiy, Shitov, Yurevich, Bordachev, Likhtarovic (Pavlov 56), Volodzo, Krivets, Nekhaichik (Bulyga 82), Skavysh (Goaryan 74), Rodionov.

Group I Table	P	W	D	L	F	A	Pts
Benfica	6	5	0	1	13	3	15
Everton	6	3	0	3	7	9	9
BATE Borisov	6	2	1	3	7	9	7
AEK Athens	6	1	1	4	5	11	4

GROUP J

Club Brugge	(0) 1	Shakhtar Donetsk	(3) 4
Partizan Belgrade	(1) 2	Toulouse	(2) 3
Shakhtar Donetsk	(2) 4	Partizan Belgrade	(0) 1
Toulouse	(0) 2	Club Brugge	(0) 2
Club Brugge	(1) 2	Partizan Belgrade	(0) 0
Shakhtar Donetsk	(3) 4	Toulouse	(0) 0
Partizan Belgrade	(0) 2	Club Brugge	(2) 4
Toulouse	(0) 0	Shakhtar Donetsk	(0) 2
Shakhtar Donetsk	(0) 0	Club Brugge	(0) 0
Toulouse	(0) 1	Partizan Belgrade	(0) 0
Club Brugge	(0) 1	Toulouse	(0) 0
Partizan Belgrade	(1) 1	Shakhtar Donetsk	(0) 0

Group J Table	P	W	D	L	F	A	Pts
Shakhtar Donetsk	6	4	1	1	14	3	13
Club Brugge	6	3	2	1	10	8	11
Toulouse	6	2	1	3	6	11	7
Partizan Belgrade	6	1	0	5	6	14	3

GROUP K

Cluj	(0) 2	FC Copenhagen	(0) 0
Sparta Prague	(0) 2	PSV Eindhoven	(0) 2
FC Copenhagen	(1) 1	Sparta Prague	(0) 0
PSV Eindhoven	(1) 1	Cluj	(0) 0
PSV Eindhoven	(0) 1	FC Copenhagen	(0) 0
Sparta Prague	(2) 2	Cluj	(0) 0
Cluj	(1) 2	Sparta Prague	(2) 3
FC Copenhagen	(1) 1	PSV Eindhoven	(0) 1
FC Copenhagen	(2) 2	Cluj	(0) 0
PSV Eindhoven	(0) 1	Sparta Prague	(0) 0
Cluj	(0) 0	PSV Eindhoven	(1) 2
Sparta Prague	(0) 0	FC Copenhagen	(2) 3

Group K Table	P	W	D	L	F	A	Pts
PSV Eindhoven	6	4	2	0	8	3	14
FC Copenhagen	6	3	1	2	7	4	10
Sparta Prague	6	2	1	3	7	9	7
Cluj	6	1	0	5	4	10	3

GROUP L

Athletic Bilbao	(2) 3	FK Austria	(0) 0
Nacional	(0) 2	Werder Bremen	(1) 3
FK Austria	(0) 1	Nacional	(1) 1
Werder Bremen	(2) 3	Athletic Bilbao	(0) 1
Athletic Bilbao	(0) 2	Nacional	(1) 1
FK Austria	(0) 2	Werder Bremen	(1) 2
Nacional	(0) 1	Athletic Bilbao	(0) 1
Werder Bremen	(0) 2	FK Austria	(0) 0
FK Austria	(0) 0	Athletic Bilbao	(1) 3
Werder Bremen	(2) 4	Nacional	(0) 1
Athletic Bilbao	(0) 0	Werder Bremen	(3) 3
Nacional	(2) 5	FK Austria	(1) 1

Group L Table	P	W	D	L	F	A	Pts
Werder Bremen	6	5	1	0	17	6	16
Athletic Bilbao	6	3	1	2	10	8	10
Nacional	6	1	2	3	11	12	5
FK Austria	6	0	2	4	4	16	2

SECOND ROUND FIRST LEG

Everton	(1) 2	Sporting Lisbon	(0) 1
Ajax	(1) 1	Juventus	(1) 2
Athletic Bilbao	(0) 1	Anderlecht	(1) 1
Atletico Madrid	(1) 1	Galatasaray	(0) 1
Club Brugge	(0) 1	Valencia	(0) 0
FC Copenhagen	(0) 1	Marseille	(0) 3
Fulham	(1) 2	Shakhtar Donetsk	(1) 1
Hamburg	(1) 1	PSV Eindhoven	(0) 0
Hertha Berlin	(1) 1	Benfica	(1) 1
Lille	(1) 2	Fenerbahce	(1) 1
Liverpool	(0) 1	Unirea	(0) 0
Panathinaikos	(0) 3	Roma	(1) 2
Rubin	(2) 3	Hapoel Tel Aviv	(0) 0
Standard Liege	(0) 3	Salzburg	(2) 2
Twente	(1) 1	Werder Bremen	(0) 0
Villarreal	(1) 2	Wolfsburg	(0) 2

Tuesday, 16 February 2010

Everton (1) 2 *(Pienaar 35, Distin 49)*

Sporting Lisbon (0) 1 *(Miguel Veloso 87 (pen))* 28,131

Everton: Howard; Neville, Baines, Yobo, Distin■, Cahill (Yakubu 62), Osman, Pienaar, Saha (Bilyaletdinov 83), Donovan, Arteta (Rodwell 78).
Sporting Lisbon: Rui Patricio; Daniel Carrico, Tonel, Grimi, Abel, Pedro Mendes, Izmailov, Matias (Saleiro 66), Miguel Veloso, Joao Moutinho (Yannick Djalo 66), Liedson.

Thursday, 18 February 2010

Fulham (1) 2 *(Gera 3, Zamora 63)*

Shakhtar Donetsk (1) 1 *(Luiz Adriano 32)* 21,832

Fulham: Schwarzer; Kelly, Baird, Murphy, Hughes, Hangeland, Duff, Etuhu, Gera (Elm 89), Zamora, Davies.
Shakhtar Donetsk: Pyatov; Hubschman (Kravchenko 79), Kucher, Rat, Fernandinho, Jadson (Douglas Costa 75), Ilsinho, Willian, Srna, Rakitskiy, Luiz Adriano.

Liverpool (0) 1 *(N'Gog 81)*

Unirea (0) 0   40,450

Liverpool: Reina; Carragher, Fabio Aurelio, Mascherano, Agger, Skrtel, Aquilani (Pacheco 75), Gerrard, N'Gog (Lucas 90), Kuyt, Riera (Babel 63).
Unirea: Arlauskis; Galamaz, Brandan, Bruno Fernandes, Maftei, Paraschiv (Viana 86), Paduretu (Rusescu 90), Frunza, Apostol, Bilasco, Onofras (Marinescu 75).

SECOND ROUND SECOND LEG

Benfica	(1) 4	Hertha Berlin	(0) 0
Anderlecht	(2) 4	Athletic Bilbao	(0) 0
Fenerbahce	(1) 1	Lille	(0) 1
Galatasaray	(0) 1	Atletico Madrid	(0) 2
Hapoel Tel Aviv	(0) 0	Rubin	(0) 0
Juventus	(0) 0	Ajax	(0) 0
Marseille	(1) 3	FC Copenhagen	(0) 1
PSV Eindhoven	(2) 3	Hamburg	(0) 2
Roma	(1) 2	Panathinaikos	(3) 3
Salzburg	(0) 0	Standard Liege	(0) 0
Shakhtar Donetsk	(0) 1	Fulham	(1) 1
Sporting Lisbon	(0) 3	Everton	(0) 0
Unirea	(1) 1	Liverpool	(2) 3
Valencia	(1) 3	Club Brugge	(0) 0
(aet.)			
Werder Bremen	(3) 4	Twente	(1) 1
Wolfsburg	(3) 4	Villarreal	(1) 1

Thursday, 25 February 2010

Shakhtar Donetsk (0) 1 *(Jadson 69)*

Fulham (1) 1 *(Hangeland 33)*   47,509

Shakhtar Donetsk: Pyatov; Hubschman (Kravchenko 46), Kucher, Rat, Fernandinho, Jadson, Ilsinho, Willian (Douglas Costa 53), Srna, Rakitskiy, Luiz Adriano (Gladkiy 76).
Fulham: Schwarzer; Kelly, Baird, Murphy▪, Hughes, Hangeland, Duff, Etuhu, Gera, Zamora (Elm 72), Davies (Riise 89).

Sporting Lisbon (0) 3 *(Miguel Veloso 64, Pedro Mendes 76, Matias 90)*

Everton (0) 0   17,609

Sporting Lisbon: Rui Patricio; Daniel Carrico, Tonel, Grimi (Saleiro 62), Abel, Pedro Mendes, Izmailov (Polga 90), Miguel Veloso, Joao Moutinho, Yannick Djalo, Liedson (Matias 90).
Everton: Howard; Neville, Baines, Yobo, Senderos (Jagielka 52), Bilyaletdinov (Rodwell 62), Osman, Pienaar, Saha, Donovan (Yakubu 73), Arteta.

Unirea (1) 1 *(Bruno Fernandes 19)*

Liverpool (2) 3 *(Mascherano 30, Babel 41, Gerrard 57)*   25,000

Unirea: Arlauskis; Galamaz (Mehmedovic 27), Bruno Fernandes, Bordeanu, Maftei, Paraschiv (Ricardo 56), Paduretu, Frunza, Apostol, Bilasco, Onofras (Semedo 62).
Liverpool: Reina; Carragher (Kelly 61), Insua, Mascherano, Agger, Skrtel (Kyrgiakos 66), Benayoun (Fabio Aurelio 77), Gerrard, N'Gog, Lucas, Babel.

THIRD ROUND FIRST LEG

Atletico Madrid	(0) 0	Sporting Lisbon	(0) 0
Benfica	(0) 1	Marseille	(0) 1
Hamburg	(2) 3	Anderlecht	(1) 1
Juventus	(3) 3	Fulham	(1) 1
Lille	(0) 1	Liverpool	(0) 0

Panathinaikos	(0) 1	Standard Liege	(2) 3
Rubin	(1) 1	Wolfsburg	(0) 1
Valencia	(0) 1	Werder Bremen	(1) 1

Thursday, 11 March 2010

Juventus (3) 3 *(Legrottaglie 9, Zebina 25, Trezeguet 45)*

Fulham (1) 1 *(Etuhu 36)*   11,406

Juventus: Manninger; Cannavaro, Grosso, Zebina, Legrottaglie, Salihamidzic (Camoranesi 46), Marchisio, Poulsen (Sissoko 76), Candreva, Diego, Trezeguet (Iaquinta 62).
Fulham: Schwarzer; Baird, Konchesky, Greening, Hughes, Hangeland, Duff, Etuhu, Gera, Zamora, Davies (Dempsey 61).

Lille (0) 1 *(Hazard 84)*

Liverpool (0) 0   17,000

Lille: Landreau; Emerson, Beria, Rami, Balmont, Cabaye (Dumont 73), Obraniak (Toure 83), Chedjou, Mavuba, Hazard, Frau (Aubameyang 77).
Liverpool: Reina; Johnson, Insua, Mascherano, Carragher, Agger, Lucas, Gerrard, Torres, Kuyt (El Zhar 88), Babel (Riera 73).

THIRD ROUND SECOND LEG

Anderlecht	(2) 4	Hamburg	(1) 3
Fulham	(2) 4	Juventus	(1) 1
Liverpool	(1) 3	Lille	(0) 0
Marseille	(0) 1	Benfica	(0) 2
Sporting Lisbon	(2) 2	Atletico Madrid	(2) 2
Standard Liege	(1) 1	Panathinaikos	(0) 0
Werder Bremen	(1) 4	Valencia	(3) 4
Wolfsburg	(0) 2	Rubin	(1) 1
(aet.)			

Thursday, 18 March 2010

Fulham (2) 4 *(Zamora 9, Gera 39, 49 (pen), Dempsey 83)*

Juventus (1) 1 *(Trezeguet 2)*   23,458

Fulham: Schwarzer; Kelly (Dempsey 72), Konchesky, Baird, Hughes, Hangeland, Duff, Etuhu, Gera (Riise 85), Zamora, Davies.
Juventus: Chimenti; Cannavaro■, Grosso (Del Piero 85), Zebina■, Felipe Melo, Salihamidzic, Camoranesi (De Ceglie 52), Sissoko, Candreva (Grygera 28), Diego, Trezeguet.

Liverpool (1) 3 *(Gerrard 9 (pen), Torres 49, 89)*

Lille (0) 0   38,139

Liverpool: Reina; Johnson, Insua, Mascherano, Carragher, Agger (Kyrgiakos 90), Lucas, Gerrard, Torres (N'Gog 90), Kuyt, Babel (Benayoun 80).
Lille: Landreau; Emerson, Beria, Rami, Balmont (Aubameyang 71), Cabaye, Obraniak, Chedjou, Mavuba, Hazard (Vandam 86), Frau (Toure 59).

QUARTER-FINALS FIRST LEG

Benfica	(0) 2	Liverpool	(1) 1
Fulham	(0) 2	Wolfsburg	(0) 1
Hamburg	(2) 2	Standard Liege	(1) 1
Valencia	(0) 2	Atletico Madrid	(0) 2

Thursday, 1 April 2010

Benfica (0) 2 *(Cardozo 59 (pen), 79 (pen))*

Liverpool (1) 1 *(Agger 9)*   62,629

Benfica: Julio Cesar; Luisao, Maxi Pereira (Nuno Gomes 66), David Luiz, Javier Garcia, Ramires, Aimar (Airton 87), Carlos Martins (Ruben Amorim 72), Fabio Coentrao, Di Maria, Cardozo.
Liverpool: Reina; Johnson, Insua, Mascherano, Carragher, Agger, Lucas, Gerrard (Benayoun 90), Torres (N'Gog 82), Kuyt, Babel■.

Fulham (0) 2 *(Zamora 59, Duff 63)*

Wolfsburg (0) 1 *(Madlung 89)*   22,307

Fulham: Schwarzer; Duff, Konchesky, Murphy (Baird 87), Hughes, Hangeland, Dempsey, Etuhu, Gera, Zamora, Davies.
Wolfsburg: Benaglio; Schafer, Madlung, Pekarik (Martins 74), Riether, Barzagli, Josue, Misimovic, Gentner (Dejagah 84), Dzeko, Grafite.

QUARTER-FINALS SECOND LEG

Atletico Madrid	(0) 0	Valencia	(0) 0
Liverpool	(2) 4	Benfica	(0) 1
Standard Liege	(1) 1	Hamburg	(2) 3
Wolfsburg	(0) 0	Fulham	(1) 1

Thursday, 8 April 2010

Liverpool (2) 4 *(Kuyt 27, Lucas 34, Torres 58, 82)*

Benfica (0) 1 *(Cardozo 70)*   42,377

Liverpool: Reina; Johnson, Kyrgiakos, Mascherano, Carragher, Agger, Benayoun (El Zhar 90), Gerrard (Aquilani 88), Torres (N'Gog 86), Kuyt, Lucas.
Benfica: Julio Cesar (Moreira 79); Luisao, David Luiz, Sidnei, Ruben Amorim, Javier Garcia, Ramires, Aimar (Fabio Coentrao 86), Carlos Martins (Kardec 67), Di Maria, Cardozo.

Wolfsburg (0) 0

Fulham (1) 1 *(Zamora 1)*   25,000

Wolfsburg: Benaglio; Schafer, Simunek (Rever 76), Pekarik (Dejagah 35), Riether, Barzagli, Josue, Misimovic, Gentner (Martins 62), Dzeko, Grafite.
Fulham: Schwarzer; Baird, Konchesky, Murphy, Hughes, Hangeland, Duff, Etuhu, Gera (Nevland 82), Zamora, Davies (Riise 86).

SEMI-FINALS FIRST LEG

| Atletico Madrid | (1) 1 | Liverpool | (0) 0 |
| Hamburg | (0) 0 | Fulham | (0) 0 |

Thursday, 22 April 2010

Atletico Madrid (1) 1 *(Forlan 9)*

Liverpool (0) 0   50,000

Atletico Madrid: De Gea; Antonio Lopez, Ujfalusi, Alvaro Dominguez, Perea, Raul Garcia, Jurado, Paulo Assuncao, Reyes (Camacho 90), Simao (Valera 78), Forlan (Salvio 85).
Liverpool: Reina; Johnson, Kyrgiakos, Mascherano, Carragher, Agger, Benayoun (El Zhar 84), Gerrard, N'Gog (Babel 64), Kuyt, Lucas.

Hamburg (0) 0

Fulham (0) 0   49,171

Hamburg: Rost; Mathijsen, Aogo, Boateng, Demel (Rincon 82), Ze Roberto, Jarolim, Trochowski, Pitroipa, Guerrero (Petric 72), Van Nistelrooy.

Fulham: Schwarzer; Baird, Konchesky, Murphy, Hughes, Hangeland, Duff, Etuhu, Gera, Zamora (Dempsey 52), Davies.

SEMI-FINALS SECOND LEG

Fulham	(0) 2	Hamburg	(1) 1
Liverpool	(1) 2	Atletico Madrid	(0) 1

(aet.)

Thursday, 29 April 2010

Fulham (0) 2 *(Davies 69, Gera 76)*

Hamburg (1) 1 *(Petric 22)* 25,700

Fulham: Schwarzer; Pantsil (Nevland 75), Konchesky, Murphy, Hughes, Hangeland, Duff, Etuhu, Gera, Zamora (Dempsey 58), Davies.
Hamburg: Rost; Mathijsen, Aogo, Boateng, Demel, Ze Roberto, Tesche (Rincon 56) (Guerrero 79), Jarolim (Rozehnal 90), Pitroipa, Petric, Van Nistelrooy

Liverpool (1) 2 *(Aquilani 44, Benayoun 95)*

Atletico Madrid (0) 1 *(Forlan 103)* 42,040

Liverpool: Reina; Mascherano (Degen 110), Johnson, Aquilani (El Zhar 89), Carragher, Agger, Benayoun (Pacheco 114), Gerrard, Babel, Kuyt, Lucas.
Atletico Madrid: De Gea; Valera, Antonio Lopez, Alvaro Dominguez, Perea, Raul Garcia, Paulo Assuncao (Jurado 99), Reyes, Simao, Forlan (Camacho 117), Aguero (Salvio 120).
aet.

UEFA EUROPA LEAGUE FINAL 2010

Wednesday, 12 May 2010

(in Hamburg, attendance 49,000)

Atletico Madrid (1) 2 *(Forlan 32, 116)*

Fulham (1) 1 *(Davies 37)*

Atletico Madrid: De Gea; Ujfalusi, Perea, Alvaro Dominguez, Antonio Lopez, Reyes (Salvio 78), Paulo Assuncao, Raul Garcia, Simao (Jurado 68), Forlan, Aguero (Valera 119).

Fulham: Schwarzer; Baird, Konchesky, Murphy (Greening 118), Hughes, Hangeland, Duff (Nevland 84), Etuhu, Gera, Zamora (Dempsey 55), Davies.

(aet.)

Referee: Rizzoli (Italy).

PAST EUROPEAN CUP FINALS

Year	Winner	Score	Runner-up	Score
1956	Real Madrid	4	Stade de Rheims	3
1957	Real Madrid	2	Fiorentina	0
1958	Real Madrid*	3	AC Milan	2
1959	Real Madrid	2	Stade de Rheims	0
1960	Real Madrid	7	Eintracht Frankfurt	3
1961	Benfica	3	Barcelona	2
1962	Benfica	5	Real Madrid	3
1963	AC Milan	2	Benfica	1
1964	Internazionale	3	Real Madrid	1
1965	Internazionale	1	SL Benfica	0
1966	Real Madrid	2	Partizan Belgrade	1
1967	Celtic	2	Internazionale	1
1968	Manchester U*	4	Benfica	1
1969	AC Milan	4	Ajax	1
1970	Feyenoord*	2	Celtic	1
1971	Ajax	2	Panathinaikos	0
1972	Ajax	2	Internazionale	0
1973	Ajax	1	Juventus	0
1974	Bayern Munich	1 4	Atletico Madrid	1 0
1975	Bayern Munich	2	Leeds U	0
1976	Bayern Munich	1	St Etienne	0
1977	Liverpool	3	Borussia Moenchengladbach	1
1978	Liverpool	1	FC Brugge	0
1979	Nottingham F	1	Malmö	0
1980	Nottingham F	1	Hamburg	0
1981	Liverpool	1	Real Madrid	0
1982	Aston Villa	1	Bayern Munich	0
1983	Hamburg	1	Juventus	0
1984	Liverpool†	1	Roma	1
1985	Juventus	1	Liverpool	0
1986	Steaua Bucharest†	0	Barcelona	0
1987	Porto	2	Bayern Munich	1
1988	PSV Eindhoven†	0	Benfica	0
1989	AC Milan	4	Steaua Bucharest	0
1990	AC Milan	1	Benfica	0
1991	Red Star Belgrade†	0	Marseille	0
1992	Barcelona	1	Sampdoria	0

PAST UEFA CHAMPIONS LEAGUE FINALS

Year	Winner	Score	Runner-up	Score
1993	Marseille	1	AC Milan	0

(Marseille subsequently stripped of title)

Year	Winner	Score	Runner-up	Score
1994	AC Milan	4	Barcelona	0
1995	Ajax	1	AC Milan	0
1996	Juventus†	1	Ajax	1
1997	Borussia Dortmund	3	Juventus	1
1998	Real Madrid	1	Juventus	0
1999	Manchester U	2	Bayern Munich	1
2000	Real Madrid	3	Valencia	0
2001	Bayern Munich†	1	Valencia	1
2002	Real Madrid	2	Leverkusen	1
2003	AC Milan†	0	Juventus	0
2004	Porto	3	Monaco	0
2005	Liverpool†	3	AC Milan	3
2006	Barcelona	2	Arsenal	1
2007	AC Milan	2	Liverpool	1
2008	Manchester U†	1	Chelsea	1
2009	Barcelona	2	Manchester U	0
2010	Internazionale	2	Bayern Munich	0

† aet; won on penalties.   * aet.

PAST UEFA CUP FINALS

Year	Winner			Runner-up		
1972	Tottenham H	2	1	Wolverhampton W	1	1
1973	Liverpool	3	0	Borussia Moenchengladbach	0	2
1974	Feyenoord	2	2	Tottenham H	2	0
1975	Borussia Moenchengladbach	0	5	Twente Enschede	0	1
1976	Liverpool	3	1	FC Brugge	2	1
1977	Juventus**	1	1	Athletic Bilbao	0	2
1978	PSV Eindhoven	0	3	SEC Bastia	0	0
1979	Borussia Moenchengladbach	1	1	Red Star Belgrade	1	0
1980	Borussia Moenchengladbach	3	0	Eintracht Frankfurt**	2	1
1981	Ipswich T	3	2	AZ 67 Alkmaar	0	4
1982	IFK Gothenburg	1	3	SV Hamburg	0	0
1983	Anderlecht	1	1	Benfica	0	1
1984	Tottenham H†	1	1	RSC Anderlecht	1	1
1985	Real Madrid	3	0	Videoton	0	1
1986	Real Madrid	5	0	Cologne	1	2
1987	IFK Gothenburg	1	1	Dundee U	0	1
1988	Bayer Leverkusen†	0	3	Espanol	0	3
1989	Napoli	2	3	Stuttgart	1	3
1990	Juventus	3	0	Fiorentina	1	0
1991	Internazionale	2	0	AS Roma	0	1
1992	Ajax**	0	2	Torino	0	2
1993	Juventus	3	3	Borussia Dortmund	1	0
1994	Internazionale	1	1	Salzburg	0	0
1995	Parma	1	1	Juventus	0	1
1996	Bayern Munich	2	3	Bordeaux	0	1
1997	Schalke*†	1	0	Internazionale	0	1
1998	Internazionale	3		Lazio	0	
1999	Parma	3		Marseille	0	
2000	Galatasaray†	0		Arsenal	0	
2001	Liverpool§	5		Alaves	4	
2002	Feyenoord	3		Borussia Dortmund	2	
2003	Porto*	3		Celtic	2	
2004	Valencia	2		Marseille	0	
2005	CSKA Moscow	3		Sporting Lisbon	1	
2006	Sevilla	4		Middlesbrough	0	
2007	Sevilla*†	2		Espanyol	2	
2008	Zenit St Petersburg	2		Rangers	0	
2009	Shakhtar Donetsk*	2		Werder Bremen	1	

UEFA EUROPA LEAGUE FINALS

Year	Winner		Runner-up	
2010	Atletico Madrid*	2	Fulham	1

*After extra time **Won on away goals †Won on penalties §Won on sudden death.

UEFA EUROPA LEAGUE 2010–2011

PARTICIPATING CLUBS
This list is provisional and subject to final confirmation from UEFA
GROUP STAGE
Club Atlético de Madrid (ESP)
PLAY-OFFS
FC Porto (POR) [CW], PFC CSKA Moskva (RUS), PSV Eindhoven (NED), FC
Steaua Bucureşti (ROU), LOSC Lille Métropole (FRA), Bayer 04 Leverkusen (GER),
Paris Saint-Germain FC (FRA) [CW], Club Brugge KV (BEL), US Città di Palermo
(ITA), Getafe CF (ESP), Manchester City FC (ENG), AEK Athens FC (GRE), Aston
Villa FC (ENG), FC Lokomotiv Moskva (RUS), FC Metalist Kharkiv (UKR),
Feyenoord (NED), RCD Mallorca (ESP), SSC Napoli (ITA), BV Borussia Dortmund
(GER), Grasshopper-Club (SUI), SC Vaslui (ROU), Trabzonspor (TUR) [CW], SC
Tavriya Simferopol (UKR) [CW], Dundee United FC (SCO) [CW]

THIRD QUALIFYING ROUND
Liverpool FC (ENG), Juventus (ITA), Sporting Clube de Portugal (POR), VfB
Stuttgart (GER), AZ Alkmaar (NED), Galatasaray AŞ (TUR), Maccabi Haifa FC
(ISR), PFC CSKA Sofia (BUL), Odense BK (DEN), FC Dnipro Dnipropetrovsk
(UKR), FK Crvena Zvezda (SRB), Aris Thessaloniki FC (GRE), FC Timişoara
(ROU), Montpellier Hérault SC (FRA), FC Sibir Novosibirsk (RUS), KRC Genk
(BEL), SK Sturm Graz (AUT) [CW], Hibernian FC (SCO), FC Luzern (SUI), FC
Nordsjælland (DEN) [CW], ŠK Slovan Bratislava (SVK) [CW], PFC Beroe Stara
Zagora (BUL) [CW], FC Viktoria Plzeň (CZE) [CW], FK Jablonec 97 (CZE), IFK
Göteborg (SWE), Apollon Limassol FC (CYP) [CW], Aalesunds FK (NOR) [CW],
HNK Hajduk Split (CRO) [CW], FC Inter Turku (FIN) [CW], Jagiellonia Białystok
(POL) [CW]

SECOND QUALIFYING ROUND
Olympiacos FC (GRE), Beşiktaş JK (TUR), FC Dinamo 1948 Bucureşti (ROU), PFC
Levski Sofia (BUL), FK Austria Wien (AUT), Brøndby IF (DEN), SK Rapid Wien
(AUT), APOEL FC (CYP), Wisła Kraków (POL), FC Karpaty Lviv (UKR), CS
Marítimo (POR), FC Baník Ostrava (CZE), IF Elfsborg (SWE), FC Utrecht (NED),
Motherwell FC (SCO), FC Lausanne-Sport (SUI) [CF], Cercle Brugge KSV (BEL)
[CF], Stabæk IF (NOR), FK Ventspils (LVA), Molde FK (NOR), Maccabi Tel-Aviv FC
(ISR), FK Dukla Banská Bystrica (SVK), FC Honka Espoo (FIN), NK Maribor (SVN)
[CW], FC Dinamo Minsk (BLR), OFK Beograd (SRB), FK Spartak Zlatibor Voda
(SRB), FK Bakı (AZE) [CW], HNK Cibalia (CRO), FK Sūduva (LTU), FC WIT
Georgia (GEO) [CW], FC Iskra-Stali (MDA), Sporting Fingal FC (IRL) [CW],
Shamrock Rovers FC (IRL), FC Vaduz (LIE) [CW], ND Gorica (SVN), FK Borac
Banja Luka (BIH) [CW], KFK Šiauliai (LTU), FK Jelgava (LVA) [CW], FC Videoton
(HUN), UE Sant Julià (AND) [CW], Breidablik (ISL) [CW], FK Teteks (MKD) [CW],
Bangor City FC (WAL) [CW], FK Atyrau (KAZ) [CW], JK Sillamäe Kalev (EST) [CW],
Mika (ARM), KS Besa (ALB) [CW], FC Differdange 03 (LUX) [CW], Valletta FC
(MLT) [CW], FK Budućnost Podgorica (MNE), Vikingur (FRO) [CW], Cliftonville FC
(NIR), SP Tre Penne (SMR)

FIRST QUALIFYING ROUND
Anorthosis Famagusta FC (CYP), Randers FC (DEN) [FP], Kalmar FF (SWE), Bnei
Yehuda Tel-Aviv FC (ISR) [CF], FC Nitra (SVK), FK Rabotnicki (MKD),
Myllykosken Pallo-47 (FIN) [FP], Gefle IF (SWE) [FP], NK Zrinjski (BIH), FK
Qarabag (AZE), KS Ruch Chorzów (POL), HNK Šibenik (CRO), FC Dnepr Mogilev
(BLR), FC Torpedo Zhodino (BLR) [CF], NK Široki Brijeg (BIH), Skonto FC (LVA),
FC Dinamo Tbilisi (GEO), KR Reykjavík (ISL), FC Dacia Chişinău (MDA) [CF],
Dundalk FC (IRL), FC TPS Turku (FIN), KF Tirana (ALB), FK Tauras (LTU), FC
Zestafoni (GEO), FC Olimpia Bălţi (MDA), FK Mogren (MNE), FC Tobol Kostanay
(KAZ), NK Olimpija Ljubljana (SVN), FC Flora (EST) [CF], EB/Streymur (FRO),
Győri ETO FC (HUN), Zalaegerszegi TE (HUN) [CF], Glentoran FC (NIR), F91
Dudelange (LUX), JK Trans Narva (EST), FK Khazar Lankaran (AZE), Fylkir (ISL),
FK Metalurg Skopje (MKD), FC Shakhtyor Karagandy (KAZ), FC Banants (ARM)
[CF], KF Laçi (ALB), Llanelli AFC (WAL), Sliema Wanderers FC (MLT), NSÍ
Runavík (FRO), FC Ulysses (ARM), Port Talbot Town FC (WAL), CS Grevenmacher
(LUX), FK Zeta (MNE), Portadown FC (NIR) [CF], UE Santa Coloma (AND), FC
Lusitans (AND), SC Faetano (SMR)

PAST EUROPEAN CHAMPIONSHIP FINALS

Year	Winners		Runners-up		Venue	Attendance
1960	USSR	2	Yugoslavia	1	Paris	17,966
1964	Spain	2	USSR	1	Madrid	120,000
1968	Italy	2	Yugoslavia	0	Rome	60,000
	(After 1-1 draw)					75,000
1972	West Germany	3	USSR	0	Brussels	43,437
1976	Czechoslovakia	2	West Germany	2	Belgrade	45,000
	(Czechoslovakia won on penalties)					
1980	West Germany	2	Belgium	1	Rome	47,864
1984	France	2	Spain	0	Paris	48,000
1988	Holland	2	USSR	0	Munich	72,308
1992	Denmark	2	Germany	0	Gothenburg	37,800
1996	Germany	2	Czech Republic	1	Wembley	73,611
	(Germany won on sudden death)					
2000	France	2	Italy	1	Rotterdam	50,000
	(France won on sudden death)					
2004	Greece	1	Portugal	0	Lisbon	62,865
2008	Spain	1	Germany	0	Vienna	51,428

PAST WORLD CUP FINALS

Year	Winners		Runners-up		Venue	Att.	Referee
1930	Uruguay	4	Argentina	2	Montevideo	90,000	Langenus (B)
1934	Italy*	2	Czechoslovakia	1	Rome	50,000	Eklind (Se)
1938	Italy	4	Hungary	2	Paris	45,000	Capdeville (F)
1950	Uruguay	2	Brazil	1	Rio de Janeiro	199,854	Reader (E)
1954	West Germany	3	Hungary	2	Berne	60,000	Ling (E)
1958	Brazil	5	Sweden	2	Stockholm	49,737	Guigue (F)
1962	Brazil	3	Czechoslovakia	1	Santiago	68,679	Latychev (USSR)
1966	England*	4	West Germany	2	Wembley	93,802	Dienst (Sw)
1970	Brazil	4	Italy	1	Mexico City	107,412	Glockner (EG)
1974	West Germany	2	Holland	1	Munich	77,833	Taylor (E)
1978	Argentina*	3	Holland	1	Buenos Aires	77,000	Gonella (I)
1982	Italy	3	West Germany	1	Madrid	90,080	Coelho (Br)
1986	Argentina	3	West Germany	2	Mexico City	114,580	Filho (Br)
1990	West Germany	1	Argentina	0	Rome	73,603	Mendez (Mex)
1994	Brazil*	0	Italy	0	Los Angeles	94,194	Puhl (H)
	(Brazil won 3-2 on penalties)						
1998	France	3	Brazil	0	St-Denis	75,000	Belqola (Mor)
2002	Brazil	2	Germany	0	Yokohama	69,029	Collina (I)
2006	Italy*	1	France	1	Berlin	69,000	Elizondo (Arg)
	(Italy won 5-3 on penalties)						
2010	Spain*	1	Holland	0	Johannesburg	84,490	Webb (E)

After extra time.

EURO 2012 FIXTURES

11 AUGUST 2010
Group C Estonia v Faeroe Islands

03 SEPTEMBER 2010
Group A Belgium v Germany
Group A Kazakhstan v Turkey
Group B Slovakia v FYR Macedonia
Group B Armenia v Republic of Ireland
Group B Andorra v Russia
Group C Slovenia v Northern Ireland
Group C Estonia v Italy
Group C Faeroe Islands v Serbia
Group D France v Belarus
Group D Romania v Albania
Group D Luxembourg v Bosnia-Herzegovina
Group E Sweden v Hungary
Group E Moldova v Finland
Group E San Marino v Netherlands
Group F Greece v Georgia
Group F Israel v Malta
Group F Latvia v Croatia
Group G England v Bulgaria
Group G Montenegro v Wales
Group H Portugal v Cyprus
Group H Iceland v Norway
Group I Lithuania v Scotland
Group I Liechtenstein v Spain

07 SEPTEMBER 2010
Group A Germany v Azerbaijan
Group A Turkey v Belgium
Group A Austria v Kazakhstan
Group B Russia v Slovakia
Group B Republic of Ireland v Andorra
Group B FYR Macedonia v Armenia
Group C Italy v Faeroe Islands
Group C Serbia v Slovenia
Group D Bosnia-Herzegovina v France
Group D Belarus v Romania
Group D Albania v Luxembourg
Group E Netherlands v Finland
Group E Sweden v San Marino
Group E Hungary v Moldova
Group F Croatia v Greece
Group F Georgia v Israel
Group F Malta v Latvia
Group G Switzerland v England
Group G Bulgaria v Montenegro
Group H Denmark v Iceland
Group H Norway v Portugal
Group I Czech Republic v Lithuania
Group I Scotland v Liechtenstein

08 OCTOBER 2010
Group A Germany v Turkey
Group A Austria v Azerbaijan
Group A Kazakhstan v Belgium
Group B Republic of Ireland v Russia
Group B Armenia v Slovakia
Group B Andorra v FYR Macedonia
Group C Serbia v Estonia
Group C Northern Ireland v Italy
Group C Slovenia v Faeroe Islands
Group D Albania v Bosnia-Herzegovina
Group D Luxembourg v Belarus
Group E Hungary v San Marino
Group E Moldova v Netherlands
Group F Greece v Latvia

Group F Georgia v Malta
Group G Wales v Bulgaria
Group G Montenegro v Switzerland
Group H Portugal v Denmark
Group H Cyprus v Norway
Group I Spain v Lithuania
Group I Czech Republic v Scotland

09 OCTOBER 2010
Group D France v Romania
Group F Israel v Croatia

12 OCTOBER 2010
Group A Belgium v Austria
Group A Kazakhstan v Germany
Group A Azerbaijan v Turkey
Group B Slovakia v Republic of Ireland
Group B FYR Macedonia v Russia
Group B Armenia v Andorra
Group C Italy v Serbia
Group C Estonia v Slovenia
Group C Faeroe Islands v Northern Ireland
Group D France v Luxembourg
Group D Belarus v Albania
Group E Netherlands v Sweden
Group E Finland v Hungary
Group E San Marino v Moldova
Group F Croatia v Malta
Group F Greece v Israel
Group F Latvia v Georgia
Group G England v Montenegro
Group G Switzerland v Wales
Group H Denmark v Cyprus
Group H Iceland v Portugal
Group I Liechtenstein v Czech Republic
Group I Scotland v Spain

17 NOVEMBER 2010
Group E Finland v San Marino

25 MARCH 2011
Group A Germany v Kazakhstan
Group A Austria v Belgium
Group C Serbia v Northern Ireland
Group C Slovenia v Italy
Group D Luxembourg v France
Group E Hungary v Netherlands
Group I Spain v Czech Republic

26 MARCH 2011
Group B Republic of Ireland v FYR Macedonia
Group B Armenia v Russia
Group B Andorra v Slovakia
Group D Bosnia-Herzegovina v Romania
Group D Albania v Belarus
Group F Israel v Latvia
Group F Georgia v Croatia
Group F Malta v Greece
Group G Bulgaria v Switzerland
Group G Wales v England
Group H Norway v Denmark
Group H Cyprus v Iceland

29 MARCH 2011
Group A Turkey v Austria
Group A Belgium v Azerbaijan
Group C Northern Ireland v Slovenia
Group C Estonia v Serbia

Group D Romania v Luxembourg
Group E Netherlands v Hungary
Group E Sweden v Moldova
Group F Israel v Georgia
Group I Czech Republic v Liechtenstein
Group I Lithuania v Spain

03 JUNE 2011
Group A Austria v Germany
Group A Belgium v Turkey
Group A Kazakhstan v Azerbaijan
Group C Italy v Estonia
Group C Faeroe Islands v Slovenia
Group D Romania v Bosnia-Herzegovina
Group D Belarus v France
Group E Moldova v Sweden
Group E San Marino v Finland
Group I Liechtenstein v Lithuania

04 JUNE 2011
Group B Russia v Armenia
Group B Slovakia v Andorra
Group B FYR Macedonia v Republic of Ireland
Group F Croatia v Georgia
Group F Greece v Malta
Group F Latvia v Israel
Group G England v Switzerland
Group G Montenegro v Bulgaria
Group H Portugal v Norway
Group H Iceland v Denmark

07 JUNE 2011
Group A Azerbaijan v Germany
Group C Faeroe Islands v Estonia
Group D Bosnia-Herzegovina v Albania
Group D Belarus v Luxembourg
Group E Sweden v Finland
Group E San Marino v Hungary

10 AUGUST 2011
Group C Northern Ireland v Faeroe Islands

02 SEPTEMBER 2011
Group A Germany v Austria
Group A Turkey v Kazakhstan
Group A Azerbaijan v Belgium
Group B Russia v FYR Macedonia
Group B Republic of Ireland v Slovakia
Group B Andorra v Armenia
Group C Northern Ireland v Serbia
Group C Slovenia v Estonia
Group C Faeroe Islands v Italy
Group D Belarus v Bosnia-Herzegovina
Group D Albania v France
Group D Luxembourg v Romania
Group E Netherlands v San Marino
Group E Finland v Moldova
Group E Hungary v Sweden
Group F Israel v Greece
Group F Georgia v Latvia
Group F Malta v Croatia
Group G Bulgaria v England
Group G Wales v Montenegro
Group H Norway v Iceland
Group H Cyprus v Portugal
Group I Lithuania v Liechtenstein

03 SEPTEMBER 2011
Group I Scotland v Czech Republic

06 SEPTEMBER 2011
Group A Austria v Turkey

Group A Azerbaijan v Kazakhstan
Group B Russia v Republic of Ireland
Group B Slovakia v Armenia
Group B FYR Macedonia v Andorra
Group C Italy v Slovenia
Group C Serbia v Faeroe Islands
Group C Estonia v Northern Ireland
Group D Romania v France
Group D Bosnia-Herzegovina v Belarus
Group D Luxembourg v Albania
Group E Finland v Netherlands
Group E Moldova v Hungary
Group E San Marino v Sweden
Group F Croatia v Israel
Group F Latvia v Greece
Group F Malta v Georgia
Group G England v Wales
Group G Switzerland v Bulgaria
Group H Denmark v Norway
Group H Iceland v Cyprus
Group I Spain v Liechtenstein
Group I Scotland v Lithuania

07 OCTOBER 2011
Group A Turkey v Germany
Group A Belgium v Kazakhstan
Group A Azerbaijan v Austria
Group E Netherlands v Moldova
Group E Finland v Sweden
Group B Slovakia v Russia
Group B Armenia v FYR Macedonia
Group B Andorra v Republic of Ireland
Group C Serbia v Italy
Group C Northern Ireland v Estonia
Group D France v Albania
Group D Romania v Belarus
Group D Bosnia-Herzegovina v Luxembourg
Group F Greece v Croatia
Group F Latvia v Malta
Group G Wales v Switzerland
Group G Montenegro v England
Group H Portugal v Iceland
Group H Cyprus v Denmark
Group I Czech Republic v Spain

08 OCTOBER 2011
Group I Liechtenstein v Scotland

11 OCTOBER 2011
Group A Germany v Belgium
Group A Turkey v Azerbaijan
Group A Kazakhstan v Austria
Group B Russia v Andorra
Group B Republic of Ireland v Armenia
Group B FYR Macedonia v Slovakia
Group C Italy v Northern Ireland
Group C Slovenia v Serbia
Group D France v Bosnia-Herzegovina
Group D Albania v Romania
Group E Sweden v Netherlands
Group E Hungary v Finland
Group E Moldova v San Marino
Group F Croatia v Latvia
Group F Georgia v Greece
Group F Malta v Israel
Group G Switzerland v Montenegro
Group G Bulgaria v Wales
Group H Denmark v Portugal
Group H Norway v Cyprus
Group I Spain v Scotland
Group I Lithuania v Czech Republic

WORLD CUP 2010 QUALIFYING RESULTS

■ *Denotes player sent off.*

EUROPE

GROUP 1

Albania	(0) 0	Sweden	(0) 0
Hungary	(0) 0	Denmark	(0) 0
Malta	(0) 0	Portugal	(1) 4
Albania	(1) 3	Malta	(0) 0
Portugal	(1) 2	Denmark	(0) 3
Sweden	(0) 2	Hungary	(0) 1
Denmark	(2) 3	Malta	(0) 0
Hungary	(0) 2	Albania	(0) 0
Sweden	(0) 0	Portugal	(0) 0
Malta	(0) 0	Hungary	(1) 1
Portugal	(0) 0	Albania	(0) 0
Malta	(0) 0	Albania	(0) 0
Albania	(0) 0	Hungary	(1) 1
Malta	(0) 0	Denmark	(2) 3
Portugal	(0) 0	Sweden	(0) 0
Denmark	(2) 3	Albania	(0) 0
Hungary	(1) 3	Malta	(0) 0
Albania	(1) 1	Portugal	(1) 2
Sweden	(0) 0	Denmark	(1) 1
Sweden	(1) 4	Malta	(0) 0
Denmark	(1) 1	Portugal	(0) 1
Hungary	(0) 1	Sweden	(1) 2
Albania	(0) 1	Denmark	(1) 1
Hungary	(0) 0	Portugal	(1) 1
Malta	(0) 0	Sweden	(0) 1
Denmark	(0) 1	Sweden	(0) 0
Portugal	(1) 3	Hungary	(0) 0
Denmark	(0) 0	Hungary	(1) 1
Portugal	(2) 4	Malta	(0) 0
Sweden	(3) 4	Albania	(0) 1

Group 1 Table	P	W	D	L	F	A	Pts
Denmark	10	6	3	1	16	5	21
Portugal	10	5	4	1	17	5	19
Sweden	10	5	3	2	13	5	18
Hungary	10	5	1	4	10	8	16
Albania	10	1	4	5	6	13	7
Malta	10	0	1	9	0	26	1

GROUP 2

Israel	(0) 2	Switzerland	(1) 2
Luxembourg	(0) 0	Greece	(2) 3
Moldova	(0) 1	Latvia	(2) 2
Latvia	(0) 0	Greece	(1) 2
Moldova	(1) 1	Israel	(2) 2
Switzerland	(1) 1	Luxembourg	(1) 2
Greece	(2) 3	Moldova	(0) 0
Luxembourg	(1) 1	Israel	(1) 3
Switzerland	(0) 2	Latvia	(0) 1

Greece	(0) 1	Switzerland	(1) 2
Latvia	(0) 1	Israel	(0) 1
Luxembourg	(0) 0	Moldova	(0) 0
Israel	(0) 1	Greece	(1) 1
Luxembourg	(0) 0	Latvia	(1) 4
Moldova	(0) 0	Switzerland	(1) 2
Greece	(1) 2	Israel	(0) 1
Latvia	(1) 2	Luxembourg	(0) 0
Switzerland	(1) 2	Moldova	(0) 0
Israel	(0) 0	Latvia	(0) 1
Moldova	(0) 0	Luxembourg	(0) 0
Switzerland	(0) 2	Greece	(0) 0
Israel	(4) 7	Luxembourg	(0) 0
Latvia	(0) 2	Switzerland	(1) 2
Moldova	(0) 1	Greece	(1) 1
Greece	(1) 5	Latvia	(2) 2
Israel	(1) 3	Moldova	(0) 1
Luxembourg	(0) 0	Switzerland	(3) 3
Greece	(2) 2	Luxembourg	(0) 1
Latvia	(2) 3	Moldova	(1) 2
Switzerland	(0) 0	Israel	(0) 0

Group 2 Table	P	W	D	L	F	A	Pts
Switzerland	10	6	3	1	18	8	21
Greece	10	6	2	2	20	10	20
Latvia	10	5	2	3	18	15	17
Israel	10	4	4	2	20	10	16
Luxembourg	10	1	2	7	4	25	5
Moldova	10	0	3	7	6	18	3

GROUP 3

Poland	(1) 1	Slovenia	(1) 1
Slovakia	(0) 2	Northern Ireland	(0) 1
Northern Ireland	(0) 0	Czech Republic	(0) 0
San Marino	(0) 0	Poland	(1) 2
Slovenia	(1) 2	Slovakia	(0) 1
Poland	(1) 2	Czech Republic	(0) 1
San Marino	(1) 1	Slovakia	(2) 3
Slovenia	(0) 2	Northern Ireland	(0) 0
Czech Republic	(0) 1	Slovenia	(0) 0
Northern Ireland	(2) 4	San Marino	(0) 0
Slovakia	(0) 2	Poland	(0) 1
San Marino	(0) 0	Czech Republic	(0) 3
San Marino	(0) 0	Northern Ireland	(2) 3
Northern Ireland	(1) 3	Poland	(1) 2
Slovenia	(0) 0	Czech Republic	(0) 0
Czech Republic	(1) 1	Slovakia	(1) 2
Northern Ireland	(0) 1	Slovenia	(0) 0
Poland	(4) 10	San Marino	(0) 0
Slovakia	(5) 7	San Marino	(0) 0
Slovenia	(2) 5	San Marino	(0) 0
Poland	(0) 1	Northern Ireland	(1) 1
Slovakia	(0) 2	Czech Republic	(0) 2
Czech Republic	(3) 7	San Marino	(0) 0
Northern Ireland	(0) 0	Slovakia	(1) 2
Slovenia	(2) 3	Poland	(0) 0
Czech Republic	(0) 2	Poland	(0) 0
Slovakia	(0) 0	Slovenia	(0) 2

Czech Republic	(0) 0	Northern Ireland	(0) 0
Poland	(0) 0	Slovakia	(1) 1
San Marino	(0) 0	Slovenia	(1) 3

Bratislava, 6 September 2008, 5445

Slovakia (0) 2 *(Skrtel 46, Hamsik 70)*

Northern Ireland (0) 1 *(Durica 81 (og))*

Slovakia: Senecky; Skrtel, Petras, Pekarik, Durica, Sapara, Kozak, Karhan (Zabavnik 75), Hamsik, Vittek (Mintal 84), Jakubko (Svento 59).
Northern Ireland: Maik Taylor; Baird (Shiels 78), McCartney, Evans, Hughes, Craigan, Davis, Clingan, Gillespie (Feeney 53), Healy, Paterson (Brunt 66).
Referee: Ivanov (Russia).

Belfast, 10 September 2008, 12,882

Northern Ireland (0) 0

Czech Republic (0) 0

Northern Ireland: Maik Taylor; Evans, Hughes, McCartney, Baird, Craigan, Brunt, Clingan (O'Connor 46), Feeney (Paterson 72), Gillespie (Shiels 83), Healy.
Czech Republic: Cech; Jankulovski, Kovac R, Rozehnal, Ujfalusi, Grygera, Plasil, Polak, Sionko (Pospech 67), Sirl, Baros (Slepicka 77).
Referee: Bebek (Croatia).

Maribor, 11 October 2008, 12,385

Slovenia (0) 2 *(Novakovic 84, Ljubijankic 85)*

Northern Ireland (0) 0

Slovenia: Handanovic; Suler, Kirm (Matic 90), Ilic, Cesar, Brecko, Koren, Komac, Sisic (Birsa 81), Novakovic, Dedic (Ljubijankic 69).
Northern Ireland: Maik Taylor; Baird, McCartney, McAuley, Hughes, Evans, Gillespie, McCann (McGivern 73), Lafferty, Healy, Davis.
Referee: Gonzalez (Spain).

Belfast, 15 October 2008, 12,957

Northern Ireland (2) 4 *(Healy 31, McCann 43, Lafferty 56, Davis 75)*

San Marino (0) 0

Northern Ireland: Maik Taylor; Baird, McCartney, McCann (Paterson 73), McAuley (McGivern 61), Hughes, Gillspie, O'Connor, Lafferty (Feeney 82), Healy, Davis.
San Marino: Valentini F; Della Valle, Vannucci, Valentini C, Bacciocchi, Albani N, Michele Marani, Mauro Marani■, Bonini (Vitaioli F 77), Selva A (Vitaioli M 46), Manuel Marani (Cibelli 86).
Referee: Kari (Finland).

Serravalle, 11 February 2009, 1942

San Marino (0) 0

Northern Ireland (2) 3 *(McAuley 7, McCann 33, Brunt 63)*

San Marino: Valentini F; Della Valle, Berretti, Bacciocchi (Vitaioli F 73), Vannucci, Valentini C, Simoncini D, Muccioli (Bugli 66), Michele Marani, Vitaioli M (Casadei 87), Manuel Marani■.
Northern Ireland: Maik Taylor; Hughes (McCourt 80), McCartney, McCann, McAuley, Craigan, Johnson, Davis, Lafferty (Brunt 55), Healy, Paterson (Feeney 77).
Referee: Stankovic (Serbia).

Belfast, 28 March 2009, 13,357

Northern Ireland (1) 3 *(Feeney 10, Evans 47, Michal Zewlakow 61 (og))*

Poland (1) 2 *(Jelen 27, Saganowski 90)*

Northern Ireland: Maik Taylor; McAuley, Evans, Craigan, Hughes, Clingan, Johnson, McCann, Feeney (Baird 84), Healy (Little 90), Brunt.
Poland: Boruc; Wasilewski, Michal Zewlakow (Bosacki 65), Wawrzyniak, Roger, Bandrowski (Blaszczykowski 60), Lewandowski M, Krzynowek, Dudka, Jelen (Saganowski 71), Lewandowski R.
Referee: Hansson (Sweden).

Belfast, 1 April 2009, 15,000

Northern Ireland (0) 1 *(Feeney 73)*

Slovenia (0) 0

Northern Ireland: Maik Taylor; Hughes, McCartney (McGivern 44), McCann, McAuley (Baird 16), Evans, Davis, Clingan, Feeney, Healy, Johnson.
Slovenia: Handanovic; Mavric, Kirm (Pecnik 77), Cesar, Brecko (Mejac 85), Koren, Komac, Jokic, Filekovic, Novakovic, Dedic (Ljubijankic 64).
Referee: Yefet (Israel).

Chorzow, 5 September 2009, 38,914

Poland (0) 1 *(Lewandowski M 80)*

Northern Ireland (1) 1 *(Lafferty 38)*

Poland: Boruc; Golanski, Zewlakow, Obraniak (Smolarek 46), Blaszczykowski, Roger, Murawski (Lewandowski R 61), Lewandowski M, Krzynowek, Dudka, Pawel Brozek.
Northern Ireland: Maik Taylor; Hughes, Craigan, Clingan, McAuley, Evans J, Davis, Johnson, Lafferty (Paterson 54), Healy, McCann.
Referee: Gonzalez (Spain).

Belfast, 9 September 2009, 13,019

Northern Ireland (0) 0

Slovakia (1) 2 *(Sestak 15, Holosko 66)*

Northern Ireland: Maik Taylor; Hughes, McAuley, Clingan (Baird 70), Evans J, Craigan, Davis, Johnson, Healy, Paterson (Brunt 76), McCann (McGinn 70).
Slovakia: Mucha; Durica, Skrtel, Pekarik, Kopunek, Strba, Zabavnik, Vittek, Stoch (Jendrisek 80), Sestak (Holosko 65), Weiss (Sapara 90).
Referee: Kuipers (Holland).

Prague, 14 October 2009, 8002

Czech Republic (0) 0

Northern Ireland (0) 0

Czech Republic: Cech; Pospech, Jankulovski, Hubschman, Hubnik, Sivok, Rosicky (Stajner 72), Plasil, Jarolim (Papadopoulos 83), Baros, Necid (Hlousek 58).
Northern Ireland: Maik Taylor; Baird, McGinn, Craigan, Hughes, McAuley, McGivern, McCann (O'Connor 80), Davis, Johnson (Kirk 83), Healy (Feeney 69).
Referee: Duhamel (France).

Group 3 Table	P	W	D	L	F	A	Pts
Slovakia	10	7	1	2	22	10	22
Slovenia	10	6	2	2	18	4	20
Czech Republic	10	4	4	2	17	6	16
Northern Ireland	10	4	3	3	13	9	15
Poland	10	3	2	5	19	14	11
San Marino	10	0	0	10	1	47	0

GROUP 4

Liechtenstein	(0) 0	Germany	(1) 6
Wales	(0) 1	Azerbaijan	(0) 0
Azerbaijan	(0) 0	Liechtenstein	(0) 0
Finland	(2) 3	Germany	(2) 3
Russia	(1) 2	Wales	(0) 1
Finland	(0) 1	Azerbaijan	(0) 0
Germany	(2) 2	Russia	(0) 1
Wales	(1) 2	Liechtenstein	(0) 0
Germany	(0) 1	Wales	(0) 0
Russia	(1) 3	Finland	(0) 0
Germany	(2) 4	Liechtenstein	(0) 0
Russia	(1) 2	Azerbaijan	(0) 0
Wales	(0) 0	Finland	(1) 2
Liechtenstein	(0) 0	Russia	(1) 1
Wales	(0) 0	Germany	(1) 2
Azerbaijan	(0) 0	Wales	(1) 1
Finland	(1) 2	Liechtenstein	(1) 1
Finland	(0) 0	Russia	(1) 3
Azerbaijan	(0) 0	Germany	(1) 2
Finland	(1) 2	Liechtenstein	(1) 1
Germany	(1) 4	Azerbaijan	(0) 0
Liechtenstein	(0) 1	Finland	(0) 1
Wales	(0) 1	Russia	(1) 3
Finland	(1) 2	Wales	(1) 1
Liechtenstein	(0) 0	Azerbaijan	(0) 2
Russia	(0) 0	Germany	(1) 1
Azerbaijan	(0) 1	Russia	(1) 1
Germany	(0) 1	Finland	(1) 1
Liechtenstein	(0) 0	Wales	(1) 2

Cardiff, 6 September 2008, 17,106

Wales (0) 1 *(Vokes 83)*

Azerbaijan (0) 0

Wales: Hennessey; Morgan C, Gunter, Williams A, Bale, Edwards D (Vokes 72), Ledley, Fletcher, Earnshaw (Evans C 62), Davies S, Koumas (Robinson 89).
Azerbaijan: Agayev; Yunisoglu, Malikov, Mammadov N (Nduka 78), Abbasov, Rashad Sadikhov, Mammadov E, Fabio■, Bakhshiyev, Subasic, Huseynov (Nabiyev 46).
Referee: Stavrev (Macedonia).

Moscow, 10 September 2008, 28,000

Russia (1) 2 *(Pavlyuchenko 22 (pen), Pogrebnyak 81)*

Wales (0) 1 *(Ledley 67)*

Russia: Akinfeev; Anyukov, Ignashevich (Bystrov 90), Kolodin, Semak (Pogrebnyak 74), Semshov, Torbinskiy (Saenko 61), Zhirkov, Zyryanov, Arshavin, Pavlyuchenko.
Wales: Hennessey; Morgan C, Gunter, Bale, Robinson (Ricketts 46), Edwards D (Evans S 76), Fletcher, Ledley, Williams A, Davies S, Vokes (Evans C 62).
Referee: Skomina (Slovenia).

Cardiff, 11 October 2008, 13,356

Wales (1) 2 *(Edwards D 42, Frick M 80 (og))*

Liechtenstein (0) 0

Wales: Hennessey; Morgan C, Gunter, Bale, Williams A, Koumas, Fletcher (Robinson 56), Edwards D, Davies S, Bellamy (Collins J 80), Vokes (Evans C 51).
Liechtenstein: Jehle; Martin Stocklasa, Ritzberger (Christen 67), D'Elia, Polverino (Buchel R 80), Gerster, Burgmeier, Buchel M, Frick M, Fischer, Beck T.
Referee: Vejlgaard (Denmark).

Moenchengladbach, 15 October 2008, 45,000

Germany (0) 1 *(Trochowski 72)*

Wales (0) 0

Germany: Adler; Westermann, Mertesacker, Lahm, Friedrich A (Fritz 65), Trochowski, Schweinsteiger, Hitzlsperger, Ballack, Podolski (Gomez 82), Klose (Helmes 46).
Wales: Hennessey; Gunter (Ricketts 86), Bale, Fletcher (Robinson 77), Morgan C, Williams A, Davies S, Collins J, Bellamy, Koumas, Edwards D (Evans C 77).
Referee: Duhamel (France).

Cardiff, 28 March 2009, 22,604

Wales (0) 0

Finland (1) 2 *(Johansson 42, Kuqi S 90)*

Wales: Hennessey; Gunter, Bale, Edwards D (Ramsey 56), Nyatanga, Collins J, Koumas, Fletcher (Robinson 65), Bellamy, Davies S, Ledley (Earnshaw 71).
Finland: Jaaskelainen; Tihinen, Pasanen, Kallio, Hyypia, Eremenko R, Heikkinen, Eremenko A (Sjolund 78), Litmanen (Porokara 90), Johansson, Forssell (Kuqi S 89).
Referee: Gonzalez (Spain).

Cardiff, 1 April 2009, 26,064

Wales (0) 0

Germany (1) 2 *(Ballack 11, Williams A 48 (og))*

Wales: Hennessey; Ricketts (Gunter 54), Bale, Williams A, Nyatanga (Cotterill 75), Collins J, Davies S, Ramsey, Vokes (Evans C 62), Earnshaw, Ledley.
Germany: Enke; Tasci, Mertesacker, Lahm, Beck, Schweinsteiger (Helmes 86), Rolfes (Westermann 79), Hitzlsperger, Ballack, Podolski (Trochowski 72), Gomez.
Referee: Hauge (Norway).

Baku, 6 June 2009, 25,000

Azerbaijan (0) 0

Wales (1) 1 *(Edwards D 41)*

Azerbaijan: Veliyev; Shukurov, Melikov, Levin, Nabiyev (Huseynov 50), Rashad Sadikhov, Fabio (Subasic 46), Zeynalov, Bakhshiyev, Javadov, Akhtyamov (Nadyrov 60).
Wales: Hennessey; Gunter, Eardley, Nyatanga, Morgan, Williams A, Ramsey, Edwards D, Ledley, Earnshaw (Vokes 70), Church (Tudur-Jones 83).
Referee: Strombergsson (Sweden).

Cardiff, 9 September 2009, 14,505

Wales (0) 1 *(Collins J 54)*

Russia (1) 3 *(Semshov 36, Ignashevich 72, Pavlyuchenko 90)*

Wales: Hennessey; Ricketts, Gunter, Gabbidon (Vokes 75), Williams A, Collins J, Ramsey, Ledley, Edwards D, Stock, Bellamy.
Russia: Akinfeev; Ignashevich, Berezutski V, Anyukov, Zyryanov, Yanbaev, Semshov (Pavlyuchenko 71), Semak, Bystrov, Kerzhakov (Rebko 84), Arshavin.
Referee: Sousa (Portugal).

Helsinki, 10 October 2009, 14,000

Finland (1) 2 *(Porokara 5, Moisander 77)*

Wales (1) 1 *(Bellamy 17)*

Finland: Jaaskelainen; Tihinen, Pasanen, Moisander, Hyypia, Sparv, Kolkka (Hamalainen 68), Eremenko R, Porokara, Litmanen (Eremenko A 90), Johansson (Kuqi S 88).
Wales: Hennessey; Gunter, Bale, Edwards D, Nyatanga (Eardley 83), Williams A, Collins J, Ramsey, Church (Vokes 63), Bellamy, Cotterill.
Referee: Mazic (Serbia).

Vaduz, 14 October 2009, 1858

Liechtenstein (0) 0

Wales (1) 2 *(Vaughan 15, Ramsey 79)*

Liechtenstein: Jehle; Ritzberger, Rechsteiner, D'Elia, Oehri, Rohrer (Beck R 36), Kieber, Eberle, Frick M, Buchel R (Polverino 70), Hasler (Christen 72).
Wales: Myhill; Gunter (Eardley 87), Bale (Nyatanga 84), Collins J, Morgan C, Williams A, Edwards D (King A 82), Ramsey, Church, Easter, Vaughan.
Referee: Kaldma (Estonia).

Group 4 Table	P	W	D	L	F	A	Pts
Germany	10	8	2	0	26	5	26
Russia	10	7	1	2	19	6	22
Finland	10	5	3	2	14	14	18
Wales	10	4	0	6	9	12	12
Azerbaijan	10	1	2	7	4	14	5
Liechtenstein	10	0	2	8	2	23	2

GROUP 5

Armenia	(0) 0	Turkey	(0) 2
Belgium	(1) 3	Estonia	(0) 2
Spain	(0) 1	Bosnia	(0) 0
Bosnia	(2) 7	Estonia	(0) 0
Spain	(2) 4	Armenia	(0) 0
Turkey	(0) 1	Belgium	(1) 1
Belgium	(2) 2	Armenia	(0) 0
Estonia	(0) 0	Spain	(2) 3
Turkey	(0) 2	Bosnia	(1) 1
Belgium	(1) 1	Spain	(1) 2
Bosnia	(2) 4	Armenia	(0) 1
Estonia	(0) 0	Turkey	(0) 0
Armenia	(1) 2	Estonia	(1) 2
Belgium	(0) 2	Bosnia	(1) 4
Spain	(0) 1	Turkey	(0) 0
Bosnia	(2) 2	Belgium	(0) 1
Estonia	(0) 1	Armenia	(0) 0
Turkey	(1) 1	Spain	(0) 2
Armenia	(0) 0	Bosnia	(1) 2
Spain	(1) 5	Belgium	(0) 0
Turkey	(2) 4	Estonia	(1) 2
Armenia	(1) 2	Belgium	(0) 1
Bosnia	(1) 1	Turkey	(1) 1
Spain	(1) 3	Estonia	(0) 0
Armenia	(0) 1	Spain	(1) 2
Belgium	(1) 2	Turkey	(0) 0
Estonia	(0) 0	Bosnia	(1) 2
Bosnia	(0) 2	Spain	(2) 5
Estonia	(1) 2	Belgium	(0) 0
Turkey	(2) 2	Armenia	(0) 0

Group 5 Table	P	W	D	L	F	A	Pts
Spain	10	10	0	0	28	5	30
Bosnia	10	6	1	3	25	13	19
Turkey	10	4	3	3	13	10	15
Belgium	10	3	1	6	13	20	10
Estonia	10	2	2	6	9	24	8
Armenia	10	1	1	8	6	22	4

GROUP 6

Kazakhstan	(3) 3	Andorra	(0) 0
Andorra	(0) 0	England	(0) 2
Croatia	(2) 3	Kazakhstan	(0) 0
Ukraine	(0) 1	Belarus	(0) 0
Andorra	(0) 1	Belarus	(1) 3
Croatia	(0) 1	England	(1) 4
Kazakhstan	(0) 1	Ukraine	(1) 3
England	(0) 5	Kazakhstan	(0) 1
Ukraine	(0) 0	Croatia	(0) 0
Belarus	(1) 1	England	(1) 3
Croatia	(2) 4	Andorra	(0) 0
Andorra	(0) 0	Croatia	(2) 2
England	(1) 2	Ukraine	(0) 1
Kazakhstan	(1) 1	Belarus	(0) 5
Belarus	(2) 5	Andorra	(0) 1
Croatia	(1) 2	Ukraine	(1) 2
Kazakhstan	(0) 0	England	(2) 4
England	(3) 6	Andorra	(0) 0
Ukraine	(1) 2	Kazakhstan	(1) 1
Belarus	(0) 1	Croatia	(1) 3
Croatia	(1) 1	Belarus	(0) 0
Ukraine	(2) 5	Andorra	(0) 0
Andorra	(0) 1	Kazakhstan	(3) 3
Belarus	(0) 0	Ukraine	(0) 0
England	(2) 5	Croatia	(0) 1
Belarus	(1) 4	Kazakhstan	(0) 0
Ukraine	(1) 1	England	(0) 0
Andorra	(0) 0	Ukraine	(1) 6
England	(1) 3	Belarus	(0) 0
Kazakhstan	(1) 1	Croatia	(1) 2

Barcelona, 6 September 2008, 10,300

Andorra (0) 0

England (0) 2 *(Cole J 48, 55)*

Andorra: Koldo; Lima T (Juli Fernandez 90), Lima I, Txema, Xavi, Vieira, Pujol (Vales 90), Ayala, Jimenez, Sonejee, Fernando Silva (Toscano 65).
England: James; Johnson G, Cole A, Barry, Terry, Lescott, Walcott, Lampard (Beckham 80), Rooney, Defoe (Heskey 46), Downing (Cole J 46).
Referee: Cuneyt (Turkey).

Zagreb, 10 September 2008, 35,218

Croatia (0) 1 *(Mandzukic 78)*

England (1) 4 *(Walcott 26, 59, 82, Rooney 63)*

Croatia: Pletikosa; Corluka, Simunic, Kovac R■, Srna, Rakitic, Pranjic, Modric, Kovac N (Pokrivac 62), Petric (Knezevic 56), Olic (Mandzukic 73).
England: James; Terry (Upson 89), Ferdinand, Cole A, Brown, Lampard, Cole J (Jenas 56), Barry, Walcott (Beckham 85), Rooney, Heskey.
Referee: Michel (Slovakia).

268

Wembley, 11 October 2008, 89,107

England (0) 5 *(Ferdinand 52, Rooney 76, 86, Defoe 90, Kuchma 64 (og))*

Kazakhstan (0) 1 *(Kukeyev 68)*

England: James; Brown, Cole A, Gerrard, Ferdinand, Upson, Walcott (Beckham 79), Lampard, Heskey, Rooney (Defoe 86), Barry (Wright-Phillips 46).
Kazakhstan: Mokin; Kuchma, Kislitsyn, Kirov (Sabalakov 85), Kukeyev, Baltiyev, Logvinenko, Ibrayev, Skorykh, Ostapenko (Maltsev 76), Nusserbayev.
Referee: Allaerts (Belgium).

Minsk, 15 October 2008, 32,000

Belarus (1) 1 *(Sitko 28)*

England (1) 3 *(Gerrard 11, Rooney 50, 74)*

Belarus: Zhevnov; Verkhovtsov, Filipenko, Omelyanchuk, Molosh, Kulchi, Sitko, Putsilo (Rodionov 67), Stasevich (Hleb V 90), Kutuzov (Strakanovich 77), Bulyga.
England: James; Brown, Bridge, Gerrard, Ferdinand, Upson, Walcott (Wright-Phillips 68), Lampard, Heskey (Crouch 70), Rooney (Beckham 87), Barry.
Referee: Hauge (Norway).

Wembley, 1 April 2009, 87,548

England (1) 2 *(Crouch 29, Terry 85)*

Ukraine (0) 1 *(Shevchenko 74)*

England: James; Johnson G, Cole A, Barry, Terry, Ferdinand (Jagielka 88), Lennon (Beckham 58), Lampard, Crouch (Wright-Phillips 79), Rooney, Gerrard.
Ukraine: Pyatov; Chigrinskiy, Shevchuk, Yarmash, Mikhalik, Valyaev (Nazarenko 61), Slyusar (Kalinichenko 89), Aliev, Tymoshchuk, Voronin (Shevchenko 55), Milevskiy.
Referee: Bo Larsen (Denmark).

Almaty, 6 June 2009, 24,000

Kazakhstan (0) 0

England (2) 4 *(Barry 39, Heskey 45, Rooney 72, Lampard 78 (pen))*

Kazakhstan: Mokin; Abdulin, Kirov, Kislitsyn, Karpovich, Logvinenko, Kukeev, Skorykh, Averchenko (Erbes 74), Ostapenko (Ibraev 27), Nuserbaev.
England: Green; Johnson G (Beckham 76), Cole A, Barry, Terry, Upson, Gerrard, Lampard, Heskey (Defoe 81), Rooney, Walcott (Wright-Phillips 46).
Referee: Jakobsson (Iceland).

Wembley, 10 June 2009, 57,897

England (3) 6 *(Rooney 4, 38, Lampard 29, Defoe 73, 75, Crouch 80)*

Andorra (0) 0

England: Green; Johnson G, Cole A (Bridge 63), Beckham, Terry, Lescott, Gerrard (Young A 46), Lampard, Crouch, Rooney (Defoe 46), Walcott.
Andorra: Koldo (Gomes 89); Lima T (Vales 47), Txema, Ayala, Lima I, Andorra, Vieira, Jimenez, Sonejee, Moreno, Fernando Silva (Juli Fernandez 79).
Referee: Nijhuis (Holland).

Wembley, 9 September 2009, 87,319

England (2) 5 *(Lampard 7 (pen), 59, Gerrard 18, 66, Rooney 77)*

Croatia (0) 1 *(Eduardo 71)*

England: Green; Johnson G, Cole A, Barry, Terry, Upson, Lennon (Milner 81), Lampard, Heskey (Defoe 60), Rooney, Gerrard (Beckham 81).
Croatia: Runje; Krizanac, Simunic, Kranjcar, Vukojevic, Srna, Pranjic, Pokrivac (Rakitic 46), Eduardo (Klasnic 73), Olic (Petric 46), Mandzukic.
Referee: Mallenco (Spain).

Dnepr, 10 October 2009, 31,000

Ukraine (1) 1 *(Nazarenko 29)*

England (0) 0

Ukraine: Pyatov; Khacheridi, Kucher, Rakitskiy, Gay, Rotan, Tymoshchuk, Nazarenko (Yarmolenko 67), Kobin, Shevchenko (Gusev 90), Milevskiy.
England: Green■; Johnson, Cole A, Carrick, Terry, Ferdinand, Lennon (James 15), Lampard, Rooney, Heskey (Cole C 72), Gerrard (Milner 46).
Referee: Skomina (Slovenia).

Wembley, 14 October 2009, 76,897

England (1) 3 *(Crouch 3, 75, Wright-Phillips 60)*

Belarus (0) 0

England: Foster; Johnson G, Bridge (Milner 78), Barry, Terry, Ferdinand, Lennon (Beckham 60), Lampard, Crouch, Agbonlahor (Cole C 66), Wright-Phillips.
Belarus: Zhevnov; Yurevich, Sosnovskiy, Shitov, Verkhovtsov, Omelyanchuk, Bordachev (Kashevski 84), Kulchiy, Kalachev, Kutuzov (Rodionov 46), Kornilenko (Kovel 77).
Referee: Batista (Portugal).

Group 6 Table	P	W	D	L	F	A	Pts
England	10	9	0	1	34	6	27
Ukraine	10	6	3	1	21	6	21
Croatia	10	6	2	2	19	13	20
Belarus	10	4	1	5	19	14	13
Kazakhstan	10	2	0	8	11	29	6
Andorra	10	0	0	10	3	39	0

GROUP 7

Austria	(2) 3	France	(0) 1
Romania	(0) 0	Lithuania	(1) 3
Serbia	(1) 2	Faeroes	(0) 0
Faeroes	(0) 0	Romania	(0) 1
France	(0) 2	Serbia	(0) 1
Lithuania	(0) 2	Austria	(0) 0
Faeroes	(0) 1	Austria	(0) 1
Romania	(2) 2	France	(1) 2
Serbia	(2) 3	Lithuania	(0) 0
Austria	(0) 1	Serbia	(3) 3
Lithuania	(1) 1	Faeroes	(0) 0
Lithuania	(0) 0	France	(0) 1
Romania	(0) 2	Serbia	(2) 3
Austria	(2) 2	Romania	(1) 1
France	(0) 1	Lithuania	(0) 0
Lithuania	(0) 0	Romania	(1) 1
Serbia	(1) 1	Austria	(0) 0
Faeroes	(0) 0	Serbia	(1) 2
Faeroes	(0) 0	France	(1) 1
Austria	(2) 3	Faeroes	(0) 1
France	(0) 1	Romania	(0) 1
Faeroes	(2) 2	Lithuania	(1) 1
Romania	(0) 1	Austria	(0) 1
Serbia	(1) 1	France	(1) 1
Austria	(1) 2	Lithuania	(0) 1
France	(2) 5	Faeroes	(0) 0

Serbia	(1) 5	Romania	(0) 0
France	(2) 3	Austria	(0) 1
Lithuania	(1) 2	Serbia	(0) 1
Romania	(1) 3	Faeroes	(0) 1

Group 7 Table	P	W	D	L	F	A	Pts
Serbia	10	7	1	2	22	8	22
France	10	6	3	1	18	9	21
Austria	10	4	2	4	14	15	14
Lithuania	10	4	0	6	10	11	12
Romania	10	3	3	4	12	18	12
Faeroes	10	1	1	8	5	20	4

GROUP 8

Cyprus	(1) 1	Italy	(1) 2
Georgia	(0) 1	Republic of Ireland	(1) 2
Montenegro	(0) 2	Bulgaria	(1) 2
Italy	(1) 2	Georgia	(0) 0
Montenegro	(0) 0	Republic of Ireland	(0) 0
Bulgaria	(0) 0	Italy	(0) 0
Georgia	(0) 1	Cyprus	(0) 1
Georgia	(0) 0	Bulgaria	(0) 0
Italy	(2) 2	Montenegro	(1) 1
Republic of Ireland	(1) 1	Cyprus	(0) 0
Republic of Ireland	(0) 2	Georgia	(1) 1
Cyprus	(1) 2	Georgia	(0) 1
Montenegro	(0) 0	Italy	(1) 2
Republic of Ireland	(1) 1	Bulgaria	(0) 1
Bulgaria	(1) 2	Cyprus	(0) 0
Georgia	(0) 0	Montenegro	(0) 0
Italy	(1) 1	Republic of Ireland	(0) 1
Bulgaria	(1) 1	Republic of Ireland	(1) 1
Cyprus	(2) 2	Montenegro	(0) 2
Bulgaria	(1) 4	Montenegro	(1) 1
Cyprus	(1) 1	Republic of Ireland	(1) 2
Georgia	(0) 0	Italy	(0) 2
Italy	(2) 2	Bulgaria	(0) 0
Montenegro	(0) 1	Cyprus	(0) 1
Cyprus	(2) 4	Bulgaria	(1) 1
Montenegro	(1) 2	Georgia	(1) 1
Republic of Ireland	(1) 2	Italy	(1) 2
Bulgaria	(6) 6	Georgia	(1) 2
Italy	(0) 3	Cyprus	(1) 2
Republic of Ireland	(0) 0	Montenegro	(0) 0

Mainz, 6 September 2008, 4500

Georgia (0) 1 *(Kenia 90)*

Republic of Ireland (1) 2 *(Doyle K 13, Whelan 70)*

Georgia: Loria; Shashiashvili, Lobjanidze, Khizanishvili (Asatiani 83), Kaladze, Odikadze, Menteshashvili, Kobiashvili, Kenia, Aleksidze (Siradze 61), Iashvili (Mchedlidze 77).
Republic of Ireland: Given; Finnan (McShane 80), O'Shea, Dunne, Rowlands, Whelan, Kilbane, Hunt, Keane, Doyle K (Miller 77), McGeady (Keogh A 87).
Referee: Szabo (Hungary).

Podgorica, 10 September 2008, 12,000

Montenegro (0) 0

Republic of Ireland (0) 0

Montenegro: Poleksic; Batak, Jovanovic, Pavicevic, Tanasijevic, Zverotic, Bozovic V (Vukcevic 54), Drincic, Pekovic, Jovetic, Vucinic.
Republic of Ireland: Given; Finnan, Hunt, Dunne, O'Shea, Whelan, Reid A, Doyle K, Keane, Kilbane, McGeady.
Referee: Kaldma (Estonia).

Dublin, 15 October 2008, 55,833

Republic of Ireland (1) 1 *(Keane 5)*

Cyprus (0) 0

Republic of Ireland: Given; McShane, Kilbane, Dunne, O'Shea, Whelan, Gibson, Doyle K (Folan 90), Keane, Duff, McGeady.
Cyprus: Georgallides; Elia, Constantinou, Marangos (Panagi 52), Charalambous, Lambrou (Papathanasiou 46), Makrides, Konstantinou (Yiasoumi 79), Garpozis, Christofi, Okkas.
Referee: Tudor (Romania).

Dublin, 11 February 2009, 45,000

Republic of Ireland (0) 2 *(Keane 73 (pen), 78)*

Georgia (1) 1 *(Iashvili 1)*

Republic of Ireland: Given; Kelly, O'Shea, Whelan, Dunne, Andrews, Duff (Hunt S 80), Doyle K, Keane, Kilbane, McGeady.
Georgia: Lomaia; Lobjanidze, Kvirkvelia, Khizanishvili, Kaladze, Siradze (Aleksidze 77), Menteshashvili (Khmaladze 70), Kobiashvili, Razmadze, Iashvili, Gotsiridze (Merebashvili 68).
Referee: Hyytia (Finland).

Dublin, 28 March 2009, 60,002

Republic of Ireland (1) 1 *(Dunne 1)*

Bulgaria (0) 1 *(Kilbane 74 (og))*

Republic of Ireland: Given; McShane, O'Shea, Whelan, Dunne, Andrews, Kilbane, Hunt S, Keane, Doyle K, McGeady (Keogh A 90).
Bulgaria: Ivankov; Manolev, Angelov S, Stoyanov I, Milanov (Kishishev 24), Tomasic, Petrov S, Georgiev (Makriev 66), Telkiyski, Popov I (Dimitrov 46), Rangelov.
Referee: Bebek (Croatia).

Bari, 1 April 2009, 41,000

Italy (1) 1 *(Iaquinta 9)*

Republic of Ireland (0) 1 *(Keane 89)*

Italy: Buffon; Grosso, Chiellini, Cannavaro, Zambrotta, Pirlo (Palombo 44), De Rossi, Brighi, Pepe (Dossena 55), Pazzini■, Iaquinta (Quagliarella 90).
Republic of Ireland: Given; McShane, O'Shea, Whelan, Dunne, Andrews (Gibson 54), Kilbane, Hunt S, Keane, Doyle K (Hunt N 63), McGeady.
Referee: Stark (Germany).

Sofia, 6 June 2009, 38,000

Bulgaria (1) 1 *(Telkiyski 29)*

Republic of Ireland (1) 1 *(Dunne 24)*

Bulgaria: Ivankov; Kishishev, Angelov S, Tomasic, Stoyanov I, Milanov, Telkiyski (Dimitrov 81), Petrov S, Petrov M (Georgiev 61), Bojinov (Makriev 59), Berbatov.
Republic of Ireland: Given; O'Shea (Kelly 82), Kilbane, Dunne, St Ledger-Hall, Whelan, Hunt S (McGeady 71), Andrews, Folan, Keane (Best 74), Duff.
Referee: Bo Larsen (Denmark).

Nicosia, 5 September 2009, 5191

Cyprus (1) 1 *(Elia 30)*

Republic of Ireland (1) 2 *(Doyle K 5, Keane 83)*

Cyprus: Avgousti; Elia, Christou, Satsias (Marangos 90), Nicolaou, Michael (Alexandrou 71), Makrides, Charalambous, Aloneftis, Okkas (Christofi 90), Avraam.
Republic of Ireland: Given; O'Shea, Kilbane, Dunne, St Ledger-Hall, Whelan, Hunt S (McGeady 67), Andrews, Doyle K (Folan 75), Keane, Duff.
Referee: Einwaller (Austria).

Dublin, 10 October 2009, 70,640

Republic of Ireland (1) 2 *(Whelan 8, St Ledger-Hall 87)*

Italy (1) 2 *(Camoranesi 25, Gilardino 90)*

Republic of Ireland: Given; O'Shea, Andrews, St Ledger-Hall, Whelan (Rowlands 70), Lawrence, Kilbane, Doyle K (Best 66), Keane, McGeady (Hunt S 78).
Italy: Buffon; Grosso (Bocchetti 76), Chiellini, Zambrotta, Legrottaglie, De Rossi, Camoranesi, Pirlo, Palombo (Pepe 89), Iaquinta, Di Natale (Gilardino 76).
Referee: Hauge (Norway).

Dublin, 14 October 2009, 50,212

Republic of Ireland (0) 0

Montenegro (0) 0

Republic of Ireland: Given; McShane, Kilbane, Dunne, St Ledger-Hall, Miller, Rowlands (O'Shea 40), Duff, Hunt N (Best 68), Keane, Hunt S (Keogh A 88).
Montenegro: Poleksic; Zverotic, Batak (Dzudovic 31), Basa, Jovanovic, Vukcevic, Pekovic, Novakovic, Drincic, Boskovic (Kascelan 81), Delibasic (Damjanovic 69).
Referee: Hrinak (Slovakia).

Group 8 Table	P	W	D	L	F	A	Pts
Italy	10	7	3	0	18	7	24
Republic of Ireland	10	4	6	0	12	8	18
Bulgaria	10	3	5	2	17	13	14
Cyprus	10	2	3	5	14	16	9
Montenegro	10	1	6	3	9	14	9
Georgia	10	0	3	7	7	19	3

GROUP 9

Macedonia	(1) 1	Scotland	(0) 0
Norway	(1) 2	Iceland	(1) 2
Iceland	(0) 1	Scotland	(1) 2
Macedonia	(0) 1	Holland	(0) 2
Holland	(1) 2	Iceland	(0) 0
Scotland	(0) 0	Norway	(0) 0
Iceland	(1) 1	Macedonia	(0) 0
Norway	(0) 0	Holland	(0) 1
Holland	(2) 3	Scotland	(0) 0
Holland	(3) 4	Macedonia	(0) 0
Scotland	(1) 2	Iceland	(0) 1
Iceland	(0) 1	Holland	(2) 2
Macedonia	(0) 0	Norway	(0) 0
Holland	(1) 2	Norway	(0) 0
Macedonia	(1) 2	Iceland	(0) 0
Norway	(2) 4	Scotland	(0) 0
Iceland	(1) 1	Norway	(1) 1
Scotland	(0) 2	Macedonia	(0) 0
Norway	(2) 2	Macedonia	(0) 1
Scotland	(0) 0	Holland	(0) 1

Skopje, 6 September 2008, 9000

Macedonia (1) 1 *(Naumoski 5)*

Scotland (0) 0

Macedonia: Milosevski; Sedloski, Petrov (Grncarov 79), Noveski, Mitreski, Lazarevski, Sumulikoski, Grozdanovski, Pandev (Tasevski 83), Naumoski (Trajanov 69), Maznov.
Scotland: Gordon; Alexander G, Naysmith, Hartley (Commons 66), Caldwell G, McManus, Fletcher D, Brown S, McFadden, Miller (Boyd 81), Robson (Maloney 76).
Referee: Kralovec (Czech Republic).

Reykjavik, 10 September 2008, 9767

Iceland (0) 1 *(Gudjohnsen E 77)*

Scotland (1) 2 *(Broadfoot 18, Robson 59)*

Iceland: Sturulson; Eiriksson (Sigurdsson I 46), Hreidarsson, Saevarsson (Gunnarsson V 78), Steinsson, Gislason S, Gunnarsson A (Palmason 64), Sigurdsson K, Hallfredsson, Gudjohnsen E, Helguson.
Scotland: Gordon; Broadfoot, Naysmith, Brown S, Caldwell G, McManus■, Fletcher D, Maloney (Alexander G 79), McFadden (Hartley 79), Robson, Commons (Miller 63).
Referee: Gumienny (Belgium).

Glasgow, 11 October 2008, 50,205

Scotland (0) 0

Norway (0) 0

Scotland: Gordon; Broadfoot, Naysmith, Morrison (Fletcher S 56), Caldwell G, Weir, Robson, Brown, Fletcher D, McFadden (Iwelumo 56), Maloney.
Norway: Knudsen; Hoiland, Waehler, Hangeland, Riise JA, Grindheim, Stromstad (Pedersen 76), Riise BH (Braaten 56), Winsnes, Carew, Iversen.
Referee: Busacca (Switzerland).

Amsterdam, 28 March 2009, 49,552

Holland (2) 3 *(Huntelaar 30, Van Persie 45, Kuyt 76 (pen))*

Scotland (0) 0

Holland: Stekelenburg; Ooijer, Mathijsen, Van der Wiel, De Jong (Afellay 79), Van Bronckhorst, Van Bommel, Kuyt, Huntelaar (Schaars 79), Van Persie (Sneijder 64), Robben.
Scotland: McGregor; Alexander G (Hutton 73), Naysmith, Berra, Caldwell G, Ferguson, Teale (Morrison 84), Fletcher D, McCormack, Miller (Fletcher S 70), Brown S.
Referee: Duhamel (France).

Glasgow, 1 April 2009, 42,259

Scotland (1) 2 *(McCormack 39, Fletcher S 65)*

Iceland (0) 1 *(Sigurdsson I 54)*

Scotland: Gordon; Hutton, Naysmith, Morrison (Rae 90), Caldwell G, McManus, Fletcher D, Brown S, Fletcher S (Teale 78), Miller, McCormack.
Iceland: Gunnleifsson; Eiriksson, Steinsson, Sigurdsson I (Bjarnason 81), Gunnarsson A (Jonsson E 70), Danielsson, Sigurdsson K, Palmason, Helguson, Gudjohnsen E, Smarason.
Referee: Einwaller (Austria).

Oslo, 12 August 2009, 24,493

Norway (2) 4 *(Riise JA 36, Pedersen 45, 90, Huseklepp 60)*

Scotland (0) 0

Norway: Knudsen; Waehler, Riise JA, Hangeland, Hogli, Hoseth, Huseklepp (Iversen 76), Grindheim, Pedersen, Riise BH (Skjelbred 85), Carew (Helstad 84).

Scotland: Marshall; Hutton, Davidson, Caldwell S (McFadden 48), Caldwell G■, Alexander G, Fletcher D, Brown S, McCormack (Berra 37) (Whittaker 78), Miller K, Commons.
Referee: Hamer (Luxembourg).

Glasgow, 5 September 2009, 50,214

Scotland (0) 2 *(Brown S 56, McFadden 81)*

Macedonia (0) 0

Scotland: Gordon; Alexander G, Hutton, Fletcher D, McManus, Davidson (Whittaker 14), Weir, Brown S (Hartley 73), Fletcher S (Maloney 68), Miller K, McFadden.
Macedonia: Nikolovski; Sedloski, Noveski, Mitreski, Georgievski (Grozdanoski 69), Popov, Despotovski, Sumulikoski, Naumoski (Tasevski 65), Stojkov (Ibraimi 80), Pandev.
Referee: Stark (Germany).

Glasgow, 9 September 2009, 51,230

Scotland (0) 0

Holland (0) 1 *(Elia 81)*

Scotland: Marshall; Hutton, Whittaker, Hartley (Commons 66), Weir, McManus, Maloney (O'Connor 81), Fletcher D, Miller K, Brown S, Naismith.
Holland: Vorm; Ooijer, Mathijsen, Van der Wiel, De Zeeuw, De Jong, Van Bronckhorst, Sneijder (Van der Vaart 77), Robben (Elia 72), Kuyt, Van Persie (Huntelaar 84).
Referee: Bo Larsen (Denmark).

Group 9 Table	P	W	D	L	F	A	Pts
Holland	8	8	0	0	17	2	24
Norway	8	2	4	2	9	7	10
Scotland	8	3	1	4	6	11	10
Macedonia	8	2	1	5	5	11	7
Iceland	8	1	2	5	7	13	5

Denmark, England, Germany, Holland, Italy, Serbia, Slovakia, Spain and Switzerland qualified.
Bosnia, France, Greece, Portugal, Republic of Ireland, Russia, Slovenia and Ukraine play-off for final four places.

SOUTH AMERICA

Argentina	(2) 2	Chile	(0) 0
Uruguay	(2) 5	Bolivia	(0) 0
Colombia	(0) 0	Brazil	(0) 0
Ecuador	(0) 0	Venezuela	(0) 1
Peru	(0) 0	Paraguay	(0) 0
Bolivia	(0) 0	Colombia	(0) 0
Venezuela	(0) 0	Argentina	(2) 2
Brazil	(1) 5	Ecuador	(0) 0
Chile	(1) 2	Peru	(0) 0
Paraguay	(1) 1	Uruguay	(0) 0
Argentina	(1) 3	Bolivia	(0) 0
Colombia	(0) 1	Venezuela	(0) 0
Paraguay	(2) 5	Ecuador	(0) 1
Peru	(0) 1	Brazil	(1) 1
Uruguay	(1) 2	Chile	(0) 2
Venezuela	(2) 5	Bolivia	(2) 3
Colombia	(0) 2	Argentina	(1) 1
Ecuador	(3) 5	Peru	(0) 1
Brazil	(1) 2	Uruguay	(1) 1
Chile	(0) 0	Paraguay	(2) 3
Uruguay	(1) 1	Venezuela	(0) 1
Argentina	(0) 1	Ecuador	(0) 1
Bolivia	(0) 0	Chile	(1) 2
Paraguay	(1) 2	Brazil	(0) 0
Peru	(1) 1	Colombia	(1) 1
Bolivia	(2) 4	Paraguay	(0) 2
Ecuador	(0) 0	Colombia	(0) 0
Uruguay	(2) 6	Peru	(0) 0
Brazil	(0) 0	Argentina	(0) 0
Venezuela	(0) 2	Chile	(0) 3
Argentina	(0) 1	Paraguay	(1) 1
Ecuador	(1) 3	Bolivia	(1) 1
Colombia	(0) 0	Uruguay	(1) 1
Peru	(1) 1	Venezuela	(0) 0
Chile	(0) 0	Brazil	(2) 3
Paraguay	(2) 2	Venezuela	(0) 0
Uruguay	(0) 0	Ecuador	(0) 0
Brazil	(0) 0	Bolivia	(0) 0
Chile	(2) 4	Colombia	(0) 0
Peru	(0) 1	Argentina	(0) 1
Argentina	(2) 2	Uruguay	(1) 1
Bolivia	(2) 3	Peru	(0) 0
Colombia	(0) 0	Paraguay	(1) 1
Ecuador	(0) 1	Chile	(0) 0
Venezuela	(0) 0	Brazil	(3) 4
Bolivia	(2) 2	Uruguay	(0) 2
Paraguay	(0) 1	Peru	(0) 0
Brazil	(0) 0	Colombia	(0) 0
Chile	(1) 1	Argentina	(0) 0
Venezuela	(0) 3	Ecuador	(1) 1
Argentina	(1) 4	Venezuela	(0) 0
Uruguay	(1) 2	Paraguay	(0) 0
Colombia	(1) 2	Bolivia	(0) 0
Ecuador	(0) 1	Brazil	(0) 1
Peru	(1) 1	Chile	(2) 3
Bolivia	(3) 6	Argentina	(1) 1
Ecuador	(0) 1	Paraguay	(0) 1

Venezuela	(0) 2	Colombia	(0) 0
Brazil	(2) 3	Peru	(0) 0
Chile	(0) 0	Uruguay	(0) 0
Argentina	(0) 1	Colombia	(0) 0
Bolivia	(0) 0	Venezuela	(1) 1
Uruguay	(0) 0	Brazil	(2) 4
Paraguay	(0) 0	Chile	(1) 2
Peru	(0) 1	Ecuador	(1) 2
Ecuador	(0) 2	Argentina	(0) 0
Brazil	(1) 2	Paraguay	(1) 1
Chile	(1) 4	Bolivia	(0) 0
Colombia	(1) 1	Peru	(0) 0
Venezuela	(1) 2	Uruguay	(0) 2
Colombia	(0) 2	Ecuador	(0) 0
Peru	(0) 1	Uruguay	(0) 0
Argentina	(0) 1	Brazil	(2) 3
Chile	(1) 2	Venezuela	(2) 2
Paraguay	(1) 1	Bolivia	(0) 0
Bolivia	(0) 1	Ecuador	(1) 3
Uruguay	(1) 3	Colombia	(0) 1
Brazil	(2) 4	Chile	(1) 2
Paraguay	(1) 1	Argentina	(0) 0
Venezuela	(1) 3	Peru	(1) 1
Argentina	(0) 2	Peru	(0) 1
Bolivia	(2) 2	Brazil	(0) 1
Colombia	(1) 2	Chile	(2) 4
Ecuador	(0) 1	Uruguay	(0) 2
Venezuela	(0) 1	Paraguay	(0) 2
Peru	(0) 1	Bolivia	(0) 0
Brazil	(0) 0	Venezuela	(0) 0
Chile	(0) 1	Ecuador	(0) 0
Paraguay	(0) 0	Colombia	(0) 2
Uruguay	(0) 0	Argentina	(0) 1

South America Table	P	W	D	L	F	A	Pts
Brazil	18	9	7	2	33	11	34
Chile	18	10	3	5	32	22	33
Paraguay	18	10	3	5	24	16	33
Argentina	18	8	4	6	23	20	28
Uruguay	18	6	6	6	28	20	24
Ecuador	18	6	5	7	22	26	23
Colombia	18	6	5	7	14	18	23
Venezuela	18	6	4	8	23	29	22
Bolivia	18	4	3	11	22	36	15
Peru	18	3	4	11	11	34	13

Brazil, Chile, Paraguay and Argentina qualified. Uruguay play-off with fourth-placed CONCACAF finalist.

WORLD CUP 2010 QUALIFYING PLAY-OFFS

EUROPEAN PLAY-OFFS FIRST LEG

Greece	(0) 0	Ukraine	(0) 0
Portugal	(1) 1	Bosnia	(0) 0
Republic of Ireland	(0) 0	France	(0) 1
Russia	(1) 2	Slovenia	(0) 1

Dublin, 14 November 2009, 74,103

Republic of Ireland (0) 0

France (0) 1 *(Anelka 72)*

Republic of Ireland: Given; St Ledger-Hall, Kilbane, O'Shea, Dunne, Whelan, Lawrence (Hunt S 80), Andrews, Doyle K (Best 71), Keane, Duff (McGeady 76).
France: Lloris; Sagna, Abidal, Gallas, Diarra L, Gourcuff, Anelka, Gignac (Malouda 90), Henry, Evra, Diarra A.
Referee: Brych (Germany).

EUROPEAN PLAY-OFFS SECOND LEG

Bosnia	(0) 0	Portugal	(0) 1
France	(0) 1	Republic of Ireland	(1) 1
(aet; France won 2-1 on aggregate.)			
Slovenia	(1) 1	Russia	(0) 0
Ukraine	(0) 0	Greece	(1) 1

Paris, 18 November 2009, 79,145

France (0) 1 *(Gallas 102)*

Republic of Ireland (1) 1 *(Keane 32)*

France: Lloris; Evra, Escude (Squillaci 9), Sagna, Gallas, Diarra L, Diarra A, Gourcuff (Malouda 88), Anelka, Henry, Gignac (Govou 57).
Republic of Ireland: Given; St Ledger-Hall, O'Shea (McShane 67), Dunne, Whelan (Gibson 63), Lawrence (McGeady 107), Kilbane, Duff, Andrews, Keane, Doyle K.
Referee: Hansson (Sweden).
aet; France won 2-1 on aggregate.

SOUTH AMERICA/CONCACAF PLAY-OFFS FIRST LEG

Costa Rica	(0) 0	Uruguay	(1) 1

SOUTH AMERICA/CONCACAF PLAY-OFFS SECOND LEG

Uruguay	(0) 1	Costa Rica	(0) 1

AFRICA PLAY-OFF

Algeria	(1) 1	Egypt	(0) 0

WORLD CUP 2010 REVIEW

Such was the final in Johannesburg that the statistics of it will remain long after the memory of the match has faded. There were fourteen yellow cards, one red to John Heitinga, just one goal by Spain. Referee Howard Webb did it his way. Paul the Octopus was right again with the result.

But it was an unpleasant affair between Spain who tried to play their normal passing game but occasionally retaliated against a physically confrontational Holland. The blessing was that with extra time drifting away, the lottery of a penalty shoot-out was something else on the cards until Andres Iniesta ended it in the 116th minute.

Real chances in the first half were limited to one apiece but after the break Arjen Robben found himself bearing down on the Spanish goalkeeper Iker Casillas. The Dutchman sent him the wrong way but his decision to place rather than bury the ball caught the Spanish captain's trailing right foot. Spain had a similar chance with substitute Cesc Fabregas but Maarten Stekelenburg saved. Fabregas made amends, however, when he made the pass for Iniesta's winner.

Neither of the finalists had previously won the competition. Indeed before Spain became champions of Europe in 2008, their achievements had been confined to their club sides, notably Real Madrid and Barcelona, from different speaking parts of the country and traditionally not the best of friends. Yet their differences are left behind for football.

Given that European countries have fared none too well when World Cup tournaments have been held outside their own continent, the venture to South Africa seemed to be tailor-made for a South American country to win in 2010. Of course it was also the first such final to be staged in Africa as a whole, so the outcome might have been less predictable.

But the group stages produced the initial shocks with the departure of both 2006 finalists, Italy the holders of the World Cup and France its runner-up, both finishing bottom of their respective sections. For the French with internal disagreements, the results were little short of humiliation.

History is full of cycles and perhaps for Italy and France who have been in the forefront of both European and World Cup challengers for many years, their reign is over, whether temporarily or for a longer period. Even Hungary who totally dominated the 1950s, did not win the World Cup which went in 1954 to West Germany as it then was designated.

So it was left to the United States of America and New Zealand to lead the surprise packets of this initial World Cup 2010 phase. The Americans held England to a merited draw, defeated Slovenia after being two goals down and then had a last minute winner against Algeria.

For the Kiwis, they could say that apart from the actual winners of the final, they left with an unbeaten record, drawing all three matches including one with Italy the reigning champions. All five South American countries qualified. Had it not been for two of them playing against each other, it could have looked even better at the quarter-final round. Argentina was arguably the best of the finalists at this point in the tournament.

The quarter-finals sorted them out. One by one they were sent packing. The Dutch surprised Brazil, Spain slowly moving into form edged out Paraguay and Germany arrogantly dismissed Argentina by four clear goals. So it left only Uruguay, the smallest country ever to win the competition.

Holland with two goals in a three-minute spell enabled them just to finish Uruguay and then Spain striking their best Euro form of two years earlier brought Germany back to earth and set up that all-European final. Even the match for third place played out in teeming rain see-sawed back and forth before Germany edged Uruguay by the odd goal in five. But Diego Forlan even hit the crossbar from a free kick, the last of the game which would have sent the match into extra time.

With the hype which had surrounded England from the moment the team qualified, there was immense disappointment when Germany gained revenge for losing the 1966 final and in more recent years the 5-1 drubbing sustained in their own country. Of course, the Germans had eliminated us in 1970 in Mexico.

Ironically just as in 1966 there was an incident in the goalmouth. This time the ball was clearly a foot over the line but no goal was given. All those years before at Wembley it was on the line, but awarded. In South Africa it produced more calls for technology to be introduced and indeed there were other incidents which proved that the human eye is being caught out too many times by the pace of the game.

The other controversies were the Vuvuzelas, the blowing horn which accompanied every match and the Jabulana ball said to be the most difficult to control. Indeed goalkeepers in particular found its flight difficult to follow and many were caught out with embarrassing results. It reacted in a different way at varying ground levels, too. At high altitude the rounder ball spun in the air alarmingly.

WORLD CUP FINALS 2010 – RESULTS

■ *Denotes player sent off.*

GROUP A

First National Bank Stadium, Johannesburg, 11 June 2010
South Africa (0) 1 *(Tshabalala 55)*
Mexico (0) 1 *(Marquez 79)*   84,490
South Africa: Khune; Gaxa, Mokoena, Thwala (Masilela 46), Khumalo, Tshabalala, Pienaar (Parker 83), Modise, Letsholonyane, Dikgacoi, Mphela.
Mexico: Perez O; Rodriguez, Salcido, Marquez, Osorio, Aguilar (Guardado 55), Torrado, Juarez, Franco (Hernandez 73), Vela (Blanco 69), Giovani.
Referee: Irmatov (Uzbekistan).

Cape Town Stadium, Cape Town, 11 June 2010
Uruguay (0) 0
France (0) 0   64,100
Uruguay: Muslera; Lugano, Godin, Victorino, Pereira M, Ignacio Gonzalez I (Lodeiro■ 63), Pereira A, Perez (Eguren 88), Arevalo, Suarez (Abreu 73), Forlan.
France: Lloris; Sagna, Abidal, Gallas, Evra, Ribery, Gourcuff (Malouda 75), Toulalan, Diaby, Govou (Gignac 85), Anelka (Henry 72).
Referee: Nishimura (Japan).

Loftus Versveld, Pretoria, 16 June 2010
South Africa (0) 0
Uruguay (1) 3 *(Forlan 24, 80 (pen), Pereira A 90)*   42,658
South Africa: Khune■; Gaxa, Masilela, Mokoena, Khumalo, Tshabalala, Pienaar (Josephs 79), Modise, Letsholonyane (Moriri 57), Dikgacoi, Mphela.
Uruguay: Muslera; Lugano, Godin, Fucile (Fernandez A 71), Pereira M, Pereira A, Perez (Gargano 90), Arevalo, Cavani (Fernandez S 89), Suarez, Forlan.
Referee: Busacca (Switzerland).

Peter Mokaba Stadium, Polokwane, 17 June 2010
France (0) 0
Mexico (0) 2 *(Hernandez 64, Blanco 79 (pen))*   35,370
France: Lloris; Sagna, Abidal, Gallas, Evra, Ribery, Toulalan, Malouda, Diaby, Govou (Valbuena 69), Anelka (Gignac 46).
Mexico: Perez O; Rodriguez, Salcido, Marquez, Osorio, Moreno, Torrado, Juarez (Hernandez 55), Franco (Blanco 62), Vela (Barrera 31), Giovani.
Referee: Al-Ghamdi (Saudi Arabia).

Free State Stadium, Bloemfontein, 22 June 2010
France (0) 1 *(Malouda 70)*
South Africa (2) 2 *(Khumalo 20, Mphela 37)*   39,415
France: Lloris; Sagna, Gallas, Squillaci, Clichy, Ribery, Gourcuff■, Diarra A (Govou 82), Diaby, Cisse (Henry 55), Gignac (Malouda 46).
South Africa: Josephs; Masilela, Mokoena, Ngconga (Gaxa 55), Khumalo, Sibaya, Tshabalala, Pienaar, Khuboni (Modise 78), Mphela, Parker (Nomvethe 68).
Referee: Ruiz (Colombia).

Royal Bafokeng, Rustenburg, 22 June 2010
Mexico (0) 0
Uruguay (0) 1 *(Suarez 43)*   33,425
Mexico: Perez O; Rodriguez, Salcido, Marquez, Osorio, Moreno (Castro 57), Torrado, Guardado (Barrera 46), Franco, Blanco (Hernandez 63), Giovani.
Uruguay: Muslera; Lugano, Fucile, Victorino, Pereira M, Pereira A (Scotti 77), Perez, Arevalo, Cavani, Suarez (Fernandez A 85), Forlan.
Referee: Kassai (Hungary).

Group A – Final Table	P	W	D	L	F	A	Pts
Uruguay	3	2	1	0	4	0	7
Mexico	3	1	1	1	3	2	4
South Africa	3	1	1	1	3	5	4
France	3	0	1	2	1	4	1

GROUP B

Ellis Park Stadium, Johannesburg, 12 June 2010
Argentina (1) 1 *(Heinze 6)*
Nigeria (0) 0   55,686
Argentina: Romero; Demichelis, Heinze, Samuel, Di Maria (Burdisso 85), Veron (Maxi Rodriguez 74), Mascherano, Gutierrez, Higuain (Milito 79), Messi, Tevez.
Nigeria: Enyeama; Yobo, Taiwo (Uche 74), Shittu, Odiah, Kaita, Haruna, Etuhu, Yakubu, Obinna (Martins 53), Ogbuke Obasi (Odemwingie 60).
Referee: Stark (Germany).

Nelson Mandela Bay, Port Elizabeth, 12 June 2010
South Korea (1) 2 *(Lee J-S 7, Park J-S 52)*
Greece (0) 0   31,513
South Korea: Jung S-R; Cho Y-H, Lee Y-P, Lee J-S, Cha D-R, Park J-S, Kim J-W, Ki S-Y (Kim N-I 75), Lee C-Y (Kim J-S 90), Park C-Y (Lee S-Y 87), Yeom K-H.
Greece: Tzorvas; Seitaridis, Vyntra, Torosidis, Tziolis, Papadopoulos A, Karagounis (Patsatzoglou 46), Katsouranis, Samaras (Salpingidis 59), Charisteas (Kapetanos 61), Gekas.
Referee: Hester (New Zealand).

First National Bank Stadium, Johannesburg, 17 June 2010
Argentina (2) 4 *(Park C-Y 17 (og), Higuain 33, 76, 80)*
South Korea (1) 1 *(Lee C-Y 45)*   82,174
Argentina: Romero; Demichelis, Heinze, Samuel (Burdisso 23), Di Maria, Mascherano, Gutierrez, Maxi Rodriguez, Higuain (Bolatti 82), Messi, Tevez (Aguero 75).
South Korea: Jung S-R; Oh B-S, Cho Y-H, Lee Y-P, Lee J-S, Park J-S, Kim J-W, Ki S-Y (Kim N-I 46), Lee C-Y, Park C-Y (Lee D-G 81), Yeom K-H.
Referee: De Bleeckere (Belgium).

Free State Stadium, Bloemfontein, 17 June 2010
Greece (1) 2 *(Salpingidis 44, Torosidis 71)*
Nigeria (1) 1 *(Uche 16)*   31,593
Greece: Tzorvas; Vyntra, Torosidis, Kyrgiakos, Papastathopoulos (Samaras 37), Tziolis, Papadopoulos A, Karagounis, Katsouranis, Salpingidis, Gekas (Ninis 79).
Nigeria: Enyeama; Yobo, Taiwo (Echiejile 55) (Afolabi 77), Shittu, Odiah, Uche, Kaita▪, Haruna, Etuhu, Yakubu, Odemwingie (Ogbuke Obasi 46).
Referee: Ruiz (Colombia).

Peter Mokaba Stadium, Polokwane, 22 June 2010
Greece (0) 0
Argentina (0) 2 *(Demichelis 77, Palermo 89)*   38,891
Greece: Tzorvas; Moras, Vyntra, Torosidis (Patsatzoglou 55), Kyrgiakos, Papastathopoulos, Tziolis, Papadopoulos A, Karagounis (Spyropoulos 46), Katsouranis (Ninis 54), Samaras.
Argentina: Romero; Demichelis, Rodriguez C, Burdisso, Otamendi, Bolatti, Veron, Maxi Rodriguez (Di Maria 63), Messi, Aguero (Pastore 77), Milito (Palermo 80).
Referee: Irmatov (Uzbekistan).

Moses Mabhida, Durban, 22 June 2010
Nigeria (1) 2 *(Uche 12, Yakubu 69 (pen))*
South Korea (1) 2 *(Lee J-S 38, Park C-Y 49)*   61,874
Nigeria: Enyeama; Yobo (Echiejile 46), Afolabi, Shittu, Odiah, Uche, Ayila, Etuhu, Kanu (Martins 57), Yakubu (Obinna 70), Ogbuke Obasi.
South Korea: Jung S-R; Cho Y-H, Lee Y-P, Lee J-S, Cha D-R, Park J-S, Kim J-W, Ki S-Y (Kim J-S 87), Lee C-Y, Park C-Y (Kim D-J 90), Yeom K-H (Kim N-I 64).
Referee: Benquerenca (Portugal).

Group B – Final Table	P	W	D	L	F	A	Pts
Argentina	3	3	0	0	7	1	9
South Korea	3	1	1	1	5	6	4
Greece	3	1	0	2	2	5	3
Nigeria	3	0	1	2	3	5	1

GROUP C

Royal Bafokeng, Rustenburg, 12 June 2010
England (1) 1 *(Gerrard 4)*
USA (1) 1 *(Dempsey 40)*   38,646
England: Green; Johnson G, Cole A, Gerrard, King (Carragher 46), Terry, Lennon, Lampard, Heskey (Crouch 79), Rooney, Milner (Wright-Phillips 30).
USA: Howard; Onyewu, Bocanegra, Cherundolo, DeMerit, Bradley, Dempsey, Donovan, Clark, Altidore (Holden 86), Findley (Buddle 77).
Referee: Simon (Brazil).

Peter Mokaba Stadium, Polokwane, 13 June 2010
Algeria (0) 0
Slovenia (0) 1 *(Koren 79)*   30,325
Algeria: Chaouchi; Bougherra, Belhadj, Yahia, Halliche, Lacen, Matmour (Saifi 81), Ziani, Yebda, Kadir (Guedioura 82), Djebbour (Ghezzal■ 58).
Slovenia: Handanovic S; Brecko, Suler, Cesar, Koren, Jokic, Kirm, Radosavljevic (Komac 87), Birsa (Pecnik 84), Novakovic, Dedic (Ljubijankic 53).
Referee: Batres (Guatemala).

Cape Town Stadium, Cape Town, 18 June 2010
England (0) 0
Algeria (0) 0   64,100
England: James; Johnson G, Cole A, Barry (Crouch 84), Carragher, Terry, Lennon (Wright-Phillips 63), Lampard, Heskey (Defoe 74), Rooney, Gerrard.
Algeria: M'Bolhi; Bougherra, Belhadj, Yahia, Halliche, Boudebouz (Abdoun 74), Lacen, Matmour, Ziani (Guedioura 80), Yebda (Mesbah 89), Kadir.
Referee: Irmatov (Uzbekistan).

Ellis Park Stadium, Johannesburg, 18 June 2010
Slovenia (2) 2 *(Birsa 13, Ljubijankic 42)*
USA (0) 2 *(Donovan 48, Bradley 82)*   45,573
Slovenia: Handanovic S; Brecko, Suler, Cesar, Koren, Jokic, Kirm, Radosavljevic, Ljubijankic (Pecnik 74) (Komac 90), Birsa (Dedic 87), Novakovic.
USA: Howard; Bocanegra, Onyewu (Gomez 80), Cherundolo, DeMerit, Bradley, Dempsey, Donovan, Torres (Feilhaber 46), Altidore, Findley (Edu 46).
Referee: Coulibaly (Mali).

Nelson Mandela Bay, Port Elizabeth, 23 June 2010
Slovenia (0) 0
England (1) 1 *(Defoe 22)*   36,893
Slovenia: Handanovic S; Brecko, Suler, Cesar, Koren, Jokic, Kirm (Matavz 79), Radosavljevic, Ljubijankic (Dedic 62), Birsa, Novakovic.
England: James; Johnson G, Cole A, Barry, Upson, Terry, Milner, Lampard, Defoe (Heskey 85), Rooney (Cole J 72), Gerrard.
Referee: Stark (Germany).

Loftus Versveld, Pretoria, 23 June 2010
USA (0) 1 *(Donovan 90)*
Algeria (0) 0   35,827
USA: Howard; Bocanegra, Cherundolo, Bornstein (Beasley 80), DeMerit, Bradley, Dempsey, Donovan, Edu (Buddle 64), Gomez (Feilhaber 46), Altidore.
Algeria: M'Bolhi; Bougherra, Belhadj, Yahia■, Halliche, Lacen, Matmour (Saifi 85), Ziani (Guedioura 69), Yebda, Kadir, Djebbour (Ghezzal 65).
Referee: De Bleeckere (Belgium).

Group C – Final Table	P	W	D	L	F	A	Pts
USA	3	1	2	0	4	3	5
England	3	1	2	0	2	1	5
Slovenia	3	1	1	1	3	3	4
Algeria	3	0	1	2	0	2	1

GROUP D

Moses Mabhida, Durban, 13 June 2010
Germany (2) 4 *(Podolski 8, Klose 26, Muller 68, Cacau 70)*
Australia (0) 0   62,660
Germany: Neuer; Friedrich, Badstuber, Lahm, Mertesacker, Khedira, Schweinsteiger, Ozil (Gomez 73), Podolski (Marin 81), Klose (Cacau 68), Muller.
Australia: Schwarzer; Neill, Moore, Chipperfield, Cahill■, Culina, Emerton (Jedinak 74), Wilkshire, Grella (Holman 46), Valeri, Garcia (Rukavytsya 64).
Referee: Rodriguez (Mexico).

Loftus Versveld, Pretoria, 13 June 2010
Serbia (0) 0
Ghana (0) 1 *(Gyan 84 (pen))*   38,833
Serbia: Stojkovic; Kolarov, Vidic, Ivanovic, Lukovic■, Stankovic, Milijas (Kuzmanovic 62), Krasic, Pantelic, Jovanovic (Subotic 76), Zigic (Lazovic 69).
Ghana: Kingson; Sarpei, Pantsil, John Mensah, Annan, Vorsah, Asamoah (Appiah 73), Boateng (Owusu-Abeyie 90), Gyan (Addy 90), Tagoe, Ayew.
Referee: Baldassi (Argentina).

Nelson Mandela Bay, Port Elizabeth, 18 June 2010
Germany (0) 0
Serbia (1) 1 *(Jovanovic 38)*   38,294
Germany: Neuer; Friedrich, Badstuber (Gomez 77), Lahm, Mertesacker, Khedira, Schweinsteiger, Ozil (Marin 70), Podolski, Klose■, Muller (Cacau 70).
Serbia: Stojkovic; Kolarov, Vidic, Ivanovic, Subotic, Stankovic, Krasic, Ninkovic (Kacar 70), Kuzmanovic (Petrovic 75), Jovanovic (Lazovic 79), Zigic.
Referee: Undiano (Spain).

Royal Bafokeng, Rustenburg, 19 June 2010
Ghana (1) 1 *(Gyan 25 (pen))*
Australia (1) 1 *(Holman 11)*   34,812
Ghana: Kingson; Sarpei, Pantsil, Jonathan Mensah, Addy, Annan, Asamoah (Ali Muntari 77), Boateng (Amoah 86), Gyan, Tagoe (Owusu-Abeyie 56), Ayew.
Australia: Schwarzer; Neill, Moore, Culina, Emerton, Wilkshire (Rukavytsya 85), Kewell■, Holman (Kennedy 68), Valeri, Carney, Bresciano (Chipperfield 66).
Referee: Rosetti (Italy).

Mbombela Stadium, Nelspruit, 23 June 2010
Australia (0) 2 *(Cahill 69, Holman 73)*
Serbia (0) 1 *(Pantelic 84)*   37,836
Australia: Schwarzer; Neill, Beauchamp, Cahill, Culina, Emerton, Wilkshire (Garcia 82), Valeri (Chipperfield 66), Carney, Bresciano (Holman 66), Kennedy.
Serbia: Stojkovic; Vidic, Ivanovic, Lukovic, Obradovic, Stankovic, Krasic (Tosic 62), Ninkovic, Kuzmanovic (Lazovic 77), Jovanovic, Zigic (Pantelic 67).
Referee: Larrionda (Uruguay).

First National Bank Stadium, Johannesburg, 23 June 2010
Ghana (0) 0
Germany (0) 1 *(Ozil 60)*   83,391
Ghana: Kingson; Sarpei, Pantsil, John Mensah, Jonathan Mensah, Annan, Asamoah, Boateng, Gyan (Amoah 81), Tagoe (Ali Muntari 63), Ayew (Adiyiah 90).
Germany: Neuer; Friedrich, Lahm, Mertesacker, Boateng (Jansen 72), Khedira, Schweinsteiger (Kroos 81), Ozil, Podolski, Muller (Trochowski 68), Cacau.
Referee: Simon (Brasil).

Group D – Final Table	P	W	D	L	F	A	Pts
Germany	3	2	0	1	5	1	6
Ghana	3	1	1	1	2	2	4
Australia	3	1	1	1	3	6	4
Serbia	3	1	0	2	2	3	3

GROUP E

First National Bank Stadium, Johannesburg, 14 June 2010
Holland (0) 2 *(Agger 46 (og), Kuyt 85)*
Denmark (0) 0 83,465
Holland: Stekelenburg; Van der Wiel, Heitinga, Mathijsen, Van Bronckhorst, Van Bommel, De Jong (De Zeeuw 88), Sneijder, Van der Vaart (Elia 67), Kuyt, Van Persie (Afellay 77).
Denmark: Sorensen; Kjaer, Agger, Jacobsen L, Poulsen S, Poulsen C, Jorgensen, Kahlenberg (Eriksen 73), Enevoldsen (Gronkjaer 56), Bendtner (Beckmann 62), Rommedahl.
Referee: Lannoy (France).

Free State Stadium, Bloemfontein, 14 June 2010
Japan (1) 1 *(Honda 39)*
Cameroon (0) 0 30,620
Japan: Kawashima; Komano, Tanaka, Nagatomo, Nakazawa, Abe, Endo, Matsui (Okazaki 69), Hasebe (Inamoto 88), Honda, Okubo (Yano 82).
Cameroon: Souleymanou; Assou-Ekotto, N'Koulou, Bassong, Matip (Emana 63), Makoun (Idrissou 74), Enoh, Mbia, Eto'o, Choupo-Moting (Geremi 75), Webo.
Referee: Benquerenca (Portugal).

Loftus Versveld, Pretoria, 19 June 2010
Cameroon (1) 1 *(Eto'o 10)*
Denmark (1) 2 *(Bendtner 33, Rommedahl 61)* 38,074
Cameroon: Souleymanou; Assou-Ekotto, N'Koulou, Bassong (Idrissou 73), Song Billong, Geremi, Emana, Enoh (Makoun 46), Mbia, Eto'o, Webo (Aboubakar 78).
Denmark: Sorensen; Kjaer, Agger, Jacobsen L, Poulsen S, Poulsen C, Gronkjaer (Kahlenberg 67), Jorgensen (Jensen D 46), Tomasson (Poulsen J 86), Bendtner, Rommedahl.
Referee: Larrionda (Uruguay).

Moses Mabhida, Durban, 19 June 2010
Holland (0) 1 *(Sneijder 53)*
Japan (0) 0 62,010
Holland: Stekelenburg; Van der Wiel, Heitinga, Mathijsen, Van Bronckhorst, Van Bommel, De Jong, Sneijder (Afellay 82), Van der Vaart (Elia 72), Kuyt, Van Persie (Huntelaar 88).
Japan: Kawashima; Komano, Tanaka, Nagatomo, Nakazawa, Abe, Endo, Matsui (Nakamura 64), Hasebe (Okazaki 77), Honda, Okubo (Tamada 77).
Referee: Baldassi (Argentina).

Cape Town Stadium, Cape Town, 24 June 2010
Cameroon (0) 1 *(Eto'o 65 (pen))*
Holland (1) 2 *(Van Persie 36, Huntelaar 83)* 63,093
Cameroon: Hamidou; Assou-Ekotto, N'Koulou (Rigobert Song 73), Bong (Aboubakar 56), N'Guemo, Geremi, Makoun, Chedjou, Mbia, Eto'o, Choupo-Moting (Idrissou 72).
Holland: Stekelenburg; Heitinga, Mathijsen, Boulahrouz, Van Bronckhorst, Van Bommel, De Jong, Sneijder, Van der Vaart (Robben 73), Kuyt (Elia 66), Van Persie (Huntelaar 59).
Referee: Pozo (Chile).

Royal Bafokeng, Rustenburg, 24 June 2010
Denmark (0) 1 *(Tomasson 81)*
Japan (2) 3 *(Honda 17, Endo 30, Okazaki 87)* 27,967
Denmark: Sorensen; Agger, Jacobsen L, Kroldrup (Larsen 56), Poulsen S, Poulsen C, Jorgensen (Poulsen J 34), Kahlenberg (Eriksen 63), Tomasson, Bendtner, Rommedahl.
Japan: Kawashima; Komano, Tanaka, Nagatomo, Nakazawa, Abe, Endo (Inamoto 90), Matsui (Okazaki 74), Hasebe, Honda, Okubo (Konno 88).
Referee: Damon (South Africa).

Group E – Final Table	P	W	D	L	F	A	Pts
Holland	3	3	0	0	5	1	9
Japan	3	2	0	1	4	2	6
Denmark	3	1	0	2	3	6	3
Cameroon	3	0	0	3	2	5	0

GROUP F

Cape Town Stadium, Cape Town, 14 June 2010
Italy (0) 1 *(De Rossi 63)*
Paraguay (1) 1 *(Alcaraz 39)*   62,869
Italy: Buffon (Marchetti 46); Criscito, Chiellini, Cannavaro, Zambrotta, De Rossi, Pepe, Marchisio (Camoranesi 59), Montolivo, Iaquinta, Gilardino (Di Natale 72).
Paraguay: Villar; Morel, Da Silva, Alcaraz, Bonet, Vera, Caceres V, Riveros, Torres (Santana 60), Valdez (Santa Cruz 68), Barrios (Cardozo 76).
Referee: Archundia (Mexico).

Royal Bafokeng, Rustenburg, 15 June 2010
New Zealand (0) 1 *(Reid 90)*
Slovakia (0) 1 *(Vittek 50)*   23,871
New Zealand: Paston; Lochhead, Reid, Nelsen, Smith, Vicelich (Christie 78), Elliott, Bertos, Smeltz, Killen (Wood 72), Fallon.
Slovakia: Mucha; Skrtel, Cech, Zabavnik, Durica, Strba, Weiss (Kucka 90), Hamsik, Sestak (Holosko 81), Vittek (Stoch 84), Jendrisek.
Referee: Damon (South Africa).

Mbombela Stadium, Nelspruit, 20 June 2010
Italy (1) 1 *(Iaquinta 29 (pen))*
New Zealand (1) 1 *(Smeltz 7)*   38,229
Italy: Marchetti; Criscito, Chiellini, Cannavaro, Zambrotta, De Rossi, Pepe (Camoranesi 46), Marchisio (Pazzini 46), Montolivo, Iaquinta, Gilardino (Di Natale 46).
New Zealand: Paston; Lochhead, Reid, Nelsen, Smith, Vicelich (Christie 81), Elliott, Bertos, Smeltz, Killen (Barron 90), Fallon (Wood 63).
Referee: Batres (Guatemala).

Free State Stadium, Bloemfontein, 20 June 2010
Slovakia (0) 0
Paraguay (1) 2 *(Vera 27, Riveros 86)*   26,643
Slovakia: Mucha; Pekarik, Skrtel, Durica, Salata (Stoch 83), Strba, Weiss, Kozak, Hamsik, Sestak (Holosko 70), Vittek.
Paraguay: Villar; Morel, Da Silva, Alcaraz, Bonet, Vera (Barreto E 88), Caceres V, Riveros, Santa Cruz, Valdez (Torres 68), Barrios (Cardozo 82).
Referee: Maillet (Seychelles).

Peter Mokaba Stadium, Polokwane, 24 June 2010
Paraguay (0) 0
New Zealand (0) 0   34,850
Paraguay: Villar; Morel, Caniza, Caceres J, Da Silva, Vera, Caceres V, Riveros, Cardozo (Barrios 66), Santa Cruz, Valdez (Benitez 67).
New Zealand: Paston; Reid, Lochhead, Nelsen, Smith, Vicelich, Elliott, Bertos, Smeltz, Killen (Brockie 79), Fallon (Wood 69).
Referee: Nishimura (Japan).

Ellis Park Stadium, Johannesburg, 24 June 2010
Slovakia (1) 3 *(Vittek 25, 73, Kopunek 89)*
Italy (0) 2 *(Di Natale 81, Quagliarella 90)*   53,412
Slovakia: Mucha; Pekarik, Skrtel, Zabavnik, Durica, Strba (Kopunek 87), Hamsik, Kucka, Vittek (Sestak 90), Stoch, Jendrisek (Petras 90).
Italy: Marchetti; Criscito (Maggio 46), Chiellini, Cannavaro, Zambrotta, De Rossi, Pepe, Gattuso (Quagliarella 46), Montolivo (Pirlo 56), Iaquinta, Di Natale.
Referee: Webb (England).

Group F – Final Table	P	W	D	L	F	A	Pts
Paraguay	3	1	2	0	3	1	5
Slovakia	3	1	1	1	4	5	4
New Zealand	3	0	3	0	2	2	3
Italy	3	0	2	1	4	5	2

GROUP G

Ellis Park Stadium, Johannesburg, 15 June 2010
Brazil (0) 2 *(Maicon 55, Elano 72)*
North Korea (0) 1 *(Ji Y-N 89)*   54,331
Brazil: Julio Cesar; Maicon, Lucio, Juan, Felipe Melo (Ramires 84), Michel Bastos,
Elano (Dani Alves 73), Gilberto Silvo, Kaka (Nilmar 78), Luis Fabiano, Robinho.
North Korea: Ri M-G; Cha J-H, Ri J-I, Ri K-C, Pak C-J, Pak N-C, Ji Y-N, Mun I-G
(Kim K-I 80), Ahn Y-H, Jeong T-S, Hong Y-J.
Referee: Kassai (Hungary).

Nelson Mandela Bay, Port Elizabeth, 15 June 2010
Ivory Coast (0) 0
Portugal (0) 0   37,430
Ivory Coast: Barry; Kolo Toure, Eboue (Romaric 88), Zokora, Tiote, Tiene, Yaya Toure,
Demel, Kalou (Drogba 66), Gervinho (Keita 82), Dindane.
Portugal: Eduardo; Bruno Alves, Paulo Ferreira, Ricardo Carvalho, Pedro Mendes,
Raul Meireles (Ruben Amorim 82), Deco (Tiago 62), Fabio Coentrao, Cristiano
Ronaldo, Liedson, Danny (Simao 55).
Referee: Larrionda (Uruguay).

First National Bank Stadium, Johannesburg, 20 June 2010
Brazil (1) 3 *(Luis Fabiano 25, 50, Elano 62)*
Ivory Coast (0) 1 *(Drogba 79)*   84,455
Brazil: Julio Cesar; Maicon, Lucio, Juan, Felipe Melo, Michel Bastos, Elano (Dani
Alves 67), Gilberto Silva, Kaka■, Luis Fabiano, Robinho (Ramires 90).
Ivory Coast: Barry; Kolo Toure, Eboue (Romaric 72), Zokora, Tiote, Tiene, Yaya Toure,
Demel, Kalou (Keita 68), Drogba, Dindane (Gervinho 54).
Referee: Lannoy (France).

Cape Town Stadium, Cape Town, 21 June 2010
Portugal (1) 7 *(Raul Meireles 29, Simao 53, Hugo Almeida 56, Tiago 60, 89, Liedson 81,
Cristiano Ronaldo 87)*
North Korea (0) 0   63,644
Portugal: Eduardo; Bruno Alves, Ricardo Carvalho, Miguel, Pedro Mendes, Raul
Meireles (Miguel Veloso 70), Tiago, Fabio Coentrao, Cristiano Ronaldo, Simao (Duda
74), Hugo Almeida (Liedson 77).
North Korea: Ri M-G; Cha J-H (Nam S-C 75), Ri J-I, Ri K-C, Pak C-J, Pak N-C (Kim
Y-J 58), Ji Y-N, Mun I-G (Kim K-I 58), Ahn Y-H, Jeong T-S, Hong Y-J.
Referee: Pozo (Chile).

Mbombela Stadium Nelspruit, 25 June 2010
North Korea (0) 0
Ivory Coast (2) 3 *(Yaya Toure 14, Romaric 20, Kalou 82)*   34,763
North Korea: Ri M-G; Cha J-H, Ri J-I, Ri K-C, Pak C-J, Pak N-C, Ji Y-N, Mun I-G
(Choe K-C 67), Ahn Y-H, Jeong T-S, Hong Y-J.
Ivory Coast: Barry; Boka, Kolo Toure, Eboue, Zokora, Tiote, Romaric (Doumbia 79),
Yaya Toure, Gervinho (Kalou 64), Drogba, Keita (Dindane 64).
Referee: Undiano (Spain).

Moses Mabhida, Durban, 25 June 2010
Portugal (0) 0
Brazil (0) 0   62,712
Portugal: Eduardo; Bruno Alves, Ricardo Carvalho, Pepe (Pedro Mendes 64), Ricardo
Costa, Duda (Simao 55), Raul Meireles (Miguel Veloso 84), Tiago, Fabio Coentrao,
Cristiano Ronaldo, Danny.
Brazil: Julio Cesar; Maicon, Lucio, Juan, Dani Alves, Felipe Melo (Josue 44), Michel
Bastos, Gilberto Silva, Julio Baptista (Ramires 82), Luis Fabiano (Grafite 85), Nilmar.
Referee: Archundia (Mexico).

Group G – Final Table	P	W	D	L	F	A	Pts
Brazil	3	2	1	0	5	2	7
Portugal	3	1	2	0	7	0	5
Ivory Coast	3	1	1	1	4	3	4
North Korea	3	0	0	3	1	12	0

GROUP H

Mbombela Stadium, Nelspruit, 16 June 2010
Honduras (0) 0
Chile (1) 1 *(Beausejour 34)* 32,664
Honduras: Valladares N; Chavez O, Figueroa, Izaguirre, Mendoza, Nunez R (Martinez 78), Palacios W, Alvarez, Guevara (Thomas 66), Pavon (Welcome 60), Espinoza.
Chile: Bravo; Ponce, Isla, Vidal (Contreras 81), Carmona, Valdivia (Gonzalez 87), Fernandez, Beausejour, Medel, Millar (Jara 52), Sanchez.
Referee: Maillet (Seychelles).

Moses Mabhida, Durban, 16 June 2010
Spain (0) 0
Switzerland (0) 1 *(Gelson 52)* 62,453
Spain: Casillas; Pique, Puyol, Capdevila, Sergio Ramos, Iniesta (Pedro 77), Xavi, Xabi Alonso, Busquets (Torres 61), David Silva (Jesus Navas 62), David Villa.
Switzerland: Benaglio; Lichtsteiner, Senderos (Von Bergen 36), Grichting, Ziegler, Huggel, Barnetta (Eggimann 90), Inler, Gelson, Nkufo, Derdiyok (Yakin 79).
Referee: Webb (England).

Nelson Mandela Bay, Port Elizabeth, 21 June 2010
Chile (0) 1 *(Gonzalez 75)*
Switzerland (0) 0 34,872
Chile: Bravo; Ponce, Isla, Vidal (Valdivia 46), Jara, Carmona, Fernandez (Paredes 65), Beausejour, Medel, Suazo (Gonzalez 46).
Switzerland: Benaglio; Lichtsteiner, Von Bergen, Grichting, Ziegler, Huggel, Inler, Behrami■, Gelson (Bunjaku 77), Frei (Barnetta 42), Nkufo (Derdiyok 68).
Referee: Al-Ghamdi (Saudi Arabia).

Ellis Park Stadium, Johannesburg, 21 June 2010
Spain (1) 2 *(David Villa 17, 51)*
Honduras (0) 0 54,386
Spain: Casillas; Pique, Puyol, Capdevila, Sergio Ramos (Arbeloa 77), Xavi (Fabregas 66), Xabi Alonso, Busquets, Jesus Navas, David Villa, Torres (Mata 70).
Honduras: Valladares N; Chavez O, Figueroa, Izaguirre, Mendoza, Palacios W, Turcios (Nunez R 63), Guevara, Suazo (Jerry Palacios 84), Espinoza (Welcome 46), Martinez.
Referee: Nishimura (Japan).

Loftus Versveld, Pretoria, 25 June 2010
Chile (0) 1 *(Millar 47)*
Spain (2) 2 *(David Villa 24, Iniesta 37)* 41,958
Chile: Bravo; Ponce, Isla, Vidal, Jara, Valdivia (Millar 46), Gonzalez (Paredes 46), Estrada■, Beausejour, Medel, Sanchez (Orellana 46).
Spain: Casillas; Pique, Puyol, Capdevila, Sergio Ramos, Iniesta, Xavi, Xabi Alonso (Martinez 73), Busquets, David Villa, Torres (Fabregas 55).
Referee: Rodriguez (Mexico).

Freestate Stadium, Bloemfontein, 25 June 2010
Switzerland (0) 0
Honduras (0) 0 28,042
Switzerland: Benaglio; Lichtsteiner, Von Bergen, Grichting, Ziegler, Huggel (Shaqiri 78), Barnetta, Inler, Gelson (Yakin 46), Nkufo (Frei 69), Derdiyok.
Honduras: Valladares N; Chavez O, Figueroa, Bernardez, Sabillon, Thomas, Nunez R (Martinez 66), Palacios W, Alvarez, Jerry Palacios (Welcome 78), Suazo (Turcios 87).
Referee: Baldassi (Argentina).

Group H – Final Table	P	W	D	L	F	A	Pts
Spain	3	2	0	1	4	2	6
Chile	3	2	0	1	3	2	6
Switzerland	3	1	1	1	1	1	4
Honduras	3	0	1	2	0	3	1

SECOND ROUND

Nelson Mandela Bay, Port Elizabeth, 26 June 2010

Uruguay (1) 2 *(Suarez 8, 80)*

South Korea (0) 1 *(Lee C-Y 68)*   30,597

Uruguay: Muslera; Lugano, Godin (Victorino 46), Fucile, Pereira M, Pereira A (Lodeiro 74), Perez, Arevalo, Cavani, Suarez (Fernandez A 84), Forlan.

South Korea: Jung S-R; Cho Y-H, Lee Y-P, Lee J-S, Cha D-R, Park J-S, Kim J-W, Kim J-S (Lee D-G 61), Ki S-Y (Yeom K-H 85), Lee C-Y, Park C-Y.

Referee: Stark (Germany).

Royal Bafokeng, Rustenburg, 26 June 2010

USA (0) 1 *(Donovan 62 (pen))*

Ghana (1) 2 *(Boateng 6, Gyan 93)*   34,976

USA: Howard; Bocanegra, Cherundolo, Bornstein, DeMerit, Bradley, Dempsey, Donovan, Clark (Edu 31), Altidore (Gomez 91), Findley (Feilhaber 46).

Ghana: Kingson; Sarpei (Addy 73), Pantsil, John Mensah, Inkoom (Ali Muntari 113), Jonathan Mensah, Annan, Asamoah, Boateng (Appiah 78), Gyan, Ayew.

Referee: Kassai (Hungary).

aet.

First National Bank Stadium, Johannesburg, 27 June 2010

Argentina (2) 3 *(Tevez 26, 52, Higuain 33)*

Mexico (0) 1 *(Hernandez 71)*   84,377

Argentina: Romero; Demichelis, Burdisso, Heinze, Otamendi, Di Maria (Gutierrez 79), Mascherano, Maxi Rodriguez (Pastore 87), Higuain, Messi, Tevez (Veron 69).

Mexico: Perez O; Rodriguez, Salcido, Marquez, Osorio, Torrado, Juarez, Guardado (Franco 61), Hernandez, Giovani, Bautista (Barrera 46).

Referee: Rossetti (Italy).

Free State Stadium, Bloemfontein, 27 June 2010

Germany (2) 4 *(Klose 20, Podolski 32, Muller 67, 70)*

England (1) 1 *(Upson 37)*   40,510

Germany: Neuer; Friedrich, Lahm, Mertesacker, Boateng, Khedira, Schweinsteiger, Ozil (Kiessling 83), Podolski, Klose (Trochowski 72), Muller (Gomez 72).

England: James; Johnson G (Wright-Phillips 87), Cole A, Barry, Terry, Upson, Milner (Cole J 64), Lampard, Defoe (Heskey 71), Rooney, Gerrard.

Referee: Larrionda (Uruguay).

Ellis Park Stadium, Johannesburg, 28 June 2010

Brazil (2) 3 *(Juan 34, Luis Fabiano 38, Robinho 59)*

Chile (0) 0   54,096

Brazil: Julio Cesar; Maicon, Lucio, Juan, Dani Alves, Michel Bastos, Gilberto Silva, Kaka (Kleberson 81), Ramires, Luis Fabiano (Nilmar 76), Robinho (Gilberto 85).

Chile: Bravo; Fuentes, Isla (Millar 62), Contreras (Valdivia 46), Vidal, Jara, Carmona, Gonzalez (Tello 46), Beausejour, Sanchez, Suazo.

Referee: Webb (England).

Moses Mabhida, Durban, 28 June 2010

Holland (1) 2 *(Robben 18, Sneijder 84)*

Slovakia (0) 1 *(Vittek 90 (pen))*   61,962

Holland: Stekelenburg; Van der Wiel, Heitinga, Mathijsen, Van Bronckhorst, Van Bommel, De Jong, Sneijder (Afellay 90), Kuyt, Van Persie (Huntelaar 80), Robben (Elia 71).

Slovakia: Mucha; Pekarik, Skrtel, Zabavnik (Sapara 87), Durica, Weiss, Hamsik (Jakubko 87), Kucka, Vittek, Stoch, Jendrisek (Kopunek 71).

Referee: Undiano (Spain).

Loftus Versveld, Pretoria, 29 June 2010
Paraguay (0) 0
Japan (0) 0   36,742
Paraguay: Villar; Morel, Da Silva, Alcaraz, Bonet, Vera, Riveros, Ortigoza (Barreto E
75), Santa Cruz (Cardozo 94), Benitez (Valdez 60), Barrios.
Japan: Kawashima; Komano, Tanaka, Nagatomo, Nakazawa, Abe (Nakamura 81),
Endo, Matsui (Okazaki 65), Hasebe, Honda, Okubo (Tamada 106).
Referee: De Bleeckere (Belgium).
*aet; Paraguay won 5-3 on penalties: Barreto E scored, Endo scored; Barrios scored, Hasebe
scored; Riveros scored, Komano hit bar; Valdez scored, Honda scored; Cardozo scored.*

Cape Town Stadium, Cape Town, 29 June 2010
Spain (0) 1 *(David Villa 63)*
Portugal (0) 0   62,955
Spain: Casillas; Pique, Puyol, Capdevila, Sergio Ramos, Iniesta, Xavi, Xabi Alonso
(Marchena 90), Busquets, David Villa (Pedro 88), Torres (Llorente 59).
Portugal: Eduardo; Bruno Alves, Ricardo Carvalho, Pepe (Pedro Mendes 72), Ricardo
Costa■, Raul Meireles, Tiago, Fabio Coentrao, Cristiano Ronaldo, Simao (Liedson 72),
Hugo Almeida (Danny 58).
Referee: Baldassi (Argentina).

QUARTER-FINALS

Nelson Mandela Bay, Port Elizabeth, 2 July 2010
Holland (0) 2 *(Felipe Melo 53 (og), Sneijder 68)*
Brazil (1) 1 *(Robinho 10)*   40,186
Holland: Stekelenburg; Van der Wiel, Heitinga, Ooijer, Van Bronckhorst, Van Bommel,
De Jong, Sneijder, Kuyt, Van Persie (Huntelaar 85), Robben.
Brazil: Julio Cesar; Maicon, Lucio, Juan, Dani Alves, Felipe Melo■, Michel Bastos
(Gilberto 62), Gilberto Silva, Kaka, Luis Fabiano (Nilmar 77), Robinho.
Referee: Nishimura (Japan).

First National Bank Stadium, Johannesburg, 2 July 2010
Uruguay (0) 1 *(Forlan 55)*
Ghana (1) 1 *(Ali Muntari 45)*   84,017
Uruguay: Muslera; Lugano (Scotti 38), Fucile, Victorino, Pereira M, Perez, Arevalo,
Fernandez A (Lodeiro 46), Cavani (Abreu 76), Suarez■, Forlan.
Ghana: Kingson; Sarpei, Pantsil, John Mensah, Inkoom (Appiah 74), Annan, Ali
Muntari (Adiyiah 88), Vorsah, Asamoah, Boateng, Gyan.
Referee: Benquerenca (Portugal).
*aet; Uruguay won 4-2 on penalties: Forlan scored, Gyan scored; Victorino scored, Appiah
scored; Scotti scored, John Mensah saved; Pereira M missed, Adiyiah saved; Abreu scored.*

Cape Town Stadium, Cape Town, 3 July 2010
Argentina (0) 0
Germany (1) 4 *(Muller 3, Klose 68, 89, Friedrich 74)*   64,100
Argentina: Romero; Demichelis, Burdisso, Heinze, Otamendi (Pastore 69), Di Maria
(Aguero 75), Mascherano, Maxi Rodriguez, Higuain, Messi, Tevez.
Germany: Neuer; Friedrich, Lahm, Mertesacker, Boateng (Jansen 72), Khedira (Kroos
78), Schweinsteiger, Ozil, Podolski, Klose, Muller (Trochowski 84).
Referee: Irmatov (Uzbekistan).

Ellis Park Stadium, Johannesburg, 3 July 2010
Paraguay (0) 0
Spain (0) 1 *(David Villa 83)*   55,395
Paraguay: Villar; Veron, Morel, Da Silva, Alcaraz, Barreto E (Vera 64), Santana, Cac-
eres V (Barrios 85), Riveros, Cardozo, Valdez (Santa Cruz 72).
Spain: Casillas; Pique, Puyol (Marchena 85), Capdevila, Sergio Ramos, Iniesta, Xavi,
Xabi Alonso (Pedro 74), Busquets, David Villa, Torres (Fabregas 57).
Referee: Batres (Guatemala).

SEMI-FINALS

Cape Town Stadium, Cape Town, 6 July 2010

Uruguay (1) 2 *(Forlan 41, Pereira M 90)*

Holland (1) 3 *(Van Bronckhorst 18, Sneijder 70, Robben 73)*   62,479

Uruguay: Muslera; Godin, Victorino, Pereira M, Caceres, Gargano, Pereira A (Abreu 78), Perez, Arevalo, Cavani, Forlan (Fernandez S 84).
Holland: Stekelenburg; Heitinga, Mathijsen, Boulahrouz, Van Bronckhorst, Van Bommel, Sneijder, De Zeeuw (Van der Vaart 46), Kuyt, Van Persie, Robben (Elia 89).
Referee: Irmatov (Uzbekistan).

Moses Mabhida, Durban, 7 July 2010

Germany (0) 0

Spain (0) 1 *(Puyol 73)*   60,960

Germany: Neuer; Friedrich, Lahm, Mertesacker, Boateng (Jansen 52), Khedira (Gomez 81), Schweinsteiger, Ozil, Trochowski (Kroos 62), Podolski, Klose.
Spain: Casillas; Pique, Puyol, Capdevila, Sergio Ramos, Iniesta, Xavi, Xabi Alonso (Marchena 90), Busquets, David Villa (Torres 81), Pedro (Silva 86).
Referee: Kassai (Hungary).

MATCH FOR THIRD PLACE

Nelson Mandela Bay, Port Elizabeth, 10 July 2010

Uruguay (1) 2 *(Cavani 28, Forlan 51)*

Germany (1) 3 *(Muller 18, Jansen 56, Khedira 82)*   36,254

Uruguay: Muslera; Lugano, Godin, Fucile, Pereira M, Caceres, Perez (Gargano 77), Arevalo, Cavani (Abreu 89), Suarez, Forlan.
Germany: Butt; Jansen (Kroos 80), Friedrich, Aogo, Mertesacker, Boateng, Khedira, Schweinsteiger, Ozil (Tasci 90), Muller, Cacau (Kiessling 73).
Referee: Archundia (Mexico).

WORLD CUP FINAL 2010

Sunday, 11 July 2010

Holland (0) 0   Spain (0) 1

(First National Bank Stadium, Johannesburg, attendance 84,490

Holland: Stekelenburg; Van der Wiel, Heitingaj, Mathijsen, Van Bronckhorst (Braafheid 105), Van Bommel, De Jong (Van der Vaart 99), Sneijder, Kuyt (Elia 71), Van Persie, Robben.

Spain: Casillas; Pique, Puyol, Capdevila, Sergio Ramos, Iniesta, Xavi, Xabi Alonso (Fabregas 87), Busquets, David Villa (Torres 106), Pedro (Jesus Navas 60).

Scorer: Iniesta 116.

aet.

Referee: Webb (England).

EUROPEAN SUPER CUP FINAL 2009

28 August 2009, Monaco (attendance 17,000)

Barcelona (0) 1 *(Rodriguez 115)*   **Shakhtar Donetsk (0) 0**

Barcelona: Victor Valdes; Daniel Alves, Pique, Puyol, Xavi, Ibrahimovic (Rodriguez 81), Messi, Henry (Bojan 96), Keita, Abidal, Toure (Busquets 100).

Shakhtar Donetsk: Pyatov; Hubschman, Kucher, Fernandinho (Jadson 80), Ilsinho, Luiz Adriano, Gay (Kobin 80), Willian (Aghahowa 91), Rat, Chygrynskiy, Srna.

Referee: De Bleeckere (Belgium).

aet.

FIFA CLUB WORLD CUP FINAL 2009

19 December 2009 (attendance 43,050)

Estudiantes (1) 1 *(Boselli 37)*   **Barcelona (0) 2** *(Pedro 89, Messi 110)*

Estudiantes: Albil; Desabato, Cellay, Perez (Nunez 79), Veron, Diaz, Re (Rojo 91), Boselli, Brana, Benitez (Sanchez 76), Rodriguez.

Barcelona: Victor Valdes; Daniel Alves, Pique, Puyol, Xavi, Ibrahimovic, Messi, Henry (Jeffren 83), Keita (Pedro 46), Busquets (Toure 79), Abidal.

aet.

AFRICAN NATIONS CUP FINAL 2009

(in Luanda, attendance 45,000)

Ghana (0) 0   **Egypt (0) 1** *(Gedo 85)*

Ghana: Kingson; Inkoom, Addy, Vorsah, Sarpei, Badu, Annan, Ayew, Asamoah, Opoku (Addo 89), Gyan (Adyiah 87).

Egypt: El Hadary; Gomaa, Said, Fathi (Moatasem 89), El Mohamady, Ghaly, Hosny, Hassan, Moawad (Abdelshafi 57), Zidan, Meteeb (Nagy 70).

Referee: K. Couibaly (Mali).

COPA SUDAMERICANA 2009

Final First Leg:
LDU Quito 5   Fluminense 1

Final Second Leg:
Fluminense 3   LDU Quito 0

MLS CUP 2009

Los Angeles Galaxy 1   Real Salt Lake 1

Real Salt Lake won 5-4 on penalties.

AFC CHALLENGE CUP 2010

North Korea 1   Turkmenistan 1

North Korea won 5-4 on penalties.

OTHER BRITISH AND IRISH INTERNATIONAL MATCHES 2009–2010

FRIENDLIES

Amsterdam, 12 August 2009, 48,000

Holland (2) 2 *(Kuyt 10, Van der Vaart 38)*

England (0) 2 *(Defoe 49, 77)*

Holland: Stekelenburg; Heitinga, Mathijsen, Ooijer, Braafheid, De Jong, Van der Vaart (Sneijder 46), Schaars (Mendes Da Silva 82), Kuyt (Huntelaar 78), Van Persie (Babel 46), Robben (Afellay 55).
England: Green; Johnson G, Cole A (Bridge 84), Barry (Carrick 46), Ferdinand, Terry, Beckham (Wright-Phillips 46), Lampard, Rooney (Cole C 59), Heskey (Defoe 46), Young A (Milner 68).
Referee: N. Rizzoli (Italy).

Wembley, 5 September 2009, 67,232

England (1) 2 *(Lampard 31 (pen), Defoe 63)*

Slovenia (0) 1 *(Ljubijankic 85)*

England: Green; Johnson G, Cole A, Barry, Terry, Upson (Lescott 64), Wright-Phillips (Lennon 46), Lampard (Milner 46), Heskey (Defoe 46), Rooney (Cole C 80), Gerrard (Carrick 46).
Slovenia: Handanovic; Brecko, Suler, Cesar (Mavric 34), Jokic, Birsa (Komac 64), Radosavljevic (Krhin 77), Koren, Kirm (Stevanovic 77), Dedic (Pecnik 71), Novakovic (Ljubijankic 55).
Referee: J. Eriksson (Sweden).

Doha, 14 November 2009, 50,000

Brazil (0) 1 *(Nilmar 47)*

England (0) 0

Brazil: Julio Cesar; Maicon, Michel Bastos, Felipe Melo, Lucio, Thiago Motta, Elano (Dani Alves 64), Kaka (Eduardo 81), Gilberto Silva, Nilmar (Julio Baptista 81), Luis Fabiano (Hulk 67).
England: Foster; Brown, Bridge, Barry (Huddlestone 82), Upson, Lescott, Wright-Phillips (Crouch 82), Jenas, Rooney, Bent (Defoe 54), Milner (Young A 87).
Referee: A. Abdou (Qatar).

Wembley, 3 March 2010, 80,602

England (0) 3 *(Crouch 56, 80, Wright-Phillips 75)*

Egypt (1) 1 *(Zidan 23)*

England: Green; Brown, Baines, Barry, Upson, Terry, Walcott (Wright-Phillips 57), Lampard (Carrick 46), Rooney (Cole C 86), Defoe (Crouch 46), Gerrard (Milner 73).
Egypt: El Hadari; Al-Muhammadi, Said (Salem 86), Fathi, Gomaa, Ghaly, Moawad (Abdelshafy 76), Hassan (Nagy 64), Abd Rabou, Zidan (Aboutreika 76), Ebdelmaby (Zaki 64).
Referee: C. Torres (Spain).

Wembley, 24 May 2010, 88,638

England (2) 3 *(King 17, Crouch 35, Johnson G 47)*

Mexico (1) 1 *(Franco 45)*

England: Green (Hart 46); Johnson G, Baines, Carrick (Huddlestone 61), Ferdinand (Carragher 46), King, Walcott (Lennon 77), Gerrard, Crouch (Defoe 46), Rooney, Milner (Johnson A 85).
Mexico: Perez; Juarez, Aguilar (Barrera 52), Marquez, Salcido, Osorio, Torrado, Rodriguez, Giovani (Blanco 72), Franco (Hernandez 46), Vela (Guardado 62).
Referee: M. Toma (Japan).

Graz, 30 May 2010, 15,326

Japan (1) 1 *(Tanaka 7)*

England (0) 2 *(Tanaka 72 (og), Nakazawa 83 (og))*

Japan: Kawashima; Nakazawa, Konno, Tanaka, Nagatomo, Endo (Tamada 86), Abe, Hasebe, Honda, Okubo (Matsui 71), Okazaki (Morimoto 65).
England: James (Hart 46); Johnson G (Wright-Phillips 46), Cole A, Huddlestone (Gerrard 46), Ferdinand, Terry, Lennon (Heskey 77), Lampard, Rooney, Bent (Cole J 46), Walcott (Carragher 46).
Referee: R. Eisner (Austria).

Podgorica, 12 August 2009, 5000

Montenegro (2) 2 *(Jovetic 31 (pen), Djalovic 45)*

Wales (0) 1 *(Vokes 52)*

Montenegro: Poleksic (Bozovic M 46); Pavicevic, Batak (Pejovic 68), Dzudovic, Jovanovic, Bozovic V (Nikolic 72), Drincic, Pekovic (Kascelan 62), Vukcevic (Novakovic 86), Djalovic (Beciraj 74), Jovetic.
Wales: Hennessey (Price 46); Gunter, Ricketts (Eardley 57), Williams A (Nyatanga 46), Collins J (Morgan C 63), Gabbidon, Collison, Ramsey (Cotterill 75), Ledley, Church (Vokes 47), Earnshaw.
Refereee: M. Mazic (Serbia).

Cardiff, 14 November 2009, 13,844

Wales (3) 3 *(Edwards 17, Church 32, Ramsey 35)*

Scotland (0) 0

Wales: Hennessey; Ricketts, Nyatanga (Gabbidon 60), Williams A, Morgan C, Bale, Ledley (King 80), Ramsey (Allen 56), Edwards (Cotterill 88), Evans C (Vokes 46), Church (Earnshaw 46).
Scotland: Marshall; Hutton, Fox (Wallace 54), Fletcher D, Caldwell G, McManus, Cowie (Riordan 78), Dorrans (Robson 71), Naismith (McCormack 62), Miller (Fletcher S 55), McFadden (Kyle 62).
Referee: C. Zimmermann (Switzerland).

Swansea, 3 March 2010, 8258

Wales (0) 0

Sweden (1) 1 *(Elmander 44)*

Wales: Myhill (Hennessey 46); Gunter, Bale (Nyatanga 67), Collins J, Morgan C, Williams A, Davies S (Cotterill 64), Collinson (Crofts 71), Church (Vokes 53), Evans C (Earnshaw 46), Vaughan.
Sweden: Gustafsson; Mellberg, Majstorovic, Safari (Wendt 62), Larsson S, Elm R (Hysen 58), Anders Svensson, Kallstrom (Elm V 80), Elmander (Wernbloom 58), Toivonen, Wilhelmsson (Lustig 73).
Referee: A. Black (Northern Ireland).

Osijek, 23 May 2010, 12,000

Croatia (1) 2 *(Rakitic 44, Gabric 82)*

Wales (0) 0

Croatia: Pletikosa; Strinic, Simunic, Lovren, Srna (Vida 75), Rakitic (Pokrivac 76), Vukojevic (Dujmovic 65), Mandzukic (Badelj 90), Jelavic (Bilic 46), Petric (Gabric 46), Modric.
Wales: Hennessey (Myhill 46); Ricketts, Williams A, Nyatanga, Gunter (Ribeiro 81), Edwards D, Morgan C, Stock (Bradley 57), Dorman (Taylor N 62), Church (Vokes 71), Earnshaw (Robson-Kanu 72).
Referee: S. Vincic (Slovenia).

Belfast, 12 August 2009, 10,250

Northern Ireland (1) 1 *(McCann 18)*

Israel (1) 1 *(Barda 26)*

Northern Ireland: Maik Taylor (Tuffey 46); Baird, Craigan, Hughes (McAuley 46), McCartney, Johnson (McGinn 46), Clingan (McGivern 70), McCann, Brunt (Davis 46), Healy (Paterson 59), Lafferty.
Israel: Awat (Davidovitch 46); Meshumar, Keinan (Ben-Haim 46), Strol (Mori 71), Ben Dayan, Cohen (Kayal 46), Baruchian, Benayoun (Toama 54), Yadin (Ziv 65), Barda, Colautti.
Referee: J. Valgeirsson (Iceland).

Belfast, 14 November 2009, 13,500

Northern Ireland (0) 0

Serbia (0) 1 *(Lazovic 57)*

Northern Ireland: Maik Taylor (Tuffey 77); Evans J (McCann 46), Hughes, Craigan, McCartney, McGinn (McCourt 71), Davis, Baird, Brunt (O'Connor 65), Feeney (Healy 65), Lafferty (Kirk 71).

Serbia: Isailovic; Rukavina, Vidic (Subotic 46), Lukovic, Kolarov (Vukovic 67), Milijas (Ninkovic 46), Kuzmanovic (Kacar 52), Petrovic, Tosic, Jovanovic (Krasic 46), Lazovic (Lekic 76).

Referee: A. Toussaint (Luxembourg).

Tirana, 3 March 2010, 7500

Albania (1) 1 *(Skela 26)*

Northern Ireland (0) 0

Albania: Hidi; Lila, Dallku, Vangjeli, Angolli (Cana 64), Lala (Hyka 64), Curri, Bulku (Kapllani 86), Duro (Bakaj 78), Skela (Vila 81), Bogdani (Salihi 46).

Northern Ireland: Maik Taylor (Tuffey 72); Little, McCartney, Craigan, McGivern, O'Connor (Evans C 46), McGinn (Shiels 46), Davis, Lafferty (Patterson 64), Healy (Kirk 78), McCann.

Referee: E. Pilav (Bosnia).

New Brittain, 26 March 2010, 4000

Turkey (0) 2 *(Sercan 47, Semih 71)*

Northern Ireland (0) 0

Turkey: Onur; Servet, Ibrahim T, Caner, Sabri, Nuri (Mehmet T 46), Selcuk, Inan (Emre B 66), Ozan (Arda 66), Kazim-Richards (Semih 62), Tuncay, Hamit Altintop (Sercan 46).

Northern Ireland: Blayney; Little, McAuley, Craigan, McGivern (Coates 76), Garrett (Lawrie 80), Mulgrew, Evans C, Braniff (McArdle 61), Gorman (Bryan 66), Patterson (Magennis 60).

Referee: T. Vaughn (USA).

Connecticut, 26 May 2010, 4000

Northern Ireland (0) 0

Turkey (0) 2 *(Yildirim 48, Semih 72)*

Northern Ireland: Blayney; Little, McAuley, Craigan, McGivern (Coates 76), Garrett (Lawrie 80), Mulgrew, Evans C, Braniff (McArdle 61), Gorman (Bryan 66), Patterson (Magennis 60).

Turkey: Kivrak; Servet, Caner (Ismail 74), Selcuk (Emre B 67), Ozan (Arda 67), Tuncay, Sabri, Ibrahim T, Hamit Altintop (Mehmet T 46), Nuri (Yildirim 46), Kazim-Richards (Semih 62).

Referee: T. Vaughn (USA).

Chillan, 30 May 2010, 12,000

Chile (1) 1 *(Paredes 30)*

Northern Ireland (0) 0

Chile: Pinto; Vidal (Ross 77), Fuentes, Isla, Cereceda, Contreras, Gonzalez (Orellana 64), Fernandez (Gutierrez 89), Fierro, Estrada, Paredes.

Northern Ireland: Blayney (McGovern 46); Little, McGivern (Coates 56), McAuley, Craigan (McArdle 46), Evans C, Garrett (Braniff 46), Patterson, Mulgrew, Gorman (Magennis 73), Bryan (Lawrie 46).

Referee: L. Prudente (Uruguay).

Limerick, 12 August 2009, 19,428

Republic of Ireland (0) 0

Australia (2) 3 *(Cahill 38, 44, Carney 90)*

Republic of Ireland: Given (Westwood 68); O'Shea, St Ledger-Hall, Dunne, Kilbane (Nolan 63), McGeady (Long 81), Whelan, Gibson (Andrews 62), Duff (Hunt S 46), Keane, Doyle K (Folan 46).

Australia: Schwarzer; Carney, North (Spiranovic 71), Williams, Kisnorbo (Madaschi 46), Jedinak (Holland 89), Wilkshire, Cahill (Holman 46), Bresciano (Carle 78), McDonald (Rukavytsya 46), Kewell.

Referee: A. Burrull (Spain).

Limerick, 8 September 2009, 14,572

Republic of Ireland (1) 1 *(Lawrence 37)*

South Africa (0) 0

Republic of Ireland: Westwood; Kelly, McShane (O'Dea 61), St Ledger-Hall, Nolan, Keogh (Duff 78), Gibson, Andrews, Lawrence, Folan, Doyle K (Best 59).
South Africa: Fernandez; Gaxa, Mokoena, Gould, Masilela (Thwala 78), Van Heerden (Khenyeza 59), Mhlongo, Dikgacoi (Ngobeni 81), Pienaar, Mphela (Henyekane 73), Parker (Tshabalala 63).
Referee: C. Gordon (Scotland).

Emirates Stadium, 2 March 2010, 40,082

Republic of Ireland (0) 0

Brazil (1) 2 *(Andrews 44 (og), Robinho 76)*

Republic of Ireland: Given; Kelly, Kilbane, Whelan (Gibson 56), St Ledger-Hall, McShane, Lawrence (McCarthy 69), Andrews, Doyle K (Best 78), Keane, Duff (McGeady 56).
Brazil: Julio Cesar; Maicon (Carlos Eduardo 84), Lucio (Luisao 82), Juan, Michel Bastos, Ramires (Dani Alves 64), Silva, Felipe Melo, Kaka, Adriano (Grafite 64), Robinho (Nilmar 77).
Referee: M. Dean (England).

Dublin, 25 May 2010, 16,722

Republic of Ireland (2) 2 *(Doyle K 7, Lawrence 39)*

Paraguay (0) 1 *(Barrios 58)*

Republic of Ireland: Westwood; Kelly, McShane, St Ledger-Hall, O'Shea, Lawrence (Foley 82), Whelan (Green 69), Andrews, Duff (Fahey 77), Keane (Sheridan 63), Doyle K (Long 87).
Paraguay: Bobadilla; Da Silva, Caniza, Alcaraz, Morel Rodriguez (Torres 65), Vera (Bonet 66), Riveros (Ortigoza 65), Santana (Aquino 82), Santa Cruz (Martinez 77), Barrios, Gamarra.
Referee: J. Lapperriere (Switzerland).

Dublin, 28 May 2010, 16,800

Republic of Ireland (1) 3 *(Green 31, Keane 52, 85 (pen))*

Algeria (0) 0

Republic of Ireland: Westwood (Murphy 86); Kelly, O'Shea (O'Dea 36), St Ledger-Hall, Cunningham, Lawrence (Long 86), Green, Whelan (Andrews 75), Duff (Fahey 65), Keane, Doyle K (Sheridan 72).
Algeria: Chaouchi (M'Bohli 66); Guedioura, Halliche, Bellaid, Mesbah, Ziani, Lacen, Mansouri (Kadir 66), Belhadj (Boudebouz 66), Djebour (Saifi 58), Ghezzal (Abdoun 77).
Referee: E. Braamhar (Holland).

Yokohama, 10 October 2009, 72,377

Japan (0) 2 *(Berra 83 (og), Honda 90)*

Scotland (0) 0

Japan: Kawashima; Iwamasa, Uchida (Okubo 65), Abe, Hashimoto (Tokunaga 67), Inamoto (Komano 81), Konno, Kengo Nakamura, Ishikawa (Matsui 67), Honda, Maeda (Morimoto 56).
Scotland: Gordon; Berra, Whittaker, Wallace L, Caldwell G, McManus, Adam (Hughes 67), Dorrans, Conway (Riordan 74), Miller (Cowie 46), Wallace R (Fletcher S 46).
Referee: S.W. Kim (South Korea).

Hampden Park, 3 March 2010, 26,530

Scotland (0) 1 *(Brown 62)*

Czech Republic (0) 0

Scotland: Gordon; Hutton, Wallace L, Brown S, Caldwell G, Webster (Berra 46), Thomson K (Hartley 46), Fletcher D (Whittaker 83), Robson (Adam 69), Miller (Boyd 63), Dorrans.
Czech Republic: Drobny; Kusnir (Pudil 86), Hubnik, Sivok, Kadlec, Plasil (Moravek 79), Holek, Hubschman (Rajnoch 79), Rosicky (Skacel 66), Necid (Blazek 67), Sverkos (Papadopoulos 67).
Referee: F. Fautrel (France).

ENGLAND UNDER-21 TEAMS 2009–2010

■*Denotes player sent off.*

Groningen, 11 August 2009, 6000

Holland (0) 0

England (0) 0

England: Loach (Fielding 46); Richards (Naughton 58), Tomkins, Mancienne, Gibbs (Bertrand 58), Rose, Stanislaus (Sears 83), Cattermole (Carroll 71), Delph (Wilshere 58), Rodwell (Smalling 58), Vaughan (Sturridge 46).

Prilep, 4 September 2009

Macdonia (1) 1 *(Ibraimi 34)*

England (0) 2 *(Sears 68, Cattermole 83 (pen))*

England: Loach; Gibbs, Mancienne, Naughton, Tomkins, Cattermole, Muamba (Sears 46), Rodwell, Rose (Wilshere 72), Sturridge, Stanislaus (Cleverley 83).

Tripoli, 8 September 2009, 2678

Greece (1) 1 *(Ninis 41)*

England (1) 1 *(Sturridge 5)*

England: Loach; Naughton, Gibbs, Muamba, Tomkins, Mancienne, Wilshere, Rodwell (Addison 56), Sturridge (Welbeck 28) (Sears 75), Rose, Cleverley.

Coventry, 9 October 2009, 20,074

England (2) 6 *(Gibbs 22, Richards 29, Carroll 54, 87, Hines 67, 90)*

Macedonia (1) 3 *(Muarem 42, Ibraimi 53, Gibbs 58 (og))*

England: Loach; Richards, Gibbs, Tomkins, Mancienne, Rodwell, Cleverley, Wilshere, Rose (Muamba 69), Carroll (Welbeck 90), Walcott (Hines 46).

Wembley, 14 November 2009, 33,833

England (1) 1 *(Rose 40)*

Portugal (0) 0

England: Loach; Mancienne (Naughton 76), Bertrand, Muamba, Richards, Smalling, Cleverley, Delph (Gosling 90), Carroll, Gibbs, Rose (Cork 76).

Vilnius, 7 November 2009

Lithuania (0) 0

England (0) 0

England: Loach; Gibbs (Bertrand 21), Mancienne, Richards, Smalling, Cleverley, Delph, Muamba (Hines 64), Rose, Carroll, Sturridge (Lansbury 79).

Doncaster, 3 March 2010, 9708

England (0) 1 *(Delfouneso 79)*

Greece (1) 2 *(Papadopoulos K 28, Papadopoulos G 48)*

England: Loach; Walker, Richards, Smalling (Delfouneso 74), Bertrand, Muamba (Sturridge 54), Wilshere, Cattermole, Rodwell, Cleverley (Gosling 87), Carroll.

ENGLAND C 2009–2010

15 Sept *(in Szekesfehervar)*

Hungary 1 *(Srekeres 26)*   **England 1** *(Briscoe 41)*

England: Roberts (Welch 80); Reynolds (Vaughan 59), Rents, Garner, Jarvis, Cadmore (McFadzean 70), Briscoe (Simpson 59), Nix, Wright, Holroyd, Knight-Percival (Green 46).

18 Nov*(in Gradiszk Wielpolski)*

Poland Under-23 1 *(Janczyk 45)*   **England 2** *(Holroyd 32, Barnes-Homer 74)*

England: Roberts (Hedge 86); Densmore, Newton, Cadmore, Charles, Howells, Porter (Reason 73), Jarvis, Wright (Shaw 60), Holroyd, Brodie (Barnes-Homer 66).

26 May *(in Waterford)*

Republic of Ireland Under-23 1 *(Madden 67)*

England 2 *(Fleming 27, Porter 63)*   1570

England: Roberts; Densmore, Cadmore, McFadzean, Newton, Morgan-Smith (Obeng 81), Gregory, Fleming (Jarvis 74), Deering (Rodman 90), Barnes-Homer, Porter (Hall 84).
Republic of Ireland: Quigley; Mulcahy, Breen, Browne (Kelly 36), Powell, Finn (Amond 86), O'Donnell (Bolger 63), Chambers, Gaynor (McCabe 59), Byrne (Madden 46), Dennehy.

ENGLAND UNDER-16 2009–2010

VICTORY SHIELD

15 Oct *(at Yeovil)*

England 1 *(Ansah 76)*

Wales 0   3700

England: Pickford; Hendrie, McFadzean (Callaghan 66), Cousins, Magri, Blackett (Henshall 41), Fanimo, Cotton, Hope (Ansah 60), Nabi (Redmond 41), Caskey (Jackson 71).

5 Nov *(at Chester)*

England 2 *(Turgott 50, Fanimo 80)*

Northern Ireland 0

England: Willis; Facey (Arthurworrey 67), McFadzean, Amenku (Barmby 41), Magri, Jackson, Redmond (Sterling 41), Powell, Ansah (Nabi 71), Fanimo, Turgott (Jordan 62).

27 Nov *(at Tynecastle)*

Scotland 1 *(Grimmer 26)*

England 2 *(Ansah 27, Turgott 60)*   2870

England: Pickford; McFadzean, Cousins, Magri (Blackett 69), Fanimo, Cotton (Henshall 60), Ansah (Hope 45), Jackson, Powell, Sterling (Amenku 45), Turgott (Hutton 74).

Northern Ireland 1, Scotland 2
Wales 0, Scotland 1
Wales 2, Northern Ireland 0

	P	W	D	L	F	A	Pts
England	3	3	0	0	5	1	9
Scotland	3	2	0	1	4	3	6
Wales	3	1	0	2	2	2	3
Northern Ireland	3	0	0	3	1	6	0

UEFA UNDER-21 CHAMPIONSHIP 2009–2011

QUALIFYING ROUND

GROUP 1
Romania 2, Andorra 0
Russia 4, Andorra 0
Latvia 4, Andorra 0
Faeroes 0, Romania 4
Faeroes 1, Russia 0
Andorra 0, Romania 2
Moldova 1, Latvia 0
Faeroes 1, Moldova 1
Latvia 0, Russia 4
Andorra 0, Russia 4
Romania 3, Moldova 0
Faeroes 1, Latvia 3
Latvia 5, Romania 1
Russia 2, Faeroes 0
Moldova 1, Andorra 0
Romania 3, Faeroes 0
Russia 3, Moldova 1
Romania 4, Latvia 1
Moldova 0, Russia 3
Latvia 0, Faeroes 1
Andorra 1, Faeroes 1
Andorra 1, Moldova 3

GROUP 2
Republic of Ireland 0, Turkey 3
Switzerland 2, Armenia 1
Armenia 2, Turkey 5
Switzerland 0, Estonia 1
Armenia 1, Switzerland 3
Estonia 2, Georgia 0
Georgia 4, Turkey 0
Estonia 1, Republic of Ireland 1
Estonia 1, Switzerland 4
Republic of Ireland 1, Georgia 1
Turkey 1, Armenia 1
Republic of Ireland 1, Switzerland 1
Georgia 1, Republic of Ireland 1
Armenia 1, Estonia 1
Turkey 1, Switzerland 3
Armenia 4, Republic of Ireland 1
Turkey 0, Estonia 0
Switzerland 1, Georgia 0
Georgia 2, Estonia 0
Republic of Ireland 1, Armenia 2
Estonia 2, Armenia 3
Estonia 1, Turkey 0
Switzerland 0, Turkey 2
Georgia 0, Switzerland 0

GROUP 3
Luxembourg 0, Wales 0

Wales 4, Luxembourg 1
Hungary 3, Luxembourg 0
Luxembourg 0, Hungary 1
Wales 4, Hungary 1
Bosnia 0, Luxembourg 1
Wales 2, Italy 1
Italy 2, Luxembourg 0
Wales 2, Bosnia 0
Italy 1, Bosnia 1
Hungary 2, Italy 0
Luxembourg 0, Italy 4
Bosnia 2, Wales 1
Luxembourg 0, Bosnia 1
Italy 2, Hungary 0

GROUP 4
Poland 2, Liechtenstein 0
Spain 2, Poland 0
Holland 2, Finland 0
Liechtenstein 0, Spain 4
Poland 2, Finland 1
Liechtenstein 0, Poland 5
Finland 0, Holland 1
Poland 0, Holland 4
Liechtenstein 0, Finland 4
Spain 1, Finland 0
Holland 3, Liechtenstein 0
Holland 2, Spain 1
Spain 3, Liechtenstein 1
Holland 3, Poland 2

GROUP 5
San Marino 0, Czech Republic 8
Iceland 0, Czech Republic 2
Germany 6, San Marino 0
Czech Republic 2, Northern Ireland 0
Germany 1, Czech Republic 2
Northern Ireland 2, Iceland 6
Iceland 8, San Marino 0
Iceland 2, Northern Ireland 1
San Marino 0, Iceland 6
Northern Ireland 1, Germany 1
San Marino 0, Germany 11
Northern Ireland 1, Czech Republic 2
Germany 2, Iceland 2
San Marino 0, Northern Ireland 3

GROUP 6
Israel 1, Kazakhstan 1
Kazakhstan 2, Bulgaria 0
Kazakhstan 0, Montenegro 2
Bulgaria 3, Israel 4
Bulgaria 3, Kazakhstan 0
Montenegro 0, Sweden 2

Kazakhstan 1, Israel 2
Sweden 2, Bulgaria 1
Bulgaria 1, Montenegro 1
Kazakhstan 1, Sweden 1
Montenegro 3, Kazakhstan 1
Montenegro 1, Israel 0
Sweden 5, Kazakhstan 1
Israel 4, Bulgaria 0
Montenegro 2, Bulgaria 0
Israel 0, Sweden 1
Sweden 2, Montenegro 0

GROUP 7
Croatia 0, Cyprus 2
Norway 2, Slovakia 2
Cyprus 1, Norway 3
Serbia 1, Slovakia 2
Norway 1, Croatia 3
Slovakia 1, Cyprus 0
Norway 0, Serbia 1
Serbia 2, Cyprus 0
Croatia 3, Serbia 1
Cyprus 0, Slovakia 1
Cyprus 1, Croatia 2
Serbia 3, Norway 2
Slovakia 1, Croatia 2
Croatia 1, Slovakia 1

GROUP 8
Malta 0, Slovenia 2
Ukraine 1, Malta 0
Malta 0, Belgium 1
Slovenia 1, France 3
Belgium 2, Slovenia 0
France 2, Ukraine 2
Ukraine 1, Belgium 1
Malta 0, France 2
Belgium 0, France 0
Slovenia 0, Ukraine 2
Slovenia 1, Malta 0

Belgium 0, Ukraine 2
France 1, Slovenia 0
Belgium 1, Malta 0
Malta 0, Ukraine 3

GROUP 9
Greece 3, Macedonia 1
Lithuania 0, Greece 1
Macedonia 1, England 2
Portugal 4, Lithuania 1
Greece 1, England 1
Macedonia 1, Lithuania 1
Greece 2, Portugal 1
England 6, Macedonia 3
Macedonia 1, Portugal 1
Greece 1, Lithuania 0
Lithuania 1, Macedonia 0
England 1, Portugal 0
Lithuania 0, England 0
Portugal 2, Greece 1
England 1, Greece 2

GROUP 10
Albania 0, Scotland 1
Scotland 5, Albania 2
Belarus 2, Austria 1
Albania 1, Azerbaijan 0
Austria 1, Scotland 0
Azerbaijan 2, Belarus 3
Austria 3, Albania 1
Azerbaijan 1, Austria 2
Scotland 1, Belarus 0
Belarus 4, Albania 2
Albania 2, Austria 2
Azerbaijan 0, Scotland 4
Albania 1, Belarus 2
Austria 4, Azerbaijan 0
Scotland 2, Azerbaijan 2

Competition still being played.

299

UEFA UNDER-19 CHAMPIONSHIP 2009–2010

Finals in Ukraine

GROUP A

England v Switzerland	1-1
Ukraine v Slovenia	0-0
Slovenia v Switzerland	1-2
Ukraine v England	2-2
Switzerland v Ukraine	0-1
Slovenia v England	1-7

GROUP B

France v Serbia	1-1
Turkey v Spain	1-2
France v Turkey	1-1
Serbia v Spain	2-1
Spain v France	0-1
Serbia v Turkey	1-0

SEMI-FINALS

England v France	3-1
Serbia v Ukraine	1-3

FINAL

2 Aug

England (0) 0

Ukraine (1) 2 *(Garmash 5, Korkishko 50)*   25,000

England: Steele; Trippier, Mattock, Gosling, Walker, Welbeck (Ranger 63), Drinkwater (Tutte 55), Delfouneso, Lansbury, Bennett, Briggs (Hoyte 56).
Ukraine: Levchenko; Kushnirov, Partsvaniya, Kryvtsov, Korkishko, Petrov (Yeremenko 90), Garmash, Shakhov, Rybalka, Kaverin (Shevchuk 80), Chaykovskiy.

UEFA UNDER-17 CHAMPIONSHIP 2009–2010

Finals in Lichtenstein

ELITE ROUND

GROUP A

France 1, Spain 2
Portugal 3, Switzerland 0
Spain 4, Switzerland 0
France 1, Portugal 0
Switzerland 1, France 3
Spain 2, Portugal 0

GROUP B

Greece 1, Turkey 3
England 3, Czech Republic 1
Turkey 1, Czech Republic 1
Greece 0, England 1
Czech Republic 0, Greece 0
Turkey 1, England 2

SEMI-FINALS

England 2, France 1
Spain 3, Turkey 1

FINAL

30 May

England (2) 2 *(Wisdom 30, Wickham 42)*

Spain (1) 1 *(Wisdom 22 (og)*   3990

England: Butland; Chalobah, Garbutt, Pilatos, Wisdom, Coady, Keane (Thorne 67), McEachran (Thorpe 79), Afobe (Hall 73), Wickham, Barkley.
Spain: Ortola; Campabadal (Bernat 73), Ramalho, Alvarez, Orti (Hervias 46), Deulofeu, Darder, Rodriguez, Campana, Alcacer, Puerto.

FIFA UNDER-17 WORLD CUP 2009–2010

Finals in Nigeria

GROUP A

Nigera 3, Germany 3
Honduras 0, Argentina 1
Argentina 2, Germany 1
Nigeria 1, Honduras 0
Germany 3, Honduras 1
Argentina 1, Nigeria 2

GROUP B

Brazil 3, Japan 2
Mexico 0, Switzerland 2
Switzerland 4, Japan 3
Brazil 0, Mexico 1
Japan 0, Mexico 2
Switzerland 1, Brazil 0

GROUP C

Iran 2, Gambia 0
Colombia 2, Holland 1
Holland 2, Gambia 1
Iran 0, Colombia 0
Gambia 2, Colombia 2
Holland 0, Iran 1

GROUP D

Turkey 1, Burkina Faso 0
Costa Rica 1, New Zealand 1
New Zealand 1, Burkina Faso 1
Turkey 4, Costa Rica 1
Burkina Faso 4, Costa Rica 1
New Zealand 1, Turkey 1

GROUP E

UAE 2, Malawi 0
Spain 2, USA 1
USA 1, Malawi 0
UAE 1, Spain 3
Malawi 1, Spain 4
USA 1, UAE 0

GROUP F

Uruguay 1, South Korea 3
Algeria 0, Italy 1
Italy 2, South Korea 1
Uruguay 2, Algeria 0
South Korea 2, Algeria 0
Italy 0, Uruguay 0

FIRST ROUND

Argentina 2, Colombia 3
Turkey 2, UAE 0
Switzerland 4, Germany 3
Italy 2, USA 1
Spain 4, Burkina Faso 1
Iran 1, Uruguay 2
Mexico 1, South Korea 1
South Korea won 5-3 on penalties.
Nigeria 5, New Zealand 0

QUARTER-FINALS

Colombia 1, Turkey 1
Colombia won 5-3 on penalties.
Switzerland 2, Italy 1
Spain 3, Uruguay 3
Spain won 4-2 on penalties.
South Korea 1, Nigeria 3

SEMI-FINALS

Colombia 0, Switzerland 4
Spain 1, Nigeria 3

MATCH FOR THIRD PLACE

Colombia 0, Spain 1

FINAL

Switzerland 1, Nigeria 0

FIFA UNDER-20 WORLD CUP 2009–2010

Finals in Egypt

GROUP A
Egypt 4, Trinidad & Tobago 1
Paraguay 0, Italy 0
Italy 2, Trinidad & Tobago 1
Egypt 1, Paraguay 2
Trinidad & Tobago 0 Paraguay 0
Italy 2, Egypt 4

GROUP B
Nigeria 0, Venezuela 1
Spain 8, Tahiti 0
Nigeria 0, Spain 2
Tahiti 0, Venezuela 8
Venezuela 0, Spain 3
Tahiti 0, Nigeria 5

GROUP C
USA 0, Germany 3
Cameroon 2, South Korea 0
South Korea 1, Germany 1
USA 4, Cameroon 1
Germany 3, Cameroon 0
South Korea 3, USA 0

GROUP D
Ghana 2, Uzbekistan 1
England 0, Uruguay 1
Uruguay 3, Uzbekistan 0
Ghana 4, England 0
Uruguay 2, Ghana 2
Uzbekistan 1, England 1

GROUP E
Brazil 5, Costa Rica 0
Czech Republic 2, Australia 1
Australia 0, Costa Rica 3
Brazil 0, Czech Republic 0
Costa Rica 2, Czech Republic 3
Australia 1, Brazil 3

GROUP F
UAE 2, South Africa 2
Honduras 3, Hungary 0
Hungary 4, South Africa 0
UAE 1, Honduras 0
Hungary 2, UAE 0
South Africa 2, Honduras 0

FIRST ROUND
Paraguay 0, South Korea 3
Ghana 2, South Africa 1
Spain 1, Italy 3
Hungary 2, Czech Republic 2
Hungary won 4-3 on penalties
Brazil 3, Uruguay 1
Germany 3, Nigeria 2
Venezuela 1, UAE 2
Egypt 0, Costa Rica 2

QUARTER-FINALS
South Korea 2, Ghana 3
Italy 2, Hungary 3
Brazil 2, Germany 1
UAE 1, Costa Rica 2

SEMI-FINALS
Ghana 3, Hungary 2
Brazil 1, Costa Rica 0

MATCH FOR THIRD PLACE
Hungary 1, Costa Rica 1
Hungary won 2-0 on penalties.

FINAL
Ghana 0, Brazil 0
Ghana won 4-3 on penalties.

POST-WAR INTERNATIONAL APPEARANCES

As at July 2010 *(Season of first cap given)*

ENGLAND

A'Court, A. (5) 1957/8 Liverpool
Adams, T. A. (66) 1986/7 Arsenal
Agbonlahor, G. (3) 2008/09 Aston Villa
Allen, C. (5) 1983/4 QPR, Tottenham H
Allen, R. (5) 1951/2 WBA
Allen, T. (3) 1959/60 Stoke C
Anderson, S. (2) 1961/2 Sunderland
Anderson, V. (30) 1978/9 Nottingham F, Arsenal, Manchester U
Anderton, D. R. (30) 1993/4 Tottenham H
Angus, J. (1) 1960/1 Burnley
Armfield, J. (43) 1958/9 Blackpool
Armstrong, D. (3) 1979/80 Middlesbrough, Southampton
Armstrong, K. (1) 1954/5 Chelsea
Ashton, D. (1) 2007/08 West Ham U
Astall, G. (2) 1955/6 Birmingham C
Astle, J. (5) 1968/9 WBA
Aston, J. (17) 1948/9 Manchester U
Atyeo, J. (6) 1955/6 Bristol C

Bailey, G. R. (2) 1984/5 Manchester U
Bailey, M. (2) 1963/4 Charlton
Baily, E. (9) 1949/50 Tottenham H
Baines, L. J. (2) 2009/10 Everton
Baker, J. (8) 1959/60 Hibernian, Arsenal
Ball, A. (72) 1964/5 Blackpool, Everton, Arsenal
Ball, M. J. (1) 2000/01 Everton
Banks, G. (73) 1962/3 Leicester C, Stoke C
Banks, T. (6) 1957/8 Bolton W
Bardsley, D. (2) 1992/3 QPR
Barham, M. (2) 1982/3 Norwich C
Barlow, R. (1) 1954/5 WBA
Barmby, N. J. (23) 1994/5 Tottenham H, Middlesbrough, Everton, Liverpool
Barnes, J. (79) 1982/3 Watford, Liverpool
Barnes, P. (22) 1977/8 Manchester C, WBA, Leeds U
Barrass, M. (3) 1951/2 Bolton W
Barrett, E. D. (3) 1990/1 Oldham Ath, Aston Villa
Barry, G. (39) 1999/00 Aston Villa, Manchester C
Barton, J. (1) 2006/07 Manchester C

Barton, W. D. (3) 1994/5 Wimbledon, Newcastle U
Batty, D. (42) 1990/1 Leeds U, Blackburn R, Newcastle U, Leeds U
Baynham, R. (3) 1955/6 Luton T
Beardsley, P. A. (59) 1985/6 Newcastle U, Liverpool, Newcastle U
Beasant, D. J. (2) 1989/90 Chelsea
Beattie, J. S. (5) 2002/03 Southampton
Beattie, T. K. (9) 1974/5 Ipswich T
Beckham, D. R. J. (115) 1996/7 Manchester U, Real Madrid, LA Galaxy
Bell, C. (48) 1967/8 Manchester C
Bent, D. A. (6) 2005/06 Charlton Ath, Tottenham H
Bentley, D. M. (7) 2007/08 Blackburn R, Tottenham H
Bentley, R. (12) 1948/9 Chelsea
Berry, J. (4) 1952/3 Manchester U
Birtles, G. (3) 1979/80 Nottingham F
Blissett, L. (14) 1982/3 Watford, AC Milan
Blockley, J. (1) 1972/3 Arsenal
Blunstone, F. (5) 1954/5 Chelsea
Bonetti, P. (7) 1965/6 Chelsea
Bould, S. A. (2) 1993/4 Arsenal
Bowles, S. (5) 1973/4 QPR
Bowyer, L. D. (1) 2002/03 Leeds U
Boyer, P. (1) 1975/6 Norwich C
Brabrook, P. (3) 1957/8 Chelsea
Bracewell, P. W. (3) 1984/5 Everton
Bradford, G. (1) 1955/6 Bristol R
Bradley, W. (3) 1958/9 Manchester U
Bridge, W. M. (36) 2001/02 Southampton, Chelsea, Manchester C
Bridges, B. (4) 1964/5 Chelsea
Broadbent, P. (7) 1957/8 Wolverhampton W
Broadis, I. (14) 1951/2 Manchester C, Newcastle U
Brooking, T. (47) 1973/4 West Ham U
Brooks, J. (3) 1956/7 Tottenham H
Brown, A. (1) 1970/1 WBA
Brown, K. (1) 1959/60 West Ham U
Brown, W. M. (23) 1998/9 Manchester U
Bull, S. G. (13) 1988/9 Wolverhampton W

Butcher, T. (77) 1979/80 Ipswich T, Rangers
Butt, N. (39) 1996/7 Manchester U, Newcastle U
Byrne, G. (2) 1962/3 Liverpool
Byrne, J. (11) 1961/2 Crystal P, West Ham U
Byrne, R. (33) 1953/4 Manchester U

Callaghan, I. (4) 1965/6 Liverpool
Campbell, S. (73) 1995/6 Tottenham H, Arsenal, Portsmouth
Carragher, J. L. (38) 1998/9 Liverpool
Carrick, M. (22) 2000/01 West Ham U, Tottenham H, Manchester U
Carson, S. P. (3) 2007/08 Liverpool, WBA
Carter, H. (7) 1946/7 Derby Co
Chamberlain, M. (8) 1982/3 Stoke C
Channon, M. (46) 1972/3 Southampton, Manchester C
Charles, G. A. (2) 1990/1 Nottingham F
Charlton, J. (35) 1964/5 Leeds U
Charlton, R. (106) 1957/8 Manchester U
Charnley, R. (1) 1962/3 Blackpool
Cherry, T. (27) 1975/6 Leeds U
Chilton, A. (2) 1950/1 Manchester U
Chivers, M. (24) 1970/1 Tottenham H
Clamp, E. (4) 1957/8 Wolverhampton W
Clapton, D. (1) 1958/9 Arsenal
Clarke, A. (19) 1969/70 Leeds U
Clarke, H. (1) 1953/4 Tottenham H
Clayton, R. (35) 1955/6 Blackburn R
Clemence, R (61) 1972/3 Liverpool, Tottenham H
Clement, D. (5) 1975/6 QPR
Clough, B. (2) 1959/60 Middlesbrough
Clough, N. H. (14) 1988/9 Nottingham F
Coates, R. (4) 1969/70 Burnley, Tottenham H
Cockburn, H. (13) 1946/7 Manchester U
Cohen, G. (37) 1963/4 Fulham
Cole, Andy (15) 1994/5 Manchester U
Cole, Ashley (82) 2000/01 Arsenal, Chelsea
Cole, C. (7) 2008/09 West Ham U
Cole, J. J. (56) 2000/01 West Ham U, Chelsea
Collymore, S. V. (3) 1994/5 Nottingham F, Aston Villa
Compton, L. (2) 1950/1 Arsenal
Connelly, J. (20) 1959/60 Burnley, Manchester U
Cooper, C. T. (2) 1994/5 Nottingham F
Cooper, T. (20) 1968/9 Leeds U
Coppell, S. (42) 1977/8 Manchester U

Corrigan, J. (9) 1975/6 Manchester C
Cottee, A. R. (7) 1986/7 West Ham U, Everton
Cowans, G. (10) 1982/3 Aston Villa, Bari, Aston Villa
Crawford, R. (2) 1961/2 Ipswich T
Crouch, P. J. (40) 2004/05 Southampton, Liverpool, Portsmouth, Tottenham H
Crowe, C. (1) 1962/3 Wolverhampton W
Cunningham, L. (6) 1978/9 WBA, Real Madrid
Curle, K. (3) 1991/2 Manchester C
Currie, A. (17) 1971/2 Sheffield U, Leeds U

Daley, A. M. (7) 1991/2 Aston Villa
Davenport, P. (1) 1984/5 Nottingham F
Deane, B. C. (3) 1990/1 Sheffield U
Deeley, N. (2) 1958/9 Wolverhampton W
Defoe, J. C. (43) 2003/04 Tottenham H, Portsmouth, Tottenham H
Devonshire, A. (8) 1979/80 West Ham U
Dickinson, J. (48) 1948/9 Portsmouth
Ditchburn, E. (6) 1948/9 Tottenham H
Dixon, K. M. (8) 1984/5 Chelsea
Dixon, L. M. (22) 1989/90 Arsenal
Dobson, M. (5) 1973/4 Burnley, Everton
Dorigo, A. R. (15) 1989/90 Chelsea, Leeds U
Douglas, B. (36) 1957/8 Blackburn R
Downing, S. (23) 2004/05 Middlesbrough
Doyle, M. (5) 1975/6 Manchester C
Dublin, D. (4) 1997/8 Coventry C, Aston Villa
Dunn, D. J. I. (1) 2002/03 Blackburn R
Duxbury, M. (10) 1983/4 Manchester U
Dyer, K. C. (33) 1999/00 Newcastle U, West Ham U

Eastham, G. (19) 1962/3 Arsenal
Eckersley, W. (17) 1949/50 Blackburn R
Edwards, D. (18) 1954/5 Manchester U
Ehiogu, U. (4) 1995/6 Aston Villa, Middlesbrough
Ellerington, W. (2) 1948/9 Southampton
Elliott, W. H. (5) 1951/2 Burnley

Fantham, J. (1) 1961/2 Sheffield W
Fashanu, J. (2) 1988/9 Wimbledon
Fenwick, T. (20) 1983/4 QPR, Tottenham H
Ferdinand, L. (17) 1992/3 QPR, Newcastle U, Tottenham H
Ferdinand, R. G. (78) 1997/8 West Ham U, Leeds U, Manchester U

Finney, T. (76) 1946/7 Preston NE
Flowers, R. (49) 1954/5
  Wolverhampton W
Flowers, T. (11) 1992/3 Southampton,
  Blackburn R
Foster, B. (4) 2006/07 Manchester U
Foster, S. (3) 1981/2 Brighton
Foulkes, W. (1) 1954/5 Manchester U
Fowler, R. B. (26) 1995/6 Liverpool,
  Leeds U
Francis, G. (12) 1974/5 QPR
Francis, T. (52) 1976/7 Birmingham C,
  Nottingham F, Manchester C,
  Sampdoria
Franklin, N. (27) 1946/7 Stoke C
Froggatt, J. (13) 1949/50 Portsmouth
Froggatt, R. (4) 1952/3 Sheffield W

Gardner, A. (1) 2003/04 Tottenham H
Garrett, T. (3) 1951/2 Blackpool
Gascoigne, P. J. (57) 1988/9 Tottenham H,
  Lazio, Rangers, Middlesbrough
Gates, E. (2) 1980/1 Ipswich T
George, F. C. (1) 1976/7 Derby Co
Gerrard, S. G. (84) 1999/00 Liverpool
Gidman, J. (1) 1976/7 Aston Villa
Gillard, I. (3) 1974/5 QPR
Goddard, P. (1) 1981/2 West Ham U
Grainger, C. (7) 1955/6 Sheffield U,
  Sunderland
Gray, A. A. (1) 1991/2 Crystal P
Gray, M. (3) 1998/9 Sunderland
Greaves, J. (57) 1958/9 Chelsea,
  Tottenham H
Green, R. P. (11) 2004/05 Norwich C,
  West Ham U
Greenhoff, B. (18) 1975/6 Manchester U,
  Leeds U
Gregory, J. (6) 1982/3 QPR
Guppy, S. (1) 1999/00 Leicester C

Hagan, J. (1) 1948/9 Sheffield U
Haines, J. (1) 1948/9 WBA
Hall, J. (17) 1955/6 Birmingham C
Hancocks, J. (3) 1948/9
  Wolverhampton W
Hardwick, G. (13) 1946/7 Middlesbrough
Harford, M. G. (2) 1987/8 Luton T
Hargreaves, O. (42) 2001/02 Bayern
  Munich, Manchester U
Harris, G. (1) 1965/6 Burnley
Harris, P. (2) 1949/50 Portsmouth
Hart, C. (3) 2007/08 Manchester C
Harvey, C. (1) 1970/1 Everton

Hassall, H. (5) 1950/1 Huddersfield T,
  Bolton W
Hateley, M. (32) 1983/4 Portsmouth,
  AC Milan, Monaco, Rangers
Haynes, J. (56) 1954/5 Fulham
Hector, K. (2) 1973/4 Derby Co
Hellawell, M. (2) 1962/3 Birmingham C
Hendrie, L. A. (1) 1998/9 Aston Villa
Henry, R. (1) 1962/3 Tottenham H
Heskey, E. W. (62) 1998/9 Leicester C,
  Liverpool, Birmingham C, Wigan Ath,
  Aston Villa
Hill, F. (2) 1962/3 Bolton W
Hill, G. (6) 1975/6 Manchester U
Hill, R. (3) 1982/3 Luton T
Hinchcliffe, A. G. (7) 1996/7 Everton,
  Sheffield W
Hinton, A. (3) 1962/3 Wolverhampton W,
  Nottingham F
Hirst, D. E. (3) 1990/1 Sheffield W
Hitchens, G. (7) 1960/1 Aston Villa,
  Internazionale
Hoddle, G. (53) 1979/80 Tottenham H,
  Monaco
Hodge, S. B. (24) 1985/6 Aston Villa,
  Tottenham H, Nottingham F
Hodgkinson, A. (5) 1956/7 Sheffield U
Holden, D. (5) 1958/9 Bolton W
Holliday, E. (3) 1959/60 Middlesbrough
Hollins, J. (1) 1966/7 Chelsea
Hopkinson, E. (14) 1957/8 Bolton W
Howe, D. (23) 1957/8 WBA
Howe, J. (3) 1947/8 Derby Co
Howey, S. N. (4) 1994/5 Newcastle U
Huddlestone, T. A. (3) 2009/10
  Tottenham H
Hudson, A. (2) 1974/5 Stoke C
Hughes, E. (62) 1969/70 Liverpool,
  Wolverhampton W
Hughes, L. (3) 1949/50 Liverpool
Hunt, R. (34) 1961/2 Liverpool
Hunt, S. (2) 1983/4 WBA
Hunter, N. (28) 1965/6 Leeds U
Hurst, G. (49) 1965/6 West Ham U

Ince, P. (53) 1992/3 Manchester U,
  Internazionale, Liverpool,
  Middlesbrough

Jagielka, P. N. (3) 2007/08 Everton
James, D. B. (53) 1996/7 Liverpool, Aston
  Villa, West Ham U, Manchester C,
  Portsmouth
Jeffers, F. (1) 2002/03 Arsenal

Jenas, J. A. (21) 2002/03 Newcastle U, Tottenham H
Jezzard, B. (2) 1953/4 Fulham
Johnson, A. (8) 2004/05 Crystal P, Everton
Johnson, A. (1) 2009/10 Manchester C
Johnson, D. (8) 1974/5 Ipswich T, Liverpool
Johnson, G. M. C. (26) 2003/04 Chelsea, Portsmouth, Liverpool
Johnson, S. A. M. (1) 2000/01 Derby Co
Johnston, H. (10) 1946/7 Blackpool
Jones, M. (3) 1964/5 Sheffield U, Leeds U
Jones, R. (8) 1991/2 Liverpool
Jones, W. H. (2) 1949/50 Liverpool

Kay, A. (1) 1962/3 Everton
Keegan, K. (63) 1972/3 Liverpool, SV Hamburg, Southampton
Kennedy, A. (2) 1983/4 Liverpool
Kennedy, R. (17) 1975/6 Liverpool
Keown, M. R. (43) 1991/2 Everton, Arsenal
Kevan, D. (14) 1956/7 WBA
Kidd, B. (2) 1969/70 Manchester U
King, L. B. (21) 2001/02 Tottenham H
Kirkland, C. E. (1) 2006/07 Liverpool
Knight, Z. (2) 2004/05 Fulham
Knowles, C. (4) 1967/8 Tottenham H
Konchesky, P. M. (2) 2002/03 Charlton Ath, West Ham U

Labone, B. (26) 1962/3 Everton
Lampard, F. J. (82) 1999/00 West Ham U, Chelsea
Lampard, F. R. G. (2) 1972/3 West Ham U
Langley, J. (3) 1957/8 Fulham
Langton, R. (11) 1946/7 Blackburn R, Preston NE, Bolton W
Latchford, R. (12) 1977/8 Everton
Lawler, C. (4) 1970/1 Liverpool
Lawton, T. (15) 1946/7 Chelsea, Notts Co
Lee, F. (27) 1968/9 Manchester C
Lee, J. (1) 1950/1 Derby C
Lee, R. M. (21) 1994/5 Newcastle U
Lee, S. (14) 1982/3 Liverpool
Lennon, A. J. (19) 2005/06 Tottenham H
Lescott, J. P. (9) 2007/08 Everton, Manchester C
Le Saux, G. P. (36) 1993/4 Blackburn R, Chelsea
Le Tissier, M. P. (8) 1993/4 Southampton
Lindsay, A. (4) 1973/4 Liverpool

Lineker, G. (80) 1983/4 Leicester C, Everton, Barcelona, Tottenham H
Little, B. (1) 1974/5 Aston Villa
Lloyd, L. (4) 1970/1 Liverpool, Nottingham F
Lofthouse, N. (33) 1950/1 Bolton W
Lowe, E. (3) 1946/7 Aston Villa

Mabbutt, G. (16) 1982/3 Tottenham H
Macdonald, M. (14) 1971/2 Newcastle U
Madeley, P. (24) 1970/1 Leeds U
Mannion, W. (26) 1946/7 Middlesbrough
Mariner, P. (35) 1976/7 Ipswich T, Arsenal
Marsh, R. (9) 1971/2 QPR, Manchester C
Martin, A. (17) 1980/1 West Ham U
Martyn, A. N. (23) 1991/2 Crystal P, Leeds U
Marwood, B. (1) 1988/9 Arsenal
Matthews, R. (5) 1955/6 Coventry C
Matthews, S. (37) 1946/7 Stoke C, Blackpool
McCann, G. P. (1) 2000/01 Sunderland
McDermott, T. (25) 1977/8 Liverpool
McDonald, C. (8) 1957/8 Burnley
McFarland, R. (28) 1970/1 Derby C
McGarry, W. (4) 1953/4 Huddersfield T
McGuinness, W. (2) 1958/9 Manchester U
McMahon, S. (17) 1987/8 Liverpool
McManaman, S. (37) 1994/5 Liverpool, Real Madrid
McNab, R. (4) 1968/9 Arsenal
McNeil, M. (9) 1960/1 Middlesbrough
Meadows, J. (1) 1954/5 Manchester C
Medley, L. (6) 1950/1 Tottenham H
Melia, J. (2) 1962/3 Liverpool
Merrick, G. (23) 1951/2 Birmingham C
Merson, P. C. (21) 1991/2 Arsenal, Middlesbrough, Aston Villa
Metcalfe, V. (2) 1950/1 Huddersfield T
Milburn, J. (13) 1948/9 Newcastle U
Miller, B. (1) 1960/1 Burnley
Mills, D. J. (19) 2000/01 Leeds U
Mills, M. (42) 1972/3 Ipswich T
Milne, G. (14) 1962/3 Liverpool
Milner, J. P. (11) 2009/10 Aston Villa
Milton, C. A. (1) 1951/2 Arsenal
Moore, R. (108) 1961/2 West Ham U
Morley, A. (6) 1981/2 Aston Villa
Morris, J. (3) 1948/9 Derby Co
Mortensen, S. (25) 1946/7 Blackpool
Mozley, B. (3) 1949/50 Derby Co
Mullen, J. (12) 1946/7 Wolverhampton W
Mullery, A. (35) 1964/5 Tottenham H

Murphy, D. B. (9) 2001/02 Liverpool

Neal, P. (50) 1975/6 Liverpool
Neville, G. A. (85) 1994/5 Manchester U
Neville, P. J. (59) 1995/6 Manchester U, Everton
Newton, K. (27) 1965/6 Blackburn R, Everton
Nicholls, J. (2) 1953/4 WBA
Nicholson, W. (1) 1950/1 Tottenham H
Nish, D. (5) 1972/3 Derby Co
Norman, M. (23) 1961/2 Tottenham H
Nugent, D. J. (1) 2006/07 Preston NE

O'Grady, M. (2) 1962/3 Huddersfield T, Leeds U
Osgood, P. (4) 1969/70 Chelsea
Osman, R. (11) 1979/80 Ipswich T
Owen, M. J. (89) 1997/8 Liverpool, Real Madrid, Newcastle U
Owen, S. (3) 1953/4 Luton T

Paine, T. (19) 1962/3 Southampton
Pallister, G. (22) 1987/8 Middlesbrough, Manchester U
Palmer, C. L. (18) 1991/2 Sheffield W
Parker, P. A. (19) 1988/9 QPR, Manchester U
Parker, S. M. (3) 2003/04 Charlton Ath, Chelsea, Newcastle U
Parkes, P. (1) 1973/4 QPR
Parlour, R. (10) 1998/9 Arsenal
Parry, R. (2) 1959/60 Bolton W
Peacock, A. (6) 1961/2 Middlesbrough, Leeds U
Pearce, S. (78) 1986/7 Nottingham F, West Ham U
Pearson, Stan (8) 1947/8 Manchester U
Pearson, Stuart (15) 1975/6 Manchester U
Pegg, D. (1) 1956/7 Manchester U
Pejic, M. (4) 1973/4 Stoke C
Perry, W. (3) 1955/6 Blackpool
Perryman, S. (1) 1981/2 Tottenham H
Peters, M. (67) 1965/6 West Ham U, Tottenham H
Phelan, M. C. (1) 1989/90 Manchester U
Phillips, K. (8) 1998/9 Sunderland
Phillips, L. (3) 1951/2 Portsmouth
Pickering, F. (3) 1963/4 Everton
Pickering, N. (1) 1982/3 Sunderland
Pilkington, B. (1) 1954/5 Burnley
Platt, D. (62) 1989/90 Aston Villa, Bari, Juventus, Sampdoria, Arsenal
Pointer, R. (3) 1961/2 Burnley
Powell, C. G. (5) 2000/01 Charlton Ath

Pye, J. (1) 1949/50 Wolverhampton W

Quixall, A. (5) 1953/4 Sheffield W

Radford, J. (2) 1968/9 Arsenal
Ramsey, A. (32) 1948/9 Southampton, Tottenham H
Reaney, P. (3) 1968/9 Leeds U
Redknapp, J. F. (17) 1995/6 Liverpool
Reeves, K. (2) 1979/80 Norwich C, Manchester C
Regis, C. (5) 1981/2 WBA, Coventry C
Reid, P. (13) 1984/5 Everton
Revie, D. (6) 1954/5 Manchester C
Richards, J. (1) 1972/3 Wolverhampton W
Richards, M. (11) 2006/07 Manchester C
Richardson, K. (1) 1993/4 Aston Villa
Richardon, K. E. (8) 2004/05 Manchester U
Rickaby, S. (1) 1953/4 WBA
Ricketts, M. B. (1) 2001/02 Bolton W
Rimmer, J. (1) 1975/6 Arsenal
Ripley, S. E. (2) 1993/4 Blackburn R
Rix, G. (17) 1980/1 Arsenal
Robb, G. (1) 1953/4 Tottenham H
Roberts, G. (6) 1982/3 Tottenham H
Robinson, P. W. (41) 2002/03 Leeds U, Tottenham H
Robson, B. (90) 1979/80 WBA, Manchester U
Robson, R. (20) 1957/8 WBA
Rocastle, D. (14) 1988/9 Arsenal
Rooney, W. (64) 2002/03 Everton, Manchester U
Rowley, J. (6) 1948/9 Manchester U
Royle, J. (6) 1970/1 Everton, Manchester C
Ruddock, N. (1) 1994/5 Liverpool

Sadler, D. (4) 1967/8 Manchester U
Salako, J. A. (5) 1990/1 Crystal P
Sansom, K. (86) 1978/9 Crystal P, Arsenal
Scales, J. R. (3) 1994/5 Liverpool
Scholes, P. (66) 1996/7 Manchester U
Scott, L. (17) 1946/7 Arsenal
Seaman, D. A. (75) 1988/9 QPR, Arsenal
Sewell, J. (6) 1951/2 Sheffield W
Shackleton, L. (5) 1948/9 Sunderland
Sharpe, L. S. (8) 1990/1 Manchester U
Shaw, G. (5) 1958/9 Sheffield U
Shearer, A. (63) 1991/2 Southampton, Blackburn R, Newcastle U
Shellito, K. (1) 1962/3 Chelsea

Sheringham, E. (51) 1992/3 Tottenham H, Manchester U, Tottenham H
Sherwood, T. A. (3) 1998/9 Tottenham H
Shilton, P. (125) 1970/1 Leicester C, Stoke C, Nottingham F, Southampton, Derby Co
Shimwell, E. (1) 1948/9 Blackpool
Shorey, N, (2) 2006/07 Reading
Sillett, P. (3) 1954/5 Chelsea
Sinclair, T. (12) 2001/02 West Ham U, Manchester C
Sinton, A. (12) 1991/2 QPR, Sheffield W
Slater, W. (12) 1954/5 Wolverhampton W
Smith, A. (19) 2000/01 Leeds U, Manchester U, Newcastle U
Smith, A. M. (13) 1988/9 Arsenal
Smith, L. (6) 1950/1 Arsenal
Smith, R. (15) 1960/1 Tottenham H
Smith, Tom (1) 1970/1 Liverpool
Smith, Trevor (2) 1959/60 Birmingham C
Southgate, G. (57) 1995/6 Aston Villa, Middlesbrough
Spink, N. (1) 1982/3 Aston Villa
Springett, R. (33) 1959/60 Sheffield W
Staniforth, R. (8) 1953/4 Huddersfield T
Statham, D. (3) 1982/3 WBA
Stein, B. (1) 1983/4 Luton T
Stepney, A. (1) 1967/8 Manchester U
Sterland, M. (1) 1988/9 Sheffield W
Steven, T. M. (36) 1984/5 Everton, Rangers, Marseille
Stevens, G. A. (7) 1984/5 Tottenham H
Stevens, M. G. (46) 1984/5 Everton, Rangers
Stewart, P. A. (3) 1991/2 Tottenham H
Stiles, N. (28) 1964/5 Manchester U
Stone, S. B. (9) 1995/6 Nottingham F
Storey-Moore, I. (1) 1969/70 Nottingham F
Storey, P. (19) 1970/1 Arsenal
Streten, B. (1) 1949/50 Luton T
Summerbee, M. (8) 1967/8 Manchester C
Sunderland, A. (1) 1979/80 Arsenal
Sutton, C. R. (1) 1997/8 Blackburn R
Swan, P. (19) 1959/60 Sheffield W
Swift, F. (19) 1946/7 Manchester C

Talbot, B. (6) 1976/7 Ipswich T, Arsenal
Tambling, R. (3) 1962/3 Chelsea
Taylor, E. (1) 1953/4 Blackpool
Taylor, J. (2) 1950/1 Fulham
Taylor, P. H. (3) 1947/8 Liverpool
Taylor, P. J. (4) 1975/6 Crystal P
Taylor, T. (19) 1952/3 Manchester U
Temple, D. (1) 1964/5 Everton

Terry, J. G. (64) 2002/03 Chelsea
Thomas, Danny (2) 1982/3 Coventry C
Thomas, Dave (8) 1974/5 QPR
Thomas, G. R. (9) 1990/1 Crystal P
Thomas, M. L. (2) 1988/9 Arsenal
Thompson, A. (1) 2003/04 Celtic
Thompson, P. (16) 1963/4 Liverpool
Thompson, P. B. (42) 1975/6 Liverpool
Thompson, T. (2) 1951/2 Aston Villa, Preston NE
Thomson, R. (8) 1963/4 Wolverhampton W
Todd, C. (27) 1971/2 Derby Co
Towers, T. (3) 1975/6 Sunderland
Tueart, D. (6) 1974/5 Manchester C

Ufton, D. (1) 1953/4 Charlton Ath
Unsworth, D. G. (1) 1994/5 Everton
Upson, M. J. (21) 2002/03 Birmingham C, West Ham U

Vassell, D. (22) 2001/02 Aston Villa
Venables, T. (2) 1964/5 Chelsea
Venison, B. (2) 1994/5 Newcastle U
Viljoen, C. (2) 1974/5 Ipswich T
Viollet, D. (2) 1959/60 Manchester U

Waddle, C. R. (62) 1984/5 Newcastle U, Tottenham H, Marseille
Waiters, A. (5) 1963/4 Blackpool
Walcott, T. J. (11) 2005/06 Arsenal
Walker, D. S. (59) 1988/9 Nottingham F, Sampdoria, Sheffield W
Walker, I. M. (4) 1995/6 Tottenham H, Leicester C
Wallace, D. L. (1) 1985/6 Southampton
Walsh, P. (5) 1982/3 Luton T
Walters, K. M. (1) 1990/1 Rangers
Ward, P. (1) 1979/80 Brighton
Ward, T. (2) 1947/8 Derby C
Warnock, S. (1) 2007/08 Blackburn R
Watson, D. (12) 1983/4 Norwich C, Everton
Watson, D. V. (65) 1973/4 Sunderland, Manchester C, Werder Bremen, Southampton, Stoke C
Watson, W. (4) 1949/50 Sunderland
Webb, N. (26) 1987/8 Nottingham F, Manchester U
Weller, K. (4) 1973/4 Leicester C
West, G. (3) 1968/9 Everton
Wheeler, J. (1) 1954/5 Bolton W
White, D. (1) 1992/3 Manchester C
Whitworth, S. (7) 1974/5 Leicester C
Whymark, T. (1) 1977/8 Ipswich T

308

Wignall, F. (2) 1964/5 Nottingham F
Wilcox, J. M. (3) 1995/6 Blackburn R, Leeds U
Wilkins, R. (84) 1975/6 Chelsea, Manchester U, AC Milan
Williams, B. (24) 1948/9 Wolverhampton W
Williams, S. (6) 1982/3 Southampton
Willis, A. (1) 1951/2 Tottenham H
Wilshaw, D. (12) 1953/4 Wolverhampton W
Wilson, R. (63) 1959/60 Huddersfield T, Everton
Winterburn, N. (2) 1989/90 Arsenal
Wise, D. F. (21) 1990/1 Chelsea
Withe, P. (11) 1980/1 Aston Villa
Wood, R. (3) 1954/5 Manchester U
Woodcock, A. (42) 1977/8 Nottingham F, FC Cologne, Arsenal
Woodgate, J. S. (8) 1998/9 Leeds U, Newcastle U, Real Madrid, Tottenham H

Woods, C. C. E. (43) 1984/5 Norwich C, Rangers, Sheffield W
Worthington, F. (8) 1973/4 Leicester C
Wright, I. E. (33) 1990/1 Crystal P, Arsenal, West Ham U
Wright, M. (45) 1983/4 Southampton, Derby C, Liverpool
Wright, R. I. (2) 1999/00 Ipswich T, Arsenal
Wright, T. (11) 1967/8 Everton
Wright, W. (105) 1946/7 Wolverhampton W
Wright-Phillips, S. C. (34) 2004/05 Manchester C, Chelsea, Manchester C

Young, A. S. (7) 2007/08 Aston Villa
Young, G. (1) 1964/5 Sheffield W
Young, L. P. (7) 2004/05 Charlton Ath

NORTHERN IRELAND

Aherne, T. (4) 1946/7 Belfast Celtic, Luton T
Anderson, T. (22) 1972/3 Manchester U, Swindon T, Peterborough U
Armstrong, G. (63) 1976/7 Tottenham H, Watford, Real Mallorca, WBA, Chesterfield

Baird, C. P. (44) 2002/03 Southampton, Fulham
Barr, H. (3) 1961/2 Linfield, Coventry C
Best, G. (37) 1963/4 Manchester U, Fulham
Bingham, W. (56) 1950/1 Sunderland, Luton T, Everton, Port Vale
Black, K. (30) 1987/8 Luton T, Nottingham F
Blair, R. (5) 1974/5 Oldham Ath
Blanchflower, D. (54) 1949/50 Barnsley, Aston Villa, Tottenham H
Blanchflower, J. (12) 1953/4 Manchester U
Blayney, A. (3) 2005/06 Doncaster R, Linfield
Bowler, G. (3) 1949/50 Hull C
Braithwaite, R. (10) 1961/2 Linfield, Middlesbrough
Braniff, K. R. (2) 2009/10 Portadown

Brennan, R. (5) 1948/9 Luton T, Birmingham C, Fulham
Briggs, R. (2) 1961/2 Manchester U, Swansea
Brotherston, N. (27) 1979/80 Blackburn R
Bruce, W. (2) 1960/1 Glentoran
Brunt, C. (26) 2004/05 Sheffield W, WBA
Bryan, M. A. (2) 2009/10 Watford

Campbell, A. (2) 1962/3 Crusaders
Campbell, D. A. (10) 1985/6 Nottingham F, Charlton Ath
Campbell, J. (2) 1950/1 Fulham
Campbell, R. M. (2) 1981/2 Bradford C
Campbell, W. (6) 1967/8 Dundee
Capaldi, A. C. (22) 2003/04 Plymouth Arg, Cardiff C
Carey, J. (7) 1946/7 Manchester U
Carroll, R. E. (19) 1996/7 Wigan Ath, Manchester U, West Ham U
Carson, S. (1) 2008/09 Coleraine
Casement, C. (1) 2008/09 Ipswich T
Casey, T. (12) 1954/5 Newcastle U, Portsmouth
Caskey, A. (8) 1978/9 Derby C, Tulsa Roughnecks
Cassidy, T. (24) 1970/1 Newcastle U, Burnley

Caughey, M. (2) 1985/6 Linfield
Clarke, C. J. (38) 1985/6 Bournemouth, Southampton, Portsmouth
Cleary, J. (5) 1981/2 Glentoran
Clements, D. (48) 1964/5 Coventry C, Sheffield W, Everton, New York Cosmos
Clingan, S. G. (24) 2005/06 Nottingham F, Norwich C, Coventry C
Clyde, M.G. (3) 2004/05 Wolverhampon W
Coates, C. (3) 2008/09 Crusaders
Cochrane, D. (10) 1946/7 Leeds U
Cochrane, T. (26) 1975/6 Coleraine, Burnley, Middlesbrough, Gillingham
Connell, T. E. (1) 1977/8 Coleraine
Coote, A. (6) 1998/9 Norwich C
Cowan, J. (1) 1969/70 Newcastle U
Coyle, F. (4) 1955/6 Coleraine, Nottingham F
Coyle, L. (1) 1988/9 Derry C
Coyle, R. (5) 1972/3 Sheffield W
Craig, D. (25) 1966/7 Newcastle U
Craigan, S. (48) 2002/03 Partick T, Motherwell
Crossan, E. (3) 1949/50 Blackburn R
Crossan, J. (24) 1959/60 Sparta Rotterdam, Sunderland, Manchester C, Middlesbrough
Cunningham, W. (30) 1950/1 St Mirren, Leicester C, Dunfermline Ath
Cush, W. (26) 1950/1 Glentoran, Leeds U, Portadown

D'Arcy, S. (5) 1951/2 Chelsea, Brentford
Davis, S. (40) 2004/05 Aston Villa, Fulham, Rangers
Davison, A. J. (3) 1995/6 Bolton W, Bradford C, Grimsby T
Dennison, R. (18) 1987/8 Wolverhampton W
Devine, J. (1) 1989/90 Glentoran
Dickson, D. (4) 1969/70 Coleraine
Dickson, T. (1) 1956/7 Linfield
Dickson, W. (12) 1950/1 Chelsea, Arsenal
Doherty, L. (2) 1984/5 Linfield
Doherty, P. (6) 1946/7 Derby Co, Huddersfield T, Doncaster R
Doherty, T. E. (9) 2002/03 Bristol C
Donaghy, M. (91) 1979/80 Luton T, Manchester U, Chelsea
Donnelly, M. (1) 2008/09 Crusaders
Dougan, D. (43) 1957/8 Portsmouth, Blackburn R, Aston Villa, Leicester C, Wolverhampton W

Douglas, J. P. (1) 1946/7 Belfast Celtic
Dowd, H. (3) 1973/4 Glenavon, Sheffield W
Dowie, I. (59) 1989/90 Luton T, West Ham U, Southampton, Crystal P, West Ham U, QPR
Duff, M. J. (22) 2001/02 Cheltenham T, Burnley
Dunlop, G. (4) 1984/5 Linfield

Eglinton, T. (6) 1946/7 Everton
Elder, A. (40) 1959/60 Burnley, Stoke C
Elliott, S. (39) 2000/01 Motherwell, Hull C
Evans, C. J. (4) 2008/09 Manchester U
Evans, J. G. (20) 2006/07 Manchester U

Farrell, P. (7) 1946/7 Everton
Feeney, J. (2) 1946/7 Linfield, Swansea T
Feeney, W. (1) 1975/6 Glentoran
Feeney, W. J. (34) 2001/02 Bournemouth, Luton T, Cardiff C
Ferguson, G. (5) 1998/9 Linfield
Ferguson, S. (1) 2008/09 Newcastle U
Ferguson, W. (2) 1965/6 Linfield
Ferris, R. (3) 1949/50 Birmingham C
Fettis, A. (25) 1991/2 Hull C, Nottingham F, Blackburn R
Finney, T. (14) 1974/5 Sunderland, Cambridge U
Fleming, J. G. (31) 1986/7 Nottingham F, Manchester C, Barnsley
Forde, T. (4) 1958/9 Ards

Gallogly, C. (2) 1950/1 Huddersfield T
Garrett, R. (3) 2008/09 Linfield
Garton, R. (1) 1968/9 Oxford U
Gault, M. (1) 2007/08 Linfield
Gillespie, K. R. (86) 1994/5 Manchester U, Newcastle U, Blackburn R, Leicester C, Sheffield U
Gorman, R. J. (2) 2009/10 Wolverhampton W
Gorman, W. (4) 1946/7 Brentford
Graham, W. (14) 1950/1 Doncaster R
Gray, P. (26) 1992/3 Luton T, Sunderland, Nancy, Luton T, Burnley, Oxford U
Gregg, H. (25) 1953/4 Doncaster R, Manchester U
Griffin, D. J. (29) 1995/6 St Johnstone, Dundee U, Stockport Co

Hamill, R. (1) 1998/9 Glentoran
Hamilton, B. (50) 1968/9 Linfield, Ipswich T, Everton, Millwall, Swindon T

Hamilton, G. (5) 2002/03 Portadown

Hamilton, W. (41) 1977/8 QPR, Burnley, Oxford U

Harkin, T. (5) 1967/8 Southport, Shrewsbury T

Harvey, M. (34) 1960/1 Sunderland

Hatton, S. (2) 1962/3 Linfield

Healy, D. J. (80) 1999/00 Manchester U, Preston NE, Leeds U, Fulham, Sunderland

Healy, P. J. (4) 1981/2 Coleraine, Glentoran

Hegan, D. (7) 1969/70 WBA, Wolverhampton W

Hill, C. F. (27) 1989/90 Sheffield U, Leicester C, Trelleborg, Northampton T

Hill, J. (7) 1958/9 Norwich C, Everton

Hinton, E. (7) 1946/7 Fulham, Millwall

Holmes, S. P. (1) 2001/02 Wrexham

Horlock, K. (32) 1994/5 Swindon T, Manchester C

Hughes, A. W. (71) 1997/8 Newcastle U, Aston Villa, Fulham

Hughes, J. (2) 2005/06 Lincoln C

Hughes, M. A. (2) 2005/06 Oldham Ath

Hughes, M. E. (71) 1991/2 Manchester C, Strasbourg, West Ham U, Wimbledon, Crystal P

Hughes, P. (3) 1986/7 Bury

Hughes, W. (1) 1950/1 Bolton W

Humphries, W. (14) 1961/2 Ards, Coventry C, Swansea T

Hunter, A. (53) 1969/70 Blackburn R, Ipswich T

Hunter, B. V. (15) 1994/5 Wrexham, Reading

Hunter, V. (2) 1961/2 Coleraine

Ingham, M. G. (3) 2004/05 Sunderland, Wrexham

Irvine, R. (8) 1961/2 Linfield, Stoke C

Irvine, W. (23) 1962/3 Burnley, Preston NE, Brighton & HA

Jackson, T. (35) 1968/9 Everton, Nottingham F, Manchester U

Jamison, A. (1) 1975/6 Glentoran

Jenkins, I. (6) 1996/7 Chester C, Dundee U

Jennings, P. (119) 1963/4 Watford, Tottenham H, Arsenal, Tottenham H

Johnson, D. M. (56) 1998/9 Blackburn R, Birmingham C

Johnston, W. (2) 1961/2 Glenavon, Oldham Ath

Jones, J. (3) 1955/6 Glenavon

Jones, S. G. (29) 2002/03 Crewe Alex, Burnley

Keane, T. (1) 1948/9 Swansea T

Kee, P. V. (9) 1989/90 Oxford U, Ards

Keith, R. (23) 1957/8 Newcastle U

Kelly, H. (4) 1949/50 Fulham, Southampton

Kelly, P. (1) 1949/50 Barnsley

Kennedy, P. H. (20) 1998/9 Watford, Wigan Ath

Kirk, A. R. (11) 1999/00 Heart of Midlothian, Boston U, Northampton T, Dunfermline Ath

Lafferty, K. (24) 2005/06 Burnley, Rangers

Lawrie, J. (3) 2008/09 Port Vale

Lawther, I. (4) 1959/60 Sunderland, Blackburn R

Lennon, N. F. (40) 1993/4 Crewe Alex, Leicester C, Celtic

Little, A. (5) 2008/09 Rangers

Lockhart, N. (8) 1946/7 Linfield, Coventry C, Aston Villa

Lomas, S. M. (45) 1993/4 Manchester C, West Ham U

Lutton, B. (6) 1969/70 Wolverhampton W, West Ham U

Magennis, J. B. D. (2) 2009/10 Cardiff C

Magill, E. (26) 1961/2 Arsenal, Brighton & HA

Magilton, J. (52) 1990/1 Oxford U, Southampton, Sheffield W, Ipswich T

Mannus, A. (4) 2003/04 Linfield

Martin, C. (6) 1946/7 Glentoran, Leeds U, Aston Villa

McAdams, W. (15) 1953/4 Manchester C, Bolton W, Leeds U

McAlinden, J. (2) 1946/7 Portsmouth, Southend U

McArdle, R. A. (2) 2009/10 Rochdale

McAuley, G. (21) 2004/05 Lincoln C, Leicester C, Ipswich T

McBride, S. (4) 1990/1 Glenavon

McCabe, J. (6) 1948/9 Leeds U

McCann, G. S. (28) 2001/02 West Ham U, Cheltenham T, Barnsley, Scunthorpe U

McCarthy, J. D. (18) 1995/6 Port Vale, Birmingham C

McCartney, G. (34) 2001/02 Sunderland, West Ham U, Sunderland

McCavana, T. (3) 1954/5 Coleraine

McCleary, J. W. (1) 1954/5 Cliftonville
McClelland, J. (6) 1960/1 Arsenal,
 Fulham
McClelland, J. (53) 1979/80 Mansfield T,
 Rangers, Watford, Leeds U
McCourt, F. (6) 1951/2 Manchester C
McCourt, P. J. (3) 2001/02 Rochdale,
 Celtic
McCoy, R. (1) 1986/7 Coleraine
McCreery, D. (67) 1975/6 Manchester U,
 QPR, Tulsa Roughnecks, Newcastle U,
 Heart of Midlothian
McCrory, S. (1) 1957/8 Southend U
McCullough, W. (10) 1960/1 Arsenal,
 Millwall
McCurdy, C. (1) 1979/80 Linfield
McDonald, A. (52) 1985/6 QPR
McElhinney, G. (6) 1983/4 Bolton W
McEvilly, L. R. (1) 2001/02 Rochdale
McFaul, I. (6) 1966/7 Linfield,
 Newcastle U
McGarry, J. K. (3) 1950/1 Cliftonville
McGaughey, M. (1) 1984/5 Linfield
McGibbon, P. C. G. (7) 1994/5
 Manchester U, Wigan Ath
McGinn, N. (7) 2009/10 Celtic
McGivern, R. (11) 2008/09 Manchester C
McGovern, M. (1) 2009/10 Ross Co
McGrath, R. (21) 1973/4 Tottenham H,
 Manchester U
McIlroy, J. (55) 1951/2 Burnley, Stoke C
McIlroy, S. B. (88) 1971/2 Manchester U,
 Stoke C, Manchester C
McKeag, W. (2) 1967/8 Glentoran
McKenna, J. (7) 1949/50 Huddersfield T
McKenzie, R. (1) 1966/7 Airdrieonians
McKinney, W. (1) 1965/6 Falkirk
McKnight, A. (10) 1987/8 Celtic,
 West Ham U
McLaughlin, J. (12) 1961/2 Shrewsbury T,
 Swansea T
McLean, B. S. (1) 2005/06 Rangers
McMahon, G. J. (17) 1994/5
 Tottenham H, Stoke C
McMichael, A. (39) 1949/50 Newcastle U
McMillan, S. (2) 1962/3 Manchester U
McMordie, E. (21) 1968/9 Middlesbrough
McMorran, E. (15) 1946/7 Belfast Celtic,
 Barnsley, Doncaster R
McNally, B. A. (5) 1985/6 Shrewsbury T
McParland, P. (34) 1953/4 Aston Villa,
 Wolverhampton W
McVeigh, P. (20) 1998/9 Tottenham H,
 Norwich C
Montgomery, F. J. (1) 1954/5 Coleraine

Moore, C. (1) 1948/9 Glentoran
Moreland, V. (6) 1978/9 Derby Co
Morgan, S. (18) 1971/2 Port Vale,
 Aston Villa, Brighton & HA,
 Sparta Rotterdam
Morrow, S. J. (39) 1989/90 Arsenal, QPR
Mulgrew, J. (2) 2009/10 Linfield
Mullan, G. (4) 1982/3 Glentoran
Mulryne, P. P. (27) 1996/7 Manchester U,
 Norwich C, Cardiff C
Murdock, C. J. (34) 1999/00 Preston NE,
 Hibernian, Crewe Alex, Rotherham U

Napier, R. (1) 1965/6 Bolton W
Neill, T. (59) 1960/1 Arsenal, Hull C
Nelson, S. (51) 1969/70 Arsenal,
 Brighton & HA
Nicholl, C. (51) 1974/5 Aston Villa,
 Southampton, Grimsby T
Nicholl, J. M. (73) 1975/6 Manchester U,
 Toronto Blizzard, Sunderland, Rangers,
 WBA
Nicholson, J. (41) 1960/1 Manchester U,
 Huddersfield T
Nolan, I. R. (18) 1996/7 Sheffield W,
 Bradford C, Wigan Ath

O'Boyle, G. (13) 1993/4
 Dunfermline Ath, St Johnstone
O'Connor, M. J. (9) 2007/08 Crewe Alex,
 Scunthorpe U
O'Doherty, A. (2) 1969/70 Coleraine
O'Driscoll, J. (3) 1948/9 Swansea T
O'Kane, L. (20) 1969/70 Nottingham F
O'Neill, C. (3) 1988/9 Motherwell
O'Neill, H. M. (64) 1971/2 Distillery,
 Nottingham F, Norwich C,
 Manchester C, Norwich C, Notts Co
O'Neill, J. (1) 1961/2 Sunderland
O'Neill, J. P. (39) 1979/80 Leicester C
O'Neill, M. A. (31) 1987/8 Newcastle U,
 Dundee U, Hibernian, Coventry C

Parke, J. (13) 1963/4 Linfield, Hibernian,
 Sunderland
Paterson, M. A. (11) 2007/08
 Scunthorpe U, Burnley
Patterson, D. J. (17) 1993/4 Crystal P,
 Luton T, Dundee U
Patterson, R. (3) 2009/10 Coleraine
Peacock, R. (31) 1951/2 Celtic, Coleraine
Penney, S. (17) 1984/5 Brighton & HA
Platt, J. A. (23) 1975/6 Middlesbrough,
 Ballymena U, Coleraine

Quinn, J. M. (46) 1984/5 Blackburn R, Swindon T, Leicester, Bradford C, West Ham U, Bournemouth, Reading
Quinn, S. J. (50) 1995/6 Blackpool, WBA, Willem II, Sheffield W, Peterborough U, Northampton T

Rafferty, P. (1) 1979/80 Linfield
Ramsey, P. (14) 1983/4 Leicester C
Rice, P. (49) 1968/9 Arsenal
Robinson, S. (7) 1996/7 Bournemouth, Luton T
Rogan, A. (18) 1987/8 Celtic, Sunderland, Millwall
Ross, E. (1) 1968/9 Newcastle U
Rowland, K. (19) 1994/5 West Ham U, QPR
Russell, A. (1) 1946/7 Linfield
Ryan, R. (1) 1949/50 WBA

Sanchez, L. P. (3) 1986/7 Wimbledon
Scott, J. (2) 1957/8 Grimsby T
Scott, P. (10) 1974/5 Everton, York C, Aldershot
Sharkey, P. (1) 1975/6 Ipswich T
Shields, J. (1) 1956/7 Southampton
Shiels, D. (9) 2005/06 Hibernian, Doncaster R
Simpson, W. (12) 1950/1 Rangers
Sloan, D. (2) 1968/9 Oxford
Sloan, T. (3) 1978/9 Manchester U
Sloan, W. (1) 1946/7 Arsenal
Smith, A. W. (18) 2002/03 Glentoran, Preston NE
Smyth, S. (9) 1947/8 Wolverhampton W, Stoke C
Smyth, W. (4) 1948/9 Distillery
Sonner, D. J. (13) 1997/8 Ipswich T, Sheffield W, Birmingham C, Nottingham F, Peterborough U
Spence, D. (29) 1974/5 Bury, Blackpool, Southend U
Sproule, I. (11) 2005/06 Hibernian, Bristol C
Stevenson, A. (3) 1946/7 Everton
Stewart, A. (7) 1966/7 Glentoran, Derby
Stewart, D. (1) 1977/8 Hull C

Stewart, I. (31) 1981/2 QPR, Newcastle U
Stewart, T. (1) 1960/1 Linfield

Taggart, G. P. (51) 1989/90 Barnsley, Bolton W, Leicester C
Taylor, M. S. (83) 1998/9 Fulham, Birmingham C
Thompson, P. (8) 2005/06 Linfield, Stockport Co
Todd, S. (11) 1965/6 Burnley, Sheffield W
Toner, C. (2) 2002/03 Leyton Orient
Trainor, D. (1) 1966/7 Crusaders
Tuffey, J. (5) 2008/09 Partick T
Tully, C. (10) 1948/9 Celtic

Uprichard, N. (18) 1951/2 Swindon T, Portsmouth

Vernon, J. (17) 1946/7 Belfast Celtic, WBA

Walker, J. (1) 1954/5 Doncaster R
Walsh, D. (9) 1946/7 WBA
Walsh, W. (5) 1947/8 Manchester C
Watson, P. (1) 1970/1 Distillery
Webb, S. M. (4) 2005/06 Ross Co
Welsh, S. (4) 1965/6 Carlisle U
Whiteside, N. (38) 1981/2 Manchester U, Everton
Whitley, Jeff (20) 1996/7 Manchester C, Sunderland, Cardiff C
Whitley, Jim (3) 1997/8 Manchester C
Williams, M. S. (36) 1998/9 Chesterfield, Watford, Wimbledon, Stoke C, Wimbledon, Milton Keynes D
Williams, P. (1) 1990/1 WBA
Wilson, D. J. (24) 1986/7 Brighton & HA, Luton, Sheffield W
Wilson, K. J. (42) 1986/7 Ipswich T, Chelsea, Notts C, Walsall
Wilson, S. (12) 1961/2 Glenavon, Falkirk, Dundee
Wood, T. J. (1) 1995/6 Walsall
Worthington, N. (66) 1983/4 Sheffield W, Leeds U, Stoke C
Wright, T. J. (31) 1988/9 Newcastle U, Nottingham F, Manchester C

SCOTLAND

Adam, C. G. (4) 2006/07 Rangers,
Blackpool
Aird, J. (4) 1953/4 Burnley
Aitken, G. G. (8) 1948/9 East Fife,
Sunderland
Aitken, R. (57) 1979/80 Celtic,
Newcastle U, St Mirren
Albiston, A. (14) 1981/2 Manchester U
Alexander, G. (40) 2001/02 Preston NE,
Burnley
Alexander, N. (3) 2005/06 Cardiff C
Allan, T. (2) 1973/4 Dundee
Anderson, J. (1) 1953/4 Leicester C
Anderson, R. (11) 2002/03 Aberdeen,
Sunderland
Archibald, S. (27) 1979/80 Aberdeen,
Tottenham H, Barcelona
Auld, B. (3) 1958/9 Celtic

Baird, H. (1) 1955/6 Airdrieonians
Baird, S. (7) 1956/7 Rangers
Bannon, E. (11) 1979/80 Dundee U
Barr, D. (1) 2008/09 Falkirk
Bauld, W. (3) 1949/50
Heart of Midlothian
Baxter, J. (34) 1960/1 Rangers,
Sunderland
Beattie, C. (7) 2005/06 Celtic, WBA
Bell, W. (2) 1965/6 Leeds U
Bernard, P. R. (2) 1994/5 Oldham Ath
Berra, C. (7) 2007/08 Heart of
Midlothian, Wolverhampton W
Bett, J. (25) 1981/2 Rangers, Lokeren,
Aberdeen
Black, E. (2) 1987/8 Metz
Black, I. (1) 1947/8 Southampton
Blacklaw, A. (3) 1962/3 Burnley
Blackley, J. (7) 1973/4 Hibernian
Blair, J. (1) 1946/7 Blackpool
Blyth, J. (2) 1977/8 Coventry C
Bone, J. (2) 1971/2 Norwich C
Booth, S. (21) 1992/3 Aberdeen,
Borussia Dortmund, Twente
Bowman, D. (6) 1991/2 Dundee U
Boyd, K. (16) 2005/06 Rangers
Boyd, T. (72) 1990/1 Motherwell,
Chelsea, Celtic
Brand, R. (8) 1960/1 Rangers
Brazil, A. (13) 1979/80 Ipswich T,
Tottenham H
Bremner, D. (1) 1975/6 Hibernian
Bremner, W. (54) 1964/5 Leeds U
Brennan, F. (7) 1946/7 Newcastle U

Broadfood, K. (3) 2008/09 Rangers
Brogan, J. (4) 1970/1 Celtic
Brown, A. (14) 1949/50 East Fife,
Blackpool
Brown, H. (3) 1946/7 Partick Th
Brown, J. (1) 1974/5 Sheffield U
Brown, R. (3) 1946/7 Rangers
Brown, S. (20) 2005/06 Hibernian, Celtic
Brown, W. (28) 1957/8 Dundee,
Tottenham H
Brownlie, J. (7) 1970/1 Hibernian
Buchan, M. (34) 1971/2 Aberdeen,
Manchester U
Buckley, P. (3) 1953/4 Aberdeen
Burchill, M. J. (6) 1999/00 Celtic
Burke, C. (2) 2005/06 Rangers
Burley, C. W. (46) 1994/5 Chelsea, Celtic,
Derby Co
Burley, G. (11) 1978/9 Ipswich T
Burns, F. (1) 1969/70 Manchester U
Burns, K. (20) 1973/4 Birmingham C,
Nottingham F
Burns, T. (8) 1980/1 Celtic

Calderwood, C. (36) 1994/5
Tottenham H, Aston Villa
Caldow, E. (40) 1956/7 Rangers
Caldwell, G. (37) 2001/02 Newcastle U,
Hibernian, Celtic, Wigan Ath
Caldwell, S. (10) 2000/01 Newcastle U,
Sunderland, Burnley
Callaghan, W. (2) 1969/70 Dunfermline
Cameron, C. (28) 1998/9 Heart of
Midlothian, Wolverhampton W
Campbell, R. (5) 1946/7 Falkirk, Chelsea
Campbell, W. (5) 1946/7 Morton
Canero, P. (1) 2003/04 Leicester C
Carr, W. (6) 1969/70 Coventry C
Chalmers, S. (5) 1964/5 Celtic
Clark, J. (4) 1965/6 Celtic
Clark, R. (17) 1967/8 Aberdeen
Clarke, S. (6) 1987/8 Chelsea
Clarkson, D. (2) 2007/08 Motherwell
Collins, J. (58) 1987/8 Hibernian, Celtic,
Monaco, Everton
Collins, R. (31) 1950/1 Celtic, Everton,
Leeds U
Colquhoun, E. (9) 1971/2 Sheffield U
Colquhoun, J. (2) 1987/8 Heart of
Midlothian
Combe, R. (3) 1947/8 Hibernian
Commons, K. (6) 2008/09 Derby Co
Conn, A. (1) 1955/6 Heart of Midlothian

Conn, A. (2) 1974/5 Tottenham H
Connachan, E. (2) 1961/2
  Dunfermline Ath
Connelly, G. (2) 1973/4 Celtic
Connolly, J. (1) 1972/3 Everton
Connor, R. (4) 1985/6 Dundee, Aberdeen
Conway, C. (1) 2009/10 Dundee U
Cooke, C. (16) 1965/6 Dundee, Chelsea
Cooper, D. (22) 1979/80 Rangers,
  Motherwell
Cormack, P. (9) 1965/6 Hibernian,
  Nottingham F
Cowan, J. (25) 1947/8 Morton
Cowie, D. (20) 1952/3 Dundee
Cowie, D. (2) 2009/10 Watford
Cox, C. (1) 1947/8 Heart of Midlothian
Cox, S. (24) 1947/8 Rangers
Craig, J. (1) 1976/7 Celtic
Craig, J. P. (1) 1967/8 Celtic
Craig, T. (1) 1975/6 Newcastle U
Crainey, S. (6) 2001/02 Celtic,
  Southampton
Crawford, S. (25) 1994/5 Raith R,
  Dunfermline Ath, Plymouth Arg
Crerand, P. (16) 1960/1 Celtic,
  Manchester U
Cropley, A. (2) 1971/2 Hibernian
Cruickshank, J. (6) 1963/4 Heart of
  Midlothian
Cullen, M. (1) 1955/6 Luton T
Cumming, J. (9) 1954/5 Heart of
  Midlothian
Cummings. W. (1) 2001/02 Chelsea
Cunningham, W. (8) 1953/4 Preston NE
Curran, H. (5) 1969/70
  Wolverhampton W

Dailly, C. (67) 1996/7 Derby Co,
  Blackburn R, West Ham U, Rangers
Dalglish, K. (102) 1971/2 Celtic,
  Liverpool
Davidson, C. I. (19) 1998/9 Blackburn R,
  Leicester C, Preston NE
Davidson, J. (8) 1953/4 Partick Th
Dawson, A. (5) 1979/80 Rangers
Deans, D. (2) 1974/5 Celtic
Delaney, J. (4) 1946/7 Manchester U
Devlin, P. J. (10) 2002/03 Birmingham C
Dick, J. (1) 1958/9 West Ham U
Dickov, P. (10) 2000/01 Manchester C,
  Leicester C, Blackburn R
Dickson, W. (5) 1969/70 Kilmarnock
Dobie, R. S. (6) 2001/02 WBA
Docherty, T. (25) 1951/2 Preston NE,
  Arsenal

Dodds, D. (2) 1983/4 Dundee U
Dodds, W. (26) 1996/7 Aberdeen,
  Dundee U, Rangers
Donachie, W. (35) 1971/2 Manchester C
Donnelly, S. (10) 1996/7 Celtic
Dorrans, G. (3) 2009/10 WBA
Dougall, C. (1) 1946/7 Birmingham C
Dougan, R. (1) 1949/50 Heart of
  Midlothian
Douglas, R. (19) 2001/02 Celtic,
  Leicester C
Doyle, J. (1) 1975/6 Ayr U
Duncan, A. (6) 1974/5 Hibernian
Duncan, D. (3) 1947/8 East Fife
Duncanson, J. (1) 1946/7 Rangers
Durie, G. S. (43) 1987/8 Chelsea,
  Tottenham H, Rangers
Durrant, I. (20) 1987/8 Rangers,
  Kilmarnock

Elliott, M. S. (18) 1997/8 Leicester C
Evans, A. (4) 1981/2 Aston Villa
Evans, R. (48) 1948/9 Celtic, Chelsea
Ewing, T. (2) 1957/8 Partick Th

Farm, G. (10) 1952/3 Blackpool
Ferguson, B. (45) 1998/9 Rangers,
  Blackburn R, Rangers
Ferguson, Derek (2) 1987/8 Rangers
Ferguson, Duncan (7) 1991/2 Dundee U,
  Everton
Ferguson, I. (9) 1988/9 Rangers
Ferguson, R. (7) 1965/6 Kilmarnock
Fernie, W. (12) 1953/4 Celtic
Flavell, R. (2) 1946/7 Airdrieonians
Fleck, R. (4) 1989/90 Norwich C
Fleming, C. (1) 1953/4 East Fife
Fletcher, D. B. (47) 2003/04
  Manchester U
Fletcher, S. (7) 2007/08 Hibernian,
  Burnley
Forbes, A. (14) 1946/7 Sheffield U,
  Arsenal
Ford, D. (3) 1973/4 Heart of Midlothian
Forrest, J. (1) 1957/8 Motherwell
Forrest, J. (5) 1965/6 Rangers, Aberdeen
Forsyth, A. (10) 1971/2 Partick Th,
  Manchester U
Forsyth, C. (4) 1963/4 Kilmarnock
Forsyth, T. (22) 1970/1 Motherwell,
  Rangers
Fox, D. (1) 2009/10 Burnley
Fraser, D. (2) 1967/8 WBA
Fraser, W. (2) 1954/5 Sunderland
Freedman, D. A. (2) 2001/02 Crystal P

Gabriel, J. (2) 1960/1 Everton
Gallacher, K. W. (53) 1987/8 Dundee U, Coventry C, Blackburn R, Newcastle U
Gallacher, P. (8) 2001/02 Dundee U
Gallagher, P. (1) 2003/04 Blackburn R
Galloway, M. (1) 1991/2 Celtic
Gardiner, W. (1) 1957/8 Motherwell
Gemmell, J. (2) 1954/5 St Mirren
Gemmell, T. (18) 1965/6 Celtic
Gemmill, A. (43) 1970/1 Derby Co, Nottingham F, Birmingham C
Gemmill, S. (26) 1994/5 Nottingham F, Everton
Gibson, D. (7) 1962/3 Leicester C
Gillespie, G. T. (13) 1987/8 Liverpool
Gilzean, A. (22) 1963/4 Dundee, Tottenham H
Glass, S. (1) 1998/9 Newcastle U
Glavin, R. (1) 1976/7 Celtic
Glen, A. (2) 1955/6 Aberdeen
Goram, A. L. (43) 1985/6 Oldham Ath, Hibernian, Rangers
Gordon, C. S. (39) 2003/04 Heart of Midlothian, Sunderland
Gough, C. R. (61) 1982/3 Dundee U, Tottenham H, Rangers
Gould, J. (2) 1999/00 Celtic
Govan, J. (6) 1947/8 Hibernian
Graham, A. (11) 1977/8 Leeds U
Graham, G. (12) 1971/2 Arsenal, Manchester U
Grant, J. (2) 1958/9 Hibernian
Grant, P. (2) 1988/9 Celtic
Gray, A. (20) 1975/6 Aston Villa, Wolverhampton W, Everton
Gray, A. D. (2) 2002/03 Bradford C
Gray, E. (12) 1968/9 Leeds U
Gray F. (32) 1975/6 Leeds U, Nottingham F, Leeds U
Green, A. (6) 1970/1 Blackpool, Newcastle U
Greig, J. (44) 1963/4 Rangers
Gunn, B. (6) 1989/90 Norwich C

Haddock, H. (6) 1954/5 Clyde
Haffey, F. (2) 1959/60 Celtic
Hamilton, A. (24) 1961/2 Dundee
Hamilton, G. (5) 1946/7 Aberdeen
Hamilton, W. (1) 1964/5 Hibernian
Hammell, S. (1) 2004/05 Motherwell
Hansen, A. (26) 1978/9 Liverpool
Hansen, J. (2) 1971/2 Partick Th
Harper, J. (4) 1972/3 Aberdeen, Hibernian, Aberdeen

Hartford, A. (50) 1971/2 WBA, Manchester C, Everton, Manchester C
Hartley, P. J. (25) 2004/05 Heart of Midlothian, Celtic, Bristol C
Harvey, D. (16) 1972/3 Leeds U
Haughney, M. (1) 1953/4 Celtic
Hay, D. (27) 1969/70 Celtic
Hegarty, P. (8) 1978/9 Dundee U
Henderson, J. (7) 1952/3 Portsmouth, Arsenal
Henderson, W. (29) 1962/3 Rangers
Hendry, E. C. J. (51) 1992/3 Blackburn R, Rangers, Coventry C, Bolton W
Herd, D. (5) 1958/9 Arsenal
Herd, G. (5) 1957/8 Clyde
Herriot, J. (8) 1968/9 Birmingham C
Hewie, J. (19) 1955/6 Charlton Ath
Holt, D. D. (5) 1962/3 Heart of Midlothian
Holt, G. J. (10) 2000/01 Kilmarnock, Norwich C
Holton, J. (15) 1972/3 Manchester U
Hope, R. (2) 1967/8 WBA
Hopkin, D. (7) 1996/7 Crystal P, Leeds U
Houliston, W. (3) 1948/9 Queen of the South
Houston, S. (1) 1975/6 Manchester U
Howie, H. (1) 1948/9 Hibernian
Hughes, J. (8) 1964/5 Celtic
Hughes, R. D. (5) 2003/04 Portsmouth
Hughes, S. D. (1) 2009/10 Norwich C
Hughes, W. (1) 1974/5 Sunderland
Humphries, W. (1) 1951/2 Motherwell
Hunter, A. (4) 1971/2 Kilmarnock, Celtic
Hunter, W. (3) 1959/60 Motherwell
Husband, J. (1) 1946/7 Partick Th
Hutchison, D. (26) 1998/9 Everton, Sunderland, West Ham U
Hutchison, T. (17) 1973/4 Coventry C
Hutton, A. (15) 2006/07 Rangers, Tottenham H

Imlach, S. (4) 1957/8 Nottingham F
Irvine, B. (9) 1990/1 Aberdeen
Iwelumo, C. R. (2) 2008/09 Wolverhampton W

Jackson, C. (8) 1974/5 Rangers
Jackson, D. (28) 1994/5 Hibernian, Celtic
Jardine, A. (38) 1970/1 Rangers
Jarvie, A. (3) 1970/1 Airdrieonians
Jess, E. (18) 1992/3 Aberdeen, Coventry C, Aberdeen
Johnston, A. (18) 1998/9 Sunderland, Rangers, Middlesbrough

Johnston, M. (38) 1983/4 Watford, Celtic, Nantes, Rangers
Johnston, L. (2) 1947/8 Clyde
Johnston, W. (22) 1965/6 Rangers, WBA
Johnstone, D. (14) 1972/3 Rangers
Johnstone, J. (23) 1964/5 Celtic
Johnstone, R. (17) 1950/1 Hibernian, Manchester C
Jordan, J. (52) 1972/3 Leeds U, Manchester U, AC Milan

Kelly, H. (1) 1951/2 Blackpool
Kelly, J. (2) 1948/9 Barnsley
Kennedy, Jim (6) 1963/4 Celtic
Kennedy, John (1) 2003/04 Celtic
Kennedy, S. (5) 1974/5 Rangers
Kennedy, S. (8) 1977/8 Aberdeen
Kerr, A. (2) 1954/5 Partick Th
Kerr, B. (3) 2002/03 Newcastle U
Kyle, K. (10) 2001/02 Sunderland, Kilmarnock

Lambert, P. (40) 1994/5 Motherwell, Borussia Dortmund, Celtic
Law, D. (55) 1958/9 Huddersfield T, Manchester C, Torino, Manchester U, Manchester C
Lawrence, T. (3) 1962/3 Liverpool
Leggat, G. (18) 1955/6 Aberdeen, Fulham
Leighton, J. (91) 1982/3 Aberdeen, Manchester U, Hibernian, Aberdeen
Lennox, R. (10) 1966/7 Celtic
Leslie, L. (5) 1960/1 Airdrieonians
Levein, C. (16) 1989/90 Heart of Midlothian
Liddell, W. (28) 1946/7 Liverpool
Linwood, A. (1) 1949/50 Clyde
Little, R. J. (1) 1952/3 Rangers
Logie, J. (1) 1952/3 Arsenal
Long, H. (1) 1946/7 Clyde
Lorimer, P. (21) 1969/70 Leeds U

Macari, L. (24) 1971/2 Celtic, Manchester U
Macaulay, A. (7) 1946/7 Brentford, Arsenal
MacDougall, E. (7) 1974/5 Norwich C
Mackay, D. (22) 1956/7 Heart of Midlothian, Tottenham H
Mackay, G. (4) 1987/8 Heart of Midlothian
Mackay, M. (5) 2003/04 Norwich C
Maloney, S. R. (17) 2005/06 Celtic, Aston Villa, Celtic
Malpas, M. (55) 1983/4 Dundee U

Marshall, D. J. (5) 2004/05 Celtic, Cardiff C
Marshall, G. (1) 1991/2 Celtic
Martin, B. (2) 1994/5 Motherwell
Martin, F. (6) 1953/4 Aberdeen
Martin, N. (3) 1964/5 Hibernian, Sunderland
Martis, J. (1) 1960/1 Motherwell
Mason, J. (7) 1948/9 Third Lanark
Masson, D. (17) 1975/6 QPR, Derby C
Mathers, D. (1) 1953/4 Partick Th
Matteo, D. (6) 2000/01 Leeds U
McAllister, B. (3) 1996/7 Wimbledon
McAllister, G. (57) 1989/90 Leicester C, Leeds U, Coventry C
McAllister, J. R. (1) 2003/04 Livingston
McAvennie, F. (5) 1985/6 West Ham U, Celtic
McBride, J. (2) 1966/7 Celtic
McCall, S. M. (40) 1989/90 Everton, Rangers
McCalliog, J. (5) 1966/7 Sheffield W, Wolverhampton W
McCann, N. D. (26) 1998/9 Heart of Midlothian, Rangers, Southampton
McCann, R. (5) 1958/9 Motherwell
McClair, B. (30) 1986/7 Celtic, Manchester U
McCloy, P. (4) 1972/3 Rangers
McCoist, A. (61) 1985/6 Rangers, Kilmarnock
McColl, I. (14) 1949/50 Rangers
McCormack, R. (5) 20007/08 Motherwell, Cardiff C
McCreadie, E. (23) 1964/5 Chelsea
McCulloch, L. (15) 2004/05 Wigan Ath, Rangers
MacDonald, A. (1) 1975/6 Rangers
McDonald, J. (2) 1955/6 Sunderland
McEveley, J. (3) 2007/08 Derby Co
McFadden, J. (45) 2001/02 Motherwell, Everton, Birmingham C
McFarlane, W. (1) 1946/7 Heart of Midlothian
McGarr, E. (2) 1969/70 Aberdeen
McGarvey, F. (7) 1978/9 Liverpool, Celtic
McGhee, M. (4) 1982/3 Aberdeen
McGinlay, J. (13) 1993/4 Bolton W
McGrain, D. (62) 1972/3 Celtic
McGregor, A. (4) 2006/07 Rangers
McGrory, J. (3) 1964/5 Kilmarnock
McInally, A. (8) 1988/9 Aston Villa, Bayern Munich
McInally, J. (10) 1986/7 Dundee U
McInnes, D. (2) 2002/03 WBA

MacKay, D. (14) 1958/9 Celtic
McKean, R. (1) 1975/6 Rangers
MacKenzie, J. (9) 1953/4 Partick Th
McKimmie, S. (40) 1988/9 Aberdeen
McKinlay, T. (22) 1995/6 Celtic
McKinlay, W. (29) 1993/4 Dundee U, Blackburn R
McKinnon, Rob (3) 1993/4 Motherwell
McKinnon, Ronnie (28) 1965/6 Rangers
McLaren, Alan (24) 1991/2 Heart of Midlothian, Rangers
McLaren, Andy (4) 1946/7 Preston NE
McLaren, Andy (1) 2000/01 Kilmarnock
McLean, G. (1) 1967/8 Dundee
McLean, T. (6) 1968/9 Kilmarnock
McLeish, A. (77) 1979/80 Aberdeen
McLeod, J. (4) 1960/1 Hibernian
MacLeod, M. (20) 1984/5 Celtic, Borussia Dortmund, Hibernian
McLintock, F. (9) 1962/3 Leicester C, Arsenal
McManus, S. (22) 2006/07 Celtic
McMillan, I. (6) 1951/2 Airdrieonians, Rangers
McNamara, J. (33) 1996/7 Celtic, Wolverhampton W
McNamee, D. (4) 2003/04 Livingston
McNaught, W. (5) 1950/1 Raith R
McNaughton, K. (4) 2001/02 Aberdeen, Cardiff C
McNeill, W. (29) 1960/1 Celtic
McPhail, J. (5) 1949/50 Celtic
McPherson, D. (27) 1988/9 Heart of Midlothian, Rangers
McQueen, G. (30) 1973/4 Leeds U, Manchester U
McStay, P. (76) 1983/4 Celtic
McSwegan, G. (2) 1999/00 Heart of Midlothian
Millar, J. (2) 1962/3 Rangers
Miller, C. (1) 2000/01 Dundee U
Miller, K. (47) 2000/01 Rangers, Wolverhampton W, Celtic, Derby Co, Rangers
Miller, L. (3) 2005/06 Dundee U, Aberdeen
Miller, W. (6) 1946/7 Celtic
Miller, W. (65) 1974/5 Aberdeen
Mitchell, R. (2) 1950/1 Newcastle U
Mochan, N. (3) 1953/4 Celtic
Moir, W. (1) 1949/50 Bolton W
Moncur, R. (16) 1967/8 Newcastle U
Morgan, W. (21) 1967/8 Burnley, Manchester U
Morris, H. (1) 1949/50 East Fife

Morrison, J. C. (5) 2007/08 WBA
Mudie, J. (17) 1956/7 Blackpool
Mulhall, G. (3) 1959/60 Aberdeen, Sunderland
Munro, F. (9) 1970/1 Wolverhampton W
Munro, I. (7) 1978/9 St Mirren
Murdoch, R. (12) 1965/6 Celtic
Murray, I. (6) 2002/03 Hibernian, Rangers
Murray, J. (5) 1957/8 Heart of Midlothian
Murray, S. (1) 1971/2 Aberdeen
Murty, G. S. (4) 2003/04 Reading

Naismith, S. J. (4) 2006/07 Kilmarnock, Rangers
Narey, D. (35) 1976/7 Dundee U
Naysmith, G. A. (46) 1999/00 Heart of Midlothian, Everton, Sheffield U
Neilson, R. (1) 2006/07 Heart of Midlothian
Nevin, P. K. F. (28) 1985/6 Chelsea, Everton, Tranmere R
Nicholas, C. (20) 1982/3 Celtic, Arsenal, Aberdeen
Nicholson, B. (3) 2000/01 Dunfermline Ath
Nicol, S. (27) 1984/5 Liverpool

O'Connor, G. (16) 2001/02 Hibernian, Lokomotiv Moscow, Birmingham C
O'Donnell, P. (1) 1993/4 Motherwell
O'Hare, J. (13) 1969/70 Derby Co
O'Neil, B. (7) 1995/6 Celtic, Wolfsburg, Derby Co, Preston NE
O'Neil, J. (1) 2000/01 Hibernian
Ormond, W. (6) 1953/4 Hibernian
Orr, T. (2) 1951/2 Morton

Parker, A. (15) 1954/5 Falkirk, Everton
Parlane, D. (12) 1972/3 Rangers
Paton, A. (2) 1951/2 Motherwell
Pearson, S. P. (10) 2003/04 Motherwell, Celtic, Derby Co
Pearson, T. (2) 1946/7 Newcastle U
Penman, A. (1) 1965/6 Dundee
Pettigrew, W. (5) 1975/6 Motherwell
Plenderleith, J. (1) 1960/1 Manchester C
Pressley, S. J. (32) 1999/00 Heart of Midlothian
Provan, David (10) 1979/80 Celtic
Provan, Davie (5) 1963/4 Rangers

Quashie, N. F. (14) 2003/04 Portsmouth, Southampton, WBA
Quinn, P. (4) 1960/1 Motherwell

Rae, G. P. (14) 2000/01 Dundee, Rangers, Cardiff C
Redpath, W. (9) 1948/9 Motherwell
Reilly, L. (38) 1948/9 Hibernian
Ring, T. (12) 1952/3 Clyde
Rioch, B. (24) 1974/5 Derby Co, Everton, Derby Co
Riordan, D. G. (3) 2005/06 Hibernian
Ritchie, P. S. (7) 1998/9 Heart of Midlothian, Bolton W, Walsall
Ritchie, W. (1) 1961/2 Rangers
Robb, D. (5) 1970/1 Aberdeen
Robertson, A. (5) 1954/5 Clyde
Robertson, D. (3) 1991/2 Rangers
Robertson, H. (1) 1961/2 Dundee
Robertson, J. (16) 1990/1 Heart of Midlothian
Robertson, J. G. (1) 1964/5 Tottenham H
Robertson, J. N. (28) 1977/8 Nottingham F, Derby Co
Robertson, S. (1) 2008/09 Dundee U
Robinson, B. (4) 1973/4 Dundee
Robson, B. G. G. (8) 2007/08 Dundee U, Celtic, Middlesbrough
Ross, M. (13) 2001/02 Rangers
Rough, A. (53) 1975/6 Partick Th, Hibernian
Rougvie, D. (1) 1983/4 Aberdeen
Rutherford, E. (1) 1947/8 Rangers

St John, I. (21) 1958/9 Motherwell, Liverpool
Schaedler, E. (1) 1973/4 Hibernian
Scott, A. (16) 1956/7 Rangers, Everton
Scott, Jimmy (1) 1965/6 Hibernian
Scott, Jocky (2) 1970/1 Dundee
Scoular, J. (9) 1950/1 Portsmouth
Severin, S. D. (15) 2001/02 Heart of Midlothian, Aberdeen
Sharp, G. M. (12) 1984/5 Everton
Shaw, D. (8) 1946/7 Hibernian
Shaw, J. (4) 1946/7 Rangers
Shearer, D. (7) 1993/4 Aberdeen
Shearer, R. (4) 1960/1 Rangers
Simpson, N. (4) 1982/3 Aberdeen
Simpson, R. (5) 1966/7 Celtic
Sinclair, J. (1) 1965/6 Leicester C
Smith, D. (2) 1965/6 Aberdeen, Rangers
Smith, E. (2) 1958/9 Celtic
Smith, G. (18) 1946/7 Hibernian
Smith, H. G. (3) 1987/8 Heart of Midlothian
Smith, J. (4) 1967/8 Aberdeen, Newcastle U
Smith, J. (2) 2002/03 Celtic

Souness, G. (54) 1974/5 Middlesbrough, Liverpool, Sampdoria
Speedie, D. R. (10) 1984/5 Chelsea, Coventry C
Spencer, J. (14) 1994/5 Chelsea, QPR
Stanton, P. (16) 1965/6 Hibernian
Steel, W. (30) 1946/7 Morton, Derby C, Dundee
Stein, C. (21) 1968/9 Rangers, Coventry C
Stephen, J. (2) 1946/7 Bradford PA
Stewart, D. (1) 1977/8 Leeds U
Stewart, J. (2) 1976/7 Kilmarnock, Middlesbrough
Stewart, M. J. (4) 2001/02 Manchester U, Heart of Midlothian
Stewart, R. (10) 1980/1 West Ham U
Stockdale, R. K. (5) 2001/02 Middlesbrough
Strachan, G. (50) 1979/80 Aberdeen, Manchester U, Leeds U
Sturrock, P. (20) 1980/1 Dundee U
Sullivan, N. (28) 1996/7 Wimbledon, Tottenham H

Teale, G. (13) 2005/06 Wigan Ath, Derby Co
Telfer, P. N. (1) 1999/00 Coventry C
Telfer, W. (1) 1953/4 St Mirren
Thompson, S. (16) 2001/02 Dundee U, Rangers
Thomson, K. (2) 2008/09 Rangers
Thomson, W. (7) 1979/80 St Mirren
Thornton, W. (7) 1946/7 Rangers
Toner, W. (2) 1958/9 Kilmarnock
Turnbull, E. (8) 1947/8 Hibernian

Ure, I. (11) 1961/2 Dundee, Arsenal

Waddell, W. (17) 1946/7 Rangers
Walker, A. (3) 1987/8 Celtic
Walker, J. N. (2) 1992/3 Heart of Midlothian, Partick Th
Wallace, I. A. (3) 1977/8 Coventry C
Wallace, L. (3) 2009/10 Heart of Midlothian
Wallace, R. (1) 2009/10 Preston NE
Wallace, W. S. B. (7) 1964/5 Heart of Midlothian, Celtic
Wardhaugh, J. (2) 1954/5 Heart of Midlothian
Wark, J. (29) 1978/9 Ipswich T, Liverpool
Watson, J. (2) 1947/8 Motherwell, Huddersfield T
Watson, R. (1) 1970/1 Motherwell

Webster, A. (23) 2002/03 Heart of Midlothian, Dundee U
Weir, A. (6) 1958/9 Motherwell
Weir, D. G. (65) 1996/7 Heart of Midlothian, Everton, Rangers
Weir, P. (6) 1979/80 St Mirren, Aberdeen
White, J. (22) 1958/9 Falkirk, Tottenham H
Whittaker, S. G. (5) 2009/10 Rangers
Whyte, D. (12) 1987/8 Celtic, Middlesbrough, Aberdeen
Wilkie, L. (11) 2001/02 Dundee
Williams, G. (5) 2001/02 Nottingham F
Wilson, A. (1) 1953/4 Portsmouth
Wilson, D. (22) 1960/1 Rangers
Wilson, I. A. (5) 1986/7 Leicester C, Everton

Wilson, P. (1) 1974/5 Celtic
Wilson, R. (2) 1971/2 Arsenal
Winters, R. (1) 1998/9 Aberdeen
Wood, G. (4) 1978/9 Everton, Arsenal
Woodburn, W. (24) 1946/7 Rangers
Wright, K. (1) 1991/2 Hibernian
Wright, S. (2) 1992/3 Aberdeen
Wright, T. (3) 1952/3 Sunderland

Yeats, R. (2) 1964/5 Liverpool
Yorston, H. (1) 1954/5 Aberdeen
Young, A. (8) 1959/60 Heart of Midlothian, Everton
Young, G. (53) 1946/7 Rangers
Younger, T. (24) 1954/5 Hibernian, Liverpool

WALES

Aizlewood, M. (39) 1985/6 Charlton Ath, Leeds U, Bradford C, Bristol C, Cardiff C
Allchurch, I. (68) 1950/1 Swansea T, Newcastle U, Cardiff C, Swansea T
Allchurch, L. (11) 1954/5 Swansea T, Sheffield U
Allen, B. (2) 1950/1 Coventry C
Allen, J. M. (2) 2008/09 Swansea C
Allen, M. (14) 1985/6 Watford, Norwich C, Millwall, Newcastle U

Baker, C. (7) 1957/8 Cardiff C
Baker, W. (1) 1947/8 Cardiff C
Bale, G. (24) 2005/06 Southampton, Tottenham H
Barnard, D. S. (22) 1997/8 Barnsley, Grimsby T
Barnes, W. (22) 1947/8 Arsenal
Bellamy, C. D. (58) 1997/8 Norwich C, Coventry C, Newcastle U, Blackburn R, Liverpool, West Ham U, Manchester C
Berry, G. (5) 1978/9 Wolverhampton W, Stoke C
Blackmore, C. G. (39) 1984/5 Manchester U, Middlesbrough
Blake, N. (29) 1993/4 Sheffield U, Bolton W, Blackburn R, Wolverhampton W
Bodin, P. J. (23) 1989/90 Swindon T, Crystal P, Swindon T
Bowen, D. (19) 1954/5 Arsenal
Bowen, J. P. (2) 1993/4 Swansea C, Birmingham C

Bowen, M. R. (41) 1985/6 Tottenham H, Norwich C, West Ham U
Boyle, T. (2) 1980/1 Crystal P
Bradley, M. S. (1) 2009/10 Walsall
Brown, J. R. (2) 2005/06 Gillingham, Blackburn R
Browning, M. T. (5) 1995/6 Bristol R, Huddersfield T
Burgess, R. (32) 1946/7 Tottenham H
Burton, O. (9) 1962/3 Norwich C, Newcastle U

Cartwright, L. (7) 1973/4 Coventry C, Wrexham
Charles, J. (38) 1949/50 Leeds U, Juventus, Leeds U, Cardiff C
Charles, J. M. (19) 1980/1 Swansea C, QPR, Oxford U
Charles, M. (31) 1954/5 Swansea T, Arsenal, Cardiff C
Church, S. R. (8) 2008/09 Reading
Clarke, R. (22) 1948/9 Manchester C
Coleman, C. (32) 1991/2 Crystal P, Blackburn R, Fulham
Collins, D. L. (7) 2004/05 Sunderland
Collins, J. M. (34) 2003/04 Cardiff C, West Ham U, Aston Villa
Collison, J. D. (7) 2007/08 West Ham U
Cornforth, J. M. (2) 1994/5 Swansea C
Cotterill, D. R. G. B. (16) 2005/06 Bristol C, Wigan Ath, Sheffield U, Swansea C

Coyne, D. (16) 1995/6 Tranmere R, Grimsby T, Leicester C, Burnley, Tranmere R

Crofts, A. L. (13) 2005/06 Gillingham, Brighton & HA

Crossley, M. G. (8) 1996/7 Nottingham F, Middlesbrough, Fulham

Crowe, V. (16) 1958/9 Aston Villa

Curtis, A. (35) 1975/6 Swansea C, Leeds U, Swansea C, Southampton, Cardiff C

Daniel, R. (21) 1950/1 Arsenal, Sunderland

Davies, A. (13) 1982/3 Manchester U, Newcastle U, Swansea C, Bradford C

Davies. A. R. (1) 2005/06 Yeovil T

Davies, C. (1) 1971/2 Charlton Ath

Davies, C. M. (5) 2005/06 Oxford U, Verona, Oldham Ath

Davies, D. (52) 1974/5 Everton, Wrexham, Swansea C

Davies, G. (16) 1979/80 Fulham, Manchester C

Davies, R. Wyn (34) 1963/4 Bolton W, Newcastle U, Manchester C, Manchester U, Blackpool

Davies, Reg (6) 1952/3 Newcastle U

Davies, Ron (29) 1963/4 Norwich C, Southampton, Portsmouth

Davies, S. (58) 2000/01 Tottenham H, Everton, Fulham

Davies, S. I. (1) 1995/6 Manchester U

Davis, G. (3) 1977/8 Wrexham

Deacy, N. (12) 1976/7 PSV Eindhoven, Beringen

Delaney, M. A. (36) 1999/00 Aston Villa

Derrett, S. (4) 1968/9 Cardiff C

Dibble, A. (3) 1985/6 Luton T, Manchester C

Dorman, A. (1) 2009/10 St Mirren

Duffy, R. M. (13) 2005/06 Portsmouth

Durban, A. (27) 1965/6 Derby C

Dwyer, P. (10) 1977/8 Cardiff C

Eardley, N. (13) 2007/08 Oldham Ath, Blackpool

Earnshaw, R. (49) 2001/02 Cardiff C, WBA, Norwich C, Derby Co, Nottingham F

Easter, J. M. (8) 2006/07 Wycombe W, Plymouth Arg, Milton Keynes D

Eastwood, F. (10) 2007/08 Wolverhampton W

Edwards, C. N. H. (1) 1995/6 Swansea C

Edwards, D. (19) 2007/08 Luton T, Wolverhampton W

Edwards, G. (12) 1946/7 Birmingham C, Cardiff C

Edwards, I. (4) 1977/8 Chester, Wrexham

Edwards, R. O. (15) 2002/03 Aston Villa, Wolverhampton W

Edwards, R. W. (4) 1997/8 Bristol C

Edwards, T. (2) 1956/7 Charlton Ath

Emanuel, J. (2) 1972/3 Bristol C

England, M. (44) 1961/2 Blackburn R, Tottenham H

Evans, B. (7) 1971/2 Swansea C, Hereford U

Evans, C. M. (12) 2007/08 Manchester C, Sheffield U

Evans, I. (13) 1975/6 Crystal P

Evans, P. S. (2) 2001/02 Brentford, Bradford C

Evans, R. (1) 1963/4 Swansea T

Evans, S. J. (7) 2006/07 Wrexham

Felgate, D. (1) 1983/4 Lincoln C

Fletcher, C. N. (36) 2003/04 Bournemouth, West Ham U, Crystal P

Flynn, B. (66) 1974/5 Burnley, Leeds U, Burnley

Ford, T. (38) 1946/7 Swansea T, Aston Villa, Sunderland, Cardiff C

Foulkes, W. (11) 1951/2 Newcastle U

Freestone, R. (1) 1999/00 Swansea C

Gabbidon, D. L. (43) 2001/02 Cardiff C, West Ham U

Garner, G. (1) 2005/06 Leyton Orient

Giggs, R. J. (64) 1991/2 Manchester U

Giles, D. (12) 1979/80 Swansea C, Crystal P

Godfrey, B. (3) 1963/4 Preston NE

Goss, J. (9) 1990/1 Norwich C

Green, C. (15) 1964/5 Birmingham C

Green, R. M. (2) 1997/8 Wolverhampton W

Griffiths, A. (17) 1970/1 Wrexham

Griffiths, H. (1) 1952/3 Swansea T

Griffiths, M. (11) 1946/7 Leicester C

Gunter, C. R. (22) 2006/07 Cardiff C, Tottenham H, Nottingham F

Hall, G. D. (9) 1987/8 Chelsea

Harrington, A. (11) 1955/6 Cardiff C

Harris, C. (24) 1975/6 Leeds U

Harris, W. (6) 1953/4 Middlesbrough

Hartson, J. (51) 1994/5 Arsenal, West Ham U, Wimbledon, Coventry C, Celtic

Haworth, S. O. (5) 1996/7 Cardiff C, Coventry C
Hennessey, T. (39) 1961/2 Birmingham C, Nottingham F, Derby Co
Hennessey, W. R. (25) 2006/07 Wolverhampton W
Hewitt, R. (5) 1957/8 Cardiff C
Hill, M. (2) 1971/2 Ipswich T
Hockey, T. (9) 1971/2 Sheffield U, Norwich C, Aston Villa
Hodges, G. (18) 1983/4 Wimbledon, Newcastle U, Watford, Sheffield U
Holden, A. (1) 1983/4 Chester C
Hole, B. (30) 1962/3 Cardiff C, Blackburn R, Aston Villa, Swansea C
Hollins, D. (11) 1961/2 Newcastle U
Hopkins, J. (16) 1982/3 Fulham, Crystal P
Hopkins, M. (34) 1955/6 Tottenham H
Horne, B. (59) 1987/8 Portsmouth, Southampton, Everton, Birmingham C
Howells, R. (2) 1953/4 Cardiff C
Hughes, C. M. (8) 1991/2 Luton T, Wimbledon
Hughes, I. (4) 1950/1 Luton T
Hughes, L. M. (72) 1983/4 Manchester U, Barcelona, Manchester U, Chelsea, Southampton
Hughes, W. (3) 1946/7 Birmingham C
Hughes, W. A. (5) 1948/9 Blackburn R
Humphreys, J. (1) 1946/7 Everton

Jackett, K. (31) 1982/3 Watford
James, G. (9) 1965/6 Blackpool
James, L. (54) 1971/2 Burnley, Derby C, QPR, Burnley, Swansea C, Sunderland
James, R. M. (47) 1978/9 Swansea C, Stoke C, QPR, Leicester C, Swansea C
Jarvis, A. (3) 1966/7 Hull C
Jenkins, S. R. (16) 1995/6 Swansea C, Huddersfield T
Johnson, A. J. (15) 1998/9 Nottingham F, WBA
Johnson, M. (1) 1963/4 Swansea T
Jones, A. (6) 1986/7 Port Vale, Charlton Ath
Jones, Barrie (15) 1962/3 Swansea T, Plymouth Argyle, Cardiff C
Jones, Bryn (4) 1946/7 Arsenal
Jones, C. (59) 1953/4 Swansea T, Tottenham H, Fulham
Jones, D. (8) 1975/6 Norwich C
Jones, E. (4) 1947/8 Swansea T, Tottenham H
Jones, J. (72) 1975/6 Liverpool, Wrexham, Chelsea, Huddersfield T

Jones, K. (1) 1949/50 Aston Villa
Jones, M. A. (2) 2006/07 Wrexham
Jones, M. G. (13) 1999/00 Leeds U, Leicester C
Jones, P. L. (2) 1996/7 Liverpool, Tranmere R
Jones, P. S. (50) 1996/7 Stockport Co, Southampton, Wolverhampton W, QPR
Jones, R. (1) 1993/4 Sheffield W
Jones, T. G. (13) 1946/7 Everton
Jones, V. P. (9) 1994/5 Wimbledon
Jones, W. (1) 1970/1 Bristol R

Kelsey, J. (41) 1953/4 Arsenal
King, A. (3) 2008/09 Leicester C
King, J. (1) 1954/5 Swansea T
Kinsey, N. (7) 1950/1 Norwich C, Birmingham C
Knill, A. R. (1) 1988/9 Swansea C
Koumas, J. (34) 2000/01 Tranmere R, WBA, Wigan Ath
Krzywicki, R. (8) 1969/70 WBA, Huddersfield T

Lambert, R. (5) 1946/7 Liverpool
Law, B. J. (1) 1989/90 QPR
Lea, C. (2) 1964/5 Ipswich T
Ledley, J. C. (32) 2005/06 Cardiff C
Leek, K. (13) 1960/1 Leicester C, Newcastle U, Birmingham C, Northampton T
Legg, A. (6) 1995/6 Birmingham C, Cardiff C
Lever, A. (1) 1952/3 Leicester C
Lewis, D. (1) 1982/3 Swansea C
Llewellyn, C. M. (6) 1997/8 Norwich C, Wrexham
Lloyd, B. (3) 1975/6 Wrexham
Lovell, S. (6) 1981/2 Crystal P, Millwall
Lowndes, S. (10) 1982/3 Newport Co, Millwall, Barnsley
Lowrie, G. (4) 1947/8 Coventry C, Newcastle U
Lucas, M. (4) 1961/2 Leyton Orient
Lucas, W. (7) 1948/9 Swansea T

Maguire, G. T. (7) 1989/90 Portsmouth
Mahoney, J. (51) 1967/8 Stoke C, Middlesbrough, Swansea C
Mardon, P. J. (1) 1995/6 WBA
Margetson, M. W. (1) 2003/04 Cardiff C
Marriott, A. (5) 1995/6 Wrexham
Marustik, C. (6) 1981/2 Swansea C
Medwin, T. (30) 1952/3 Swansea T, Tottenham H

Melville, A. K. (65) 1989/90 Swansea C,
Oxford U, Sunderland, Fulham,
West Ham U
Mielczarek, R. (1) 1970/1 Rotherham U
Millington, A. (21) 1962/3 WBA,
Crystal P, Peterborough U, Swansea C
Moore, G. (21) 1959/60 Cardiff C,
Chelsea, Manchester U, Northampton
T, Charlton Ath
Morgan, C. (20) 2006/07 Milton Keynes D,
Peterborough U
Morris, W. (5) 1946/7 Burnley
Myhill, G. O. (8) 2007/08 Hull C

Nardiello, D. (2) 1977/8 Coventry C
Nardiello, D. A. (3) 2006/07 Barnsley,
QPR
Neilson, A. B. (5) 1991/2 Newcastle U,
Southampton
Nicholas, P. (73) 1978/9 Crystal P,
Arsenal, Crystal P, Luton T, Aberdeen,
Chelsea, Watford
Niedzwiecki, E. A. (2) 1984/5 Chelsea
Nogan, L. M. (2) 1991/2 Watford,
Reading
Norman, A. J. (5) 1985/6 Hull C
Nurse, M. T. G. (12) 1959/60 Swansea T,
Middlesbrough
Nyatanga, L. J. (33) 2005/06 Derby Co,
Bristol C

O'Sullivan, P. (3) 1972/3 Brighton & HA
Oster, J. M. (13) 1997/8 Everton,
Sunderland

Page, M. (28) 1970/1 Birmingham C
Page, R. J. (41) 1996/7 Watford,
Sheffield U, Cardiff C, Coventry C
Palmer, D. (3) 1956/7 Swansea T
Parry, J. (1) 1950/1 Swansea T
Parry, P. I. (12) 2003/04 Cardiff C
Partridge, D. W. (7) 2004/05 Motherwell,
Bristol C
Pascoe, C. (10) 1983/4 Swansea C,
Sunderland
Paul, R. (33) 1948/9 Swansea T,
Manchester C
Pembridge, M. A. (54) 1991/2 Luton T,
Derby C, Sheffield W, Benfica, Everton,
Fulham
Perry, J. (1) 1993/4 Cardiff C
Phillips, D. (62) 1983/4 Plymouth Argyle,
Manchester C, Coventry C, Norwich C,
Nottingham F
Phillips, J. (4) 1972/3 Chelsea

Phillips, L. (58) 1970/1 Cardff C,
Aston Villa, Swansea C, Charlton Ath
Pipe, D. R. (1) 2002/03 Coventry C
Pontin, K. (2) 1979/80 Cardiff C
Powell, A. (8) 1946/7 Leeds U, Everton,
Birmingham C
Powell, D. (11) 1967/8 Wrexham,
Sheffield U
Powell, I. (8) 1946/7 QPR, Aston Villa
Price, L. P. (7) 2005/06 Ipswich T,
Derby Co
Price, P. (25) 1979/80 Luton T,
Tottenham H
Pring, K. (3) 1965/6 Rotherham U
Pritchard, H. K. (1) 1984/5 Bristol C

Ramsey, A. (11) 2008/09 Arsenal
Rankmore, F. (l) 1965/6 Peterborough U
Ratcliffe, K. (59) 1980/1 Everton,
Cardiff C
Ready, K. (5) 1996/7 QPR
Reece, G. (29) 1965/6 Sheffield U,
Cardiff C
Reed, W. (2) 1954/5 Ipswich T
Rees, A. (1) 1983/4 Birmingham C
Rees, J. M. (1) 1991/2 Luton T
Rees, R. (39) 1964/5 Coventry C, WBA,
Nottingham F
Rees, W. (4) 1948/9 Cardiff C,
Tottenham H
Ribeiro, C. M. (1) 2009/10 Bristol C
Richards, S. (1) 1946/7 Cardiff C
Ricketts, S. (38) 2004/05 Swansea C,
Hull C, Bolton W
Roberts, A. M. (2) 1992/3 QPR
Roberts, D. (17) 1972/3 Oxford U, Hull C
Roberts, G. W. (9) 1999/00 Tranmere R
Roberts, I. W. (15) 1989/90 Watford,
Huddersfield T, Leicester C, Norwich C
Roberts, J. G. (22) 1970/1 Arsenal,
Birmingham C
Roberts, J. H. (1) 1948/9 Bolton W
Roberts, N. W. (4) 1999/00 Wrexham,
Wigan Ath
Roberts, P. (4) 1973/4 Portsmouth
Roberts, S. W. (1) 2004/05 Wrexham
Robinson, C. P. (52) 1999/00
Wolverhampton W, Portsmouth,
Sunderland, Norwich C, Toronto Lynx
Robinson, J. R. C. (30) 1995/6
Charlton Ath
Robson-Kanu, H. (1) 2009/10 Reading
Rodrigues, P. (40) 1964/5 Cardiff C,
Leicester C, Sheffield W
Rouse, V. (1) 1958/9 Crystal P

Rowley, T. (1) 1958/9 Tranmere R

Rush, I. (73) 1979/80 Liverpool, Juventus, Liverpool

Saunders, D. (75) 1985/6 Brighton & HA, Oxford U, Derby C, Liverpool, Aston Villa, Galatasaray, Nottingham F, Sheffield U, Benfica, Bradford C

Savage, R. W. (39) 1995/6 Crewe Alexandra, Leicester C, Birmingham C

Sayer, P. (1) 1976/7 Cardiff C

Scrine, F. (2) 1949/50 Swansea T

Sear, C. (1) 1962/3 Manchester C

Sherwood, A. (41) 1946/7 Cardiff C, Newport C

Shortt, W. (12) 1946/7 Plymouth Argyle

Showers, D. (2) 1974/5 Cardiff C

Sidlow, C. (7) 1946/7 Liverpool

Slatter, N. (22) 1982/3 Bristol R, Oxford U

Smallman, D. (7) 1973/4 Wrexham, Everton

Southall, N. (92) 1981/2 Everton

Speed, G. A. (85) 1989/90 Leeds U, Everton, Newcastle U, Bolton W

Sprake, G. (37) 1963/4 Leeds U, Birmingham C

Stansfield, F. (1) 1948/9 Cardiff C

Stevenson, B. (15) 1977/8 Leeds U, Birmingham C

Stevenson, N. (4) 1981/2 Swansea C

Stitfall, R. (2) 1952/3 Cardiff C

Stock, B. B. (2) 2009/10 Doncaster R

Sullivan, D. (17) 1952/3 Cardiff C

Symons, C. J. (37) 1991/2 Portsmouth, Manchester C, Fulham, Crystal P

Tapscott, D. (14) 1953/4 Arsenal, Cardiff C

Taylor, G. K. (15) 1995/6 Crystal P, Sheffield U, Burnley, Nottingham F

Taylor, N. J. (1) 2009/10 Wrexham

Thatcher, B. D. (7) 2003/04 Leicester C, Manchester C

Thomas, D. (2) 1956/7 Swansea T

Thomas, M. (51) 1976/7 Wrexham, Manchester U, Everton, Brighton & HA, Stoke C, Chelsea, WBA

Thomas, M. R. (1) 1986/7 Newcastle U

Thomas, R. (50) 1966/7 Swindon T, Derby C, Cardiff C

Thomas, S. (4) 1947/8 Fulham

Toshack, J. (40) 1968/9 Cardiff C, Liverpool, Swansea C

Trollope, P. J. (9) 1996/7 Derby Co, Fulham, Coventry C, Northampton T

Tudur-Jones, O. (4) 2007/08 Swansea C

Van Den Hauwe, P. W. R. (13) 1984/5 Everton

Vaughan, D. O. (17) 2002/03 Crewe Alex, Real Sociedad, Blackpool

Vaughan, N. (10) 1982/3 Newport Co, Cardiff C

Vearncombe, G. (2) 1957/8 Cardiff C

Vernon, R. (32) 1956/7 Blackburn R, Everton, Stoke C

Villars, A. (3) 1973/4 Cardiff C

Vokes, S. M. (16) 2007/08 Bournemouth, Wolverhampton W

Walley, T. (1) 1970/1 Watford

Walsh, I. (18) 1979/80 Crystal P, Swansea C

Ward, D. (2) 1958/9 Bristol R, Cardiff C

Ward, D. (5) 1999/00 Notts Co, Nottingham F

Webster, C. (4) 1956/7 Manchester U

Weston, R. D. (7) 1999/00 Arsenal, Cardiff C

Williams, A. (13) 1993/4 Reading, Wolverhampton W, Reading

Williams, A. E. (20) 2007/08 Stockport Co, Swansea C

Williams, A. P. (2) 1997/8 Southampton

Williams, D. G. 1987/8 13, Derby Co, Ipswich T

Williams, D. M. (5) 1985/6 Norwich C

Williams, G. (1) 1950/1 Cardiff C

Williams, G. E. (26) 1959/60 WBA

Williams, G. G. (5) 1960/1 Swansea T

Williams, G. J. (2) 2005/06 West Ham U, Ipswich T

Williams, H. (4) 1948/9 Newport Co, Leeds U

Williams, Herbert (3) 1064/5 Swansea T

Williams, S. (43) 1953/4 WBA, Southampton

Witcomb, D. (3) 1946/7 WBA, Sheffield W

Woosnam, P. (17) 1958/9 Leyton Orient, West Ham U, Aston Villa

Yorath, T. (59) 1969/70 Leeds U, Coventry C, Tottenham H, Vancouver Whitecaps

Young, E. (21) 1989/90 Wimbledon, Crystal P, Wolverhampton W

REPUBLIC OF IRELAND

Aherne, T. (16) 1945/6 Belfast Celtic, Luton T

Aldridge, J. W. (69) 1985/6 Oxford U, Liverpool, Real Sociedad, Tranmere R

Ambrose, P. (5) 1954/5 Shamrock R

Anderson, J. (16) 1979/80 Preston NE, Newcastle U

Andrews, K. J. (15) 2008/09 Blackburn R

Babb, P. (35) 1993/4 Coventry C, Liverpool, Sunderland

Bailham, E. (1) 1963/4 Shamrock R

Barber, E. (2) 1965/6 Shelbourne, Birmingham C

Barrett, G. (6) 2002/03 Arsenal, Coventry C

Beglin, J. (15) 1983/4 Liverpool

Bennett, A. J. (2) 2006/07 Reading

Best, L. J. B. (7) 2008/09 Coventry C, Newcastle U

Bonner, P. (80) 1980/1 Celtic

Braddish, S. (1) 1977/8 Dundalk

Brady, T. R. (6) 1963/4 QPR

Brady, W. L. (72) 1974/5 Arsenal, Juventus, Sampdoria, Internazionale, Ascoli, West Ham U

Branagan, K. G. (1) 1996/7 Bolton W

Breen, G. (63) 1995/6 Birmingham C, Coventry C, West Ham U, Sunderland

Breen, T. (3) 1946/7 Shamrock R

Brennan, F. (1) 1964/5 Drumcondra

Brennan, S. A. (19) 1964/5 Manchester U, Waterford

Browne, W. (3) 1963/4 Bohemians

Bruce, A. (2) 2006/07 Ipswich T

Buckley, L. (2) 1983/4 Shamrock R, Waregem

Burke, F. (1) 1951/2 Cork Ath

Butler, P. J. (1) 1999/00 Sunderland

Butler, T. (2) 2002/03 Sunderland

Byrne, A. B. (14) 1969/70 Southampton

Byrne, J. (23) 1984/5 QPR, Le Havre, Brighton & HA, Sunderland, Millwall

Byrne, J. (2) 2003/04 Shelbourne

Byrne, P. (8) 1983/4 Shamrock R

Campbell, A. (3) 1984/5 Santander

Campbell, N. (11) 1970/1 St Patrick's Ath, Fortuna Cologne

Cantwell, N. (36) 1953/4 West Ham U, Manchester U

Carey, B. P. (3) 1991/2 Manchester U, Leicester C

Carey, J. J. (21) 1945/6 Manchester U

Carolan, J. (2) 1959/60 Manchester U

Carr, S. (44) 1998/9 Tottenham H, Newcastle U

Carroll, B. (2) 1948/9 Shelbourne

Carroll, T. R. (17) 1967/8 Ipswich T, Birmingham C

Carsley, L. K. (39) 1997/8 Derby Co, Blackburn R, Coventry C, Everton

Cascarino, A. G. (88) 1985/6 Gillingham, Millwall, Aston Villa, Celtic, Chelsea, Marseille, Nancy

Chandler, J. (2) 1979/80 Leeds U

Clarke, C. R. (2) 2003/04 Stoke C

Clarke, J. (1) 1977/8 Drogheda U

Clarke, K. (2) 1947/8 Drumcondra

Clarke, M. (1) 1949/50 Shamrock R

Clinton, T. J. (3) 1950/1 Everton

Coad, P. (11) 1946/7 Shamrock R

Coffey, T. (1) 1949/50 Drumcondra

Colfer, M. D. (2) 1949/50 Shelbourne

Colgan, N. (9) 2001/02 Hibernian, Barnsley

Conmy, O. M. (5) 1964/5 Peterborough U

Connolly, D. J. (41) 1995/6 Watford, Feyenoord, Wolverhampton W, Excelsior, Wimbledon, West Ham U, Wigan Ath

Conroy, G. A. (27) 1969/70 Stoke C

Conway, J. P. (20) 1966/7 Fulham, Manchester C

Corr, P. J. (4) 1948/9 Everton

Courtney, E. (1) 1945/6 Cork U

Coyle, O. (1) 1993/4 Bolton W

Coyne, T. (22) 1991/2 Celtic, Tranmere R, Motherwell

Crowe, G. (2) 2002/03 Bohemians

Cummins, G. P. (19) 1953/4 Luton T

Cuneen, T. (1) 1950/1 Limerick

Cunningham, G. R. (1) 2009/10 Manchester C

Cunningham, K. (72) 1995/6 Wimbledon, Birmingham C

Curtis, D. P. (17) 1956/7 Shelbourne, Bristol C, Ipswich T, Exeter C

Cusack, S. (1) 1952/3 Limerick

Daish, L. S. (5) 1991/2 Cambridge U, Coventry C

Daly, G. A. (48) 1972/3 Manchester U, Derby C, Coventry C, Birmingham C, Shrewsbury T

Daly, M. (2) 1977/8 Wolverhampton W

Daly, P. (1) 1949/50 Shamrock R
Deacy, E. (4) 1981/2 Aston Villa
Delaney, D. F. (2) 2007/08 QPR
Delap, R. J. (11) 1997/8 Derby Co,
Southampton
De Mange, K. J. P. P. (2) 1986/7
Liverpool, Hull C
Dempsey, J. T. (19) 1966/7 Fulham,
Chelsea
Dennehy, J. (11) 1971/2 Cork Hibernian,
Nottingham F, Walsall
Desmond, P. (4) 1949/50 Middlesbrough
Devine, J. (13) 1979/80 Arsenal,
Norwich C
Doherty, G. M. T. (34) 1999/00 Luton T,
Tottenham H, Norwich C
Donovan, D. C. (5) 1954/5 Everton
Donovan, T. (1) 1979/80 Aston Villa
Douglas, J. (8) 2003/04 Blackburn R,
Leeds U
Doyle, C. (1) 1958/9 Shelbourne
Doyle, Colin (1) 2006/07 Birmingham C
Doyle, K. E. (35) 2005/06 Reading,
Wolverhampton W
Doyle, M. P. (1) 2003/04 Coventry C
Duff, D. A. (83) 1997/8 Blackburn R,
Chelsea, Newcastle U, Fulham
Duffy, B. (1) 1949/50 Shamrock R
Dunne, A. P. (33) 1961/2 Manchester U,
Bolton W
Dunne, J. C. (1) 1970/1 Fulham
Dunne, P. A. J. (5) 1964/5 Manchester U
Dunne, R. P. (58) 1999/00 Everton,
Manchester C, Aston Villa
Dunne, S. (15) 1952/3 Luton T
Dunne, T. (3) 1955/6 St Patrick's Ath
Dunning, P. (2) 1970/1 Shelbourne
Dunphy, E. M. (23) 1965/6 York C,
Millwall
Dwyer, N. M. (14) 1959/60 West Ham U,
Swansea T

Eccles, P. (1) 1985/6 Shamrock R
Eglington, T. J. (24) 1945/6 Shamrock R,
Everton
Elliott, S. W. (9) 2004/05 Sunderland
Evans, M. J. (1) 1997/8 Southampton

Fagan, E. (1) 1972/3 Shamrock R
Fagan, F. (8) 1954/5 Manchester C,
Derby C
Fahey, K. D. (2) 2009/10 Birmingham C
Fairclough, M. (2) 1981/2 Dundalk
Fallon, S. (8) 1950/1 Celtic

Farrell, P. D. (28) 1945/6 Shamrock R,
Everton
Farrelly, G. (6) 1995/6 Aston Villa,
Everton, Bolton W
Finnan, S. (53) 1999/00 Fulham,
Liverpool
Finucane, A. (11) 1966/7 Limerick
Fitzgerald, F. J. (2) 1954/5 Waterford
Fitzgerald, P. J. (5) 1960/1 Leeds U,
Chester
Fitzpatrick, K. (1) 1969/70 Limerick
Fitzsimons, A. G. (26) 1949/50
Middlesbrough, Lincoln C
Fleming, C. (10) 1995/6 Middlesbrough
Fogarty, A. (11) 1959/60 Sunderland,
Hartlepool U
Folan, C. C. (7) 2008/09 Hull C
Foley, D. J. (6) 1999/00 Watford
Foley, K. P. (2) 2008/09
Wolverhampton W
Foley, T. C. (9) 1963/4 Northampton T
Fullam, J. 1960/1 Preston NE,
Shamrock R

Gallagher, C. (2) 1966/7 Celtic
Gallagher, M. (1) 1953/4 Hibernian
Galvin, A. (29) 1982/3 Tottenham H,
Sheffield W, Swindon T
Gamble, J. (2) 2006/07 Cork C
Gannon, E. (14) 1948/9 Notts Co,
Sheffield W, Shelbourne K
Gannon, M. (1) 1971/2 Shelbourne
Gavin, J. T. (7) 1949/50 Norwich C,
Tottenham H, Norwich C
Gibbons, A. (4) 1951/2 St Patrick's Ath
Gibson, D. T. D. (9) 2007/08
Manchester U
Gilbert, R. (1) 1965/6 Shamrock R
Giles, C. (1) 1950/1 Doncaster R
Giles, M. J. (59) 1959/60 Manchester U,
Leeds U, WBA, Shamrock R
Given, S. J. J. (103) 1995/6 Blackburn R,
Newcastle U, Manchester C
Givens, D. J. (56) 1968/9 Manchester U,
Luton T, QPR, Birmingham C,
Neuchatel Xamax
Gleeson, S. M. (2) 2006/07
Wolverhampton W
Glynn, D. (2) 1951/2 Drumcondra
Godwin, T. F. (13) 1948/9 Shamrock R,
Leicester C, Bournemouth
Goodman, J. (4) 1996/7 Wimbledon
Goodwin, J. (1) 2002/03 Stockport Co
Gorman, W. C. (2) 1946/7 Brentford

Grealish, A. (45) 1975/6 Orient, Luton T,
Brighton & HA, WBA
Green, P. J. (2) 2009/10 Derby Co
Gregg, E. (8) 1977/8 Bohemians
Grimes, A. A. (18) 1977/8 Manchester U,
Coventry C, Luton T

Hale, A. (13) 1961/2 Aston Villa,
Doncaster R, Waterford
Hamilton, T. (2) 1958/9 Shamrock R
Hand, E. K. (20) 1968/9 Portsmouth
Harte, I. P. (64) 1995/6 Leeds U, Levante
Hartnett, J. B. (2) 1948/9 Middlesbrough
Haverty, J. (32) 1955/6 Arsenal,
Blackburn R, Millwall, Celtic, Bristol
R, Shelbourne
Hayes, A. W. P. (1) 1978/9 Southampton
Hayes, W. E. (2) 1946/7 Huddersfield T
Hayes, W. J. (1) 1948/9 Limerick
Healey, R. (2) 1976/7 Cardiff C
Healy, C. (13) 2001/02 Celtic, Sunderland
Heighway, S. D. (34) 1970/1 Liverpool,
Minnesota Kicks
Henderson, B. (2) 1947/8 Drumcondra
Henderson, W. C. P. (6) 2005/06
Brighton & HA, Preston NE
Hennessy, J. (5) 1964/5 Shelbourne, St
Patrick's Ath
Herrick, J. (3) 1971/2 Cork Hibernians,
Shamrock R
Higgins, J. (1) 1950/1 Birmingham C
Holland, M. R. (49) 1999/00 Ipswich T,
Charlton Ath
Holmes, J. (30) 1970/1 Coventry C,
Tottenham H, Vancouver Whitecaps
Hoolahan, W. (1) 2007/08 Blackpool
Houghton, R. J. (73) 1985/6 Oxford U,
Liverpool, Aston Villa, Crystal P,
Reading
Howlett, G. (1) 1983/4 Brighton & HA
Hughton, C. (53) 1979/80 Tottenham H,
West Ham U
Hunt, N. (3) 2008/09 Reading
Hunt, S. P. (25) 2006/07 Reading, Hull C
Hurley, C. J. (40) 1956/7 Millwall,
Sunderland, Bolton W

Ireland, S. J. (6) 2005/06 Manchester C
Irwin, D. J. (56) 1990/1 Manchester U

Kavanagh, G. A. (16) 1997/8 Stoke C,
Cardiff C, Wigan Ath

Keane, R. D. (99) 1997/8
Wolverhampton W, Coventry C,
Internazionale, Leeds U, Tottenham H,
Liverpool, Tottenham H
Keane, R. M. (67) 1990/1 Nottingham F,
Manchester U
Keane, T. R. (4) 1948/9 Swansea T
Kearin, M. (1) 1971/2 Shamrock R
Kearns, F. T. (1) 1953/4 West Ham U
Kearns, M. (18) 1969/70 Oxford U,
Walsall, Wolverhampton W
Kelly, A. T. (34) 1992/3 Sheffield U,
Blackburn R
Kelly, D. T. (26) 1987/8 Walsall,
West Ham U, Leicester C, Newcastle U,
Wolverhampton W, Sunderland,
Tranmere R
Kelly, G. (52) 1993/4 Leeds U
Kelly, J. A. (48) 1956/7 Drumcondra,
Preston NE
Kelly, J. P. V. (5) 1960/1
Wolverhampton W
Kelly, M. J. (4) 1987/8 Portsmouth
Kelly, N. (1) 1953/4 Nottingham F
Kelly, S. M. (18) 2005/06 Tottenham H,
Birmingham C, Fulham
Kenna, J. J. (27) 1994/5 Blackburn R
Kennedy, M. (34) 1995/6 Liverpool,
Wimbledon, Manchester C,
Wolverhampton W
Kennedy, M. F. (2) 1985/6 Portsmouth
Kenny, P. (7) 2003/04 Sheffield U
Keogh, A. D. (13) 2006/07
Wolverhampton W
Keogh, J. (1) 1965/6 Shamrock R
Keogh, S. (1) 1958/9 Shamrock R
Kernaghan, A. N. (22) 1992/3
Middlesbrough, Manchester C
Kiely, D. L. (11) 1999/00 Charlton Ath,
WBA
Kiernan, F. W. (5) 1950/1 Shamrock R,
Southampton
Kilbane, K. D. (103) 1997/8 WBA,
Sunderland, Everton, Wigan Ath,
Hull C
Kinnear, J. P. (26) 1966/7 Tottenham H,
Brighton & HA
Kinsella, M. A. (48) 1997/8 Charlton Ath,
Aston Villa, WBA

Langan, D. (26) 1977/8 Derby Co,
Birmingham C, Oxford U
Lapira, J. (1) 2006/07 Notre Dame
Lawler, J. F. (8) 1952/3 Fulham

Lawlor, J. C. (3) 1948/9 Drumcondra, Doncaster R
Lawlor, M. (5) 1970/1 Shamrock R
Lawrence, L. (8) 2008/09 Stoke C
Lawrenson, M. (39) 1976/7 Preston NE, Brighton & HA, Liverpool
Lee, A. L. (10) 2002/03 Rotherham U, Cardiff C, Ipswich T
Leech, M. (8) 1968/9 Shamrock R
Long, S. P. (13) 2006/07 Reading
Lowry, D. (1) 1961/2 St Patrick's Ath

McAlinden, J. (2) 1945/6 Portsmouth
McAteer, J. W. (52) 1993/4 Bolton W, Liverpool, Blackburn R, Sunderland
McCann, J. (1) 1956/7 Shamrock R
McCarthy, J. (1) 2009/10 Wigan Ath
McCarthy, M. (57) 1983/4 Manchester C, Celtic, Lyon, Millwall
McConville, T. (6) 1971/2 Dundalk, Waterford
McDonagh, Jim (25) 1980/1 Everton, Bolton W, Notts C
McDonagh, Jacko (3) 1983/4 Shamrock R
McEvoy, M. A. (17) 1960/1 Blackburn R
McGeady, A. (32) 2003/04 Celtic
McGee, P. (15) 1977/8 QPR, Preston NE
McGoldrick, E. J. (15) 1991/2 Crystal P, Arsenal
McGowan, D. (3) 1948/9 West Ham U
McGowan, J. (1) 1946/7 Cork U
McGrath, M. (22) 1957/8 Blackburn R, Bradford Park Avenue
McGrath, P. (83) 1984/5 Manchester U, Aston Villa, Derby C
McLoughlin, A. F. (42) 1989/90 Swindon T, Southampton, Portsmouth
McMillan, W. (2) 1945/6 Belfast Celtic
McNally, J. B. (3) 1958/9 Luton T
McPhail, S. (10) 1999/00 Leeds U
McShane, P. D. (22) 2006/07 WBA, Sunderland, Hull C
Macken, A. (1) 1976/7 Derby Co
Macken, J. P. (1) 2004/05 Manchester C
Mackey, G. (3) 1956/7 Shamrock R
Mahon, A. J. (2) 1999/00 Tranmere R
Malone, G. (1) 1948/9 Shelbourne
Mancini, T. J. (5) 1973/4 QPR, Arsenal
Martin, C. J. (30) 1945/6 Glentoran, Leeds U, Aston Villa
Martin, M. P. (52) 1971/2 Bohemians, Manchester U, WBA, Newcastle U
Maybury, A. (10) 1997/8 Leeds U, Heart of Midlothian, Leicester C

Meagan, M. K. (17) 1960/1 Everton, Huddersfield T, Drogheda
Miller, L. W. P. (21) 2003/04 Celtic, Manchester U, Sunderland, Hibernian
Milligan, M. J. (1) 1991/2 Oldham Ath
Mooney, J. (2) 1964/5 Shamrock R
Moore, A. (8) 1995/6 Middlesbrough
Moran, K. (71) 1979/80 Manchester U, Sporting Gijon, Blackburn R
Moroney, T. (12) 1947/8 West Ham U, Evergreen U
Morris, C. B. (35) 1987/8 Celtic, Middlesbrough
Morrison, C. H. (36) 2001/02 Crystal P, Birmingham C, Crystal P
Moulson, G. B. (3) 1947/8 Lincoln C
Mucklan, C. (1) 1977/8 Drogheda
Mulligan, P. M. (50) 1968/9 Shamrock R, Chelsea, Crystal P, WBA, Shamrock R
Munroe, L. (1) 1953/4 Shamrock R
Murphy, A. (1) 1955/6 Clyde
Murphy, B. (1) 1985/6 Bohemians
Murphy, D. (9) 2006/07 Sunderland
Murphy, Jerry (1) 1979/80 Crystal P
Murphy, Joe (2) 2003/04 WBA, Scunthorpe U
Murphy, P. M. (1) 2006/07 Carlisle U
Murray, T. (1) 1949/50 Dundalk

Newman, W. (1) 1968/9 Shelbourne
Nolan, E. W. (3) 2008/09 Preston NE
Nolan, R. (10) 1956/7 Shamrock R

O'Brien, A. (5) 2006/07 Newcastle U
O'Brien, A. J. (26) 2000/01 Newcastle U, Portsmouth
O'Brien, F. (3) 1979/80 Philadelphia Fury
O'Brien, J. M. (3) 2005/06 Bolton W
O'Brien, L. (16) 1985/6 Shamrock R, Manchester U, Newcastle U, Tranmere R
O'Brien, R. (5) 1975/6 Notts Co
O'Byrne, L. B. (1) 1948/9 Shamrock R
O'Callaghan, B. R. (6) 1978/9 Stoke C
O'Callaghan, K. (21) 1980/1 Ipswich T, Portsmouth
O'Cearuill, J. (2) 2006/07 Arsenal
O'Connnell, A. (2) 1966/7 Dundalk, Bohemians
O'Connor, T. (4) 1949/50 Shamrock R
O'Connor, T. (7) 1967/8 Fulham, Dundalk, Bohemians
O'Dea, D. (2) 2009/10 Celtic
O'Driscoll, J. F. (3) 1948/9 Swansea T
O'Driscoll, S. (3) 1981/2 Fulham

O'Farrell, F. (9) 1951/2 West Ham U, Preston NE
O'Flanagan, K. P. (3) 1946/7 Arsenal
O'Flanagan, M. (1) 1946/7 Bohemians
O'Halloran, S. E. (2) 2006/07 Aston Villa
O'Hanlon, K. G. (1) 1987/8 Rotherham U
O'Keefe, E. (5) 1980/1 Everton, Port Vale
O'Leary, D. (68) 1976/7 Arsenal
O'Leary, P. (7) 1979/80 Shamrock R
O'Neill, F. S. (20) 1961/2 Shamrock R
O'Neill, J. (17) 1951/2 Everton
O'Neill, J. (1) 1960/1 Preston NE
O'Neill, K. P. (13) 1995/6 Norwich C, Middlesbrough
O'Regan, K. (4) 1983/4 Brighton & HA
O'Reilly, J. (2) 1945/6 Cork U
O'Shea, J. F. (62) 2001/02 Manchester U

Peyton, G. (33) 1976/7 Fulham, Bournemouth, Everton
Peyton, N. (6) 1956/7 Shamrock R, Leeds U
Phelan, T. (42) 1991/2 Wimbledon, Manchester C, Chelsea, Everton, Fulham
Potter, D. M. (5) 2006/07 Wolverhampton W

Quinn, A. (8) 2002/03 Sheffield W, Sheffield U
Quinn, B. S. (4) 1999/00 Coventry C
Quinn, N. J. (91) 1985/6 Arsenal, Manchester C, Sunderland

Reid, A. M. (27) 2003/04 Nottingham F, Tottenham H, Charlton Ath, Sunderland
Reid, S. J. (23) 2001/02 Millwall, Blackburn R
Richardson, D. J. (3) 1971/2 Shamrock R, Gillingham
Ringstead, A. (20) 1950/1 Sheffield U
Robinson, M. (24) 1980/1 Brighton & HA, Liverpool, QPR
Roche, P. J. (8) 1971/2 Shelbourne, Manchester U
Rogers, E. (19) 1967/8 Blackburn R, Charlton Ath
Rowlands, M. C. (5) 2003/04 QPR
Ryan, G. (18) 1977/8 Derby Co, Brighton & HA
Ryan, R. A. (16) 1949/50 WBA, Derby C

Sadlier, R. T. (1) 2001/02 Millwall
Savage, D. P. T. (5) 1995/6 Millwall

Saward, P. (18) 1953/4 Millwall, Aston Villa, Huddersfield T
Scannell, T. (1) 1953/4 Southend U
Scully, P. J. (1) 1988/9 Arsenal
Sheedy, K. (46) 1983/4 Everton, Newcastle U
Sheridan, C. (2) 2009/10 Celtic
Sheridan, J. J. (34) 1987/8 Leeds U, Sheffield W
Slaven, B. (7) 1989/90 Middlesbrough
Sloan, J. W. (2) 1945/6 Arsenal
Smyth, M. (1) 1968/9 Shamrock R
Stapleton, F. (71) 1976/7 Arsenal, Manchester U, Ajax, Le Havre, Blackburn R
Staunton, S. (102) 1988/9 Liverpool, Aston Villa, Liverpool, Aston Villa
St. Ledger-Hall, S. P. (12) 2008/09 Preston NE
Stevenson, A. E. (6) 1946/7 Everton
Stokes, A. (3) 2006/07 Sunderland
Strahan, F. (5) 1963/4 Shelbourne
Swan, M. M. G. (1) 1959/60 Drumcondra
Synott, N. (3) 1977/8 Shamrock R

Taylor T. (1) 1958/9 Waterford
Thomas, P. (2) 1973/4 Waterford
Thompson, J. (1) 2003/04 Nottingham F
Townsend, A. D. (70) 1988/9 Norwich C, Chelsea, Aston Villa, Middlesbrough
Traynor, T. J. (8) 1953/4 Southampton
Treacy, R. C. P. (42) 1965/6 WBA, Charlton Ath, Swindon T, Preston NE, WBA, Shamrock R
Tuohy, L. (8) 1955/6 Shamrock R, Newcastle U, Shamrock R
Turner, P. (2) 1962/3 Celtic

Vernon, J. (2) 1945/6 Belfast Celtic

Waddock, G. (21) 1979/80 QPR, Millwall
Walsh, D. J. (20) 1945/6 Linfield, WBA, Aston Villa
Walsh, J. (1) 1981/2 Limerick
Walsh, M. (21) 1975/6 Blackpool, Everton, QPR, Porto
Walsh, M. (4) 1981/2 Everton
Walsh, W. (9) 1946/7 Manchester C
Waters, J. (2) 1976/7 Grimsby T
Westwood, K. (5) 2008/09 Coventry C
Whelan, G. D. (20) 2007/08 Stoke C
Whelan, R. (2) 1963/4 St Patrick's Ath
Whelan, R. (53) 1980/1 Liverpool, Southend U
Whelan, W. (4) 1955/6 Manchester U
Whittaker, R. (1) 1958/9 Chelsea

BRITISH ISLES INTERNATIONAL GOALSCORERS SINCE 1946

ENGLAND

Name	Goals
A'Court, A.	1
Adams, T.A.	5
Allen, R.	2
Anderson, V.	2
Anderton, D.R.	7
Astall, G.	1
Atyeo, P.J.W.	5
Baily, E.F.	5
Baker, J.H.	3
Ball, A.J.	8
Barmby, N.J.	4
Barnes, J.	11
Barnes, P.S.	4
Barry, G.	2
Beardsley, P.A.	9
Beattie, J.K.	1
Beckham, D.R.J.	17
Bell, C.	9
Bentley, R.T.F.	9
Blissett, L.	3
Bowles, S.	1
Bradford, G.R.W.	1
Bradley, W.	2
Bridge, W.M.	1
Bridges, B.J.	1
Broadbent, P.F.	2
Broadis, I.A.	8
Brooking, T.D.	5
Brooks, J.	2
Brown, W.M.	1
Bull, S.G.	4
Butcher, T.	3
Byrne, J.J.	8
Campbell, S.J.	1
Carter, H.S.	5
Chamberlain, M.	1
Channon, M.R.	21
Charlton, J.	6
Charlton, R.	49
Chivers, M.	13
Clarke, A.J.	10
Cole, A.	1
Cole, J.J.	10
Connelly, J.M.	7
Coppell, S.J.	7
Cowans, G.	2
Crawford, R.	1
Crouch, P.J.	21
Currie, A.W.	3
Defoe, J.C.	12
Dixon, L.M.	1
Dixon, K.M.	4
Douglas, B.	11
Eastham, G.	2
Edwards, D.	5
Ehiogu, U.	1
Elliott, W.H.	3
Ferdinand, L.	5
Ferdinand, R.G.	3
Finney, T.	30
Flowers, R.	10
Fowler, R.B.	7
Francis, G.C.J.	3
Francis, T.	12
Froggatt, J.	2
Froggatt, R.	2
Gascoigne, P.J.	10
Gerrard, S.G.	17
Goddard, P.	1
Grainger, C.	3
Greaves, J.	44
Haines, J.T.W.	2
Hancocks, J.	2
Hassall, H.W.	4
Hateley, M.	9
Haynes, J.N.	18
Heskey, E.W.	7
Hirst, D.E.	1
Hitchens, G.A.	5
Hoddle, G.	8
Hughes, E.W.	1
Hunt, R.	18
Hunter, N.	2
Hurst, G.C.	24
Ince P.E.C.	2
Jeffers, F.	1
Jenas, J.A.	1
Johnson, D.E.	6
Johnson, G.M.C.	1
Kay, A.H.	1
Keegan, J.K.	21
Kennedy, R.	3
Keown, M.R.	2
Kevan, D.T.	8
Kidd, B.	1
King, L.B.	2
Lampard, F.J.	20
Langton, R.	1
Latchford, R.D.	5
Lawler, C.	1
Lawton, T.	16
Lee, F.	10
Lee, J.	1
Lee, R.M.	2
Lee, S.	2
Le Saux, G.P.	1
Lineker, G.	48
Lofthouse, N.	30
Mabbutt, G.	1
McDermott, T.	3
Macdonald, M.	6
McManaman, S.	3
Mannion, W.J.	11
Mariner, P.	13
Marsh, R.W.	1
Matthews, S.	3
Medley, L.D.	1
Melia, J.	1
Merson, P.C.	3
Milburn, J.E.T.	10
Moore, R.F.	2
Morris, J.	3
Mortensen, S.H.	23
Mullen, J.	6
Mullery, A.P.	1
Murphy, D.B.	1
Neal, P.G.	5
Nicholls, J.	1
Nicholson, W.E.	1
Nugent, D.J.	1
O'Grady, M.	3
Owen, M.J.	40
Own goals	31
Paine, T.L.	7
Palmer, C.L.	1
Parry, R.A.	1
Peacock, A.	3
Pearce, S.	5
Pearson, J.S.	5
Pearson, S.C.	5
Perry, W.	2
Peters, M.	20
Pickering, F.	5
Platt, D.	27
Pointer, R.	2

Liddell, W.	6	Ormond, W.E.	2	Blackmore, C.G.	1
Linwood, A.B.	1	Orr, T.	1	Blake, N.A.	4
Lorimer, P.	4	Own goals	9	Bodin, P.J.	3
				Bowen, D.I.	3
Macari, L.	5	Parlane, D.	1	Bowen, M.	2
MacDougall, E.J.	3	Pettigrew, W.	2	Boyle, T.	1
MacKay, D.C.	4	Provan, D.	1	Burgess, W.A.R.	1
Mackay, G.	1				
MacKenzie, J.A.	1	Quashie, N.F.	1	Charles, J.	1
MacLeod, M.	1	Quinn, J.	7	Charles, M.	6
McAllister, G.	5	Quinn, P.	1	Charles, W.J.	15
McAvennie, F.	1			Church, S.R.	1
McCall, S.M.	1	Reilly, L.	22	Clarke, R.J.	5
McCalliog, J.	1	Ring, T.	2	Coleman, C.	4
McCann, N.	3	Rioch, B.D.	6	Collins, J.	2
McClair, B.	2	Ritchie, P.S.	1	Curtis, A.	6
McCoist, A.	19	Robertson, A.	2		
McCormack, R.	1	Robertson, J.	3	Davies, G.	2
McCulloch, L.	1	Robertson, J.N.	8	Davies, R.T.	9
McFadden, J.	15*	Robson, B.	1	Davies, R.W.	6
McGhee, M.	2			Davies, Simon	6
McGinlay, J.	3	St John, I.	9	Deacy, N.	4
McInally, A.	3	Scott, A.S.	5	Durban, A.	2
McKimmie, S.I.	1	Sharp, G.	1	Dwyer, P.	2
McKinlay, W.	4	Shearer, D.	2		
McKinnon, R.	1	Smith, G.	4	Earnshaw, R.	14
McLaren, A.	4	Souness, G.J.	4	Eastwood, F.	4
McLean, T.	1	Steel, W.	12	Edwards, D.	3
McLintock, F.	1	Stein, C.	10	Edwards, G.	2
McManus S.	1	Stewart, R.	1	Edwards, R.I.	4
McMillan, I.L.	2	Strachan, G.	5	England, H.M.	4
McNeill, W.	3	Sturrock, P.	3	Evans, C.	2
McPhail, J.	3			Evans, I.	1
McQueen, G.	5	Thompson, S.	3		
McStay, P.	9	Thornton, W.	1	Fletcher, C.	1
McSwegan, G.J.	1			Flynn, B.	7
Maloney, S.	1			Ford, T.	23
Mason, J.	4	Waddell, W.	6	Foulkes, W.J.	1
Masson, D.S.	5	Wallace, I.A.	1		
Miller, K.	11	Wark, J.	7	Giggs, R.J.	12
Miller, W.	1	Webster, A.	1	Giles, D.	2
Mitchell, R.C.	1	Weir, A.	1	Godfrey, B.C.	2
Morgan, W.	1	Weir, D.	1	Griffiths, A.T.	6
Morris, H.	3	White, J.A.	3	Griffiths, M.W.	2
Mudie, J.K.	9	Wilkie, L.	1		
Mulhall, G.	1	Wilson, D.	9	Harris, C.S.	1
Murdoch, R.	5			Hartson, J.	14
Murray, J.	1	Young, A.	2	Hewitt, R.	1
				Hockey, T.	1
Narey, D.	1	**WALES**		Hodges, G.	2
Naysmith, G.A.	1	Allchurch, I.J.	23	Horne, B.	2
Nevin, P.K.F.	5	Allen, M.	3	Hughes, L.M.	16
Nicholas, C.	5				
		Bale, G.	2	James, L.	10
O'Connor, G.	4	Barnes, W.	1	James, R.	7
O'Hare, J.	5	Bellamy, C.D.	17	Jones, A.	1

The Scottish FA officially changed Robsons's goal against Iceland on 10 September 2008 to McFadden.

Jones, B.S. 2
Jones, Cliff 16
Jones, D.E. 1
Jones, J.P. 1

Koumas, J. 10
Kryzwicki, R.I. 1

Ledley, J. 2
Leek, K. 5
Llewelyn, C.M 1
Lovell, S. 1
Lowrie, G. 2

Mahoney, J.F. 1
Medwin, T.C. 6
Melville, A.K. 3
Moore, G. 1

Nicholas, P. 2

O'Sullivan, P.A. 1
Own goals 8

Palmer, D. 1
Parry, P.I. 1
Paul, R. 1
Pembridge, M.A. 6
Phillips, D. 2
Powell, A. 1
Powell, D. 1
Price, P. 1

Ramsay, A. 2
Reece, G.I. 2
Rees, R.R. 3
Roberts, P.S. 1
Robinson, C.P. 1
Robinson, J.R.C. 3
Rush, I. 28

Saunders, D. 22
Savage R.W. 2
Slatter, N. 2
Smallman, D.P. 1
Speed, G.A. 7
Symons, C.J. 2

Tapscott, D.R. 4
Taylor, G.J. 1
Thomas, M. 4
Toshack, J.B. 12

Vaughan, D.O. 1
Vernon, T.R. 8
Vokes, S.M. 2

Walsh, I. 7
Williams, A. 1

Williams, G.E. 1
Williams, G.G. 1
Woosnam, A.P. 3

Yorath, T.C. 2
Young, E. 1

NORTHERN IRELAND

Anderson, T. 4
Armstrong, G. 12

Barr, H.H. 1
Best, G. 9
Bingham, W.L. 10
Black, K. 1
Blanchflower, D. 2
Blanchflower, J. 1
Brennan, R.A. 1
Brotherston, N. 3
Brunt, C. 1

Campbell, W.G. 1
Casey, T. 2
Caskey, W. 1
Cassidy, T. 1
Clarke, C.J. 13
Clements, D. 2
Cochrane, T. 1
Crossan, E. 1
Crossan, J.A. 10
Cush, W.W. 5

Davis S. 2
D'Arcy, S.D. 1
Doherty, I. 1
Doherty, P.D. 2
Dougan, A.D. 8
Dowie, I. 12

Elder, A.R. 1
Elliott, S. 4
Evans, J.G. 1

Feeney, W. 1
Feeney, W.J. 5
Ferguson, W. 1
Ferris, R.O. 1
Finney, T. 2

Gibson, W. 1
Gillespie, K.R. 2
Gray, P. 6
Griffin, D.J. 1

Hamilton, B. 4
Hamilton, W. 5
Harkin, J.T. 2

Harvey, M. 3
Healy, D.J. 35
Hill, C.F. 1
Humphries, W. 1
Hughes, M.E. 5
Hunter, A. 1
Hunter, B.V. 1

Irvine, W.J. 8

Johnston, W.C. 1
Jones, J. 1
Jones, S. 1

Lafferty, K. 7
Lennon, N.F. 2
Lockhart, N. 3
Lomas, S.M. 3

Magilton, J. 5
McAdams, W.J. 7
McAuley, G. 1
McCann, G.S. 4
McCartney, G. 1
McClelland, J. 1
McCrory, S. 1
McCurdy, C. 1
McDonald, A. 3
McGarry, J.K. 1
McGrath, R.C. 4
McIlroy, J. 10
McIlroy, S.B. 5
McLaughlin, J.C. 6
McMahon, G.J. 2
McMordie, A.S. 3
McMorran, E.J. 4
McParland, P.J. 10
Moreland, V. 1
Morgan, S. 3
Morrow, S.J. 1
Mulryne, P.P. 3
Murdoch, C.J. 1

Neill, W.J.T. 2
Nelson, S. 1
Nicholl, C.J. 3
Nicholl, J.M. 1
Nicholson, J.J. 6

O'Boyle, G. 1
O'Kane, W.J. 1
O'Neill, J. 2
O'Neill, M.A. 4
O'Neill, M.H. 8
Own goals 9

Patterson, D.J. 1
Peacock, R. 2
Penney, S. 2

Quinn, J.M. 12
Quinn, S.J. 4

Rowland, K. 1

Simpson, W.J. 5
Smyth, S. 5
Spence, D.W. 3
Sproule, I. 1
Stewart, I. 2

Taggart, G.P. 7
Tully, C.P. 3

Walker, J. 1
Walsh, D.J. 5
Welsh, E. 1
Whiteside, N. 9
Whitley, Jeff 2
Williams, M.S. 1
Wilson, D.J. 1
Wilson, K.J. 6
Wilson, S.J. 7

EIRE

Aldridge, J. 19
Ambrose, P. 1
Anderson, J. 1
Andrews, K. 1

Barrett, G. 2
Brady, L. 9
Breen, G. 7
Byrne, J. 4

Cantwell, J. 14
Carey, J. 3
Carroll, T. 1
Cascarino, A. 19
Coad, P. 3
Connolly, D.J. 9
Conroy, T. 2
Conway, J. 3
Coyne, T. 6
Cummins, G. 5
Curtis, D. 8

Daly, G. 13
Dempsey, J. 1
Dennehy, M. 2
Doherty, G.M.T. 4
Doyle, K.E. 8
Duff, D.A. 7
Duffy, B. 1
Dunne, R.P. 7

Eglinton, T. 2

Elliott, S.W. 1

Fagan, F. 5
Fallon, S. 2
Farrell, P. 3
Finnan, S. 2
Fitzgerald, J. 1
Fitzgerald, P. 2
Fitzsimons, A. 7
Fogarty, A. 3
Foley, D. 2
Fullam, J. 1

Galvin, A. 1
Gavin, J. 2
Giles, J. 5
Givens, D. 19
Glynn, D. 1
Grealish, T. 8
Green, P.J. 1
Grimes, A.A. 1

Hale, A. 2
Hand, E. 2
Harte, I.P. 11
Haverty, J. 3
Healy, C. 1
Holland, M.R. 5
Holmes, J. 1
Houghton, R. 6
Hughton, C. 1
Hunt, S.P. 1
Hurley, C. 2

Ireland, S.J. 4
Irwin, D. 4

Kavanagh, G.A. 1
Keane, R.D. 43
Keane, R.M. 9
Kelly, D. 9
Kelly, G. 2
Kennedy, M. 4
Keogh, A. 1
Kernaghan, A. 1
Kilbane, K.D. 7
Kinsella, M.A. 3

Lawrence, L. 2
Lawrenson, M. 5
Leech, M. 2
Long, S.P. 3

McAteer, J.W. 3
McCann, J. 1
McCarthy, M. 2
McEvoy, A. 6

McGee, P. 4
McGrath, P. 8
McLoughlin, A. 2
McPhail, S. 1
Mancini, T. 1
Martin, C. 6
Martin, M. 4
Miller, L.W.P. 1
Mooney, J. 1
Moran, K. 6
Moroney, T. 1
Morrison, C.H. 9
Mulligan, P. 1

O'Brien, A.J. 1
O'Callaghan, K. 1
O'Connor, T. 2
O'Farrell, F. 2
O'Keefe, E. 1
O'Leary, D.A. 1
O'Neill, F. 1
O'Neill, K.P. 4
O'Reilly, J. 1
O'Shea, J.F. 1
Own goals 10

Quinn, N. 21

Reid, A.M. 4
Reid, S.J. 2
Ringstead, A. 7
Robinson, M. 4
Rogers, E. 5
Ryan, G. 1
Ryan, R. 3

St Ledger-Hall, S.P. 1
Sheedy, K. 9
Sheridan, J. 5
Slaven, B. 1
Sloan, J. 1
Stapleton, F. 20
Staunton, S. 7
Strahan, F. 1

Townsend, A.D. 7
Treacy, R. 5
Tuohy, L. 4

Waddock, G. 3
Walsh, D. 5
Walsh, M. 3
Waters, J. 1
Whelan, G.D. 2
Whelan, R. 3

BLUE SQUARE PREMIER 2009–2010

		Home					Away					Total						
		P	W	D	L	F	A	W	D	L	F	A	W	D	L	F	A	GD	Pts
1	Stevenage B	44	16	5	1	44	11	14	4	4	35	13	30	9	5	79	24	55	99
2	Luton T (R)	44	14	3	5	54	22	12	7	3	30	18	26	10	8	84	40	44	88
3	Oxford U¶	44	16	4	2	37	10	9	7	6	27	21	25	11	8	64	31	33	86
4	Rushden & D	44	12	6	4	40	21	10	7	5	37	18	22	13	9	77	39	38	79
5	York C	44	13	7	2	40	15	9	5	8	22	20	22	12	10	62	35	27	78
6	Kettering T	44	6	8	8	27	23	12	4	6	24	18	18	12	14	51	41	10	66
7	Crawley T	44	14	3	5	33	24	5	6	11	17	33	19	9	16	50	57	–7	66
8	AFC Wimbledon (P)	44	8	5	9	30	19	10	5	7	31	28	18	10	16	61	47	14	64
9	Mansfield T	44	9	8	5	34	22	8	3	11	35	38	17	11	16	69	60	9	62
10	Cambridge U	44	11	4	7	44	24	4	10	8	21	29	15	14	15	65	53	12	59
11	Wrexham	44	9	7	6	26	17	6	6	10	19	22	15	13	16	45	39	6	58
12	Salisbury C*	44	11	5	6	33	21	10	0	12	25	42	21	5	18	58	63	–5	58
13	Kidderminster H	44	11	3	8	31	21	4	9	9	26	31	15	12	17	57	52	5	57
14	Altrincham	44	7	7	8	29	25	6	8	8	24	26	13	15	16	53	51	2	54
15	Barrow	44	7	9	6	27	29	6	4	12	23	38	13	13	18	50	67	–17	52
16	Tamworth (P)	44	7	6	9	26	30	4	10	8	16	22	11	16	17	42	52	–10	49
17	Hayes & Yeading U (P)	44	7	7	8	38	38	5	5	12	21	47	12	12	20	59	85	–26	48
18	Histon	44	6	9	7	24	28	5	4	13	20	39	11	13	20	44	67	–23	46
19	Eastbourne B	44	8	7	7	26	29	3	6	13	16	43	11	13	20	42	72	–30	46
20	Gateshead* (P)	44	10	3	9	24	23	3	4	15	22	46	13	7	24	46	69	–23	45
21	Forest Green R	44	9	5	8	27	29	3	4	15	23	47	12	9	23	50	76	–26	45
22	Ebbsfleet U	44	7	4	11	25	36	5	4	13	25	46	12	8	24	50	82	–32	44
23	Grays Ath	44	4	5	13	16	41	1	8	13	19	50	5	13	26	35	91	–56	28

Chester City (R) – record expunged.

*Salisbury City deducted 10 points, Gateshead deducted 1 point.

¶Oxford United promoted via play-offs.

Leading Goalscorers 2009–10

	Club	League	Play-Offs	FA Cup	Total
Matt Tubbs	(Salisbury City)	27	0	4	31
Richard Brodie	(York City)	26	1	4	31
James Constable	(Oxford United)	22	3	1	26
Tom Craddock	(Luton Town)	22	0	1	23
Danny Kedwell	(AFC Wimbledon)	21	0	1	22
Danny Crow	(Cambridge United)	19	0	0	19
Jake Speight	(Mansfield Town)	17	0	0	17
Kevin Gallen	(Luton Town)	16	0	2	18
Magno Vieira	(Ebbsfleet United)	16	0	0	16
Chris Senior	(Altrincham)	15	0	0	15

BLUE SQUARE PREMIER RESULTS 2009–2010

	AFC Wimbledon	Altrincham	Barrow	Cambridge U	Crawley T	Eastbourne B	Ebbsfleet U	Forest Green R	Gateshead	Grays Ath	Hayes & Yeading U	Histon	Kettering T	Kidderminster H	Luton T	Mansfield T	Oxford U	Rushden & D	Salisbury C	Stevenage B	Tamworth	Wrexham	York C
AFC Wimbledon	—	1-1	0-2	0-0	1-1	2-0	3-0	2-0	2-0	0-2	5-2	4-0	1-2	0-1	1-1	2-0	0-1	2-2	4-0	0-3	0-1	2-2	0-1
Altrincham	0-1	—	0-1	0-2	0-0	3-0	1-1	2-2	3-2	1-1	3-1	2-1	2-0	3-2	0-1	1-2	0-1	2-2	5-0	0-3	0-0	1-3	0-0
Barrow	2-2	0-3	—	0-1	4-1	3-2	4-0	1-0	3-3	2-2	1-1	0-0	0-2	1-0	2-1	3-1	1-1	1-6	3-1	0-0	1-0	2-1	0-0
Cambridge U	2-2	0-2	0-1	—	1-0	2-0	2-1	7-0	3-0	2-0	4-1	2-0	0-2	1-0	3-4	3-1	1-1	2-2	1-1	1-3	2-0	2-0	0-1
Crawley T	2-1	1-0	4-1	0-2	—	2-2	1-2	3-1	1-4	1-1	1-0	1-1	2-1	2-2	2-1	0-2	1-2	2-1	2-0	0-3	2-0	1-0	3-1
Eastbourne B	1-0	2-2	2-1	2-1	2-2	—	1-2	1-3	2-1	2-2	3-1	0-1	0-1	2-2	0-1	1-2	1-0	1-1	0-1	0-6	1-1	2-1	3-1
Ebbsfleet U	2-2	1-2	1-4	1-3	4-0	2-2	—	4-3	2-0	2-1	1-2	1-2	1-2	0-0	0-1	1-2	0-1	0-0	1-2	2-1	0-1	2-1	1-0
Forest Green R	2-5	4-3	1-0	1-0	3-1	1-1	0-0	—	1-0	2-1	0-0	0-1	1-2	1-1	1-6	1-4	0-1	3-4	2-1	1-1	3-4	0-2	1-0
Gateshead	1-0	1-0	2-1	2-0	2-3	1-0	1-3	3-1	—	3-0	0-0	0-3	0-2	0-1	0-1	1-3	0-1	1-1	0-2	0-0	1-1	1-0	1-2
Grays Ath	2-4	0-3	3-3	2-0	2-1	1-1	0-3	2-1	4-0	—	0-0	0-1	0-0	0-2	0-1	1-1	0-4	1-0	3-4	1-2	1-0	0-2	0-4
Hayes & Yeading U	1-0	0-0	2-2	3-0	1-1	4-0	4-2	2-3	3-2	4-0	—	0-2	1-0	1-3	0-2	0-5	2-1	0-3	0-2	1-1	2-2	0-1	1-1
Histon	1-3	2-0	1-1	2-1	0-1	0-2	1-0	5-2	0-0	0-1	3-3	—	1-0	2-2	2-3	2-2	3-4	1-6	1-2	0-2	0-0	1-1	1-1
Kettering T	1-2	2-0	2-0	1-0	1-1	4-1	3-0	0-2	4-0	2-0	1-0	1-1	—	1-1	0-2	3-1	1-1	0-3	4-0	1-1	2-1	0-0	0-1
Kidderminster H	0-1	3-0	1-0	2-2	1-0	2-3	2-3	2-1	3-2	4-1	1-3	3-0	0-1	—	0-0	4-1	3-1	0-2	4-2	1-0	0-0	2-2	0-1
Luton T	1-2	1-2	4-1	3-0	3-0	4-0	3-0	2-1	2-1	6-0	0-2	6-3	0-2	1-2	—	0-0	2-1	0-3	1-0	0-1	2-1	1-0	0-1
Mansfield T	0-1	1-1	1-0	4-0	4-0	2-0	4-2	1-0	0-2	0-2	3-1	2-0	0-0	3-1	1-2	—	1-1	3-2	2-1	2-3	3-2	0-1	2-1
Oxford U	2-0	1-1	1-0	0-0	3-1	4-2	2-3	0-0	5-0	5-0	2-1	3-0	1-1	3-3	0-1	2-0	—	1-3	3-1	2-1	0-0	0-1	1-1
Rushden & D	0-1	0-1	0-0	3-1	1-1	2-0	3-1	4-2	8-0	5-4	2-1	1-0	2-0	0-0	0-0	1-0	1-1	—	1-3	0-1	1-1	2-1	0-1
Salisbury C	0-2	4-1	1-1	2-2	2-2	3-1	3-0	1-3	5-4	0-1	3-1	3-0	2-0	4-2	1-0	2-1	3-1	1-3	—	1-0	1-1	0-0	2-1
Stevenage B	0-0	3-0	4-0	2-0	2-0	3-0	4-2	1-3	1-1	1-1	4-0	1-3	2-0	1-0	1-1	2-4	1-0	0-1	2-0	—	1-0	1-1	1-1
Tamworth	2-2	1-1	0-2	0-0	0-1	1-1	1-1	0-0	0-1	2-1	2-2	0-0	1-3	0-0	0-1	2-1	0-1	0-1	1-0	1-0	—	0-0	1-0
Wrexham	1-0	0-2	3-0	2-2	3-0	3-0	0-1	1-0	2-1	2-1	0-2	3-1	2-0	2-1	1-0	2-1	0-1	0-1	1-2	1-1	0-0	—	2-1
York C	5-0	2-1	3-0	2-2	2-0	0-1	0-1	2-0	1-0	1-1	1-1	1-1	0-1	0-1	3-0	3-0	1-1	0-0	1-2	1-1	1-1	2-1	—

BLUE SQUARE PREMIER
PLAY-OFFS 2009–2010

BLUE SQUARE PREMIER SEMI-FINALS FIRST LEG

Rushden & D	(0) 1	Oxford U	(1) 1
York C	(0) 1	Luton T	(0) 0

BLUE SQUARE PREMIER SEMI-FINALS SECOND LEG

Luton T	(0) 0	York C	(0) 1
Oxford U	(0) 2	Rushden & D	(0) 0

BLUE SQUARE PREMIER FINAL (at Wembley)

Sunday, 16 May 2010

Oxford U (2) 3 *(Green M 15, Constable 21, Potter 90)*

York C (1) 1 *(Clarke 42 (og))* 38,857

Oxford U: Clarke; Batt, Tonkin, Bulman, Creighton, Wright, Chapman (Day), Midson (Deering), Constable, Green M (Potter), Clist.
York C: Ingham; Purkiss, Meredith, Mackin, McGurk, Graham, Lawless, Barrett (Sangare), Rankine (Gash), Brodie, Carruthers (Pitt).
Referee: M. Naylor (Sheffield).

ATTENDANCES BY CLUB 2009–2010

	Aggregate 2009–10	Average 2009–10	Highest Attendance 2009–10
Luton Town	152,851	6,947	8,860 v Oxford United
Oxford United	132,084	6,003	10,613 v Luton Town
AFC Wimbledon	77,963	3,543	4,688 v Luton Town
Mansfield Town	70,540	3,206	7,261 v Gateshead
Cambridge United	67,701	3,077	4,870 v Luton Town
Wrexham	62,923	2,860	5,672 v Rushden & Diamonds
York City	58,619	2,664	4,587 v Mansfield Town
Stevenage Borough	56,968	2,589	7,024 v Luton Town
Rushden & Diamonds	36,918	1,678	4,820 v Luton Town
Kidderminster Harriers	34,054	1,547	3,569 v Oxford United
Kettering Town	30,506	1,386	3,266 v Luton Town
Barrow	27,580	1,253	1,969 v Altrincham
Eastbourne Borough	26,774	1,217	3,108 v AFC Wimbledon
Tamworth	24,012	1,091	2,246 v Luton Town
Ebbsfleet United	23,505	1,068	2,005 v AFC Wimbledon
Altrincham	23,457	1,066	1,821 v Wrexham
Salisbury City	22,873	1,039	2,677 v Oxford United
Forest Green Rovers	22,269	1,012	1,921 v AFC Wimbledon
Crawley Town	22,061	1,002	2,118 v Luton Town
Histon	18,684	849	2,371 v Cambridge United
Grays Athletic	15,057	684	1,762 v AFC Wimbledon
Gateshead	14,679	667	1,304 v AFC Wimbledon
Hayes & Yeading	13,900	631	1,881 v Luton Town
Chester City	15,087	1,160	1,757 v Cambridge United

APPEARANCES AND GOALSCORERS 2009–2010

AFC WIMBLEDON
League Appearances: Adjei, 17(5); Blanchett, 11; Brown, 17(1); Conroy, J. 21(11); Cumbers, 2(2); Duncan, 13(9); Elder, 12(6); Gerrard, 5(1); Godfrey, 7(10); Gregory, 35(2); Harmsworth, (3); Hatton, 34(6); Hendry, 17(2); Hussey, 15; Inns, 5(2); Jackson, 2(1); Johnson, 36(1); Judge, B. 21(5); Kedwell, 39; Lorraine, 37; Main, 19(8); Montague, 5(11); Moore, 25(6); Parker, (2); Poole, 12(5); Pullen, 26; Rapson, (2); Stafford, (2); Stenning, (1); Taylor, 29(3); Turner, 1; Wellard, 21(11).
Goals – League (61): Kedwell 21 (3 pens), Main 11 (3 pens), Moore 7, Taylor 5, Elder 3, Poole 3 (1 pen), Montague 2, Cumbers 1, Godfrey 1, Gregory 1, Hatton 1, Hendry 1, Johnson 1, Judge 1, Wellard 1, own goal 1.
FA Cup (5): Hatton 1, Kedwell 1, Main 1, Moore 1, Taylor 1.

ALTRINCHAM
League Appearances: Brown, R. 13(4); Bryan, 1; Burns, 5(2); Carden, 3(12); Clee, 24(11); Coburn, 40; Crowell, 5; Danylyk, 38(2); Denham, 28(10); Densmore, 42; Doran, 14(3); Doughty, 23(1); Heffernan, D. 3(6); Johnson, 9(1); Kearney, 29(1); Lawton, 20(8); Little, 12(19); McAliskey, 14(6); Moffatt, 1; Moyo, (4); Owens, (1); Pearson, (5); Saunders, 4; Senior, 40(1); Sheridan, 4(1); Smith, 34(1); Thaker, (2); Thornley, (1); Welch, 2(10); Williams, 39(4); Young, 37(3).
Goals – League (53): Senior 15 (2 pens), Denham 10, Young 5, Densmore 4 (2 pens), Doughty 3 (2 pens), Williams 3, Kearney 2, Little 2, McAliskey 2, Burns 1, Clee 1, Crowell 1, Danylyk 1, Doran 1, Johnson 1, own goal 1.
FA Cup (0).

BARROW
League Appearances: Blundell, 10(9); Bolland, P. 31(1); Bond, 36(4); Bowery, 1(3); Boyd, 19(10); Brown, (2); Chadwick, 17(3); Cook, 1(2); Deasy, 24; Dugdale, 10(1); Edwards, 12; Foley, 3; Goodfellow, 1(1); Green, 2; Hulbert, 34(3); Jelleyman, 25(1); Jones, 30(2); Kamara, 6; Logan, 22(13); McEvilly, 1(5); Morris, (1); Nelthorpe, 6; Newton, 4; Owen, 1(2); Pearson, 29(3); Powell, (2); Rogan, 1(4); Rothery, (2); Rutherford, 29(9); Shaw, 13(1); Sheridan, 7; Spender, 41; Taylor, 2(3); Tomlinson, 20; Wainwright, 5; Walker, 32(4); Wiles, 9(9).
Goals – League (50): Walker 14 (4 pens), Chadwick 8, Shaw 5, Bond 4 (2 pens), Blundell 2, Bolland 2, Jones 2, Kamara 2, Nelthorpe 2, Wiles 2, Boyd 1, Cook 1, Goodfellow 1, Logan 1, own goals 3.
FA Cup (11): Bond 3 (1 pen), Cook 2, Walker 2 (1 pen), Bolland 1, Goodfellow 1, Logan 1, Rutherford 1.

CAMBRIDGE UNITED
League Appearances: Beesley, 4(13); Berry, (1); Brown, S. 17; Carden, 38; Challinor, (2); Coakley, 5(2); Coulson, 22(1); Crow, 37(4); Gleeson, 31(1); Hatswell, 23; Holroyd, 24(1); Hudson, 2; Ives, 9(16); Marriott, 2(7); McAuley, 21(6); Murray, 6(6); Nielson, 14; Palmer, 14(1); Parkinson, 15(3); Partridge, 11; Patrick, (2); Phillips, 16(16); Pitt, 11(5); Potter, 26; Reason, 31(7); Roberts, 5(1); Russell, 13(2); Saah, 35; Tonkin, 19(1); Walker, 1; Willmott, 27(2); Willock, 5(8).
Goals – League (65): Crow 19 (5 pens), Holroyd 12 (3 pens), Marriott 4, Hatswell 3, Nielson 3, Saah 3, Beesley 2, Carden 2, Coulson 2, Ives 2, Phillips 2, Pitt 2, Reason 2, Willmott 2, Hudson 1, McAuley 1, Murray 1, Parkinson 1, own goal 1.
FA Cup (8): Hatswell 1, Holroyd 1, McAuley 1, Marriott 1, Pitt 1, Reason 1, Tonkin 1, Willmott 1.

CHESTER CITY
League Appearances: Alessandra, 4; Ashton, N. 19; Barry, A. 11(3); Beesley, 8; Blundell, 10(9); Chadwick, N. 21(2); Coulson, 5; Coulter, 2(1); Danby, J. 28; Davidson, 2(3); Ellams, L. 9(7); Flynn, 3; Freeman, 1; Jones, B. 4; Kay, 13(3); Kelly, S. 15(3); Keltie, 11; Lea, M. 18(1); Lynch, 10; Meynell, R. 11(6); Murphy, (1); Owen, J. 7(5); Platt, K. 2(3);

Rawlinson, C. (3); Rea, 3(1); Roberts, K. 27(1); Rule, G. 14(3); Ryan, T. 24; Vaughan, J. 1; Vaughan, S. 6; Wilkinson , B. 19(7).
Goals – League (23): Chadwick 7, Blundell 3 (2 pens), Wilkinson 3, Beesley 2, Roberts 2, Barry 1, Coulson 1, Kelly 1, Rea 1, Rule 1, own goal 1.
FA Cup (1): Flynn 1.

CRAWLEY TOWN
League Appearances: Ademeno, 26(6); Barton, 1(1); Broadhurst, 32(2); Carruthers, 6(1); Carter, 2(4); Cogan, 31(6); Collins, 2; Cook, 6; Djilali, 5; Forrest, 17(16); Giles, 9; Hutchinson, 34(5); Jordan, 9(1); Killeen, 19(10); King, (2); Langston, 8; Lokanbo, 1(1); Louis, 10(8); Malcolm, 22(17); Napper, (7); Pinault, 38(2); Powell, 1(2); Quinn, 28; Rayner, 35; Rents, 39; Rusk, 36(2); Smith, 27(7); Willock, 12(4); Wilson, 28(4).
Goals – League (50): Ademeno 11, Smith 7, Forrest 6 (3 pens), Louis 5, Cogan 3, Cook 3, Malcolm 3, Wilson 3, Hutchinson 2, Killeen 2, Willock 2, Carruthers 1, Pinault 1, Rents 1.
FA Cup (2): Forrest 1, Louis 1.

EASTBOURNE BOROUGH
League Appearances: Armstrong, 27(2); Atkin, 16(16); Austin, 41; Baker, 27(5); Benjamin, 16(5); Brown, 25(5); Crabb, N. 8(14); Crabb, M. 40(1); Elphick, G. 38(1); Enver-Marum, 28(12); Fraser, 2(2); Jenkins, 27(2); Johnson, 18(10); Jordan, 9(1); Knowles, 33; Lightwood, (1); McLaggon, 3; Nessling, 1; Opinel, 2; Pullan, 31(2); Rooney, 8; Rowe, 1(3); Smart, 15(13); Smith, 5(10); Taylor, 39(4); Treleavan, (1); Walker, 1; Weatherstone, S. 23(7).
Goals – League (42): Enver-Marum 10, Taylor 10, Weatherstone 5 (3 pens), Atkin 3, Crabb M 3, Crabb N 2, Rooney 2, Armstrong 1, Austin 1, Benjamin 1, Jenkins 1, McLaggon 1, Smart 1, own goal 1.
FA Cup (6): Elphick 2, Armstrong 1 (pen), Austin 1, Crabb M 1, Taylor 1.

EBBSFLEET UNITED
League Appearances: Abbey, (1); Ashikodi, 15; Bailey, 30(3); Charles, D. 39; Charles, E. 2(1); Collins, 16(1); Cronin, 44; Crooks, 41; Cumbers, 6; Easton, 7(2); Forshaw, 2(11); Ginty, 2(28); Heeroo, 28(4); Henry, 2; Holmes, 28; Lindie, 3(3); McCarthy, 5; Pooley, 27(1); Salmon, 27(4); Shakes, 35(7); Shulton, 8(2); Smith, 6; Stavrinou, 19(2); Thomas, 6; Vieira, 38(3); Welsh, 22(8); West, 13(9); Wills, 13(13).
Goals – League (50): Vieira 16 (1 pen), Ashikodi 10 (1 pen), Ginty 6, Bailey 4, Shakes 4, Crooks 2, Holmes 2, Cumbers 1, Lindie 1, McCarthy 1, Stavrinou 1, Thomas 1, own goal 1.
FA Cup (0).

FOREST GREEN ROVERS
League Appearances: Adams, S. 7; Ameobi, T. 25(2); Armstrong, 13; Ayres, 6(2); Berry, (2); Brown, 33(8); Burton, 25(1); Challinor, 7; Curran, 1(1); Davies, 10(8); Ellis, M. 7; Else, 3(3); Ford, (1); Fowler, (2); Hodgkiss, 31; Imudia, 3; Ireland, 11; Joyce, 1(1); King, 1(3); Lloyd, 3(10); Maxwell, (1); McDonald, 14(2); Morris, 1(8); O'Cearuill, 13(1); Palmer, (1); Pass, 1(1); Platt, 34(6); Powell, 19(5); Preece, 37; Pugh, 1(2); Rankin, 17(2); Rigg, 15; Rocastle, 14(1); Smith, 39(1); Spence, 6; Stearn, R. 2(5); Stonehouse, 40(3); Styche, 13(5); Taylor, 6; Thorne, O. 18(5); Wilkinson, 7.
Goals – League (50): Smith 7, Powell 6, Rigg 6, Styche 5, Ameobi 4, Brown 4 (3 pens), Platt 4 (2 pens), Preece 3, Rankin 3 (1 pen), Morris 2, Davies 1, Hodgkiss 1, Stearn 1, Stonehouse 1, Thorne 1, own goal 1.
FA Cup (8): Platt 2, Brown 1 (pen), Davies 1, Hodgkiss 1, Preece 1, Rankin 1, Smith 1.

GATESHEAD
League Appearances: Armstrong, 23(15); Ascherl, 1; Ascherl, 1; Bains, 4(1); Baxter, 42; Brittain, 6; Buchanan, 2; Cave, 17(1); Clare, 26; Curtis, 38; Farman, P. 33; Ferrell, 14(2); Forsyth, 2(3); Francis, 7(19); Gate, 30; Harwood, J. 3(3); Haworth, 5(1); Heckingbottom, 15; Hurren, 2(4); Jones, 9(1); Keltie, 3; Mackay, 14(3); McDermott, 4(7); One, 7(5); Parkinson, 12(2); Pelonde, 3; Phillips, 18(17); Provett, 11; Richardson, 9(10); Robinson, 15(2); Shaw, 1; Sinclair, 3(2); Swailes, C. 22(1); Turnbull, 36(5); Wake, 9(9); Williams, D. 14(2); Winn, 23(1).

Goals – League (46): Clare 13 (2 pens), Armstrong 7, Gate 4, Winn 4, Turnbull 3, Wake 3, Baxter 2, Brittain 2 (2 pens), Francis 2, Mackay 2, Harwood 1, McDermott 1, Richardson 1, own goal 1.
FA Cup (7): Armstrong 2, Turnbull 2, Baxter 1, Winn 1, own goal 1.

GRAYS ATHLETIC
League Appearances: Agumbar, 6(11); Anderson, 1; Baker, 4; Bayowa, 8(2); Beavan, 5(1); Bingham, 4(1); Black, T. (2); Braham-Barrett, C. 9(3); Bull, R. 4; Bunce, 22(2); Butcher, 5; Charge, D. 10(2); Cissoko, 20(1); Clarey, 13; Conteh, (5); Crowther, 7(3); Cutler, S. 6(3); Davis, 33(1); Dean, 23; Dos Santos, J. (1); Edwards, P. 19(1); Garner, 12; Gaughran, 2; Glowacki, 3(3); Graham, R. 33(4); Gray, 6(2); Guy, 15; Harvey, T. 12(2); Hickie, 3; Hoyte, G. 27; Hudson-Odoi, 1(1); Hunt, 4; James, 5(1); Jeffrey, 1(3); Leahy, 1; Lechmere, 2(1); Logombe, 5(1); Long, S. 1(2); Makofo, 1; Mallmann, 1; Martin, 3; Mawer, C. 23; Morgan , D. 2; Obaze, 3; Obersteller, 3(1); Onibuje, 6(2); Osborn, 3(7); Poole, 13(1); Reed, 1; Reid, 3; Reynolds, 14; Rhodes, 12(3); Rigoglioso, A. 4; Rnkovic, P. 6(2); Robinson, 4; Robson, 6(1); Slabber, 11(4); Sweeney, (1); Taylor, 3(8); Terry, P. 3; Uddin, 11; Vernazza, 11; Wilson, 4(6); Zola, 2.
Goals – League (35): Slabber 4, Charge 3, Guy 3 (2 pens), Rnkovic 3, Cissoko 2, Davis 2, James 2, Onibuje 2, Osborn 2, Poole 2 (1 pen), Dean 1, Gaughran 1, Graham 1, Gray 1, Morgan 1, Obersteller 1, Reid 1 (1 pen), Reynolds 1, Taylor 1, Uddin 1.
FA Cup (0).

HAYES & YEADING UNITED
League Appearances: Allen-Page, 36; Basham, 13(1); Binns, 29(9); Cadmore, 39; Canham, M. 30(6); Canham, S. 14; Cochrane, 29(2); Daly, G. 6(10); El-Abd, S. 9(6); Fitzgerald, 16(13); Fraser-Allen, (1); Gradwell, 4(4); Green, 43; Harris, 13; Ide, 2(2); James, 20(7); Little, T. 15(8); Marwa, 32(8); Masters, 15; Mehmet, (1); Mulley, 31(5); Overland, 29(1); Palmer, (3); Preddie, D. (1); Ruby, 39(2); Stolcers, 4(5); Wassmer, 1(1); Watkins, 11(6); Webb, 2(2); Wishart, 2(9).
Goals – League (59): Fitzgerald 11, Basham 8 (2 pens), Canham S 6 (3 pens), James 4, Marwa 4, Allen-Page 3, Binns 3, Green 3, Little 3, Watkins 3, Cadmore 2, Cochrane 2, Daly 2 (1 pen), Mulley 2, Gradwell 1, Ruby 1, Stolcers 1.
FA Cup (0).

HISTON
League Appearances: Andrews, 8(6); Barker, 21(1); Bygrave, 28(5); Cox, 2; Crook, 2(3); Farrell, B. 4(1); Frew, 13(9); Gwillim, 35; Hammond, C. (5); Hudson-Odoi, 10(9); Joseph-Dubois, (1); Kennedy, 15(3); Knight, 12; Knight-Percival, 43; Langston, 31; Leabon, K. 1(3); Long, 2(4); Naisbitt, 27; Okay, 21(4); Oyebanjo, 23(4); Pope, 10(3); Pugh, 5(1); Sheringham, 10(5); Simpson, 17; Smith, 24; Southam, 19; Sparkes, 11(3); Stewart, 5(5); Taffe, (2); Tann, 40(1); Tidswell, 6(11); Verma, 7(1); Welch, 5(1); Werndly, (1); Wright, 26; York, 1(4).
Goals – League (44): Wright 8 (1 pen), Knight-Percival 7, Simpson 7 (1 pen), Smith 4, Hudson-Odoi 3, Langston 3, Barker 2, Southam 2 (1 pen), Frew 1, Hammond 1, Pugh 1, Sparkes 1, Tann 1, Tidswell 1, own goals 2.
FA Cup (1): Oyebanjo 1.

KETTERING TOWN
League Appearances: Abbey, 17; Appiah, 9(6); Ashikodi, 12(2); Bain, 2; Boucaud, 29(7); Bussey, 1; Carayol, 4(1); Carrillo, (2); Charles, 2(5); Dance, 23(1); Davis, 3; Dempster, 39(3); Dobson, 1; Eaden, 9; Ebigbo, 4(5); Elding, 7(1); Fowler, 16(1); Geohaghan, 17(2); Green, 19(1); Hadfield, 12(3); Harper, 26; Heslop, 8; Jennings, 34(2); Kelly, 15(2); Marna, 15(21); McPike, J. 1(1); Noubissie, P. 35(3); Partridge, 2; Pryor, 1; Robinson, (4); Roper, 38; Seddon, 4(3); Spencer, 10(8); Taylor, 28(4); Thelwell, 6(2); Thomas, D. 18(16); Wrack, 17(10).
Goals – League (51): Marna 11 (6 pens), Ashikodi 6 (1 pen), Green 4, Dance 3, Elding 3 (1 pen), Jennings 3, Thomas 3, Appiah 2, Dempster 2, Kelly 2, Spencer 2, Ebigbo 1, Fowler 1, Noubissie 1, Partridge 1, Roper 1, Taylor 1, Wrack 1, own goals 3.
FA Cup (5): Ashikodi 2, Elding 1, Marna 1, Roper 1.

KIDDERMINSTER HARRIERS
League Appearances: Andrew, 8; Atkins, 10; Baker, 33(1); Barnes-Homer, 21; Bennett, 36(2); Bignot, 2(1); Boyes, 1(2); Byrne, 10(2); Caines, 29(2); Charles, 1(2); Coleman, 29; Courtney, 39(2); Dolman, 2(5); Farrell, 3(10); Finnigan, 20(3); Goodfellow, 5(5); Hadley, 3(11); Hayward, 1(8); Kerry, 4(5); Knights, 31(11); Lawrie, 3(7); Matthews, 28(5); McDermott, 13(10); McPhee, 40; Prosser, 9; Riley, 42(1); Sharpe, T. 9(6); Singh, 5; Smikle, 42(1); Spencer, 5(3).

Goals – League (57): Smikle 12, McPhee 11 (2 pens), Barnes-Homer 9, Matthews 6, Knights 4, Finnigan 3, Caines 2, Spencer 2, Bennett 1, Byrne 1, Courtney 1, Lawrie 1, McDermott 1, Riley 1, own goals 2.

FA Cup (1): Caines 1.

LUTON TOWN
League Appearances: Asafu-Adjaye, E. 18(2); Barnes-Homer, 8(14); Basham, (5); Blackett, 13(10); Burgess, 5(1); Charles, R. (6); Craddock, T. 40(4); Donnelly, (4); Emanuel, L. 1(1); Gallen, K. 30(1); Gnakpa, C. 26(9); Gore, (1); Hall, A. 27(5); Hatch, 10(10); Heslop, 11; Howells, J. 21(10); Jarvis, 21(6); Keane, 33; Kovacs, 17; Murray, F. 38(2); Nelthorpe, (8); Newton, 32(3); Nicholls, K. 22; Nwokeji, (7); Pilkington, G. 44; Pilkington, A. 7; Reynolds, 3(2); Tyler, 37; White, A. 16; Wright, B. 4(1).

Goals – League (84): Craddock 22 (4 pens), Gallen 16 (1 pen), Gnakpa 8 (1 pen), Howells 6, Pilkington G 6, Hall 5, Barnes-Homer 4, Hatch 4, Newton 3 (1 pen), Jarvis 2, Keane 2, Charles 1, Heslop 1, Kovacs 1, Wright 1, own goals 2.

FA Cup (13): Basham 2, Gallen 2, Newton 2, Blackett 1, Craddock 1 (pen), Gnakpa 1, Hall 1, Nwokeji 1, White 1, own goal 1.

Play-Offs (0).

MANSFIELD TOWN
League Appearances: Armstrong, 15(2); Briscoe, 29(8); Brough, 18(2); Burgess, 14(3); Challinor, 19(1); Clare, 3(8); Dobson, 1(2); Duffy, 34(3); Foster, 16; Gardner, 4; Garner, 31; Graham, 6(1); Heckingbottom, 11; Hotchkiss, 5(3); Istead, S. 3(11); Jones, 24(1); Marriott, 44; Mills, 25(1); Morris, 2(3); Nicholas, 14; Nix, 16(7); Perry, 28(12); Porter, (2); Shaw, 6(8); Silk, 39; Somner, 25(3); Speight, 15(19); Sturrock, 10(14); Williams, 27(8).

Goals – League (69): Speight 17, Duffy 14 (6 pens), Perry 9, Briscoe 3, Challinor 3, Shaw 3, Sturrock 3, Burgess 2, Clare 2 (2 pens), Garner 2, Jones 2, Nix 2, Williams 2, Heckingbottom 1, Hotchkiss 1, Morris 1, Nicholas 1, Silk 1.

FA Cup (5): Duffy 2, Perry 2, Garner 1.

OXFORD UNITED
League Appearances: Batt, 31(6); Bulman, 41(1); Cain, (1); Carruthers, 1; Chalmers, 6(2); Chapman, 21(15); Clarke, R. 43; Clist, 40(1); Constable, 35(2); Cook, 14(2); Creighton, 31(3); Day, 15(3); Deering, 15(8); Foster, 20(1); Grant, 4(4); Green, M. 26(15); Green, F. 8(3); Hargreaves, 9(1); Kelly, 2(1); Kinniburgh, 12; Midson, 18(17); Murray, 21; Perry, 4(4); Potter, 12(10); Rhodes, (3); Sandwith, 16(5); Sodje, 1(3); Tonkin, 17; Turley, 1(1); Woodley, A. (3); Wright, 20.

Goals – League (64): Constable 22 (2 pens), Green M 10, Clist 5, Potter 5, Midson 4 (1 pen), Chapman 3 (1 pen), Cook 3, Deering 2, Sandwith 2, Batt 1, Creighton 1, Foster 1, Green F 1, Kinniburgh 1, Murray 1, Sodje 1, own goal 1.

FA Cup (5): Clist 1, Constable 1, Cook 1, Creighton 1, Midson 1.

Play-Offs (6): Constable 3, Green M 2, Potter 1.

RUSHDEN & DIAMONDS
League Appearances: Abbey, 10; Ainsley, (1); Akurang, 16(17); Beecroft, 1; Byrne, 36(4); Corcoran, 22(2); Cousins, 4(4); Day, 1; Downer, 26(3); Farrell, 26(15); Huke, 5(2); Louis, 20(4); McDonald, (1); McNamara, 7(3); Mills, G. 1(); O'Connor, 29(9); Osano, 39(2); Pattison, 17(8); Porter, 34(9); Reid, 4(7); Roberts, 33; Robinson, 39(1); Smith, 3(16); Stuart, 41; Terry, 29(2); Tomlin, L. 34(1); Wolleaston, 8(9).

Goals – League (77): Tomlin L 14 (2 pens), Farrell 11, O'Connor 10, Akurang 8, Louis 7, Byrne 5, Porter 3, Stuart 3, Corcoran 2, Pattison 2, Reid 2, Terry 2, Cousins 1, Downer 1, Smith 1, Wolleaston 1, own goals 4.

FA Cup (8): O'Connor 4, Corcoran 2 (1 pen), Byrne 1, Tomlin L. 1.

Play-Offs (1): Byrne 1.

SALISBURY CITY

League Appearances: Adelsbury, 19; Anderson, 33(2); Bittner, 40; Brown, 11(2); Bull, 8(1); Bush, 6(1); Clarke, 43; Clohessy, 39(1); Connolly, 8(3); Cox, 10(2); Flood, 26(16); Franks, (1); Giles, 11(1); Glover, D. 2(5); Gray, B. 13(12); Lester, 1; Martin, 14; Matthews, 1; O'Hara, 10(6); Oastler, 8(3); Osman, T. (11); Porter, 1; Prosser, L. 10(1); Pryce, 2(1); Reid, 6(6); Robinson, 1; Ruddick, 23(8); Shephard, 9; Sinclair, 20(3); Spence, 10(1); Tafazolli, 5; Todd, 4; Tubbs, 39(3); Turley, 29(2); Webb, 22(7); Widdrington, (2).
Goals – League (58): Tubbs 27 (4 pens), Flood 6, Adelsbury 3, Clarke 3, Connolly 3, Reid 3, Anderson 2, Clohessy 2, Shephard 2, Webb 2, Giles 1, Martin 1, Todd 1, Turley 1, own goal 1.
FA Cup (5): Tubbs 4, Flood 1.

STEVENAGE BOROUGH

League Appearances: Albrighton, 8(6); Anaclet, (1); Anderson, 1; Ashton, 32(3); Bayes, 4; Beardsley, C. 30(7); Bostwick, 42; Boylan, 14(7); Bridges, 24(3); Brough, 6; Byrom, 28(11); Cole, 19(13); Day, 40; Drury, 21(8); Griffin, 17(9); Henry, 37; Laird, 42; Long, 14(7); Murphy, 20; Odhiambo, 5(10); Odubade, 24(13); Roberts, 38; Sills, 9(8); Vincenti, 2(19); Wilson, 7(5).
Goals – League (79): Odubade 14 (1 pen), Griffin 13 (1 pen), Boylan 7 (2 pens), Beardsley 6, Bostwick 6, Laird 6 (3 pens), Byrom 5, Cole 4 (1 pen), Roberts 4, Ashton 3, Bridges 2, Drury 2, Long 2, Wilson 2, Henry 1, Odhiambo 1, own goal 1.
FA Cup (3): Griffin 2, Vincenti 1.

TAMWORTH

League Appearances: Alcock, 43; Andrew, (5); Benjamin, (4); Blackwood, 29(4); Briscoe, 29(5); Brown, 7; Christie, 20(4); Fankem, 1; Gaughran, 1; Hurren, 2(1); Koranteng, (1); Lake-Gaskin, S. 12(14); Langdon, 3(1); Lyttle, 19(4); MacKenzie, 21(7); Mills, 1(1); Mitchell, 6(2); Murdock, 3(11); Nicholson, S. (4); Pritchard, 40(1); Rodman, 23; Russell, 10(1); Shaw, 33(3); Sheridan, 38(3); Smith, C. 33; Smith, J. 15(1); Tait, 41(1); Ulker, (3); Wright, 23(2); Wylde, 31(2).
Goals – League (42): Christie 6, Sheridan 6, Pritchard 5, Smith C 4, Wright 4, Wylde 4, Tait 3, Blackwood 2, Rodman 2, Benjamin 1, Briscoe 1, Lyttle 1, Mitchell 1, Murdock 1, Shaw 1 (1 pen).
FA Cup (0).

WREXHAM

League Appearances: Anoruo, (6); Assoumani, 38(1); Baynes, W. 24(14); Brown, 8; Cieslewicz, 8(14); Edwards, (1); Fairhurst, 6(3); Fleming, A. 35(2); Holden, 13(2); Hunt, 1(1); Jones, Mark 28(6); Mangan, 23; Maxwell, 26; McCluskey, 6(7); Mitchley, 3(3); O'Leary, 8; Obeng, C. 27(6); Russell, 18; Sakho, 14(4); Sinclair, 18; Smith, 26(4); Spann, S. 24(2); Taboubi, 10(2); Taylor, N. 20(3); Taylor, G. 24(3); Tsiaklis, 1; Walker, 1; Westwood, 33; Williams, Marc 10(6); Williams, Mike 25(5); Williamson, 2; Wolfenden, 4(11).
Goals – League (45): Taylor G 9 (2 pens), Baynes W 7, Mangan 7 (1 pen), Mark Jones, 4, Mike Williams, 4, Smith 3, Westwood 2, Assoumani 1, Fleming A 1, Holden 1, Sakho 1, Taboubi 1, Taylor N. 1, Wolfenden 1, own goals 2.
FA Cup (2): Baynes W. 1, Taylor G 1.

YORK CITY

League Appearances: Barrett, 39(2); Boyes, 1(2); Brodie, 36(4); Carruthers, 22(4); Clarke, 7; Ferrell, 16(6); Gall, (5); Gash, 21(15); Graham, 25; Harsley, 7(2); Ingham, 43; Lawless, 31(4); Mackin, 29(5); McGurk, 28(6); McWilliams, (3); Meredith, 42(1); Mimms, 1; Nelthorpe, (6); Pacquette, 3(10); Parslow, 33; Pitt, 6(5); Purkiss, 34(2); Rankine, 29(14); Sangare, 18(4); Smith, A. 13(13).
Goals – League (62): Brodie 26 (7 pens), Rankine 8 (2 pens), Gash 7, Barrett 4, Sangare 3, Carruthers 2, Smith A 2, Ferrell 1, Gall 1, Graham 1, Harsley 1, Lawless 1, Mackin 1, McGurk 1, Pacquette 1, Pitt 1, Purkiss 1.
FA Cup (8): Brodie 4 (1 pen), Rankine 2, Barrett 1, Pacquette 1.
Play-Offs (3): Brodie 1, Carruthers 1, own goal 1.

BLUE SQUARE NORTH 2009–2010

FINAL LEAGUE TABLE

		Home					Away					Total						
	P	W	D	L	F	A	W	D	L	F	A	W	D	L	F	A	GD	Pts
1 Southport	40	15	4	1	54	19	10	7	3	37	26	25	11	4	91	45	46	86
2 Fleetwood T¶	40	15	4	1	58	21	11	3	6	28	23	26	7	7	86	44	42	85
3 Alfreton T	40	15	3	2	49	20	6	8	6	28	25	21	11	8	77	45	32	74
4 Workington	40	9	7	4	20	14	11	3	6	26	23	20	10	10	46	37	9	70
5 Droylsden	40	11	4	5	47	25	7	6	7	35	37	18	10	12	82	62	20	64
6 Corby T (P)	40	8	6	6	38	31	10	3	7	35	31	18	9	13	73	62	11	63
7 Hinckley U	40	9	7	4	30	20	7	7	6	30	32	16	14	10	60	52	8	62
8 Ilkeston T (P)	40	10	6	4	31	23	6	7	7	22	22	16	13	11	53	45	8	61
9 Stalybridge Celtic	40	8	5	7	34	28	8	2	10	37	36	16	7	17	71	64	7	55
10 Eastwood T (P)	40	9	4	7	22	24	6	5	9	28	31	15	9	16	50	55	–5	54
11 AFC Telford U	40	7	7	6	29	21	7	2	11	23	34	14	9	17	52	55	–3	51
12 Northwich Vic* (R)	40	9	5	6	36	30	6	8	6	26	25	15	13	12	62	55	7	48
13 Blyth Spartans	40	10	3	7	38	30	3	6	11	29	42	13	9	18	67	72	–5	48
14 Gainsborough Trinity	40	9	4	7	29	27	3	7	10	21	30	12	11	17	50	57	–7	47
15 Hyde U	40	9	7	4	28	30	2	5	13	17	42	11	12	17	45	72	–27	45
16 Stafford Rangers	40	6	7	7	28	28	4	7	9	31	42	10	14	16	59	70	–11	44
17 Solihull Moors	40	5	6	9	26	26	6	3	11	21	32	11	9	20	47	58	–11	42
18 Gloucester C (P)	40	7	1	12	23	29	5	5	10	24	30	12	6	22	47	59	–12	42
19 Redditch U	40	6	7	7	28	31	4	1	15	21	52	10	8	22	49	83	–34	38
20 Vauxhall Motors	40	7	7	6	30	34	0	7	13	15	47	7	14	19	45	81	–36	35
21 Harrogate T	40	6	2	12	24	40	2	4	14	17	40	8	6	26	41	80	–39	30

*Northwich Victoria deducted 10 points. ¶Fleetwood Town promoted via play-offs.

BLUE SQUARE SOUTH 2009–2010

FINAL LEAGUE TABLE

		Home					Away					Total						
	P	W	D	L	F	A	W	D	L	F	A	W	D	L	F	A	GD	Pts
1 Newport Co	42	18	3	0	50	8	14	4	3	43	18	32	7	3	93	26	67	103
2 Dover Ath (P)	42	12	4	5	36	20	10	5	6	30	27	22	9	11	66	47	19	75
3 Chelmsford C	42	10	7	4	30	21	12	2	7	32	27	22	9	11	62	48	14	75
4 Bath C¶	42	10	8	3	30	19	10	4	7	36	27	20	12	10	66	46	20	72
5 Woking (R)	42	11	4	6	29	20	10	5	6	28	24	21	9	12	57	44	13	72
6 Havant & Waterlooville	42	10	8	3	40	23	9	6	6	25	21	19	14	9	65	44	21	71
7 Braintree T	42	12	5	4	32	17	6	12	3	24	24	18	17	7	56	41	15	71
8 Staines T (P)	42	10	6	5	37	20	8	7	6	22	20	18	13	11	59	40	19	67
9 Welling U	42	9	4	8	30	23	9	5	7	36	28	18	9	15	66	51	15	63
10 Thurrock	42	9	7	5	37	33	7	6	8	29	27	16	13	13	66	60	6	61
11 Eastleigh	42	8	4	9	37	32	9	5	7	34	34	17	9	16	71	66	5	60
12 Bromley	42	8	5	8	37	27	7	5	9	31	37	15	10	17	68	64	4	55
13 St Albans C	42	9	3	9	25	25	6	7	8	20	30	15	10	17	45	55	–10	55
14 Hampton & Richmond B	42	7	5	9	34	36	7	4	10	22	30	14	9	19	56	66	–10	51
15 Basingstoke T	42	5	5	11	19	33	8	5	8	30	35	13	10	19	49	68	–19	49
16 Maidenhead U	42	6	6	9	24	28	6	6	9	28	31	12	12	18	52	59	–7	48
17 Dorchester T	42	9	8	4	41	26	4	1	16	15	48	13	9	20	56	74	–18	48
18 Bishop's Stortford	42	6	5	10	17	25	6	6	9	31	34	12	11	19	48	59	–11	47
19 Lewes (R)	42	7	7	7	31	28	2	8	11	18	35	9	15	18	49	63	–14	42
20 Worcester C	42	7	4	10	29	28	3	6	12	19	32	10	10	22	48	60	–12	40
21 Weston Super Mare	42	4	5	12	30	42	1	3	17	18	51	5	8	29	48	93	–45	23
22 Weymouth (R)	42	4	3	14	17	51	1	4	16	14	52	5	7	30	31	103	–72	22

¶Bath City promoted via play-offs.

UNIBOND PREMIER DIVISION 2009–10

		Home					Away					Total						
	P	W	D	L	F	A	W	D	L	F	A	W	D	L	F	A	GD	Pts
1 Guiseley	38	12	3	4	32	17	13	1	5	41	24	25	4	9	73	41	32	79
2 Bradford Park Avenue	38	12	2	5	42	25	12	4	3	52	26	24	6	8	94	51	43	78
3 Boston United	38	12	5	2	53	17	11	3	5	37	17	23	8	7	90	34	56	77
4 North Ferriby United	38	11	5	3	38	16	11	4	4	32	22	22	9	7	70	38	32	75
5 Kendal Town	38	12	5	2	38	17	9	3	7	37	30	21	8	9	75	47	28	71
6 Retford United	38	5	8	6	36	27	13	3	3	37	19	18	11	9	73	46	27	65
7 Matlock Town	38	11	3	5	44	23	6	6	7	28	26	17	9	12	72	49	23	60
8 Buxton	38	8	7	4	34	21	8	5	6	32	22	16	12	10	66	43	23	60
9 Marine	38	9	4	6	34	27	8	2	9	26	28	17	6	15	60	55	5	57
10 Nantwich Town	38	10	2	7	40	37	6	4	9	24	32	16	6	16	64	69	–5	54
11 Stocksbridge PS	38	10	3	6	49	33	5	4	10	31	35	15	7	16	80	68	12	52
12 Ashton United	38	7	3	9	25	30	8	3	8	23	33	15	6	17	48	63	–15	51
13 FC United	38	8	3	8	33	31	5	5	9	29	34	13	8	17	62	65	–3	47
14 Whitby Town	38	8	5	6	32	28	4	5	10	24	34	12	10	16	56	62	–6	46
15 Frickley Athletic	38	8	5	6	23	19	4	4	11	27	47	12	9	17	50	66	–16	45
16 Burscough	38	9	1	9	31	23	4	4	11	24	42	13	5	20	55	65	–10	44
17 Hucknall Town	38	8	4	7	42	38	4	4	11	23	43	12	8	18	65	81	–16	44
18 Worksop Town	38	4	5	10	22	34	3	4	12	23	34	7	9	22	45	68	–23	30
19 Ossett Town	38	4	1	14	27	46	2	6	11	19	46	6	7	25	46	92	–46	25
20 Durham City*	38	1	0	18	16	71	1	0	18	11	97	2	0	36	27	168	–141	0

*Durham City deducted 6 points.

ZAMARETTO PREMIER DIVISION 2009–10

		Home					Away					Total						
	P	W	D	L	F	A	W	D	L	F	A	W	D	L	F	A	GD	Pts
1 Farnborough	42	17	2	2	54	20	11	7	3	46	24	28	9	5	100	44	56	93
2 Nuneaton Town	42	13	7	1	47	16	13	3	5	43	21	26	10	6	90	37	53	88
3 Chippenham Town	42	14	2	5	46	24	7	9	5	21	19	21	11	10	67	43	24	74
4 Hednesford Town	42	9	8	4	40	29	11	5	5	39	22	20	13	9	79	51	28	73
5 Brackley Town	42	12	3	6	38	24	9	6	6	45	37	21	9	12	83	61	22	72
6 Cambridge City	42	10	9	2	45	23	8	8	5	28	21	18	17	7	73	44	29	71
7 Bashley	42	12	2	7	41	33	8	9	4	38	28	20	11	11	79	61	18	71
8 Halesowen Town	42	12	8	1	44	29	9	3	9	40	29	21	11	4	84	53	31	70
9 Stourbridge	42	14	4	3	46	22	5	9	7	34	43	19	13	10	80	65	15	70
10 Leamington	42	10	3	8	46	38	9	5	7	38	37	19	8	15	84	75	9	65
11 Truro City	42	7	7	7	39	31	10	4	7	39	34	17	11	14	78	65	13	62
12 Banbury United	42	9	7	5	28	26	5	6	10	25	41	14	13	15	53	67	–14	55
13 Oxford City	42	6	10	5	33	28	7	5	9	32	39	13	15	14	65	67	–2	54
14 Swindon Supermarine	42	4	9	8	30	47	6	5	10	18	29	10	14	18	48	76	–28	44
15 Didcot Town	42	4	7	10	24	31	6	4	11	32	39	10	11	21	56	70	–14	41
16 Evesham United	42	3	10	8	14	21	6	4	11	21	31	9	14	19	35	52	–17	41
17 Merthyr Tydfil	42	8	4	9	30	32	4	7	10	32	41	12	11	19	62	73	–11	37
18 Bedford Town	42	6	5	10	31	38	3	5	13	19	50	9	10	23	50	88	–38	37
19 Tiverton Town	42	4	7	10	16	27	4	5	12	19	34	8	12	22	35	61	–26	36
20 Hemel Hempstead Town	42	6	5	10	32	35	2	5	14	18	46	8	10	24	50	81	–31	34
21 Clevedon Town	42	2	4	15	18	49	4	7	10	30	43	6	11	25	48	92	–44	29
22 Rugby Town	42	3	6	12	26	54	1	2	18	15	60	4	8	30	41	114	–73	20

*Halesowen Town deducted 10 points, Merthyr Tydfil deducted 10 points.

RYMAN PREMIER LEAGUE 2009–10

		Home					Away					Total						
	P	W	D	L	F	A	W	D	L	F	A	W	D	L	F	A	GD	Pts
1 Dartford	42	11	5	5	44	29	18	1	2	57	16	29	6	7	101	45	56	93
2 Sutton United	42	10	5	6	37	26	12	4	5	28	19	22	9	11	65	45	20	75
3 Aveley	42	11	3	7	38	27	10	4	7	45	35	21	7	14	83	62	21	70
4 Boreham Wood	42	10	4	7	32	24	10	4	7	22	20	20	8	14	54	44	10	68
5 Kingstonian	42	11	4	6	41	37	9	4	8	32	32	20	8	14	73	69	4	68
6 Wealdstone	42	10	5	6	29	27	7	9	5	36	38	17	14	11	65	65	0	65
7 Hastings United	42	10	5	6	36	27	8	4	9	32	29	18	9	15	68	56	12	63
8 Tonbridge Angels	42	11	3	7	36	31	7	5	9	33	36	18	8	16	69	67	2	62
9 AFC Hornchurch	42	11	7	3	29	19	5	6	10	22	28	16	13	13	51	47	4	61
10 Hendon	42	10	3	8	30	25	8	3	10	31	34	18	6	18	61	59	2	60
11 Horsham	42	10	2	9	35	33	6	6	9	30	34	16	8	18	65	67	–2	56
12 Tooting and Mitcham	42	7	5	9	33	37	8	5	8	27	27	15	10	17	60	64	–4	55
13 Billericay Town	42	8	6	7	23	23	6	6	9	21	19	14	12	16	44	42	2	54
14 Harrow Borough	42	7	8	6	32	30	6	6	9	34	33	13	14	15	66	63	3	53
15 Cray Wanderers	42	7	3	11	25	33	7	6	8	29	37	14	9	19	54	70	–16	51
16 Canvey Island	42	6	6	9	28	31	7	5	9	29	31	13	11	18	57	62	–5	50
17 Carshalton Athletic	42	8	5	8	27	26	4	8	9	31	38	12	13	17	58	64	–6	49
18 Maidstone United	42	6	4	11	20	34	7	6	8	19	23	13	10	19	39	57	–18	49
19 Margate	42	4	7	10	21	36	7	5	9	28	35	11	12	19	49	71	–22	45
20 Ashford Town (Middx)	42	6	8	7	34	40	5	3	13	28	40	11	11	20	62	80	–18	44
21 Waltham Abbey	42	6	3	12	21	35	6	5	10	28	39	12	8	22	49	74	–25	44
22 Bognor Regis Town	42	5	9	7	27	30	4	5	12	18	35	9	14	19	45	65	–20	41

FA PREMIER RESERVE LEAGUE

NORTH SECTION	P	W	D	L	GD	Pts	SOUTH SECTION	P	W	D	L	GD	Pts
Manchester U	18	13	2	3	25	41	Aston Villa	16	11	4	1	22	37
Manchester C	18	10	5	3	14	35	Arsenal	16	10	2	4	14	32
Liverpool	18	10	2	6	8	32	Fulham	16	8	4	4	6	28
Blackburn R	18	8	5	5	11	29	Chelsea	16	7	1	8	1	22
Sunderland	18	7	1	10	–7	22	Portsmouth	16	6	3	7	–6	21
Wigan Ath	18	6	3	9	–7	21	West Ham U	16	5	4	7	–1	19
Burnley	18	6	3	9	–14	21	Birmingham C	16	4	3	9	–20	15
Hull C	18	6	2	10	–4	20	Wolverhampton W	16	3	4	9	–11	13
Everton	18	5	3	10	–13	18							
Bolton W	18	5	2	11	–13	17							

PREMIER RESERVE LEAGUE PLAY-OFF FINAL

Manchester U (1) (3) *(Diouf 43, 88, Macheda 60 (pen))*

Aston Villa (1) 3 *(Delfouneso 22, 55, Clarke 82)*　　　　　　　　　　2165

Manchester U won 3-2 on penalties.

at Old Trafford.

Manchester U: Foster; Rafael, Dudgeon, Evans C, De Laet, Gill, Stewart (Obertan 56) (Keane 75), Possebon, Diouf, Norwood (Pogba 86), Macheda.

Aston Villa: Marshall; Roome, O'Halloran, Hogg, Clarke, Baker (Collins J 46), Albrighton, Welmann, Delfouneso, Bannan, Hofbauer.

Referee: L. Mason.

FA ACADEMY UNDER-18 LEAGUE 2009–2010

GROUP A	P	W	D	L	F	A	GD	Pts
Arsenal	28	17	5	6	72	41	31	56
Crystal Palace	28	13	8	7	49	31	18	47
Chelsea	28	14	5	9	51	43	8	47
Norwich C	28	11	6	11	50	57	–7	39
West Ham U	28	10	8	10	52	44	8	38
Fulham	28	12	2	14	59	59	0	38
Southampton	28	10	5	13	46	59	–13	35
Charlton Ath	28	10	4	14	41	58	–17	34
Ipswich T	28	8	9	11	39	48	–9	33
Portsmouth	28	4	3	21	31	68	–37	15

GROUP B	P	W	D	L	F	A	GD	Pts
Leicester C	28	22	6	0	79	31	48	72
Tottenham H	28	19	2	7	94	45	49	59
Aston Villa	28	16	5	7	71	31	40	53
Reading	28	11	7	10	65	63	2	40
Birmingham C	28	11	5	12	39	54	–15	38
Watford	28	10	4	14	53	58	–5	34
Cardiff C	28	10	4	14	37	46	–9	34
Bristol C	28	9	5	14	40	60	–20	32
Coventry C	28	7	9	12	44	54	–10	30
Milton Keynes D	28	2	7	19	27	84	–57	13

GROUP C	P	W	D	L	F	A	GD	Pts
Manchester U	28	16	7	5	58	31	27	55
Everton	28	15	5	8	55	34	21	50
WBA	28	12	9	7	55	34	21	45
Liverpool	28	14	3	11	45	41	4	45
Wolverhampton W	28	13	5	10	47	46	1	44
Manchester C	28	12	6	10	64	45	19	42
Blackburn R	28	11	9	8	42	44	–2	42
Stoke C	28	9	10	9	32	38	–6	37
Crewe Alex	28	10	6	12	45	54	–9	36
Bolton W	28	5	8	15	28	49	–21	23

GROUP D	P	W	D	L	F	A	GD	Pts
Nottingham F	28	18	5	5	63	36	27	59
Sunderland	28	17	4	7	66	29	37	55
Newcastle U	28	14	7	7	58	41	17	49
Middlesbrough	28	9	9	10	42	49	–7	36
Leeds U	28	10	5	13	38	53	–15	35
Barnsley	28	8	5	15	31	52	–21	29
Derby Co	28	7	6	15	42	63	–21	27
Sheffield U	28	5	11	12	36	52	–16	26
Huddersfield T	28	4	7	17	30	58	–28	19
Sheffield Wednesday	28	3	8	17	24	57	–33	17

ACADEMY SEMI-FINALS

Manchester United 1, Arsenal 1 *Arsenal won 5-3 on penalties.*
Leicester City 1, Nottingham Forest 1 *Nottingham Forest won 2-1 on penalties.*

ACADEMY FINAL

Arsenal 5 *(Afobe 31, 41, 65 (pen), Freeman 72 (pen), 81)*

Nottingham Forest 3 *(Elliot 5, Thompson 61, Mullen 73)*

Arsenal: Shea; Yennaris, Evina, Boateng, Miquel, Frimpong, Ozyakup, Aneke, Henderson, Afobe, Freeman.

Nottingham Forest: Mytides; Sibson, Freeman, Elliot, Diagne, Watson, Meadows, Gibbons (McCashin 72), Thomson, Mullen, Sykes (Bamford 65).

TOTESPORT.COM LEAGUE 2009–2010

CENTRAL DIVISION

	P	W	D	L	GD	Pts
Derby Co	16	9	2	5	9	29
Burton Alb	16	8	4	4	1	28
WBA	16	7	6	3	16	27
Port Vale	16	6	5	5	6	23
Shrewsbury T	16	6	5	5	2	23
Sheffield U	16	6	2	8	–6	20
Walsall	16	5	4	7	–2	19
Macclesfield T	16	5	1	10	–17	16
Sheffield W	16	4	3	9	–9	15

WEST DIVISION

	P	W	D	L	GD	Pts
Wrexham	16	9	6	1	19	33
Carlisle U	16	9	4	3	20	31
Preston NE	16	8	3	5	5	27
Rochdale	16	8	2	6	3	26
Oldham Ath	16	7	2	7	2	23
Morecambe	16	6	3	7	–4	21
Blackpool	16	6	1	9	0	19
Tranmere R	16	6	1	9	–5	19
Accrington S	16	2	0	14	–40	6

EAST DIVISION

	P	W	D	L	GD	Pts
Leeds U	18	11	3	4	24	36
Hartlepool U	18	11	2	5	16	35
Middlesbrough	18	11	2	5	13	35
Huddersfield T	18	10	0	8	8	30
Rotherham U	18	9	0	9	0	27
Newcastle U	18	7	4	7	5	25
Lincoln C	18	7	4	7	–6	25
Grimsby T	18	5	3	10	–19	18
Bradford C	18	4	3	11	–15	15
Scunthorpe U	18	3	3	12	–26	12

TOTESPORT.COM COMBINATION 2009–2010

CENTRAL DIVISION

	P	W	D	L	GD	Pts
Brighton & HA	18	13	4	1	29	43
Crystal Palace	18	13	4	1	25	43
QPR	18	8	8	2	10	32
Aldershot T	18	8	4	6	8	28
Leyton Orient	18	7	5	6	–9	26
Brentford	18	6	3	9	–5	21
Crawley T	18	5	5	8	–4	20
Gillingham	18	3	6	9	–12	15
Millwall	18	2	4	12	–17	10
Eastbourne B	18	1	5	12	–25	8

EAST DIVISION

	P	W	D	L	GD	Pts
Watford	18	13	2	3	30	41
Ipswich T	18	10	3	5	16	33
Norwich C	18	9	3	6	14	30
Wycombe W	18	7	7	4	4	28
Peterborough U	18	8	3	7	10	27
Luton T	18	8	0	10	–5	24
Colchester U	18	5	8	5	8	23
Northampton T	18	5	5	8	–10	20
Stevenage B	18	3	4	11	–35	13
Southend U	18	2	5	11	–32	11

WALES & WEST DIVISION

	P	W	D	L	GD	Pts
Exeter C	18	10	5	3	4	35
Swansea C	18	10	2	6	9	32
Reading	18	10	1	7	14	31
Swindon T	18	9	4	5	12	31
Bristol C	17	9	2	6	23	29
Southampton	18	9	2	7	11	29
Plymouth Arg	17	7	4	6	16	25
Forest Green R	18	4	5	9	–16	17
Salisbury C	18	4	3	11	–38	15
AFC Bournemouth	18	2	2	14	–35	8

TOTESPORT.COM LEAGUE CUP 2009–2010

GROUP ONE

	P	W	D	L	GD	Pts
Leicester C	3	2	0	1	5	6
Walsall	3	2	0	1	–2	6
Sheffield U	3	1	0	2	0	3
Tranmere R	3	1	0	2	–3	3

GROUP TWO

	P	W	D	L	GD	Pts
Preston NE	4	3	0	1	3	9
Oldham Ath	4	2	1	1	0	7
Bradford C	4	2	0	2	0	6
Middlesbrough	4	1	1	2	–4	4
Morecambe	4	1	0	3	1	3

GROUP THREE

	P	W	D	L	GD	Pts
Scunthorpe U	3	2	0	1	5	6
Sunderland	3	2	0	1	1	6
Hartlepool U	3	1	1	1	0	4
Grimsby T	3	0	1	2	–6	1

SEMI-FINALS

Preston NE v Oldham Ath *(to be played pre-season 2010–11)*.
Leicester C 5, Scunthorpe U 0

FINAL

Leicester C v Preston NE or Oldham Ath *(to be played pre-season 2010–11)*.

WOMEN'S FOOTBALL 2009–2010

NATIONAL DIVISION

			Home				Away					Total					
	P	W	D	L	F	A	W	D	L	F	A	W	D	L	F	A	GD	Pts
1 Arsenal	22	11	0	0	53	11	9	1	1	26	8	20	1	1	79	19	60	61
2 Everton	22	8	0	3	33	11	8	2	1	34	8	16	2	4	67	19	48	50
3 Chelsea	22	8	0	3	27	16	8	1	2	33	11	16	1	5	60	27	33	49
4 Leeds Carnegie	22	7	1	3	23	9	8	1	2	27	7	15	2	5	50	16	34	47
5 Sunderland	22	6	1	4	18	17	6	0	5	18	18	12	1	9	36	35	1	37
6 Doncaster Rovers Belles	22	3	6	2	18	17	6	1	4	18	20	9	7	6	36	37	–1	34
7 Blackburn Rovers	22	2	2	7	11	25	5	1	5	16	20	7	3	12	27	45	–18	24
8 Millwall Lionesses	22	4	1	6	11	22	2	2	7	13	21	6	3	13	24	43	–19	21
9 Watford	22	3	4	4	10	19	1	1	9	13	41	4	5	13	23	60	–37	17
10 Birmingham City	22	4	0	7	11	16	0	4	7	10	25	4	4	14	21	41	–20	16
11 Nottingham Forest	22	0	2	9	9	34	3	2	6	7	17	3	4	15	16	51	–35	13
12 Bristol Academy	22	2	0	9	5	25	1	1	9	7	33	3	1	18	12	58	–46	10

NORTHERN DIVISION

	P	W	D	L	F	A	W	D	L	F	A	W	D	L	F	A	GD	Pts
1 Liverpool	22	9	1	1	31	9	10	1	0	28	10	19	2	1	59	19	40	59
2 OOH Lincoln	22	8	1	2	22	10	7	3	1	24	12	15	4	3	46	22	24	49
3 Leicester City	22	6	3	2	30	17	5	3	3	23	18	11	6	5	53	35	18	39
4 Manchester City	22	3	4	4	20	18	7	2	2	16	7	10	6	6	36	25	11	36
5 Curzon Ashton	22	5	3	3	18	15	4	1	6	19	24	9	4	9	37	39	–2	31
6 Aston Villa	22	4	3	4	15	15	3	5	3	22	20	7	8	7	37	35	2	29
7 Leeds City Vixens	22	4	2	5	21	26	5	0	6	20	22	9	2	11	41	48	–7	29
8 Newcastle United	22	3	3	5	16	20	4	3	4	22	28	7	6	9	38	48	–10	27
9 Preston North End	22	5	2	4	38	27	1	4	6	18	27	6	6	10	56	54	2	24
10 Derby County	22	3	3	5	15	20	2	2	7	15	31	5	5	12	30	51	–21	20
11 Sheffield Wednesday	22	4	3	4	20	22	0	3	8	9	28	4	6	12	29	50	–21	18
12 Luton Town	22	1	1	9	6	23	0	2	9	6	25	1	3	18	12	48	–36	6

SOUTHERN DIVISION

	P	W	D	L	F	A	W	D	L	F	A	W	D	L	F	A	GD	Pts
1 Barnet	22	9	2	0	35	8	7	2	2	18	10	16	4	2	53	18	35	52
2 Reading	22	5	5	1	20	14	8	0	3	23	14	13	5	4	43	28	15	44
3 Keynsham Town	22	7	3	1	27	13	5	2	4	28	23	12	5	5	55	36	19	41
4 Portsmouth	22	7	1	3	21	13	4	5	2	21	19	11	6	5	42	32	10	39
5 West Ham United	22	5	4	2	22	12	4	5	2	16	12	9	9	4	38	24	14	36
6 Cardiff City	22	7	2	2	24	17	3	3	5	20	15	10	5	7	44	32	12	35
7 Charlton Athletic	22	6	2	3	11	7	4	2	5	13	13	10	4	8	24	20	4	34
8 Brighton & HA	22	3	4	4	20	19	3	4	4	13	14	6	8	8	33	33	0	26
9 Colchester United	22	4	3	4	10	13	2	2	7	9	27	6	5	11	19	40	–21	23
10 Queens Park Rangers	22	3	2	6	26	20	2	3	6	16	23	5	5	12	42	43	–1	20
11 WFC Fulham	22	0	2	9	8	27	2	0	9	6	36	2	2	18	14	63	–49	8
12 Crystal Palace	22	0	1	10	5	27	1	3	7	7	23	1	4	17	12	50	–38	7

FA WOMEN'S CUP FINAL 2009–2010

Monday, 3 May 2010

(at Nottingham Forest)

Arsenal (1) 2 (*Little 43 (pen), Fleeting 54*)   17,505

Everton (2) 3 (*Dowie 16, 119, White 45 (og)*)

Arsenal: Byrne; Yorston, Flaherty, White, Grant, Fleeting (Carter 70), Yankey, Davison, Beattie, Little, Fahey.

Everton: Brown; Easton, Unitt (Whelan 63), Williams, Westwood, Johnson, Handley, Scott, Dowie, Hinnigan (Chaplen 77), Duggan (Evans 111).

aet.

Referee: U. Hon.

ENGLAND WOMEN'S INTERNATIONAL MATCHES 2009–2010

EUROPEAN CHAMPIONSHIP FINAL TOURNAMENT (in Finland)

GROUP C – 25 Aug *(in Lahti)*

England 1 *(Williams 38 (pen))*   **Italy 2** *(Panico 56, Tuttino 80)*   2950

England: Brown; Scott A, Stoney■, Williams F, Asante (Unitt 73), Carney, Chapman, Aluko (Smith K 46), Smith S (Sanderson 85), Scott J, White F.

GROUP C – 28 Aug *(in Helsinki)*

England 3 *(Carney 24, Aluko 32, Smith K 42)*   **Russia 2** *(Tsybutovich 2, Kurochkina 22)*
                                                                                          1462

England: Brown; Scott A, Williams F, Johnson, Carney, Chapman, Aluko, Smith K, Smith S (Clarke 66), White F, Unitt.

GROUP C – 31 Aug*(in Turku)*

Sweden 1 *(Svensson 40 (pen))*   **England 1** *(White 28)*   6142

England: Brown; Scott A, Stoney, Williams F, Johnson, Carney, Chapman, Aluko (Westwood 65), Smith K, Smith S (Clarke 90), White F.

QUARTER-FINAL – 3 Sept *(in Turku)*

Finland 2 *(Sjolund 66, Sallstrom 79)*   **England 3** *(Aluko 14, 67, Williams F 49)*   7247

England: Brown; Stoney, Williams F, Johnson (Bassett 68), Asante, Carney, Chapman, Aluko, Smith K, Smith S, White F(Scott J 41).

SEMI-FINAL – 6 Sept *(in Tampere)*

England 2 *(Smith K 61, Scott J 116)*   **Holland 1** *(Pieete 64)*   4621

England: Brown; Scott A, Stoney, Williams F, Johnson, Asante, Chapman, Aluko (Sanderson 70), Smith K, Smith S (Carney 46), Clarke (Scott J 91).

FINAL 10 Sept *(in Helsinki)*

England 2 *(Carney 24, Smith K 55)*   **Germany 6** *(Prinz 19, 76, Behringer 22, Kulig 50, Grings 62, 73)*

                                                                                          15,877

England: Brown; Scott A, Stoney, Williams F, Asante, White F, Carney, Scott J, Chapman (Westwood 86), Aluko (Sanderson 81), Smith K.

FRIENDLIES

16 July *(at Colchester)*

England 0   Iceland 2 *(Magmusdottir 25, Vidarsodottir 81)*   4170

England: Chamberlain (Telford 46); Unitt, Yorston (Susi 65), White F, Bassett, Buet, Clarke (Davison 79), Scott J (Williams R 65), Westwood, Aluko, Yankey.

22 July *(at Swindon)*

England 1 *(Handley 87)*   **Denmark 0**   4177

England: Bardsley; Scott A, Stoney, Chapman, Johnson, Asante, Carney, Scott J (Westwood 90), Sanderson (Handley 46), Williams F, Smith S.

CYPRUS CUP

24 Feb *(in Larnaca)*

England 1 *(Scott J 5)*   **South Africa 0**

England: Brown (Chamberlain 46); Susi, Stoney, Buet (Bassett 58), White F (Unitt 67), Johnson, Clarke (Yankey 76), Scott J, Westwood, Handley, Smith S.

27 Feb *(in Larnaca)*

England 0   Canada 1 *(Julien 10)*

England: Bardsley; Scott A, Stoney, Williams F, White F, Bassett (Susi 59), Clarke, Scott J, Unitt, Sanderson (Westwood 59), Yankey.

1 Mar *(in Larnaca)*

England 2 *(Stoney 56, Sanderson 76)*   **Switzerland 2** *(Dickenmann 27, 84)*

England: Chamberlain; Susi (Clarke 80), Unitt, Buet, Johnson, Stoney, Scott A, Scott J, Handley (Sanderson 46), Westwood (Smith K 73), Smith S.

3 Mar *(in Nicosia)*

England 3 *(Scott A 8, 58, White 90)*   **Italy 2** *(Brown 43 (og), Camporese 64)*

England: Brown (Bardsley 68); Susi, White F, Stoney, Unitt, Bassett, Scott J, Smith K (Sanderson 46), Scott A, Clarke, Yankey.

FIFA 2011 WOMEN'S WORLD CUP QUALIFYING COMPETITION

25 Oct *(at Blackpool)*

England 8 *(White F 5, Williams F 20, 37, 65, Clarke 35, 75, Westwood 77, Unitt 88)*
Malta 0   3681

England: Bardsley; Scott A, Unitt, Buet, White F (Johnson 59), Bassett, Clarke, Scott J, Sanderson (Handley 53), Williams F (Westwood 68), Smith S.

26 Nov *(in Izmir)*

Turkey 0   England 3 *(Scott A 76, Sanderson 80, Unitt 84)*

England: Bardsley; Scott A, Unitt, Williams F, White F, Bassett, Clarke (Sanderson 76), Buet (Carney 62), Handley (Dowie 84), Westwood, Smith S.

25 Mar *(at QPR)*

England 3 *(Sanderson 15, Aluko 68, White E 90)*   **Austria 0**   3980

England: Bardsley; Susi (White E 62), Unitt (Rafferty 87), Chapman, White F, Stoney, Scott A, Williams F, Aluko, Sanderson, Yankey (Smith S 87).

1 Apr *(at Millwall)*

England 1 *(Chapman 29)*   **Spain 0**   5041

England: Brown; Scott A, Unitt, Chapman, White F, Stoney, Clarke, Williams F, Aluko (White E 69), Smith K (Scott J 59), Yankey (Smith S 83).

20 May *(in Ta'Qali)*

Malta 0   England 6 *(White F 7, Smith K 15, Williams F 29, 82, Clarke 56, White E 67)*

England: Brown; Scott A (Susi 46), Stoney, White F (Dowie 74), Chapman, Williams F, Yankey (Carney 64), Clarke, Smith K, Rafferty, White E.

19 June *(in Aranda de Duero)*

Spain 2 *(Martin 16, Bermudez 67)*   **England 2** *(Unitt 78, White F 88)*

England: Brown; Scott A, Stoney, Unitt, White F, Chapman, Williams F, Yankey (Scott J 46), Smith K, Carney, Aluko (White E 73).

THE FA TROPHY 2009–2010

FINAL (at Wembley) – Saturday, 8 May 2010
Barrow (0) 2 (*McEvilly 79, Walker 107*)

Stevenage Borough (1) 1 (*Drury 10*)   17,500
Barrow: Tomlinson; Spender, Edwards, Jones, Bolland, Hulbert, Bond, Rutherford (Boyd 110), Walker, Blundell (McEvilly 74), Wiles (Logan 64).
Stevenage Borough: Day (Bayes 90); Henry, Laird, Roberts, Ashton, Bostwick, Drury, Bridges, Beardsley (Griffin 66), Odubade, Byrom (Wilson 59).
aet.
Referee: L. Probert (Wiltshire).

THE FA VASE 2009–2010
FINAL (at Wembley) – Sunday, 9 May 2010
Whitley Bay (2) 6 (*Chow 1, Eastaugh 16 (og), Kerr 46, Johnston 50, Robinson 76, Gillies 85*)

Wroxham (1) 1 (*Cook 12*)   8920
Whitley Bay: Burke; McFarlane, Anderson, Hodgson (Picton 69), Timmons, Ryan, Johnston (Gillies 77), Robson, Kerr, Chow (Bell 62), Robinson.
Wroxham: Howie; Pauling (Durrant 58), Howes, Challen, McNeil (Carus 46), Eastaugh (Paynter 69), Spriggs, Lemmon, Cook, White, Gilmore.
Referee: A. Taylor (Cheshire).

THE FA YOUTH CUP 2009–2010

FINAL (First Leg) – Thursday, 29 April 2010
Aston Villa (1) 1 (*Devine 19*)

Chelsea (0) 1 (*Bruma 64*)   3359
Aston Villa: Siegrist; Berry, Devine, Williams, Deeney, Nelson-Addy, Blythe, Carruthers, Roberts, Simmonds (Halfhuid 82), Poyser (Darkin 79).
Chelsea: Walker; Clifford B, Ince, Bruma, Conteh (Sampayo 90), Djalo, McEachran, Clifford C (Lalkovic 71), Sala, Mitrovic, Tore.
Referee: K. Friend (Leicestershire).

FINAL (Second Leg) – Tuesday, 4 May 2010
Chelsea (0) 2 (*Mitrovic 65, Clifford C 86*)

Aston Villa (1) 1 (*Poyser 33*)   10,464
Chelsea: Walker; Clifford B, Ince, Bruma, Conteh, Clifford C, Sala, Djalo (Saville 90), Mitrovic, McEachran, Tore (Lalkovic 89).
Aston Villa: Siegrist; Berry, Deeney, Devine, Williams (Darkin 72), Blythe (Halfhuid 89), Carruthers, Nelson-Addy, Poyser, Simmonds, Roberts.
Referee: K. Friend (Leicestershire).

THE FA SUNDAY CUP 2009–2010
FINAL (at Liverpool FC)
Hetton Lions Cricket Club (1) 4 (*Cogden, Rae 2, Lawther*)
Magnet Tavern (1) 2 (*Sozo, Coulson*)   856

THE FA COUNTY YOUTH CUP 2009–2010
FINAL (at Gillingham FC)
Kent (0) 1 (*Miller 79*)
Sheffield & Hallamshire (0) 0

NATIONAL LIST OF REFEREES FOR SEASON 2010–2011

As at 2009–2010

Atkinson, M (Martin) – W. Yorkshire
Attwell, SB (Stuart) – Warwickshire
Bates, A (Tony) – Staffordshire
Bennett, SG (Steve) – Kent
Booth, R (Russell) – Nottinghamshire
Boyeson, C (Carl) – E. Yorkshire
Bratt, SJ (Steve) – West Midlands
Clattenburg, M (Mark) – Tyne & Wear
Cook, SD (Steven) – Surrey
Crossley, PT (Phil) – Kent
Deadman, D (Darren) – Cambs.
Dean, ML (Mike) – Wirral
Dowd, P (Phil) – Staffordshire
D'urso, AP (Andy) – Essex
East, R (Roger) – Wiltshire
Eltringham, G (Geoff) – Tyne & Wear
Evans, KG (Karl) – Lancashire
Foster, D (David) – Tyne & Wear
Foy, CJ (Chris) – Merseyside
Friend, KA (Kevin) – Leicestershire
Gibbs, PN (Phil) – W. Midlands
Graham, F (Fred) – Essex
Haines, A (Andy) – Tyne & Wear
Hall, AR (Andy) – W. Midlands
Halsey, MR (Mark) – Lancashire
Haywood, M (Mark) – W. Yorkshire
Hegley, GK (Grant) – Hertfordshire
Hill, KD (Keith) – Hertfordshire
Hooper, SA (Simon) – Wiltshire
Horwood, GD (Graham) – Bedfordshire
Ilderton, EL (Eddie) – Tyne & Wear
Jones, MJ (Michael) – Cheshire
Kettle, TM (Trevor) – Rutland
Langford, O (Oliver) – W. Midlands
Laws, G (Graham) – Tyne & Wear
Linington, JJ (James) – Isle of Wight
McDermid, D (Danny) – Middlesex
Marriner, AM (Andre) – W. Midlands
Mason, LS (Lee) – Lancashire

Mathieson, SW (Scott) – Cheshire
Miller, NS (Nigel) – Co. Durham
Miller, P (Pat) – Bedfordshire
Moss, J (Jon) – W. Yorkshire
Oliver, CW (Clive) – Northumberland
Oliver, M (Michael) – Northumberland
Pawson, CL (Craig) – S. Yorkshire
Penn, AM (Andy) – W. Midlands
Phillips, DJ (David) – W. Sussex
Probert, LW (Lee) – Wiltshire
Quinn, P (Peter) – Cleveland
Rushton, SJ (Steve) – Staffordshire
Russell, MP (Mike) – Hertfordshire
Salisbury, G (Graham) – Lancashire
Sarginson, CD (Chris) – Staffordshire
Scott, GD (Graham) – Oxfordshire
Sheldrake, D (Darren) – Surrey
Shoebridge, RL (Rob) – Derbyshire
Singh, J (Jarnail) – Middlesex
Stroud, KP (Keith) – Hampshire
Sutton, GJ (Gary) – Lincolnshire
Swarbrick, ND (Neil) – Lancashire
Tanner, SJ (Steve) – Somerset
Taylor, A (Anthony) – Cheshire
Taylor, P (Paul) – Hertfordshire
Thorpe, M (Mike) – Suffolk
Tierney, P (Paul) – Lancashire
Walton, P (Peter) – Northamptonshire
Ward, GL (Gavin) – Surrey
Waugh, J (Jock) – S. Yorkshire
Webb, D (David) – Co. Durham
Webb, HM (Howard) – S. Yorkshire
Webster, CH (Colin) – Tyne & Wear
Whitestone, D (Dean) –
  Northamptonshire
Wiley, AG (Alan) – Staffordshire
Williamson, IG (Iain) – Berkshire
Woolmer, KA (Andy) – Northamptonshire
Wright, KK (Kevin) – Cambridgeshire

ENGLISH LEAGUE FIXTURES 2010–2011

*Sky Sports   All fixtures subject to change.

Friday, 6 August 2010
npower Football League Championship
Norwich C v Watford* (7.45)

Saturday, 7 August 2010
npower Football League Championship
Bristol C v Millwall
Burnley v Nottingham F
Coventry C v Portsmouth
Crystal Palace v Leicester C
Hull C v Swansea C
Leeds U v Derby Co
Middlesbrough v Ipswich T
Preston NE v Doncaster R
QPR v Barnsley
Reading v Scunthorpe U

npower Football League One
Carlisle U v Brentford
Charlton Ath v Bournemouth
Exeter C v Colchester U
Notts Co v Huddersfield T
Peterborough U v Bristol R
Rochdale v Hartlepool U
Sheffield W v Dagenham & R
Southampton v Plymouth Arg* (12.15)
Swindon T v Brighton & HA
Tranmere R v Oldham Ath
Walsall v Milton Keynes D
Yeovil T v Leyton Orient

npower Football League Two
Accrington S v Aldershot T
Burton Alb v Oxford U
Bury v Port Vale
Chesterfield v Barnet
Crewe Alex v Hereford U
Gillingham v Cheltenham T
Rotherham U v Lincoln C City
Shrewsbury T v Bradford C
Southend U v Stockport Co
Stevenage v Macclesfield T
Torquay U v Northampton T
Wycombe W v Morecambe

Sunday, 8 August 2010
npower Football League Championship
Cardiff C v Sheffield U* (12.35)

Friday, 13 August 2010
npower Football League One
Leyton Orient v Charlton Ath* (7.45)

Saturday, 14 August 2010
Barclays Premier League
Aston Villa v West Ham U
Blackburn R v Everton
Wigan Ath v Blackpool
Bolton W v Fulham
Chelsea v WBA
Sunderland v Birmingham C
Tottenham H v Manchester C* (12.45)
Wolverhampton W v Stoke C

npower Football League Championship
Barnsley v Crystal Palace
Derby Co v Cardiff C
Doncaster R v Bristol C
Ipswich T v Burnley
Leicester C v Middlesbrough
Millwall v Hull C
Portsmouth v Reading
Scunthorpe U v Norwich C
Sheffield U v QPR
Swansea C v Preston NE
Watford v Coventry C

npower Football League One
Bournemouth v Peterborough U
Brentford v Walsall
Brighton & HA v Rochdale
Bristol R v Yeovil T
Colchester U v Sheffield W
Dagenham & R v Exeter C
Hartlepool U v Swindon T
Huddersfield T v Tranmere R
Milton Keynes D v Southampton
Oldham Ath v Notts Co
Plymouth Arg v Carlisle U

npower Football League Two
Aldershot T v Southend U
Barnet v Burton Alb
Bradford C v Stevenage
Cheltenham T v Crewe Alex
Hereford U v Gillingham
Lincoln C City v Torquay U
Macclesfield T v Shrewsbury T
Morecambe v Rotherham U
Northampton T v Accrington S
Oxford U v Bury
Port Vale v Chesterfield
Stockport Co v Wycombe W

Sunday, 15 August 2010
Barclays Premier League
Liverpool v Arsenal* (4.00)

npower Football League Championship
Nottingham F v Leeds U* (1.15)

Monday, 16 August 2010
Barclays Premier League
Manchester U v Newcastle U* (8.00) 3-0

Saturday, 21 August 2010 BARTON
Barclays Premier League
Arsenal v Blackpool NOLAN 2
Birmingham C v Blackburn R CARROLL 3
Everton v Wolverhampton W
Newcastle U v Aston Villa 6-0
Stoke C v Tottenham H
WBA v Sunderland
West Ham U v Bolton W
Wigan Ath v Chelsea* (5.15)

npower Football League Championship
Bristol C v Barnsley
Burnley v Leicester C
Cardiff C v Doncaster R
Coventry C v Derby Co* (12.15)
Crystal Palace v Ipswich T
Hull C v Watford
Leeds U v Millwall
Norwich C v Swansea C
Preston NE v Portsmouth
QPR v Scunthorpe U
Reading v Nottingham F

npower Football League One
Carlisle U v Milton Keynes D
Charlton Ath v Oldham Ath
Exeter C v Bristol R
Notts Co v Dagenham & R
Peterborough U v Huddersfield T
Rochdale v Colchester U
Sheffield W v Brighton & HA
Southampton v Leyton Orient
Swindon T v Brentford
Tranmere R v Bournemouth
Walsall v Plymouth Arg
Yeovil T v Hartlepool U

npower Football League Two
Accrington S v Macclesfield T
Burton Alb v Morecambe
Bury v Northampton T
Chesterfield v Hereford U
Crewe Alex v Barnet
Gillingham v Lincoln C City
Rotherham U v Cheltenham T
Shrewsbury T v Aldershot T
Southend U v Port Vale
Stevenage v Stockport Co
Torquay U v Bradford C
Wycombe W v Oxford U

Sunday, 22 August 2010
Barclays Premier League
Fulham v Manchester U* (4.00)

npower Football League Championship
Middlesbrough v Sheffield U* (1.15)

Monday, 23 August 2010
Barclays Premier League
Manchester C v Liverpool* (8.00)

Saturday, 28 August 2010
Barclays Premier League
Blackburn R v Arsenal* (12.45)
Blackpool v Fulham
Chelsea v Stoke C
Liverpool v WBA
Manchester U v West Ham U
Sunderland v Manchester C CARROLL
Tottenham H v Wigan Ath
Wolverhampton W v Newcastle U 1-1

npower Football League Championship
Barnsley v Middlesbrough
Derby Co v QPR
Doncaster R v Hull C
Ipswich T v Bristol C
Leicester C v Reading* (5.20)
Millwall v Coventry C
Nottingham F v Norwich C
Portsmouth v Cardiff C
Scunthorpe U v Crystal Palace
Sheffield U v Preston NE
Swansea C v Burnley
Watford v Leeds U

npower Football League One
Bournemouth v Notts Co
Brentford v Rochdale
Brighton & HA v Walsall
Bristol R v Southampton
Colchester U v Carlisle U
Dagenham & R v Tranmere R
Hartlepool U v Sheffield W
Huddersfield T v Charlton Ath
Leyton Orient v Exeter C
Milton Keynes D v Swindon T
Oldham Ath v Yeovil T
Plymouth Arg v Peterborough U

npower Football League Two
Aldershot T v Stevenage
Barnet v Bury
Bradford C v Southend U
Cheltenham T v Burton Alb
Hereford U v Rotherham U
Lincoln C City v Crewe Alex
Macclesfield T v Chesterfield
Morecambe v Gillingham
Northampton T v Wycombe W
Oxford U v Accrington S
Port Vale v Torquay U
Stockport Co v Shrewsbury T

Sunday, 29 August 2010
Barclays Premier League
Bolton W v Birmingham C* (1.30)
Aston Villa v Everton* (4.00)

Saturday, 4 September 2010
npower Football League One
Carlisle U v Swindon T
Dagenham & R v Leyton Orient
Exeter C v Charlton Ath
Huddersfield T v Bournemouth
Milton Keynes D v Hartlepool U* (12.15)
Notts Co v Yeovil T
Oldham Ath v Bristol R
Plymouth Arg v Brighton & HA
Southampton v Rochdale
Tranmere R v Peterborough U
Walsall v Colchester U

npower Football League Two
Accrington S v Wycombe W
Aldershot T v Northampton T
Barnet v Cheltenham T
Bradford C v Port Vale
Burton Alb v Hereford U
Bury v Gillingham
Chesterfield v Lincoln C City
Macclesfield T v Stockport Co
Oxford U v Morecambe
Shrewsbury T v Rotherham U
Southend U v Torquay U
Stevenage v Crewe Alex

Sunday, 5 September 2010
npower Football League One
Brentford v Sheffield W* (12.00)

Saturday, 11 September 2010
Barclays Premier League
Arsenal v Bolton W
Fulham v Wolverhampton W
Manchester C v Blackburn R
Newcastle U v Blackpool 0-2
WBA v Tottenham H
West Ham U v Chelsea
Wigan Ath v Sunderland

npower Football League Championship
Burnley v Preston NE
Cardiff C v Hull C
Coventry C v Leicester C
Derby Co v Sheffield U
Leeds U v Swansea C
Norwich C v Barnsley
Nottingham F v Millwall
Portsmouth v Ipswich T
QPR v Middlesbrough
Reading v Crystal Palace
Scunthorpe U v Bristol C
Watford v Doncaster R

npower Football League One
Bournemouth v Dagenham & R
Brighton & HA v Milton Keynes D
Bristol R v Brentford
Charlton Ath v Notts Co
Colchester U v Plymouth Arg
Hartlepool U v Exeter C
Leyton Orient v Huddersfield T
Peterborough U v Oldham Ath
Rochdale v Walsall
Sheffield W v Carlisle U
Swindon T v Southampton
Yeovil T v Tranmere R

npower Football League Two
Cheltenham T v Stevenage
Crewe Alex v Bury
Gillingham v Shrewsbury T
Hereford U v Oxford U
Lincoln C City v Barnet
Morecambe v Chesterfield
Northampton T v Southend U
Port Vale v Aldershot T
Rotherham U v Burton Alb
Stockport Co v Bradford C
Torquay U v Accrington S
Wycombe W v Macclesfield T

Sunday, 12 September 2010
Barclays Premier League
Everton v Manchester U* (1.30)
Birmingham C v Liverpool* (4.00)

Monday, 13 September 2010
Barclays Premier League
Stoke C v Aston Villa* (8.00)

Tuesday, 14 September 2010
npower Football League Championship
Barnsley v Leeds U
Bristol C v Watford
Crystal Palace v Portsmouth
Doncaster R v Norwich C
Hull C v Derby Co
Ipswich T v QPR
Leicester C v Cardiff C
Middlesbrough v Burnley
Millwall v Reading

Preston NE v Nottingham F
Sheffield U v Scunthorpe U
Swansea C v Coventry C

Friday, 17 September 2010
npower Football League Championship
Doncaster R v Leeds U* (7.45)

Saturday, 18 September 2010
Barclays Premier League
Aston Villa v Bolton W   BEN ARFA
Blackburn R v Fulham
Everton v Newcastle U   0—1
Stoke C v West Ham U* (12.45)
Sunderland v Arsenal
Tottenham H v Wolverhampton W
WBA v Birmingham C
Wigan Ath v Manchester C

npower Football League Championship
Barnsley v Derby Co
Bristol C v Coventry C
Crystal Palace v Burnley
Hull C v Nottingham F* (5.20)
Ipswich T v Cardiff C
Leicester C v QPR
Middlesbrough v Reading
Millwall v Watford
Preston NE v Norwich C
Sheffield U v Portsmouth
Swansea C v Scunthorpe U

npower Football League One
Brentford v Hartlepool U
Carlisle U v Brighton & HA
Dagenham & R v Bristol R
Exeter C v Peterborough U
Huddersfield T v Yeovil T
Milton Keynes D v Rochdale
Notts Co v Leyton Orient
Oldham Ath v Bournemouth
Plymouth Arg v Sheffield W
Southampton v Colchester U
Tranmere R v Charlton Ath
Walsall v Swindon T

npower Football League Two
Accrington S v Lincoln C City
Aldershot T v Wycombe W
Barnet v Rotherham U
Bradford C v Gillingham
Burton Alb v Crewe Alex
Bury v Hereford U
Chesterfield v Cheltenham T
Macclesfield T v Port Vale
Oxford U v Stockport Co
Shrewsbury T v Northampton T
Southend U v Morecambe
Stevenage v Torquay U

Sunday, 19 September 2010
Barclays Premier League
Manchester U v Liverpool* (1.30)
Chelsea v Blackpool* (4.00)

Friday, 24 September 2010
npower Football League Championship
Portsmouth v Leicester C* (7.45)

Saturday, 25 September 2010
Barclays Premier League
Arsenal v WBA
Birmingham C v Wigan Ath
Blackpool v Blackburn R
Bolton W v Manchester U
Fulham v Everton
Liverpool v Sunderland
Manchester C v Chelsea* (12.45)
West Ham U v Tottenham H

npower Football League Championship
Burnley v Bristol C
Cardiff C v Millwall
Coventry C v Preston NE
Derby Co v Crystal Palace
Leeds U v Sheffield U
Norwich C v Hull C
Nottingham F v Swansea C
QPR v Doncaster R
Reading v Barnsley
Scunthorpe U v Ipswich T
Watford v Middlesbrough

npower Football League One
Bournemouth v Carlisle U
Brighton & HA v Oldham Ath
Bristol R v Notts Co
Charlton Ath v Dagenham & R
Colchester U v Tranmere R
Hartlepool U v Walsall
Leyton Orient v Brentford
Peterborough U v Milton Keynes D
Rochdale v Plymouth Arg
Sheffield W v Southampton
Swindon T v Huddersfield T
Yeovil T v Exeter C

npower Football League Two
Cheltenham T v Bury
Crewe Alex v Oxford U
Gillingham v Burton Alb
Hereford U v Southend U
Lincoln C City v Stevenage
Morecambe v Barnet
Northampton T v Bradford C
Port Vale v Accrington S
Rotherham U v Chesterfield
Stockport Co v Aldershot T
Torquay U v Macclesfield T
Wycombe W v Shrewsbury T

Sunday, 26 September 2010
Barclays Premier League
Wolverhampton W v Aston Villa* (2.00)
Newcastle U v Stoke C* (4.10) 1-2

Tuesday, 28 September 2010
npower Football League Championship
Burnley v Hull C
Cardiff C v Crystal Palace
Coventry C v Doncaster R
Derby Co v Middlesbrough
Leeds U v Preston NE
Norwich C v Leicester C
Nottingham F v Sheffield U
Portsmouth v Bristol C
QPR v Millwall
Reading v Ipswich T
Scunthorpe U v Barnsley
Watford v Swansea C

npower Football League One
Bournemouth v Exeter C
Brighton & HA v Brentford
Bristol R v Tranmere R
Charlton Ath v Milton Keynes D
Colchester U v Dagenham & R
Hartlepool U v Carlisle U
Leyton Orient v Walsall
Peterborough U v Notts Co
Rochdale v Huddersfield T
Sheffield W v Oldham Ath
Swindon T v Plymouth Arg
Yeovil T v Southampton

npower Football League Two
Cheltenham T v Oxford U
Crewe Alex v Macclesfield T
Gillingham v Southend U
Hereford U v Stevenage
Lincoln C City v Burton Alb
Morecambe v Bury
Northampton T v Chesterfield
Port Vale v Shrewsbury T
Rotherham U v Bradford C
Stockport Co v Accrington S
Torquay U v Aldershot T
Wycombe W v Barnet

Saturday, 2 October 2010
Barclays Premier League
Birmingham C v Everton
Liverpool v Blackpool
Manchester C v Newcastle U 1-2
Stoke C v Blackburn R
Sunderland v Manchester U GUITTAEZ
Tottenham H v Aston Villa
WBA v Bolton W
West Ham U v Fulham

npower Football League Championship
Barnsley v Cardiff C
Bristol C v Norwich C

Crystal Palace v QPR
Doncaster R v Nottingham F
Hull C v Coventry C
Ipswich T v Leeds U
Leicester C v Scunthorpe U
Middlesbrough v Portsmouth
Millwall v Burnley
Preston NE v Reading
Sheffield U v Watford
Swansea C v Derby Co

npower Football League One
Brentford v Charlton Ath
Carlisle U v Peterborough U
Dagenham & R v Swindon T
Exeter C v Rochdale
Huddersfield T v Bristol R
Milton Keynes D v Colchester U
Notts Co v Sheffield W
Oldham Ath v Leyton Orient
Plymouth Arg v Hartlepool U
Southampton v Bournemouth
Tranmere R v Brighton & HA
Walsall v Yeovil T

npower Football League Two
Accrington S v Gillingham
Aldershot T v Cheltenham T
Barnet v Hereford U
Bradford C v Morecambe
Burton Alb v Stockport Co
Bury v Rotherham U
Chesterfield v Crewe Alex
Macclesfield T v Northampton T
Oxford U v Port Vale
Shrewsbury T v Torquay U
Southend U v Lincoln C City
Stevenage v Wycombe W

Sunday, 3 October 2010
Barclays Premier League
Chelsea v Arsenal* (4.00)

Monday, 4 October 2010
Barclays Premier League
Wigan Ath v Wolverhampton W* (8.00)

Saturday, 9 October 2010
npower Football League One
Brentford v Oldham Ath
Brighton & HA v Bournemouth* (12.15)
Carlisle U v Notts Co
Colchester U v Huddersfield T
Hartlepool U v Peterborough U
Milton Keynes D v Dagenham & R
Plymouth Arg v Charlton Ath
Rochdale v Yeovil T
Sheffield W v Leyton Orient
Southampton v Tranmere R
Walsall v Exeter C

npower Football League Two
Barnet v Bradford C
Burton Alb v Wycombe W
Bury v Accrington S
Cheltenham T v Northampton T
Chesterfield v Southend U
Crewe Alex v Torquay U
Gillingham v Stockport Co
Hereford U v Port Vale
Lincoln C City v Macclesfield T
Morecambe v Shrewsbury T
Oxford U v Aldershot T
Rotherham U v Stevenage

Monday, 11 October 2010
npower Football League One
Swindon T v Bristol R* (7.45)

Saturday, 16 October 2010
Barclays Premier League
Arsenal v Birmingham C
Aston Villa v Chelsea
Bolton W v Stoke C
Fulham v Tottenham H
Manchester U v WBA
Newcastle U v Wigan Ath
Wolverhampton W v West Ham U

AMEdi
(gucinni
2 - 2

npower Football League Championship
Barnsley v Nottingham F
Cardiff C v Bristol C
Crystal Palace v Millwall
Derby Co v Preston NE
Ipswich T v Coventry C
Leicester C v Hull C
Middlesbrough v Leeds U* (5.20)
Portsmouth v Watford
QPR v Norwich C
Reading v Swansea C
Scunthorpe U v Doncaster R
Sheffield U v Burnley

npower Football League One
Bournemouth v Milton Keynes D
Bristol R v Rochdale
Charlton Ath v Brighton & HA
Dagenham & R v Walsall
Exeter C v Carlisle U
Huddersfield T v Southampton
Leyton Orient v Hartlepool U
Notts Co v Plymouth Arg
Oldham Ath v Colchester U
Peterborough U v Swindon T
Tranmere R v Brentford
Yeovil T v Sheffield W

npower Football League Two
Accrington S v Rotherham U
Aldershot T v Morecambe
Bradford C v Cheltenham T
Macclesfield T v Oxford U
Northampton T v Hereford U

Port Vale v Gillingham
Shrewsbury T v Lincoln C City
Southend U v Crewe Alex
Stevenage v Burton Alb
Stockport Co v Barnet
Torquay U v Bury
Wycombe W v Chesterfield

Sunday, 17 October 2010
Barclays Premier League
Blackpool v Manchester C* (4.00)
Everton v Liverpool* (1.30)

Monday, 18 October 2010
Barclays Premier League
Blackburn R v Sunderland* (8.00)

Tuesday, 19 October 2010
npower Football League Championship
Bristol C v Reading
Burnley v Barnsley
Coventry C v Cardiff C
Doncaster R v Derby Co
Hull C v Sheffield U
Leeds U v Leicester C
Millwall v Portsmouth
Norwich C v Crystal Palace
Nottingham F v Middlesbrough
Preston NE v Scunthorpe U
Swansea C v QPR
Watford v Ipswich T

Friday, 22 October 2010
npower Football League Championship
Bristol C v QPR* (7.45)

Saturday, 23 October 2010
Barclays Premier League
Birmingham C v Blackpool
Chelsea v Wolverhampton W
Liverpool v Blackburn R
Sunderland v Aston Villa
Tottenham H v Everton* (12.45)
WBA v Fulham
West Ham U v Newcastle U* (5.30)
Wigan Ath v Bolton W

2 - 1
NOLAN, CARR

npower Football League Championship
Burnley v Reading
Coventry C v Barnsley
Doncaster R v Sheffield U
Hull C v Portsmouth
Leeds U v Cardiff C
Millwall v Derby Co
Norwich C v Middlesbrough
Nottingham F v Ipswich T
Preston NE v Crystal Palace
Watford v Scunthorpe U

npower Football League One
Brentford v Peterborough U
Brighton & HA v Yeovil T
Carlisle U v Charlton Ath

Colchester U v Notts Co
Hartlepool U v Bristol R
Milton Keynes D v Exeter C
Plymouth Arg v Huddersfield T
Rochdale v Dagenham & R
Sheffield W v Bournemouth
Southampton v Oldham Ath
Swindon T v Leyton Orient
Walsall v Tranmere R

npower Football League Two
Barnet v Macclesfield T
Burton Alb v Bradford C
Bury v Southend U
Cheltenham T v Port Vale
Chesterfield v Shrewsbury T
Crewe Alex v Aldershot T
Gillingham v Torquay U
Hereford U v Accrington S
Lincoln C City v Stockport Co
Morecambe v Stevenage
Oxford U v Northampton T
Rotherham U v Wycombe W

Sunday, 24 October 2010
Barclays Premier League
Stoke C v Manchester U* (1.30)
Manchester C v Arsenal* (4.00)

Monday, 25 October 2010
npower Football League Championship
Swansea C v Leicester C* (7.45)

Saturday, 30 October 2010
Barclays Premier League
Arsenal v West Ham U
Aston Villa v Birmingham C
Blackburn R v Chelsea
Everton v Stoke C
Fulham v Wigan Ath
Manchester U v Tottenham H
Wolverhampton W v Manchester C

npower Football League Championship
Barnsley v Hull C* (5.20)
Cardiff C v Norwich C
Crystal Palace v Swansea C
Derby Co v Watford
Ipswich T v Millwall
Leicester C v Preston NE
Middlesbrough v Bristol C
Portsmouth v Nottingham F
QPR v Burnley
Reading v Doncaster R
Scunthorpe U v Leeds U
Sheffield U v Coventry C

npower Football League One
Bournemouth v Colchester U
Bristol R v Carlisle U
Charlton Ath v Sheffield W
Dagenham & R v Hartlepool U

Exeter C v Brentford
Huddersfield T v Walsall
Leyton Orient v Rochdale
Notts Co v Southampton
Oldham Ath v Plymouth Arg
Peterborough U v Brighton & HA
Tranmere R v Milton Keynes D
Yeovil T v Swindon T

npower Football League Two
Accrington S v Cheltenham T
Aldershot T v Bury
Bradford C v Oxford U
Macclesfield T v Burton Alb
Northampton T v Gillingham
Port Vale v Crewe Alex
Shrewsbury T v Barnet
Southend U v Rotherham U
Stevenage v Chesterfield
Stockport Co v Hereford U
Torquay U v Morecambe
Wycombe W v Lincoln C City

Sunday, 31 October 2010
Barclays Premier League
Bolton W v Liverpool* (1.30)
Newcastle U v Sunderland* (4.00)

Monday, 1 November 2010
Barclays Premier League
Blackpool v WBA* (8.00)

Tuesday, 2 November 2010
npower Football League One
Brentford v Bournemouth
Brighton & HA v Exeter C
Carlisle U v Tranmere R
Colchester U v Leyton Orient
Hartlepool U v Notts Co
Milton Keynes D v Yeovil T
Plymouth Arg v Bristol R
Rochdale v Oldham Ath
Sheffield W v Huddersfield T
Southampton v Dagenham & R
Swindon T v Charlton Ath
Walsall v Peterborough U

npower Football League Two
Barnet v Stevenage
Burton Alb v Port Vale
Bury v Bradford C
Cheltenham T v Southend U
Chesterfield v Accrington S
Crewe Alex v Shrewsbury T
Gillingham v Wycombe W
Hereford U v Aldershot T
Lincoln C City v Northampton T
Morecambe v Stockport Co
Oxford U v Torquay U
Rotherham U v Macclesfield T

Saturday, 6 November 2010
Barclays Premier League
Birmingham C v West Ham U
Blackburn R v Wigan Ath
Blackpool v Everton
Bolton W v Tottenham H* (12.45)
Fulham v Aston Villa
Manchester U v Wolverhampton W
Sunderland v Stoke C
WBA v Manchester C

npower Football League Championship
Barnsley v Leicester C
Bristol C v Preston NE
Cardiff C v Swansea C
Coventry C v Leeds U
Derby Co v Portsmouth* (5.20)
Doncaster R v Millwall
Hull C v Scunthorpe U
Middlesbrough v Crystal Palace
Norwich C v Burnley
QPR v Reading
Sheffield U v Ipswich T
Watford v Nottingham F

Sunday, 7 November 2010
Barclays Premier League
Arsenal v Newcastle U* (1.30) 0-1
Liverpool v Chelsea* (4.00)
CARROLL

Tuesday, 9 November 2010
Barclays Premier League
Stoke C v Birmingham C
Tottenham H v Sunderland
West Ham U v WBA* (8.00)
Wigan Ath v Liverpool
Wolverhampton W v Arsenal

npower Football League Championship
Burnley v Doncaster R
Crystal Palace v Watford
Ipswich T v Derby Co
Leeds U v Hull C
Leicester C v Sheffield U
Millwall v Norwich C
Nottingham F v Coventry C
Portsmouth v QPR
Preston NE v Barnsley
Reading v Cardiff C
Scunthorpe U v Middlesbrough
Swansea C v Bristol C

Wednesday, 10 November 2010
Barclays Premier League
Aston Villa v Blackpool
Chelsea v Fulham
Everton v Bolton W
Manchester C v Manchester U* (8.00)
Newcastle U v Blackburn R   1-2

Friday, 12 November 2010
npower Football League Championship
Preston NE v Hull C* (7.45)

Saturday, 13 November 2010
Barclays Premier League
Aston Villa v Manchester U* (12.45)
Manchester C v Birmingham C
Newcastle U v Fulham   0-0
Stoke C v Liverpool
Tottenham H v Blackburn R
West Ham U v Blackpool
Wigan Ath v WBA
Wolverhampton W v Bolton W

npower Football League Championship
Burnley v Watford
Crystal Palace v Coventry C
Ipswich T v Barnsley
Leeds U v Bristol C
Leicester C v Derby Co
Millwall v Sheffield U
Nottingham F v QPR
Portsmouth v Doncaster R
Reading v Norwich C* (5.20)
Scunthorpe U v Cardiff C
Swansea C v Middlesbrough

npower Football League One
Bournemouth v Walsall
Brentford v Milton Keynes D
Bristol R v Leyton Orient
Carlisle U v Southampton
Exeter C v Notts Co
Hartlepool U v Brighton & HA
Oldham Ath v Huddersfield T
Peterborough U v Charlton Ath
Sheffield W v Rochdale
Swindon T v Colchester U
Tranmere R v Plymouth Arg
Yeovil T v Dagenham & R

npower Football League Two
Bury v Stockport Co
Chesterfield v Burton Alb
Gillingham v Crewe Alex
Hereford U v Cheltenham T
Macclesfield T v Aldershot T
Morecambe v Lincoln C City
Northampton T v Port Vale
Rotherham U v Oxford U
Southend U v Accrington S
Stevenage v Shrewsbury T
Torquay U v Barnet
Wycombe W v Bradford C

Sunday, 14 November 2010
Barclays Premier League
Everton v Arsenal* (2.00)
Chelsea v Sunderland* (4.10)

Saturday, 20 November 2010
Barclays Premier League
Birmingham C v Chelsea
Blackburn R v Aston Villa
Blackpool v Wolverhampton W
Bolton W v Newcastle U
Liverpool v West Ham U
Manchester U v Wigan Ath
WBA v Stoke C

npower Football League Championship
Barnsley v Portsmouth
Bristol C v Leicester C
Cardiff C v Nottingham F
Coventry C v Burnley
Derby Co v Scunthorpe U
Doncaster R v Swansea C
Hull C v Ipswich T
Middlesbrough v Millwall
Norwich C v Leeds U
QPR v Preston NE
Sheffield U v Crystal Palace* (5.20)
Watford v Reading

npower Football League One
Brighton & HA v Bristol R
Charlton Ath v Yeovil T
Colchester U v Hartlepool U
Dagenham & R v Oldham Ath
Huddersfield T v Exeter C
Leyton Orient v Bournemouth
Milton Keynes D v Sheffield W
Notts Co v Tranmere R
Plymouth Arg v Brentford
Rochdale v Swindon T
Southampton v Peterborough U
Walsall v Carlisle U

npower Football League Two
Accrington S v Stevenage
Aldershot T v Chesterfield
Barnet v Northampton T
Bradford C v Macclesfield T
Burton Alb v Bury
Cheltenham T v Morecambe
Crewe Alex v Rotherham U
Lincoln C City v Hereford U
Oxford U v Gillingham
Port Vale v Wycombe W
Shrewsbury T v Southend U
Stockport Co v Torquay U

Sunday, 21 November 2010
Barclays Premier League
Arsenal v Tottenham H* (1.30)
Fulham v Manchester C* (4.00)

Monday, 22 November 2010
Barclays Premier League
Sunderland v Everton* (8.00)

Tuesday, 23 November 2010
npower Football League One
Bournemouth v Yeovil T
Carlisle U v Rochdale
Charlton Ath v Bristol R
Colchester U v Brentford
Huddersfield T v Milton Keynes D
Notts Co v Swindon T
Oldham Ath v Exeter C
Peterborough U v Leyton Orient
Plymouth Arg v Dagenham & R
Sheffield W v Walsall
Southampton v Brighton & HA
Tranmere R v Hartlepool U

npower Football League Two
Barnet v Gillingham
Bradford C v Accrington S
Burton Alb v Aldershot T
Chesterfield v Oxford U
Lincoln C City v Bury
Macclesfield T v Cheltenham T
Morecambe v Crewe Alex
Rotherham U v Northampton T
Shrewsbury T v Hereford U
Stevenage v Southend U
Stockport Co v Port Vale
Wycombe W v Torquay U

Saturday, 27 November 2010
Barclays Premier League
Aston Villa v Arsenal* (12.45)
Bolton W v Blackpool
Everton v WBA
Fulham v Birmingham C
Manchester U v Blackburn R
Stoke C v Manchester C
West Ham U v Wigan Ath
Wolverhampton W v Sunderland

npower Football League Championship
Barnsley v Watford
Bristol C v Sheffield U
Burnley v Derby Co
Crystal Palace v Doncaster R
Middlesbrough v Hull C
Norwich C v Ipswich T
Preston NE v Millwall
QPR v Cardiff C
Reading v Leeds U
Scunthorpe U v Coventry C
Swansea C v Portsmouth

Sunday, 28 November 2010
Barclays Premier League
Newcastle U v Chelsea* (1.30)
Tottenham H v Liverpool* (4.00)

Monday, 29 November 2010
npower Football League Championship
Leicester C v Nottingham F* (7.45)

Saturday, 4 December 2010
Barclays Premier League
Arsenal v Fulham
Birmingham C v Tottenham H
Blackburn R v Wolverhampton W
Blackpool v Manchester U
Chelsea v Everton
Liverpool v Aston Villa
Manchester C v Bolton W
Sunderland v West Ham U
WBA v Newcastle U ~~3-1~~
Wigan Ath v Stoke C *LOVENKRANS*

npower Football League Championship
Cardiff C v Preston NE
Coventry C v Middlesbrough
Derby Co v Norwich C
Doncaster R v Barnsley
Hull C v QPR
Ipswich T v Swansea C
Leeds U v Crystal Palace
Millwall v Scunthorpe U
Nottingham F v Bristol C
Portsmouth v Burnley
Sheffield U v Reading
Watford v Leicester C

npower Football League One
Brentford v Notts Co
Brighton & HA v Colchester U
Bristol R v Bournemouth
Dagenham & R v Huddersfield T
Exeter C v Tranmere R
Hartlepool U v Southampton
Leyton Orient v Carlisle U
Milton Keynes D v Plymouth Arg
Rochdale v Charlton Ath
Swindon T v Sheffield W
Walsall v Oldham Ath
Yeovil T v Peterborough U

npower Football League Two
Accrington S v Shrewsbury T
Aldershot T v Bradford C
Bury v Chesterfield
Cheltenham T v Lincoln C City
Crewe Alex v Wycombe W
Gillingham v Rotherham U
Hereford U v Morecambe
Northampton T v Stockport Co
Oxford U v Barnet
Port Vale v Stevenage
Southend U v Macclesfield T
Torquay U v Burton Alb

Saturday, 11 December 2010
Barclays Premier League
Aston Villa v WBA
Bolton W v Blackburn R
Everton v Wigan Ath
Fulham v Sunderland
Manchester U v Arsenal

Newcastle U v Liverpool *3-1 NOLAN, PART CARROL*
Stoke C v Blackpool
Tottenham H v Chelsea
West Ham U v Manchester C
Wolverhampton W v Birmingham C

npower Football League Championship
Barnsley v Sheffield U
Bristol C v Derby Co
Burnley v Leeds U
Crystal Palace v Hull C
Leicester C v Doncaster R
Middlesbrough v Cardiff C
Norwich C v Portsmouth
Preston NE v Ipswich T
QPR v Watford
Reading v Coventry C
Scunthorpe U v Nottingham F
Swansea C v Millwall

npower Football League One
Bournemouth v Hartlepool U
Carlisle U v Dagenham & R
Charlton Ath v Walsall
Colchester U v Yeovil T
Huddersfield T v Brighton & HA
Notts Co v Milton Keynes D
Oldham Ath v Swindon T
Peterborough U v Rochdale
Plymouth Arg v Exeter C
Sheffield W v Bristol R
Southampton v Brentford
Tranmere R v Leyton Orient

npower Football League Two
Barnet v Accrington S
Bradford C v Hereford U
Burton Alb v Southend U
Chesterfield v Torquay U
Lincoln C City v Oxford U
Macclesfield T v Gillingham
Morecambe v Port Vale
Rotherham U v Aldershot T
Shrewsbury T v Cheltenham T
Stevenage v Northampton T
Stockport Co v Crewe Alex
Wycombe W v Bury

Saturday, 18 December 2010
Barclays Premier League
Arsenal v Stoke C
Birmingham C v Newcastle U
Blackburn R v West Ham U *2-0*
Blackpool v Tottenham H
Chelsea v Manchester U
Liverpool v Fulham
Manchester C v Everton *LOVKLAND BESt.*
Sunderland v Bolton W
WBA v Wolverhampton W
Wigan Ath v Aston Villa

npower Football League Championship
Cardiff C v Burnley
Coventry C v Norwich C
Derby Co v Reading
Doncaster R v Middlesbrough
Hull C v Bristol C
Ipswich T v Leicester C
Leeds U v QPR
Millwall v Barnsley
Nottingham F v Crystal Palace
Portsmouth v Scunthorpe U
Sheffield U v Swansea C
Watford v Preston NE

npower Football League One
Brentford v Huddersfield T
Brighton & HA v Notts Co
Bristol R v Colchester U
Dagenham & R v Peterborough U
Exeter C v Sheffield W
Hartlepool U v Charlton Ath
Leyton Orient v Plymouth Arg
Milton Keynes D v Oldham Ath
Rochdale v Bournemouth
Swindon T v Tranmere R
Walsall v Southampton
Yeovil T v Carlisle U

npower Football League Two
Accrington S v Burton Alb
Aldershot T v Lincoln C City
Bury v Stevenage
Cheltenham T v Stockport Co
Crewe Alex v Bradford C
Gillingham v Chesterfield
Hereford U v Macclesfield T
Northampton T v Morecambe
Oxford U v Shrewsbury T
Port Vale v Barnet
Southend U v Wycombe W
Torquay U v Rotherham U

Sunday, 26 December 2010
Barclays Premier League
Arsenal v Chelsea
Aston Villa v Tottenham H
Blackburn R v Stoke C
Blackpool v Liverpool
Bolton W v WBA   GMMoll
Everton v Birmingham C
Fulham v West Ham U
Manchester U v Sunderland
Newcastle U v Manchester C   1-3
Wolverhampton W v Wigan Ath

npower Football League Championship
Barnsley v Burnley
Cardiff C v Coventry C
Crystal Palace v Norwich C
Derby Co v Doncaster R
Ipswich T v Watford
Leicester C v Leeds U

Middlesbrough v Nottingham F
Portsmouth v Millwall
QPR v Swansea C
Reading v Bristol C
Scunthorpe U v Preston NE
Sheffield U v Hull C

npower Football League One
Bournemouth v Plymouth Arg
Bristol R v Walsall
Charlton Ath v Southampton
Dagenham & R v Brighton & HA
Exeter C v Swindon T
Huddersfield T v Hartlepool U
Leyton Orient v Milton Keynes D
Notts Co v Rochdale
Oldham Ath v Carlisle U
Peterborough U v Colchester U
Tranmere R v Sheffield W
Yeovil T v Brentford

npower Football League Two
Accrington S v Crewe Alex
Aldershot T v Gillingham
Bradford C v Chesterfield
Macclesfield T v Morecambe
Northampton T v Burton Alb
Port Vale v Lincoln C City
Shrewsbury T v Bury
Southend U v Barnet
Stevenage v Oxford U
Stockport Co v Rotherham U
Torquay U v Cheltenham T
Wycombe W v Hereford U

Tuesday, 28 December 2010
Barclays Premier League
Birmingham C v Manchester U
Chelsea v Bolton W
Liverpool v Wolverhampton W
Manchester C v Aston Villa
Stoke C v Fulham
Sunderland v Blackpool
Tottenham H v Newcastle U   2-0
WBA v Blackburn R
West Ham U v Everton
Wigan Ath v Arsenal

npower Football League Championship
Bristol C v Crystal Palace
Burnley v Scunthorpe U
Coventry C v QPR
Doncaster R v Ipswich T
Hull C v Reading
Leeds U v Portsmouth
Millwall v Leicester C
Norwich C v Sheffield U
Nottingham F v Derby Co
Preston NE v Middlesbrough
Swansea C v Barnsley
Watford v Cardiff C

363

npower Football League One
Brentford v Tranmere R
Brighton & HA v Charlton Ath
Carlisle U v Exeter C
Colchester U v Oldham Ath
Hartlepool U v Leyton Orient
Milton Keynes D v Bournemouth
Plymouth Arg v Notts Co
Rochdale v Bristol R
Sheffield W v Yeovil T
Southampton v Huddersfield T
Swindon T v Peterborough U
Walsall v Dagenham & R

npower Football League Two
Barnet v Stockport Co
Burton Alb v Stevenage
Bury v Torquay U
Cheltenham T v Bradford C
Chesterfield v Wycombe W
Crewe Alex v Southend U
Gillingham v Port Vale
Hereford U v Northampton T
Lincoln C City v Shrewsbury T
Morecambe v Aldershot T
Oxford U v Macclesfield T
Rotherham U v Accrington S

Saturday, 1 January 2011
Barclays Premier League
Birmingham C v Arsenal
Chelsea v Aston Villa
Liverpool v Bolton W
Manchester C v Blackpool
Stoke C v Everton
Sunderland v Blackburn R
Tottenham H v Fulham
WBA v Manchester U
West Ham U v Wolverhampton W
Wigan Ath v Newcastle U

npower Football League Championship
Bristol C v Cardiff C
Burnley v Sheffield U
Coventry C v Ipswich T
Doncaster R v Scunthorpe U
Hull C v Leicester C
Leeds U v Middlesbrough
Millwall v Crystal Palace
Norwich C v QPR
Nottingham F v Barnsley
Preston NE v Derby Co
Swansea C v Reading
Watford v Portsmouth

npower Football League One
Brentford v Dagenham & R
Brighton & HA v Leyton Orient
Carlisle U v Huddersfield T
Colchester U v Charlton Ath
Hartlepool U v Oldham Ath
Milton Keynes D v Bristol R

Plymouth Arg v Yeovil T
Rochdale v Tranmere R
Sheffield W v Peterborough U
Southampton v Exeter C
Swindon T v Bournemouth
Walsall v Notts Co

npower Football League Two
Barnet v Aldershot T
Burton Alb v Shrewsbury T
Bury v Macclesfield T
Cheltenham T v Wycombe W
Chesterfield v Stockport Co
Crewe Alex v Northampton T
Gillingham v Stevenage
Hereford U v Torquay U
Lincoln C City v Bradford C
Morecambe v Accrington S
Oxford U v Southend U
Rotherham U v Port Vale

Monday, 3 January 2011
npower Football League Championship
Barnsley v Coventry C
Cardiff C v Leeds U
Crystal Palace v Preston NE
Derby Co v Millwall
Ipswich T v Nottingham F
Leicester C v Swansea C
Middlesbrough v Norwich C
Portsmouth v Hull C
QPR v Bristol C
Reading v Burnley
Scunthorpe U v Watford
Sheffield U v Doncaster R

npower Football League One
Bournemouth v Brentford
Bristol R v Plymouth Arg
Charlton Ath v Swindon T
Dagenham & R v Southampton
Exeter C v Brighton & HA
Huddersfield T v Sheffield W
Leyton Orient v Colchester U
Notts Co v Hartlepool U
Oldham Ath v Rochdale
Peterborough U v Walsall
Tranmere R v Carlisle U
Yeovil T v Milton Keynes D

npower Football League Two
Accrington S v Chesterfield
Aldershot T v Hereford U
Bradford C v Bury
Macclesfield T v Rotherham U
Northampton T v Lincoln C City
Port Vale v Burton Alb
Shrewsbury T v Crewe Alex
Southend U v Cheltenham T
Stevenage v Barnet
Stockport Co v Morecambe

Torquay U v Oxford U
Wycombe W v Gillingham

Tuesday, 4 January 2011
Barclays Premier League
Arsenal v Manchester C
Blackpool v Birmingham C
Bolton W v Wigan Ath
Manchester U v Stoke C
Wolverhampton W v Chelsea

Wednesday, 5 January 2011
Barclays Premier League
Aston Villa v Sunderland
Blackburn R v Liverpool
Everton v Tottenham H
Fulham v WBA
Newcastle U v West Ham U

Saturday, 8 January 2011
npower Football League One
Bournemouth v Sheffield W
Bristol R v Hartlepool U
Charlton Ath v Carlisle U
Dagenham & R v Rochdale
Exeter C v Milton Keynes D
Huddersfield T v Plymouth Arg
Leyton Orient v Swindon T
Notts Co v Colchester U
Oldham Ath v Southampton
Peterborough U v Brentford
Tranmere R v Walsall
Yeovil T v Brighton & HA

npower Football League Two
Accrington S v Bury
Aldershot T v Oxford U
Bradford C v Barnet
Macclesfield T v Lincoln C City
Northampton T v Cheltenham T
Port Vale v Hereford U
Shrewsbury T v Morecambe
Southend U v Chesterfield
Stevenage v Rotherham U
Stockport Co v Gillingham
Torquay U v Crewe Alex
Wycombe W v Burton Alb

Saturday, 15 January 2011
Barclays Premier League
Birmingham C v Aston Villa
Chelsea v Blackburn R
Liverpool v Everton
Manchester C v Wolverhampton W
Stoke C v Bolton W
Sunderland v Newcastle U
Tottenham H v Manchester U
WBA v Blackpool
West Ham U v Arsenal
Wigan Ath v Fulham

npower Football League Championship
Bristol C v Middlesbrough
Burnley v QPR
Coventry C v Sheffield U
Doncaster R v Reading
Hull C v Barnsley
Leeds U v Scunthorpe U
Millwall v Ipswich T
Norwich C v Cardiff C
Nottingham F v Portsmouth
Preston NE v Leicester C
Swansea C v Crystal Palace
Watford v Derby Co

npower Football League One
Brentford v Exeter C
Brighton & HA v Peterborough U
Carlisle U v Bristol R
Colchester U v Bournemouth
Hartlepool U v Dagenham & R
Milton Keynes D v Tranmere R
Plymouth Arg v Oldham Ath
Rochdale v Leyton Orient
Sheffield W v Charlton Ath
Southampton v Notts Co
Swindon T v Yeovil T
Walsall v Huddersfield T

npower Football League Two
Barnet v Shrewsbury T
Burton Alb v Macclesfield T
Bury v Aldershot T
Cheltenham T v Accrington S
Chesterfield v Stevenage
Crewe Alex v Port Vale
Gillingham v Northampton T
Hereford U v Stockport Co
Lincoln C City v Wycombe W
Morecambe v Torquay U
Oxford U v Bradford C
Rotherham U v Southend U

Saturday, 22 January 2011
Barclays Premier League
Arsenal v Wigan Ath
Aston Villa v Manchester C
Blackburn R v WBA
Blackpool v Sunderland
Bolton W v Chelsea
Everton v West Ham U
Fulham v Stoke C
Manchester U v Birmingham C
Newcastle U v Tottenham H
Wolverhampton W v Liverpool

npower Football League Championship
Barnsley v Swansea C
Cardiff C v Watford
Crystal Palace v Bristol C
Derby Co v Nottingham F
Ipswich T v Doncaster R
Leicester C v Millwall

Middlesbrough v Preston NE
Portsmouth v Leeds U
QPR v Coventry C
Reading v Hull C
Scunthorpe U v Burnley
Sheffield U v Norwich C

npower Football League One
Bournemouth v Brighton & HA
Bristol R v Swindon T
Charlton Ath v Plymouth Arg
Dagenham & R v Milton Keynes D
Exeter C v Walsall
Huddersfield T v Colchester U
Leyton Orient v Sheffield W
Notts Co v Carlisle U
Oldham Ath v Brentford
Peterborough U v Hartlepool U
Tranmere R v Southampton
Yeovil T v Rochdale

npower Football League Two
Accrington S v Hereford U
Aldershot T v Crewe Alex
Bradford C v Burton Alb
Macclesfield T v Barnet
Northampton T v Oxford U
Port Vale v Cheltenham T
Shrewsbury T v Chesterfield
Southend U v Bury
Stevenage v Morecambe
Stockport Co v Lincoln C City
Torquay U v Gillingham
Wycombe W v Rotherham U

Saturday, 29 January 2011
npower Football League One
Brentford v Yeovil T
Brighton & HA v Dagenham & R
Carlisle U v Oldham Ath
Colchester U v Peterborough U
Hartlepool U v Huddersfield T
Milton Keynes D v Leyton Orient
Plymouth Arg v Bournemouth
Rochdale v Notts Co
Sheffield W v Tranmere R
Southampton v Charlton Ath
Swindon T v Exeter C
Walsall v Bristol R

npower Football League Two
Barnet v Southend U
Burton Alb v Northampton T
Bury v Shrewsbury T
Cheltenham T v Torquay U
Chesterfield v Bradford C
Crewe Alex v Accrington S
Gillingham v Aldershot T
Hereford U v Wycombe W
Lincoln C City v Port Vale
Morecambe v Macclesfield T
Oxford U v Stevenage

Rotherham U v Stockport Co

Tuesday, 1 February 2011
Barclays Premier League
Arsenal v Everton
Birmingham C v Manchester C
Blackpool v West Ham U
Bolton W v Wolverhampton W
Manchester U v Aston Villa
Sunderland v Chelsea
WBA v Wigan Ath

npower Football League Championship
Barnsley v Preston NE
Bristol C v Swansea C
Cardiff C v Reading
Coventry C v Nottingham F
Derby Co v Ipswich T
Doncaster R v Burnley
Hull C v Leeds U
Middlesbrough v Scunthorpe U
Norwich C v Millwall
QPR v Portsmouth
Sheffield U v Leicester C
Watford v Crystal Palace

npower Football League One
Bournemouth v Swindon T
Bristol R v Milton Keynes D
Charlton Ath v Colchester U
Dagenham & R v Brentford
Exeter C v Southampton
Huddersfield T v Carlisle U
Leyton Orient v Brighton & HA
Notts Co v Walsall
Oldham Ath v Hartlepool U
Peterborough U v Sheffield W
Tranmere R v Rochdale
Yeovil T v Plymouth Arg

npower Football League Two
Accrington S v Morecambe
Aldershot T v Barnet
Bradford C v Lincoln C City
Macclesfield T v Bury
Northampton T v Crewe Alex
Port Vale v Rotherham U
Shrewsbury T v Burton Alb
Southend U v Oxford U
Stevenage v Gillingham
Stockport Co v Chesterfield
Torquay U v Hereford U
Wycombe W v Cheltenham T

Wednesday, 2 February 2011
Barclays Premier League
Blackburn R v Tottenham H
Fulham v Newcastle U
Liverpool v Stoke C

Saturday, 5 February 2011
Barclays Premier League
Aston Villa v Fulham
Chelsea v Liverpool
Everton v Blackpool
Manchester C v WBA
Newcastle U v Arsenal
Stoke C v Sunderland
Tottenham H v Bolton W
West Ham U v Birmingham C
Wigan Ath v Blackburn R
Wolverhampton W v Manchester U

[handwritten: BARTON (2) PENS / TIOTE / BEST / 4-4]

npower Football League Championship
Burnley v Norwich C
Crystal Palace v Middlesbrough
Ipswich T v Sheffield U
Leeds U v Coventry C
Leicester C v Barnsley
Millwall v Doncaster R
Nottingham F v Watford
Portsmouth v Derby Co
Preston NE v Bristol C
Reading v QPR
Scunthorpe U v Hull C
Swansea C v Cardiff C

npower Football League One
Bournemouth v Leyton Orient
Brentford v Plymouth Arg
Bristol R v Brighton & HA
Carlisle U v Walsall
Exeter C v Huddersfield T
Hartlepool U v Colchester U
Oldham Ath v Dagenham & R
Peterborough U v Southampton
Sheffield W v Milton Keynes D
Swindon T v Rochdale
Tranmere R v Notts Co
Yeovil T v Charlton Ath

npower Football League Two
Bury v Burton Alb
Chesterfield v Aldershot T
Gillingham v Oxford U
Hereford U v Lincoln C City
Macclesfield T v Bradford C
Morecambe v Cheltenham T
Northampton T v Barnet
Rotherham U v Crewe Alex
Southend U v Shrewsbury T
Stevenage v Accrington S
Torquay U v Stockport Co
Wycombe W v Port Vale

Saturday, 12 February 2011
Barclays Premier League
Arsenal v Wolverhampton W
Birmingham C v Stoke C
Blackburn R v Newcastle U
Blackpool v Aston Villa
Bolton W v Everton

[handwritten: 0-0]

Fulham v Chelsea
Liverpool v Wigan Ath
Manchester U v Manchester C
Sunderland v Tottenham H
WBA v West Ham U

npower Football League Championship
Barnsley v Ipswich T
Bristol C v Leeds U
Cardiff C v Scunthorpe U
Coventry C v Crystal Palace
Derby Co v Leicester C
Doncaster R v Portsmouth
Hull C v Preston NE
Middlesbrough v Swansea C
Norwich C v Reading
QPR v Nottingham F
Sheffield U v Millwall
Watford v Burnley

npower Football League One
Brighton & HA v Hartlepool U
Charlton Ath v Peterborough U
Colchester U v Swindon T
Dagenham & R v Yeovil T
Huddersfield T v Oldham Ath
Leyton Orient v Bristol R
Milton Keynes D v Brentford
Notts Co v Exeter C
Plymouth Arg v Tranmere R
Rochdale v Sheffield W
Southampton v Carlisle U
Walsall v Bournemouth

npower Football League Two
Accrington S v Southend U
Aldershot T v Macclesfield T
Barnet v Torquay U
Bradford C v Wycombe W
Burton Alb v Chesterfield
Cheltenham T v Hereford U
Crewe Alex v Gillingham
Lincoln C City v Morecambe
Oxford U v Rotherham U
Port Vale v Northampton T
Shrewsbury T v Stevenage
Stockport Co v Bury

Saturday, 19 February 2011
npower Football League Championship
Burnley v Coventry C
Crystal Palace v Sheffield U
Ipswich T v Hull C
Leeds U v Norwich C
Leicester C v Bristol C
Millwall v Middlesbrough
Nottingham F v Cardiff C
Portsmouth v Barnsley
Preston NE v QPR
Reading v Watford
Scunthorpe U v Derby Co
Swansea C v Doncaster R

npower Football League One
Bournemouth v Huddersfield T
Brighton & HA v Plymouth Arg
Bristol R v Oldham Ath
Charlton Ath v Exeter C
Colchester U v Walsall
Hartlepool U v Milton Keynes D
Leyton Orient v Dagenham & R
Peterborough U v Tranmere R
Rochdale v Southampton
Sheffield W v Brentford
Swindon T v Carlisle U
Yeovil T v Notts Co

npower Football League Two
Cheltenham T v Barnet
Crewe Alex v Stevenage
Gillingham v Bury
Hereford U v Burton Alb
Lincoln C City v Chesterfield
Morecambe v Oxford U
Northampton T v Aldershot T
Port Vale v Bradford C
Rotherham U v Shrewsbury T
Stockport Co v Macclesfield T
Torquay U v Southend U
Wycombe W v Accrington S

Tuesday, 22 February 2011
npower Football League Championship
Burnley v Middlesbrough
Cardiff C v Leicester C
Coventry C v Swansea C
Derby Co v Hull C
Leeds U v Barnsley
Norwich C v Doncaster R
Nottingham F v Preston NE
Portsmouth v Crystal Palace
QPR v Ipswich T
Reading v Millwall
Scunthorpe U v Sheffield U
Watford v Bristol C

Saturday, 26 February 2011
Barclays Premier League
Aston Villa v Blackburn R   NORN
Chelsea v Birmingham C
Everton v Sunderland
Manchester C v Fulham
Newcastle U v Bolton W   1-1
Stoke C v WBA
Tottenham H v Arsenal
West Ham U v Liverpool
Wigan Ath v Manchester U
Wolverhampton W v Blackpool

npower Football League Championship
Barnsley v Norwich C
Bristol C v Scunthorpe U
Crystal Palace v Reading
Doncaster R v Watford
Hull C v Cardiff C

Ipswich T v Portsmouth
Leicester C v Coventry C
Middlesbrough v QPR
Millwall v Nottingham F
Preston NE v Burnley
Sheffield U v Derby Co
Swansea C v Leeds U

npower Football League One
Brentford v Bristol R
Carlisle U v Sheffield W
Dagenham & R v Bournemouth
Exeter C v Hartlepool U
Huddersfield T v Leyton Orient
Milton Keynes D v Brighton & HA
Notts Co v Charlton Ath
Oldham Ath v Peterborough U
Plymouth Arg v Colchester U
Southampton v Swindon T
Tranmere R v Yeovil T
Walsall v Rochdale

npower Football League Two
Accrington S v Torquay U
Aldershot T v Port Vale
Barnet v Lincoln C City
Bradford C v Stockport Co
Burton Alb v Rotherham U
Bury v Crewe Alex
Chesterfield v Morecambe
Macclesfield T v Wycombe W
Oxford U v Hereford U
Shrewsbury T v Gillingham
Southend U v Northampton T
Stevenage v Cheltenham T

Saturday, 5 March 2011
Barclays Premier League
Arsenal v Sunderland
Birmingham C v WBA
Blackpool v Chelsea   BEST
Bolton W v Aston Villa
Fulham v Blackburn R
Liverpool v Manchester U
Manchester C v Wigan Ath
Newcastle U v Everton   1-2
West Ham U v Stoke C
Wolverhampton W v Tottenham H

npower Football League Championship
Burnley v Crystal Palace
Cardiff C v Ipswich T
Coventry C v Bristol C
Derby Co v Barnsley
Leeds U v Doncaster R
Norwich C v Preston NE
Nottingham F v Hull C
Portsmouth v Sheffield U
QPR v Leicester C
Reading v Middlesbrough
Scunthorpe U v Swansea C
Watford v Millwall

npower Football League One
Bournemouth v Oldham Ath
Brighton & HA v Carlisle U
Bristol R v Dagenham & R
Charlton Ath v Tranmere R
Colchester U v Southampton
Hartlepool U v Brentford
Leyton Orient v Notts Co
Peterborough U v Exeter C
Rochdale v Milton Keynes D
Sheffield W v Plymouth Arg
Swindon T v Walsall
Yeovil T v Huddersfield T

npower Football League Two
Cheltenham T v Chesterfield
Crewe Alex v Burton Alb
Gillingham v Bradford C
Hereford U v Bury
Lincoln C City v Accrington S
Morecambe v Southend U
Northampton T v Shrewsbury T
Port Vale v Macclesfield T
Rotherham U v Barnet
Stockport Co v Oxford U
Torquay U v Stevenage
Wycombe W v Aldershot T

Tuesday, 8 March 2011
npower Football League Championship
Barnsley v Scunthorpe U
Bristol C v Portsmouth
Crystal Palace v Cardiff C
Doncaster R v Coventry C
Hull C v Burnley
Ipswich T v Reading
Leicester C v Norwich C
Middlesbrough v Derby Co
Millwall v QPR
Preston NE v Leeds U
Sheffield U v Nottingham F
Swansea C v Watford

npower Football League One
Brentford v Brighton & HA
Carlisle U v Hartlepool U
Dagenham & R v Colchester U
Exeter C v Bournemouth
Huddersfield T v Rochdale
Milton Keynes D v Charlton Ath
Notts Co v Peterborough U
Oldham Ath v Sheffield W
Plymouth Arg v Swindon T
Southampton v Yeovil T
Tranmere R v Bristol R
Walsall v Leyton Orient

npower Football League Two
Accrington S v Stockport Co
Aldershot T v Torquay U
Barnet v Wycombe W
Bradford C v Rotherham U

Burton Alb v Lincoln C City
Bury v Morecambe
Chesterfield v Northampton T
Macclesfield T v Crewe Alex
Oxford U v Cheltenham T
Shrewsbury T v Port Vale
Southend U v Gillingham
Stevenage v Hereford U

Saturday, 12 March 2011
npower Football League Championship
Burnley v Millwall
Cardiff C v Barnsley
Coventry C v Hull C
Derby Co v Swansea C
Leeds U v Ipswich T
Norwich C v Bristol C
Nottingham F v Doncaster R
Portsmouth v Middlesbrough
QPR v Crystal Palace
Reading v Preston NE
Scunthorpe U v Leicester C
Watford v Sheffield U

npower Football League One
Bournemouth v Southampton
Brighton & HA v Tranmere R
Bristol R v Huddersfield T
Charlton Ath v Brentford
Colchester U v Milton Keynes D
Hartlepool U v Plymouth Arg
Leyton Orient v Oldham Ath
Peterborough U v Carlisle U
Rochdale v Exeter C
Sheffield W v Notts Co
Swindon T v Dagenham & R
Yeovil T v Walsall

npower Football League Two
Cheltenham T v Aldershot T
Crewe Alex v Chesterfield
Gillingham v Accrington S
Hereford U v Barnet
Lincoln C City v Southend U
Morecambe v Bradford C
Northampton T v Macclesfield T
Port Vale v Oxford U
Rotherham U v Bury
Stockport Co v Burton Alb
Torquay U v Shrewsbury T
Wycombe W v Stevenage

Saturday, 19 March 2011
Barclays Premier League
Aston Villa v Wolverhampton W
Blackburn R v Blackpool
Chelsea v Manchester C
Everton v Fulham
Manchester U v Bolton W
Stoke C v Newcastle U
Sunderland v Liverpool
Tottenham H v West Ham U

369

WBA v Arsenal
Wigan Ath v Birmingham C

npower Football League Championship
Barnsley v Reading
Bristol C v Burnley
Crystal Palace v Derby Co
Doncaster R v QPR
Hull C v Norwich C
Ipswich T v Scunthorpe U
Leicester C v Portsmouth
Middlesbrough v Watford
Millwall v Cardiff C
Preston NE v Coventry C
Sheffield U v Leeds U
Swansea C v Nottingham F

npower Football League One
Brentford v Leyton Orient
Carlisle U v Bournemouth
Dagenham & R v Charlton Ath
Exeter C v Yeovil T
Huddersfield T v Swindon T
Milton Keynes D v Peterborough U
Notts Co v Bristol R
Oldham Ath v Brighton & HA
Plymouth Arg v Rochdale
Southampton v Sheffield W
Tranmere R v Colchester U
Walsall v Hartlepool U

npower Football League Two
Accrington S v Port Vale
Aldershot T v Stockport Co
Barnet v Morecambe
Bradford C v Northampton T
Burton Alb v Gillingham
Bury v Cheltenham T
Chesterfield v Rotherham U
Macclesfield T v Torquay U
Oxford U v Crewe Alex
Shrewsbury T v Wycombe W
Southend U v Hereford U
Stevenage v Lincoln C City

Saturday, 26 March 2011
npower Football League One
Bournemouth v Charlton Ath
Brentford v Carlisle U
Brighton & HA v Swindon T
Bristol R v Peterborough U
Colchester U v Exeter C
Dagenham & R v Sheffield W
Hartlepool U v Rochdale
Huddersfield T v Notts Co
Leyton Orient v Yeovil T
Milton Keynes D v Walsall
Oldham Ath v Tranmere R
Plymouth Arg v Southampton

npower Football League Two
Aldershot T v Accrington S

Barnet v Chesterfield
Bradford C v Shrewsbury T
Cheltenham T v Gillingham
Hereford U v Crewe Alex
Lincoln C City v Rotherham U
Macclesfield T v Stevenage
Morecambe v Wycombe W
Northampton T v Torquay U
Oxford U v Burton Alb
Port Vale v Bury
Stockport Co v Southend U

Saturday, 2 April 2011
Barclays Premier League
Arsenal v Blackburn R
Birmingham C v Bolton W
Everton v Aston Villa
Fulham v Blackpool
Manchester C v Sunderland
Newcastle U v Wolverhampton W
Stoke C v Chelsea
WBA v Liverpool
West Ham U v Manchester U
Wigan Ath v Tottenham H

npower Football League Championship
Bristol C v Doncaster R
Burnley v Ipswich T
Cardiff C v Derby Co
Coventry C v Watford
Crystal Palace v Barnsley
Hull C v Millwall
Leeds U v Nottingham F
Middlesbrough v Leicester C
Norwich C v Scunthorpe U
Preston NE v Swansea C
QPR v Sheffield U
Reading v Portsmouth

npower Football League One
Carlisle U v Plymouth Arg
Charlton Ath v Leyton Orient
Exeter C v Dagenham & R
Notts Co v Oldham Ath
Peterborough U v Bournemouth
Rochdale v Brighton & HA
Sheffield W v Colchester U
Southampton v Milton Keynes D
Swindon T v Hartlepool U
Tranmere R v Huddersfield T
Walsall v Brentford
Yeovil T v Bristol R

npower Football League Two
Accrington S v Northampton T
Burton Alb v Barnet
Bury v Oxford U
Chesterfield v Port Vale
Crewe Alex v Cheltenham T
Gillingham v Hereford U
Rotherham U v Morecambe
Shrewsbury T v Macclesfield T

Southend U v Aldershot T
Stevenage v Bradford C
Torquay U v Lincoln C City
Wycombe W v Stockport Co

Saturday, 9 April 2011
Barclays Premier League
Aston Villa v Newcastle U
Blackburn R v Birmingham C
Blackpool v Arsenal
Bolton W v West Ham U
Chelsea v Wigan Ath
Liverpool v Manchester C
Manchester U v Fulham
Sunderland v WBA
Tottenham H v Stoke C
Wolverhampton W v Everton

npower Football League Championship
Barnsley v Bristol C
Derby Co v Coventry C
Doncaster R v Cardiff C
Ipswich T v Crystal Palace
Leicester C v Burnley
Millwall v Leeds U
Nottingham F v Reading
Portsmouth v Preston NE
Scunthorpe U v QPR
Sheffield U v Middlesbrough
Swansea C v Norwich C
Watford v Hull C

npower Football League One
Bournemouth v Tranmere R
Brentford v Swindon T
Brighton & HA v Sheffield W
Bristol R v Exeter C
Colchester U v Rochdale
Dagenham & R v Notts Co
Hartlepool U v Yeovil T
Huddersfield T v Peterborough U
Leyton Orient v Southampton
Milton Keynes D v Carlisle U
Oldham Ath v Charlton Ath
Plymouth Arg v Walsall

npower Football League Two
Aldershot T v Shrewsbury T
Barnet v Crewe Alex
Bradford C v Torquay U
Cheltenham T v Rotherham U
Hereford U v Chesterfield
Lincoln C City v Gillingham
Macclesfield T v Accrington S
Morecambe v Burton Alb
Northampton T v Bury
Oxford U v Wycombe W
Port Vale v Southend U
Stockport Co v Stevenage

Tuesday, 12 April 2011
npower Football League Championship
Barnsley v QPR
Derby Co v Leeds U
Doncaster R v Preston NE
Ipswich T v Middlesbrough
Leicester C v Crystal Palace
Millwall v Bristol C
Nottingham F v Burnley
Portsmouth v Coventry C
Scunthorpe U v Reading
Sheffield U v Cardiff C
Swansea C v Hull C
Watford v Norwich C

Saturday, 16 April 2011
Barclays Premier League
Arsenal v Liverpool
Birmingham C v Sunderland
Everton v Blackburn R
Fulham v Bolton W
Manchester C v Tottenham H
Newcastle U v Manchester U
Stoke C v Wolverhampton W
WBA v Chelsea
West Ham U v Aston Villa
Blackpool v Wigan Ath

npower Football League Championship
Bristol C v Ipswich T
Burnley v Swansea C
Cardiff C v Portsmouth
Coventry C v Millwall
Crystal Palace v Scunthorpe U
Hull C v Doncaster R
Leeds U v Watford
Middlesbrough v Barnsley
Norwich C v Nottingham F
Preston NE v Sheffield U
QPR v Derby Co
Reading v Leicester C

npower Football League One
Carlisle U v Colchester U
Charlton Ath v Huddersfield T
Exeter C v Leyton Orient
Notts Co v Bournemouth
Peterborough U v Plymouth Arg
Rochdale v Brentford
Sheffield W v Hartlepool U
Southampton v Bristol R
Swindon T v Milton Keynes D
Tranmere R v Dagenham & R
Walsall v Brighton & HA
Yeovil T v Oldham Ath

npower Football League Two
Accrington S v Oxford U
Burton Alb v Cheltenham T
Bury v Barnet
Chesterfield v Macclesfield T
Crewe Alex v Lincoln C City

Gillingham v Morecambe
Rotherham U v Hereford U
Shrewsbury T v Stockport Co
Southend U v Bradford C
Stevenage v Aldershot T
Torquay U v Port Vale
Wycombe W v Northampton T

Saturday, 23 April 2011
Barclays Premier League
Aston Villa v Stoke C
Blackburn R v Manchester C   1-1
Blackpool v Newcastle U
Bolton W v Arsenal
Chelsea v West Ham U
Liverpool v Birmingham C
Manchester U v Everton
Sunderland v Wigan Ath
Tottenham H v WBA
Wolverhampton W v Fulham

npower Football League Championship
Cardiff C v QPR
Coventry C v Scunthorpe U
Derby Co v Burnley
Doncaster R v Crystal Palace
Hull C v Middlesbrough
Ipswich T v Norwich C
Leeds U v Reading
Millwall v Preston NE
Nottingham F v Leicester C
Portsmouth v Swansea C
Sheffield U v Bristol C
Watford v Barnsley

npower Football League One
Brentford v Colchester U
Brighton & HA v Southampton
Bristol R v Charlton Ath
Dagenham & R v Plymouth Arg
Exeter C v Oldham Ath
Hartlepool U v Tranmere R
Leyton Orient v Peterborough U
Milton Keynes D v Huddersfield T
Rochdale v Carlisle U
Swindon T v Notts Co
Walsall v Sheffield W
Yeovil T v Bournemouth

npower Football League Two
Accrington S v Bradford C
Aldershot T v Burton Alb
Bury v Lincoln C City
Cheltenham T v Macclesfield T
Crewe Alex v Morecambe
Gillingham v Barnet
Hereford U v Shrewsbury T
Northampton T v Rotherham U
Oxford U v Chesterfield
Port Vale v Stockport Co
Southend U v Stevenage
Torquay U v Wycombe W

Monday, 25 April 2011
npower Football League Championship
Barnsley v Doncaster R
Bristol C v Nottingham F
Burnley v Portsmouth
Crystal Palace v Leeds U
Leicester C v Watford
Middlesbrough v Coventry C
Norwich C v Derby Co
Preston NE v Cardiff C
QPR v Hull C
Reading v Sheffield U
Scunthorpe U v Millwall
Swansea C v Ipswich T

npower Football League One
Bournemouth v Bristol R
Carlisle U v Leyton Orient
Charlton Ath v Rochdale
Colchester U v Brighton & HA
Huddersfield T v Dagenham & R
Notts Co v Brentford
Oldham Ath v Walsall
Peterborough U v Yeovil T
Plymouth Arg v Milton Keynes D
Sheffield W v Swindon T
Southampton v Hartlepool U
Tranmere R v Exeter C

npower Football League Two
Barnet v Oxford U
Bradford C v Aldershot T
Burton Alb v Torquay U
Chesterfield v Bury
Lincoln C City v Cheltenham T
Macclesfield T v Southend U
Morecambe v Hereford U
Rotherham U v Gillingham
Shrewsbury T v Accrington S
Stevenage v Port Vale
Stockport Co v Northampton T
Wycombe W v Crewe Alex

Saturday, 30 April 2011
Barclays Premier League
Arsenal v Manchester U
Birmingham C v Wolverhampton W
Blackburn R v Bolton W
Blackpool v Stoke C
Chelsea v Tottenham H
Liverpool v Newcastle U
Manchester C v West Ham U   3-0
Sunderland v Fulham
WBA v Aston Villa
Wigan Ath v Everton

npower Football League Championship
Cardiff C v Middlesbrough
Coventry C v Reading
Derby Co v Bristol C
Doncaster R v Leicester C
Hull C v Crystal Palace

Ipswich T v Preston NE
Leeds U v Burnley
Millwall v Swansea C
Nottingham F v Scunthorpe U
Portsmouth v Norwich C
Sheffield U v Barnsley
Watford v QPR

npower Football League One
Brentford v Southampton
Brighton & HA v Huddersfield T
Bristol R v Sheffield W
Dagenham & R v Carlisle U
Exeter C v Plymouth Arg
Hartlepool U v Bournemouth
Leyton Orient v Tranmere R
Milton Keynes D v Notts Co
Rochdale v Peterborough U
Swindon T v Oldham Ath
Walsall v Charlton Ath
Yeovil T v Colchester U

npower Football League Two
Accrington S v Barnet
Aldershot T v Rotherham U
Bury v Wycombe W
Cheltenham T v Shrewsbury T
Crewe Alex v Stockport Co
Gillingham v Macclesfield T
Hereford U v Bradford C
Northampton T v Stevenage
Oxford U v Lincoln C City
Port Vale v Morecambe
Southend U v Burton Alb
Torquay U v Chesterfield

Saturday, 7 May 2011
Barclays Premier League
Aston Villa v Wigan Ath
Bolton W v Sunderland
Everton v Manchester C
Fulham v Liverpool
Manchester U v Chelsea   2~1
Newcastle U v Birmingham C
Stoke C v Arsenal   *AMEOBI (P)*
Tottenham H v Blackpool
West Ham U v Blackburn R   *J.TAYLOR*
Wolverhampton W v WBA

npower Football League One
Bournemouth v Rochdale
Carlisle U v Yeovil T
Charlton Ath v Hartlepool U
Colchester U v Bristol R
Huddersfield T v Brentford
Notts Co v Brighton & HA
Oldham Ath v Milton Keynes D
Peterborough U v Dagenham & R
Plymouth Arg v Leyton Orient

Sheffield W v Exeter C
Southampton v Walsall
Tranmere R v Swindon T

npower Football League Two
Barnet v Port Vale
Bradford C v Crewe Alex
Burton Alb v Accrington S
Chesterfield v Gillingham
Lincoln C City v Aldershot T
Macclesfield T v Hereford U
Morecambe v Northampton T
Rotherham U v Torquay U
Shrewsbury T v Oxford U
Stevenage v Bury
Stockport Co v Cheltenham T
Wycombe W v Southend U

Sunday, 8 May 2011
npower Football League Championship
Barnsley v Millwall
Bristol C v Hull C
Burnley v Cardiff C
Crystal Palace v Nottingham F
Leicester C v Ipswich T
Middlesbrough v Doncaster R
Norwich C v Coventry C
Preston NE v Watford
QPR v Leeds U
Reading v Derby Co
Scunthorpe U v Portsmouth
Swansea C v Sheffield U

Saturday, 14 May 2011
Barclays Premier League
Arsenal v Aston Villa   *SUN*
Birmingham C v Fulham   *13pm*
Blackburn R v Manchester U
Blackpool v Bolton W   2-2
Chelsea v Newcastle U   S.TAYLOR,
Liverpool v Tottenham H
Manchester C v Stoke C   S.TAYLOR,
Sunderland v Wolverhampton W
WBA v Everton   CROTTIERS
Wigan Ath v West Ham U

Sunday, 22 May 2011
Barclays Premier League
Aston Villa v Liverpool
Bolton W v Manchester C   3-3
Everton v Chelsea
Fulham v Arsenal   S.TAYLOR
Manchester U v Blackpool   LOWENK,
Newcastle U v WBA   O.G.
Stoke C v Wigan Ath
Tottenham H v Birmingham C
West Ham U v Sunderland
Wolverhampton W v Blackburn R

BLUE SQUARE PREMIER LEAGUE FIXTURES 2010–2011

Saturday, 14 August 2010
Crawley T v Grimsby T
Darlington v Newport Co
Gateshead v Kettering T
Hayes & Yeading U v Bath C
Histon v Barrow
Luton T v Altrincham
Mansfield T v Forest Green R
Rushden & D v Fleetwood T
Southport v AFC Wimbledon
Tamworth v Eastbourne B
Wrexham v Cambridge U
York C v Kidderminster H

Tuesday, 17 August 2010
AFC Wimbledon v Histon
Altrincham v Darlington
Barrow v Gateshead
Bath C v Rushden & D
Cambridge U v Crawley T
Eastbourne B v Hayes & Yeading U
Fleetwood T v Mansfield T
Forest Green R v Wrexham
Grimsby T v York C
Kettering T v Luton T
Kidderminster H v Southport
Newport Co v Tamworth

Saturday, 21 August 2010
AFC Wimbledon v Tamworth
Altrincham v Crawley T
Barrow v Rushden & D
Bath C v York C
Cambridge U v Southport
Eastbourne B v Wrexham
Fleetwood T v Luton T
Forest Green R v Gateshead
Grimsby T v Hayes & Yeading U
Kettering T v Darlington
Kidderminster H v Mansfield T
Newport Co v Histon

Tuesday, 24 August 2010
Crawley T v Bath C
Darlington v Grimsby T
Gateshead v Fleetwood T
Hayes & Yeading U v Forest Green R
Histon v Eastbourne B
Luton T v Newport Co
Mansfield T v Kettering T
Rushden & D v AFC Wimbledon

Southport v Altrincham
Tamworth v Cambridge U
Wrexham v Kidderminster H
York C v Barrow

Saturday, 28 August 2010
Darlington v Gateshead
Eastbourne B v AFC Wimbledon
Forest Green R v Bath C
Hayes & Yeading U v Crawley T
Histon v Kettering T
Mansfield T v Cambridge U
Newport Co v Kidderminster H
Rushden & D v Grimsby T
Southport v Fleetwood T
Tamworth v Luton T
Wrexham v Barrow
York C v Altrincham

Monday, 30 August 2010
AFC Wimbledon v Newport Co
Altrincham v Mansfield T
Barrow v Darlington
Bath C v Wrexham
Cambridge U v Eastbourne B
Crawley T v Forest Green R
Fleetwood T v York C
Grimsby T v Histon
Kettering T v Rushden & D
Kidderminster H v Tamworth
Luton T v Hayes & Yeading U

Saturday, 4 September 2010
Altrincham v Kidderminster H
Bath C v Barrow
Cambridge U v Gateshead
Crawley T v Fleetwood T
Eastbourne B v Darlington
Forest Green R v Southport
Grimsby T v Luton T
Hayes & Yeading U v Histon
Kettering T v AFC Wimbledon
Mansfield T v Tamworth
Newport Co v Wrexham
York C v Rushden & D

Tuesday, 7 September 2010
Gateshead v Southport

Saturday, 11 September 2010
AFC Wimbledon v Bath C
Barrow v Eastbourne B

Darlington v Forest Green R
Fleetwood T v Kettering T
Gateshead v Altrincham
Histon v Crawley T
Kidderminster H v
  Hayes & Yeading U
Luton T v Cambridge U
Rushden & D v Newport Co
Southport v Mansfield T
Tamworth v Grimsby T
Wrexham v York C

Saturday, 18 September 2010
Barrow v Forest Green R
Bath C v Darlington
Crawley T v Gateshead
Eastbourne B v Altrincham
Grimsby T v Fleetwood T
Histon v Tamworth
Kettering T v Wrexham
Kidderminster H v Cambridge U
Luton T v AFC Wimbledon
Newport Co v Mansfield T
Southport v Rushden & D
York C v Hayes & Yeading U

Tuesday, 21 September 2010
AFC Wimbledon v Crawley T
Altrincham v Barrow
Cambridge U v Kettering T
Darlington v Luton T
Fleetwood T v Kidderminster H
Forest Green R v Eastbourne B
Gateshead v Grimsby T
Hayes & Yeading U v Newport Co
Mansfield T v York C
Rushden & D v Histon
Tamworth v Bath C
Wrexham v Southport

Saturday, 25 September 2010
Altrincham v Grimsby T
Cambridge U v Newport Co
Darlington v Southport
Fleetwood T v Bath C
Forest Green R v Kettering T
Gateshead v Luton T
Hayes & Yeading U v Barrow
Kidderminster H v AFC Wimbledon
Mansfield T v Eastbourne B
Rushden & D v Crawley T
Tamworth v York C
Wrexham v Histon

Tuesday, 28 September 2010
AFC Wimbledon v Cambridge U

Barrow v Fleetwood T
Bath C v Kidderminster H
Crawley T v Tamworth
Eastbourne B v Rushden & D
Grimsby T v Wrexham
Histon v Gateshead
Kettering T v Altrincham
Luton T v Mansfield T
Newport Co v Forest Green R
Southport v Hayes & Yeading U
York C v Darlington

Saturday, 2 October 2010
AFC Wimbledon v Forest Green R
Altrincham v Rushden & D
Barrow v Luton T
Cambridge U v Bath C
Crawley T v Kidderminster H
Darlington v Wrexham
Eastbourne B v York C
Fleetwood T v Histon
Gateshead v Mansfield T
Grimsby T v Newport Co
Kettering T v Hayes & Yeading U
Southport v Tamworth

Tuesday, 5 October 2010
Bath C v Altrincham
Forest Green R v Grimsby T
Hayes & Yeading U v Cambridge U
Histon v Southport
Kidderminster H v Gateshead
Luton T v Crawley T
Mansfield T v AFC Wimbledon
Newport Co v Eastbourne B
Rushden & D v Darlington
Tamworth v Barrow
Wrexham v Fleetwood T
York C v Kettering T

Saturday, 9 October 2010
Barrow v Crawley T
Bath C v Eastbourne B
Darlington v Hayes & Yeading U
Fleetwood T v Cambridge U
Gateshead v Tamworth
Histon v Altrincham
Kidderminster H v Grimsby T
Luton T v Forest Green R
Newport Co v York C
Rushden & D v Mansfield T
Southport v Kettering T
Wrexham v AFC Wimbledon

Saturday, 16 October 2010
AFC Wimbledon v Gateshead

Altrincham v Fleetwood T
Cambridge U v Barrow
Crawley T v Newport Co
Eastbourne B v Luton T
Forest Green R v Histon
Grimsby T v Southport
Hayes & Yeading U v Wrexham
Kettering T v Kidderminster H
Mansfield T v Darlington
Tamworth v Rushden & D
York C v Bath C

Saturday, 30 October 2010
AFC Wimbledon v Darlington
Forest Green R v York C
Gateshead v Cambridge U
Grimsby T v Eastbourne B
Hayes & Yeading U v Altrincham
Histon v Wrexham
Luton T v Bath C
Mansfield T v Crawley T
Newport Co v Kettering T
Rushden & D v Barrow
Southport v Kidderminster H
Tamworth v Fleetwood T

Tuesday, 9 November 2010
Altrincham v AFC Wimbledon
Barrow v Newport Co
Bath C v Hayes & Yeading U
Cambridge U v Grimsby T
Darlington v Tamworth
Eastbourne B v Forest Green R
Fleetwood T v Gateshead
Kettering T v Mansfield T
Kidderminster H v Rushden & D
Wrexham v Luton T
York C v Southport

Saturday, 13 November 2010
Altrincham v Luton T
Barrow v AFC Wimbledon
Darlington v Crawley T
Eastbourne B v Newport Co
Fleetwood T v Rushden & D
Forest Green R v Mansfield T
Hayes & Yeading U v Grimsby T
Histon v Kidderminster H
Kettering T v Cambridge U
Southport v Bath C
Tamworth v Gateshead
York C v Wrexham

Saturday, 20 November 2010
AFC Wimbledon v Kettering T
Bath C v Fleetwood T

Cambridge U v Tamworth
Crawley T v Altrincham
Gateshead v Forest Green R
Grimsby T v Barrow
Kidderminster H v Eastbourne B
Luton T v Histon
Mansfield T v Hayes & Yeading U
Newport Co v Southport
Rushden & D v York C
Wrexham v Darlington

Saturday, 27 November 2010
Barrow v Kidderminster H
Cambridge U v Altrincham
Crawley T v Southport
Eastbourne B v Tamworth
Fleetwood T v AFC Wimbledon
Forest Green R v Rushden & D
Histon v Bath C
Kettering T v Gateshead
Luton T v Darlington
Newport Co v Hayes & Yeading U
Wrexham v Mansfield T
York C v Grimsby T

Tuesday, 30 November 2010
AFC Wimbledon v Luton T
Altrincham v Forest Green R
Bath C v Crawley T
Darlington v Histon
Gateshead v Barrow
Grimsby T v Kettering T
Hayes & Yeading U v Eastbourne B
Kidderminster H v York C
Mansfield T v Fleetwood T
Rushden & D v Cambridge U
Southport v Wrexham
Tamworth v Newport Co

Saturday, 4 December 2010
Darlington v Kidderminster H
Eastbourne B v Gateshead
Forest Green R v Luton T
Hayes & Yeading U v Rushden & D
Histon v Fleetwood T
Kettering T v Bath C
Mansfield T v Barrow
Newport Co v Cambridge U
Southport v Grimsby T
Tamworth v Altrincham
Wrexham v Crawley T
York C v AFC Wimbledon

Saturday, 18 December 2010
AFC Wimbledon v Wrexham
Altrincham v Histon

376

Barrow v Tamworth
Bath C v Southport
Cambridge U v Darlington
Crawley T v Mansfield T
Fleetwood T v Newport Co
Gateshead v Hayes & Yeading U
Grimsby T v Forest Green R
Kidderminster H v Kettering T
Luton T v York C
Rushden & D v Eastbourne B

Sunday, 26 December 2010
Darlington v Fleetwood T
Eastbourne B v Crawley T
Forest Green R v Kidderminster H
Hayes & Yeading U v AFC Wimbledon
Histon v Cambridge U
Mansfield T v Grimsby T
Newport Co v Bath C
Rushden & D v Luton T
Southport v Barrow
Tamworth v Kettering T
Wrexham v Altrincham
York C v Gateshead

Tuesday, 28 December 2010
AFC Wimbledon v Eastbourne B
Altrincham v York C
Barrow v Wrexham
Bath C v Forest Green R
Cambridge U v Mansfield T
Crawley T v Hayes & Yeading U
Fleetwood T v Southport
Gateshead v Darlington
Grimsby T v Rushden & D
Kettering T v Histon
Kidderminster H v Newport Co
Luton T v Tamworth

Saturday, 1 January 2011
AFC Wimbledon v Hayes & Yeading U
Altrincham v Wrexham
Barrow v Southport
Bath C v Newport Co
Cambridge U v Histon
Crawley T v Eastbourne B
Fleetwood T v Darlington
Gateshead v York C
Grimsby T v Mansfield T
Kettering T v Tamworth
Kidderminster H v Forest Green R
Luton T v Rushden & D

Monday, 3 January 2011
Darlington v Barrow
Eastbourne B v Cambridge U

Forest Green R v Crawley T
Hayes & Yeading U v Luton T
Histon v Grimsby T
Mansfield T v Altrincham
Newport Co v AFC Wimbledon
Rushden & D v Kettering T
Southport v Gateshead
Tamworth v Kidderminster H
Wrexham v Bath C
York C v Fleetwood T

Saturday, 8 January 2011
Barrow v Cambridge U
Bath C v Luton T
Crawley T v Kettering T
Darlington v AFC Wimbledon
Eastbourne B v Mansfield T
Forest Green R v Fleetwood T
Gateshead v Kidderminster H
Hayes & Yeading U v Tamworth
Histon v York C
Rushden & D v Altrincham
Southport v Newport Co
Wrexham v Grimsby T

Saturday, 22 January 2011
AFC Wimbledon v Southport
Altrincham v Bath C
Cambridge U v Wrexham
Fleetwood T v Hayes & Yeading U
Grimsby T v Crawley T
Kettering T v Eastbourne B
Kidderminster H v Barrow
Luton T v Gateshead
Mansfield T v Histon
Newport Co v Rushden & D
Tamworth v Darlington
York C v Forest Green R

Tuesday, 25 January 2011
Altrincham v Hayes & Yeading U
Barrow v Histon
Bath C v AFC Wimbledon
Crawley T v Cambridge U
Darlington v Mansfield T
Kettering T v Fleetwood T
Luton T v Grimsby T

Saturday, 29 January 2011
Barrow v Altrincham
Bath C v Cambridge U
Crawley T v Luton T
Darlington v Kettering T
Eastbourne B v Grimsby T
Fleetwood T v Forest Green R
Gateshead v AFC Wimbledon

Hayes & Yeading U v Kidderminster H
Histon v Newport Co
Mansfield T v Wrexham
Rushden & D v Tamworth
Southport v York C

Saturday, 5 February 2011
AFC Wimbledon v Fleetwood T
Altrincham v Southport
Cambridge U v Rushden & D
Forest Green R v Hayes & Yeading U
Grimsby T v Gateshead
Kettering T v Crawley T
Kidderminster H v Bath C
Luton T v Barrow
Newport Co v Darlington
Tamworth v Histon
Wrexham v Eastbourne B
York C v Mansfield T

Saturday, 12 February 2011
AFC Wimbledon v York C
Bath C v Tamworth
Crawley T v Wrexham
Darlington v Eastbourne B
Gateshead v Rushden & D
Grimsby T v Cambridge U
Histon v Hayes & Yeading U
Kettering T v Barrow
Kidderminster H v Altrincham
Luton T v Fleetwood T
Mansfield T v Newport Co
Southport v Forest Green R

Saturday, 19 February 2011
Altrincham v Kettering T
Barrow v Mansfield T
Cambridge U v Kidderminster H
Eastbourne B v Histon
Fleetwood T v Grimsby T
Forest Green R v Darlington
Hayes & Yeading U v Southport
Newport Co v Luton T
Rushden & D v Bath C
Tamworth v AFC Wimbledon
Wrexham v Gateshead
York C v Crawley T

Saturday, 26 February 2011
AFC Wimbledon v Altrincham
Cambridge U v Luton T
Crawley T v Barrow
Fleetwood T v Eastbourne B
Forest Green R v Tamworth
Gateshead v Bath C
Grimsby T v Darlington

Hayes & Yeading U v York C
Histon v Rushden & D
Kettering T v Newport Co
Kidderminster H v Wrexham
Mansfield T v Southport

Tuesday, 1 March 2011
Southport v Histon

Saturday, 5 March 2011
Altrincham v Gateshead
Barrow v York C
Bath C v Kettering T
Crawley T v Histon
Darlington v Cambridge U
Eastbourne B v Southport
Grimsby T v AFC Wimbledon
Luton T v Kidderminster H
Newport Co v Fleetwood T
Rushden & D v Hayes & Yeading U
Tamworth v Mansfield T
Wrexham v Forest Green R

Tuesday, 8 March 2011
Kidderminster H v Crawley T
Rushden & D v Forest Green R

Saturday, 12 March 2011
AFC Wimbledon v Kidderminster H
Fleetwood T v Crawley T
Forest Green R v Barrow
Gateshead v Eastbourne B
Histon v Darlington
Kettering T v Grimsby T
Mansfield T v Bath C
Newport Co v Altrincham
Southport v Cambridge U
Tamworth v Hayes & Yeading U
Wrexham v Rushden & D
York C v Luton T

Saturday, 19 March 2011
Altrincham v Tamworth
Bath C v Grimsby T
Cambridge U v York C
Crawley T v AFC Wimbledon
Eastbourne B v Barrow
Fleetwood T v Wrexham
Forest Green R v Newport Co
Hayes & Yeading U v Gateshead
Histon v Mansfield T
Kidderminster H v Darlington
Luton T v Kettering T
Rushden & D v Southport

Saturday, 26 March 2011
AFC Wimbledon v Rushden & D

Barrow v Bath C
Cambridge U v Forest Green R
Darlington v Altrincham
Eastbourne B v Kettering T
Gateshead v Crawley T
Grimsby T v Tamworth
Hayes & Yeading U v Fleetwood T
Mansfield T v Kidderminster H
Southport v Luton T
Wrexham v Newport Co
York C v Histon

Tuesday, 29 March 2011
Newport Co v Gateshead
Tamworth v Wrexham
York C v Eastbourne B

Saturday, 2 April 2011
AFC Wimbledon v Barrow
Altrincham v Cambridge U
Bath C v Gateshead
Crawley T v Darlington
Fleetwood T v Tamworth
Histon v Forest Green R
Kettering T v York C
Kidderminster H v Luton T
Mansfield T v Rushden & D
Newport Co v Grimsby T
Southport v Eastbourne B
Wrexham v Hayes & Yeading U

Saturday, 9 April 2011
Barrow v Kettering T
Cambridge U v AFC Wimbledon
Darlington v Bath C
Eastbourne B v Fleetwood T
Forest Green R v Altrincham
Gateshead v Histon
Grimsby T v Kidderminster H
Hayes & Yeading U v Mansfield T
Luton T v Southport
Rushden & D v Wrexham
Tamworth v Crawley T
York C v Newport Co

Saturday, 16 April 2011
Eastbourne B v Kidderminster H
Fleetwood T v Altrincham
Forest Green R v Cambridge U
Grimsby T v Bath C

Hayes & Yeading U v Darlington
Histon v AFC Wimbledon
Mansfield T v Luton T
Newport Co v Barrow
Rushden & D v Gateshead
Southport v Crawley T
Wrexham v Kettering T
York C v Tamworth

Saturday, 23 April 2011
AFC Wimbledon v Mansfield T
Altrincham v Newport Co
Barrow v Grimsby T
Bath C v Histon
Cambridge U v Hayes & Yeading U
Crawley T v Rushden & D
Darlington v York C
Gateshead v Wrexham
Kettering T v Forest Green R
Kidderminster H v Fleetwood T
Luton T v Eastbourne B
Tamworth v Southport

Monday, 25 April 2011
Eastbourne B v Bath C
Fleetwood T v Barrow
Forest Green R v AFC Wimbledon
Grimsby T v Altrincham
Hayes & Yeading U v Kettering T
Histon v Luton T
Mansfield T v Gateshead
Newport Co v Crawley T
Rushden & D v Kidderminster H
Southport v Darlington
Wrexham v Tamworth
York C v Cambridge U

Saturday, 30 April 2011
AFC Wimbledon v Grimsby T
Altrincham v Eastbourne B
Barrow v Hayes & Yeading U
Bath C v Mansfield T
Cambridge U v Fleetwood T
Crawley T v York C
Darlington v Rushden & D
Gateshead v Newport Co
Kettering T v Southport
Kidderminster H v Histon
Luton T v Wrexham
Tamworth v Forest Green R

OTHER FIXTURES — SEASON 2010–2011

July 2010

14 Wed	UEFA Champions League 2Q (1)
	UEFA Europa League 2Q (1)
21 Wed	UEFA Champions League 2Q (2)
	UEFA Europa League 2Q (2)
28 Wed	UEFA Champions League 3Q (1)
	UEFA Europa League 3Q (1)

August 2010

04 Wed	UEFA Champions League 3Q (2)
	UEFA Europa League 3Q (2)
11 Wed	International Friendly
	Football League Cup 1
14 Sat	FA Cup EP
18 Wed	UEFA Champions League Play-Off (1)
	UEFA Europa League Play-Off (1)
25 Wed	UEFA Champions League Play-Off (2)
	UEFA Europa League Play-Off (2)
	Football League Cup 2
27 Fri	UEFA Super Cup
28 Sat	FA Cup P
30 Mon	Bank Holiday

September 2010

01 Wed	Football League Trophy 1
03 Fri	England v Bulgaria – Euro 2012 Qualifier
04 Sat	FA Vase 1Q
06 Mon	FA Youth Cup P†
07 Tue	Switzerland v England – Euro 2012 Qualifier
11 Sat	FA Cup 1Q
15 Wed	UEFA Champions League MD1
	UEFA Europa League MD1
18 Sat	FA Vase 2Q
20 Mon	FA Youth Cup 1Q†
22 Wed	Football League Cup 3
25 Sat	FA Cup 2Q
26 Sun	FA Sunday Cup P
29 Wed	UEFA Champions League MD2
	UEFA Europa League MD2

October 2010

02 Sat	FA Trophy P
	FA Vase 1P
04 Mon	FA Youth Cup 2Q†
06 Wed	Football League Trophy 2
09 Sat	International Qualifier
	FA Cup 3Q
12 Tue	England v Montenegro – Euro 2012 Qualifier
16 Sat	FA Trophy 1Q
17 Sun	FA County Youth Cup 1*
	FA Sunday Cup 1
18 Mon	FA Youth Cup 3Q†
20 Wed	UEFA Champions League MD3
	UEFA Europa League MD3
23 Sat	FA Cup 4Q
27 Wed	Football League Cup 4
30 Sat	FA Trophy 2Q

November 2010

03 Wed	UEFA Champions League MD4
	UEFA Europa League MD4
06 Sat	FA Cup 1P
	FA Youth Cup 1P*
10 Wed	Football League Trophy AQF
13 Sat	FA Vase 2P
14 Sun	FA County Youth Cup 2*
17 Wed	International Qualifier
	FA Cup 1P Replay
20 Sat	FA Trophy 3Q
	FA Youth Cup 2P*
21 Sun	FA Sunday Cup 2
24 Wed	UEFA Champions League MD5
27 Sat	FA Cup 2P

December 2010

01 Wed	UEFA Europa League MD5
	Football League Cup 5
	Football League Trophy ASF
04 Sat	FA Vase 3P
08 Wed	UEFA Champions League MD6
	FA Cup 2P Replay
11 Sat	FA Trophy 1P
	FA Youth Cup 3P*
12 Sun	FA Sunday Cup 3
15 Wed	UEFA Europa League MD6
	FIFA World Club Cup
18 Sat	FIFA World Club Cup
19 Sun	FA County Youth Cup 3*

January 2011
08 Sat	FA Cup 3P
12 Wed	Football League Cup SF 1
15 Sat	FA Trophy 2P
	FA Youth Cup 4P*
19 Wed	FA Cup 3P Replay
	Football League Trophy AF1
22 Sat	FA Vase 4P
23 Sun	FA Sunday Cup 4
26 Wed	Football League Cup SF 2
29 Sat	FA Cup 4P
	FA Youth Cup P*
30 Sun	FA County Youth Cup 4*

February 2011
05 Sat	FA Trophy 3P
09 Wed	International Friendly
	FA Cup 4P Replay
	Football League Trophy AF2
12 Sat	FA Vase 5P
	FA Youth Cup 6P*
16 Wed	UEFA Champions League 16 (1)
	UEFA Europa League 32 (1)
19 Sat	FA Cup 5P
20 Sun	FA Sunday Cup 5
23 Wed	UEFA Champions League 16 (1)
	UEFA Europa League 32 (2)
26 Sat	FA Trophy 4P
27 Sun	FA County Youth Cup SF*
	Football League Cup Final

March 2011
02 Wed	FA Cup 5P Replay
05 Sat	FA Vase 6P
	FA Youth Cup SF (1)*
09 Wed	UEFA Champions League 16 (2)
	UEFA Europa League 16 (1)
12 Sat	FA Cup 6P
	FA Trophy SF (1)
16 Wed	UEFA Champions League 16 (2)
	UEFA Europa League 16 (2)
19 Sat	FA Trophy SF (2)
	FA Youth Cup SF (2)*

20 Sun	FA Sunday Cup SF
23 Wed	FA Cup 6p Replay
26 Sat	Wales v England – Euro 2012 Qualifier
	FA Vase SF (1)
29 Tue	International Qualifier

April 2011
02 Sat	FA Vase SF (2)
03 Sun	Football League Trophy Final
06 Wed	UEFA Champions League QF (1)
	UEFA Europa League QF (1)
13 Wed	UEFA Champions League QF (2)
	UEFA Europa League QF (2)
16 Sat	FA Cup SF
17 Sun	FA Cup SF
27 Wed	UEFA Champions League SF (1)
	UEFA Europa League SF (1)
30 Sat	FA County Youth Cup Final (Prov)

May 2011
01 Sun	FA Sunday Cup Final
02 Mon	Bank Holiday
04 Wed	UEFA Champions League SF (2)
	UEFA Europa League SF (2)
07 Sat	FA Trophy Final
	Football League Season Finishes
08 Sun	FA Vase Final
14 Sat	FA Cup Final
18 Wed	UEFA Europa League Final
22 Sun	Premier League Season Finishes
28 Sat	UEFA Champions League Final
	League 2 Play-Off Final
29 Sun	League 1 Play-Off Final
30 Mon	Championship Play-Off Final

June 2011
04 Sat	England v Switzerland – Euro 2012 Qualifier

† *Ties to be played in week commencing.*
* *Closing date of round.*
FA Youth Cup Final 1st and 2nd leg – dates to be confirmed.
FA Women's Cup – dates to be confirmed.

STOP PRESS

Summer transfers completed and pending:

Premier League: Arsenal: Laurent Koscielny (Lorient) undisclosed; Marouane Chamakh (Bordeaux) Free. **Birmingham C:** Nikola Zigic (Valencia) undisclosed; Enric Vales (NAC Breda) Free; Ben Foster (Manchester U) undisclosed. **Bolton W:** Robbie Blake (Burnley) Free; Martin Petrov (Manchester C) Free. **Chelsea:** Yossi Benayoun (Liverpool) undisclosed. **Everton:** Jermaine Beckford (Leeds U) Free. **Fulham:** Philippe Senderos (Arsenal) Free. **Liverpool:** Milan Jovanovic (Standard Liege) Free. **Manchester C:** Yaya Toure (Barcelona) undisclosed; David Silva (Valencia) undisclosed; Jerome Boateng (Hamburg) undisclosed. **Manchester U:** Chris Smalling (Fulham) undisclosed; Javier Hernandez (*Chicarito*) (Guadalajara) undisclosed. **Newcastle U:** James Perch (Nottingham F) undisclosed. **Stoke C:** Florent Cuvelier (Portsmouth) undisclosed. **Sunderland:** Ahmed Al-Muhammadi (ENPPI) Loan; Simon Mignolet (St Truiden) undisclosed; Christian Riveros (Cruz Azul) Free. **WBA:** Pablo Ibanez (Atletico Madrid) Free; Gabriel Tamas (Auxerre) £800,000. **West Ham U:** Thomas Hitzlsperger (Lazio) Free. **Wigan Ath:** Mauro Boselli (Estudiantes) undisclosed. **Wolverhampton W:** Stephen Nolan (Hull C) undisclosed; Steven Mouyokolo (Hull C) undisclosed; Steven Fletcher (Burnley) undisclosed; Jelle van Damme (Anderlecht) undisclosed.

Football League Championship: Barnsley: James McEveley (Derby Co) Free; Goran Lovre (Groningen) undisclosed; Liam Dickinson (Brighton & HA) undisclosed; Diego Arismendi (Stoke C) Loan. **Bristol C:** Kalifa Cisse (Reading) undisclosed. **Burnley:** Ross Wallace (Preston NE) undisclosed; Dean Marney (Hull C) undisclosed; Chris Iwelumo (Wolverhampton W) undisclosed. **Cardiff C:** Tom Heaton (Manchester U) Free. **Coventry C:** Roy O'Donovan (Sunderland) Free; Gary McSheffrey (Birmingham C) Free. **Crystal Palace:** Andy Dorman (St Mirren) Free; Adam Barrett (Southend U) Free; David Wright (Ipswich T) Free. **Derby Co:** James Bailey (Crewe Alex) undisclosed: John Brayford (Crewe Alex) undisclosed; Gareth Roberts (Doncaster R) Free. **Doncaster R:** Billy Sharp (Sheffield U) undisclosed; George Friend (Wolverhampton W) Free. **Hull C:** James Harper (Sheffield U) Free; Nolberto Solano (Leicester C) Free. **Leeds U:** Lloyd Sam (Charlton Ath) Free; Neill Collins (Preston NE) undisclosed; Federico Bessone (Swansea C) Free; Paul Connolly (Derby Co) Free; Billy Paynter (Swindon T) Free; Kasper Schmeichel (Notts Co) Free. **Middlesbrough:** Nicky Bailey (Charlton Ath) £1,400,000; Kris Boyd (Rangers) Free; Andrew Halliday (Livingston) undisclosed. **Norwich C:** John Ruddy (Everton) undisclosed; Andrew Surman (Wolverhampton W) undisclosed; Andrew Crofts (Brighton & HA) undisclosed; Elliott Ward (Coventry C) Free; David Fox (Colchester U) undisclosed. **Preston NE:** Wayne Brown (Leicester C) Free; Craig Morgan (Peterborough U) £400,000. **Reading:** Marcus Williams (Scunthorpe U) Free. **Scunthorpe U:** Eddie Nolan (Preston NE) (loan); Michael Collins (Huddersfield T) undisclosed; Chris Dagnall (Rochdale) Free. **Sheffield U:** Simon Walton (Plymouth Arg) Loan; Leon Britton (Swansea C) Free; Daniel Bogdanovic (Barnsley) Free. **Swansea C:** Scott Donnelly (Aldershot T) undisclosed; Neil Taylor (Wrexham) undisclosed. **Watford:** Rene Gilmartin (Walsall) undisclosed; Tom Aldred (Carlisle U) undisclosed.

Football League 1: Bournemouth: Steve Lovell (Partick T) Free; Michael Symes (Accrington S) Free; Marc Pugh (Hereford U) Free; Harry Arter (Woking) undisclosed. **Brentford:** Craig Woodman (Wycombe W) undisclosed; Kirk Hudson (Aldershot T) Free; Nicky Forster (Brighton & HA) Free. **Brighton & HA:** Ashley Barnes (Plymouth Arg) undisclosed. **Bristol R:** Will Hoskins (Watford) Free; Gary Sawyer (Plymouth Arg) Free; Harry Pell (Charlton Ath) Free. **Carlisle U:** Jason Price (Millwall) Free; Sean McDaid (Doncaster R) Free; Craig Curran (Tranmere R) undisclosed. **Charlton Ath:** Johnnie Jackson (Notts Co) Free; Alan McCormack (Southend U) Free; Gary Doherty (Norwich C) Free; Akpo Sodje (Sheffield W) undisclosed. **Colchester U:** Andrew Bond (Barrow) undisclosed. **Dagenham & R:** Luke Wilkinson (Portsmouth) undisclosed; Gavin Tomlin (Yeovil T) Free; Gareth Gwillim (Histon) Free; Stuart Lewis (Gillingham) Free; Alex Osborn (Grays Ath) undisclosed. **Exeter C:** Artur Krysiak (Birmingham C) Free; Daniel Nardiello (Blackpool) Free. **Huddersfield T:** Lee Croft (Derby Co) Loan; Gary Naysmith (Sheffield U) Free; Joey Gudjonsson (Burnley) Free. **Leyton Orient:** Elliot Omozusi (Fulham) Free; Aaron Brown (Aldershot T) Free; Terrell Forbes (Yeovil T) Free; Alex Revell (Southend U) Free; Lee Butcher (Tottenham H) undisclosed.